REGENTS COLLEGE EXAMINATIONS
OFFICIAL STUDY GUIDE

2001 EDITION

The College Board

New York

This guide was prepared by Regents College in conjunction with the College Board, which produced the book.

Regents College is the originator and now sole administrator of Regents College Examinations (formerly known as ACT PEP: Regents College Examinations). Regents College Examinations are recognized by the American Council on Education (ACE), Center for Adult Learning and Educational Credentials, for the award of college-level credit. Regents College Examinations in nursing are the only nursing exams approved by ACE.

Regents College does not discriminate on the basis of age, color, religion, creed, disability, marital status, veteran status, national origin, race, gender, or sexual orientation in the educational programs and activities which it operates.

If you have questions about Regents College Examinations (RCEs) that are not answered in this publication, write to the Dean of Assessment, Regents College, 7 Columbia Circle, Albany, NY 12203. For questions about Regents College in general, write to the Dean of Enrollment Management at the same address.

The College Board is a national nonprofit membership association dedicated to preparing, inspiring, and connecting students to college and opportunity. Founded in 1900, the association is composed of more than 3,800 schools, colleges, universities, and other educational organizations. Each year, the College Board serves over three million students and their parents, 22,000 high schools, and 3,500 colleges, through major programs and services in college admission, guidance, assessment, financial aid, enrollment, and teaching and learning. Among its best-known programs are the SAT®, the PSAT/NMSQT™, the Advanced Placement Program® (AP®), and Pacesetter®. The College Board is committed to the principles of equity and excellence, and that commitment is embodied in all of its programs, services, activities, and concerns.

For more information on the College Board, visit our Web site at www.collegeboard.com.

Additional copies of this book (item number 006518) may be obtained by sending $18.95 plus $4.00 for postage and handling to College Board Publications, Dept. GPC0199A, Box 886, New York, NY 10101-0886. Please allow two weeks for delivery. For credit card orders, call 1 (800) 323-7155. Visa, Mastercard, American Express, and Discover are accepted. Purchase orders above $25.00 are accepted.

Copyright © 2000 by Regents College. All rights reserved.

College Board, Advanced Placement Program, AP, College-Level Examination Program, CLEP, Pacesetter, SAT, and the acorn logo are registered trademarks of the College Entrance Examination Board. PSAT/NMSQT is a joint trademark owned by the College Entrance Examination Board and the National Merit Scholarship Corporation. The Regents College globe logo is a registered trademark of Regents College. Microsoft Internet Explorer, PowerPoint, Windows, and Windows NT are registered trademarks of Microsoft Corporation. Adobe and Acrobat are registered trademarks of Adobe Systems Incorporated. Macintosh is a registered trademark of Apple Computer, Inc. Netscape Navigator is a registered trademark of Netscape Communications Corporation. College Video is a trademark of Learningforce, Inc. SuperStar Teachers is a trademark of The Teaching Company.

Library of Congress Catalog Card Number: 00-132932

ISBN: 0-87447-651-8

Printed in the United States of America.

Contents

Introduction 1
For Your Benefit: A Word of Caution 2
Regents College Examinations 3
Registering for and Scheduling a Regents College Examination 5
How to Use the Regents College Examinations Study Guides 6
Guided Learning Packages 8
Regents College Bookstore 9
Computer-Delivered Testing 10
On the Day of Your Exam 11
Test Development and Scoring 12
About Regents College 13
How Regents College Works 15
Sources of Credit 16
Earning Credit Through Distance Learning 17
Degree Programs 18
    General Education Outcomes 18
    Regents College Liberal Arts Degrees 18
    Regents College Nursing Degrees 20
    Regents College Business Degrees 22
    Regents College Technology Degrees 22
How Will a Regents College Degree Help Me? 24
Enrolled Students Reap All the Benefits of Regents College 25
Arts and Sciences Examinations 28
    Abnormal Psychology 29
    Anatomy & Physiology 36
    Ethics: Theory & Practice 51
    Foundations of Gerontology 59
    Life Span Developmental Psychology 72
    Microbiology 88
    Pathophysiology 103
    Psychology of Adulthood & Aging 123
    Research Methods in Psychology 134
    Statistics 148
    World Population 161
    English Composition 171

The Upper-Level Examination Series 179
American Dream 181
History of Nazi Germany 188
Religions of the World 195

Business Examinations 201
Human Resource Management 202
Labor Relations 212
Organizational Behavior 223
Production/Operations Management 233
Business Policy & Strategy 240

Education Examination 249
Reading Instruction in the Elementary School 250

Examinations for the Regents College Degree Programs in Nursing 261
Suggestions for Success on the Written Nursing Examinations 262

Associate Degree Nursing Examinations Series 264
Nursing Concepts 1 (Associate Level) 267
Nursing Concepts 2 (Associate Level) 294
Nursing Concepts 3 (Associate Level) 320
Differences in Nursing Care: Area A (modified) (Associate Level) 359
Differences in Nursing Care: Area B (Associate Level) 373
Differences in Nursing Care: Area C (Associate Level) 396
Occupational Strategies in Nursing (Associate Level) 415

Bacccalaureate Degree Nursing Examinations Series 432
Health Restoration: Area I (Bacccalaureate Level) 434
Health Restoration: Area II (Bacccalaureate Level) 455
Health Support A: Health Promotion & Health Protection
(Bacccalaureate Level) 474
Health Support B: Community Health Nursing (Bacccalaureate Level) . 490
Professional Strategies in Nursing (Bacccalaureate Level) 510
Research in Nursing (Bacccalaureate Level) 525

Classical Curriculum Nursing Examinations 543
Fundamentals of Nursing 544
Maternal & Child Nursing (associate) 564
Maternity Nursing 590
Adult Nursing 593
Maternal & Child Nursing (bacccalaureate) 607
Psychiatric/Mental Health Nursing 619

Answer Rationales 631

Contents

Introduction

With Regents College Examinations, you can *show what you know and earn the college-level credit you deserve.* If you're like many adults today, you've worked hard to get where you are personally and professionally, and are working even harder to improve your situation. You're looking for a way to earn the college degree you've always wanted, and want your learning gained from past training and experiences to apply toward that degree. Or perhaps you are interested in pursuing independent study in a subject for which Regents College Examinations offer credit. Either way, when you're ready, you can earn three or more credit hours with each Regents College Examination you take.

You don't have to be enrolled in Regents College to gain credit by examination. Credit earned by taking Regents College Examinations may be used at more than 900 other colleges and universities in the United States.

Now Regents College Examinations are more accessible than ever before!
Now Regents College Examinations are offered at Sylvan Technology Centers® in the U.S., Canada, American Samoa, Guam, Puerto Rico, Saipan (Northern Mariana Islands), and the Virgin Islands, so you can pick the location nearest you and the time most convenient for you to test. Most Sylvan Technology Centers are available up to six days a week. In February 2000, availability of computer-delivered Regents College Examinations expanded to international sites in Africa, Asia, the Middle East, Europe, and South America. You can call toll free 888-RCEXAMS for the Sylvan Technology Center nearest you, or visit our Web site for a full listing: www.regents.edu/828.htm.

Consider applying your college credits toward a Regents College degree.
Individuals taking examinations with the intention of earning a Regents College degree should consider enrolling in the program of their choice when they begin testing, so that they can take advantage of the myriad of services available to enrolled Regents College students. Degree program information begins on page 18.

For Your Benefit: A Word of Caution

Be sure to work directly with Regents College when considering enrolling in the college or taking Regents College Examinations. There are many for-profit publishers and consultants who claim they can assist you in earning a Regents College degree. Some will tell you that their materials and services will provide you with a special advantage in completing degree requirements. Despite these representations, the materials and services offered by these organizations do not, in fact, provide any special advantage, and you may be charged hundreds, even thousands, of dollars for them. Enrollment in Regents College ensures that you'll receive the professional academic advice and full depth of resources you need to chart a path toward finishing your degree.

Regents College does have an authorized network of affiliated organizations offering assistance and support to our students. The network includes our own Graduate Resource Network and the staffs of our nursing program's Regional Performance Assessment Centers, located throughout the United States. We also have authorized affiliates outside the United States.

If you are approached by or are considering using a non–Regents College organization to help you earn your degree, be sure to ask if this organization is an authorized representative of Regents College. Look for the symbol below and call us to verify the organization's status. Make sure your dollars and time are spent wisely: come directly to the source for your Regents College degree.

Regents College Examinations

Regents College Examinations are college-level examinations that are used by more than 900 colleges and universities in the United States to award credit or advanced placement. Regents College Examinations provide flexible opportunities for adults to demonstrate their college-level knowledge in the arts and sciences, business, education, and nursing. They enable colleges to offer students options such as advanced placement and exemption from course requirements, and give employers a means to allow employees to earn credit toward job advancement or to pursue a college education without interrupting work schedules. Regents College Examinations credit has also been used toward teacher certification or advancement and in fulfillment of civil service qualifications and continuing education requirements.

Regents College Examinations are offered in computer-delivered testing format at Sylvan Technology Centers throughout the United States and in Canada, American Samoa, Guam, Puerto Rico, Saipan (Northern Mariana Islands), and the Virgin Islands. With the new computer-delivered testing system, you can schedule your examinations when it's convenient for you (including Saturdays). Paper-and-pencil testing is available for those examinees who test at international locations or who qualify for reasonable accommodation as defined in the Registration Guide for Regents College Examinations. Regents College Examinations are also available to the U.S. military worldwide through the Defense Activity for Non-Traditional Education Support (DANTES) program.

In addition to our written examinations that are detailed in this book, Regents College offers several other types of assessments:

Performance Examinations in Nursing: The nursing performance examinations are available only to students enrolled in Regents College degree programs in nursing or in programs that have contracted for the use of these examinations. The performance examinations test the ability to perform nursing care activities in actual and simulated clinical settings. They range from one to three days in length and are scheduled individually, usually on weekends. The examinations are administered through Regional Performance Assessment Center offices in New York, California, Georgia, and Wisconsin. The examinations are the Clinical Performance in Nursing Examination (CPNE), taken by all students enrolled in associate-level nursing degree programs and by students enrolled in the baccalaureate degree program who do not possess an RN license, and three examinations required of all students enrolled in the baccalaureate degree programs: Health Assessment Performance Examination (HAPE), Teaching Performance Examination (TPE), and Professional Role Performance Examination (PRPE). For each examination, a comprehensive study guide is provided that describes the examination requirements in detail. Guided learning resources such as videotapes, workshops, and teleconferences are also available for students preparing for the nursing performance exams.

Special Assessment: A Special Assessment is an individualized examination used to assess learning in an area where standardized proficiency examinations do not exist or are not appropriate. It is an evaluation of knowledge and understanding of college-level subject matter. Special Assessments are available only to students enrolled in Regents College, and are usually administered in Albany, New York. Each Special Assessment is individually arranged and its content is mutually agreed upon prior to the evaluation. A student desiring a Special Assessment usually proposes a list of specific courses whose content corresponds to the learning to be assessed. A Special Assessment is generally limited to content taught within a single academic department. Special Assessments are generally conducted before a panel of evaluators who are experts in the subject area being assessed and who usually hold faculty status at a leading college or university. A Special Assessment always includes oral questioning and may also include written sections, demonstrations, performances, and exhibitions of work, depending on the learning being evaluated.

Registering for and Scheduling a Regents College Examination

Registering for your Regents College Examination and scheduling your test date are easier than ever. Just contact us in one of the convenient ways listed below. Once registered, you will be sent an Authorization to Test letter (ATT letter) that will admit you to the Sylvan Technology Center you choose. The ATT letter will indicate your one-year "window," that is, the one-year timeframe during which you can take your exam.

Study at your own pace in your own place, preparing with this guide and other learning resources available from Regents College. When you know when you will be ready to test, schedule your exam at the time and place most convenient for you.

To request information or to register for your exam by phone call toll free 888-RCEXAMS (888-723-9267). From outside the United States dial the international access code and 518-464-8500. TDD is 518-464-8501.

To request information or a registration packet by mail write to:

Regents College
Test Administration
7 Columbia Circle
Albany, NY 12203-5159

You can also e-mail testadmn@regents.edu or fax to 518-464-8777.

Now you can register on-line. Our new Web service allows you to register for your Regents College Examinations at the time and place most convenient for you. Simply log on from the Regents College Web site, 24 hours a day, seven days a week. Follow the simple on-line registration instructions to register for your exams. Be sure to have your Visa, MasterCard, or Discover card on hand to pay for the exams you choose.

To find the Sylvan Technology Center nearest to you and to schedule your exam, call toll free 800-479-5606. Or use the Web: www.regents.edu/100.htm.

How to Use the Regents College Examinations Study Guides

It is a good idea to read the introductory material for the section in which your chosen exam appears. There may be special information about the applicability of the exam to your Regents College degree, advice on sequencing and overlap of exam topics, or information on special features such as the availability of guided learning packages or variations from the standard computer-delivered testing practice.

Each individual exam study guide begins with a display of basic information about the test: the official title and administration number (used when you register for the exam); the number of credits (stated in semester hours) and designation as lower or upper level; type(s) of questions included; and a validity date. It's especially important to check the validity date before you actually register to take the examination. You will want to be sure that you have studied the appropriate material for the exam you will be taking. If some time has elapsed between your purchase of this book and your sitting for the exam, it is possible that the content outline has changed substantially. Feel free to call Regents College to verify the timeliness of your content outline.

How Long Will It Take Me to Study?

Each Regents College Examination is a means to document that you have learned material comparable to the content of one or more college-level courses. To prepare, you should study and review just as you would if you were taking a college course. Remember, as an independent student, you are acting as your own teacher. To fully prepare for a Regents College Examination requires self-direction and discipline.

When preparing for the examination, be certain to allow sufficient time for both study and review. Study is an in-depth activity involving careful reading and reflection. When planning how much time to spend preparing for your examination, consider the time needed both to attend class and to study at home for the equivalent college course(s). College professors advise that in each week of the semester, you should plan on spending three hours studying for every semester hour of credit you will be earning. For example, for a three-credit course, you can expect to study for nine hours in each week of a 15-week semester. Use this system to determine how much time you should plan to spend studying and reviewing for your Regents College Examination.

The Content Outline

At the core of each RCE study guide is a highly detailed content outline. It is important that you structure your study using this content outline along with the recommended resources. If you encounter topics in the content outline that are not covered in the resource you are using, you should supplement your study with one of the additional resources.

The first piece of the content outline for a multiple-choice examination is a content/percent chart that shows the weight of each major content area on the exam. Because of the methods used to determine your grade on the exam, it is not possible to use the content/percent chart to predict the precise number of questions related to each content area. However, the weightings may be useful to you as you allocate your study time.

Most of the content outlines contain many examples to illustrate the types of information you should be studying. Although these examples are very numerous, you should not assume that everything on the exam will come from these examples only. Conversely, you should not expect that every detail you have studied will be directly tested on the exam. Any exam is only a broad sample of all the questions that could be asked about a given subject matter.

Using the Textbooks and Other Study Resources

Every Regents College Examination has recommended books, which may be regular college textbooks, primary and secondary source materials, or publications prepared especially by Regents College staff to support your exam preparation. At times, audiovisual materials or journal articles are among the recommended resources. A category for Additional or Other Resources is sometimes used to list resources that may provide clarification for some of the topics on the content outline or provide enrichment in areas of interest. Check individual listings to determine how many of the resources you should expect to use. The textbooks in each category are listed in alphabetical order, not in order of preference. Many of the study guides provide a brief description of the materials that may assist you in choosing among alternatives.

You should be an active reader of the textbook material. For example, you should preview or survey each chapter; highlight or underline text you believe is important; write questions or comments in the margins; and try to determine how what you are reading relates to the chapter title, section headings, and other organizing elements of the textbook. The more active and involved you are when you study, the more likely you will be not just to retain the information but to better understand and appropriately apply it.

You may find it helpful to study with a partner or a small group. If you cannot locate another person or group to study with, you may be able to find a good listener who will help you reflect on what you have studied. Some publishers sell workbooks or study guides to accompany their textbooks. If the committee developing your examination has evaluated such workbooks, you will find them listed in the study guide. Some students also find it helpful to review notes that they have recorded on cards or audiotapes.

When you feel confident that you understand a content area, review what you have learned. Review involves taking a second look at the material to evaluate how well you have learned it. If you have a study partner, you can review by explaining the content to your partner. Review questions often provided at the end of textbook chapters may be helpful for partner or individual study, as well.

Using the Sample Questions and Rationales

For each multiple-choice examination in this book, sample questions are provided. These sample questions illustrate those typically found on the particular examination. The order in which the questions are presented corresponds with the presentation of their main idea or topic in the content outline. Sample questions are also provided for the extended response (essay) exams. The sample questions are <u>not</u> intended to be a readiness or diagnostic test.

In the last section of this book, you will find the answers (keys) to all multiple-choice sample questions, along with rationales explaining why the key is the correct answer and what is wrong with the other answer choices. In addition, each question is referenced to the content outline. Especially if you chose one of the wrong answers, you may want to return to its section of the content outline for additional study.

Guided Learning Packages

Regents College offers Guided Learning Packages to help prepare for selected exams. Each Guided Learning Package has been carefully developed to provide thorough, integrated learning resources for you. Most of the packages include Course Guides that lead you through the study materials step-by-step with questions, commentary, and examples written by faculty who developed the examinations. These guides also give insight on the examination format and scoring, and list textbooks and associated materials recommended by faculty.

Each Guided Learning Package also includes one or more of the following: books of readings, textbooks, audiotapes, videotapes, computer software, and links to on-line study groups.

Guided Learning Packages are available for these Regents College Examinations:

Upper Level
- American Dream—6 credits
- Ethics: Theory & Practice
- History of Nazi Germany
- Religions of the World
- Research in Nursing
- Research Methods in Psychology
- World Population

Lower Level
- English Composition—6 credits
- Statistics

You can order your Guided Learning Packages from the Regents College Bookstore. Contact information is on the next page.

Regents College Bookstore

Regents College has teamed up with Specialty Books, one of the nation's leading collegiate bookstore operators, to bring the best in bookstore services to its students. The Regents College Bookstore stocks the current editions of recommended textbooks for all examinations. In some cases, current editions will be more recent than those listed in this guide. Regents College-developed course guides, Guided Learning Packages, and books of readings are available only from the Regents College Bookstore. The bookstore also offers resources in areas such as study strategies, personal planning, and stress reduction.

If you're on-line, with a couple of mouse-clicks you can order the textbooks you need—any time of the day, every day of the week—and your order will be shipped within 24 hours. And, if you're taking a course at another college toward your Regents College degree, chances are that our Bookstore will have what you need. After all, Specialty stocks nearly 600,000 titles! Plus, you won't have to wait in line at that campus store.

You'll find more than just textbooks at the Regents College Bookstore. You can also purchase the latest in software at special educational discounts. And if you simply want to sit back and read a bestseller or need a reference book, you'll find them here, too.

To request your free copy of the **Regents College Bookstore flyer,** which provides a full listing of resources available to help you prepare for your exams, call Regents College toll free at 888-647-2388 (at the automated greeting press 1, 2).

Ordering Information

It's easy to contact the Regents College Bookstore. Once you've selected the resources you need, choose the most convenient way to order:

- **To place your order by phone** call the Regents College Bookstore toll free at 800-466-1365. (When calling from Ohio or from outside the United States please call 740-594-2274.) We're available by phone Monday through Friday from 8:30 AM until 8:00 PM, Saturday from 8:00 AM until 12:00 noon, Eastern Time.

- **We're open 24 hours a day via fax, e-mail, and our Web site:**
  Fax toll free to 800-466-7132 (in Ohio and from outside the United States, fax 740-593-3045); e-mail order@specialty-books.com; or order on-line at www.regents.edu/bookstore.htm.

- **To order by mail** please use the order form and instructions in the Regents College Bookstore flyer.

Other Sources of Study Materials

You may also find resource materials in the libraries of colleges, schools of business, schools of nursing, medical schools, and hospitals. Public libraries may have some of the materials or may be able to obtain them through an interlibrary loan program.

Wherever you go for your study resources, be sure that you allow sufficient time to obtain materials and to study before taking any examination.

Computer-Delivered Testing

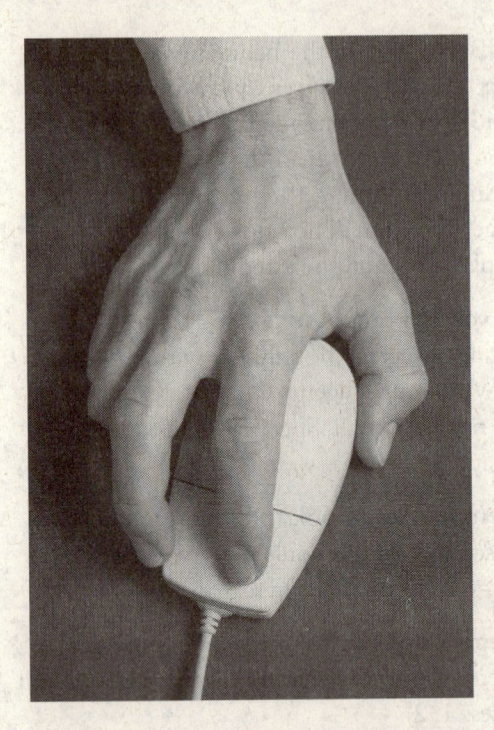

If you are testing at a Sylvan Technology Center, your examination will be delivered by computer. For all of the multiple-choice exams, you will enter your answers on the computer using either the keyboard or the mouse. If you are taking an extended response (essay) or mixed format (multiple-choice and free response) exam, look for further information about computer-delivered testing in the individual exam study guide section.

The system used for our computer-delivered testing is designed to be as user-friendly as possible, even for those with little or no computer experience. Instructions provided on-screen are similar to those you would receive in a paper examination booklet. In addition, before the timed portion of your examination begins, you may choose to complete a tutorial that orients you to the computer testing environment and gives you the opportunity to try each feature before using it in questions that will be scored. You will be instructed in how to use the mouse, the keyboard, and different parts of the screen. We encourage you to take advantage of this tutorial.

A copy of the tutorial that you can actually practice with on your own computer is included on the CD-ROM that came with this book. If you are unable to use Windows® files, but have a Web browser (Netscape or Internet Explorer) installed, you can view (but not practice with) the screens that you will see in the tutorial by following the screenshot links rather than downloading.

On the Day of Your Exam

On the testing day, be sure to allow sufficient time for travel, for parking, and for locating the test center. Be sure to bring current photo identification and your Authorization To Test letter. Consult individual exam guides to determine if you are expected to bring any other materials, such as a calculator or pens or pencils. Be prepared for possible variations in temperature at the test center due to changes in the weather or energy conservation measures.

Three (3) hours of testing time are allowed for each examination. If you are taking a computer-delivered Regents College Examination, you may also spend some time working through the tutorial. Neither the tutorial nor the exit survey (during which you may comment on the experience of preparing for the exam and order further materials) will be counted against your three hour testing time. Time remaining is always displayed in the upper right-hand corner of your computer screen.

Regents College Examinations measure not only your factual knowledge, but also your ability to use that knowledge effectively. For this reason, you should try to prepare for all content areas covered by the test you are taking. The questions on each multiple-choice examination cover a wider range than any one person would usually study. You should not, therefore, expect to be able to answer all the questions on the multiple-choice examinations correctly, but if you are well prepared, you should find you have sufficient time to complete all the questions. If you are taking an extended response examination, it is essential that you think through answers carefully and outline your thoughts before you write. Since you will probably not have time to reconstruct or recopy extended response answers, you should keep track of the time closely and not linger over any one question.

Test Development and Scoring

A committee of faculty determined the content to be tested on each Regents College Examination. Committee members are teaching faculty and practicing professionals in the field covered by the exam. Regents College Assessment Unit staff oversee the technical aspects of test construction in accordance with current professional standards.

Multiple-choice examinations may contain anywhere from 80 to 160 four-option multiple-choice questions, some of which are unscored, experimental questions. Extended response and mixed format examinations will have fewer questions that you must answer at some length. Since you will not be able to tell which questions are experimental, you should do your best on all of them. Scores are based on ability level as defined in the item response theory (IRT) method of examination development, rather than simply your total number of correct answers. Your score will be reported as a letter grade. Your grade report will also include a bar graph that indicates where your score falls on a grade scale of A to F. The location of the score within the grade zone shows how close you come to the minimum or maximum required for that grade.

Regents College awards credit for scores that correspond to or exceed a letter grade of C. Most other institutions will grant credit when the content of a test matches or closely parallels the content of courses that the institution offers. Colleges are not required to grant the amount of credit suggested in the individual exam's study guide. Faculty of the appropriate college academic department decide whether and how much credit to grant. Colleges may request additional proof of competency in a subject area. For instance, faculty members may want students to present evidence that they can prepare a research paper, complete a laboratory assignment, or take a performance test before granting credit. If you wish to transfer from one college to another, the second college may reevaluate the credit being transferred in, including that awarded for proficiency examinations.

Institutions also use Regents College Examinations as a basis for assigning students to course sections, for placing students at appropriate levels in a curriculum, for waiving degree or elective requirements, and for evaluating the effectiveness of programs and curricula. High school students may use Regents College Examinations to earn advanced placement in college. Regents College Examinations should not be used for admission or selection purposes.

About Regents College

Founded on the belief that *what you know is more important than where or how you learned it,* Regents College has been providing access to higher education for nearly three decades. We offer a flexible, affordable way to earn a respected Regents College degree.

Regents College was established in 1971 by the New York State Board of Regents as its external degree program. In 1998, the Board of Regents granted the college a charter to operate as a private, independent college. All academic programs are registered (i.e., approved) by the New York State Education Department. The college is governed by a board of trustees composed of individuals prominent in the fields of business, education, and the professions.

Regents College is accredited by the Commission on Higher Education of the Middle States Association of Colleges and Schools, 3624 Market Street, Philadelphia, PA 19104, 215-662-5606. The Commission on Higher Education is an institutional accrediting agency recognized by the U.S. Secretary of Education and the Council for Higher Education Accreditation (CHEA).

The associate and baccalaureate degree programs in nursing at Regents College are accredited by the National League for Nursing Accrediting Commission (NLNAC), 61 Broadway, New York, NY 10006, 800-669-9656. The NLNAC is a specialized accrediting agency recognized by the U.S. Secretary of Education.

The baccalaureate degree programs in electronics engineering technology and nuclear engineering technology are accredited by the Technology Accreditation Commission of the Accreditation Board for Engineering and Technology (TAC/ABET), 111 Market Place, Suite 1050, Baltimore, MD 21202, 410-347-7700. TAC/ABET is a specialized accrediting agency recognized by the U.S. Secretary of Education.

Regents College Examinations are recognized by the American Council on Education (ACE), Center for Adult Learning and Educational Credentials, for the award of college-level credit. Regents College Examinations in nursing are the only nursing exams approved by ACE.

The faculty of Regents College are drawn from many colleges and universities as well as from industry and the professions. They establish and monitor academic policies and standards, determine degree requirements and the ways in which credit can be earned, develop the content for all examinations, review the records of students to verify their degree requirement completion, and recommend degree conferral to the Board of Trustees.

Our Mission Statement

Regents College affirms that what individuals know is more important than how or where they acquired the knowledge, and believes that students can demonstrate their knowledge and competencies through a variety of methods. The College exists to advance the learning of students, primarily adults, who for personal, economic, family, or other reasons, choose to pursue their education in a flexible, self-paced manner. While remaining open to all, the College ensures academic quality through rigorous programs, student-centered advisement, and careful assessment. By offering high-quality innovative educational opportunities to those desiring an alternative to traditional institutions of higher education, the College strives to broaden individual horizons, develop intellectual autonomy and respect for inquiry, expand career interests and options, and inspire a commitment to lifelong learning.

Regents College exists to increase access to education with excellence and economy, particularly for those historically underserved by higher education. The College seeks to meet the needs of a pluralistic society that is increasingly dependent upon an informed and educated citizenry. The College is an international resource and, by example and by advocacy, a major force in expanding access to higher education. As a leader in innovative education, the College works in active partnership with other colleges and universities, employers and organizations to remove barriers to educational opportunity. The College complements the academic offerings of more conventional institutions of higher learning in the interest of equity, economy, and efficiency.

How Regents College Works

Regents College helps you apply credit from many traditional and nontraditional sources toward a respected degree. More than 83,000 satisfied graduates from every state in the U.S. and from many countries around the world have earned a Regents College degree without residency requirements. No matter where you live, no matter how busy you are, Regents College offers the flexibility you need to finish your college degree. We offer adult learners 32 highly respected degree programs in Business, Liberal Arts, Nursing, and Technology, including a Master of Science in Nursing and a Master of Arts degree in Liberal Studies.

Regents College Provides Many Avenues to Reach Your Degree Goal

If you've started college coursework, but never had the chance to complete your degree, Regents College gives you affordable options and the opportunity to apply credits you've already earned. Our advisors can provide you with a credit evaluation to determine how the credits you've already earned may apply toward your degree, such as:

- College-level proficiency exams, including Regents College Examinations, CLEP®, and DANTES
- Regular classroom courses taken at regionally accredited colleges or universities in the U.S. or abroad
- Distance courses, telecourses, on-line computer and video courses
- Portfolio assessment of experiential learning
- Credit from ACE-evaluated training completed on the job, in the military or other settings approved by the American Council on Education
- Credit that other colleges may reject due to residency requirements. *Regents College has no residency requirement.*

Find Out How Close You Are to Earning a Regents College Degree

The Regents College concept is not for everyone, and you may already be in a program that works well for you. But if the opportunity to earn your degree *at your own pace and in your own place,* outside a traditional college setting, appeals to your lifestyle today, we encourage you to consider Regents College. Find out how close you are to earning the degree you have always wanted. **Call toll free 888-647-2388** (at the prompt press 2, 7) to speak with an experienced Admissions Counselor. Or e-mail admissions@regents.edu.

Sources of Credit

When you enroll in Regents College, you receive the most current edition of *A Student Guide to Credit by Examination at Regents College,* a publication that lists examinations from the following sources and briefly identifies how they might apply to your degree program:

- Regents College Examinations
- College-Level Examination Program® (CLEP)
- Defense Activity for Non-Traditional Education Support (DANTES)
- Graduate Record Examinations Subject Tests (GREs)
- Advanced Placement Program® (AP®) Examinations
- Ohio University Examinations
- University of North Carolina Examinations
- New York University Foreign Language Proficiency Tests
- Thomas Edison College Examination Program (TECEP)

A copy of the 1999–2000 guide is provided on the CD-ROM that came with this book.

In addition, Regents College grants credit for all examinations recommended by the American Council on Education (ACE), Center for Adult Learning and Educational Credentials. These are listed in the annual ACE *Guide to Educational Credit by Examination.*

Business, industry, military, and other noncollegiate training programs reviewed by the ACE College Credit Recommendation Service (formerly called ACE/PONSI) are also a source of Regents College credit.

Transfer of degree-level credit from regionally accredited colleges and universities includes not only traditional on-campus course credits but also many computer and video courses, telecourses, and independent study programs that are college based but delivered at a distance. See page 17 for information on our DistanceLearn database. Before you enroll for a college course, whether on campus or at a distance, check with your academic adviser to be sure that the college and course are approved for credit toward your Regents College degree program.

Earning Credit Through Distance Learning

Distance learning courses and proficiency examinations are challenging and rewarding ways to earn college-level credit. These courses and examinations provide a means for you to study at your own pace and in your own place, while continually moving toward the college degree you have always wanted.

Regents College lets you apply credit you have already earned at other accredited colleges and universities toward our degree programs. We also accept credit earned through accredited distance learning courses and examinations. More than 75 percent of Regents College students have used proficiency examinations to complete various portions of their degree requirements. The average graduate earns more than 40 credits from proficiency tests. We offer our own series of college-level proficiency examinations (Regents College Examinations) in business, liberal arts and sciences, education, technology, and nursing subjects, at both the lower and upper levels. This guide contains detailed information about the 40 undergraduate-level exams in business, arts and sciences, education, and nursing. Information on technology exams and exams in support of our graduate programs must be obtained separately from the college.

To help you locate distance learning courses and examinations that meet your needs, Regents College provides students with **DistanceLearn**, a searchable computer database of college-level learning opportunities available at a distance. If you are interested in a particular subject area and can't find a course locally, or if you need to earn credit but can't (or choose not to) attend a class, **DistanceLearn** may provide the answer. Over 10,000 distance courses and examinations are included in the **DistanceLearn** database. These courses and examinations are delivered through video, audio, computer, and print. They are catalogued by subject, level, delivery system, and key words, making the program easy to use. The entire **DistanceLearn** database has been incorporated into an on-line resource developed in partnership with Peterson's, the country's leading education information provider. You can link to LifeLongLearning.com[SM] from the Regents College Web site.

Degree Programs

General Education Outcomes

We expect that as a Regents College graduate, you will be able to

- Read analytically and critically in a range of fields.
- Write clear, grammatical, and effective prose.
- Think critically in making judgments and identifying and posing solutions to problems.
- Develop cohesive arguments using appropriate supporting evidence.
- Interpret events using more than one perspective, such as historical, economic, biological, social, or global.
- Explain the role of culture in shaping diverse societies.
- Identify elements of artistic and creative expression.
- Apply knowledge of mathematics/natural sciences in different contexts.
- Demonstrate an awareness of the ethical implications of actions.

Regents College Liberal Arts Degrees

Regents College liberal arts programs offer a range of major concentrations similar to those offered at many traditional institutions. Our faculty believe the primary purpose of an undergraduate education is to expose students to a broad vision of human experience and to help them gain a full and rich understanding of the complexity of human life. A breadth of academic experience enriches you, allowing you to become a more informed citizen of an increasingly complex world. It enables you to communicate more effectively, think more creatively, and demonstrate increased purpose. Such studies enhance awareness of the ethical consequences of actions and a commitment to learning as a lifelong endeavor. An undergraduate education will assist you in developing the skills to attain the highest level of accomplishment in your career and personal life.

Each undergraduate liberal arts degree program requires the completion of general education requirements in the arts and sciences. Beyond these requirements, each degree program allows for additional study in the arts and sciences and for professional applied study. On the baccalaureate level, you will explore two subject areas or disciplines in greater depth.

Choose from these Liberal Arts degree programs
Associate in Arts
Associate in Science
Bachelor of Arts

Bachelor of Science
Master of Arts degree in Liberal Studies

Baccalaureate Concentrations
- Area Studies
- Biology
- Chemistry
- Communication
- Economics
- Geography
- Geology
- History
- Literature in English
- Mathematics
- Music
- Philosophy
- Physics
- Political Science
- Psychology
- Sociology
- World Language and Literature

Master of Arts Degree in Liberal Studies (MLS)

Earned at a distance, the 33-credit Master of Arts degree in Liberal Studies (MLS) provides access to interdisciplinary study in the arts and sciences through a flexible program of study delivered through assessment, guided learning, and technology. Students enjoy a robust course of learning designed for serious, graduate-level learners with an abiding interest in achieving a depth of understanding of our world and the people who inhabit it.

Students start with a strong interdisciplinary core, comprising two 6-credit courses. They build on the core with individualized study based on their special interests, satisfying the 15-credit requirement through a combination of coursework taken at other institutions, independent learning contracts with Regents College faculty, assessments of graduate-level learning acquired through life experience or nontraditional means, and even credits previously earned. This study is capped off with a thesis that includes research into a focus topic.

If you would like to know more about the program and how it works, call toll free 888-647-2388 (at the prompt press 2, 7) or e-mail mls@regents.edu.

Regents College Nursing Degrees

The Regents College Nursing programs are designed specifically for adult learners who have significant health care clinical experience. Our associate and baccalaureate nursing programs enable you to learn independently, at your own pace and in your own place, through the use of guided study materials, on-line discussion, and advisers available by phone, mail, or e-mail. You are then provided with the opportunity to demonstrate nursing knowledge and clinical proficiency through a series of written and clinical performance nursing examinations.

We encourage you to review the information in this book thoroughly, write down your questions, and then call Regents College and make an appointment to speak with a prospective student adviser. This process will help to ensure that Regents College is the right choice for you.

Goals of the Regents College Nursing programs

- To provide comprehensive professionally accredited degree programs in nursing in which the requirements can be met by objective documentation of learning.

- To provide a foundation for lifelong learning.

- To ensure academically sound nursing programs through the incorporation of research findings into the development of academic programs.

- To provide valid and reliable performance measures of clinical competency in nursing.

- To provide direction and focus for the program of learning through program objectives, specific degree requirements, related study guides, and other program materials.

- To provide academic and career planning advisement to both enrolled and prospective students in nursing.

- To provide access to qualified students from diverse backgrounds by removing barriers to education and providing opportunities for students with disabilities.

- To create and implement innovative learning opportunities to assist students in earning Regents College nursing degrees.

- To meet the needs of health care providers in an environment of changing opportunities for practice through the development of distance certificate programs.

- To serve as a resource to other educational and health care institutions by assisting them in the development of competency-based evaluation models.

- To disseminate research findings to appropriate audiences.

- To engage in development activities designed to generate funding in support of nursing programs.

Choose from these Nursing degree programs
- Associate in Applied Science (Nursing)
- Associate in Science (Nursing)
- Bachelor of Science in Nursing
- Master of Science (Nursing)

Nursing Minors available in the BSN program:
- Human Resource Management
- Biology
- Psychology
- Sociology

Other programs of interest to health care professionals:

Home Health Nursing Certificate (HHCC): This program is designed to assist registered nurses in making the transition from hospital care to home-based care. The program includes self-study modules and an 80-hour precepted clinical experience.

Graduate Programs in Nursing and Health Care: Move into the next generation of health care, updating your knowledge of clinical systems management and health care informatics with two new graduate programs from Regents College, the most experienced provider of nursing education offered at a distance.

The new 44-credit Master of Science, Nursing and the 17-credit Certificate Program in Health Care Informatics are forward-thinking programs developed to provide health care professionals with a firm grounding in theory and technology. Both "next generation" curricula, developed by many of the most published and respected names in the field, are delivered via computer-based Guided Learning programs so you can work from home at your own pace. The programs are delivered almost exclusively on-line.

For more information contact a Regents College Admissions Counselor about these state-of-the-art programs:

- Master of Science, Nursing, with a major in clinical systems management
- RN to MSN program
- Certificate in Health Care Informatics for health care professionals with a baccalaureate degree in any field.

Call toll free 888-647-2388 (at the prompt press 2, 7) or e-mail msn@regents.edu.

Regents College Business Degrees

Unlike traditional business degree programs, the Regents College business programs allow you to choose to meet your business component requirements, and all of the arts and sciences course requirements, by passing college-level proficiency exams rather than attending classes. Examinations are both cost-effective and time-saving, offering you a distinct advantage if you have significant work or life experience in a test subject area, if you live in a location where college-level course offerings are limited or nonexistent, or if your ACE College Credit Recommendation Service (formerly ACE/PONSI) courses do not fully meet your degree requirements. Business component requirements can also be fulfilled with coursework, as long as that coursework has been completed within 20 years of your enrollment. If you prefer to pursue independent study and pace your degree studies according to your needs, the Regents College business program will work well for you.

Choose from these Business degree programs
 Associate in Applied Science in Administrative/Management Studies★
 Associate in Science in Business (fully articulates into a Regents College baccalaureate degree)
 Bachelor of Science in Accounting
 Bachelor of Science in Accounting with a NYS CPA Track
 Bachelor of Science in Finance
 Bachelor of Science in International Business
 Bachelor of Science in Management of Human Resources
 Bachelor of Science in Management Information Systems
 Bachelor of Science in Marketing
 Bachelor of Science in Operations Management

 ★These degree programs are designed specifically to meet the needs of servicemembers by formally recognizing their military training for academic credit.

Regents College Technology Degrees

Regents College offers technology degree programs that enable students to earn credit and complete degree requirements at a distance, fostering enhanced career opportunities for motivated individuals while increasing opportunities for professional organizations and corporations to develop a more technologically literate work force. The Regents College technology curricula are rigorous, designed to provide both breadth and depth of content. In order to ensure currency in a field that changes at varying rates, each technology degree program has specific time limits applied to certain technology component courses submitted for transfer credit. We will help you identify and evaluate college-level learning you have already acquired and develop a plan to obtain the additional credits you need.

In addition to our Regents College Examinations appropriate for completing general education requirements or electives, Regents College now offers examinations in Computer Technology. The CIS degree can now be completed entirely by exam. And for the IT professional, academic credit is being awarded for certification exams like MCSE and CompTIA. Some of the Technology degrees <u>cannot</u> be completed entirely by exam. We strongly recommend that you contact an admissions counselor for specific details.

Choose from these Technology degree programs

Associate in Applied Science in Aviation Studies★
Associate in Applied Science in Technical Studies (with Specialty)★
Associate in Occupational Studies in Aviation★
Associate in Science in Computer Software
Associate in Science in Electronics Technology
Associate in Science in Nuclear Technology
Associate in Science in Technology (with Specialty)
Bachelor of Science in Computer Information Systems
Bachelor of Science in Computer Technology
Bachelor of Science in Electronics Engineering Technology
Bachelor of Science in Nuclear Engineering Technology
Bachelor of Science in Technology (with Specialty)

Specialty choices:
  Chemical Technologies
  Computer Technologies
  Electromechanical Technologies
  Electronic/Instrumentation Technologies
  Manufacturing Technologies
  Mechanical/Welding Technologies
  Nuclear Technologies
  Optical Technologies

★These degree programs are designed specifically to meet the needs of servicemembers by formally recognizing their military training for academic credit.

The baccalaureate degree programs in electronics engineering technology and nuclear engineering technology are accredited by the Technology Accreditation Commission of the Accreditation Board for Engineering and Technology (TAC/ABET), a specialized accrediting agency recognized by the U.S. Secretary of Education.

How Will a Regents College Degree Help Me?

A Regents College degree can help you get ahead in your career, increase your salary, boost your self-confidence, prepare for success in graduate school, and achieve personal satisfaction in completing what you started.

You could be one of the more than 5,000 adults who graduate from Regents College each year, motivated individuals who achieve their goals and move forward in their lives. A recent survey of the college's baccalaureate degree graduates showed that 38 percent went on immediately to graduate and professional schools. Over 250 graduate institutions have admitted Regents College graduates. These include many of the most competitive and prestigious schools in the country, among them Columbia University, Harvard University, Ohio State University, University of California–Los Angeles, and Yale University. Ninety-five percent of graduate programs in nursing accept Regents College graduates.

Many of our graduates say that the independence and motivation required for success at Regents College proved to be equally valuable assets for success in graduate school. A large number of graduates report that through their Regents College studies they have enjoyed significant intellectual growth, enhanced their critical thinking abilities, improved their oral and written communication skills, and experienced personal growth and fulfillment. Workers and employers alike believe that the Regents College experience provides excellent preparation for jobs and career growth.

Enrolled Students Reap All the Benefits of Regents College

Enrolled students have the benefit of ongoing team advising; support from peers, alumni, and faculty; and access to information not available to those who are not enrolled. For example, the enrolled student Web page is a great place for you to learn first about new services, new sources of credit, changes in academic policies, and other vital information, all designed to help you meet your educational goals and complete your Regents College degree.

Most important, enrolled students are assigned a team of advisers to help you complete your degree in the most efficient manner. If you are like most of the students enrolled at Regents College, time is your most precious commodity, followed by money. Your team of advisers makes sure the courses and examinations you intend to take will count toward your degree. In this way you don't take time out of your schedule or dollars out of your pocket unnecessarily.

Enrolled Students Gain Access to the Electronic Peer Network

Enrolled Regents College students are eligible to join the Regents College Electronic Peer Network (EPN). The EPN is a Web-based environment that enables enrolled students to interact academically and socially. In establishing the EPN, Regents College has acknowledged the obstacles faced by adults who must complete challenging degree programs while continuing to meet commitments at work, at home, and in their communities. We know that peer collaboration and support can play a significant role in overcoming these obstacles while enriching and deepening learning. As an EPN member, you will be able to locate a study partner, join an on-line study group for your exam, chat in real time with other students or join a facilitated chat, and access other resources that may be helpful to students preparing for Regents College Examinations. Enrolled students can join the EPN by visiting the Regents College home page (www.regents.edu) and clicking on Electronic Peer Network.

EPN Components: Following is an overview of the components of the EPN.

- **What's New**
  This component of the EPN is used by the Office of Learning Services to communicate new information about the EPN. Check this area whenever you arrive at the EPN homepage, as it is updated weekly.

- **Discussion Groups**
  EPN discussion groups allow members to participate in a variety of threaded discussions related to examinations or special interests. While these discussion groups are primarily peer oriented, Regents College staff members monitor the groups periodically and comment on discussions or answer students' questions as time and duties permit. Sample discussion groups include **Ethics: Theory & Practice, English Composition, HATPE, CPNE, CLEP Examinations,** and **International Students.**

- **Chat Rooms**

    Chat rooms enable students to participate in real-time discussions with other students anytime and with Regents College staff during scheduled facilitated chat sessions. Chat transcripts are provided for review for anyone who can't participate in real time. Students can link directly to the chat schedule and transcripts from the EPN homepage.

- **Student Directory**

    The student directory is a searchable database that will help you contact other EPN members with similar interests. Students can search the directory to find e-mail addresses and other contact information about students who are willing to share information about exam preparation, give you study tips, or discuss shared interests with you.

- **Book Exchange**

    The book exchange is used by EPN members to buy, sell, and trade used study materials such as textbooks, videotapes, and calculators. As Regents College provides the EPN only as a clearinghouse, students who post messages on the book exchange are responsible for carrying out the details of their transactions.

- **Career Resources**

    Regents College wants to assist you with your career development by providing resources to help you explore your career possibilities. Career Resources provides information on self-assessment, career exploration, graduate school, and the job search. Links to information about writing résumés and cover letters are included.

- **Web Resources**

    Regents College believes that its students benefit significantly from the convenient availability of a wide range of on-line resources. Visit Web Resources for links to on-line writing labs, library services, and links to assist in preparation for Regents College examinations, CLEP, GRE, and DANTES information.

- **DistanceLearn Center**

    The DistanceLearn Center assists students by helping them locate distance courses, review student evaluations of distance courses, and use a variety of distance learning resources. The DistanceLearn database compiles information on available distance courses and proficiency examinations from regionally accredited colleges and universities. Students enrolled in Regents degree programs take advantage of the database of 12,000 courses/exams through searches executed by their advisors and then read student reviews. Resources such as "How to Study Independently" will be available also.

- **EPN Photo Gallery**

    Our gallery contains photographs of Regents College staff who are actively involved in supporting students on the EPN. The Photo Gallery also features such Regents events as commencement exercises.

- **Guided Learning Packages**

    Guided learning packages have been developed to help you successfully prepare for Regents College Examinations. Students can order selected guided learning packages which include such resources as textbooks, study guides, books of readings, CD-ROMs, computer disks, videotapes or audiocassettes, and special equipment.

- **New Materials**

    Students can visit this area to preview or test new Regents College products under development to help students prepare for our examinations. EPN members can try out the new guided learning package for the Regents College Examination in **Research Methods in Psychology,** which includes 140 self-test questions.

- **Frequently Asked Questions (FAQ)**

    Use this area to search for answers to commonly asked questions regarding the EPN. Whether you have a technical question or wonder how to get started on the EPN, click on FAQ for help.

- **EPN Newsletter**

    EPN members are welcome to subscribe to a newsletter called *EPN News* that students receive by e-mail. New activities, updates, services, and products are featured in the new electronic newsletter.

Technical Requirements

Students will need to meet the following minimum technical requirements to take advantage of all the features of the EPN:

- A computer running Windows 95, 98, or NT, or Mac OS 7.5 or greater
- A connection to the Internet (28.8 or higher modem speed recommended)
- A graphical Web browser (Netscape 3.x, 4.x, or newer versions, Internet Explorer 4.x or newer versions, etc.)

How to Join the EPN

Currently enrolled Regents College students and alumni can join the EPN by clicking on a button on the Web site and answering a series of questions. Your registration will be processed immediately.

NOTE: If you experience any problems with the registration process, send an e-mail to: epn_admin@regents.edu.

If you would like to comment on the contents of the EPN, send an e-mail to the Office of Learning Services at epn@regents.edu.

Arts and Sciences Examinations

General education requirements—central to the curriculum of most U.S. undergraduate degree programs—ensure that you have a good foundation in the natural sciences, the humanities, and the social sciences. In addition, colleges may expect you to demonstrate quantitative skills, to be able to communicate effectively in writing and speech, and to understand the evolution of Western culture and the relationship of its development with that of other ethnic and cultural groups. The Regents College Examinations in the Arts & Sciences category can help you to fulfill such general education requirements.

In the **humanities**, you consider the nature, meaning, and value of human existence in subjects such as art, comparative literature, drama, English, foreign language, music, philosophy, and religion. Among the Regents College Examinations that may meet humanities requirements are American Dream, Ethics: Theory & Practice, English Composition, and Religions of the World.

In the **social sciences**, you consider human behavior and interaction in subjects such as anthropology, economics, geography, government, history, political science, psychology, and sociology. The Regents College Examinations program is especially rich in this area, with **four** psychology examinations (Abnormal Psychology, Life Span Developmental Psychology, Psychology of Adulthood & Aging, and Research Methods in Psychology) and the following additional examinations: American Dream, Foundations of Gerontology, History of Nazi Germany, and World Population. Some colleges, including Regents College, will also accept our Organizational Behavior examination (listed in the Business section) as fulfilling a social science requirement.

In the **natural sciences**, you analyze, measure, and investigate the natural world in subjects such as biology, chemistry, geology, mathematics, and physics. There are three Regents College Examinations in the natural sciences: Anatomy & Physiology, Microbiology, and Pathophysiology. Our Statistics examination may meet a mathematics or quantitative reasoning requirement and/or fulfill the statistics requirement for students majoring in sociology, psychology, or nursing.

As you can see, then, the group of examinations in this section offers an enormous breadth of study for the adult learner.

Study Guide
Abnormal Psychology (459)

Credit Hours: 3 **Credit Level:** Upper
Question Type(s): Multiple-choice

The information in this study guide is valid until Summer 2001.
If you will be taking the examination after that date, be sure to check for a new edition of this guide before you complete your preparation for the exam.

General Description of the Examination

The Regents College Examination in Abnormal Psychology is based on material typically taught in an undergraduate course in abnormal psychology. A knowledge of concepts usually learned in an introductory psychology course is assumed.

The examination tests for knowledge and understanding of the historical background of abnormal psychology, major conceptualizations in the field, and the nature and descriptions of psychological disorders, as well as their definitions, classification, etiology, and major treatments.

Content Outline

Content Area	Percent of Examination
I. Introduction and Basic Issues	25%
II. Disorders	60%
III. Treatment, Prevention, and Legal Issues	15%
	Total 100%

I. Introduction and Basic Issues (25%)

A. **Historical development**
   1. History of abnormal psychology from early demonology through humanitarian reforms
   2. The mental health professions

B. **Definitions and changing conceptions of "abnormal" behavior**

C. **Research approaches in abnormal psychology (for example: methods, strengths and weaknesses, applications, interpretations, and ethical issues)**

D. Theories, paradigms, and perspectives
1. Biological
2. Psychodynamic
3. Behavioral/learning
4. Cognitive
5. Humanistic/existential
6. Sociocultural
7. Diathesis-stress

E. Classifications and diagnoses
1. Current classifications: DSM-IV (1994) Multiaxial diagnosis
2. Issues in classification (for example: reliability, validity, problems of labeling)

F. Assessment
1. Interviewing
2. Psychological testing
3. Behavioral and cognitive assessments
4. Biological, medical, psychophysiological, and neuropsychological assessments
5. Issues in assessment (for example: reliability, validity, bias)

II. Disorders (60%)

Note: You should be familiar with descriptions, current and historical views of major causal factors, and treatments for the disorders listed in this section.

A. Anxiety disorders
1. Panic disorder and agoraphobia
2. Specific and social phobias
3. Obsessive-compulsive disorder
4. Post-traumatic stress disorder
5. Generalized anxiety disorder

B. Mood disorders
1. Depressive disorders
2. Bipolar disorders
3. Suicide

C. Somatoform disorders (for example: conversion disorder, hypochondriasis, somatization disorder)

D. Dissociative disorders (for example: amnesia, fugue, dissociative identity disorder, depersonalization disorder)

E. Psychological factors affecting physical conditions (for example: essential hypertension, asthma)

F. Eating disorders (for example: anorexia nervosa, bulimia nervosa)

G. Sexual and gender identity disorders
1. Gender identity disorders (for example: transsexualism)
2. Paraphilias (for example: exhibitionism, fetishism, transvestism)
3. Sexual dysfunctions

H. **Substance use disorders**
   1. Dependence on and abuse of alcohol
   2. Dependence on and abuse of other substances (for example: tranquilizers, narcotics

I. **Psychotic disorders**
   1. Schizophrenia (including etiological models, subtypes, positive and negative symptomology, genetic and environmental influences, and social functioning)
   2. Delusional disorders
   3. Other (for example: schizoaffective disorder, brief psychotic disorder)

J. **Delirium, dementia, amnestic and other cognitive disorders**

K. **Life-span developmental disorders**
   1. Disorders that are usually first evident in childhood and adolescence (for example: autistic disorder, attention-deficit hyperactivity disorder, conduct disorder)
   2. Mental retardation
   3. Problems associated with aging

L. **Factitious disorders**

M. **Personality disorders**
   1. Cluster A: eccentric types (paranoid, schizoid, schizotypal)
   2. Cluster B: erratic types (antisocial, borderline, narcissistic, histrionic)
   3. Cluster C: fearful types (avoidant, dependent, obsessive-compulsive)
   4. Issues in diagnosis (for example: gender or class bias in classification)

III. Treatment, Prevention, and Legal Issues (15%)

A. **Approaches to treatment** (for example: psychoanalytic; cognitive/behavioral; social learning; humanistic/existential; group, marital, and family therapy; biological)

B. **Issues of treatment** (for example: efficacy, effectiveness, empirical validation, cultural and ethnic factors)

C. **Specific community approaches**
   1. Prevention and crisis intervention
   2. Deinstitutionalization and community mental health

D. **Legal and ethical issues**
   1. The law and abnormal behavior (for example: commitment, the insanity defense)
   2. Ethical issues (for example: the right to treatment, informed consent, confidentiality)

Sample Questions: Abnormal Psychology

1. The idea that intellectual genius represents abnormality illustrates which definition of abnormality?
   1) medical
   2) personal discomfort
   3) social
   4) statistical

2. Which research method in abnormal psychology should be used for identifying cause and effect relationships?
   1) epidemiological
   2) correlational
   3) experimental
   4) observational

3. Which concept is central to understanding the relationship between the psychodynamic therapist and the patient?
   1) anxiety threshold
   2) transference
   3) empathy
   4) response hierarchy

4. According to Sigmund Freud's psychoanalytic paradigm, what is the source of most of the important determinants of human behavior?
   1) conscious
   2) preconscious
   3) superego
   4) unconscious

5. Which course of action by a therapist illustrates a cognitive-behavioral approach?
   1) encouraging the client to explore early-life experiences
   2) helping the client to change mistaken assumptions and increase self-efficacy
   3) providing the client with insight about unconscious motives
   4) using hypnosis to help the client forget painful life experiences

6. What is the essential feature of borderline personality disorder?
   A pervasive pattern of
   1) instability in a variety of areas
   2) inflexibility and perfectionism
   3) constant attention seeking
   4) callousness in interpersonal relationships

7. A person is diagnosed as having an avoidant personality disorder, a major depression, and hypertension. How would these diagnoses be recorded using the multiaxial system of DSM?

	Axis I	Axis II	Axis III
1)	avoidant personality	major depression	hypertension
2)	major depression	avoidant personality	no diagnosis
3)	major depression	avoidant personality	hypertension
4)	hypertension	major depression	avoidant personality

Sample Questions: Abnormal Psychology

8. How were items for the clinical scales of the Minnesota Multiphasic Personality Inventory (MMPI) ultimately selected?
    Item selection was based on
    1) the judgments made by clinicians familiar with the symptoms included in the diagnostic categories.
    2) how well items differentiated between groups of individuals without psychiatric diagnoses and a group with a specific diagnosis.
    3) specific theories of personality related to behavioral traits.
    4) the diagnostic criteria of the DSM.

9. What is the most common complication of panic disorder?
    1) agoraphobia
    2) cardiovascular disease
    3) bipolar disorder
    4) migraine headache

10. A child acquires a phobia after being bitten by a dog. The initial fear most likely developed through which process?
    1) classical conditioning
    2) operant conditioning
    3) cognitive dissonance
    4) social learning

11. What is a persistent, irrational thought or impulse that is very difficult to dismiss or control?
    1) a compulsion
    2) a delusion
    3) an illusion
    4) an obsession

12. What is the key feature of conversion disorder and somatization disorder?
    1) depression
    2) dissociation
    3) loose associations
    4) physical symptoms

13. How is dissociative identity disorder best defined?
    1) two or more loosely organized, incomplete personalities or personality states
    2) two or more distinct, well-developed personalities or personality states
    3) two or more personalities, each with well-developed thought processes, but loosely organized emotional processes
    4) two or more personalities, each with well-developed emotional processes, but loosely organized thought processes

14. Compared to patients with hypochondriasis, patients with conversion disorders are likely to have which manifestation?
    1) heightened awareness of new symptoms
    2) preoccupation with bodily processes
    3) specific physical symptoms
    4) fear of real illness

Sample Questions: Abnormal Psychology

15. An individual leaves a family without warning, moves to a new town, assumes a new identity, and takes a new name. Once the family locates the individual, the individual denies ever having known them. This behavior is consistent with which diagnosis?
    1) depersonalization disorder
    2) dissociative fugue
    3) somnambulism
    4) dissociative identity disorder

16. Which statement exemplifies depersonalization?
    1) "I sometimes feel like I'm not in control of myself, like I'm just watching myself from the outside."
    2) "I hear voices telling me what to do. I'm afraid I will die if I don't obey the voices."
    3) "Life is so impersonal and meaningless that I feel like ending it all."
    4) "I secretly think I was born into the body of the wrong sex."

17. Which stress-related disorder is most common among children?
    1) asthma
    2) hypertension
    3) migraine headaches
    4) ulcer

18. What personality pattern is seemingly shared by men who engage in voyeurism or exhibitionism?
    1) fearfulness, social immaturity, and avoidance of direct social contact
    2) deep-seated rage directed at women, with wishes for revenge
    3) latent homosexual strivings
    4) great social confidence and many brief sexual encounters

19. A male client experiences recurrent urges to wear women's clothing and sexual arousal when wearing women's clothing. These symptoms are most consistent with which diagnosis?
    1) transsexualism
    2) hypoactive sexual desire disorder
    3) frotteurism
    4) transvestic fetishism

20. Which is the most effective treatment for bipolar disorder?
    1) implosion
    2) lithium carbonate
    3) psychoanalysis
    4) electroconvulsive therapy (ECT)

21. A person says that "thoughts are leaking out of his neuro-hole." Which characteristic of schizophrenia is this person displaying?
    The person is
    1) exhibiting overinclusiveness.
    2) expressing a delusion of grandeur.

3) using a neologism.
4) experiencing thought broadcasting.

22. Low-birth-weight infants and children who are malnourished are at higher risk for which condition?
    1) separation anxiety disorder
    2) conduct disorder
    3) anorexia nervosa
    4) mental retardation

23. Which symptom would a person who has Alzheimer's disease be most likely to display?
    1) delirium
    2) delusions
    3) dementia
    4) dysthymia

24. A therapist is treating a client's depression by helping the client to learn how to initiate and end conversations, make small talk, and maintain eye contact. The therapist's treatment is most likely based on the belief that depression is caused by which factor? The client's inability to
    1) feel physically attractive
    2) openly express anger
    3) obtain social reinforcers
    4) focus on the problems of others

25. What class of medication is commonly used to treat schizophrenia?
    1) antipsychotics
    2) monoamine oxidase inhibitors
    3) stimulants
    4) tricyclics

Reference Materials

Barlow, D.H., & Durand, V.M. (1999). Abnormal psychology (2nd ed.). Pacific Grove, CA: Brooks/Cole.

Davison, G.C., & Neale, J.M. (1998). Abnormal psychology (7th ed.). New York: Wiley.

Study Guide
Anatomy & Physiology (506)

Credit Hours: 6
Credit Level: Lower
Question Type(s): Multiple-choice

The information in this study guide is valid until Summer 2001.
If you will be taking the examination after that date, be sure to check for a new edition of this guide before you complete your preparation for the exam.

General Description of the Examination

The Anatomy & Physiology examination is based on material normally taught in an introductory, two-semester course in anatomy and physiology. The examination measures knowledge and understanding of the integrative mechanisms that contribute to the functioning of the human body.

Content Outline

Content Area	Percent of Examination
I. The Human Body: An Overview	5%
II. Chemical Basis of Life	5%
III. Dynamics of Support and Motion	12%
IV. Integration and Regulatory Mechanisms	23%
V. Maintenance of the Human Body	33%
VI. Urinary System	10%
VII. Fluid and Electrolyte Balance	5%
VIII. Reproduction and Development	7%
	Total 100%

I. The Human Body: An Overview (5%)

A. Basic anatomical terminology
1. Body cavities and regions
2. Anatomical position, planes, and directional terms

B. General organization of the body
1. Cell structure and function as revealed by electron microscopy (including cell membrane receptor sites)
2. Fundamental body tissues
   a. Epithelial
   b. Connective
   c. Muscle
   d. Nervous
3. Organs: definition and examples
4. Systems: definition and examples

C. Skin (Integument)
1. Epidermis
2. Dermis (receptors, glands, hair follicles, nails)

D. Maintenance of the internal environment
1. Homeostasis
2. Cellular fluid dynamics
   a. Osmosis
   b. Filtration
   c. Diffusion
   d. Active transport
   e. Endocytosis and exocytosis

II. Chemical Basis of Life (5%)

A. Atomic structure
1. Elements and isotopes
2. Atomic weights

B. Chemical bonds
1. Ionic bonds
2. Covalent bonds
3. Hydrogen bonds

C. Types of reactions
1. Decomposition
2. Synthesis
3. Reversible reactions
4. Enzymes and chemical reactions

D. Inorganic compounds
1. Water and its properties
2. Aqueous solutions
3. Colloids and suspensions
4. Hydrogen ions in body fluids

  5. Inorganic acids and bases
  6. Salts
  7. Buffers and pH control
- **E. Organic compounds**
    1. Carbohydrates
        a. Monosaccharides
        b. Disaccharides
        c. Polysaccharides
    2. Lipids
        a. Fatty acids
        b. Glycerol
        c. Steroids
        d. Phospholipids
    3. Proteins
        a. Structure of proteins
        b. Protein shape
        c. Enzyme function
    4. Nucleic acids
        a. Structure of nucleic acids
        b. RNA and DNA

III. The Dynamics of Support and Motion (12%)

- **A. Supporting tissue**
    1. Anatomy
        a. Gross anatomy
            (1) Bone
                (a) Types: long, short, flat, irregular, sesamoid
                (b) Markings (processes): elevations (for example: ridge or crest, tubercle, tuberosity, malleolus, trochanter, spine, head, condyles), depressions (for example: pit or fovea, fossa, groove or sulcus), openings (for example: foramen, canal or meatus, fissure)
            (2) Cartilage: hyaline, white fibrous, elastic
        b. Microscopic anatomy
            (1) Bone (osseous tissue): osteoblasts, osteocytes, osteoclasts, periosteum, Sharpey's fibers, osteon (Haversian) system, lacunae, canaliculi, Haversian canal, lamellae, Volkmann's canal, interstitial lamellae, endosteum, bone marrow (yellow and red), organic and inorganic constituents
            (2) Cartilage: cells in intercellular matrix, chondrogenic layer (chondroblasts and chondrocytes), perichondrium
    2. Development and growth
        a. Intramembranous ossification
        b. Intracartilaginous or endochondral ossification
        c. Hormonal influences: for example: growth hormone (GH) (somatotropin), thyroxine, adrenocorticotropic hormone, parathyroid hormone, calcitonin, estrogen, testosterone
        d. Other chemical influences: vitamins and minerals

B. Skeletal system
   1. Divisions
      a. Axial: skull (cranial and facial bones), hyoid, vertebral column, sternum, ribs
      b. Appendicular (girdles and extremities)
         (1) Upper limb: pectoral girdle (clavicles, scapulae), humerus, radius, ulna, carpals, metacarpals, phalanges
         (2) Lower limb: pelvic girdle (hip bones), femur, patella, fibula, tibia, tarsals, metatarsals, phalanges
   2. Articulations
      a. Types
         (1) Synarthrosis (immovable): for example: sutures
         (2) Amphiarthrosis (slightly moveable): for example: symphysis pubis, intervertebral disks
         (3) Diarthrosis (fully moveable): gliding, hinge joint (ginglymus), condyloid joint, saddle joint, pivot joint, ball-and-socket joint
      b. Movements: flexion, extension, adduction, abduction, circumduction, rotation

C. Muscle tissue
   1. Types and characteristics
      a. Skeletal (striated, voluntary)
      b. Smooth (nonstriated, involuntary)
      c. Cardiac (striated, involuntary)
   2. Gross anatomy
      a. Attachment: origins, insertions (for example: by tendons and aponeuroses)
      b. Levers: first class, second class, third class (fulcrum, effort, resistance)
      c. Location and function of major muscles (Textbooks identify these muscles.)

D. Muscle physiology
   1. Contractions: muscle twitch, tetanus (complete vs. incomplete), summation (temporal, spatial)
   2. Mechanism of contraction
      a. Electrical and mechanical aspects: for example: stimuli (subthreshold, threshold), action potential, latent period, period of contraction, relaxation, all-or-none principle, graded strength principle, absolute and relative refractory period, tonus, motor unit, excitation-contraction coupling, calcium effect, summation (temporal, spatial)
      b. Chemical and thermal aspects: for example: sliding filament theory (actin, myosin, regulating proteins), energy sources (ATP-creatine phosphate-glycogen), heat formation, oxygen debt, fatigue
   3. Exercise physiology: isometric and isotonic contractions, white and red fibers, strength vs. endurance

IV. Integration and Regulatory Mechanisms (23%)

A. Nervous system
   1. Cell types
      a. Neuron: cell body, dendrites, axon, neurofibrils, myelin sheath, nodes of Ranvier, telodendria

(1) Structural classification: unipolar, bipolar, multipolar
(2) Functional classification: afferent (sensory), efferent (motor), association (interneuron)
   b. Supportive cells
      (1) CNS: neuroglia or glial cells (astrocytes, oligodendrocytes, microglia, ependymal cells)
      (2) PNS: Schwann cells
2. Nerve impulse: membrane excitation (graded, voltage-regulated potential), membrane inhibition, facilitation, saltatory conduction
3. Synapse: excitation (EPSP), inhibition (IPSP), convergence, divergence, calcium modulation, neurotransmitters, MAO, specificity of receptors (adrenergic, cholinergic), fatigue
4. Reflexes (knee jerk, stretch, withdrawal)
5. Development and growth
   a. Ectoderm: neural (medullary) plate, neural tube (brain and spinal cord)
   b. Brain: forebrain, midbrain, hindbrain
6. Divisions
   a. Central nervous system
      (1) Brain: gray and white matter
         (a) Forebrain (prosencephalon): telencephalon (lateral ventricles, cerebral cortex, basal nuclei, rhinencephalon), diencephalon (third ventricle, epithalamus, thalamus, metathalamus, hypothalamus)
         (b) Midbrain (mesencephalon): cerebral aqueduct, cerebral peduncles, corpora quadrigemina
         (c) Hindbrain (rhombencephalon): fourth ventricle, metencephalon (cerebellum, pons), myelencephalon (medulla oblongata)
      (2) Spinal cord: gray and white matter
         (a) Ascending tracts (sensory): for example: posterior columns, spinothalamic pathways, spinocerebellar pathways
         (b) Descending tracts (motor): for example: pyramidal pathways (corticospinal tracts), extrapyramidal pathways (rubrospinal and reticulospinal)
      (3) Meninges: dura mater, arachnoid, pia mater
      (4) Cerebrospinal fluid (formation, flow, reabsorption, and function)
   b. Peripheral nervous system
      (1) Cranial nerves (12 pairs): name, number, type, function
      (2) Spinal nerves
         (a) Thirty-one pairs (8 cervical, 12 thoracic, 5 lumbar, 5 sacral, 1 coccygeal): dorsal root, ventral root
         (b) Plexi: cervical, brachial, lumbar, sacral
   c. Autonomic nervous system (visceral efferent system)
      (1) Sympathetic division (thoracolumbar)
      (2) Parasympathetic division (craniosacral)
      (3) Anatomical and functional aspects
         (a) Preganglionic (white rami root) and postganglionic (gray rami root) fibers: for example: adrenergics, cholinergics
         (b) Autonomic plexus

B. **Senses**
   1. General senses
      a. Exteroceptors: free nerve endings, Pacinian corpuscles, Meissner's corpuscles, Ruffini end organ, Krause end organ
      b. Chemoreceptors (carotid and aortic bodies)
      c. Baroreceptors (carotid and aortic sinuses)
      d. Stretch receptors of the lung (Hering-Breuer reflex)
      e. Proprioceptors: muscle spindles, tendon organ, joints
   2. Special senses
      a. Visual
         (1) Anatomy of eye: for example: layers of eyeball, extraocular muscles
         (2) Physiology of vision and errors of refraction (CNII)
      b. Auditory
         (1) Anatomy of ear: external ear, middle ear, inner ear
         (2) Physiology of hearing (mechanics, organ of Corti) (CNVIII)
      c. Olfactory: olfactory nerves, olfactory membrane, conchae (CNI)
      d. Gustatory: tongue, taste buds (papillae of tongue), classes of taste (CNXI, XII)
      e. Balance and equilibrium
         (1) Anatomy of semicircular canals (utricle and saccule)
         (2) Physiology of balance (static vs. dynamic equilibrium) (CNVIII)

C. **Endocrine system**
   1. Hormones
      a. Amino acid derivatives
      b. Peptide hormones
      c. Proteins
      d. Steroids
   2. Mechanisms of hormonal action: first and second messengers
      a. Plasma membrane: adenyl cyclase mechanisms, c-AMP
      b. Cytosol: nuclear membrane receptor mechanism
   3. Endocrine glands: structure and function
      a. Pituitary (hypophysis cerebri)
         (1) Neurohypophysis (pars nervosa): ADH, oxytocin
         (2) Adenohypophysis (pars distalis): ACTH, GH, TSH, FSH, LH (ICSH)
         (3) Relationship to hypothalamus (hypothalamic-hypophyseal portal system and tract)
      b. Thyroid: thyroxine (T_4), triiodothyronine (T_3), calcitonin
      c. Parathyroid: parathormone (PTH)
      d. Adrenal (suprarenal)
         (1) Medulla: epinephrine, norepinephrine, relationship to the sympathetic division of the autonomic nervous system
         (2) Cortex: glucocorticoids, mineralocorticoids, sex hormones
      e. Pancreas: islets of Langerhans, insulin, glucagon
      f. Gonads
         (1) Ovaries: estrogens and progesterone
         (2) Testes: androgens (testosterone)
      g. Thymus (role in T_4 and T_8 synthesis)
      h. Pineal gland: melatonin

      i. Placenta: estrogens, progesterone, human chorionic gonadotropin (HCG)
  4. Other secretory tissue
     a. Gastrointestinal mucosa (enteroendocrine cells): gastrin, secretin, cholecystokinin (CCK)
     b. Kidney: for example: renin, erythropoietin
  5. Hypothalamus
     a. Releasing factors and inhibiting factors
     b. Posterior pituitary hormones (ADH, oxytocin)

V. Maintenance of the Human Body (33%)

A. Circulatory system
  1. Blood
     a. Characteristics: color, specific gravity, pH, temperature
     b. Formed elements: characteristics, life cycle, number, function
        (1) Erythrocytes (red blood cells)
        (2) Leukocytes (white blood cells)
        (3) Thrombocytes (platelets)
     c. Nonformed elements (plasma): components and characteristics
        (1) Water
        (2) Proteins (albumin, globulin, fibrinogen)
        (3) Salts
        (4) Gases
        (5) Nutrients
        (6) Enzymes and hormones
        (7) Waste products
     d. Blood typing (agglutinins, agglutinogens)
        (1) ABO groups
        (2) Rh factor
     e. Hemostasis: vessel constriction, platelet plugging, coagulation (intrinsic and extrinsic)
  2. The heart: a dual pressure pump
     a. Structure
        (1) Layers: pericardium, endocardium, myocardium, epicardium
        (2) Chambers: atria, ventricles
        (3) Valves: tricuspid, bicuspid (mitral), aortic and pulmonic semilunar
        (4) Coronary circulation: coronary arteries, cardiac veins, coronary sinus
        (5) Conduction system
            (a) Intrinsic (S-A node, A-V node, Bundle of His, left and right bundle branches, Purkinje fibers)
            (b) Extrinsic (vagal and cardiac nerve modulation)
     b. Function
        (1) Properties of cardiac muscle: automaticity, intercellular conductivity (gap junctions)
        (2) Origin of heartbeat and conduction pathway
        (3) Cardiac cycle: phases (systole, diastole), pressure and volume changes, heart sounds, ECG
        (4) Control of cardiac output
            (a) Nervous control: vagus and cardiac nerve

(b) Autoregulation
(c) Role of receptors: baroreceptors (Bainbridge reflex, aortic sinus reflex, carotid sinus reflex)
(d) Other factors affecting frequency and strength of heart action: for example: blood pressure, emotional excitement, blood temperature, physical factors (size, age, gender)
3. Vascular system
   a. Divisions: systemic, pulmonary
   b. Vessels: histology and function
      (1) Arteries: layers, elastic arteries, muscular arteries, vasa vasorum
      (2) Veins: layers, valves, vasa vasorum
      (3) Capillaries: distribution
   c. Location of major vessels (Textbooks identify these vessels.)
   d. Special circuits
      (1) Hepatic portal system
      (2) Coronary
      (3) Cerebral (circle of Willis)
      (4) Renal
      (5) Fetal
      (6) Hypothalamic and hypophyseal portal systems
4. Cardiovascular physiology
   a. Pressure dynamics: blood distribution to body organs and organ needs
   b. Regulation and maintenance of blood pressure
      (1) Cardiac output (stroke volume times heart rate)
      (2) Resistance to blood flow: vasodilation, vasoconstriction, blood viscosity
      (3) Role of chemoreceptors and baroreceptors
      (4) Effect of nervous stimulation
   c. Capillaries exchange
      (1) Fluid exchange: a result of the balance between
         (a) Hydrostatic pressure
         (b) Osmotic (oncotic) pressure
      (2) Diffusion (nutrients, gases)
5. Lymphatic system
   a. Anatomical organization: lymph capillaries, right lymphatic duct, thoracic duct, lymph nodes
   b. Lymph fluid: origin, composition, flow, function
   c. Structure of lymph vessels and organs: spleen, thymus, tonsillar tissue, pharyngeal tissue (adenoid)
6. Immune responses
   a. Nonspecific resistance to disease
   b. Specific resistance to disease
      (1) Antigens and antibodies
      (2) Cellular and humoral immunity
         (a) T lymphocytes (helper, cytotoxic, suppressor, memory)
         (b) B lymphocytes (active and memory)
         (c) Types of immunity: active and passive

B. **Respiratory system**
   1. Anatomy

a. Respiratory tract (conducting and respiratory portions—changes in histology)
b. Respiratory muscles: diaphragm and intercostals
c. Pleura (visceral and parietal layers)
2. Physiology
   a. Diffusion of gases: pressure (intraalveolar and intrapleural)
      (1) Boyle's Law
      (2) Charles' Law
      (3) Dalton's Law
      (4) Henry's Law
   b. Mechanisms of ventilation
      (1) Inspiration
      (2) Expiration
      (3) Lung volumes and capacities: for example: tidal volume, inspiratory reserve, expiratory reserve, residual volume, vital capacity
   c. Gas exchange and transport
      (1) Oxygen, carbon dioxide
      (2) Hemoglobin dissociation curve
   d. Control ventilation
      (1) Nervous control
         (a) Medulla oblongata (inspiration, expiration)
         (b) Pons varolii (apneustic area and pneumotaxic area)
         (c) Lungs (Hering-Breuer reflex)
      (2) Chemical control: pH, carbon dioxide (PCO_2), hypoxia (PO_2)
      (3) Other controls: temperature change, pressure change, voluntary (cerebrum)

C. Digestive system
1. Anatomy and functions of the alimentary canal
   a. Microscopic anatomy: serosa, muscular layers, submucosa, mucosa, lymph nodes (Peyer's patches)
   b. Gross anatomy
      (1) Alimentary tract: mouth, pharynx, esophagus, cardiac (esophageal) sphincter, stomach, pyloric sphincter, small intestine (duodenum, jejunum, ileum), ileocecal valve, large intestine (caecum, vermiform appendix, ascending colon, transverse colon, descending colon, sigmoid colon, rectum, anal canal)
      (2) Accessory organs: tongue, teeth, salivary glands, pancreas, liver, gallbladder
2. Physiology of the digestive process
   a. Physical (mechanical) digestion: ingestion, mastication, deglutition, peristalsis, segmentation, pendular movement, defecation
   b. Chemical digestion: Catalytic enzymes and hydrolysis of carbohydrates, lipids, proteins
   c. Control of digestion
      (1) Nervous control: autonomic nervous system (parasympathetic and sympathetic), myenteric and submucosal plexus
      (2) Hormonal control: gastrin, enterogastrone (GIP), secretin, cholecystokinin (CCK)

        d. Mechanisms of absorption: simple diffusion, facilitated diffusion, osmosis, active transport, endocytosis, physical factors (particle size, concentration of materials, lipid solubility, surface area)

  D. Metabolism
      1. Nutrient metabolism of carbohydrates, proteins, and lipids
        a. Anabolism (glycogenesis, gluconeogenesis, lipogenesis, protein synthesis)
        b. Catabolism (glycogenolysis, glycolysis, lipolysis, protein degradation)
      2. Energy metabolism (aerobic and anaerobic): role of enzymes and phosphorylation, TCA (Krebs) cycle, oxidative phosphorylation, electron transport chain, role of NAD and FAD (Students are not responsible for the individual biochemical events of above processes.)
      3. Daily calorie requirement, nutritional needs, body heat
      4. Calorimetry: basal metabolic rate (BMR)

VI. Urinary System (10%)

A. Gross anatomy: kidney (capsule, pelvis, calyces, medulla, cortex, renal columns, renal pyramids), ureters, bladder, urethra, blood supply

B. Microscopic anatomy: nephron (glomerulus, podocytes, renal [Bowman's] capsule, proximal convoluted tubule, loop of Henle, distal convoluted tubule), collecting duct

C. Nephron dynamics (homeostatic maintenance)
    1. Glomeruli (GFR, GFP)
      a. Hydrostatic pressure
      b. Osmotic pressure
      c. Fluid exchange
    2. Tubular reabsorption
    3. Tubular secretion
    4. Countercurrent multiplier/exchanger
    5. JGA (renin-angiotensinogen mechanism)

D. Control of renal function
    1. Hormonal: antidiuretic hormone (ADH or vasopressin), aldosterone
    2. Nervous: autonomic nerves

E. Micturition reflex and voluntary control

F. Urine composition
    1. Physical characteristics: color, transparency, pH, specific gravity, quantity
    2. Constituents
      a. Inorganic: chlorides; sulphates; phosphates of sodium, potassium, magnesium and calcium; water; ammonium salts
      b. Organic: creatinine, urea, uric acid

VII. Fluid and Electrolyte Balance (5%)

A. Fluid compartments: distribution of water and electrolytes in the body, movement of water, water intake and output, adjustment of excess fluid intake, regulation by hormones, stress situations, reserve body water, milliequivalents, important cations and anions
1. Extracellular (interstitial fluid, plasma)
2. Intracellular

B. Acid-base balance: normal pH range, pH regulation, sources of acid and base
1. Blood buffers
2. Respiratory regulation
3. Renal regulation
4. Acid-base disturbances (acidosis, alkalosis)

VIII. Reproduction and Development (7%)

A. Anatomy
1. Primary reproductive organs
   a. Male: testes
   b. Female: ovaries
2. Accessory reproductive organs
   a. Male: epididymis, vas deferens (ductus deferens), seminal vesicles, ejaculatory ducts, prostate gland, bulbourethral (Cowper's) glands, urethra, penis
   b. Female: fallopian tubes (oviducts), uterus, vagina, greater vestibular (Bartholin's) glands, external genitalia

B. Physiology of reproductive system
1. Gametogenesis: reduction division
   a. Spermatogenesis
   b. Oogenesis
2. Hormonal control
   a. Female: oogenesis, menstrual cycle (FSH, LH, estrogen, progesterone)
   b. Male: spermatogenesis, gonadotropins (FSH, LH [ICSH]), testosterone
3. Nervous control
   a. Erection (parasympathetic)
   b. Ejaculation (sympathetic)
4. Fertilization and implantation
5. Pregnancy
   a. Hormonal control: corpus luteum (estrogen, progesterone), placenta (HCG)
   b. Development
      (1) Egg stage
      (2) Embryonic stages
      (3) Fetal stage
6. Parturition: stages, hormonal control (oxytocin, relaxin)
7. Lactation: nervous and hormonal control, nutritional aspects

Sample Questions: Anatomy & Physiology

1. What is the name given to an imaginary plane that divides the body into right and left halves?
    1) coronal
    2) frontal
    3) sagittal
    4) transverse

2. Which statement best explains what happens when oxygen and hydrogen combine to form water (H_2O)?
    1) Hydrogen becomes weakly negative.
    2) Oxygen remains in an unstable state.
    3) Oxygen loses its high electronegativity.
    4) There is unequal sharing of electrons.

3. Which cordlike structure attaches muscle to bone?
    1) aponeurosis
    2) fascicle
    3) ligament
    4) tendon

4. Which property of cardiac muscle prevents tetanic contractions?
    1) sliding of actin and myosin
    2) branching muscle fibers
    3) long refractory period
    4) low extracellular calcium

5. Which component of the spinal reflex arc is responsible for delivering an efferent impulse to either a muscle or a gland?
    1) association neuron
    2) postganglion neuron
    3) motor neuron
    4) sensory neuron

6. Which is a function of the cerebellum?
    1) control of voluntary scanning movements of the eyes
    2) production of coordinated movement
    3) regulation of autonomic body functions
    4) regulation of emotions

7. What results from sectioning the corpus callosum?
    1) The brain ceases to function and death occurs.
    2) The capacity for abstract thought is lost.
    3) Information transfer between the cerebral hemispheres is lost.
    4) Control of autonomic functions is lost.

8. Which ability would be impaired by damage to hair cells at the basal end of the cochlea?
    1) discriminating loudness
    2) discriminating the direction of sound

Anatomy & Physiology 47

Sample Questions: Anatomy & Physiology

    3) hearing high-frequency sounds
    4) hearing low-frequency sounds

9. Which compensatory response is likely to occur when the blood calcium level is low?
   1) Fecal calcium will be higher than normal.
   2) Urine calcium will be higher than normal.
   3) Osteoclast activity will be greater than normal.
   4) Calcium deposition in bone will be greater than normal.

10. When does ejection of blood from the ventricles occur during an ECG trace?
    1) between the QRS and T waves
    2) right after the P wave
    3) between the T and P waves
    4) right after the T wave

11. During which phase of the cardiac cycle is the pressure in the aorta the highest?
    1) early atrial diastole
    2) atrial systole
    3) early ventricular diastole
    4) ventricular systole

12. In a normal heart, which of the following decreases cardiac output?
    1) increased stroke volume
    2) increased heart rate
    3) increased venous return to the heart
    4) increased parasympathetic stimulation of the heart

13. Which cells in the islets of Langerhans produce insulin?
    1) alpha cells
    2) beta cells
    3) delta cells
    4) F cells

14. Which statement best explains why stimulating the sympathetic nervous system will increase arterial blood pressure?
    1) Cardiac output will increase and total peripheral resistance will remain unchanged.
    2) Cardiac output will remain unchanged and total peripheral resistance will increase.
    3) Cardiac output will increase and stroke volume will decrease.
    4) Cardiac output and total peripheral resistance will both increase.

15. Which condition may result from the hypersecretion of gastric juices?
    1) acute pancreatitis
    2) cirrhosis
    3) peptic ulcers
    4) peritonitis

Sample Questions: Anatomy & Physiology

16. What is the effect of the Hering-Breuer reflex?
    1) It controls the basic rhythm of respiration.
    2) It constricts terminal bronchioles.
    3) It stimulates inspiration.
    4) It prevents overinflation of the lungs.

17. Which is the correct pathway of filtrate through the nephron?
    1) Bowman's capsule, proximal convoluted tubule, loop of Henle, distal convoluted tubule
    2) Bowman's capsule, loop of Henle, proximal convoluted tubule, collecting tubule
    3) Bowman's capsule, collecting tubule, proximal convoluted tubule, loop of Henle
    4) collecting tubule, Bowman's capsule, loop of Henle, distal convoluted tubule

18. During cellular respiration, a diminished supply of oxygen will result in the storage of hydrogen as which acid?
    1) acetic
    2) citric
    3) lactic
    4) pyruvic

19. Which hormone increases the reabsorption of sodium and the secretion of potassium by the kidney?
    1) aldosterone
    2) antidiuretic hormone (ADH)
    3) thyroxine
    4) cortisol

20. The renin-angiotensin mechanism regulates the production of which hormone?
    1) aldosterone
    2) cortisol
    3) glucagon
    4) insulin

21. An increase in renal bicarbonate reabsorption would tend to have which effect on body fluids?
    1) increased acidity
    2) increased pH
    3) decreased buffering capacity
    4) decreased osmolarity

22. Which would be the effect of afferent impulses from lactating breasts to the hypothalamus?
    1) Release of posterior pituitary hormones would increase.
    2) Lactiferous ducts would not develop.
    3) The milk let-down reflex would not occur.
    4) Prolactin levels would increase.

23. What is the main source of progesterone following degeneration of the corpus luteum during pregnancy?
    1) corpus albicans
    2) follicular epithelial cells
    3) placenta
    4) thecal cells

Reference Materials

Marieb, E. (1998). Human anatomy and physiology (4th ed.). Redwood City, CA: Benjamin-Cummings.

Martini, F. (1992). Fundamentals of anatomy and physiology (2nd ed.). Englewood Cliffs, NJ: Prentice Hall.

Tortora, G.J., & Grabowski, S.R. (1996). Principles of anatomy and physiology (8th ed.). New York: HarperCollins.

Study Guide

Ethics: Theory & Practice (484)

Credit Hours: 3
Question Type(s): Multiple-choice
Credit Level: Upper

The information in this study guide is valid until Summer 2001.
If you will be taking the examination after that date, be sure to check for a new edition of this guide before you complete your preparation for the exam.

General Description of the Examination

The Regents College Examination in Ethics: Theory & Practice is based on material normally presented in a one-semester course in applied ethics. The examination measures understanding of ethical theories and concepts, metaethics, and the principles of moral deliberation, as they apply to practical ethical situations. Testing for the application of knowledge about ethics is accomplished through the use of case studies or situations and their related sets of multiple-choice questions. The content category for theories and concepts includes theories such as utilitarianism, natural law, and Kantianism, and concepts such as justice, duties and obligations, and rights. The metaethics category includes topics relating to subjectivism/objectivism, naturalistic fallacy, and genealogical subjects; moral deliberation covers topics such as moral sensitivity, status of moral judgments, and implications of moral concepts. Knowledge from the broad categories is then applied to practical ethical concerns such as social and personal issues, medical issues, professional and business issues, and environmental issues. A familiarity with the content generally taught in an introductory ethics course is required.

You can prepare for this examination by following an independent program of study based on directed readings in selected textbooks. This program of study is fully outlined in the Regents College *Course Guide for Ethics: Theory & Practice*. The course guide is described in detail on page 53, immediately following the content outline.

Content Outline

Content Area	Percent of Examination
I. Theory	33%
II. Practice	67%
	Total 100%

I. Theory (33%)

A. Basic theories
1. Natural law
2. Social contract
3. Deontological
4. Utilitarianism/consequentialism
5. Virtue
6. Egoism
   a. Psychological egoism
   b. Ethical egoism
7. Divine Command
8. Intuitionism
9. Feminism
10. Existentialism

B. Basic concepts
1. Justice
2. Rights
3. Values and goods
4. Duties and obligations, including *prima facie* vs. actual
5. Respect for persons
6. Moral agency
7. Moral standing
8. Moral relations
9. Autonomy and parentalism
10. Beneficence and nonmaleficence
11. Double effect
12. Equal opportunity and discrimination

C. Metaethics
1. Subjectivism/objectivism
2. Value theory
3. Genealogical
4. Skepticism/nihilism
5. Naturalistic fallacy

D. Moral deliberation
1. Moral reasoning
2. Implications of moral concepts
3. Status of moral judgments (self-interest, immediate self-interest)
4. Why be moral?

II. Practice (67%)

A. Social and personal issues: for example, personal behavior and relationships, including friendship, marital fidelity and loyalty, sexual harassment, and divorce; social and political issues, including censorship, privacy, pornography, and treatment of minorities

B. Medical issues: for example, autonomy and informed consent, including treatment decisions and competence; death and dying, including withholding and withdrawing care and active and passive euthanasia; reproduction and genetics, including reproductive technologies and risks, abortion, and genetic engineering

C. Professional and business issues: for example, professional/client and employee/employer relationships, including employee loyalty and whistle-blowing; equal opportunity and affirmative action; business and consumers, including health and safety issues; business regulation and moral/legal issues, including insider trading and use of insider knowledge

D. Environmental Issues: for example, ecocentrism and anthropocentrism; resource use, global justice, and future generations; sentience, animals, and vegetarianism

Course Guide for Ethics: Theory & Practice

The examination development committee strongly recommends that you order the Regents College *Course Guide for Ethics: Theory & Practice* for guidance in preparing for this examination. The course guide is designed to help you structure your own study and preparation and includes suggestions for successful independent study. To help you learn the content of this examination, the plan of study divides your efforts into units covering the major content topics. The topical sessions provide some general discussion to assist your reading or use of reference materials. The sessions are designed to direct and focus your learning.

The course guide also provides sample questions to familiarize you with the structure of the examination, and tips on preparing to take the examination. The course guide may be purchased only from the Regents College Bookstore.

Sample Questions: Ethics: Theory & Practice

1. According to Aristotle, what is a moral virtue?
   1) an inclination to obey the laws of one's society
   2) using a combination of intelligence and prudence
   3) a disposition to choose the mean
   4) acting nobly and admirably

2. Which theory is characterized by the claim, "Whatever contributes to the overall well-being of the social unit is good; whatever detracts from it is bad"?
   1) ethical egoism
   2) cultural relativism
   3) Kantianism
   4) utilitarianism

3. What is one of the most fundamental objections to intuitionism?
   1) It gives women a moral advantage over men.
   2) It fails to consider the pragmatic consequences of behavior.
   3) What maximizes pleasure may not be intuitive.
   4) What is self-evident to one may not be self-evident to another.

4. Ethical egoism and utilitarianism are correctly described in which statement?
   1) Ethical egoism is based on the belief that pleasure is the only intrinsic good; utilitarianism is based on the view that the future is beyond human control.
   2) Ethical egoism is concerned with promoting only one's own good; utilitarianism is concerned with promoting the greatest good for the greatest number.
   3) Ethical egoism is concerned with universal principles; utilitarianism is concerned with duties as opposed to inclination.
   4) Ethical egoism is based on the belief that feelings determine morality; utilitarianism is based on the belief that a higher being determines all.

5. According to a Kantian moralist, why should one always tell the truth? Truth telling
   1) will maximize social utility.
   2) shows respect for persons.
   3) is the best policy.
   4) is a basic human inclination.

6. What is the formal principle of justice?
   1) The form of the distribution of resources is as important as the actual distribution.
   2) However we distribute resources, we ought to follow rules.
   3) Like cases are to be treated alike and unlike cases unalike.
   4) What matters in justice is that we respect the forms of society.

Sample Questions: Ethics: Theory & Practice

7. An actual duty is what one actually ought to do in some particular situation. What is a *prima facie* duty?
    1) what it appears one ought to do, but not what one actually ought to do
    2) what one ought to do if other moral considerations do not intervene
    3) what one ought to do first
    4) what one ought to do if no one interferes

8. According to emotivism, what does it mean to say that an act is right?
    1) The act makes most people feel good.
    2) The act is objectively right.
    3) One sees a reason for the act.
    4) One approves of the act.

9. Which best describes the emotivist position?
    1) Utterances like "Stealing is wrong" are mere expressions of human sentiment and, as such, are neither true nor false.
    2) Moral wisdom may be found only by listening to the dictates of the human heart.
    3) Because morality is more properly a matter of reason than emotion, human sentiment must be tamed if we are ever to reach moral perfection.
    4) One's spirit may be willing, but humanity is generally weak.

10. To avoid the is/ought problem, what must be true of a deductively valid argument with a normative conclusion?
    1) It contains at least one normative premise.
    2) It contains a link between the normative and non-normative premises.
    3) There is a clear separation between the factual and normative premises.
    4) The context of the argument is given.

11. Which feature is a necessary condition for a judgment to be a moral judgment?
    1) Its realization maximizes well-being.
    2) It conforms with intuition.
    3) It expresses one's deepest convictions.
    4) It is universalizable.

12. According to Plato, a person who possesses the Ring of Gyges still ought to be moral for which reason?
    1) Harmony within self and society will be achieved.
    2) Self-control will lead to control of others.
    3) Seeming to be moral is the road to success.
    4) What exists is what ought to be.

Sample Case Study and Associated Questions

Marie is a 42-year-old teacher who has been waiting for a heart transplant for nearly 18 months. She has no other medical problems that would cause the transplant to be rejected. Early this morning, she was rushed to the hospital. She is conscious and lucid, but her survival depends on the availability of a suitable donor organ.

Dr. Johnson, a cardiologist, has taken a scientific and personal interest in Marie's case. Marie's age, tissue type, and positive attitude make her a perfect candidate for an experimental transplant using the heart of a young mammal. Although she expresses a strong preference for a human heart, Marie has not ruled out the procedure.

Marie's daughter, Susan, is a college sophomore. Four months ago, Susan unexpectedly became pregnant. Marie is not happy about the circumstances, but is looking forward to becoming a grandmother. She has begged God to let her live long enough to be present for the delivery of Susan's baby.

On her way to the hospital to see her mother, Susan lost control of her car and rammed into an embankment. Now doctors and nurses have gathered to discuss both situations.

Dr. Osborne, Susan's obstetrician, begins. "Susan has suffered severe brain trauma and is unable to breathe without a respirator. Her heart is strong and the fetus remains unharmed. We can and therefore should maintain life support for 8 to 10 weeks. There is no chance of Susan's recovery, but the fetus's odds of survival increase daily."

"Is she a potential organ donor?" asks Dr. Johnson.

"Yes," Dr. Carrigan, chief of surgery, replies. "She is a perfect match for Marie, whose chances of survival with a human heart are at least three times better than your most optimistic estimate. I intend to talk with Marie about transplanting Susan's heart to Marie. Your experiment will just have to wait."

"You cannot assess an experimental procedure in terms of its initial patients' survival," Dr. Johnson objects. "The long-term benefits for the human race surely outweigh any disadvantage which may apply to this particular case."

"These are people," interjects Nurse Beamer, "not objects you can manipulate to suit your own research interests! Marie keeps asking for Susan. What am I supposed to tell her?"

13. Which person pursues a line of reasoning and concern most clearly associated with rule utilitarianism?
    1) Beamer
    2) Carrigan
    3) Johnson
    4) Osborne

Sample Case Study and Associated Questions: Ethics: Theory & Practice

14. Which person pursues a line of reasoning and concern most clearly associated with Kantianism?
    1) Beamer
    2) Carrigan
    3) Johnson
    4) Osborne

15. Which of the following judgments is indicative of an approach that emphasizes individual autonomy?
    1) Susan should be kept on life support long enough to allow her fetus to develop.
    2) Susan's heart should be transplanted into Marie as soon as possible to maximize Marie's chance of survival.
    3) Marie should be allowed to make an informed decision based on her own beliefs.
    4) Due to the unusual circumstances of the case, the hospital should consult both religious and legal counsel before proceeding further.

16. Which ethical theory would be most likely to assign significance to the fact that Marie is a teacher?
    1) egoism
    2) utilitarianism
    3) Divine Command
    4) Kantianism

17. Which pair would be most likely to agree on a course of action?
    1) Johnson and Osborne
    2) Johnson and Carrigan
    3) Osborne and Carrigan
    4) Johnson and Beamer

18. Which claim would be characteristic of a person who strongly opposes all forms of euthanasia?
    1) Susan should be kept on life support long enough to allow her fetus to develop.
    2) Susan should be kept on life support indefinitely.
    3) Susan's heart should be transplanted into Marie as soon as possible to maximize Marie's chance of survival.
    4) Doctors should ask Marie if Susan ever expressed her beliefs about organ transplantation.

Recommended Resources

The committee recommends that you purchase all of the resources listed below. The textbooks listed are those around which the course guide has been developed.

Arthur, J. (Ed.). (1996). Morality and moral controversies *(4th ed.). Upper Saddle River, NJ: Prentice Hall.*

Beauchamp, T.L. (1991). Philosophical ethics *(2nd ed.). New York: McGraw-Hill.*

Holmes, R.L. (1998). Basic moral philosophy *(2nd ed.). Belmont, CA: Wadsworth.*

Regents College. (1999). Course guide for Ethics: Theory & Practice *(3rd ed.).*

Additional Resources

The committee has also listed the following anthologies in applied ethics, which may provide further clarification of the content. You may wish to have at least one resource from an area of interest available through purchase or library borrowing.

Social and Personal Issues

Luper-Foy, S., & Brown, C. (Eds.). (1992). The moral life. *Orlando, FL: Harcourt Brace.*

Medical Issues

Arras, J., & Steinbock, B. (1995). Ethical issues in modern medicine *(4th ed.). Mountain View, CA: Mayfield.*

Mappes, T.A., & Zembaty, J.S. (1991). Biomedical ethics *(3rd ed.). New York: McGraw-Hill.*

Munson, R. (1992). Intervention and reflection: Basic issues in medical ethics *(4th ed.). Belmont, CA: Wadsworth.*

Professional and Business Issues

Beauchamp, T. (1993). Case studies in business, society, and ethics *(3rd ed.). Englewood Cliffs, NJ: Prentice Hall.*

DeGeorge, R. (1990). Business ethics *(3rd ed.). New York: Macmillan.*

Shaw, W.H., & Barry, V. (1992). Moral issues in business *(5th ed.). Belmont, CA: Wadsworth.*

Environmental Issues

Armstrong, S., & Botzler, R. (Eds.). (1993). Environmental ethics: Divergence and convergence. *New York: McGraw-Hill.*

Pojman, L. (1994). Environmental ethics: Readings in theory and application. *Boston: Jones and Bartlett.*

Study Guide

Foundations of Gerontology (407)

Credit Hours: 3
Question Type(s): Multiple-choice
Credit Level: Upper

The information in this study guide is valid until Summer 2001.
If you will be taking the examination after that date, be sure to check for a new edition of this guide before you complete your preparation for the exam.

General Description of the Examination

The Foundations of Gerontology examination is based on material usually taught in a one-semester course in gerontology. The examination tests for knowledge and understanding of the biological, psychological, and social aspects of aging. It measures the ability to describe, understand, and analyze issues pertaining to the functioning and well-being of older people. In addition to a knowledge base, you will be expected to have an awareness of the needs and realities involved in the aging process and the implications of population aging for society. Emphasis is placed on both typical aspects of aging and problems associated with aging. The content of the examination is multidisciplinary in nature and covers theories, concepts, empirical patterns, and their implications for policy and practice.

Unless otherwise specified, all of the questions on the examination refer to the situation of older people in the United States today. In addition, the term "older people" refers to persons age 65 and older. This information is not repeated in individual questions.

Content Outline

Content Area	Percent of Examination
I. Important Concepts of Gerontology	10%
II. Demography of Aging: Trends and Projections	9%
III. Biology and Physical Health	17%
IV. Psychology and Mental Health	17%
V. Sociology	14%
VI. Economics, Work, and Retirement	14%
VII. Political Behavior and Public Policy	14%
VIII. Death and Dying	5%
Total	**100%**

I. Important Concepts of Gerontology (10%)

A. Definition of gerontology
1. The importance of gerontology
2. Study of aging as a normal developmental process over the life span
3. Study of aging from a societal perspective
4. Gerontology as a multidisciplinary field of study
5. Gerontology as a professional field: development and current status

B. Definitions of aging
1. Chronological aging
2. Biological aging
3. Functional aging
4. Psychological aging
5. Sociological aging

C. Variables involved in the aging process—similarities and differences
1. Intrinsic, age-related effects (for example: genetics, physiological changes, susceptibility to illness)
2. External, reactive effects (for example: social, cultural, and personal expectations)
3. Cohort effects: age differences vs. age change

D. Ageism
1. Definition and identification
2. Myths, stereotypes, and misconceptions concerning aging
   a. Sources
   b. Impact

E. Research issues
1. Cross-sectional vs. longitudinal designs
2. Validity and reliability of findings

II. Demography of Aging: Trends and Projections (9%)

A. Population age structure (for example: numbers and percentages of older people, life expectancy, mortality, fertility, dependency ratio)
1. Cross-cultural similarities and differences
2. Historical views of aging and impact of modernization

B. Description of the older population and comparison across age groups
1. Demographic characteristics (for example: sex ratio, race, geographic location, mobility)
2. Social characteristics (for example: marital status, housing and living arrangements, education, income and poverty, labor force participation)
3. Health characteristics (for example: general patterns of acute and chronic illness, functional health, institutionalization, those over 85)

C. Sources of variation within the older population—implications for policy and programs
   1. Cohort differences (for example: baby boom)
   2. Age differences (for example: young-old vs. old-old)
   3. Gender differences (for example: income, marital status, housing and living arrangements)
   4. Racial and ethnic differences (for example: health and longevity, income, family, multiple jeopardy)
   5. Locational differences (for example: urban, suburban, rural, and states)
   6. Other groups (for example: homosexuals, prisoners, developmentally disabled, homeless)

III. Biology and Physical Health (17%)

A. General considerations
   1. Universality of aging
      a. Cells, animals, plants, microbes, chemical, nonliving
      b. Senescence as end stage of aging
      c. Inter- and intraindividual differences in senescence; commonalities in aging
   2. Life span/life expectancy
   3. Length of life and relationship to physiological parameters (for example: body weight, brain weight, DNA repair rate)
   4. Aging vs. disease
   5. Aging in populations

B. Age changes
   1. Physiological vs. chronological
   2. Control systems: nervous, endocrine, immune
   3. Sensory systems
      a. Internal (for example: stretch and pressure, chemical)
      b. External (for example: vision, hearing, pressure, pain, taste, smell)
   4. Structural systems: bone, muscle, skin
   5. Other organ systems: cardiovascular, respiratory, gastrointestinal, reproductive, urinary

C. Theories of aging
   1. Genetic program
      a. Hayflick cellular clock
      b. Gene coding for specific changes
   2. Wear-and-tear
   3. Cellular garbage and free radical
   4. Error
   5. Stress-induction
   6. Immunity-autoimmunity and autoaggressiveness
   7. Somatic mutation and radiation
   8. Brain-endocrine aging

D. Factors affecting aging and/or senescence (for example: nutrition, stress, exercise, lifestyle, substance abuse, genetics, radiation)

Foundations of Gerontology

E. **General concepts of health**
   1. Definition of health: World Health Organization definition, objective health, subjective health, functional health
   2. Chronic vs. acute disease
      a. Distinction
      b. Relationship to age
      c. Incidence in older people
   3. Presence of multiple chronic conditions

F. **Causes of illness and death among older people**
   1. Major diseases (for example: arteriosclerosis, arthritis, cancer, cardiovascular disease, cerebrovascular disease, diabetes)
   2. Stress-induced causes (for example: alcoholism, suicide)

G. **Psychosocial effects of illness**
   1. Disability, excess disability, and impact on lifestyle
   2. The sick role and secondary gains
   3. Coping mechanisms
   4. Potential impact on family
   5. Value dilemmas

H. **Health care:** Awareness and attitudes about health care; availability, accessibility, and use and effectiveness of health care
   1. Prevention (for example: nutrition, drugs and interactions, physical activity, smoking, knowledge and beliefs about health, life satisfaction)
   2. Community-based services (for example: health maintenance organizations, geriatric screening teams, visiting nurses, in-home services, informal network of care)

I. **Institutional care**
   1. Levels of care
   2. Causes of institutionalization
   3. Psychological effects of institutionalization
   4. Trends
   5. Quality of care

IV. Psychology and Mental Health (17%)

A. **Cognitive functioning in later life**
   1. Reaction time/psychomotor performance
      a. Physiological correlates (for example: CNS, sensory system)
      b. Causes of age-related slowing of reaction times (for example: individual variations)
      c. Effects of exercise and daily activities on reaction time
   2. Learning and memory
      a. Information processing
         (1) Conditions affecting the learning of older people (for example: pacing, motivation, anxiety, disease)
         (2) Age differences and learning ability
         (3) Cautiousness vs. rigidity
      b. Short- and long-term memory over the life span: continuity and change

  c. Implications for life-long learning
 3. Intellectual ability
  a. Definition of intelligence
   (1) Crystallized vs. fluid
   (2) Performance vs. capacity
  b. Measurements of intelligence (for example: classic cross-sectional vs. longitudinal studies)
  c. Factors affecting intelligence (for example: health, education, cohort differences, activity patterns)
  d. Terminal drop
 4. Creativity: needs and abilities
 5. Motivation

B. Personality—continuity and change
 1. Definition, types, and measurement of personality
 2. Factors affecting personality (for example: personal resources, cognitive abilities, self-concept, physical status, sense of control, social competence)
 3. Theories of personality
  a. Psychoanalytic viewpoint
  b. Erikson: psychosocial development
  c. Havighurst: developmental tasks
  d. Peck: developmental tasks

C. Measures of well-being
 1. Dimensions of successful aging (for example: life satisfaction, morale, self-esteem)
 2. Theories (for example: disengagement vs. activity, exchange)
 3. Correlates and predictors

D. Mental health and aging
 1. Psychopathology in later life
  a. Affective disorders (for example: major depression)
  b. Other disorders (for example: functional, anxiety, paranoid, somatization, substance abuse)
  c. Organic brain disorders
   (1) The myth of senility
   (2) Reversible vs. irreversible brain disorders (for example: acute disorders vs. dementias)
   (3) Causes, symptoms, progression, and treatment of organic disorders
   (4) Differentiation between dementia and depression
 2. Social factors affecting the mental health status of older people
  a. Situational (for example: socioeconomic status, marital status, specific life events)
  b. Social breakdown syndrome, labeling
  c. Stress and coping
 3. Approaches to mental health intervention
  a. Psychotherapies (for example: group, activity, milieu, reality orientation, pet therapy)
  b. Pharmacotherapy/medical intervention
  c. Institutionalization
  d. Community-based services

V. Sociology (14%)

A. The social context for aging—basic perspectives and concepts
   1. Life course perspective: intersection of history, society, and individual biography
   2. Age stratification: age-grading of roles, age norms, and socialization
   3. Person-environment congruence: implications for housing and services
   4. Support systems
      a. Relationship between formal and informal support
      b. Types and sources of informal support

B. Sources of variation in aging—aging and the life cycle as social constructions
   1. Historical and cross-cultural patterns: the impact of modernization
   2. Cohort flow and social change
   3. Population subgroups (for example: gender, race and ethnicity, socioeconomic status)

C. Housing and community context
   1. Housing and neighborhood quality
      a. Patterns
      b. Sources
      c. Variation (for example: urban, suburban, rural)
   2. Friends and neighbors
      a. Patterns of involvement
      b. Role in support networks
      c. Variation (for example: gender, socioeconomic status)
   3. Age density of housing: advantages and disadvantages of age-segregated and age-integrated settings
   4. Fear of crime and victimization
      a. Age-related patterns
      b. Consequences

D. Family roles and relationships over the life cycle—patterns and trends
   1. Marital roles, marital satisfaction, and role realignments (for example: empty nest, retirement, blended families)
   2. Unmarried older persons: widowed, divorced, never married, homosexual
      a. Trends
      b. Consequences of unmarried status
      c. Variations (for example: cohort and gender differences)
   3. Sexual interest and activity
      a. Age and cohort differences
      b. Normal aging vs. disease processes
   4. Extended family
      a. Intergenerational exchange: patterns of interaction and assistance (for example: informal support, strains of caregiving, elder abuse)
      b. Historical trends and future projections
      c. Sources of variation (for example: gender, socioeconomic status, race and ethnicity)
   5. Grandparent role

E. Other roles and activities—patterns and trends, age and cohort differences, sources of variation (for example: gender, socioeconomic status, health)
   1. Leisure activities and pets
   2. Voluntary associations and senior centers
   3. Volunteer roles
   4. Participation in education
   5. Religious involvement

VI. Economics, Work, and Retirement (14%)

A. Income
   1. Sources of income
   2. Comparisons with younger age groups
   3. Changes in income since the 1950s (for example: poverty)

B. Consumer patterns
   1. Expenditure patterns
   2. Experiences: inflation, fraud
   3. Growing private sector interest in older consumers (for example: AoA initiatives, marketplace responses)

C. Work
   1. Age-related patterns of work
      a. Performance
      b. Attitudes toward work
   2. Job prospects and economic realities: retraining, redesign, part-time vs. full-time work, flexible careers
   3. Age discrimination
      a. Sources
      b. Types
      c. Legal status

D. Retirement
   1. The retirement process—as a role, an event, and a phase of life
   2. Decision to retire
      a. Patterns and trends: individual and societal factors
      b. Mandatory retirement: status in law and practice
   3. Attitudes toward retirement: individual and cultural
   4. Individual responses and adjustments to retirement
      a. Impact on income, housing, morale, health, activity
      b. Variation by gender, socioeconomic status
   5. Retirement income
      a. Social Security
         (1) Development, financing, and current status
         (2) Future issues and proposals
      b. Private pensions
         (1) Development
         (2) Provisions
         (3) Legislation
   6. Preretirement programs
   7. Cross-cultural variations in retirement patterns and policies

VII. Political Behavior and Public Policy (14%)

A. Political participation—age and cohort effects
1. Voting behavior
2. Political identification
3. Political attitudes: conservatism, liberalism, alienation

B. Older adult movements
1. History, background, and impact
2. Advocacy
   a. National organizations (for example: AARP, NCOA, NCBA, NCSC, Gray Panthers)
   b. AoA network

C. Policies and programs
1. Major public policies
   a. Social Security Act of 1935: the three-pronged approach
   b. Older Americans Act of 1965 and amendments: provisions and results
   c. Supplemental Security Income (SSI)
2. Health care policy issues
   a. Medicare and Medicaid
      (1) Basic elements, coverage
      (2) Present and future problems
      (3) Costs and financing
   b. Long-term care alternatives
3. Housing
   a. Alternatives (for example: public housing, nonprofit programs, congregate housing, foster homes, day care)
   b. Factors affecting selection
4. White House Conferences on Aging: 1961, 1971, 1981
5. Private programs (for example: United Way, churches, senior centers, EAP)
6. Factors affecting service delivery and utilization (for example: awareness, availability, responsiveness, staffing)

D. Contemporary policy issues
1. Age vs. need
2. Intergenerational equity
3. Intergenerational linkages
4. Public vs. private sector approaches
5. Future older adults

VIII. Death and Dying (5%)

A. Responses to death and dying
1. Attitudes of older people toward death
2. Responses of the dying (for example: Kübler-Ross)

B. Care for the dying
1. Quality of life of the dying
2. Roles and responses of the caregiver (for example: family, clergy, physicians, nurses)
3. Care settings for the dying (for example: hospitals, hospice, home)
4. Respite

C. Bereavement
1. Effects of bereavement
   a. Normal responses
   b. Abnormal responses
2. Adjustment to bereavement
   a. Functions of the funeral
   b. Support networks
3. Sources of variation (for example: individual resources and experiences, nature of death)

D. Issues concerning death and dying
1. Definitions of death and dying
2. Legal issues
   a. Patient's right to know
   b. Options
3. Euthanasia
4. Suicide

E. Multicultural perspectives on death and dying

Sample Questions: Foundations of Gerontology

1. Which is the best experimental design for studying the way intelligence varies with age?
    1) cross-sectional
    2) longitudinal
    3) period analysis
    4) time series analysis

2. In 1960, a study of parents of children with developmental disabilities was conducted. A gerontological researcher is now planning to study possible personality changes in those parents. What would be an appropriate research methodology for the researcher to employ?
    1) cross-sectional design
    2) longitudinal design
    3) period analysis
    4) time series analysis

3. Why is the ratio of males to females in the population over age 65 less than one to one?
    1) higher male birthrate
    2) higher female birthrate
    3) higher male mortality rate
    4) higher female mortality rate

4. Which two public systems are facing the greatest pressure from growth in the number and proportion of older people?
    1) health care and housing
    2) health care and income
    3) transportation and housing
    4) transportation and education

5. Which variables are used to determine the age dependency ratio?
    1) older adults and nursing home beds
    2) grandparents and grandchildren
    3) retirement-age persons and working-age persons
    4) old (65+) persons and old-old (85+) persons

6. What do population projections of the baby boom cohort indicate about the future older population?

    The older population will most likely be
    1) a smaller percentage of the U.S. population.
    2) better educated.
    3) less politically active.
    4) in worse health.

7. What is the primary reason that the search for universal factors associated with senescence is complicated?
    1) Aging is variable.
    2) Older people die before studies are completed.
    3) Funds for research on aging are limited.
    4) Gerontologists are unable to agree on a definition of senescence.

Sample Questions: Foundations of Gerontology

8. Which is a criterion for differentiating between biological aging and other biological processes, such as disease?
    1) Aging will occur in most members of a species.
    2) Aging may have both positive and negative effects on physical functioning.
    3) A functional change affects older adults more that it affects persons in other age groups.
    4) Aging comes from within the body rather than from outside environmental factors.

9. Based on the free radical theory of aging, what would be an appropriate behavior that might increase one's life expectancy?
    1) Exercise for 45 minutes at least three times a week.
    2) Eat foods rich in antioxidants.
    3) Eat a low-calorie, high-protein diet.
    4) Do nothing. Life expectancy is determined through genetic programming.

10. Which procedure would best minimize the negative effects associated with relocating an older person from one nursing home to another?
    1) Involve the person in planning the move.
    2) Accomplish the relocation as quickly as possible.
    3) Ensure that the new nursing home differs substantially from the old one.
    4) Anticipate the person's needs and make decisions accordingly.

11. Which finding resulted from research on older people's response time for complex tasks? Older people
    1) process stimuli quickly.
    2) can no longer perform complex tasks.
    3) use trial and error to solve timed complex tasks.
    4) use strategies to help them perform complex tasks.

12. Erikson's psychosocial stage of ego integrity versus despair most closely corresponds to which of Levinson's developmental stages?
    1) early adult transition
    2) midlife transition
    3) middle adulthood
    4) late adulthood

13. Which theory suggests that older people who have low levels of social activity have a high degree of life satisfaction?
    1) activity
    2) age stratification
    3) disengagement
    4) exchange

14. An older person with a chronic mental disorder enters the mental health system. Which type of treatment will the person most likely receive?
    1) medication
    2) psychotherapy

Sample Questions: Foundations of Gerontology

3) group therapy
4) nutritional modification

15. Which term represents the idea that older people from historically underrepresented groups experience discrimination on the basis of age and race?
    1) age stratification
    2) double jeopardy
    3) ethnocentrism
    4) new ageism

16. Which best explains why people move to retirement communities?
    1) development of a major disability
    2) desire for low-cost housing
    3) easy access to public transportation
    4) interest in age-homogeneous settings

17. Which view does the concept of an extended family emphasize?
    Older people
    1) develop family-like ties with friends and neighbors.
    2) live near and interact regularly with family members.
    3) seldom see or receive assistance from their children.
    4) wish to live with their children during widowhood.

18. Which was the first federal legislation to address the needs of the aged?
    1) Age Discrimination in Employment Act
    2) Older Americans Act
    3) Social Security Act
    4) Medicare Health Insurance Program

19. Which is most likely to show a decline immediately after retirement?
    1) community involvement
    2) family relationships
    3) health
    4) income

20. Which is the main function of retirement in the United States?
    1) reducing the workforce
    2) rewarding people for service rendered
    3) supporting people too old for employment
    4) supporting people physically unable to hold jobs

21. Which pattern of political participation by older people is accurate?
    Older people
    1) are less likely to hold opinions on current national issues than their younger counterparts.
    2) become politically conservative with age and tend to vote Republican.
    3) are underrepresented among those holding political office.
    4) are more likely to vote than their younger counterparts.

Sample Questions: Foundations of Gerontology

22. What is the major reason why the Supplemental Security Income (SSI) program is underutilized?
    1) There is too much red tape involved in the income eligibility verification process.
    2) SSI eligibility requirements vary from state to state.
    3) The older cohort is unwilling to participate in entitlement programs.
    4) Many older people are not aware that they are eligible for SSI benefits.

23. Which statement accurately compares the Medicare and Medicaid programs?
    1) Medicare is the main source of payment for nursing home costs; Medicaid pays for nursing home costs in only a small number of cases.
    2) Medicare is an age-based program; Medicaid is a needs-based program.
    3) Medicare is financed by general tax revenues; Medicaid is financed by the Social Security trust fund.
    4) Medicare does not require the insured to pay a significant amount for co-insurance and deductibles; Medicaid requires the insured to pay.

24. Which of the following federal programs requires a means test?
    1) Medicare
    2) Senior Nutrition Program
    3) Social Security
    4) Supplemental Security Income

25. In Kübler-Ross's theory of dying, which stage is characterized by a sense of loss?
    1) anger
    2) bargaining
    3) denial
    4) depression

Recommended Resources

Atchley, R.C. (1997). Social forces and aging: An introduction to social gerontology *(8th ed.). Belmont, CA: Wadsworth.*

Cox, H. (1996). Later life: The realities of aging *(4th ed.). Upper Saddle River, NJ: Prentice Hall.*

Supplementary Resource

Spence, A. (1995). Biology of human aging *(2nd ed.). Upper Saddle River, NJ: Prentice Hall.*

Study Guide
Life Span Developmental Psychology (583)

Credit Hours: 3
Question Type(s): Multiple-choice
Credit Level: Lower

The information in this study guide is valid until Summer 2001.
If you will be taking the examination after that date, be sure to check for a new edition of this guide before you complete your preparation for the exam.

General Description of the Examination

The Regents College Examination in Life Span Developmental Psychology is based on material usually taught in an undergraduate course in life span development. The examination measures understanding of the concepts, principles, and theories associated with life span development as well as the ability to apply this understanding in specific situations. You will be expected to integrate content across the stages of the life span. A course in life span development typically has introductory psychology as a prerequisite.

Content Outline

Content Area	Percent of Examination
I. The Study of Life Span Development	15%
II. Genetics, Prenatal Development, and Childbirth	10%
III. Infancy and Toddlerhood	10%
IV. Early Childhood	10%
V. Middle Childhood	10%
VI. Adolescence	10%
VII. Early Adulthood	10%
VIII. Middle Adulthood	10%
IX. Late Adulthood	10%
X. Death and Dying	5%
Total	**100%**

I. The Study of Life Span Developmental Psychology (15%)

A. Concepts related to the study of life span development
1. Defining development and the life span approach
2. Domains of development
   a. Physical, biological, and evolutionary
   b. Cognitive
   c. Social and emotional (psychosocial, personality)
3. The complex nature of development (including the influence of growth, maturation, and learning; heredity and environment)
4. Continuity and discontinuity
5. Contexts of development and individual differences (for example: society, culture, home, school, race, gender, socioeconomic status)

B. Research methods in the study of life span development
1. The scientific method (formulate a research question, develop a hypothesis, test the hypothesis, draw conclusions, make findings available)
2. Types of research
   a. Naturalistic observation and field experiments
   b. Controlled experiment (independent and dependent variables)
   c. Surveys
   d. Interviews
   e. Case studies
3. Developmental research designs
   a. Longitudinal
   b. Cross-sectional
   c. Sequential
4. Interpretation of results
   a. Correlation vs. causation
   b. Cohort effects
   c. Issues related to generalizability (for example: sex, culture, socioeconomic status, ecological validity)
5. Ethical considerations (for example: ability to give informed consent, privacy, deception)

C. Theoretical foundations for life span developmental psychology
1. Ethological perspectives (for example: Bowlby)
2. Psychodynamic perspectives (for example: Freud, Erikson, Levinson, Vaillant)
3. Learning perspectives
   a. Classical conditioning (for example: Pavlov, Watson)
   b. Operant conditioning (for example: Skinner, Thorndike)
   c. Social learning (for example: Bandura)
4. Cognitive perspectives (for example: Piaget, Case, Bruner)
5. Humanistic perspectives (for example: Maslow, Rogers)
6. Ecological and social-contextual perspectives (for example: Bronfenbrenner, Vygotsky)

II. Genetics, Prenatal Development, and Childbirth (10%)

A. Basic concepts of genetics
1. Genes and chromosomes
2. Genotype, phenotype, and reaction range
3. Dominant and recessive traits
4. Sex-linked traits
5. Polygenic traits
6. Behavior genetics (for example: twin and adoption studies)
7. Genetic and chromosomal abnormalities (for example: phenylketonuria, Turner syndrome, Down syndrome, Huntington's disease)
8. Natural selection

B. Prenatal development
1. Conception
2. Prenatal critical periods and stages (germinal, embryonic, fetal)
3. Prenatal environment (for example: maternal nutrition, illness, and stress; teratogens)
4. Prenatal life-support systems (placenta, umbilical cord, amnion)

C. Childbirth
1. Preparation for, and methods of, childbirth
2. Stages of childbirth
3. Complications (for example: prematurity, postmaturity, low birth weight)
4. Neonatal assessment (for example: Apgar scale, Brazelton scale)

D. Issues (for example: genetic assessment and counseling, cultural differences)

III. Infancy and Toddlerhood (10%)

A. Characteristics of the newborn
1. Reflexes
2. States and behaviors (for example: sleep/wake cycles)

B. Development in infancy and toddlerhood
1. Physical development
   a. Principles of growth (for example: cephalocaudal, proximodistal, individual differences)
   b. Motor development
   c. Sensory development
   d. Brain development
   e. Nutrition
2. Cognitive development
   a. Methods of studying (for example: habituation)
   b. Sensorimotor intelligence (for example: object permanence, imitation)
   c. Perceptual development (for example: cross-modal perception)
   d. Early language development

    3. Social and emotional development
        a. Temperament and personality
        b. Attachment to caregivers
        c. Self-awareness and independence
        d. Emotions and emotional expression
        e. Family processes
    4. Issues (for example: attachment vs. bonding, sudden infant death syndrome [SIDS], child abuse and neglect, day care)

IV. Early Childhood (10%)

A. Physical development
  1. Physical growth
  2. Motor development
  3. Brain development
  4. Nutrition
  5. Health and safety

B. Cognitive development
  1. Preoperational and symbolic thought
  2. Zone of proximal development (Vygotsky)
  3. Language development
  4. Memory development
  5. Early childhood education (for example: Head Start)

C. Social and emotional development
  1. The developing self (for example: self-concept, self-awareness, autonomy, initiative)
  2. Gender identity and gender roles
  3. Moral development and prosocial behavior
  4. Family (for example: parenting styles, sibling relationships, extended families)
  5. Peers and play
  6. Culture, school, and media (for example: television, aggression)
  7. Childhood fears

D. Issues (for example: working parents, divorce, day care, sexual abuse)

V. Middle Childhood (10%)

A. Physical development
  1. Physical growth and motor skill development
  2. Health and fitness (for example: sports, exercise, childhood obesity)

B. Cognitive development
  1. Concrete operational thought
  2. Language development and communication (for example: vocabulary, grammar, bilingualism)
  3. Memory development and metacognition
  4. Intelligence testing and theories (Gardner, Sternberg)
  5. Children with specific educational needs (for example: learning disabilities, gifted and talented, attention-deficit hyperactivity disorder)

Life Span Developmental Psychology

C. **Social and emotional development**
 1. Self-concept and self-esteem
 2. Moral development and prosocial behavior
 3. Family (for example: changing definitions of the family, family interaction, extended families)
 4. Peer relationships and social cognition (for example: conformity, popularity, rejection, friendship patterns)
 5. The school setting (for example: achievement and motivation, mainstreaming, gender differences)
 6. Problems of adjustment (for example: childhood depression, school phobia, aggressive and antisocial behavior, stress and resilience)

D. **Issues** (for example: after-school care [self-care children], divorce, families who are homeless, poverty, cultural differences in schooling)

VI. Adolescence (10%)

A. **Physical development**
 1. Physical growth (for example: individual and gender differences, growth spurt)
 2. Sexual maturation and puberty
 3. Health and fitness (for example: sports and exercise, nutrition)

B. **Cognitive development**
 1. Formal operational thought
 2. Adolescent egocentrism
 3. Decision making
 4. Metacognition

C. **Social and emotional development**
 1. Self-concept and identity (for example: Marcia's theory, cultural and gender differences, body image, risk-taking behavior)
    a. Moral development and behavior (for example: Kohlberg, Gilligan)
 2. Sexuality (for example: attitudes, knowledge, behavior, values, birth control, sexual harassment and abuse, sexually transmitted diseases, adolescent pregnancy)
 3. Family (for example: shared and nonshared values, autonomy and interdependence, relationships with parents and siblings)
 4. Peers (for example: adolescent subculture, conformity, cliques and crowds, shared and nonshared values)
 5. The school setting (for example: transitions in school, dropping out of school, achievement and socioeconomic status)
 6. Problems of adjustment (for example: substance abuse, violence, depression, suicide, eating disorders)

D. **Issues** (for example: stereotypes about adolescents, cross-cultural perspectives, adolescents who leave home, adolescents who have jobs)

VII. Early Adulthood (10%)

A. Physical development
   1. Physical changes
   2. Health and fitness (for example: nutrition, exercise, lifestyle, stress)
   3. Sexual reproductive systems (for example: fertility, pregnancy)

B. Cognitive development
   1. Postformal thought and intelligence (for example: relativistic thinking, dialectical thought)
   2. Influences of life events, occupation, and higher education on cognitive development

C. Social and emotional development
   1. Models of adult development (for example: Erikson, Gould, Levinson, Loevinger, Schaie, Vaillant)
   2. Affiliation and intimacy
      a. Friendship (for example: gender differences)
      b. Marriage, cohabitation, and love (for example: Sternberg's triangular theory of love)
      c. Parenthood and the family life cycle (for example: birth, adoption, becoming a parent)
      d. Couples with no children
      e. Divorce
      f. Single adults
   3. Achievement
      a. Education
      b. Importance of work
      c. Vocational development
      d. Mentoring
      e. Career changes
      f. Employment and parenthood
      g. Dual-earner couples

D. Issues (for example: gender identity and roles, spouse abuse, unemployment)

VIII. Middle Adulthood (10%)

A. Physical development
   1. Physical changes (for example: hearing, vision, reaction time, menopause and the climacteric)
   2. Health and fitness (for example: lifestyle, environment, heredity, physiology, stress, personality type [A and B], cardiovascular disorders, cancer)
   3. Changes in sexual functioning

B. Cognitive development
   1. Memory and learning
   2. Intelligence (for example: fluid, crystallized, practical)
   3. Wisdom and expertise

C. Social and emotional development
   1. Affiliation and intimacy
      a. Midlife crisis/shift/transitions (for example: empty nest, intergenerational relationships)
      b. Stability of personality
      c. Family configurations (for example: returning adult children, "sandwich generation")
      d. Divorce and remarriage
      e. Grandparenthood
      f. Changes in gender roles
   2. Achievement and generativity
      a. Career satisfaction and change
      b. Job performance
      c. Work-related problems (for example: alienation, burnout, reevaluation)

D. Issues (for example: unemployment, cultural differences, gender differences)

IX. Late Adulthood (10%)

A. **Basic concepts—life expectancy, periods of late adulthood, causal theories of aging (cellular, genetic, wear and tear)**

B. **Physical development**
   1. Physical changes (for example: sensory, motor, sleep patterns, reaction time, physical appearance, physiological reactions, organ reserve)
   2. Health and fitness (for example: nutrition, exercise)
   3. Health problems (for example: depression, dementia, multi-infarct dementia, Alzheimer's disease, Pick's disease)
   4. Sexuality

C. **Cognitive development**
   1. Intellectual changes in information processing
   2. Memory and problem solving in the real world
   3. Intelligence (age influences, history influences, and nonnormative influences; terminal decline)
   4. Emerging cognitive interests (for example: aesthetics, spirituality)

D. **Social and emotional development**
   1. Affiliation and intimacy
      a. Psychosocial theories of aging (for example: activity theory, disengagement theory)
      b. Relationships with friends and neighbors
      c. Divorce and remarriage
      d. The single older adult
      e. Family relationships
      f. Living arrangements

      2. Achievement and generativity
         a. Work
         b. Retirement
         c. Leisure
         d. Education
      3. Life review, integrity vs. despair

E. Issues (for example: health treatment and costs; elder abuse; social and economic issues; poverty; ageism and stereotypes; cross-cultural perspectives; use of alcohol, drugs, and prescription medications)

X. Death and Dying (5%)

A. Conceptions of death and dying (for example: across the life span, in different cultures)

B. Confronting one's own death (stages of adjustment)

C. The hospice movement

D. Grief, mourning, and bereavement
        1. The grieving process
        2. Rituals and customs

E. Issues (for example: euthanasia, living wills, suicide)

Sample Questions: Life Span Developmental Psychology

1. Which aspect is central in the Lamaze method of childbirth?
    1) Childbirth occurs at home, rather than in a hospital.
    2) Anesthetics and cesarean sections are not used.
    3) The mother learns breathing and other exercises to help manage labor pains.
    4) The mother and infant are submerged in a warm bath.

2. A 23-year-old patient is terminally ill. After a long struggle, she realizes that death is inevitable and begins to make preparations for her funeral and burial. This patient is most likely in which of Kübler-Ross's stages of dying?
    1) acceptance
    2) bargaining
    3) denial
    4) depression

3. A child who is in first grade has messy handwriting, does not know the alphabet, and is easily distracted during class. He has difficulty sitting still for more than a few minutes at a time and his parents describe him as very fidgety. These findings are characteristic of which childhood problem?
    1) attention-deficit hyperactivity disorder
    2) dysgraphia
    3) dyslexia
    4) emotional disturbance

4. A researcher studies language development by collecting data from a specific group of infants starting when they are six months old and continuing at six-month intervals for the next five years. This is an example of which developmental research design?
    1) cross-sectional
    2) experimental
    3) longitudinal
    4) sequential

5. A 60-year-old man runs a 100-yard dash and feels very short of breath. This never happened to him 20 years ago. This reflects which common physiological change that occurs with aging?
    1) lower hormone levels
    2) less cardiovascular efficiency
    3) declining agility
    4) slower neural conduction

6. What is the leading cause of death among preschool children in the United States?
    1) accidents
    2) diarrhea
    3) diphtheria
    4) pneumonia

Sample Questions: Life Span Developmental Psychology

7. A 14-year-old acts responsibly, makes decisions independently, and accepts the consequences of inappropriate behavior. The parents of this adolescent probably relied most upon which parenting style?
    1) authoritarian
    2) authoritative
    3) permissive
    4) restrictive

8. Water from one of two identical full glasses is poured into a taller glass of a different shape. Which child will know that the taller glass contains the same amount of water as the shorter glass?
A child at the
    1) concrete operational stage who hears the procedure described verbally
    2) preoperational stage who hears the procedure described verbally
    3) concrete operational stage who observes the procedure
    4) preoperational stage who observes the procedure

9. Which is the main factor accounting for the high correlations between IQ and personality traits in identical twins who grew up in different environments?
    1) They shared the same prenatal environment.
    2) They have identical genotypes.
    3) They have identical phenotypes.
    4) Fifty percent of their genes are identical.

10. According to David Elkind, what is one form of adolescent egocentrism?
    1) excessive self-esteem
    2) fear of taking risks
    3) use of concrete operations
    4) imaginary audience

11. How is "grief" best defined?
    1) a change in status and role
    2) the burial rituals used in a culture
    3) an abnormal reaction to death
    4) an emotional response to loss

12. How does Levinson describe adulthood?
    1) a long, stable period
    2) process of continuous change
    3) rapid changes between stable periods
    4) stable periods alternating with transitional periods

13. Which early form of communication consists of only two or more essential words?
    1) functional grammar
    2) overextension
    3) telegraphic speech
    4) underextension

Sample Questions: Life Span Developmental Psychology

14. Infants who are deaf usually begin to babble at the same age as infants who can hear, even though their vocal language development does <u>not</u> continue. Which concept is illustrated by this situation?
    1) learning
    2) maturation
    3) modeling
    4) reinforcement

15. What usually happens to hearing in middle adulthood?
    1) Females and males both experience very little hearing loss.
    2) Females and males both experience the same amount of hearing loss.
    3) Males experience more hearing loss than females do.
    4) Females experience more hearing loss than males do.

16. A two year old struggles to button his shirt and angrily refuses help from his father. According to Erikson's theory, this child is most likely in which stage of psychosocial development?
    1) autonomy versus shame and doubt
    2) industry versus inferiority
    3) initiative versus guilt
    4) trust versus mistrust

17. What is the relationship between age and plasticity in the brain?
Plasticity is
    1) greater at younger ages.
    2) greater at older ages.
    3) greatest at age 35 and then declines.
    4) constant throughout the life span.

18. When a one-week-old infant is held upright so that her feet just touch a surface, which reflex is most likely to occur?
    1) Babinski
    2) Moro
    3) plantar
    4) stepping

19. Which statement best describes research findings regarding personality traits, such as neuroticism and openness, throughout adulthood?
    1) Personality traits are generally stable over the life span.
    2) Personality traits usually change dramatically as a function of an adult's experiences.
    3) There is greater stability of personality traits in childhood than in adulthood.
    4) There is more variation of personality traits in late adulthood than in early adulthood.

Sample Questions: Life Span Developmental Psychology

20. A researcher is interested in whether the type of preschool program that children attend affects the children's grades when they are in elementary school. What is the dependent variable in this study?
    1) age of the child
    2) grades received in elementary school
    3) type of preschool program attended
    4) placement in elementary school

21. Which technique is used to study perceptual development during infancy?
    1) conservation studies
    2) double-blind studies
    3) equilibration studies
    4) habituation studies

22. The process of putting life in perspective occurs in which of Erikson's stages of psychosocial development?
    1) autonomy versus shame and doubt
    2) integrity versus despair
    3) intimacy versus isolation
    4) generativity versus stagnation

23. Both work and parenthood help to address which psychosocial conflict for most adults?
    1) identity versus role confusion
    2) generativity versus stagnation
    3) integrity versus despair
    4) intimacy versus isolation

24. Carol Gilligan's theory of moral development emphasizes the importance of which factor?
    1) the rules of society
    2) the rights of individuals
    3) the individual's level of cognitive development
    4) interpersonal communication and relationships

25. According to Piaget's theory, which statement best describes the preoperational stage of cognitive development in children?
    1) Children are able to solve problems logically, if the problems are focused on the present.
    2) Children begin to learn about themselves and the world around them, and begin to form concepts.
    3) Children are able to think about objects, events, or people that are not physically present.
    4) Children begin to think in abstract terms with little or no help from adults.

Sample Questions: Life Span Developmental Psychology

26. A couple has been informed that their newborn daughter has stubby fingers and a "webbed" neck. The parents are told that, in the future, their child may have difficulty with spatial and mathematical reasoning, be shorter than average, and probably will not be able to have children. These characteristics are typical of which sex chromosome abnormality?
    1) the triple X pattern
    2) phenylketonuria (PKU)
    3) Klinefelter syndrome
    4) Turner syndrome

27. An adolescent's process of developing an ethnic identity may entail an active "ethnic identity search." This process is similar to which process in James Marcia's theory of identity formation?
    1) achievement
    2) diffusion
    3) foreclosure
    4) moratorium

28. Which biological theory of aging holds that all human genes are programmed to produce changes that bring about death?
    1) cross-linkage theory
    2) endocrine theory
    3) Hayflick theory
    4) wear-and-tear theory

29. At what age do infants typically first display the ability to turn the head in the direction of a sound?
    1) at birth
    2) one week
    3) two weeks
    4) three weeks

30. Which stage does Vaillant add to Erikson's description of human development during early adulthood?
    1) career consolidation
    2) early adult transition
    3) keeping the meaning
    4) postformal thought

31. Which developmental theorist emphasized that children's cognitive development is optimized by having adults or skilled peers actively assist them through the process of solving problems just beyond the child's ability level?
    1) Noam Chomsky
    2) Jean Piaget
    3) B.F. Skinner
    4) Lev Vygotsky

Sample Questions: Life Span Developmental Psychology

32. Cross-sectional research on fluid and crystallized intelligence supports which conclusion?
    1) Fluid intelligence peaks during young adulthood.
    2) Crystallized intelligence peaks during young adulthood.
    3) Fluid intelligence first declines in late adulthood.
    4) Crystallized intelligence first declines in middle adulthood.

33. Which term is used to describe children's emerging awareness and control of their intellectual skills and abilities?
    1) intelligence quotient
    2) metacognition
    3) operational thought
    4) self-awareness

34. The second stage of labor in the birth process is characterized by which occurrence?
    1) The cervix starts to dilate.
    2) Contractions expel the placenta.
    3) The newborn is delivered.
    4) The amniotic sac breaks.

35. Which type of thought has been characterized as relativistic and integrative in nature?
    1) concrete operational
    2) postformal
    3) preoperational
    4) sensorimotor

Recommended Resources

The examination development committee recommends that you obtain one of the textbooks listed below for use in preparing for the examination. All three of these textbooks are comprehensive, well written, and up-to-date. Each of them provides excellent coverage of most of the material in the content outline. In addition, each of these textbooks has a companion study guide. If you would like assistance in organizing your study and reviewing the material in the textbooks, the committee recommends that you purchase the study guide that was designed to accompany the text you are using.

Berger, K. (1994). The developing person through the life span *(3rd ed.). NY: Worth.*

Study Guide: Straub, R., & Brown, J.W. (1994). Study guide to accompany Berger: The developing person through the life span *(3rd ed.). NY: Worth.*

> The content of this textbook is presented chronologically. For your reference, a topical table of contents is also included. Each chapter begins with an overview and a set of questions to stimulate thought. Each chapter concludes with a summary, a list of key terms, and review questions. At the end of each major age span, an overview of the period is presented. The textbook contains many color photographs, tables, and charts that illustrate the content and provide visual interest. You may need to refer to a second textbook to cover all of the material in this study guide's content outline.

Sample Questions: Life Span Developmental Psychology

The study guide that accompanies the Berger text is excellent. Each chapter includes a review of the key concepts, guided study questions, section reviews, and lists of key terms. Multiple-choice, true-false, and matching exercises appear in each chapter. The correct answers to test questions are explained to ensure understanding. The fill-in-the-blank sections may not be as useful.

OR

Santrock, J. (1997). Life-span development *(6th ed.). Dubuque, IA: Brown & Benchmark.*

Study Guide: Peden, B., Santrock, J., & Keniston, A. (1997). Student study guide to accompany Life-span development—Santrock *(6th ed.). Dubuque, IA: Brown & Benchmark.*

The content of this textbook is presented chronologically. The book is visually interesting, with many well selected color illustrations. Each chapter has concept tables that summarize the main points. Each chapter also contains an outline, an overview, critical thinking exercises, and a list of key terms. Most chapters contain boxed features including themes of sociocultural variations and current issues, as well as reviews of popular books on child-rearing and life span issues. You may need to refer to a second textbook to cover all of the material in this study guide's content outline.

The study guide that accompanies the Santrock text is comprehensive. Each chapter contains learning objectives and a guided review. Self-test exercises are open-ended and multiple-choice. The fill-in-the-blank sections in the guided review may not be as useful.

An electronic study guide is available that contains interactive quizzes in addition to the material that appears in the printed study guide. A student audiotape is also available.

Two other supplements are available that help the student understand human development from specific professional perspectives:

> *Guide to life-span development for future nurses*
> *Guide to life-span development for future educators*

OR

Sigelman, C., & Shaffer, D. (1995). Life-span human development *(2nd ed.). Pacific Grove, CA: Brooks/Cole.*

Study Guide: Rider, E. (1995). Study guide for Sigelman and Shaffer's Life-span human development *(2nd ed.). Pacific Grove, CA: Brooks/Cole.*

This textbook may appeal to you if you wish to address the content topically rather than chronologically. The book is presented in a single color, black-and-white format. It may not be as visually interesting to you as the other two textbooks. Many tables, charts, and figures are presented to illustrate the content. Each chapter begins with an outline and concludes with summary points and a list of key terms. Most chapters contain boxed features that offer a closer look at topics of interest. You may need to refer to a second textbook to cover all of the material in this study guide's content outline.

Sample Questions: Life Span Developmental Psychology

The study guide that accompanies Sigelman and Shaffer is designed to promote active learning through a guided review of the important principles and concepts in the textbook. Each chapter begins with a set of learning objectives. Each chapter also contains a comprehensive multiple-choice test, matching exercises, and a number of exercises designed to challenge you to think about and apply what you have learned. The fill-in-the-blank summary may not be as useful.

Audiovisual Resources

The examination development committee has also identified the following audiovisual resources. Some of these resources may provide you with an overview of the material; others provide enrichment in areas of interest. You may be able to locate these resources through a college library, a local library, or interlibrary loan. Some of them may be available for rental in a local video store. It is not necessary to purchase these resources.

WQED/Pittsburgh, & the University of Michigan (Producers). (1990). Seasons of Life *[video series]. (Available from the Annenberg/CPB Multimedia Collection, P.O. Box 2345, So. Burlington VT 05407-9920, phone 1-800-LEARNER [1-800-532-7637], fax 1-802-864-9846.) The five video programs in this series are listed below. The series is also available as 26 audio programs.*

1. Infancy and Early Childhood
2. Childhood and Adolescence (Ages 6–20)
3. Early Adulthood (Ages 20–40)
4. Middle Adulthood (Ages 40–60)
5. Late Adulthood (Ages 60+)

WGBH/Boston (with the American Psychological Association) (Producers). (1990). Discovering Psychology *[video series]. (Available from the Annenberg/CPB Multimedia Collection, P.O. Box 2345, So. Burlington, VT 05407-9920, phone 1-800-LEARNER [1-800-532-7637], fax 1-802-864-9846.) The video programs in this series that are related to life-span development are listed below.*

5. The Developing Child
6. Language Development
17. Sex and Gender
18. Maturing and Aging

Genesis Film Production in association with WNET (Educational Broadcasting Corporation) (Producers). (1983). Miracle of Life *[Primal Instinct Nature Series video]. Available from Time-Life, 1450 E. Paraham Road, Richmond, VA 23280-2300, 1-800-621-7026.*

Study Guide
Microbiology (558)

Credit Hours: 3 **Credit Level:** Lower
Question Type(s): Multiple-choice

The information in this study guide is valid until Summer 2001.
If you will be taking the examination after that date, be sure to check for a new edition of this guide before you complete your preparation for the exam.

General Description of the Examination

The Microbiology examination measures knowledge and understanding of bacteria, algae, fungi, protozoa, and viruses, and their relationships with humans. It is based on material typically taught in a one-semester course in Microbiology at the undergraduate level. A general knowledge of chemistry, as well as biology or anatomy and physiology, is assumed.

Content Outline

Content Area	Percent of Examination
I. Introduction to Microbiology	5%
II. Biology of Microorganisms	25%
III. Control of Microorganisms	15%
IV. Disease, Resistance, and the Immune System	20%
V. Biology of Infectious Disease	25%
VI. Environmental, Food, and Industrial Microbiology	10%
Total	**100%**

I. Introduction to Microbiology (5%)

A. Early history
1. Discovery of microorganisms
2. Disproving spontaneous generation
3. Development of germ theory of disease
4. Discovery of immunity
5. Discovery of viruses
6. Development of chemotherapeutic agents

B. Place of microorganisms in the world
1. Prokaryotes vs. eukaryotes
2. Prokaryotes
   a. Bacteria
   b. Cyanobacteria
3. Archaeobacteria
4. Eukaryotes
   a. Protista
      (1) Protozoa
      (2) Simple algae
   b. Fungi
5. Viruses

C. Microbial laboratory techniques
1. Microscopy
2. Stain procedures
3. Media preparation and growth
4. Pure culture and aseptic techniques

II. Biology of Microorganisms (25%)

A. Anatomy
1. Prokaryotes
   a. Bacteria
      (1) Gross morphology—cell size, shape, and arrangement
      (2) Component parts—name, chemistry, function, and importance
         (a) Cell envelope
            i) Capsule
            ii) Cell wall
            iii) Cell membrane
         (b) Cytoplasm
            i) Chromosome and plasmids
            ii) Ribosomes
            iii) Cell inclusions
         (c) Spores
         (d) Appendages
            i) Flagella
            ii) Pili
   b. Cyanobacteria—special features

2. Eukaryotes (fungi, algae, and protozoa)
    a. Fungi
        (1) Cellular and vegetative structures
        (2) Reproductive structures
    b. Algae
        (1) Cellular structure
        (2) Photosynthetic apparatus
    c. Protozoa
        (1) Structures for locomotion—flagella, cilia, pseudopodia
        (2) Vacuoles

B. Growth and nutrition
1. Patterns of nutrition
2. Requirements for growth (increase in numbers/mass)
    a. Physical—pH, temperature
    b. Chemical—N, C, energy sources; vitamins; trace elements
    c. Gaseous—anaerobic, aerobic, facultative
3. Cultivation
    a. Selective, enrichment, and differential media
    b. Mixed and pure cultures
    c. Culture techniques—solid and liquid media
4. Dynamics of populations
    a. Growth mechanisms—binary fission, mycelial growth, budding
    b. Growth rates, generation times
    c. Growth curve: lag, exponential growth, and stationary phases
    d. Enumeration of cell number and culture mass—viable and total counts; turbidity

C. Metabolism—basic mechanisms of metabolism and energy conversion
1. Enzymes (mediators of all reactions)
    a. Structures and function
    b. Factors that influence enzyme activity
2. Photosynthetic vs. chemosynthetic metabolism
3. Cellular respiration
    a. Aerobic
    b. Anaerobic
    c. Fermentation
4. Photosynthesis
5. Biosynthetic mechanisms
    a. Macromolecular synthesis
        (1) Nucleic acid
        (2) Gene expression and protein synthesis
    b. Regulation
        (1) Control of enzyme activity (feedback regulation)
        (2) Control of enzyme synthesis

D. Genetics
1. Variation in populations of cells and viruses
   a. Genotype and phenotype
   b. Haploidy and diploidy
   c. Asexual and sexual
2. Mutations
   a. Spontaneous and induced
   b. Selection of mutants
   c. Types of mutations
3. Recombination
   a. Transformation
   b. Transduction (generalized; specialized)
   c. Conjugation
4. Gene manipulation
   a. Plasmids
   b. Genetic elements
   c. Genetic engineering/recombinant DNA techniques
   d. Applications of genetic engineering

E. Viruses
1. Structure
   a. Type of nucleic acid
   b. Capsid, envelope, specialized structures
2. Multiplication of viruses
   a. Lytic cycle
   b. Lysogenic cycle
   c. Retroviruses
3. Effects of viruses on cells
   a. Isolation and detection of viruses
   b. Cytopathologic effects
   c. Transformation and oncogenesis
   d. Control of viral replication

III. Control of Microorganisms (15%)

A. Principles of microbial control
1. Factors influencing success of control methods
   a. Number and nature of microorganisms
   b. Strength of control agent
   c. Time, temperature, and pH
2. General methods of control
   a. Bactericidal vs. bacteriostatic
   b. Sterilization
   c. Asepsis
   d. Disinfection and antisepsis
   e. Sanitation
   f. Antibiosis and chemotherapy

B. Physical methods of control
   1. Incineration
   2. Dry heat
   3. Moist heat
      a. Boiling water
      b. Pressurized steam—autoclave
      c. Pasteurization
   4. Radiation
      a. Ultraviolet
      b. Ionizing
   5. Filtration

C. Chemical methods of control
   1. Chemical agents
      a. Halogens
      b. Alcohols
      c. Phenols
      d. Heavy metals
      e. Aldehydes
      f. Gases
      g. Detergents
      h. Peroxides
      i. Dyes
   2. Tests for effectiveness of antiseptics and disinfectants
      a. Phenol coefficient test
      b. Use-dilution test

D. Chemotherapeutic agents and antibiotics
   1. Modes of action
   2. Chemotherapeutic agents (nucleic acid analogs and others)
      a. Antiviral agents
      b. Antifungal agents
      c. Antiparasitic agents
   3. Antibiotics (penicillin and others)
      a. The problem of antibiotic resistance
      b. Antibiotic sensitivity assays

IV. Disease, Resistance, and the Immune System (20%)

A. The disease process
   1. Host-parasite relationships
      a. The concepts of infection and disease
      b. The normal flora
      c. Commensalism
      d. Mutualism
      e. Antibiosis
      f. Opportunists
      g. Virulence

2. Progress of disease
    a. Periods of disease
    b. Clinical and subclinical disease
3. Types of diseases
    a. Communicable and noncommunicable diseases
    b. Endemic, epidemic, and pandemic diseases
    c. Acute and chronic diseases
    d. Primary and secondary diseases
    e. Local and systemic diseases
    f. Nosocomial diseases
4. Establishment of disease
    a. Transmission
    b. Portal of entry
    c. Dose
    d. Virulence factors

B. Nonspecific resistance to disease
1. Mechanical and chemical factors
    a. Skin
    b. Mucous membranes
    c. pH (cell, tissue, organ)
    d. Lysozyme
2. Phagocytosis
    a. Types of phagocytes
    b. Mechanism of phagocytosis
    c. Reticuloendothelial system (mononuclear phagocytic system)
3. Inflammation
4. Individual, species, and racial immunities

C. Principles of immunology
1. Antigens
    a. Definition, composition, and types of antigens
    b. Haptens
    c. Immunologic tolerance
    d. Self vs. nonself
2. The immune system
    a. B lymphocytes
    b. T lymphocytes
    c. Location and operation of the immune system
    d. Cell-mediated immunity—process, stimulation, lymphokines
    e. Antibody-mediated (humoral) immunity—antibody structure and origin, five types of antibodies, primary and secondary antibody responses, opsonization, antigen-antibody reactions, neutralization, precipitation, agglutination
    f. The complement system
    g. The alternative pathway
3. Types of immunity
    a. Naturally acquired, active immunity
    b. Artificially acquired, active immunity

c. Naturally acquired, passive immunity
d. Artificially acquired, passive immunity
4. Serological and diagnostic reactions
   a. Radioimmunoassays
   b. Neutralization reactions
   c. Precipitation and agglutination
   d. Complement fixation
   e. Monoclonal antibody
   f. Fluorescent antibody tests
   g. Enzyme-linked immunosorbent assay (ELISA)
   h. Western-blot analysis
   i. Polymerase chain reaction (PCR)
   j. Gene probe

D. Disorders of the immune system
1. Type I anaphylactic hypersensitivity
   a. Allergens and IgE
   b. Basophils and mast cells
   c. Degranulation and mediator release
   d. Atopic diseases
2. Type II cytotoxic hypersensitivity
   a. Transfusion reactions
   b. Hemolytic disease of the newborn
   c. Autoimmune reactions
3. Type III immune complex hypersensitivity
   a. Immune complex formation
   b. Serum sickness
   c. Systemic lupus erythematosus (SLE)
4. Type IV cellular hypersensitivity
   a. Infection allergy
   b. Contact dermatitis
   c. Tuberculin skin test
5. Immune-deficiency diseases

V. Biology of Infectious Diseases (25%)

Parameters for the study of infectious disease:

—Recognition of the disease syndrome (symptoms)
—Etiology of the disease
  —unique morphological characteristics of the agent(s)
  —unique physiological characteristics of the agent(s)
  —unique cultural characteristics of the agent(s)
—Mode of transmission and portal of entry
—Methods of immunization
—Methods of prevention, control, and/or treatment

A. Respiratory tract diseases
1. Bacterial diseases
   a. Tuberculosis
   b. Diphtheria

  c. Pertussis
  d. Streptococcal diseases
  e. Bacterial pneumonias
  f. Primary atypical pneumonia
  g. Legionnaires' disease
  h. Bacterial meningitis
  i. Chlamydial diseases
 2. Viral diseases
  a. Common cold
  b. Influenza
  c. Measles
  d. Mumps
  e. Chickenpox
  f. Rubella
  g. Viral pneumonia
 3. Fungal diseases
  a. Cryptococcosis
  b. Histoplasmosis
  c. Aspergillosis
 4. Protozoal diseases—*Pneumocystis carinii* pneumonia

B. Gastrointestinal tract diseases and intoxications
 1. Bacterial diseases and intoxications
  a. Typhoid fever
  b. Cholera
  c. Salmonellosis
  d. *E. coli* disease
  e. *Campylobacter* disease
  f. *H. pylori* disease
  g. Shigellosis
  h. Botulism
  i. Staphylococcal food poisoning
  j. *Clostridium perfringens* food poisoning
  k. Brucellosis
 2. Viral diseases
  a. Hepatitis A
  b. Enteroviral infections
 3. Protozoal diseases
  a. Amoebiasis
  b. Giardiasis
  c. Cryptosporidiosis

C. Urogenital tract diseases
 1. Bacterial diseases
  a. Gonorrhea
  b. Syphilis
  c. Chlamydia
 2. Viral diseases
  a. Genital herpes
  b. Genital warts

3. Fungal diseases—candidiasis
4. Protozoal diseases—trichomoniasis

D. Skin and wound diseases
1. Bacterial diseases
   a. Tetanus
   b. Staphylococcal diseases
   c. Anthrax
   d. Leprosy
   e. Gas gangrene
2. Viral diseases
   a. Smallpox
   b. Rabies
   c. Warts
   d. Herpes simplex infections
3. Fungal diseases
   a. Ringworm (tinea)
   b. Candidiasis

E. Blood diseases
1. Bacterial diseases
   a. Plague
   b. Tularemia
   c. Spotted fevers
   d. Typhus fevers
   e. Q fever
   f. Lyme disease
   g. Toxic shock syndrome
2. Viral diseases
   a. Yellow fever
   b. Viral encephalitis
   c. Hepatitis B and hepatitis C
   d. Infectious mononucleosis
   e. Hemorrhagic fevers
3. Protozoal diseases
   a. Malaria
   b. Sleeping sickness
   c. Toxoplasmosis

F. Nosocomial diseases

G. Acquired immunodeficiency syndrome (AIDS)
1. Human immunodeficiency virus (HIV)
2. Transmission and epidemiology
3. Pathology (including opportunistic infections)
4. Diagnosis
5. Treatment

VI. Environmental, Food, and Industrial Microbiology (10%)

A. **Environmental (ecological) microbiology**
   1. Terrestrial environment (soils)
      a. Flora of soil
      b. Biogeochemical cycles (carbon, nitrogen, sulfur, phosphorus)
      c. Biodegradation and recycling
   2. Aquatic environment
      a. Fresh water and marine environment
      b. Aquatic pollution (eutrophy, human waste, food waste, industrial waste)
      c. Pollution abatement
         (1) Waste water treatment
         (2) Preparation of drinking water

B. **Food microbiology**
   1. Foods produced using microorganisms
   2. Spoilage of food by microorganisms
   3. Preservation methods

C. **Industrial microbiology**
   1. Alcoholic beverages (beer, wine, distilled spirits)
   2. Production of organic compounds (organic acids, amino acids, vitamins, enzymes, steroids, antibiotics, other pharmaceuticals)
   3. Biological insecticides
   4. Genetically engineered or recombinant DNA products

Sample Questions: Microbiology

1. Which microorganisms are classified as prokaryotes?
    1) algae
    2) archaeobacteria
    3) protozoans
    4) yeasts

2. The Gram stain is an example of which type of stain?
    1) differential
    2) lipid granule
    3) negative
    4) simple

3. The presence of a spore in a vegetative bacterial cell helps establish that the organism is of which genus?
    1) *Bacillus*
    2) *Erwinia*
    3) *Pseudomonas*
    4) *Salmonella*

4. The nutrition of *Euglena gracilis* is generally classified as being
    1) autotrophic
    2) heterotrophic
    3) parasitic
    4) saprophytic

5. In a mixed culture, a bacterial species is found as 0.01% of the total cell population. What is the best way to isolate this species in a pure culture?
    1) Use the pour plate isolation method.
    2) Grow the culture on a minimal medium.
    3) Grow the culture on an enrichment medium and then use the streak plate method.
    4) Use the streak plate method directly.

6. A barrier that prevents the passage of bacteria, but not smaller particles, is placed between a genetic donor and a genetic recipient. Which gene transfer will be stopped by this barrier?
    1) conjugation
    2) generalized transduction
    3) specialized transduction
    4) transformation

7. If a bacterial gene coding for a repressor protein were to be mutated so that it no longer binds to the operator site in the DNA, what would happen to the structural genes controlled by that repressor?
    They would be
    1) permanently turned on.
    2) turned on only in the presence of the inducer.

Sample Questions: Microbiology

3) turned on only in the absence of the inducer.
4) turned off.

8. What can be determined from the one-step growth curve exhibited by lytic bacteriophage?
    1) the extent of recombination during the latent period
    2) the site of the virion particles
    3) the average number of viruses released per infected cell
    4) the evolutionary relatedness of bacteriophage and animal viruses

9. Which method ensures sterilization because of its high sporicidal activity?
    1) desiccation
    2) pasteurization
    3) pressurized steam
    4) ultraviolet light

10. How does moist heat kill bacteria?
    1) by causing hemolysis of the cell
    2) by denaturing proteins in the cell
    3) by dissolving lipids in the cell
    4) by extracting water from the cell

11. In which form of radiation does the killing of cells result from inactivation of sensitive macromolecules by free radicals such as the hydroxyl radical (OH•)?
    1) infrared
    2) ionizing
    3) ultraviolet
    4) visible

12. Why is the practice of adding antibiotics to animal feed controversial? The practice
    1) inflates the cost of meat.
    2) limits the supply of antibiotics for humans.
    3) lowers the natural resistance of the animal to disease.
    4) promotes development of bacterial resistance.

13. Which microorganism is a common, normal inhabitant of the human intestine?
    1) *Escherichia coli*
    2) *Pseudomonas aeruginosa*
    3) *Staphylococcus aureus*
    4) *Vibrio cholerae*

14. Which enzyme, found in tears and saliva, destroys the cell walls of gram-positive bacteria?
    1) catalase
    2) coagulase
    3) lysozyme
    4) penicillinase

Sample Questions: Microbiology

15. How do tears and saliva disrupt the cell walls of gram-positive bacteria?
    Tears and saliva
    1) contain lysozyme, which weakens the cell wall.
    2) are basic and hydrolyze the cell wall.
    3) deprive the bacteria of oxygen.
    4) lower the ionic strength of the fluid in which the bacteria are suspended.

16. What do high serum titers of IgM indicate?
    1) the typical primary response to an antigen
    2) a typical secondary response to an antigen
    3) the inability to produce IgG
    4) a disorder of the immune system

17. A child immunized with a polio vaccine will develop which type of immunity?
    1) artificially acquired, active
    2) artificially acquired, passive
    3) naturally acquired, active
    4) naturally acquired, passive

18. Why is a pneumococcus resistant to destruction by phagocytes?
    The resistance is due largely to the
    1) presence of a capsule.
    2) chemical nature of the cell membrane.
    3) secretion of an exotoxin.
    4) secretion of an endotoxin.

19. A newborn in an intensive care nursery has low birth weight and shows signs of cataracts and a heart murmur. A history reveals that the mother had contracted an undiagnosed upper respiratory tract infection with a low-grade fever and a mild skin rash during the third week of pregnancy. Which microbial agent would most likely be responsible for these occurrences in both mother and newborn?
    1) beta-hemolytic streptococci
    2) *Haemophilus influenzae*
    3) *Mycoplasma pneumoniae*
    4) rubella virus

20. A poultry processor comes to the clinic complaining of chronic cough and general malaise. Lung X rays show calcified nodules. A tuberculin test and acid-fast test are negative. Sputum samples show large fungus-like oval cells, often inside leukocytes. What is the most probable cause of the person's signs and symptoms?
    1) an adenovirus
    2) *Histoplasma capsulatum*
    3) *Mycobacterium tuberculosis*
    4) *Treponema pallidum*

Sample Questions: Microbiology

21. What is the mechanism that leads to death in patients with cholera?
    1) cardiomyopathy
    2) endotoxin poisoning
    3) fluid and electrolyte losses
    4) renal failure

22. Why are there more female than male carriers of gonorrhea in the United States?
    1) Acidity of the female reproductive tract enhances infectivity and growth of the gonococcus.
    2) Females are often asymptomatic and therefore fail to seek treatment.
    3) Increased use of condoms usually prevents male exposure.
    4) Males are more easily treated and cured than females.

23. What does the detection of coliform bacteria in a drinking water supply reveal? The water is
    1) safe to drink, because coliform bacteria are not usually pathogenic.
    2) potentially dangerous to drink, because the water is contaminated with bacteriophage.
    3) potentially dangerous to drink, because the water is contaminated with soil or sewage.
    4) dangerous to drink, because coliform bacteria cause fatal intestinal disease.

24. Which disease may be prevented by immunizing with a toxoid?
    1) smallpox
    2) tetanus
    3) tuberculosis
    4) typhoid fever

25. A microorganism used in an industrial setting to produce antibiotics should ideally exhibit which characteristic?
    The microorganism should
    1) be a small, slowly growing cell.
    2) grow at low temperatures.
    3) excrete the secondary metabolite.
    4) produce large amounts of polysaccharide.

26. The conversion of ethanol in wine to acetic acid occurs when
    1) organisms are present that carry out malolactic fermentation
    2) the ethanol concentration is too low to inhibit the growth of acetic acid bacteria
    3) too much fermentable carbohydrate is present
    4) the wine has been exposed too long to aerobic conditions

Study Materials

Alcamo, I.E. (1997). Fundamentals of microbiology *(5th ed.). Reading, MA: Benjamin/Cummings (distributed by Addison Wesley).*

Black, J. (1998). Microbiology: Principles and exploration *(4th ed.). Upper Saddle River, NJ: Prentice Hall.*

Madigan, M. et al. (1997). Brock Biology of microorganisms *(8th ed.). Upper Saddle River, NJ: Prentice Hall.*

Talaro, K.P., & Talaro, A. (1999). Foundations in Microbiology *(3rd ed.). Boston: McGraw Hill.*

Tortora, G. et al. (1998). Microbiology: An introduction *(6th ed.). Reading, MA: Benjamin/Cummings (distributed by Addison Wesley).*

Study Guide
Pathophysiology (584)

Credit Hours: 3 **Credit Level:** Upper
Question Type(s): Multiple-choice

The information in this study guide is valid until Summer 2001.
If you will be taking the examination after that date, be sure to check for a new edition of this guide before you complete your preparation for the exam.

General Description of the Examination

The Regents College Examination in Pathophysiology is based on material usually presented in a one-semester course in pathophysiology. The examination measures understanding of the physiologic mechanisms altered by disease in the living organism. The primary focus of the examination is on the altered health states of adults, including clinical presentation, signs and symptoms, appropriate diagnostic studies, and global concepts of treatment. A familiarity with normal anatomy and physiology and microbiology is assumed. A familiarity with concepts of biochemistry and immunology would also be useful.

Content Outline

Content Area	Percent of Examination
I. Cell Biology/Mechanisms of Cell Injury/Neoplasia	10%
II. Host Defense/Hematology	16%
III. The Cardiovascular System	15%
IV. The Respiratory System	11%
V. The Renal System/Fluids and Electrolytes/Acid–Base	12%
VI. Neurology and the Musculoskeletal System	10%
VII. The Gastrointestinal System/Nutrition/The Endocrine System/The Reproductive System	16%
VIII. Clinical Applications Related to the Various Systems	10%
Total	**100%**

I. Cell Biology/Mechanisms of Cell Injury/Neoplasia (10%)

A. **Cellular adaptation**
   1. Atrophy
   2. Hypertrophy
   3. Hyperplasia
   4. Metaplasia
   5. Dysplasia

B. **Cellular injury**
   1. Reversible (for example: swelling)
   2. Irreversible
      a. Necrosis
      b. Apoptosis
      c. Fatty changes
   3. Mechanisms
      a. Hypoxia
      b. Hyperoxia/free radical
      c. Nutritional deficits
      d. Chemical injury
      e. Infectious agents
      f. Physical and mechanical injury (trauma)
   4. Intracellular accumulation (for example: Tay-Sachs, glycogen storage, hemochromatosis)

C. **Genetic disorders**
   1. Chromosomal abnormalities (for example: Down syndrome)
   2. Mutations (for example: sickle cell anemia, thalassemias, cystic fibrosis)

D. **Neoplasia**
   1. Nomenclature/classification/naming of neoplasias
      a. Characteristics of benign neoplasms
      b. Characteristics of malignant neoplasms
      c. Mechanisms of metastasis
   2. Mechanisms of oncogenesis
      a. Viral oncogenesis
         (1) Oncogenes
         (2) Tumor suppressor genes
      b. Radiation-induced oncogenesis (for example: UV radiation)
      c. Chemical-induced oncogenesis (for example: cigarette smoking and asbestos)
   3. Tumor markers
      a. Prostate-specific antigen (PSA)
      b. a-fetoprotein (AFP)
      c. Carcinoembryonic antigen (CEA)
   4. Effects of the tumor on the host
      a. Paraneoplastic syndromes
      b. Thrombosis/hemorrhage
      c. Pain

II. Host Defense/Hematology (16%)

A. Alterations in integument function
1. Mechanical barriers
   a. Burns
   b. Trauma (for example: abrasions)
2. Disorders of the skin
   a. Inflammatory response (for example: psoriasis, acne, lupus)
   b. Allergic response
   c. Neoplastic (for example: basal cells, malignant melanoma, and associated risk factors, such as fair skin, UV light exposure, heredity, moles, etc.)

B. Inflammation
1. Local manifestation (chemical/cellular response)
   a. Acute (hemodynamic changes and inflammatory mediators)
   b. Chronic (granuloma and inflammatory mediators)
   c. Healing
   d. Exudates
2. Systemic manifestation
   a. Chemical/cellular response
   b. Fever/pain
   c. Global immune response

C. Alterations in wound healing
1. Dysfunction in inflammatory response
2. Nutritional factors
3. Congenital factors
4. Complicating factors (for example: diabetes, autoimmune)
5. Impaired perfusion (for example: surgical wounds, stasis and decubitus ulcers)

D. Alterations in immune function
1. Primary immune deficiencies (congenital)
   a. Severe combined immunodeficiency
   b. Wiskott-Aldrich syndrome
   c. T-cell disorders
   d. B-cell disorders
2. Secondary immune deficiencies (acquired)
   a. HIV
   b. AIDS
   c. Iatrogenic immune deficiency (for example: trauma, stress, chemo-radiation)
3. Autoimmunity disease
   a. Localized (for example: Graves' disorder and Hashimoto's thyroiditis)
   b. Generalized or systemic (for example: lupus scleroderma)
4. Hypersensitivity reactions
   a. Type I: atopic hypersensitivity or anaphylactic allergic reaction
   b. Type II: cytotoxic or cytolytic hypersensitivity
   c. Type III: immune complex or Arthus reaction
   d. Type IV: delayed hypersensitivity

5. Immunization/vaccination
   a. Active
   b. Passive
   c. Immunomodulating agents/adjuvants (for example: BCG—bacille Calmette-Guérin colony stimulating factors)
   d. Immunotherapy (for example: interferon, monoclonal antibodies)
6. Immunocompromised host
   a. Etiology
      1) Primary, such as HIV and diabetes
      2) Secondary due to chemotherapy or steroid therapy
   b. Risks (for example: opportunistic infections)
   c. Preventive measures (for example: avoiding crowds in flu season)
7. Transplantation reactions
   a. Graft-versus-host disease (GvHD)
   b. Rejection
   c. Blood transfusion reactions

E. **Alterations in the hematologic system**
   1. Disorders of red blood cells
      a. Anemia
         1) Due to decreased RBC production (for example: iron deficiency, vitamin B_{12} and folic acid deficiencies)
         2) Due to blood loss
         3) Due to increased destruction (for example: hemolytic anemia, sickle cell anemia)
      b. Polycythemia
         1) Primary
         2) Secondary
   2. Disorders of white blood cells
      a. Leukopenia
      b. Leukocytosis
      c. Leukemia
         1) Acute lymphocytic
         2) Chronic lymphocytic
         3) Acute myelogenous
         4) Chronic myelogenous
      d. Multiple myeloma
   3. Disorders of platelets
      a. Thrombocytopenia
      b. Alterations in platelet function
   4. Disorders of plasma and hemostasis
      a. Nutritional deficiencies
      b. Hemophilia A
      c. Hemophilia B
      d. Other coagulation deficiencies (for example: vitamin K deficiency)
      e. Factors predisposing to thrombosis
      f. Clinical determination of coagulation value
      g. Disseminated intravascular coagulation (DIC)

III. The Cardiovascular System (15%)

A. **Cardiac excitation/rhythmic disturbances**
1. Action potentials (fast response/slow response)
2. Disorders of conduction
   a. Atrial (for example: tachycardia)
   b. Ventricular (for example: tachycardia, bradycardia)
3. Enhanced automaticity/ectopy (for example: PVC)
4. Re-entry (for example: SVT)
5. Abnormal conduction pathways (for example: heart block, Wolff-Parkinson-White syndrome)

B. **Valvular function/dysfunction**
1. Mitral stenosis/regurgitation
2. Aortic stenosis/regurgitation
3. Tricuspid/pulmonic disease

C. **Cardiac mechanics/heart failure**
1. Congestive heart failure
   a. Etiology
   b. Basic mechanism
   c. Compensatory responses
   d. Clinical manifestations
      1) Right-sided heart failure
      2) Left-sided heart failure
      3) Backward failure (low-output failure) vs. forward failure (high-output failure)
2. Cardiogenic shock
3. Transplant

D. **Atherosclerosis**
1. Risk factors
2. Vascular disease
3. Coronary artery disease
   a. Clinical presentation/angina
   b. Cardiac ischemia
   c. Cardiac injury
   d. Cardiac infarct
   e. Complications/sequelae

E. **Hypertension**
1. Renin-angiotensin-aldosterone system
2. Risk factors
3. Classification
   a. Primary
   b. Secondary
4. End organ effects (for example: left ventricular hypertrophy)

F. **Congenital heart disease**
   1. Acyanotic defects (for example: septal defects)
   2. Cyanotic defects (for example: tetralogy of Fallot)

G. **Pericardial disease**
   1. Effusion
   2. Pericarditis

H. **Peripheral vascular disease**
   1. Arterial
      a. Occlusive arterial disease
      b. Aneurysmal arterial disease
      c. Aortic dissection
   2. Venous
      a. Thromboembolic venous disease
      b. Superficial thrombophlebitis
      c. Acute deep vein thrombosis
      d. Varicose veins

I. **Embolic disease**
   1. Etiology
   2. Sequelae

J. **Shock**
   1. Hypovolemic
   2. Septic

K. **Infection**
   1. Rheumatic heart disease
   2. Infective endocarditis

IV. The Respiratory System (11%)

A. **Obstructive diseases**
   1. Chronic obstructive pulmonary disease (COPD)
      a. Asthma
         1) Extrinsic
         2) Intrinsic
      b. Chronic bronchitis
      c. Emphysema
   2. Bronchiectasis
   3. Cystic fibrosis

B. **Restrictive diseases**
   1. Extrinsic
      a. Pneumothorax
      b. Pleural effusion
      c. Kyphoscoliosis
      d. Ankylosing spondylitis
      e. Neuromuscular disease
         1) Guillain-Barré syndrome
         2) Myasthenia gravis
      f. Pickwickian syndrome/sleep apnea
   2. Intrinsic
      a. Sarcoidosis
      b. Pulmonary fibrosis (for example: pneumoconiosis)

C. **Cardiovascular diseases of the lung**
   1. Pulmonary embolism
   2. Pulmonary hypertension
   3. Cor pulmonale

D. **Alterations in gas exchange**
   1. Hypoxemia
   2. Hypoxia
   3. Hypercapnia
   4. Ventilation-perfusion mismatch

E. **Respiratory failure**
   1. Acute respiratory failure
   2. Adult respiratory distress syndrome (ARDS)
   3. Infant respiratory distress syndrome

F. **Infection**
   1. Atelectasis
   2. Pneumonia (for example: bacterial, viral, pneumocystis)
   3. Tuberculosis

G. **Neoplasia**
   1. Small (oat) cell
   2. Large cell
   3. Squamous cell
   4. Adenocarcinoma
   5. Oral laryngeal cancer/bronchogenic cancer

H. **Risk factors**

V. The Renal System/Fluids and Electrolytes/Acid-Base (12%)

A. **Fluid imbalance**
   1. Control of fluid volume
   2. Deficit
   3. Excess

B. **Electrolyte imbalance, including etiology, effect, and clinical manifestation of imbalances in the following:**
   1. Potassium
   2. Sodium
   3. Calcium
   4. Magnesium
   5. Phosphate
   6. Chloride

C. **Acid-base imbalance**
   1. Acidosis
   2. Alkalosis
   3. Buffers
   4. Compensatory mechanisms

D. **Acute renal failure**
   1. Prerenal
   2. Intrarenal
   3. Postrenal

E. **Chronic renal failure**
   1. Electrolyte imbalances
   2. Physiologic changes
   3. Dialysis
   4. Transplant

F. **End-stage renal disease**

G. **Infection**
   1. Pyelonephritis
   2. Urogenital infection
   3. Glomerulonephritis

H. **Disorders of the bladder**
   1. Cystitis
   2. Neurogenic bladder

I. **Nephrotic syndrome**

J. **Neoplasia**

K. **Stone formation**

VI. Neurology and the Musculoskeletal System (10%)

A. Traumatic injury
1. Head
    a. Blunt trauma (concussion)
    b. Increased intracranial pressure (cerebral edema)
    c. Hematoma
    d. Craniofacial trauma
2. Spinal cord: Mechanisms of injury
    a. Spinal shock
    b. Autonomic dysreflexia
    c. Chronic injury consideration

B. Seizure disorders
1. Epilepsy
    a. Partial (focal) (for example: temporal lobe)
    b. Generalized (absence, tonic-clonic, petit and grand mal seizures)
    c. Status epilepticus
2. Other (drug, febrile, traumatic, tumor)

C. Vascular insult
1. Cerebrovascular accident (CVA)
    a. Hemorrhagic
    b. Thromboembolic
    c. AV malformations and aneurysms
2. Transient ischemic attack (TIA)

D. Infections/inflammation
1. Meningitis
2. Guillain-Barré syndrome
3. Encephalitis
4. Reye's syndrome
5. Polio
6. Abscess

E. Alterations in neural psychological function
1. Alzheimer's disease
2. Psychotic illness (for example: schizophrenia, major affective disease, delusional disorder)
3. Nonpsychotic illness (for example: anxiety disorders, personality disorders)

F. Alterations in neuromuscular function
1. Parkinson's disease
2. Multiple sclerosis
3. Myasthenia gravis
4. Amyotrophic lateral sclerosis (ALS)

G. **Pain**
1. Types of pain
2. Pain assessment
3. Mechanisms (pathways)
4. Endorphins-opioid receptors
5. Management of pain

H. **Alterations of the musculoskeletal system**
1. Muscle disorders
   a. Muscular dystrophy
   b. Myopathies
2. Joint disorders
   a. Noninflammatory joint disorders, such as osteoarthritis
   b. Inflammatory joint disorders
      1) Noninfectious joint disorders
         (a) Rheumatoid arthritis
         (b) Ankylosing spondylitis
         (c) Gout
         (d) Psoriatic arthritis
      2) Infectious joint disorders
         (a) Septic arthritis
         (b) Lyme disease
3. Bone disorders
   a. Osteomyelitis
   b. Paget's disease
   c. Osteoporosis
   d. Osteomalacia
   e. Rickets
   f. Trauma (for example: fractures)
      1) Complete—closed, open, comminuted
      2) Incomplete—greenstick, stress
      3) Dislocation/subluxation

I. **Neoplasia**
1. Tumors of the brain and spinal cord (for example: gliomas, meningiomas, neurofibroma, angioma)
2. Tumors of the skeletal system (for example: osteosarcoma, fibrosarcoma)
3. Tumors of the muscular system (for example: rhabdomyosarcoma)

VII. The Gastrointestinal System/Nutrition/The Endocrine System/The Reproductive System (16%)

A. **Disorders of motility**
1. Nausea and vomiting
2. Achalasia (cardiospasm)
3. Reflux esophagitis/gastroesophageal reflux disease (GERD)
4. Hiatal hernia
5. Diarrhea/constipation

B. Disorders of absorption
   1. Malabsorption syndromes
   2. Sprue (celiac disease)

C. Peptic ulcer disease
   1. Types
      a. Gastric
      b. Duodenal
   2. Pathogenesis (for example: back diffusion, *Helicobacter pylori*)
   3. Clinical manifestations

D. Inflammatory bowel disease
   1. Ulcerative colitis/Crohn's disease
   2. Pathogenesis
   3. Clinical manifestations

E. Hepatic/gallbladder disorders
   1. Jaundice (prehepatic such as hemolytic, intrahepatic, posthepatic)
   2. Viral hepatitis
   3. Cirrhosis
      a. Necrotic
      b. Toxic
      c. Alcoholic
      d. Pathogenetic
   4. Cholecystitis/cholelithiasis
   5. Clinical manifestations
      a. Liver disease
      b. Gallbladder disease
      c. Alcoholism

F. Disorders of the pancreas
   1. Exocrine (pancreatitis—acute and chronic)
   2. Endocrine—Diabetes mellitus
      a. Risk factors
      b. Insulin-dependent vs. noninsulin-dependent
      c. Long-term effects
      d. Complications such as diabetic ketoacidosis

G. Alterations of hypothalamic-pituitary function
   1. Panhypopituitarism (Simmonds' disease, Sheehan's syndrome)
   2. Pituitary adenoma and consequences
   3. Acromegaly and galactorrhea/amenorrhea
   4. Diabetes insipidus
   5. Syndrome of inappropriate ADH secretion

H. Alterations of thyroid function and parathyroid function
   1. Thyrotoxicosis (hyperthyroidism)
   2. Graves' disease
   3. Toxic nodular goiter
   4. Hashimoto's thyroiditis
   5. Complications resulting from T_4/T_3 excess and deficiency

6. Hyperparathyroidism (primary and secondary)
7. Hypoparathyroidism

I. **Alterations of adrenal function** (cortex and medulla)
1. Cushing's syndrome
2. Addison's disease
3. Aldosteronism and primary hyperaldosteronism
4. Androgen excess/virilization (adrenal-genital hyperplasia)
5. Pheochromocytoma
6. Drug-induced alteration (for example: steroids)

J. **Female reproductive system**
1. Endometriosis
2. Amenorrhea/dysmenorrhea
3. Leiomyomas
4. Fibrocystic breast disease
5. Infertility
6. Ovarian cysts

K. **Male reproductive system**
1. Hypogonadism
2. Cryptorchidism
3. Benign prostatic hyperplasia
4. Infertility

VIII. Clinical Applications Related to the Various Systems (10%)

A. **Signs and symptoms** (patient clinical presentation)
(For all systems—pain, and in addition, for GI, etc. section—jaundice)

B. **Diagnostic studies, including normal values**
For hematology—transfusion reaction
For cardiovascular—cardiac enzymes
For renal—urinalysis
For GI, etc. section—direct and indirect bilirubin, amylase, lipase, liver enzymes, blood sugar, hormones
For neurology, etc.—Glasgow Coma Scale, brain stem function

C. **Treatment**
For hematology—blood transfusion, anti-coagulation therapy, thrombolytic therapy
For respiratory—bronchodilators
For cardiovascular—lifestyle modification, diet, exercise
For renal—fluid intake, dialysis
For GI, etc.—H_2 blockers, Pepto-Bismol
For neurology, etc.—hormone replacement therapy, calcium supplements

Sample Questions: Pathophysiology

1. What process occurs in endocrine-dependent organs when hormonal stimulation decreases?
    1) atrophy
    2) dysplasia
    3) hyperplasia
    4) hypertrophy

2. Which cells are capable of hyperplastic growth?
    1) cardiac muscle
    2) epithelial
    3) nerve
    4) skeletal muscle

3. A patient with carrier status for cystic fibrosis marries another person with carrier status for the disease. What are the consequences for the children of this couple?
    1) All of their children will be carriers.
    2) Some of their children will have the disease, others will carry the trait, and others will not have the disease.
    3) All of their children will either carry the trait or present with the disease.
    4) None of the children will be affected as the disorder skips every other generation.

4. Why are corticosteroids used to treat skin disorders such as seborrheic dermatitis?
    1) to reduce inflammation
    2) to minimize pain
    3) to enhance collagen production
    4) to prevent infection

5. Which factor is related to a high incidence of malignant melanoma?
    1) steroid hormone activity
    2) excess solar radiation
    3) long-term antibiotic use
    4) fungal infection

6. Hyperthyroidism, enlarged thyroid glands, and exophthalmos are symptoms associated with which disorder?
    1) myxedema
    2) myasthenia gravis
    3) Hashimoto's disease
    4) Graves' disease

7. Angioedema, bronchial wheezing, and cutaneous itching within minutes of exposure to an allergen are typical of which type of hypersensitivity reaction?
    1) type I: anaphylactic
    2) type II: cytotoxic
    3) type III: immune complex
    4) type IV: delayed

Sample Questions: Pathophysiology

8. What is the major distinguishing characteristic of Mobitz type I (Wenckebach) second degree heart block?
   1) Impulses are not conducted from the atria to the ventricles and a ventricular escape rhythm is present.
   2) P waves are nonconducted and there is a consistent P-R interval.
   3) There is a prolonged P-R interval, but each P wave is associated with a QRS complex.
   4) There is a progressively lengthening P-R interval until one P wave is not conducted.

9. Preload, afterload, contractility, and heart rate affect which action in the cardiovascular system?
   1) cardiac cycle
   2) myocardial conduction
   3) cardiac output
   4) atrial systole

10. What congenital circulatory problem results in the bypassing of the lungs and the recirculating of blood into the pulmonary circuit?
    1) patent foramen ovale
    2) ventricular septal defect
    3) transposition of the great arteries
    4) atrioventricular septal defect

11. Chest pain, friction rub, and serial electrocardiogram (ECG) abnormalities are found in which disorder?
    1) myocardial infarction
    2) angina pectoris
    3) cardiac tamponade
    4) acute pericarditis

12. Chronic dilation of the medium-sized bronchi and bronchioles is most likely to be associated with which disease?
    1) bronchiectasis
    2) emphysema
    3) chronic bronchitis
    4) cystic fibrosis

13. What is the primary mode of transmission of tuberculosis (TB)?
    1) airborne droplets
    2) contaminated blood
    3) fecal-oral contamination
    4) sexual contact

Sample Questions: Pathophysiology

14. Which is an accurate statement regarding extracellular fluid volume deficit? It is the result of
    1) addition of sodium into the body.
    2) removal of a sodium-containing fluid from the body.
    3) excessive aldosterone secretion in the body.
    4) inadequate sodium and water losses from the body.

15. What blood test results are consistent with a diagnosis of respiratory acidosis?
    1) PaO$_2$ 65 mm Hg; PaCO$_2$ 58 mm Hg; pH 7.1; anion gap 8 mEq/L
    2) PaO$_2$ 99 mm Hg; PaCO$_2$ 25 mm Hg; pH 7.2; anion gap 25 mEq/L
    3) PaO$_2$ 100 mm Hg; PaCO$_2$ 29 mm Hg; pH 7.7; anion gap 10 mEq/L
    4) PaO$_2$ 94 mm Hg; PaCO$_2$ 50 mm Hg; pH 7.5; anion gap 7 mEq/L

16. Which of the following can be expected in the late stages of chronic renal failure when the glomerular filtration rate (GFR) declines to 25%?
    1) hypocalcemia and phosphaturia
    2) hypercalcemia and decreased calcium deposition
    3) hypocalcemia and phosphate retention in kidneys
    4) hypercalcemia and decreased serum calcium levels

17. A painless chancre is the most common symptom associated with which urogenital disorder?
    1) chlamydia
    2) gonorrhea
    3) syphilis
    4) nonspecific urogenital infection

18. Which signs and symptoms are indicative of autonomic dysreflexia (hyperreflexia)?
    1) tachycardia, hyperthermia, and urticaria, with pain and spasm below the level of the lesion
    2) hypoventilation and absence of deep tendon reflexes, with flaccid paralysis bilaterally below the level of the lesion
    3) hypotension, hypothermia, and paresthesia, with pallor and goose bumps above the level of the lesion
    4) hypertension, bradycardia, and severe headache, with sweating and flushing of the skin above the level of the lesion

19. Why are pain-reducing measures such as acupuncture and transcutaneous electrical nerve stimulation (TENS) thought to alleviate pain?
    1) They inhibit the release of endogenous opioids and enkephalins.
    2) They are morphine antagonists that moderate pain.
    3) They stimulate the release of substance P.
    4) They close the pain gate and recruit large fibers.

20. Which joint structure is involved in the initial stage of degenerative joint disease?
    1) synovial membrane
    2) articular cartilage
    3) epiphyseal plate
    4) joint cavity

Sample Questions: Pathophysiology

21. What factor causes exacerbation of a sliding hiatal hernia?
    1) an increase in intrathoracic pressure
    2) an increase in intra-abdominal pressure
    3) a decrease in intra-abdominal pressure
    4) a decrease in intrathoracic pressure

22. What is the primary damage seen with gluten intolerance (celiac disease)?
    1) edema of the mucous membrane
    2) hyperplasia of lymphoid tissue
    3) atrophy or loss of epithelial villi
    4) increased cell production

23. Which treatment is recommended for the syndrome of inappropriate antidiuretic hormone secretion (SIADH)?
    1) administration of hypotonic saline
    2) infusion of 0.9% saline
    3) injection of posterior pituitary extract
    4) restriction of fluid intake

24. Which laboratory test result would indicate thyroid hypofunction?
    1) low levels of ACTH
    2) high levels of T_4 and T_3
    3) low levels of parathyroid hormone
    4) high levels of TSH

25. Avoidance of caffeine is typically recommended for individuals with which pair of disorders?
    1) ovarian cysts and endometriosis
    2) mastitis and amenorrhea
    3) fibrocystic breast disease and premenstrual syndrome
    4) pelvic inflammatory disease and leiomyomas

26. Which disease is most likely to be diagnosed in a 37-year-old individual who presents with joint pain, fever, morning stiffness, proteinuria, and a red rash across the bridge of the nose and cheeks?
    1) gout
    2) rheumatoid arthritis
    3) systemic lupus erythematosus
    4) ankylosing spondylitis

27. Which arterial blood gas result indicates that a patient is hyperventilating?
    1) pH 7.32, $PaCO_2$ 45, PaO_2 82, HCO_3- 20
    2) pH 7.48, $PaCO_2$ 30, PaO_2 98, HCO_3- 22
    3) pH 7.20, $PaCO_2$ 60, PaO_2 60, HCO_3- 27
    4) pH 7.51, $PaCO_2$ 52, PaO_2 95, HCO_3- 33

Sample Questions: Pathophysiology

28. What is the ultimate goal when treating hepatic encephalopathy?
    1) to decrease urea production
    2) to eliminate carbohydrate intake
    3) to reduce serum ammonia level
    4) to prevent secondary infection

Recommended Textbook

The Recommended Textbook is essential to your understanding of the content of the examination, and the examination development committee suggests that you use it as your primary study aid. It will be to your advantage to use a combination of the Recommended Textbook and at least one Additional Resource in your study.

Copstead, L.-E. (1995). Perspectives on pathophysiology. *Philadelphia: W.B. Saunders.*

Study aids include chapter overviews, definitions of key terms, highlighted key concepts, and chapter summaries.

Additional Resources

To further assist you in learning the content, the examination development committee suggests that you supplement your understanding of specific topics or concepts related to the content outlined earlier by using at least one of the additional textbooks listed below, in conjunction with the CONTENT CHART FOR SPECIFIC TOPICS on pages 120–122. You may be able to locate the resource(s) you prefer to use through a public or college library.

McCance, K.L., & Heuther, S.E. (1998). Pathophysiology: The biologic basis for disease in adults and children *(3rd. ed.). St. Louis: Mosby.*

Porth, C.M. (1998). Pathophysiology: Concepts of altered health states *(5th ed.). Philadelphia: Lippincott.*

Price, S.A., & Wilson, L.M. (1997). Pathophysiology: Clinical concepts of disease processes *(5th ed.). St. Louis: Mosby.*

Content Chart for Specific Topics

The following content chart is organized so that topics associated with broad content areas are grouped together. For example, topics related to neoplasia are grouped together so that you can study general concepts about tumors and then proceed to more detailed concepts about specific tumors.

In general, the content chart is intended to complement the presentation of the material in the Recommended Textbook. The listed topics can be studied in conjunction with and/or at about the same point as the associated topic is presented in the Copstead textbook.

Topic	McCance & Huether (3rd ed., 1998)	Price & Wilson (5th ed., 1997)	Porth (5th ed., 1998)
Neoplasia Tumor Markers	pp. 313–315, Table 10-3 (314)	not indexed (discussed with each tumor)	pp. 98, 1167 (Testicular), 1172 (Prostate)
Mechanisms of Metastasis	pp. 350–357	pp. 111–112	pp. 87–88
Angiogenesis	pp. 355–356	not indexed	p. 88 (limited discussion)
Neoplasia Nomenclature	pp. 309–311, Table 10-2 (310)	pp. 116–117, Table 8-1 (117)	Table 5-1 (83)
Lung Cancers	pp. 1191–1197 Table 32-4 (1193)	pp. 638–641	pp. 516–518
Brain Cancers	pp. 540–546, Table 16-10 (542)	pp. 897–905, Table 57-1 (898)	pp. 907–910
Musculoskeletal Cancers (Rhabdomyosarcoma)	pp. 1482–1483, 1511–1514 (in relation to a child)	pp. 1034–1036	pp. 1116–1117 (Osteosarcoma), 1198–1199 (Leiomyoma)
Oral and Laryngeal Cancers	pp. 1190–1191	not indexed	not indexed
Paraneoplastic Syndromes (Hormone Expression, etc.)	pp. 356–360 (not called paraneoplastic)	not indexed	pp. 90, 517
Systemic Lupus Erythematosus	pp. 250–252, 1534–1535 (in relation to skin)	pp. 1049–1051	pp. 1127–1129
Wound Healing	pp. 228–234	pp. 54–57	pp. 43–47
Pelvic Inflammatory Disease	pp. 754–756	pp. 978–979	pp. 1199–1200

Pathophysiology

Topic	McCance & Huether (3rd ed., 1998)	Price & Wilson (5th ed., 1997)	Porth (5th ed., 1998)
Fractures and Fracture Repair	pp. 1435–1441, Table 41-1 (1436)	pp. 1027–1031	pp. 1083–1090
Irritable Bowel Syndrome	Table 41-9 (1478)	not indexed	pp. 729–730
Crohn's Disease	p. 1343	pp. 350–351	pp. 730–731
Ulcerative Colitis	pp. 1342–1343	pp. 362–365	pp. 731–732
Peptic Ulcer Disease: Gastric and Duodenal Ulcers	pp. 1334–1338	pp. 331–339, Table 24-2 (332)	pp. 725–728
Lactose Intolerance: Treatment	p. 1341	p. 349	p. 717
Sprue	pp. 1390–1393 Gluten-sensitive Enteropathy	p. 349	pp. 740–742
Use of Corticosteroids	pp. 955, 1063, 1178, 1278, 1470	pp. 213, 1081	pp. 537–538, 680, 887, 1126–1129
Diabetes: Causes of Death	pp. 673–694, Table 20-11 (685)	pp. 956–962	pp. 821–828
Common Lab Values	Table 24-1 (846), Inside back cover	Table 16-1 (194), Table 16-2 (194), Table 36-1 (580)	Table 8-1 (136)
Bilirubin (Direct and Indirect)	pp. 1309–1311, Fig. 37-21 (1311), Table 37-6 (1316)	Table 27-2 (377), pp. 380–383	pp. 146–147, 750–752
Interpretation of Blood Gases	Table 24-1 (846), Table 31-4 (1154)	pp. 579–581, Table 36-3 (580)	p. 631
Acid-Base Disorders and Interpretation of Lab Values	pp. 101–111	Table 36-4 (580)	pp. 625–642
Plasma Proteins	pp. 210–217, Inside back cover	Table 27-2 (377)	pp. 330–331
Chart of Cardiac Enzymes	p. 1056 (no chart)	pp. 470–471, Fig. 31-12 (470)	Fig. 19-12 (400)
Chart of Coagulation (Clotting) Factors	Table 24-7 (868), Fig. 24-17 (869)	Fig. 19-1 (227), Table 19-1 (229)	Fig. 7-3 (123)

Sample Questions: Pathophysiology

Topic	McCance & Huether (3rd ed., 1998)	Price & Wilson (5th ed., 1997)	Porth (5th ed., 1998)
Assessment Signs:			
Kernig's sign	p. 537	not indexed	p. 906
Brudzinski's sign	p. 537	not indexed	p. 906
Homans' sign	p. 1187	p. 545	p. 355
Trousseau's sign	p. 99	Fig. 21-7 (276)	p. 615
Chvostek's sign	p. 99	Fig. 21-7 (276)	p. 615
Influenza	pp. 257, 609 (Reye's syndrome)	pp. 608–609	pp. 505–506
Lyme Disease	pp. 1542–1543	pp. 1107–1108	pp. 172, 284
Primary Organisms (Beta-hemolytic Streptococci, etc.)	Table 8-7 (255), Table 8-8 (257)	p. 488	pp. 297, 658–659
Hepatitis Chart	pp. 1355–1358 Table 38-8 (1355)	pp. 383–389, Table 27-5 (384)	pp. 753–759
Schedule of Vaccinations and Immunizations	Table 8-10 (261), pp. 1258–1260	not indexed	pp. 505–506 (no table), 1308–1309
Nephritic and Nephrotic Syndromes	pp. 1253–1255 (under glomerulonephritis), 1258–1260	pp. 701–708	pp. 657–659
Relation of Creatine Kinase to Muscular Dystrophy	pp. 1503–1508	p. 19 (in relation to genetics)	p. 928 (no creatine kinase)
Head Injury (Concussion, etc.)	pp. 510–519	pp. 888–892 (no chart)	pp. 902–903
Intracranial Pressure	pp. 489–491, 517–518	pp. 884–888	pp. 883–884
Coma Scale	pp. 460–469 (no Glasgow Scale)	Table 51-1 (805)	pp. 889–892, Table 38-3 (890)
Epilepsy	pp. 606–608	pp. 877–883	pp. 910–914, Chart 38-2 (911)
Seizure Terms Chart	Table 15-10 (474–476)	Table 55-1 (879)	Chart 38-2 (911)
Pain	pp. 423–432	pp. 818–844	pp. 967–976
Pain Relief: Acupuncture Transcutaneous Electrical Nerve Stimulation	not indexed	pp. 833–836	pp. 976–989

Study Guide

Psychology of Adulthood & Aging (485)

Credit Hours: 3
Credit Level: Upper
Question Type(s): Multiple-choice

The information in this study guide is valid until Summer 2001.
If you will be taking the examination after that date, be sure to check for a new edition of this guide before you complete your preparation for the exam.

General Description of the Examination

The Regents College Examination in Psychology of Adulthood & Aging is based on material usually presented in a one-semester course in psychology of adulthood and aging. The examination measures understanding of the psychological, biological, and social aspects of aging throughout adulthood. The examination includes both classic and contemporary research and theory related to adult development and aging. A familiarity with the content typically presented in a general introductory-level psychology course is required.

Content Outline

Content Area	Percent of Examination
I. Concepts of Age and Demographics	10%
II. Research Methods and Designs	7%
III. Personality and Adjustment	11%
IV. Biology, Physiology, Health, and Chronic Conditions	21%
V. Cognitive Aspects	13%
VI. Work, Retirement, Leisure, and Relationships	17%
VII. Death, Dying, and Bereavement	7%
VIII. Mental Health and Psychopathology	14%
Total	**100%**

I. Concepts of Age and Demographics (10%)

A. Concepts of age
1. Models of aging
   a. Mechanistic
   b. Organismic
   c. Contextual
   d. Normative/nonnormative/history-graded factors
2. Definitions of age
   a. Chronological
   b. Biological
   c. Psychological
   d. Functional
   e. Social
3. Ageism

B. Demographics
1. History
   a. Changes in family/economic structure
   b. Changes in numbers/percentages in different age groups
   c. Maximum life span, life expectancy, and longevity present vs. past (for example: rectangularization)
2. Gender/ethnic/cultural differences in demographics, including the racial crossover effect
3. Housing arrangements, including institutional and group living

II. Research Methods and Designs (7%)

A. Research methods and designs
1. Correlational vs. experimental research
2. Qualitative/interview research
3. Cross-sectional designs
4. Longitudinal designs
5. Unconfounding age, period, and cohort effects
   a. Cohort-sequential
   b. Time-sequential
   c. Cross-sequential
   d. Schaie's "most efficient design"
6. Problems with these designs, including ecological validity

B. Practical and ethical issues when studying older adults

III. Personality and Adjustment (11%)

A. Costa and McCrae's trait theory

B. Stage theories
1. Erikson
2. Levinson
3. Jung

C. Social theories
   1. Activity
   2. Disengagement
   3. Social clock

IV. Biology, Physiology, Health, and Chronic Conditions (21%)

A. Biology and physiology
   1. Cellular theories of aging
      a. Genetic theories
         1) DNA damage (mutation) theory
         2) Genetic switching theory
         3) Error theory
         4) Hayflick's aging clock
      b. Nongenetic theories
         1) Wear-and-tear theory
         2) Accumulation theory
         3) Free radical theory
         4) Cross-linkage theory
   2. Physiological theories and system changes
      a. Aging vs. disease (primary and secondary aging)
      b. Stress theory (Selye)
      c. Nervous system, including changes in sleep
      d. Endocrine system
      e. Immune system
      f. Cardiovascular and respiratory system
      g. Muscular/skeletal system
      h. Skin changes
      i. Sexual changes, such as menopause
   3. Sensation/perception
      a. Vision
      b. Hearing
      c. Olfactory
      d. Balance
      e. Skin senses
      f. Environmental effects and variability

B. Factors affecting health and chronic conditions
   1. Diet
   2. Exercise
   3. Alcohol
   4. Smoking
   5. Family history/genetic issues
   6. Socioeconomic issues, including health care costs, access to health care, SSI, Medicaid, and Medicare
   7. Stress—amount of and personality types
   8. Personal control
   9. Ethnic and gender factors
   10. Causes of death across the life cycle

V. Cognitive Aspects (13%)

A. Age changes in information processing
1. Sensory registers
   a. Timing of responses/reaction time
   b. Attention
2. Short-term memory
3. Working memory
4. Long-term memory
   a. Types of memory: semantic, episodic, procedural, and autobiographical
   b. Recognition vs. recall (cued/noncued)
   c. Acquisition, consolidation, retrieval
   d. Implicit/explicit
5. Factors influencing memory
   a. Anxiety
   b. Pacing
   c. Motivation
   d. Expertise—compensation for losses
   e. Interventions
   f. Ecological validity—meaningfulness of information (laboratory vs. everyday problem solving, for example: driving)
   g. Normal vs. pathological losses
   h. Memory aids

B. Intelligence, creativity, and wisdom
1. Types of intelligence measures
   a. Primary abilities
   b. Fluid and crystallized intelligence and changes with age, including classic aging patterns
   c. Other measures of intelligence
2. Factors influencing performance
   a. Cohort effects/educational effects
   b. Test-taking anxiety
   c. Cautiousness
   d. Timed tests
   e. Motivation
   f. Terminal drop
3. Creativity, including measures of, and changes in, creativity vs. productivity
4. Wisdom
   a. Formal and postformal operations
   b. Practical and philosophical wisdom, for example: Baltes

VI. Work, Retirement, Leisure, and Relationships (17%)

A. Work, retirement, and leisure
1. Work
   a. Occupational cycle—normative and nonnormative
   b. Job satisfaction
   c. Gender and class issues in the occupational cycle

        d. Stereotypes and evidence concerning age differences in job performance
        e. Unemployment across age
        f. Postretirement employment
    2. Retirement—factors that influence the timing of, and adjustment to, retirement
        a. Age
        b. Socioeconomic status (SES)
        c. Health
        d. Gradual vs. abrupt retirement
        e. Phases of retirement (Atchley)
        f. Gender and racial differences
        g. Sense of control
        h. Community involvement, including volunteerism, politics, religion, and Elderhostels
    3. Leisure/recreation across the life cycle

B. Relationships
    1. Family life cycle, including racial, gender, and ethnic differences
        a. Marital satisfaction
        b. Pre-children
        c. Midlife issues, for example: sandwich generation, empty nest, revolving door
        d. Divorce
        e. Reconstituted family
        f. Post-children
        g. Widowhood adjustment
        h. Caregiver burden
        i. Elder abuse
        j. Grandparenting, including styles such as surrogate or primary caregiver (Neugarten's work)
    2. Never-married
    3. Gay and lesbian families
    4. Friendship
    5. Sexuality

VII. Death, Dying, and Bereavement (7%)

A. Ethical, medical, and legal issues
    1. Definitions of death, for example: brain, clinical, cortical, psychic, and social
    2. Context of dying, for example: advance directives, euthanasia, hospices

B. Reactions to death
    1. Death anxiety across the life span
    2. Attitudes toward death across the life span
    3. Kübler-Ross's stages

C. Grief and mourning
   1. Process of grief, including rituals and religion
   2. Coping with dying and death
      a. Stages
      b. Normal grief reactions

VIII. Mental Health and Psychopathology (14%)

A. Mental health
   1. Life satisfaction (for example: health, social support, religion)
   2. Stress and adaptation
      a. Negative life events
      b. Defense mechanisms (for example: Vaillant's theory)
      c. Coping strategies

B. Psychopathology—distinctions between normal and psychopathological aging, including diagnosis, prognosis, symptoms, and treatment of the following:
   1. Dementias
      a. Irreversible
         1) Alzheimer's
         2) Others: multi-infarct, Parkinson's disease, and AIDS dementia
      b. Reversible or apparent (for example: pseudodementia)
         1) Drug interactions
         2) Nutrition deficits
      c. Delirium
   2. Depression
      a. Differences across adulthood
      b. Treatment issues (for example: cognitive therapy)
      c. Suicide
   3. Anxiety disorders
   4. Alcohol and drug problems
   5. Paranoia and relationships with sensory changes

C. Treatments that are unique to the older population
   1. Sensory training
   2. Reality orientation
   3. Remotivation
   4. Life review therapy
   5. Pet therapy

Sample Questions: Psychology of Adulthood & Aging

1. A 40-year-old first-year college student could be considered young by which definition of age?
   1) biological
   2) chronological
   3) psychological
   4) social

2. Which is an example of a normative age-graded event?
   1) taking early retirement
   2) reaching menopause at 50
   3) winning a lottery
   4) testing positive for AIDS

3. Which statement most accurately describes the housing situation for the majority of persons over age 65?
   They live in
   1) age-segregated congregate housing.
   2) institutional settings.
   3) retirement communities.
   4) their own homes or apartments.

4. Which pair of variables is confounded in longitudinal research?
   1) age changes and cohort
   2) cohort and selective dropout
   3) time of measurement and cohort
   4) age changes and time of measurement

5. Which statement is consistent with current research ethics?
   1) Subjects must be informed of risks that might influence their participation.
   2) Compensation can be withheld if a subject prematurely withdraws from a study.
   3) Language or cultural barriers do not have to be considered when seeking informed consent from possible participants.
   4) Informed consent should be obtained from subjects after they participate in research.

6. Mark is happy one moment and irritable the next, whereas Dorothy is even-tempered most of the time. As defined by Costa and McCrae, these two individuals differ along which dimension of personality?
   1) conscientiousness
   2) extroversion
   3) neuroticism
   4) openness to experience

Sample Questions: Psychology of Adulthood & Aging

7. According to Erikson, which struggle has been resolved by an older adult who can look back on life and be satisfied with what has been accomplished?
    1) autonomy versus shame and doubt
    2) generativity versus stagnation
    3) integrity versus despair
    4) intimacy versus isolation

8. According to disengagement theory, what is the result of the voluntary withdrawal of an older adult from society?
    1) loneliness and depression
    2) better health
    3) increased life satisfaction
    4) social isolation and rejection

9. What is the most likely cause of an older adult's increased difficulty in hearing higher pitched sounds?
    1) presbycusis
    2) presbyopia
    3) presbystasis
    4) tinnitus

10. Why would a physician recommend that a 30-year-old woman take a calcium and vitamin D supplement for her future health?
    To reduce the
    1) night sweats associated with menopause
    2) possibility of osteoporosis
    3) likelihood of pregnancy
    4) possibility of Alzheimer's disease

11. Which genetic theory predicts the maximum life span of humans to be 110 to 120 years?
    1) Hayflick's aging clock
    2) wear-and-tear theory
    3) free radical theory
    4) cross-linkage theory

12. An older adult must enter a nursing home because of chronic health problems. Which action would best help this individual to adapt to the new setting?
    The individual should be
    1) encouraged to take an active role in selecting and moving into the facility.
    2) encouraged to allow family members to select the facility and plan for the move.
    3) told that the move to the facility is necessary and given enough time to accept the idea.
    4) provided with many details, pictures, and descriptions of the activities of the facility.

Sample Questions: Psychology of Adulthood & Aging

13. Which behavior change would have the greatest impact on improving health in the United States?
    1) increasing exercise
    2) quitting smoking
    3) eating healthier foods
    4) reducing levels of stress

14. Which memory task shows the most decline with age?
    1) holding information in the sensory store
    2) visualizing stimuli in iconic memory
    3) retrieving information from long-term memory
    4) manipulating information in short-term memory

15. Which type of intelligence most often increases with age?
    1) crystallized
    2) fluid
    3) full-scale
    4) performance

16. Which characterizes postformal thought?
    1) using logical, hypothetical-deductive reasoning
    2) distinguishing between mental symbols and real-life objects
    3) committing oneself to absolute truths
    4) understanding ideas within frames of reference

17. Which of the following is the most accurate conclusion that can be drawn from the research on the effect of job loss on men?
    Job loss
    1) has its greatest effect on older men.
    2) has its greatest effect on middle-aged men.
    3) has its greatest effect on young men.
    4) affects all age groups equally.

18. Which statement is true regarding recent trends in retirement patterns?
    1) Most people retire at age 65.
    2) The percentage of males age 65 or older working full-time has increased.
    3) The percentage of people choosing early retirement has increased.
    4) The percentage of people choosing early retirement has decreased.

19. A married couple have three grandchildren whom they baby-sit, occasionally indulge, and express strong interest in. The couple also believe that childrearing is the responsibility of parents and rarely give advice unless asked. What type of grandparenting does this represent?
    1) distant
    2) formal
    3) fun seeker
    4) surrogate

Sample Questions: Psychology of Adulthood & Aging

20. Gabriella's parents are in their late seventies and rely on her to help with shopping and transportation to medical appointments and social functions. Gabriella also has two adult children who frequently rely on her to help care for their young children. This situation best illustrates which midlife concept?
    1) empty nest
    2) kinkeepers
    3) revolving door
    4) sandwich generation

21. What is the purpose of the hospice movement?
    1) to assist individuals to determine how and when to end their lives
    2) to use any means necessary to prolong life
    3) to preserve the dignity and relieve the pain of individuals who are dying
    4) to provide medical care comparable to that given in hospitals

22. A man goes to the doctor for a checkup and some tests. When the test results come back, he is told that he has advanced cancer. According to Kübler-Ross's stage theory of dying, what is the man most likely to do now?
    1) insist that a mistake was made
    2) become very depressed
    3) accept the diagnosis and plan for death
    4) become angry with those who will go on living

23. According to research, which factor plays no significant role in life satisfaction?
    1) age
    2) income
    3) marital status
    4) social support

24. Which disorder is characterized by a series of small strokes in the brain?
    1) Alzheimer's disease
    2) multi-infarct dementia
    3) Parkinson's disease
    4) pseudodementia

25. Which of the following causes dementia symptoms that are reversible with proper treatment?
    1) Alzheimer's disease
    2) multi-infarct dementia
    3) nutritional deficiencies
    4) Pick's disease

26. A nursing home resident has been having therapy that stresses efforts to identify her actual abilities and to discover activities that she once found pleasurable. The woman had been recommended for therapy because she was apathetic, withdrawn from the other residents, and seemed confused. What form of therapy is she receiving?
   1) cognitive
   2) sensory training
   3) remotivation
   4) reality orientation

Recommended Resources

Cavanaugh, J. (1997). Adult development and aging. (3rd ed.). Belmont, CA: Brooks/Cole. (A study guide is available to supplement this textbook.)

Hoyer, W., Rybash, J., & Roodin, P. (1995). Adult development and aging. (4th ed.) New York: McGraw Hill.

Papalia, D., Camp, C., & Feldman, R. (1996). Adult development and aging. New York: McGraw Hill.

Other Resources

Cox, H. (Ed.). Aging (Annual editions). Guilford, CT: Dushkin.

Fries, J.F., & Crapo, L.M. (1981). Vitality and aging. San Francisco: Freeman.

Hayflick, L. (1994). How and why we age. New York: Ballantine.

Seasons of life. A video series with study guide. (Available from the Annenberg/CPB Multimedia Collection, P.O. Box 2345, So. Burlington VT 05407-9920, phone 1-800-LEARNER [1-800-532-7637], fax 1-802-864-9846.)

Study Guide
Research Methods in Psychology (436)

Credit Hours: 3 **Credit Level:** Upper
Question Type(s): multiple-choice

The information in this study guide is valid until Summer 2001.
If you will be taking the examination after that date, be sure to check for a new edition of this guide before you complete your preparation for the exam.

General Description of the Examination

The Regents College Examination in Research Methods in Psychology is based on material normally taught in a one-semester undergraduate course in research methods. The examination measures understanding of the course material as well as the ability to apply this understanding in specific research situations. The examination assumes a background in introductory psychology and elementary statistics.

We recommend that you prepare for this examination by following an independent program of study based on the study materials included in this guide. This program of study is fully outlined in the Regents College Course Guide for the Research Methods in Psychology Examination. The course guide is described on page 140, immediately following the content outline.

This examination satisfies the research requirement in the sociology concentration of the Regents College Baccalaureate Degrees in Liberal Arts. Regents College B.S.(n) students should consult their advisors regarding duplication of credit with the Research in Nursing exam.

Content Outline

Content Area	Percent of Examination
I. Experimental Psychology and the Scientific Method	5%
II. Research Ethics (APA Guidelines)	7%
III. Alternatives to Experimentation (Nonexperimental Designs)	25%
IV. Basic Concepts of Experimental Research	25%
V. Experimental Research Designs	20%
VI. Data Analysis and Interpretation	10%
VII. Writing Research Reports	8%
Total	**100%**

NOTE: The chapter numbers and titles provided at the beginning of each content area refer to specific chapters in the recommended textbook for this examination (see page 147, Recommended Resources). Chapter numbers and titles may differ in subsequent editions.

I. Experimental Psychology and the Scientific Method (5%)

Myers and Hansen (1997): Chapter 1, Experimental Psychology and the Scientific Method
Chapter 5, Formulating the Hypothesis

A. Nonscientific vs. scientific methodology (Chapter 1)
 1. Nonscientific sources of data
 2. Characteristics of the scientific method

B. The tools of psychological science (Chapter 1)
 1. Observation
 2. Measurement
 3. Experimentation (establishing cause and effect)

C. Formulating the research hypothesis (Chapter 5)
 1. Characteristics of a good hypothesis
 2. Induction vs. deduction
 3. Review of previous research

II. Research Ethics (American Psychological Association Guidelines) (7%)

Myers and Hansen, 1997: Chapter 2, Research Ethics

A. Research with human participants
 1. Informed consent
 2. Deception and debriefing
 3. Institutional review boards

B. Research with animal subjects

C. Fraud and plagiarism

III. Alternatives to Experimentation (Nonexperimental designs) (25%)

Myers and Hansen (1997): Chapter 3, Alternatives to Experimentation: Nonexperimental Designs
Chapter 4, Alternatives to Experimentation: Correlational and Quasi-Experimental Designs

A. Survey research (Chapter 3)
 1. Characteristics of surveys (for example, interview, questionnaire)
 2. Response styles
 3. Sampling issues
  a. Probability sampling
  b. Nonprobability sampling

B. **Correlational research** (Chapter 4)
 1. Direction and strength of relationships
    a. Correlation coefficient
    b. Scatterplots
 2. Limitations
    a. Correlation does not prove causation.
    b. Direction of causality
    c. Third variable problems

C. **Quasi-experimental designs** (Chapter 4)
 1. Definition and characteristics of quasi-experimental designs
 2. Types of quasi-experimental designs
    a. Ex post facto designs
    b. Longitudinal designs
    c. Cross-sectional designs
    d. Pretest/posttest design
 3. Advantages and disadvantages of quasi-experimental designs

D. **Other types of nonexperimental research** (Chapter 3)
 1. Observational research/field studies
 2. Case studies
 3. Archival research/secondary records

E. **Advantages and disadvantages of nonexperimental designs**

IV. Basic Concepts of Experimental Research (25%)

Myers and Hansen (1997): Chapter 6, The Basics of Experimentation
Chapter 11, Solving Problems: Controlling Extraneous Variables
Chapter 15, Drawing Conclusions: The Search for the Elusive Bottom Line

A. **Measurement issues** (Chapter 6)
 1. Independent and dependent variables
 2. Operational definitions and hypothetical constructs
 3. Scales of measurement
    a. Nominal
    b. Ordinal
    c. Interval
    d. Ratio
 4. Reliability of measurement
    a. Interitem reliability
    b. Interrater reliability
    c. Test-retest reliability
 5. Validity of measurement
    a. Construct validity
    b. Content validity
    c. Face validity
    d. Predictive validity

B. **Internal validity** (Chapters 6 and 11)
    1. Definition of internal validity
    2. Concepts related to internal validity—extraneous and confounding variables
        a. Characteristics of the setting (physical variables)
        b. Characteristics of the experimenter
            1) Experimenter bias
            2) Experimenter personality
            3) Selection of subjects
        c. Characteristics of the participants (subjects)
            1) Demand characteristics
            2) Volunteers
            3) "Good subject" bias
            4) Social desirability
    3. Specific threats to internal validity
        a. History
        b. Instrumentation
        c. Maturation
        d. Selection
        e. Selection interaction
        f. Statistical regression
        g. Subject mortality
        h. Testing
    4. Controlling for extraneous variables
        a. Single blind
        b. Double blind
        c. Placebo

C. **External validity of experiments** (Chapter 15)
    1. Definition of external validity
    2. Basic requirements for external validity
        a. Internal validity
        b. Replication
    3. Important external validity issues
        a. Generalizing across subjects
        b. Generalizing from procedures to concepts
        c. Generalizing beyond the lab
        d. Increasing external validity (five approaches)
            1) Aggregation
            2) Multivariate designs
            3) Nonreactive measures
            4) Field experiments
            5) Naturalistic observation

V. Experimental Research Designs (20%)

Myers and Hansen (1997): Chapter 7, Basic Between-Subjects Designs
Chapter 8, Between-Subjects Factorial Designs
Chapter 9, Within-Subjects Designs
Chapter 10, Within-Subjects Designs: Small N

A. Between-subjects designs (Chapter 7)
1. One independent variable
   a. Two independent groups
      1) Random assignment
      2) Experimental group–control group design
      3) Two-experimental-groups design
   b. Two matched groups
   c. Multiple groups
2. Factorial Designs (Chapter 8)
   a. Types of factorial designs—definitions/descriptions
   b. Main effects
   c. Interaction effects
   d. Describing the design (notation)

B. Within-subjects designs (Chapter 9)
1. Types of within-subjects designs
   a. Definitions/descriptions
   b. One independent variable
   c. Multiple independent variables (factorial designs)
   d. Mixed designs
2. Problems of within-subjects designs: order effects
   a. Carryover effects
   b. Fatigue and practice effects
3. Controlling for order effects: counterbalancing

C. Small N Designs (Chapter 10)
1. *ABA* designs
2. Multiple-baseline design

D. Advantages and disadvantages of the various experimental designs

VI. Data Analysis and Interpretation (10%)

Myers and Hansen (1997): Chapter 12, Why We Need Statistics
Chapter 13, Analyzing Results: Two-Group Examples
Chapter 14, Analyzing Results: Multiple Groups and Factorial Experiments
Chapter 15, Drawing Conclusions: The Search for the Elusive Bottom Line

(**NOTE:** The focus in this section will be on selecting the appropriate analysis technique and interpreting the results of a data analysis. Questions will <u>not</u> focus on computation of statistics.)

A. **Descriptive statistics—organizing and summarizing data (Chapter 12)**
    1. Frequency distributions
    2. Measures of central tendency
        a. Mean
        b. Median
        c. Mode
    3. Measures of variability
        a. Range
        b. Variance
        c. Standard deviation

B. **Inferential Statistics/Hypothesis Testing**
    1. Null vs. alternative hypotheses (Chapter 12)
    2. Odds of finding significance (Chapter 12)
        a. Significance levels
            1) Type I errors
            2) Type II errors
        b. Critical regions
        c. One-tailed vs. two-tailed tests (directional vs. nondirectional hypotheses)
    3. Comparing two groups (Chapter 13)
        a. Chi-square test
        b. *t* test
    4. Comparing multiple groups (Chapter 14)
        a. One-way between-subjects ANOVA (one independent variable)
        b. One-way repeated measures ANOVA (one independent variable within subjects)
        c. Two-way ANOVA (between subjects, multiple independent variables)
        d. Repeated measures and mixed factorial designs

C. **Evaluating research findings (Chapter 15)**
    1. Internal validity
    2. External validity
    3. Interpreting a nonsignificant outcome

VII. Writing Research Reports (8%)

Myers and Hansen, (1997):   Chapter 16, Writing the Research Report

A. **Purpose and format**

B. **Major sections**
    1. Descriptive title
    2. Abstract
    3. Introduction
    4. Method
    5. Results
    6. Discussion
    7. References

Research Methods in Psychology

Course Guide for the Research Methods in Psychology Examination

The examination development committee strongly recommends that you order the Regents College *Course Guide and Computerized Resource for Research Methods in Psychology* for additional guidance in preparing for this exam.

The course guide will help you structure your own exam preparation. It is designed to help you learn the content of this examination. The guide is part of an integrated guided learning package. It includes study suggestions and approaches for learning the content of the examination. A computer disk containing multiple-choice self-assessment questions on each textbook chapter accompanies the course guide. Using the disk requires a computer running Windows 95 or Windows 98 and a graphical Web browser. The course guide can be purchased only from the Regents College Bookstore.

Sample Questions

1. A researcher uses the same methods as those employed in a previous experiment and then determines if the results are the same. Which concept does this situation best illustrate?
    1) correlation
    2) observation
    3) publication
    4) replication

2. In which model of hypothesis formation is the accumulation of data used to form general explanatory principles?
    1) correlational
    2) deductive
    3) inductive
    4) scientific

3. What is the primary reason for debriefing individuals following their participation in a research study?
    1) to adhere to scientific guidelines
    2) to protect the reputations of the institution and department
    3) to avoid possible legal action by participants as a result of the study
    4) to ensure that there are no harmful consequences for participants

Sample Questions: Research Methods in Psychology

4. A researcher proposes to conduct an experiment that exposes participants to possible physical, social, or psychological injury. What should the institutional review board require of this researcher?
   The researcher must
   1) obtain informed consent from potential participants.
   2) receive approval from the American Psychological Association.
   3) provide payment to the research participants.
   4) conduct a less risky pilot study before proceeding.

5. Which example constitutes fraud by a psychological researcher?
   The researcher fails to
   1) obtain informed consent from all prospective participants in a study.
   2) conduct a risk/benefit analysis prior to conducting an experiment.
   3) include data in the research report that are inconsistent with the hypothesis.
   4) debrief all of the participants at the end of an experiment.

6. Which research method would be most useful to study the attitudes held by adolescents about cigarette smoking?
   1) case study
   2) experimental
   3) observation
   4) survey

7. Which is an example of a person's position preference in responding to a questionnaire? When uncertain, the respondent always
   1) selects answers at random.
   2) selects the last option in multiple-choice questions.
   3) chooses the answer by the manifest content.
   4) answers all questions conservatively.

8. Which sampling method selects participants in such a manner that the odds of an individual's being selected are known?
   1) convenience
   2) nonprobability
   3) probability
   4) quota

9. What is a disadvantage of quota sampling?
   1) The procedure for selecting participants is not random.
   2) The findings are valid only when the sample is large.
   3) Only alternate participants can be selected.
   4) The procedure is valid only when the sample is large.

Sample Questions: Research Methods in Psychology

10. An observed correlation between two variables of interest may be the result of an unknown or unmeasured variable that is moderately associated with both measured variables. What term is used in correlational research to refer to this alternative explanation?
    1) bidirectional causation
    2) causal modeling
    3) multiple correlation
    4) third variable problem

11. What can be concluded about the cause and effect relationship between two variables that have a highly significant correlation?
    1) No conclusion can be drawn about the cause and effect relationship.
    2) The cause and effect relationship is significant if the correlation is positive.
    3) The cause and effect relationship is significant if the correlation is negative.
    4) There is a significant cause and effect relationship between the two variables.

12. What is a <u>disadvantage</u> of cross-sectional studies as compared to longitudinal studies? Cross-sectional studies
    1) require a larger number of participants.
    2) require more time for data collection.
    3) have higher participant attrition rates.
    4) do not allow for causal inferences.

13. A researcher learns that a university is about to implement a new program designed to reduce racial tension on campus. Because the researcher knows about this event before it occurs, which design would be most appropriate?
    1) case study
    2) cross-sectional
    3) observational
    4) pretest/posttest

14. A researcher collects a lengthy and detailed description of an individual's experiences and behaviors. This situation illustrates which type of research?
    1) case study
    2) correlational study
    3) quasi-experiment
    4) true experiment

15. Which situation is an example of an archival study?
    A researcher
    1) joins a college fraternity to learn about its initiation rituals.
    2) unobtrusively observes the behavior of shoppers at a local mall.
    3) uses existing court records to investigate variables that influence plea bargaining.
    4) investigates and describes three individuals who have a rare form of mental illness.

Sample Questions: Research Methods in Psychology

16. Under which condition is an experimental hypothesis supported?
    1) Holding the independent variable constant brings about a change in the dependent variable.
    2) Manipulating the independent variable brings about a change in the dependent variable.
    3) Holding the dependent variable constant brings about a change in the independent variable.
    4) Manipulating the dependent variable brings about a change in the independent variable.

17. A researcher hypothesizes that there will be a significant difference in the concerns expressed by pregnant women during the first, second, or third trimester of pregnancy. What is the independent variable in this hypothesis?
    1) difference in concerns
    2) expressed concerns
    3) pregnant women
    4) trimester of pregnancy

18. What feature distinguishes a ratio scale from other scales of measurement?
    1) It allows for the use of negative numbers.
    2) It possesses a true zero point.
    3) There are equal intervals between the values.
    4) More powerful statistical tests can be used.

19. Two observers have separately scored a child's play behaviors for aggressiveness. Which measurement concept assesses the level of agreement between the two observers?
    1) face validity
    2) criterion validity
    3) interrater reliability
    4) test-retest reliability

20. Researchers are studying whether the safety level of a person's driving varies depending upon the type of vehicle driven. The researchers have designed a safe driving practices questionnaire. They have asked a panel of driving instructors to review their questionnaire to determine whether it measures the important aspects of driving safety. The process of soliciting feedback from the driving instructors is intended to improve which aspect of the questionnaire's validity?
    1) content
    2) external
    3) face
    4) internal

21. Rats are randomly divided into three groups for a study on the effects of diet on maze-learning time. Through a mechanical malfunction, one of the groups receives much less water with their food than the other two groups. Why is this factor a threat to internal validity?
    1) An extraneous variable has systematically affected all groups in the study.
    2) An extraneous variable has systematically affected one group, but not the other groups.
    3) The independent variable has been changed for one group, but not for the other groups.
    4) The dependent variable has been changed for one group, but not for the other groups.

22. In which research situation would the experiment be confounded?
    1) The dependent variable varies systematically with the independent variable.
    2) The dependent variable fails to vary systematically with the independent variable.
    3) An extraneous variable varies systematically with the independent variable.
    4) An extraneous variable fails to vary systematically with the independent variable.

23. A middle-school student designs a science project to determine whether female cats prefer scented or unscented kitty litter (cat-box filler). The student buys a box of unscented, brown kitty litter and a box of scented, blue kitty litter for the project. The student finds that the sample of cats used the brown, unscented kitty litter more frequently and concludes that cats prefer unscented kitty litter. Which two variables are confounded in this experiment?
    1) kitty litter color and cat's gender
    2) kitty litter color and kitty litter scent
    3) kitty litter scent and frequency of use
    4) cat's gender and frequency of use

24. Which is a strategy for avoiding the threat of maturation to the internal validity of a study?
    1) Ensure appropriate number of subjects in the study group.
    2) Ensure that all subjects are from the same cohort or age group.
    3) Minimize the time between administering pretest and posttest measures.
    4) Minimize the impact of treatment ordering effects.

25. What aspect of a research study can be enhanced by using measures such as aggregation, multivariate designs, nonreactive measurements, field experiments, and naturalistic observations?
    1) external validity
    2) operational definitions
    3) reliability
    4) statistical power

Sample Questions: Research Methods in Psychology

26. Which statement best characterizes a between-subjects experimental design?
    1) Participants are sampled from two different populations.
    2) Participants are asked to choose between two experimental conditions.
    3) Participants are each assigned to at least two levels of the independent variable.
    4) Participants are each assigned to a single experimental condition.

27. What is the rationale for randomly assigning each research participant to one of two groups?
    1) to eliminate systematic bias in the groups
    2) to manipulate the independent variables in the groups
    3) to protect the privacy of the participants
    4) to ensure representative sampling

28. A researcher wants to determine if listening to familiar music causes people to become more or less contented than they are when listening to unfamiliar music. Hoping to control for the potential effects of age, the researcher randomly assigns students of the same age to listen to either familiar music or unfamiliar music. What kind of experimental design is this researcher using?
    1) mixed design
    2) multiple-independent-groups design
    3) two-matched-groups design
    4) factorial design

29. A researcher is studying the effects of a new drug on the treatment of migraine headaches. The researcher believes that the drug will be most effective if taken at night rather than during the day. The researcher randomly assigns participants to different drug level/time-of-day treatment combinations. Which type of experimental design is the researcher using?
    1) mixed design
    2) two-matched-groups design
    3) between-subjects factorial design
    4) within-subjects factorial design

30. A researcher tests the effects of sleep deprivation on memory. Ten participants are asked to memorize a list of 20 words. They are then allowed to sleep for four hours, at which point they are awakened and asked to recall the 20 words. The next night, the subjects are allowed to sleep two hours, at which point they are awakened and asked to recall the 20 words. What design did the researcher use?
    1) between-subjects one independent variable design
    2) within-subjects one independent variable design
    3) between-subjects multiple independent variable design
    4) within-subjects multiple independent variable design

Sample Questions: Research Methods in Psychology

31. In within-subjects designs, what confounds may result from administering the conditions in the same order to all participants?
    1) history effects
    2) practice effects
    3) selection effects
    4) mortality effects

32. Which technique is used to control progressive error in within-subjects designs?
    1) block randomization
    2) counterbalancing
    3) random assignment
    4) statistical regression

33. The number of problem behaviors that a child displays is counted for six weeks. For the next six weeks, the number of problem behaviors is counted while the child undergoes behavior modification therapy. Next, the number of problem behaviors is counted for six weeks after the therapy is discontinued. Which type of experimental design is being used in this study?
    1) ABA
    2) BAB
    3) ABAB
    4) ABABA

34. Which statement is true of the frequency distribution illustrated below?

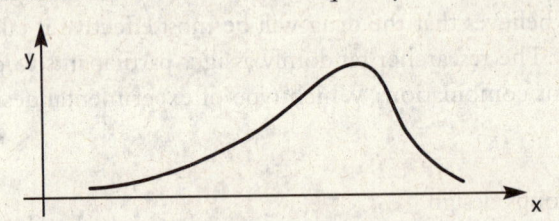

    1) The mean will be greater than the mode.
    2) The mean will be less than the mode.
    3) The median will be greater than the mode.
    4) The median will be less than the mean.

35. Random samples of 100 full-time and 100 part-time undergraduate students are asked to rate the usefulness of a new computer network at the college library. The full-time students rate the facilities as more useful than do the part-time students. Which conclusion illustrates the concept of statistical inference?
    The full-time students
    1) sampled find the facilities more useful than do the part-time students sampled.
    2) at the college find the facilities more useful than do the part-time students at the college.
    3) sampled have greater opportunity to use the facilities than do the part-time students sampled.
    4) at the college have greater opportunity to use the facilities than do the part-time students at the college.

Sample Questions: Research Methods in Psychology

36. A researcher is examining the effect of caffeine on memory. Participants are placed in one of three treatment groups that differ as follows: twenty minutes prior to taking a short-term memory test, participants in Group 1 ingest 200 mg of caffeine, participants in Group 2 ingest 100 mg of caffeine, and participants in Group 3 ingest a placebo. What statistic should be used to determine whether caffeine affects short-term memory?
    1) one-way between-subjects ANOVA
    2) one-way repeated-measures ANOVA
    3) two-way between-subjects ANOVA
    4) two-way repeated-measures ANOVA

37. A researcher is evaluating a set of research findings. Why would the researcher want to replicate the findings?
    Replication will promote the
    1) interaction of the variables.
    2) reactivity of the participants.
    3) internal validity of the study.
    4) external validity of the study.

38. Psychological research reports should be written in a style similar to which document?
    1) an article in a popular magazine
    2) an editorial in a newspaper
    3) a study published in a medical journal
    4) a chapter in a textbook

39. When is the abstract for a psychological research report usually written?
    1) first, before any other part of the paper
    2) immediately after the data are collected
    3) after the title page is formulated
    4) last, after the entire paper is complete

40. A researcher is studying the relationship between social support and stress among young mothers during the transition to parenthood. Which statement should appear in the procedure subsection of the research report?
    1) "The average age of the participants was 20.3 years."
    2) "The participants were interviewed in their homes during their third trimester of pregnancy."
    3) "The participants were found to have higher levels of stress after becoming parents."
    4) "Previous research suggests that social support can buffer stress for young mothers."

Recommended Resources

Hansen, C. (1997). Study guide and workbook for Myers & Hansen's Experimental psychology (4th ed.). Pacific Grove, CA: Brooks/Cole.

Myers., A., & Hansen, C. (1997). Experimental psychology (4th ed.). Pacific Grove, CA: Brooks/Cole.

Regents College (1998). Course guide and computerized resource for Research methods in psychology.

Study Guide
Statistics (408)

Credit Hours: 3   **Credit Level:** Lower
Question Type(s): Multiple-choice

The information in this study guide is valid until Summer 2001.
If you will be taking the examination after that date, be sure to check for a new edition of this guide before you complete your preparation for the exam.

General Description of the Examination

The Statistics examination measures knowledge and understanding of the fundamental concepts of descriptive and inferential statistics. It tests for the ability to interpret various types of data, to determine implications and consequences, and to perform statistical calculations. The examination is based on material typically taught in a one-semester course in statistics. It is designed to correspond to a service course applicable to different majors. A basic knowledge of algebra is assumed.

We recommend that you prepare for this examination by following an independent course of study based on the study materials included in this guide. This course of study is fully outlined in the Regents College *Course Guide for the Statistics Examination*. The course guide is described on page 153, immediately following the content outline.

You will be permitted to use only the authorized Regents College Examinations calculator in answering questions on this examination. The formulas and tables referred to in this guide will be provided with the examination.

Content Outline

Content Area	Percent of Examination
I. Overview of Statistics	5%
II. Summarizing, Organizing, and Describing Data	20%
III. Regression and Correlation	10%
IV. Basic Probability Theory	10%
V. Probability Distributions	10%
VI. Sampling	10%
VII. Statistical Estimation	15%
VIII. Hypothesis Testing	20%
Total	**100%**

I. Overview of Statistics (5%)

A. Descriptive vs. inferential statistics (populations—samples, parameters—statistics)

B. Uses and misuses of statistics

C. Counting and measuring
  1. Measurement scales (nominal, ordinal, interval, ratio)
  2. Discrete vs. continuous variables

D. Collection of data (random samples, probability samples, samples of convenience)

II. Summarizing, Organizing, and Describing Data (20%)

A. Measures of central tendency
  1. Mean (population and sample)
  2. Median
  3. Mode

B. Measures of variation
  1. Range
  2. Variance (population and sample)
  3. Standard deviation (population and sample)
  4. Interquartile range

C. Organizing data
  1. Ordering or ranking
  2. Distributions
     a. Frequency
     b. Relative frequency
     c. Cumulative frequency
  3. Pictorial displays (quantitative, qualitative)
     a. Histogram
     b. Frequency polygon
     c. Box-and-whisker plot
     d. Stem-and-leaf display

D. Measures of relative position
  1. Rank
  2. Quartiles
  3. Percentiles
  4. Standardized scores (z-scores)

E. Interpreting descriptive measures
  1. Symmetry and skewness
  2. Comparative characteristics of measures of central tendency
  3. Unimodal vs. bimodal distributions
  4. Coding data/effects of adding and multiplying by constants
  5. Effects of outliers on descriptive measures

III. Regression and Correlation (10%)

A. Scatterplots/diagrams

B. Least squares regression line
1. Calculation of coefficients
2. Prediction

C. Correlation coefficient r and coefficient of determination (R^2)—calculation and interpretation

IV. Basic Probability Theory (10%)

A. Possibilities and probabilities
1. Counting principles
   a. Basic counting rule—multiplication principle
   b. Permutations
   c. Combinations
2. Sample spaces
3. Events
   a. Mutually exclusive
   b. Union, intersection, complement
4. The concept of a probability
   a. Relative frequency
   b. Theoretical (classical) probability
   c. Conditional probability

B. Rules of probability
1. Complement rule
2. Addition rules
   a. Mutually exclusive events
   b. Non-mutually exclusive events
3. Multiplication rules
   a. Independent events
   b. Dependent events

V. Probability Distributions (10%)

A. Discrete random variables and their distributions
1. Basic concepts
   a. Probability distributions and probability functions
   b. Mean (expected value)
   c. Variance and standard deviation
2. Binomial distributions
   a. Properties of a binomial experiment
   b. Parameters of binomial distributions (n, p)
   c. Calculation of binomial probabilities
      1) Formula
      2) Use of table
   d. Mean and standard deviation
   e. Related word problems

B. **Continuous random variables and their distributions**
   1. Basic concepts
      a. Probability as area under the curve
      b. Interpretation of mean and standard deviation
   2. Normal distributions
      a. Properties of the normal curve
      b. Parameters of the normal distribution—mean (μ) and standard deviation (σ)
      c. Standard normal distributions
      d. Use of table of areas for standard normal distribution
      e. Standardized units (standardized scores, z-scores)
      f. Use of area tables to solve general normal distribution problems
      g. Normal approximation of binomial distribution (using continuity correction)

VI. Sampling (10%)

A. **Simple random sampling**
   1. Concept of a random sample
   2. Obtaining a simple random sample

B. **Sampling distribution of the sample means**
   1. Shape of sampling distribution
   2. Expected value (mean) of the sample mean
   3. Standard deviation (standard error) and variance of the sample mean
   4. Probabilities based on sampling distribution
   5. Central limit theorem and applications

C. **Other sampling schemes** (for example: stratified, cluster, systematic)

VII. Statistical Estimation (15%)

A. **Estimation of a single population mean**
   1. Large sample or sample with known variance (using z-statistic)
      a. Point estimation
      b. Interval estimation (confidence intervals)
   2. Small sample from normal populations (using t-statistic)
      a. Point estimation
      b. Student's t distribution
      c. Interval estimation (confidence intervals)

B. **Estimation of population proportions using the normal approximation** (for large samples, only)
   1. Point estimate (sample proportion)
   2. Mean and standard deviation of sample proportion
   3. Interval estimation (confidence intervals)

C. **Estimation of the difference between two population means**
   1. Matched pairs (dependent samples)
      a. Point estimate
      b. Confidence interval

2. Large independent samples or samples with known variances
   a. Point estimate
   b. Confidence interval
3. Small independent samples from normal distributions with equal variances
   a. Point estimate
   b. Confidence interval

D. **Estimation of the difference between two population proportions** (for large samples, only)
   1. Point estimate of difference
   2. Mean and standard deviation of differences of proportions
   3. Interval estimate of differences of proportions

VIII. Hypothesis Testing (20%)

A. **Testing hypotheses for a single population mean**
   1. Formulating hypotheses (null vs. alternative)
      a. Large sample case (using z test)
      b. Small sample case (using t test)
   2. Decisions based on P-values or critical values
   3. Type I and Type II errors

B. **Testing hypotheses for population proportions** (for large samples, only)
   1. Formulating hypotheses (null vs. alternative)
   2. Decisions based on P-values or critical values
   3. Type I and Type II errors

C. **Testing hypotheses for the difference between two population means**
   1. Large independent samples or samples with known population variances (z test)
   2. Small independent samples from normal distributions with unknown, but assumed equal variance (t test)
   3. Matched-pairs samples (t test)

D. **Testing hypotheses for the difference between two population proportions** (for large samples, only)

E. **Chi-square tests**
   1. Goodness of fit
   2. Independence in two-way contingency tables

Sample Questions: Statistics

Course Guide for the Statistics Examination

The examination development committee strongly recommends that you order the Regents College *Course Guide for the Statistics Examination* for additional guidance in preparing for this exam.

The course guide will help you structure your own exam preparation. It is designed to help you learn the content of this examination. The guide is part of an integrated guided learning package. It includes study suggestions and approaches for learning statistics and will direct you on how to best use the other recommended resources. Supplementary exercises on content not thoroughly covered in the recommended textbook are also provided. The guide also includes the formulas that will be provided for your use during the examination. The course guide can be purchased only from the Regents College Bookstore.

On the testing day, be sure to bring your Regents College Examinations calculator. Make sure that your calculator is in good working order before the day of the examination. No replacement calculators will be provided. Sharing a calculator will not be permitted.

Sample Questions

1. What is the mean of the set of data below?
   1, 1, 2, 2, 2, 4, 6, 7, 9, 10, 11
   1) 5
   2) 2
   3) 6
   4) 4

2. A random sample of 5 test scores has a mean of 82 points on a scale of 0–100, with a variance of zero. What is the range of these test scores?
   1) 0
   2) 50
   3) 82
   4) 100

3. A stem-and-leaf display of a set of data is shown below:
   ```
   2 | 3 4 5
   3 | 0 1 1 2
   4 | 1 2 5 5 5 7 8 9
   5 | 1 1 2 3 5
   6 | 2 3 5
   7 | 0 2
   ```
   Leaf Unit = 1.0

   What is the median of the data set?
   1) 45
   2) 45.5
   3) 47
   4) 49

Sample Questions: Statistics

4. A set of scores has a mean of 70 and a standard deviation of 4. Which score has a standardized score of −2.5?
   1) 55
   2) 60
   3) 65
   4) 80

5. If the number k were added to each value in a set of data, which measure would remain unchanged?
   1) mean
   2) median
   3) mode
   4) range

6. Which of the following scatterplots would have a correlation coefficient closest to zero?
   1) 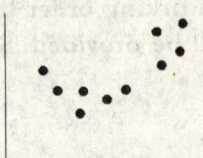
   2) 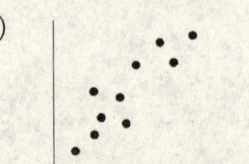
   3) 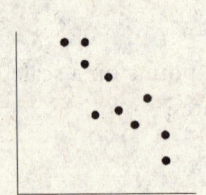
   4)

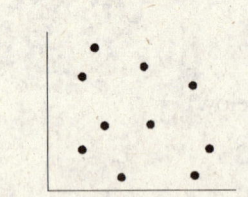

7. Given the regression equation $y = -3 + 0.5x$, which is true?
   1) The value of y increases 1 unit for every 2 units of increase in x.
   2) The value of y increases 2 units for every 1 unit of increase in x.
   3) The value of $\overline{y}$ is 3 units less than $\overline{x}$.
   4) The correlation between x and y is negative.

Sample Questions: Statistics

8. Base your answer to this question on the scatter diagram below:

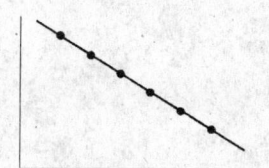

   If the regression line $\bar{y} = 3 - 0.5x$ fits the points on the scatter diagram perfectly, what is the value of the correlation coefficient r?
   1) 1
   2) −1
   3) 0.5
   4) −0.5

9. How many different radio station call letter combinations could there be if the first letter must be a W or a K and the whole station name must have three letters?
   1) 54
   2) 676
   3) 1352
   4) 17,576

10. Assume that events A and B are mutually exclusive, with $P(A) = .4$ and $P(B) = .5$. What is $P(A \text{ or } B)$?
    1) 0
    2) .2
    3) .7
    4) .9

11. Which of the following is a probability distribution for a discrete random variable?

    1) | x | $P(x)$ |
       |---|---|
       | 0 | 0.6 |
       | 1 | 0.6 |
       | 2 | −0.2 |

    2) | x | $P(x)$ |
       |---|---|
       | 0 | 0.7 |
       | 1 | −0.2 |
       | 2 | −0.1 |

    3) | x | $P(x)$ |
       |---|---|
       | 0 | 0.1 |
       | 1 | 0.3 |
       | 2 | 0.6 |

    4) | x | $P(x)$ |
       |---|---|
       | 0 | 0.3 |
       | 1 | 0.3 |
       | 2 | 0.3 |

Sample Questions: Statistics

12. What are the mean (μ) and standard deviation (σ) of a binomial distribution where $n = 60$ and $p = 1/6$?
    1) $\mu = 10$ and $\sigma = 2.89$
    2) $\mu = 10$ and $\sigma = 8.33$
    3) $\mu = 30$ and $\sigma = 3.87$
    4) $\mu = 30$ and $\sigma = 15$

13. Assume that the grades of individuals taking a proficiency examination are distributed normally with an average score of 75 and a standard deviation of 5. The minimum passing grade on the examination is 70. What is the approximate proportion of individuals who fail the examination?
    1) .16
    2) .34
    3) .68
    4) .84

14. Which is an accurate statement with regard to a simple random sample?
    1) The population is divided into stratified groups.
    2) The sample consists of every nth subject.
    3) The sample uses only subjects that have been screened for common traits.
    4) Samples of the same size have the same probability of being selected.

15. Given a normally distributed population with a mean of 72 and a standard deviation of 12, what is the standard error for the distribution of sample means for samples of size 36?
    1) 12
    2) 2
    3) 36
    4) 72

16. To get a sample of size 20 from the Fortune 500 companies, a statistician began by choosing a random integer (which turned out to be 16) from among the integers 1 to 25. The sample consisted of the companies with the following rankings:

    | 16 | 41 | 66 | 91 | 116 | 141 | 166 | 191 | 216 | 241 |
    | 266 | 291 | 316 | 341 | 366 | 391 | 416 | 441 | 466 | 491 |

    Which sampling scheme was used?
    1) cluster
    2) simple random
    3) stratified
    4) systematic

17. A change in which value would move the midpoint of the confidence interval for the population mean?
    1) sample size
    2) sample mean
    3) sample standard deviation
    4) confidence level

Sample Questions: Statistics

18. Which of the following pair of procedures would increase the length of a confidence interval for the population mean? (Assume σ remains constant.)
    1) increasing the confidence level and decreasing the sample size
    2) decreasing the confidence level and increasing the sample size
    3) increasing both the confidence level and sample size
    4) decreasing both the confidence level and sample size

19. A random sample of size 5 from a normal distribution, whose mean and variance are unknown, yields a sample mean of 27.75 and a sample variance of 16. Which of the following is closest to a 95% confidence interval for the true mean?
    1) 27.75 ± 3.51
    2) 27.75 ± 4.60
    3) 27.75 ± 4.97
    4) 27.75 ± 14.02

20. A college's past experience is that 46% of students accepted for admission will actually enroll at the college. It is assumed that the students act independently and that the 46% probability of acceptance still holds. If 5490 students are accepted, what is a 99% confidence interval for the number who will enroll?
    1) (2430, 2620)
    2) (2453, 2597)
    3) (2465, 2585)
    4) (0.443, 0.477)

21. In testing the hypotheses $H_0: \mu = \mu_0$ and $H_a: \mu \neq \mu_0$ based on a sample of size $n = 36$, assume that the population standard deviation is known and the value of the test statistic is $z = 1.71$. What is the approximate P-value?
    1) .044
    2) .050
    3) .087
    4) .100

22. A group of researchers plan to test the null hypothesis $H_0: \mu_1 - \mu_2 = 0$ by drawing independent samples of size $n = 15$ and $n = 12$, respectively, from two normally distributed populations. The population variances are unknown, but are assumed to be equal. Which statement best describes part of the test procedures?
    1) Use test statistic t and the pooled variance calculated from the sample variances.
    2) Use test statistic t but not the pooled variance calculated from the sample variances.
    3) Use test statistic z and the pooled variance calculated from the sample variances.
    4) Use test statistic z but not the pooled variance calculated from the sample variances.

Sample Questions: Statistics

23. An insurance company that currently sells only automobile insurance is planning to introduce homeowners insurance to its customers. The management has indicated that they will introduce homeowners insurance if more than 40% of their current customers indicate that they will purchase the new insurance. A random sample of 500 customers was used to test $H_a: p > .40$. The value of the test statistic was computed to be 2.8. Let α be the significance level. What is the appropriate conclusion?
    At $\alpha = 0.05$,
    1) there is sufficient evidence to conclude that homeowners insurance should not be introduced.
    2) there is insufficient evidence to conclude that homeowners insurance should be introduced.
    3) there is sufficient evidence to conclude that homeowners insurance should be introduced.
    4) there is insufficient evidence to conclude that more than 80% of current customers will purchase homeowners insurance.

24. A researcher developed a method to treat stomach ulcers. The researcher found that 47% of patients in the treatment group (sample size = 82) were cured, and that 38% of patients in the control group (sample size = 78) were cured. Let P_1 = the proportion cured in the population represented by the control group. Let P_2 = the proportion cured in the population of those taking treatment. The z test for $H_0: p_1 = p_2$ is closest to which value?
    1) 0.7
    2) 1.15
    3) 1.6
    4) 2.53

25. A researcher wishes to know if there is a relationship between gender and a person's preference of color in an automobile. Male and female customers at a car dealership are shown a particular model of car in each of four colors and are asked to state their preference. Which would be the most appropriate test to determine whether men and women have different preferences?
    1) chi-square test for goodness of fit
    2) chi-square test for independence of effects
    3) two-sample t test for comparing means
    4) z test for comparing means

Recommended Resources

Regents College. (1999). *Course guide for the Statistics examination* (2nd ed.).

Moore, D., & McCabe, G. (1993). *Introduction to the practice of statistics* (2nd ed.). New York: W.H. Freeman.

Against All Odds: Inside Statistics *telecourse (a series of 26 half-hour television shows).*

Moore, D. (1993). Telecourse study guide for Against all odds: Inside statistics and Introduction to the practice of statistics. (2nd ed.). New York: W.H. Freeman.

Regents College Examinations calculator. This calculator may be purchased from the Regents College Bookstore and is the only calculator you will be permitted to use during the examination.

Sample Questions: Statistics

Additional Resource

Rowntree, D. (1981). Statistics without tears: A primer for non-mathematicians. *New York: Charles Scribner's Sons.*

Formulas and Tables

The formulas and tables listed below will be provided for your use during the examination. The tables and most of the formulas appear in the 2nd edition of Moore and McCabe's *Introduction to the Practice of Statistics.*

Formulas

1. Mean
2. Variance
3. Standard deviation
4. Formula for converting to standardized units
5. Number of permutations of *n* objects taken *r* at a time
6. Number of combinations of *n* objects taken *r* at a time
7. Complement rule
8. General addition rule
9. Addition rule for mutually exclusive (disjoint) events
10. General multiplication rule
11. Multiplication rule for independent events
12. Mean of a discrete random variable
13. Variance of a discrete random variable
14. Binomial distribution
15. Mean (expected value) and standard deviation of a binomial distribution
16. Standard error of the mean
17. Large-sample level C confidence interval for μ
18. Level C confidence interval for *p*
19. Level C confidence interval for $\mu_1 - \mu_2$ if both populations are normal with equal unknown variances (independent samples)
20. Level C confidence interval for $p_1 - p_2$ if both sample sizes are large
21. Level C confidence interval for $\mu_1 - \mu_2$ for matched paired samples
22. Variance of difference of two independent means $\bar{x}_1 - \bar{x}_2$
23. Large-sample level C confidence interval for difference of two means
24. Test statistic for test concerning mean with known variance
25. Test statistic for small-sample test concerning mean of normal population with unknown variance
26. Test statistic for large independent sample test concerning $(\mu_1 - \mu_2)$ difference of two means
27. Test statistic for small independent sample test concerning $(\mu_1 - \mu_2)$ difference of two means of two normal populations with equal variance
28. Statistic for large-sample test concerning $(p_1 - p_2)$ difference of two proportions of two populations

29. Chi-square statistic for test of goodness of fit
30. Coefficients of least squares line $\hat{y} = a + bx$
31. Computing formula for linear correlation coefficient

Table I Standard Normal Probabilities
Table II Binomial Probabilities
Table III t Distribution Critical Values
Table IV Chi-square Critical Values

Study Guide
World Population (487)

Credit Hours: 3 **Credit Level:** Upper
Question Type(s): Multiple-choice

The information in this study guide is valid until Summer 2001.
If you will be taking the examination after that date, be sure to check for a new edition of this guide before you complete your preparation for the exam.

General Description of the Examination

The Regents College Examination in World Population measures knowledge and understanding of material typically taught in a course in world population offered in a department of sociology or geography. The examination assumes a knowledge of content included in lower-level arts and sciences courses, and requires basic college-level mathematical skills. Familiarity with the content of lower-level social sciences courses (for example: sociology, geography, economics) is helpful in learning the content of the examination.

The examination tests for a knowledge and understanding of the subject matter and of interrelationships among human population, society, and the environment. It tests for the ability to demonstrate interpretive skills, including the interpretation of tabular and graphed data; to analyze information; and to apply critical thinking.

You can prepare for this examination by following an independent program of study based on directed readings in a selected textbook and other resources. This program of study is fully outlined in the Regents College *Course Guide for World Population*. The course guide is described in detail on page 165, immediately following the content outline.

Content Outline

Content Area	Percent of Examination
I. Overview of the World's Population	15%
II. Demographic Perspectives	10%
III. Fertility	20%
IV. Mortality	10%
V. Migration and Urbanization	15%
VI. Case Studies and the Future of Population	15%
VII. Population Issues	15%
Total	**100%**

I. Overview of the World's Population (15%)

A. Brief history of world population

B. The world's most populous countries

C. Sources of data
1. Population censuses
2. Vital statistics
3. Sample surveys

D. Population composition and structure
1. Sex ratio
2. Population pyramids
3. Age stratification and cohort flow
4. Dependency ratio
5. Population projections

II. Demographic Perspectives (10%)

A. Malthus

B. Marx

C. Boserup

D. Demographic transition

E. Other perspectives

III. Fertility (20%)

A. Measures of fertility
1. Crude birth rate (CBR)
2. General fertility rate (GFR)
3. Child-woman ratio (CWR)
4. Age-specific fertility rates (ASFR)
5. Total fertility rate (TFR)
6. Gross reproduction rate (GRR)
7. Net reproduction rate (NRR)

B. Determinants of fertility
1. Biological component (age, health, nutrition, environment)
2. Social component (marriage, contraception, abortion)

C. Explanations for the fertility transition
1. The supply-demand framework
2. The innovation/diffusion and "cultural" perspective
3. Preconditions for a fertility decline

D. Explanations for high fertility—case studies (India, Ghana, Jordan)
1. Need to replenish society
2. Children as security and labor
3. Desire for sons

E. **Explanations for low fertility—case studies** (England, Japan, United States)
   1. Wealth, prestige, and fertility
   2. Income and fertility
   3. Education and fertility
   4. Other factors

IV. Mortality (10%)

A. **Measures**
   1. Crude death rate (CDR)
   2. Age/sex-specific death rate (ASDR)
   3. Infant mortality rate (IMR)
   4. Life expectancy

B. **Determinants of mortality**
   1. Causes of death
   2. The epidemiological transition (from communicable to degenerative)

C. **Mortality differentials**
   1. Urban and rural
   2. Social status
   3. Gender
   4. Age

V. Migration and Urbanization (15%)

A. **Basic concepts**

B. **Measures of migration**
   1. Immigration rate
   2. Emigration rate
   3. Net migration rate

C. **Why people migrate**
   1. Push-pull theory
   2. Selectivity of migration
   3. Conceptualizing the migration process

D. **International migration**

E. **Internal migration** (excluding rural-to-urban)

F. **Urbanization**

VI. Case Studies and the Future of World Population (15%)

A. China

B. India

C. The future of world population

VII. Population Issues (15%)

A. **Gender, household, and family**
   1. Household composition
   2. Explaining the transformation of households
   3. Consequences of demographic shifts in household composition

B. **Population and development**
   1. Growth as stimulus
   2. Growth as obstacle
   3. Growth as unrelated
   4. Case study: Mexico

C. **Population, resources, and the environment**
   1. Role of the agricultural and industrial revolutions
   2. Agricultural productivity
   3. Environmental issues

D. **Population policies** (including ethical dimensions)
   1. Fertility policies
   2. Mortality policies
   3. Migration policies

E. **Demographics**
   1. Geographic information system (GIS)
   2. Business planning
   3. Social planning
   4. Political planning

Course Guide for the World Population Examination

The examination development committee strongly recommends that you order the Regents College *Course Guide for World Population* for guidance in preparing for this examination. The course guide is designed to help you structure your own study and preparation, and includes suggestions for successful independent study. It contains five (5) units with over 25 study sessions and self-assessment activities. The course guide may be purchased only from the Regents College Bookstore.

Sample Questions: World Population

1. If 1995 national growth rates continue, which country will have the largest population in 2050?
    1) Brazil
    2) China
    3) India
    4) United States

2. Which mortality and fertility pattern is found in most economically developing countries of the world?
    1) low mortality and low fertility
    2) low mortality and high fertility
    3) high mortality and low fertility
    4) high mortality and high fertility

3. Which policy would a country choose if it followed the Malthusian perspective in attempting to solve the problem of rapid population growth?
   The country would
    1) raise the legal age of marriage.
    2) raise wages.
    3) subsidize education.
    4) tax wealthy incomes.

4. Which theorist would most likely have seen class differences as a major factor in economic development?
    1) Charles Darwin
    2) Thomas Malthus
    3) Karl Marx
    4) John Stuart Mill

5. If it is easy for individuals to rise in their professions, they are more likely to marry early and have several children. This concept is associated with which theorist?
    1) Ester Boserup
    2) Richard Easterlin
    3) Abdel Omran
    4) E.G. Ravenstein

6. What is the term for the number of live births in a given year for every one thousand people?
    1) crude birth rate (CBR)
    2) general fertility rate (GFR)
    3) gross reproduction rate (GRR)
    4) total fertility rate (TFR)

7. How is the child-woman ratio (CWR) measured?
   Based on census data, it is the ratio of
    1) children age 0–4 to the number of women, multiplied by 1,000.
    2) children age 0–4 to the number of women age 15–49, multiplied by 1,000.
    3) all children to the number of women, multiplied by 1,000.
    4) all children to the number of women age 15–49, multiplied by 1,000.

Sample Questions: World Population

8. Which fertility measure is concerned with female births, only?
    1) child-woman ratio (CWR)
    2) general fertility rate (GFR)
    3) gross reproduction rate (GRR)
    4) total fertility rate (TFR)

9. Which information is required to calculate the age/sex-specific death rate (ASDR)?
    1) census data, only
    2) vital registration data, only
    3) both census and vital registration data
    4) sample survey data and population pyramid data

10. Which category comprises the leading causes of death in the United States?
    1) accidents
    2) communicable disease
    3) degenerative illness
    4) homicide

BASE YOUR ANSWERS TO QUESTIONS 11–15 ON THE TABLE BELOW:
Basic Demographic Characteristics for Selected Countries—1996

Country	Crude Population (millions)	Crude Birth Rate	Infant Death Rate	Total Mortality Rate	Fertility Rate
A	9.5	50	20	134.0	6.7
B	8.1	11	10	5.5	1.4
C	24.0	29	7	60.0	3.5
D	18.4	20	5	18.4	2.3
E	11.7	29	6	40.0	3.6

11. Which country has demographic characteristics associated with economically developed nations?
    1) A
    2) B
    3) C
    4) D

12. Which country has the largest annual growth rate?
    1) A
    2) B
    3) D
    4) E

13. Which country has demographic characteristics associated with sub-Saharan African nations?
    1) A
    2) B
    3) C
    4) E

Sample Questions: World Population

14. Which country is likely to have the greatest gender inequality?
    1) A
    2) B
    3) D
    4) E

15. Which country has the lowest natural increase?
    1) A
    2) B
    3) D
    4) E

16. Which measure of migration is calculated by the equation below?

    $$\frac{\text{Total in-migrants} - \text{Total out-migrants}}{\text{Total midyear population}} \times 1{,}000$$

    1) migration ratio
    2) crude net migration rate
    3) in-migration rate
    4) out-migration rate

17. What is the major determinant of migration?
    1) climate
    2) employment
    3) family
    4) housing

18. According to U.S. census data, who is most likely to migrate?
    People who
    1) have not completed high school
    2) have completed high school, only
    3) have attended college but did not graduate
    4) have completed college

19. Which theory of international migration is represented when a rich nation exploits the resources of a poorer nation?
    1) dual labor market theory
    2) neoclassical economic theory
    3) network theory
    4) world systems theory

20. As part of its efforts to slow population growth, which country initiated a one-child policy for married couples?
    1) China
    2) India
    3) Japan
    4) Thailand

Sample Questions: World Population

21. If India's current demographic trends continue, which event will occur during the mid-21st century?
    1) India's population will surpass that of China.
    2) India's population rank will drop to third place behind that of the United States.
    3) Fertility rates will drop sharply, and the country will attain zero population growth.
    4) Immigration will exceed births as the primary source of population growth.

22. Which region of the world is likely to show the greatest increase in its share of the world's population by 2030?
    1) Africa
    2) Asia
    3) Latin America
    4) Western Europe

23. Which situation is consistently associated with lower fertility?
    1) higher educational status for men
    2) lower educational status for men
    3) higher educational status for women
    4) lower educational status for women

24. What is the most commonly used index for a nation's income?
    1) consumer price index (CPI)
    2) stock market performance
    3) gross reproduction rate (GRR)
    4) gross national product (GNP)

25. Which theoretical position argues that population growth is detrimental to economic development?
    1) capitalist
    2) nationalist
    3) neo-Malthusian
    4) neo-Marxist

26. Which statement best describes core nations?
Core nations
    1) are self-sufficient with respect to energy sources.
    2) have high incomes and low rates of consumption.
    3) experience higher rates of emigration.
    4) dictate economic terms to the rest of the world.

27. What is the fundamental premise of a Marxist perspective on population growth and economic development?
    1) Capitalist economic structure has no effect on overpopulation.
    2) Development will be stimulated by population growth among society's more educated classes.
    3) Development can occur only with a reduction in population size and a lower demand for food resources.
    4) Development emerges from society's political and economic structure, not from population change.

Sample Questions: World Population

28. Which best describes the green revolution?
    1) the rebellion of tenant farmers in Latin America against the landowners
    2) the rise in levels of food per capita in economically developing countries as a result of falling birth rates
    3) increases in food production that resulted from the development of new varieties of wheat and rice
    4) a worldwide program aimed at converting pastures and forests into cropland in economically developing countries

29. What was emphasized in the Programme of Action developed at the 1994 World Population Conference?
    1) immigration policies
    2) China's fertility policy and its potential for implementation elsewhere
    3) high mortality rates as a means of reducing population
    4) empowering women in order to limit fertility

30. Which is an example of market segmentation?
    1) advertising expensive cars in the mass media
    2) starting a college radio station that plays only current Top 40 songs
    3) using population data to determine the number of televisions to stock at an appliance store
    4) hiring department store salespersons with different ethnic and racial backgrounds

Recommended Resources

Regents College (1999). Course Guide for World Population.

Weeks, J. (1996). Population *(6th ed.). New York: Wadsworth.*

Population Reference Bureau (PRB) Bulletins:

   Yuan Tien, H. et al. (1992). China's Demographic Dilemmas.

   Visaria, L., & Visaria, P. (1995). India's Population in Transition.

   Lutz, W. (1994). The Future of World Population.

Other Resources

Population Reference Bureau (PRB) Bulletins and Publications:

   Haupt, A., & Kane, T. (1991). Population Handbook–International Edition.

   Martin, P., & Widgren, J. (1996). International Migration: A Global Challenge.

Study Guide
English Composition (434)

Credit Hours: 6 **Credit Level: Lower**
Question Type(s): Extended response

The information in this study guide is valid until Summer 2001.
If you will be taking the examination after that date, be sure to check for a new edition of this guide before you complete your preparation for the exam.

General Description of the Examination

The English Composition examination corresponds to an introductory, two-semester course in English Composition. It measures the ability to persuade a reader to pursue a specified course of action, using personal knowledge and experience to support a proposal; to analyze and respond appropriately to written texts that represent opposing viewpoints, using the Modern Language Association (MLA) style of citation; and to recognize and write about the strengths and weaknesses of a piece of writing. In general, the examination measures the ability to organize knowledge, ideas, and information; to adopt rhetorical strategies (such as narration, illustration, explanation, and description) in appropriate ways; to adopt and maintain a tone and point of view appropriate for a specified audience and rhetorical situation; to develop and maintain a controlling idea and a coherent organization; and to write within the rhetorical, syntactic, and mechanical conventions of Standard Written American English.

You can prepare for this examination by following a program of study based on a guided independent study package. This program of study is fully outlined in the Regents College *Course Guide for English Composition*. The course guide is described in detail on page 172, immediately following the descriptions of the writing prompts.

This examination can be used to fulfill the written English requirement (WER) of Regents College degree programs. (Three credits may be applied to the WER and three credits toward lower-level humanities requirements.) If you enrolled in Regents College on or after September 1, 1997, you may satisfy the WER by passing this English Composition examination, the Advanced Placement (AP) English exam, or a Regents College Special Assessment examination. A maximum of six semester hours of credit in English Composition/Freshmen English courses from traditional colleges will continue to apply toward degree requirements.

Descriptions of Questions

The examination includes three types of writing prompts as described below. Each type of prompt requires you to demonstrate a number of interrelated writing abilities.

Proposal Writing

This type of prompt tests your ability to persuade a reader to pursue a specified course of action, using your knowledge and experience to support your proposal. It tests your ability to select and effectively use such rhetorical strategies as narration, illustration, explanation, and description to support your proposal.

Analysis and Response

This type of prompt tests your ability to summarize and analyze two texts that present opposing viewpoints; to respond to a controversy effectively; to use sources inventively and responsibly by quoting and/or paraphrasing; to use the Modern Language Association (MLA) style of citation when referring to the words and/or ideas of others; and to write within the rhetorical, syntactic, and mechanical conventions of Standard Written American English.

You are directed to read two texts presented in the prompt and to write an essay in which you identify each author's position on an issue, analyze and evaluate these positions, and respond to the issue. You are asked to assume that your audience does not have access to the texts, so that part of your task is to summarize the arguments in such a way that your audience will understand them. You may choose how to respond to the issue. You may, for instance, defend the position of one of the authors, find a compromise position between them, explain why the controversy cannot be resolved, or suggest a way to resolve the controversy.

Response to Writing Sample

This type of prompt tests your ability to recognize and write about the strengths and weaknesses of a piece of writing within a specified rhetorical context. The prompt examines your awareness of the writing process, understanding of strategies for revising, and knowledge of the effective use of rhetorical, syntactic, and mechanical conventions of Standard Written American English.

You are directed to read a sample of writing presented to you and to write an essay in which you critique the writing sample. In your essay, you are directed to offer an overall assessment of the piece of writing, pointing out specific strengths and weaknesses; to assess the effectiveness of the writing in the context of the situation; to identify patterns of error in punctuation, spelling, usage, syntax, etc., and provide examples of each kind of error you identify; to comment on any issues that you think the writer should consider as he or she revises the piece; and to offer specific advice for revision that you think would make it a more effective piece of writing.

Course Guide for the English Composition Examination

The examination development committee strongly recommends that you order the Regents College *Course Guide for English Composition* for guidance in preparing for this examination. The course guide is organized into three major sections:

Part I provides a brief introduction to the recommended course of study, as well as study objectives and information about the resource materials, including the organization of the course guide.

Part II includes tools for evaluating your readiness for guided independent study and suggestions on creating a study plan and selecting appropriate learning strategies.

Part III Section A includes basic skills units that address different types of writing. It suggests ways to get started through journal writing; provides reading assignments from the textbooks, with discussion to help you understand the assignments; presents techniques for preparing to write; and presents guidelines for writing and revising, editing and proofreading, and evaluating your work.

Part III Section B provides information on how best to prepare for the questions on this examination. It includes strategies for planning your responses, sample essay responses, scoring guidelines, and analyses of the responses.

The course guide may be purchased only from the Regents College Bookstore.

Computer-Delivered Testing: Specific Information for the English Composition Examination

The questions for your examination—including stimulus material such as the texts for analysis and the writing sample—will be presented on the computer screen. Scrap paper will be provided for taking notes. You will handwrite your answers in separate answer booklets. You will also receive a General Instructions card containing the objectives for each prompt.

If you are used to analyzing or critiquing a text by marking it up, you will need to prepare yourself to handle text presented to you on a computer screen. You may want to develop a system for indicating what part of the text your note applies to, using screen number, location on screen, etc. If possible, spend some time reading from a computer workstation if this is not something you are accustomed to doing.

The essay questions (writing prompts) that follow illustrate those typically found on this examination. These sample questions are included to familiarize you with the types of questions you will find on the examination. The course guide includes scoring guidelines and examples of student answers for each type of prompt.

Sample Questions: English Composition

Proposal Writing

Your community's planning committee has set aside funding for the renovation of a vacant building or lot to be used for the whole community. The goal is for this new public space to be used frequently and by as many people as possible. The committee is asking people to suggest a site in their community and recommend a use for it.

Write a letter to the community planners. Be sure that you:

- propose that they purchase a specific vacant building or lot, explain why it is the best location for a community space, and describe how it should be used to achieve their goals;

- explain carefully and in detail why your proposal should be accepted;

- argue persuasively to the community planners that the proposal you have suggested is a wise investment.

Analysis and Response

Read the two texts presented on the following pages. The texts give different opinions on the language that college students and professors use when speaking to each other, and whether or not their speech should be regulated. The first text is taken from the editorial page of a newspaper; the second is a letter to the editor.

Write an essay for an audience of college students in which you

- *identify* each author's position on the issue "university speech codes." You should assume that your audience does not have access to these texts, so part of your task will be to summarize the arguments in such a way that your audience will understand them;

- *analyze* and *evaluate* these positions;

- *respond* to the issue. You may choose how to respond to the issue. You may, for instance, defend the position of one of the authors, find a compromise position between them, explain why the controversy cannot be resolved, or suggest a way to resolve the controversy.

Be careful to avoid plagiarism. These texts represent sources, so when paraphrasing or quoting from them, you should use the Modern Language Association (MLA) system of citation. You do not need to prepare a list of works cited.

P.C. University Goes Too Far

If you are heading for college or graduate school and are sensitive about being male, female, black, white, Asian, young, old, married, unmarried, gay, straight, Catholic, Jewish, evangelical Protestant or a veteran, think about going to the University of Massachusetts at Amherst. You will be protected there against offense to your group sensibilities.

That is the purpose of a new code of behavior proposed by the university's administration and its union of graduate student employees. It would punish as "harassment" a wide range of speech by faculty members or students—including "epithets, slurs and negative stereotyping"—that may offend groups....

The proposed code, circulated at the Amherst campus last month, would ban speech that offends "on the basis of race, color, national or ethnic origin, gender, sexual orientation, age, religion, marital status, veteran status or disability." The graduate students' union said it would add to that list "citizenship, culture, HIV status, language, parental status, political affiliation or belief and pregnancy status."

Orwell is the name that comes to mind as one reads this proposal. It would create a totalitarian atmosphere in which everyone would have to guard his tongue all the time lest he say something that someone finds offensive. (The code would let anyone who heard a doubtful remark about some group bring a complaint, even if he was not a member of the group.)

Do the drafters have no knowledge of history? One wonders. No understanding that freedom requires, as Justice Oliver Wendell Holmes said, "freedom for the thought that we hate"? And if not, what are they doing at a university? ...

The chancellor at the Amherst campus, David K. Scott, responded to criticism by suggesting that a code was required by federal Department of Education regulations. They threaten to withhold federal aid from any university with a "hostile environment" in terms of race—and similar gender rules are being prepared.

If so, the federal regulations need revision. It is time to stop letting the elastic concept of a "hostile environment" menace freedom of speech, at universities of all places.

(Lewis, Anthony. "P.C. University Goes Too Far." *The Oregonian* 28 Nov. 1995: C7.)

Response to "P.C. University Goes Too Far"

To the Editor:

I am writing in response to Anthony Lewis's recent editorial regarding the University of Massachusetts at Amherst's proposed speech code. Anthony Lewis is wrong. Such a speech code is not an "Orwellian" or "Nazi" tactic. Rather, it is a directive asking that people speak with politeness and consideration for others. How can that be wrong?

I am a female student at Astoria State University, and I have quite often felt the stings of harassment in the speech of others. I once had a professor say to me, "Why don't you stay home and have children? That's all you're suited to do." Maybe he was joking—he said it with a laugh—but I was devastated. More than once I have heard male students refer to females using terms that your newspaper wouldn't print.

I have heard other students refer to African Americans using racial epithets. Because this speech was not corrected or checked, fraternities have also engaged in outright racist behavior, such as dressing in white sheets imitating the Ku Klux Klan. What does it take for the administration to see that there is a problem—a lynching?

A college campus should provide a safe environment for learning. If students feel that they are hated by others or that their presence is not wanted, how can that student begin to learn and grow as a person? We are all entitled to an education in the United States, not just white males who resemble Anthony Lewis.

Student retention at universities like UMass is usually worse for students who are minorities of one type or another. Perhaps it is time to create a safe place for *all* of us to learn.

Nadine Williams
Astoria, Oregon

(Williams, Nadine. *Astorian Journal* 2 Dec. 1995: B12.)

For Response to Writing Sample, see next page.

Sample Questions: English Composition

Response to Writing Sample
A college is considering a graduation requirement mandating a minimum number of unpaid community service hours for all undergraduates. The community service hours would be devoted to helping individuals, organizations, and agencies in the community. While the school has not determined details such as the number of required hours, the amount of school supervision, the necessary relevance to academic majors, etc., it looks as if the administration and most of the faculty are in favor of instituting some type of community service requirement.

Some students are against required service hours and have drafted a letter to the school's administration providing reasons why the requirement should not be adopted.

Write an essay in which you critique the letter. In your essay, be sure to:

- offer an overall assessment of the letter, pointing out specific strengths and weaknesses;

- assess the effectiveness of the letter in the context of the situation;

- identify patterns of error in punctuation, spelling, usage, syntax, etc., and provide examples of each kind of error you identify;

- comment on any issues that you think the writers should consider as they revise the letter;

- offer specific advice for revising the letter that you think would make it a more effective piece of writing.

Writing Sample
Dear Administrators:
   We, a group of students here want to urge you not to add a community service requirement. Their are many reasons why community service should not be mandatory: college students are already too busy, community service is a waist of time, your unfairly making us, community service is only valuable if it is provided voluntarily, and, because we're so busy, many of us will do a bad job.
   We aren't obligated to help the community, and it really doesn't even need help from us. And requiring community service lessons the meaning and the benefit to the student. Its useful only if its voluntary.
   If you make college students volunteer in the community some of us will do a good job, but many of them will fail to show up. Or will do work poorly. This will reflect badly on the school. It will provide negative P.R.
   Community service seems pointless for us. Our job is to get an education, and thats what we're paying for, not to help others, thats what we pay taxes for. And we're not yet ready to help others—we don't have the skills or knowledge. Once we graduate and get jobs, we'll be able to help if we want to.

Sample Questions: English Composition

Now students are too busy. Their in class at least fifteen hours a week, and many of them have long labs, too. Their involved in collegiate and intramural athletics and many of them work to. They need time to relax and unwind to watch TV and refresh themselves. We've also got to have time for social activities. Belonging to organizations, parties to go to, and having dates are among the most important parts of college life. This is there time to have fun—to relax and socialize. To still be kids before we go out into the real world. We need to develop our social skill's. We should be allowed to take advantage of this time and enjoy ourselves and should not be made to work at community service.

Community service is slave labor. We cant be made to work without pay its unAmerican. It's also unfair because those who run the school don't do community service. An the faculty doesn't do community service, so we shouldn't either.

In conclusion, we should be concentrating on our studies to prepare for life in today's society. A community service requirement would make it harder to do that. For that reason we urge you not to make community service a requirement.

Sincerely,

Outraged students

Recommended Resources

The examination development committee recommends that you obtain the resources listed below.

Axelrod, Rise B. and Charles R. Cooper. The St. Martin's Guide to Writing. *5th ed. New York: St. Martin's Press, 1997.*

Behrens, Laurence and Leonard J. Rosen. Writing and Reading Across the Curriculum. *6th ed. New York: Longman, 1997.*

Ede, Lisa. Work in Progress: A Guide to Writing and Revising. *3rd ed. New York: St. Martin's Press, 1995.*

Hacker, Diana. A Writer's Reference. *3rd ed. Boston: Bedford Books of St. Martin's Press, 1995.*

Hacker, Diana. Exercises to Accompany A Writer's Reference. *3rd ed. Boston: Bedford Books of St. Martin's Press, 1995.*

Hacker, Diana. Exercises to Accompany A Writer's Reference: Answer Key. *3rd ed. Boston: Bedford Books of St. Martin's Press, 1995.*

Harnack, Andrew and Gene Kleppinger. Online! A Reference Guide to Using Internet Sources. *Boston: Bedford Books of St. Martin's Press, 1998.*

Regents College. Course Guide for English Composition.

The Upper-Level Examination Series

As part of a drive to better meet students' need for upper-level credit, Regents College developed a group of extended response (essay) examinations that are distinctly interdisciplinary in scope: American Dream, History of Nazi Germany, and Religions of the World. You can prepare for each of these examinations by following an independent program of study based on directed readings and other resources, such as audiotapes or videotapes. This program of study is fully outlined in the Regents College course guide for the particular exam.

The examination development committee strongly recommends that you order the appropriate Regents College course guide for guidance in preparing for an exam in this group. The course guide is organized into three major sections:

Part I   Introduction
Part II   Mastering the Content
Part III   Preparing for the Examination

Part I of the course guide is designed to help you structure your own study and preparation and includes suggestions for successful independent study.

Part II is designed to help you master the content of this examination. The content outline is displayed along with specific reading or other assignments for each topic. The Plan of Study divides your efforts into several units covering the major content topics. For each topic, the guide provides a list of objectives or issues to consider as you study, some general discussion to assist your reading or use of the other reference materials, and study questions to guide your thinking. The Plan of Study is designed to direct and focus your learning.

Part III is designed to assist you in writing well-organized, cogent essays on the content you have learned during your independent study. Part III provides guidance in writing an essay, and includes scoring guidelines, a sample question, and additional help such as analyses of good and poor essay responses, so that you can practice working your way through a question.

The course guides may be purchased only from the Regents College Bookstore. (See page 9 for information on ordering publications from the bookstore.)

Achieving Success on an Extended Response Exam

Achieving success on an extended response examination requires more than just learning content. You must be able to convey your understanding of that content through the writing of effective responses. An extended response examination requires you to generate ideas, develop relationships among ideas, and supply supporting facts and concepts. You may find it helpful to supplement the material in Part III of the course guide with a reference guide or college textbook on writing a good essay. The resources recommended for our English Composition examination (see page 178) may be used for this purpose.

Computer-Delivered Testing: The Upper-Level Exam Series

The questions for your examination will be presented on the computer screen. You will have the choice of entering your answers on the computer, using a simple word-processing function, or writing them in answer booklets. If you wish to handwrite your answers, you are responsible for bringing several blue or black ballpoint pens with you to your examination appointment.

The tutorial for these exams provides practice in using the built-in word processor. We encourage you to take advantage of this tutorial. A copy of the tutorial that you can actually practice with is included on the CD-ROM that came with this book. If you are unable to use Windows files but have a Web browser (Netscape or Internet Explorer) installed, you can view (but not practice with) the screens that you will see in the tutorial by following the screenshot links rather than downloading.

Study Guide
American Dream (460)

Credit Hours: 6 **Credit Level: Upper**
Question Type(s): Extended response

The information in this study guide is valid until Summer 2001.
If you will be taking the examination after that date, be sure to check for a new edition of this guide before you complete your preparation for the exam.

General Description of the Examination

The Regents College Examination in American Dream measures understanding of material appropriate to a two-semester interdisciplinary humanities course in American studies.

The content is composed of elements drawn from traditional subjects such as American literature, American history, and political science from the period prior to the Civil War. Although the content is structured chronologically, the examination is comparative and thematic in its approach and calls for the student to demonstrate comprehension of the emerging nature of an American culture that is marked by both conflict and consensus.

The American Dream means many things to many people. Students will be asked to focus on the role that both conflict and consensus played in shaping the American Dream.

Content Outline

Content Area

I. Colonial America

II. Revolution and Nation Building

III. The Antebellum Period: Revolution and Reform

NOTE: *Specific reading and listening assignments useful for learning the content outlined in the first column are listed in the second column. These resources can all be found in one of the print or other media resources described on page 187. Because the resources build on previously assigned material, it is important that the assignments be studied in the order presented.*

I. Colonial America

Reading/Listening

A. The quest for wealth and success

Christopher Columbus, from *Journal of the First Voyage to America*; Samuel de Champlain, from *The Voyages of Samuel de Champlain, 1604–1618*, "An Encounter with the Iroquois"; John Smith, "A Description of New England"; William Bradford, from *Of Plymouth Plantation*; Cotton Mather, from *Magnalia Christi Americana*; William Cronon, "Indians, Colonists, and Property Rights"

B. The individual and the community

John Smith, "Advertisements for the Unexperienced Planters of New-England, or Anywhere, or the Pathway to Experience to Erect a Plantation"; John Winthrop, "On Trade"; Thomas Morton, from *New English Canaan*; Roger Williams, "To the Town of Providence"; *The New England Primer*; Jonathan Edwards, from *Personal Narrative*, "Sinners in the Hands of an Angry God"

C. The role of government

William Bradford, from *Of Plymouth Plantation*

D. Forging an American identity

Sean Wilentz, "Artisan Republicanism"; Ira Berlin, "Time, Space, and the Evolution of Afro-American Society"

E. Addendum: A look west

"The Coming of the Spanish and the Pueblo Revolt"; Don Antonio de Otermìn, "Letter on the Pueblo Revolt of 1680"; Don Diego de Vargas, "Letter on the Reconquest of New Mexico"; Rev. Father Fray Carlos Delgado, "Report made by Rev. Father Fray Carlos Delgado to our Rev. Father Ximeno"

II. Revolution and Nation Building

A. The quest for wealth and success

Thomas Jefferson, from *Notes on the State of Virginia*; Alexander Hamilton, "Report on the Subject of Manufactures"; Max Weber, from The Spirit of Capitalism; Richard Bushman, "Family Security in the Transition from Farm to City, 1750–1850"; Washington Irving, "Style, at Ballston"

B.	**The individual and the community**	Olaudah Equiano (Gustavus Vassa), from "The Interesting Narrative of the Life of Olaudah Equiano, or Gustavus Vassa, The African. Written by Himself"; Phillis Wheatley, Poetry; Jupiter Hammon, "An Address to Miss Phillis Wheatly [sic]"; Francisco Palou, from *Life of Junípero Serra*; Thomas Paine, from *An Occasional Letter on the Female Sex*; Abigail Adams, Letter to John Adams, 3/31/76; David Walker, from *Appeal &c*
C.	**The role of government**	from *The Federalist Papers*, #6, #10; "An Anti-Federalist Paper"; Thomas Jefferson, Letters to John Adams and James Madison
D.	**Forging an American identity**	Thomas Paine, from *The American Crisis*, "Number 1"; Patriot and Loyalist Songs and Ballads; James Fenimore Cooper, "An Aristocrat and a Democrat"; J. Hector St. John de Crèvecoeur, from *Letters from an American Farmer*; Thomas Archdeacon, "Natives and Newcomers: Confrontation"

III. The Antebellum Period: Revolution and Reform

A.	**The quest for wealth and success**	Mariano Guadalupe Vallejo, from *Recuerdos históricos y personales tocante a la alta California*, "An Account of the Gold Rush"; Fanny Fern (Sara Willis Parton), "The Working-Girls of New York"; Herman Melville, "Bartleby, the Scrivener," "The Paradise of Bachelors and the Tartarus of Maids"
B.	**The individual and the community**	Harriet Ann Jacobs, from *Incidents in the Life of a Slave Girl*; William Lloyd Garrison, from *William Lloyd Garrison: The Story of His Life*; Elizabeth Cady Stanton, "Declaration of Sentiments"; Henry David Thoreau, from *Walden*, "Where I Lived, and What I Lived For"; "Reminiscences by Frances D. Gage of Sojourner Truth, for May 28-29, 1851"; Margaret Fuller, from *Woman in the Nineteenth Century*; Bret Harte, "The Outcasts of Poker Flat," "Tennessee's Partner"; Emily Dickinson, Poem #324, Poem #508; Herbert Storing, from *The Moral Foundations of the American Republic*; Jacqueline Jones, "Black Women, Work, and the Family Under Slavery"; Mary P. Ryan, "Women, Revival, and Reform"

C. **The role of government** Ralph Waldo Emerson, "Concord Hymn"; Henry David Thoreau, "Resistance to Civil Government"; David Christy, from *Cotton is King*; Eric L. McKitrick, "The Defense of Slavery"; Edmund Ruffin, "The Political Economy of Slavery"; Abraham Lincoln, "Address at the Dedication of the Gettysburg National Cemetery," "Second Inaugural Address"

D. **Forging an American identity** George Washington Harris, "Sut Lovingood's Adventures in New York," "Sut Lovingood, on the Puritan Yankee"; Ralph Waldo Emerson, "The American Scholar"; Nathaniel Hawthorne, "My Kinsman, Major Molineux"; George Washington Harris, from *The Crockett Almanacs*; Harriet Beecher Stowe, from *Uncle Tom's Cabin*; Frederick Douglass, "What to the Slave is the Fourth of July?"; Caroline Kirkland, from *A New Home—Who'll Follow?*; Fanny Fern (Sara Willis Parton), "Independence"; John Rollin Ridge, "Oppression of Digger Indians"; Henry Wadsworth Longfellow, "The Jewish Cemetery at Newport"; Walt Whitman, "Song of Myself"; Winthrop Jordan and Leon Litwack, "The Last American West"; William Kephart and William Zellner, "The Oneida Community"; Leonard Arrington and Davis Bitton, "Brigham Young Leads the Mormons into the West"; Jean Baker, "Learning to Be Americans: Schooling and Political Culture"; Emily Dickinson, Poem #341, Poem #657

Sample Questions: American Dream

The search for wealth and success brought many people to the Americas. Their competing definitions of wealth and success led to, and were shaped by, the conflicts that resulted when these definitions were put into practice (for example, if wealth is defined as land ownership, land must be obtained).

QUESTION:

Using specific examples from the readings, discuss the following:

- how native populations and colonists defined wealth and success;
- how the practices that followed from these definitions led to conflict; and
- how the resulting conflicts were resolved.

Scoring Guidelines

The three questions on the examination are weighted equally. Each response is rated on the basis of ten points. In general, the following criteria apply:

Score	Criteria
9–10	**Factual Material**

Excellent command of individual readings and authors; makes reference to readings and authors throughout the answer; distinguishes between works and the regions and traditions they represent; displays an understanding of the chronological, ideological, and literary connections that exist among the various readings and authors; makes clear references to the taped lectures when appropriate.

Analysis

Well-crafted analysis based on a collection of specific readings. Points are developed moving from the general topic of the question toward a discussion of a single theme or idea based on a specific set of readings.

Answer demonstrates an ability to consider the relationships that exist among the readings and displays a sound understanding of how individual examples relate to the topic.

A mix of primary and secondary sources are called upon throughout the answer; demonstrates an understanding of the relation between primary and secondary materials to each other and to the topic.

8   **Factual material**

A good command of individual readings and authors; refers to specific readings and authors throughout the essay; brings in material from the taped lectures when appropriate.

Analysis

Offers a complete and coherent answer that looks at several aspects of the topic and uses several examples to highlight each aspect. Uses clear transitions to move from one point to another.

Identifies specific primary and secondary works; demonstrates their connection to the topic.

Sample Questions: American Dream

7 **Factual material**
A good command of individual readings and authors; is generally accurate when citing specific sources; limited reference to the taped lectures when appropriate.

Analysis
Offers a complete answer, although the response may be choppy or introduce unrelated ideas or themes.

Uses a minimum of specific examples from the reading but is accurate when citing sources; deals with issues on a general level.

6 **Factual material**
Limited use and command of individual readings.

Analysis
Offers a complete answer to the question; however, the response is not logically developed; offers broad and unsupported general statements.

Limited reference to specific examples from the reading; few, if any, references to secondary sources or tapes.

5 **Factual material**
Frequent mistakes regarding individual readings.

Analysis
Refers to the full question but does not respond to each aspect.

Offers a series of general statements with few attempts to bring in specific examples in support; references to primary sources are vague or inaccurate; response is poorly organized.

4 **Factual material**
Few, if any, references to specific readings; frequent mistakes with factual material.

Analysis
Attempts to answer only one section of the question.
Highly general.

1–3 **Factual material**
No evidence of having completed any of the readings or having listened to the tapes; facts and generalizations inaccurate.

Analysis
Incoherent; no evidence of reading or listening to taped lectures.

0 **No response or off the topic.**

Sample Questions: American Dream

Study Materials

Unlike other examinations for which you can prepare using any assortment of textbooks, the American Dream examination is based on the textbooks and *Book of Readings* listed below. The new edition of the course guide even includes a computer disk with all the study questions formatted so you can enter your answers using a word processor. It will be to your advantage to use these materials in your study, rather than to attempt to learn the same content using comparable material prepared by other publishers.

Print Materials

The Declaration of Independence and the Constitution of the United States of America.

Frazier, T.R. (Ed.). (1987). The underside of American history. Volume 1: to 1877 (5th ed.). San Diego: Harcourt Brace Jovanovich.

Lauter, P. et al. (Eds.). (1994). The Heath anthology of American literature. Volume 1. (2nd ed.). Lexington, MA: D.C. Heath.

Regents College. (1993). The American dream (Part I): A book of readings. Acton, MA: Copley.

Regents College. (2000). Course guide for the American dream examination (2nd ed.).

Other Media

The audiocassette lecture series with which this exam is correlated is now available for purchase only from the Regents College Bookstore. You might be able to find these resources through a library, as well.

The American dream, *Dr. John K. Roth. SuperStar Teachers™, The Teaching Company.*

Study Guide

History of Nazi Germany (432)

Credit Hours: 3 **Credit Level: Upper**
Question Type(s): Extended response

The information in this study guide is valid until Summer 2001.
If you will be taking the examination after that date, be sure to check for a new edition of this guide before you complete your preparation for the exam.

General Description of the Examination

The History of Nazi Germany examination measures knowledge and understanding of material appropriate to an undergraduate course in the history of Nazi Germany.

The examination tests for knowledge and understanding of the historical evidence and the historical debates surrounding Nazi Germany and the student's ability to interpret this history. The examination content is drawn from that commonly included in courses with such titles as History of National Socialism (Nazism), Modern German History, History of the Holocaust, and History of World War II.

The examination measures understanding of the background of the history of Nazi Germany, Hitler and the rise of National Socialism, Nazi seizure of power, life in Nazi Germany, the origins of World War II, the home front during World War II, the Holocaust, and the legacy of National Socialism.

Content Outline

Content Area

I. Background

II. The Seizure of Power

III. Aspects of Life in Nazi Germany

IV. Foreign Policy to 1939

V. War and Society, 1939–1942

VI. War and Society, 1942–1945

VII. Legacy

I. Background

A. Introduction
1. Enduring impact of National Socialism (Nazism)
2. Primary and secondary sources for study of National Socialism
3. Introductory issues of Nazism and German history
   a. Continuity and change
   b. *Sonderweg* thesis ("the special path")
   c. Historical roots of Nazism

B. The Great War (World War I), 1914–1918
1. Causes
2. Impact on Germany
3. Revolution

C. Peace of Versailles

D. Weimar Germany
1. Political framework
   a. Constitution
   b. Parties
2. The new regime's poor start
3. Periodization—connection of economic and political developments
   a. Inflation and political instability—1919–1924
   b. Stabilization—1924–1929
   c. Depression, renewed political instability, and collapse—1929–1933

E. Hitler and the rise of National Socialism
1. The connection between the rise of National Socialism and the fall of the Weimar Republic
2. Nazi electoral politics through 1932

II. The Seizure of Power

A. The NSDAP (Nazi party) gains strength
1. Cooperation with other parties
2. Respectability and financial support

B. Nazi propaganda
1. Role in making NSDAP a party of mass appeal
2. Main target: Weimar Republic
3. Joseph Goebbels as Propaganda Chief
4. Strengths of Nazi propaganda

C. The decline of the Weimar Republic, 1930–1932
1. Presidential dictatorship under Brüning
2. Hindenburg's acceptance of authoritarian methods
3. Increasing use of "emergency" decrees
4. NSDAP successes in September 1930 elections
5. Papen solicits NSDA support
6. Hitler solicits support of industrialists
7. Presidential elections of 1932

8. Paralysis following July 1932 Parliamentary elections
9. Parliamentary elections of November 1932

D. January 1933 Elections: Hitler becomes Chancellor

E. Interpretations of Hitler's personality and the rise of National Socialism

F. The March 1933 election
1. Reichstag fire and suspension of civil liberties
2. Coercion and terror in the campaign
3. NSDAP gets 43.9 percent of the vote
4. Enabling Act: Legal foundation of the Third Reich

III. Aspects of Life in Nazi Germany

A. *Gleichschaltung* (forced coordination of German society by National Socialism)
1. The method of *Gleichschaltung*
2. Public reaction
3. The partnership between National Socialists and conservative elites

B. The Hitler state
1. Hitler's role
2. The polycratic state

C. National Socialist ideology
1. Race and ideology
   a. Theory
   b. Practice
2. The *Volksgemeinschaft* (people's community)
   a. The concept of the *Volksgemeinschaft*
   b. Aspects of the *Volksgemeinschaft*
      1) Business and industry
      2) Women
      3) The working class
      4) Farmers
3. Youth under National Socialism
   a. Education
   b. The Hitler Youth
4. Art, science, and medicine under National Socialism

IV. Foreign Policy to 1939

A. Basic historiographical issues

B. The aftermath of World War I

C. Hitler and Nazi foreign policy
1. Hitler: Opportunist or planner?
2. Interrelated policies
   a. Expansionism (living space)
   b. Racial policy (creating a racially pure Reich)
   c. Crusade against Bolshevism
   d. Economic self-sufficiency

3. Perceived British threat to German hegemony
4. Hitler's use of the "Stab in the Back" theory
5. Impact of domestic affairs
6. The Hossbach Memorandum: Hitler's plans for aggression?

D. Aggression and appeasement in the 1930s: Undoing the Treaty of Versailles
1. Authoritarianism and expansionism
2. 1933: German successes
   a. Resignation from Geneva Disarmament Conference
   b. Resignation from League of Nations
   c. Secret plans to triple the size of the army
3. 1934: Assassination of Austrian Chancellor
4. 1935: Repudiation of military and naval clauses of Treaty of Versailles
5. 1936: The Rhineland and war plans
   a. German remilitarization of Rhineland
   b. Four-year plan to prepare economy for war
   c. 1937: The Hossbach Memorandum

E. 1938: Austria and Czechoslovakia
1. Anschluss: German annexation of Austria
2. The crisis over the Sudetenland
3. The Munich Pact: September 29, 1938
4. Evaluating the Munich Pact

F. 1939: The Nazi-Soviet Pact and Poland
1. The "domestic crisis" and the beginning of war
2. Annexation of the rest of Czechoslovakia
3. British guarantee of Greek, Romanian, and Polish sovereignty
4. German-Soviet nonaggression pact
   a. The Pact and the isolation of Poland
   b. German invasion of Poland
5. Britain and France declare war on Germany

V. War and Society, 1939–1942

A. The *Blitzkrieg*: The height of German expansion

B. The origins of the SS

C. The SS/police complex

D. Racial and anti-Semitic policy

VI. War and Society, 1942–1945

A. The changing tide of military fortune
1. From military stalemate to defeat
2. Personal experiences of war
   a. Soldiers
   b. Civilians and the home front
3. Resistance, accommodation, and criticism at home

- B. **The Holocaust**
    1. Personal experiences
    2. Planning and implementations
    3. Timing and motivations
    4. Varieties of Jewish response: Collaboration, appeasement, resistance, uprising
    5. What could (or should) have been done?

- C. **The Holocaust as part of general ideological war and barbarization of warfare**
    1. The perpetrators: Not only the Nazis
    2. The victims: Not only the Jews

- D. *Götterdämmerung*: **The end of the Third Reich**

VII. Legacy

- A. **Hitler, National Socialism, and World War II**
    1. Reconsidering the origins of Nazism
    2. Reconsidering the issue of responsibility

- B. **West German historians and the attempt to escape from the Nazi past**

- C. **Continuity and change**

Sample Questions: History of Nazi Germany

Focusing on different social groups in Germany, analyze how membership in and levels of support for the National Socialist movement changed between 1920 and 1945. In your answer, be sure to examine the following periods:

- from the founding of the Nazi Party to the Beer Hall Putsch
- from the refounding of the party based on the strategy of legality to the eve of the Great Depression
- from the Great Depression to the "seizure of power"
- during the period of *Gleichschaltung* (mid-1933–1939)
- during the Lightning War (September 1939–December 1941)
- during the period of total war

For each of these periods, identify and analyze which social groups joined or supported the National Socialist movement, why they joined, and how political and economic factors influenced levels of support.

After completing your analysis of the individual time periods, provide a general explanation for the changing appeal of National Socialism over time.

Your analysis should conclude with a brief discussion of what it meant after World War II for particular social groups to have supported National Socialism.

Scoring Guidelines

The three questions on the examination are weighted equally. Each response is rated on the basis of ten points. In general, the following criteria apply:

Score	Criteria
9–10	Excellent command of factual material; answers entire question in a coherent, well-thought-out essay; factual material and generalizations based on it well balanced, with accurate examples backing up each general point; includes several specific references to the literature and lectures that support the response.
8	Good command of factual material; answers entire question in coherent essay; some attempt to back up general points with specific examples; includes general references to the literature and lectures that support the response.
7	Good command of factual material; answers entire question coherently, although the response may not flow well; focuses primarily on either generalizations or specific examples, but, in either case, does so accurately; few if any references, however general, to the literature or lectures that support the response.
6	Limited command of factual material; answers entire question, although not necessarily in an orderly fashion; focuses primarily on either generalization or specific examples with occasional, minor inaccuracies; usually no references to supporting literature or lectures.

Sample Questions: History of Nazi Germany

5   Makes frequent mistakes with factual material; at least tries to answer all of question; focuses on generalizations; specific examples often inaccurate; usually no references to supporting lectures or literature, and, if they are there, they are either very general or inaccurate.

4   Frequent mistakes with factual material; answers only one or two parts of question; overly general; no references to literature.

1–3   Incoherent, with both facts and generalizations inaccurate; no evidence that any of reading or listening done.

0   No response or off the topic.

Print Materials

Eubank, K. (1992). World War II: Roots and causes *(2nd ed.). Lexington, MA: D.C. Heath.*

Kershaw, I. (1991). Profiles in power: Hitler. *New York: Longman.*

Mitchell, A. (1990). The Nazi revolution: Hitler's dictatorship and the German nation. *(3rd ed.). Lexington, MA: D.C. Heath.*

Niewyk, D.L. (1992). The holocaust: Problems and perspectives of interpretation *(1st ed.). Lexington, MA: D.C. Heath.*

Regents College. (1992). The history of Nazi Germany: A book of readings. Acton, MA: *Copley.*

Regents College. (1994). Course guide for History of Nazi Germany.

Sax, B., and Kuntz, D. (1992). Inside Hitler's Germany. *Lexington, MA: D.C. Heath.*

Other Media

A history of Hitler's empire, *Professor Thomas Childers. SuperStar Teachers™, The Teaching Company.*

To purchase the audiocassettes or videocassettes, please contact:
    The Teaching Company
    7405 Alban Station Court
    Suite A-107
    Springfield, VA 22150
    Telephone: 800-832-2412

Study Guide
Religions of the World (509)

Credit Hours: 3 **Credit Level: Upper**
Question Type(s): Extended response

The information in this study guide is valid until Summer 2001.
If you will be taking the examination after that date, be sure to check for a new edition of this guide before you complete your preparation for the exam.

General Description of the Examination

The Religions of the World examination measures knowledge and understanding of the major world religions as viewed in their social and historical context. It is based on material that would typically be taught in an interdisciplinary course at the undergraduate level. The examination tests for the ability to apply concepts drawn from sociology, psychology, and philosophy and to compare and analyze religious beliefs and practices.

Content Outline

Content Area

I. Theoretical Framework

II. Disciplinary Perspectives: Sociology, Psychology, Philosophy

III. Historical and Cultural Framework

IV. Selected Topics for Comparative and Interpretive Analysis

I. Theoretical Framework

A. The nature of religion
1. Definitions of religion
2. Organized structures and personal belief systems
3. Variety of religions
4. Types of religious experience and expression
   a. The sacred and the profane
   b. Ceremony, rituals, and rites of worship
   c. The individual and the group

B. Ways of studying religion
1. Examining religious phenomena
   a. Religious dimensions of culture
   b. Representatives of religious life
   c. "Inside" and "outside" descriptions
   d. Bias and objectivity
2. Constructing the history of a religion
   a. Historical sources
   b. Data and interpretation
   c. Historical methods
3. Reading religious texts
   a. Texts and interpretation
   b. Languages and cultures
   c. Privileged interpretations

C. Religions of prehistoric and primal cultures

D. Tools for study: Vocabulary and pronunciation

II. Disciplinary Perspectives: Sociology, Psychology, Philosophy

A. General introduction

B. Sociology and religion
1. Sociological perspective on religion
2. Social functions of religion
3. Types of religious organizations
4. Religious communities as organizations
5. Religion and issues of class, race, and gender

C. Psychology and religion

D. Philosophy and religion
1. Using reason as a tool for the study of religion
2. Thinking religiously—as a believer

III. Historical and Cultural Framework

NOTE: For content area III, the following topics apply to each religion:

The world in which the religion developed
- The land and its people
  - Culture
- Religious traditions
  - Religious artifacts
  - Ideas of the supernatural

Traditions of the founder

Historical development of the religion
- Formative stage
  - Sacred writings/literature
  - Teachings
    - Theology and cosmology
    - Ethics
  - Worship
    - Sacred spaces
    - Rituals and ceremonies
    - Symbolic objects
  - Cultural roles
    - Religious institutions
    - Social and political institutions
- Developmental and mature stages
  - Topics listed above, as well as interaction with other religions
- Modern configurations
  - Challenges to this tradition
  - Varieties of response

A. Hinduism

B. Jainism

C. Buddhism

D. Confucianism

E. Taoism (Daoism)

F. Shinto

G. Judaism

H. Christianity

I. Islam

IV. Selected Topics for Comparative and Interpretive Analysis

A. Cosmology and world view
 1. Origin and nature of the world
 2. Time, space, and order
 3. Change, permanence, and purpose

B. Religion and religious writing

C. Life goals and ultimate aims
 1. The ordinary, the good, and the perfect
 2. Enlightenment, peace, and salvation

D. Self and community
 1. Experience and practice alone and in groups
 2. Belonging, supporting, and dissenting
 3. Identity formation through, or in opposition to, the community
 4. Religious uniformity, diversity, and tolerance

Sample Questions: Religions of the World

In religions that begin with an individual as leader, there is a significant stage when the original leader or "prophet" dies and successive generations of leadership take over.

Assess to what degree any two (2) of the following religions (Buddhism, Christianity, Islam) changed within 500 years after the death of the founder. For each religion you select, identify specific changes that occurred in each of the following areas:

- cosmology and world view
- defined life goals and ultimate aims
- beliefs about the founder

After you have identified specific changes that occurred for each religion, evaluate the overall significance of these changes for the structure and practices of the religion.

Scoring Guidelines

The three questions on the examination are weighted equally. Each response is rated on the basis of six points. In general, the following scores apply:

Score	Criteria
6	Excellent command of factual material, both in scope and accuracy; responds fully to all parts (tasks) of the question; answer well-structured, coherent, with insightful use of specific detail; references to source materials always provided when required; coherent argument when required to support a position.
5	Good command of factual material, few if any inaccuracies; responds adequately to all parts (tasks) of the question; answer adequately structured, with a balance between specific detail and generalization; sufficient references (where required) to supporting materials; coherent argument when required to support a position.
4	Adequate, but clearly limited, command of factual material; inaccuracies that do not affect the substance of the answer; responds (at least minimally) to all parts (tasks) of the question; answer inadequately structured, with more generalization than specific detail; no references (where required) to supporting materials; weak argument when required to support a position.
3	Inadequate command of factual material; minor inaccuracies that affect the substance of the answer; does not respond to all parts (tasks) of the question; no argument (where required) to support a position; answer relies mostly on generalizations rather than specific detail.
2	Inadequate command of factual material; major factual errors; does not respond adequately to any part (task) of the question; relies entirely on unsupported generalization.
1	No response OR off topic entirely OR answer cannot be evaluated due to logical self-contradiction, lack of content, or failure to make a coherent statement.

Print Materials

Carmody, D. (1989). Women and world religions *(2nd ed.). Englewood Cliffs, NJ: Prentice Hall.*

Ellwood, R. (Ed.). (1993). Introducing religion: From inside and outside *(3rd ed.). Englewood Cliffs, NJ: Prentice Hall.*

Hinnells, J. (Ed.). (1984). The Penguin dictionary of religions. *New York: Penguin.*

Noss, D. & Noss, J. (1994). A history of the world's religions *(9th ed.). New York: MacMillan.*

Regents College. (1993). Religions of the world: A book of readings. *Acton, MA: Copley.*

Regents College. (1994). Course guide for Religions of the world.

Videocassettes
The long search. *College Video*™

To rent *The Long Search* videocassettes, please contact:
    Learningforce, Inc.
    1027 33rd St., NW
    Washington, DC 20007
    Telephone: 800-852-5277

Business Examinations

The Regents College Examinations in business subjects meet several specific needs for students. They provide upper-level business credit opportunities that may otherwise be difficult to find, and they may meet core requirements within the Regents College Business degree programs or meet Regents College concentration requirements in Management of Human Resources.

Regents College has targeted these exams to address subjects that complement the lower-level business exams currently offered by the College-Level Examination Program (CLEP).

The Management of Human Resources Cluster

The Human Resources Management, Labor Relations, and Organizational Behavior examinations are a group of three examinations in management of human resources offered by Regents College. A small number of individual topics may appear in more than one of the examinations. Treatment of any overlapping topics will differ in emphasis, detail, and depth, as defined and specified in the individual content outlines.

The three examinations fulfill the requirement in, respectively, personnel administration, labor relations, or organizational behavior for Regents College students enrolled in the Bachelor of Science degree in Management of Human Resources. The examinations also fulfill the requirement in personnel administration, labor relations, or organizational behavior for nursing students pursuing a minor in Management of Human Resources. The examinations may be used as business electives by Regents College students enrolled in the Bachelor of Science degree in general business or the Associate in Science degree in business, and as free electives for all other Regents College degrees that allow for free electives.

If you wish to be successful on one of these examinations, it is essential that you study from the recommended textbooks, rather than just rely on practical experience in the workplace. All Regents College business examinations require the integration of theoretical knowledge with real-world application.

Study Guide
Human Resource Management (486)

Credit Hours: 3 **Credit Level:** Upper
Question Type(s): Multiple-choice

The information in this study guide is valid until Summer 2001.
If you will be taking the examination after that date, be sure to check for a new edition of this guide before you complete your preparation for the exam.

General Description of the Examination

The Human Resource Management examination measures knowledge and understanding of material typically taught in a one-semester survey course. The examination corresponds to a course required of management majors and usually taken in the junior or senior year. Examination content is drawn from that commonly included in courses titled Human Resources, Human Resource Management, or Personnel Administration. The examination tests for a knowledge of facts and terminology, an understanding of personnel management concepts and principles, and the ability to apply these concepts to typical personnel management situations. A knowledge of basic management concepts is assumed.

Content Outline

Content Area	Percent of Examination
I. The Role and Context of Human Resource Management	10%
II. Fair Employment Practices	10%
III. Human Resource Planning	10%
IV. Human Resource Staffing	15%
V. Performance Management	15%
VI. Employee Development	15%
VII. Employee Compensation	15%
VIII. Labor Relations	10%
Total	**100%**

I. The Role and Context of Human Resource Management (10%)

A. Role of human resource management in organizational strategy
1. Evolution of human resource management
   a. Functions
   b. Relationship to the organization
   c. Value to the organization
2. Human resource decision making (for example: diagnostic model, strategic management process)

B. Human resource information systems (HRISs)
1. Record keeping and administration
2. Decision support
3. Security, privacy, and employee access

C. Labor force
1. Labor market data and trends
   a. Changing demographics
   b. Diversity
   c. Use of temporary employees
2. Employee values and attitudes

D. Global issues for human resource management
1. The global workforce
2. Competitive advantage
3. International assignments

E. Importance of the legal environment
1. Regulation of human resource management
2. Human resource management's role in compliance

II. Fair Employment Practices (10%)

A. History and nature of illegal discrimination in employment

B. Major federal legislation (who is covered, basic provisions)
1. Civil Rights Act of 1964, Title VII (as amended) and Civil Rights Act of 1991
2. Age Discrimination in Employment Act (ADEA) of 1967
3. Americans with Disabilities Act (ADA) of 1990 and Vocational Rehabilitation Act of 1973
4. Equal Pay Act of 1963
5. Immigration Reform and Control Act of 1986
6. Executive Order 11246
7. Pregnancy Discrimination Act of 1978 and Family and Medical Leave Act of 1993

C. Equal employment opportunity (EEO) issues
1. Disparate treatment and adverse impact
2. Roles of the Equal Employment Opportunity Commission (EEOC)
3. Job relatedness in human resource management decision making

D. Affirmative action
  1. Role of the Office of Federal Contract Compliance Programs
  2. Affirmative action planning
  3. Preferential selection and reverse discrimination

E. Sexual harassment
  1. Definition
  2. Policies and practices

III. Human Resource Planning (10%)

A. Role in organizational strategy

B. Planning process
  1. Forecasting
     a. Determining needs—internal and external demand
     b. Analyzing internal and external supply
  2. Action planning
  3. Implementation and evaluation
  4. Special issues related to downsizing

C. Job analysis
  1. Uses and purposes
  2. Methods and techniques

IV. Human Resource Staffing (15%)

A. Recruitment
  1. Internal and external sources
  2. Methods
  3. Evaluation and control
  4. Matching applicant job choice and organizational needs

B. Selection
  1. Methods
     a. Application forms and resumes
     b. Employment tests and work samples
     c. Interviews
     d. References, biographical data, and background checks
     e. Other selection methods
  2. Decision making
     a. Reliability
     b. Validity
     c. Evaluating the utility of selection practices

C. EEO and affirmative action implications
  1. Staffing implications of EEO and affirmative action (see topics in IIC and IID)
  2. Physical examinations and drug testing

V. Performance Management (15%)

A. Performance appraisal
1. Purposes and uses
2. Requirements for effective design
   a. Relevance (accuracy, validity)
   b. Reliability
   c. Acceptability and practicality
   d. Reduction of rater errors
3. Appraisal methods
4. Sources of performance information
   a. Supervisors, peers, subordinates, self, customers
   b. Team-based approaches
5. Communicating results
   a. Evaluation and feedback
   b. Goal setting
6. Training raters

B. Productivity programs
1. Total quality management (TQM)
2. Organizational design and development
3. Job design
4. Quality of Work Life (QWL)
   a. Self-managed (autonomous) work teams
   b. Employee involvement/empowerment
5. Work schedule patterns and hours of work
6. Other productivity programs

VI. Employee Development (15%)

A. Training
1. Strategy and purposes
2. Training program design
   a. Needs assessment
   b. Methods and techniques
   c. Evaluation
   d. Cost benefit analysis

B. Orientation and socialization

C. Career planning
1. Planning
   a. Mentoring
   b. Preparing for international assignments
   c. Succession planning
2. Issues
   a. Psychological contract
   b. Skills obsolescence and career plateauing
   c. Work/family conflict

D. Special issues
1. Job loss and outplacement
2. Dealing with the difficult employee (for example: discipline problems)
3. Employee assistance programs (EAPs)
4. Organizational due process—grievance and appeal procedures
5. Workforce diversity

E. Safety and health issues
1. AIDS in the workplace
2. Occupational Safety and Health Act of 1970
   a. Management's obligations
   b. Employee rights
3. Safety programs
4. Stress and wellness programs

VII. Employee Compensation (15%)

A. Direct compensation—pay level and pay structure
1. Compensation strategy
   a. External and internal equity
   b. Legal issues (Equal Pay Act of 1963 and Fair Labor Standards Act [FLSA] of 1938)
2. Determining pay level (pay surveys)
3. Determining pay structure
   a. Method of job evaluation
   b. Administration of the pay structure
4. The comparable worth debate

B. Special compensation programs
1. Individual
   a. Merit pay
   b. Skill-based pay
   c. Incentive pay
2. Group- and organization-wide incentive plans
   a. Gainsharing
   b. Profit sharing
   c. Ownership
3. Executive pay

C. Indirect compensation—employee benefits
1. Mandatory
   a. Social Security
   b. Unemployment insurance
   c. Workers' compensation
2. Discretionary
   a. Insurance programs
   b. Paid time away from work
   c. Retirement plans
   d. Employee services (for example: family care, educational programs)

3. Benefits administration and strategy
    a. Surveys and benchmarking
    b. Determining and controlling costs
    c. Communicating employee benefits
    d. Trends (for example: employee contributions vs. entitlement, flexible benefits)
    e. Consolidated Omnibus Budget Reconciliation Act (COBRA) of 1985 and Employee Retirement Income Security Act (ERISA) of 1974

VIII. Labor Relations (10%)

A. History and organization of organized labor
1. AFL-CIO
2. National and local unions

B. Labor legislation and regulation
1. National Labor Relations Act of 1935 (for example: unfair labor practices—employers, National Labor Relations Board [NLRB])
2. Taft-Hartley Act of 1947 and Landrum-Griffin Act of 1959 (for example: right to work, unfair labor practices—unions)

C. Organizing and representation
1. Why employees join unions
2. Organizing campaign

D. Collective bargaining
1. Contract negotiation
2. Contract administration
    a. Issues (for example: discipline and discharge, seniority, security arrangement)
    b. Grievance procedures
3. Impasses
    a. Mediation and arbitration
    b. Direct action (strike, lockout, boycott, picket)
4. Trends
    a. Labor-management cooperation
    b. Union avoidance
    c. Union membership changes

Sample Questions: Human Resource Management

1. During the human resource management strategy formulation, which of the following must be determined first?
   1) the internal strengths and weaknesses
   2) the external opportunities and threats
   3) the organization's mission and goals
   4) the knowledge, skills, and abilities of employees

2. A company that relies on a differentiation strategy requires which type of employees? Employees who
   1) are reluctant to take risks
   2) are focused on short-term results
   3) have a high concern for quantity
   4) have a tolerance for ambiguity

3. When writing job descriptions, an employer should focus on which component to facilitate compliance with the Americans with Disabilities Act (ADA) of 1990?
   1) Identify why a job should be done.
   2) Identify essential job tasks.
   3) Provide generic job descriptors.
   4) Provide reasonable job descriptors.

4. The human resource manager in a company needs to hire a number of people. The applicant pool consists of 70 white applicants and 30 black applicants. If 35 white applicants are selected, using the four-fifths rule, what is the minimum number of black applicants that should be selected to avoid disparate impact?
   1) 12
   2) 24
   3) 28
   4) 30

5. Which term is defined as a written document outlining specific goals and timetables to reflect relevant labor force demographics?
   1) bona fide occupational qualification (BFOQ)
   2) EEO-1 report
   3) quota system
   4) affirmative action plan

6. An organization has completed a workforce analysis and has projected employee activity changes and employee quantity changes. These activities are part of which human resource forecast?
   1) external supply
   2) business activity
   3) labor demand
   4) internal labor supply

7. Which is a statistical technique used to assess the likelihood that employees will change jobs during a specific time period in the future?
   1) Delphi technique
   2) nominal group technique
   3) labor force participation rate
   4) transitional matrix

Sample Questions: Human Resource Management

8. Which type of selection interview is the most valid and reliable?
   1) narrative
   2) nondirective
   3) structured
   4) unstructured

9. Which selection tool is used to minimize the risk of negligent hiring?
   1) reference checks
   2) honesty tests
   3) job experience questionnaires
   4) ability tests

10. Which type of analysis identifies the percentage of men, members of historically underrepresented groups, and women employed in an organization?
    1) job analysis
    2) utilization analysis
    3) availability analysis
    4) yield ratio analysis

11. Which legislation states that employers may require medical examinations only after an offer of employment has been made to the applicant?
    1) Title VII of the Civil Rights Act of 1964
    2) Age Discrimination in Employment Act (ADEA) of 1967
    3) Vocational Rehabilitation Act of 1973
    4) Americans with Disabilities Act (ADA) of 1990

12. Which is an important criterion in evaluating the success of a performance appraisal system in a company?
    1) endorsement by customers
    2) acceptance by employees
    3) use in determining pension levels
    4) use in assessing profitability

13. In which performance appraisal method is an employee's performance judged on the basis of goals established through consultation between the employee and the employee's supervisor?
    1) behaviorally anchored rating scales (BARS)
    2) critical incidents
    3) management by objectives (MBO)
    4) assessment centers

14. In a training program for supervisors, the human resource manager gives the supervisors examples of the most common types of problems that occur in employee evaluations. The human resource manager also solicits suggestions from the supervisors on how to avoid these problems. Which evaluator training technique is the human resource manager using?
    1) decision-making training
    2) observation training
    3) rater error training
    4) frame-of-reference training

Sample Questions: Human Resource Management

15. What is a likely advantage to redesigning jobs according to the job enrichment approach?
    1) greater work satisfaction
    2) lower training requirements
    3) lower physical requirements
    4) increased performance feedback

16. For three years, a trainee attends classes on auto mechanics and participates in on-the-job training with an experienced auto mechanic. What type of training is the trainee receiving?
    1) apprenticeship
    2) action learning
    3) behavior modeling
    4) cooperation training

17. In a training needs assessment, what is the purpose of an individual analysis?
    1) to determine where in the organization individuals need to be trained
    2) to determine how well a specific employee is carrying out the tasks that comprise a job
    3) to determine the current skills and knowledge of the employees to be trained
    4) to establish what the individual knowledge, skills, and abilities are for a particular job

18. Which human resource program is aimed at identifying and tracking employees that an organization believes will be successful in higher-level managerial positions?
    1) career planning
    2) management forecasting
    3) succession planning
    4) trend analysis

19. The Occupational Safety and Health Act of 1970 grants which right to employees? The right to
    1) insist that management shut down a dangerous work site
    2) request an OSHA inspection of a working condition believed to be unsafe
    3) have the employer pay damages to employees exposed to dangerous substances
    4) have an OSHA inspector remove dangerous substances from the workplace

20. A job evaluation is conducted in a company using the point method and two different jobs are found to have approximately equal points. The company can use this information to establish which type of equity?
    1) external
    2) individual
    3) internal
    4) interorganizational

Sample Questions: Human Resource Management

21. What is the purpose of a wage and salary survey?
    1) to report the rates paid for specific jobs by an organization's relevant competitors
    2) to determine the employees' level of satisfaction with an organization's pay policy
    3) to determine the internal equity of jobs in an organization
    4) to discover the individuals in an organization who are the most underpaid or the most overpaid

22. Organizations are most likely to adopt gainsharing plans for which reason?
    1) improvement in productivity
    2) union avoidance
    3) bargaining trade-off
    4) reduction in turnover and absenteeism

23. Which organization determines the appropriate bargaining unit for a union representation election?
    1) American Arbitration Association (AAA)
    2) National Labor Relations Board (NLRB)
    3) Department of Labor (DOL)
    4) Federal Mediation and Conciliation Service (FMCS)

24. Which management activity is legally allowed during a union election campaign?
    1) Management states its opinion to workers about the ramifications of unionization.
    2) Management discharges employees for union activity before the union is recognized.
    3) Management questions employees individually about their personal union preferences.
    4) Management promises to provide additional benefits if the union is rejected.

25. Which type of bargaining is referred to as win-lose or zero-sum negotiation?
    1) integrative
    2) distributive
    3) multiemployer
    4) intraorganizational

Recommended Resources

The examination development committee recommends that you obtain one of the textbooks listed below to use in preparing for the examination. Either textbook will provide the theoretical basis for your study and very good coverage of the topics on the content outline.

Fisher, C.D., Schoenfeldt, L.F., & Shaw, J.B. (1999). *Human resource management* (4th ed.). Boston: Houghton Mifflin.

Noe, R., Hollenbeck, J., Gerhart, B., & Wright, P. (1997). *Human resource management: Gaining a competitive advantage* (2nd ed.). Burr Ridge, IL: Richard D. Irwin.

Study Guide
Labor Relations (538)

Credit Hours: 3 **Credit Level:** Upper
Question Type(s): Multiple-choice

The information in this study guide is valid until Summer 2001.
If you will be taking the examination after that date, be sure to check for a new edition of this guide before you complete your preparation for the exam.

General Description of the Examination

The Labor Relations examination measures knowledge and understanding of material typically taught in a one-semester survey course usually taken in the junior or senior year of a business, industrial relations, or economics program. Examination content is drawn from that commonly included in courses with such titles as Labor Relations, Labor-Management Relations, Industrial and Labor Relations, or Collective Bargaining. The examination tests for a knowledge of facts and terminology, an understanding of basic concepts, and the ability to apply this knowledge and understanding.

Content Outline

Content Area	Percent of Examination
I. Labor Relations in the United States	15%
II. American Labor Law	20%
III. The Organizing Process	15%
IV. Collective Bargaining	25%
V. Contract Administration	15%
VI. Miscellaneous Topics	10%
Total	**100%**

I. Labor Relations in the United States (15%)

A. The industrial relations system
1. Industrial relations actors
2. Attitudes towards unions
   a. Social factors
   b. Political factors
3. Trends
   a. Rate of unionization over time
   b. Service vs. manufacturing
   c. Public vs. private
   d. Geographic differences
   e. The internationalization of American business

B. Labor history
1. Early union activity
   a. Conspiracy doctrine
   b. Use of the injunction (anti-trust)
   c. Boycott legislation
   d. Yellow-dog contracts
2. Emergence of national unions
   a. Knights of Labor
   b. American Federation of Labor (AFL)
   c. Radical unionism/Industrial Workers of the World (IWW)
3. Emergence of industrial unions
   a. Congress of Industrial Organizations (CIO)
   b. United Mine Workers, United Auto Workers, United Steel Workers, etc.
4. Consolidation of unions
   a. Merger of the AFL and the CIO
   b. Merger of international/national unions

C. Union structure and organization
1. Hierarchy
   a. Local unions
   b. National and international unions
   c. AFL-CIO
2. Union
   a. Governance
      (1) Member participation
      (2) Leadership selection
   b. Functions
      (1) Organizing
      (2) Collective bargaining
      (3) Contract administration
      (4) Political activity
   c. Finances
      (1) Dues
      (2) Strike funds
      (3) Political action

II. American Labor Law (20%)

A. Early labor law
1. Railway Labor Act
   a. Historical perspective
   b. Employee groups covered
   c. Dispute settlement mechanisms
2. Norris-LaGuardia Act
   a. Historical perspective
   b. Employee groups covered
   c. Injunction and the right to strike

B. The National Labor Relations Act as amended
1. Historical perspective
   a. Wagner Act
   b. Taft-Hartley Act
2. Status of current law
   a. Administration
      1) NLRB (judgment)
      2) Office of the General Counsel (prosecution)
   b. Rights of employees (Section 7)
   c. Resolving questions concerning representation
      1) Organizing rules
      2) Determining the appropriate bargaining unit
         (a) Community of interest
         (b) Treatment of supervisors and professionals
      3) Election rules
      4) Election certification
   d. Unfair labor practices (Section 8)
      1) Employer
         (a) Discrimination
         (b) Coercion of employees
         (c) Domination of the union
         (d) Bargaining in good faith
      2) Union
         (a) Discrimination
         (b) Coercion of employees
         (c) Coercion of employers
         (d) Bargaining in good faith
         (e) Hot cargo
   e. Union security provisions and right-to-work laws
      1) Union shop
      2) Agency shop
      3) Closed shop
      4) Right-to-work laws

- C. Public-sector labor law
    1. Federal employees
        a. Historical perspective
        b. Civil Service Reform Act of 1978
            1) Administration
            2) Impasse procedures
    2. State and local government employees
        a. Historical perspective
        b. Key differences in state laws
            1) Employees covered
            2) Impasse procedures
            3) Right to strike
- D. Other laws affecting labor relations
    1. Landrum-Griffin Act (Labor-Management Reporting and Disclosure Act [LMRDA])
        a. Historical perspective
        b. Coverage
        c. Major provisions
            1) "Bill of rights" for union members
            2) Reporting requirements (for example: financial disclosure)
            3) Election of union officers
            4) Fiduciary responsibility
    2. Discrimination laws (for example: Title VII of the Civil Rights Act of 1964, Americans with Disabilities Act of 1990 [ADA])
    3. Occupational Safety and Health Act (OSHA)
    4. Employee Retirement Income Security Act (ERISA)

III. The Organizing Process (See also content area IIB2) (15%)

- A. How organizing begins
- B. The employee decision to join a union
- C. Determining the appropriate bargaining unit
- D. Organizing campaign
    1. Union rights and strategies
    2. Employer rights and strategies
- E. The election process
    1. Authorization cards
    2. Certification/decertification

IV. Collective Bargaining (25%)

- A. Factors affecting the bargaining process
    1. Economic and market considerations
    2. Industry characteristics
    3. Employer interests
    4. Union interests

5. Employee interests
6. Political environment
   a. Public sector
   b. Private sector

B. **The bargaining process**
   1. Legal definition of collective bargaining (Section 8)
   2. Duty to bargain
      a. Good faith requirement
      b. Issues (for example: mandatory, permissive or voluntary, illegal)

C. **Bargaining structures**
   1. Centralized, decentralized
   2. Single-employer, multi-employer
   3. Pattern

D. **Management and union preparation for bargaining**
   1. Selecting a negotiating team
   2. Conducting research for bargaining
   3. Preparing demands
   4. Developing bargaining positions
   5. Developing a settlement range
   6. Costing an agreement

E. **Conducting bargaining**
   1. Analyzing power relationships (for example: bargaining power)
   2. Distributive vs. integrative bargaining (for example: win-win bargaining, collaborative)
   3. Intraorganizational bargaining and attitudinal structuring
   4. Tactics
   5. Ratifying an agreement

F. **Bargaining issues**
   1. Wages
      a. Factors affecting wage determination
      b. Theories of wage determination
      c. Alternative pay systems (for example: incentives)
   2. Benefits (for example: health insurance, pension plans)
   3. Noneconomic issues
      a. Management rights (for example: subcontracting, work transfer, discipline and discharge)
      b. Union rights (for example: union security, seniority, grievance procedure, successorship)

G. **Impasse strategies and processes**
   1. Concerted activities
      a. Strikes and lockouts
         1) Unfair labor practice strikes
         2) Economic strikes
         3) Wildcat strikes
      b. Boycotts and picketing

    c. Trends
    d. Alternatives to strikes
  2. Private sector
    a. Mediation
    b. Strike/lockout
  3. Public sector
    a. Limitations on the right to strike
    b. Mediation
    c. Fact-finding
    d. Interest arbitration

H. Impact of collective bargaining
  1. On organizational performance
    a. Wage effects
    b. Non-wage effects
  2. On society
    a. Economic effects
    b. Non-wage effects

V. Contract Administration (15%)

A. Issues in contract administration (for example: seniority, work rules, discipline and discharge, management rights, past practices)

B. Grievances
  1. Definition of grievances
  2. Reasons for grievances
    a. Contract interpretation (for example: seniority, work rules)
    b. Discipline and discharge
  3. Grievance procedure
    a. Purpose
    b. Duty of fair representation
    c. Steps

C. Rights arbitration (grievance arbitration)
  1. The legal status of arbitration
    a. *Lincoln Mills* Supreme Court decision
    b. Steelworkers' Trilogy Supreme Court decisions
    c. NLRB deferral policy (*Collyer* case)
    d. Recent decisions
  2. Source and selection of arbitrators
    a. Federal Mediation and Conciliation Service (FMCS)
    b. American Arbitration Association (AAA)
    c. Other (for example: state agencies, permanent arbitrators)
  3. Arbitration procedures
    a. Preparation
    b. Hearing
  4. Arbitrator decision-making criteria

VI. Miscellaneous Topics (10%)

A. Industrial relations systems abroad

B. Union-management cooperation
   1. Employee involvement and participation
   2. Quality of Work Life programs
   3. Labor-management committees (*Electromation* decision)
   4. Productivity bargaining
   5. Trends in union-management cooperation

C. Employee relations in nonunion organizations
   1. Application of labor law
   2. Union avoidance strategies
   3. Employee involvement (voice) systems

D. Challenges to collective bargaining
   1. Future climate of labor relations
   2. Impact of global economy

Sample Questions: Labor Relations

1. In recent years, which type of union has been particularly effective in political action at the state and local levels?
   1) industrial
   2) craft
   3) public sector
   4) private sector

2. Which union federation suffered government repression because of its antiwar stance during World War I?
   1) American Federation of Labor (AFL)
   2) Congress of Industrial Organizations (CIO)
   3) Knights of Labor (KOL)
   4) Industrial Workers of the World (IWW)

3. What is the most common governance process used by local unions?
   1) autocratic
   2) bureaucratic
   3) democratic
   4) theocratic

4. For which reason may strike benefits be withheld?
   Failure to
   1) attend 50 percent of the local meetings
   2) vote for the union
   3) support union leadership
   4) participate in strike activities

5. Which act first prohibited unfair labor practices by unions?
   1) Norris-LaGuardia Act
   2) Taft-Hartley Act
   3) Wagner Act
   4) Clayton Act

6. What legal principle is established under right-to-work laws?
   1) Union membership as a condition of continued employment is prohibited.
   2) Contract clauses requiring union membership as a precondition to employment are permitted.
   3) An employee may decline union membership, but still must pay dues and fees.
   4) An employee has a right to work, even if the union strikes.

7. Which employer action is a clear violation of Section 8(a) of the National Labor Relations Act?
   1) providing financial assistance to a union to help with union administrative costs
   2) urging assembled employees to vote against union representation
   3) speaking to individual employees about the advantages of not joining a union
   4) refusing to grant a cost-of-living pay raise demanded by a union

Sample Questions: Labor Relations

8. The National Labor Relations Board (NLRB) determines that a company refused to bargain in good faith. What is a possible remedy?
    1) An arbitrator makes a binding decision on the contract.
    2) The NLRB makes a binding decision on the contract.
    3) The NLRB issues a cease-and-desist order.
    4) At the NLRB's request, the courts determine an appropriate remedy.

9. Which act established criteria to resolve questions involving the right of federal employee unions to consultation and exclusive recognition?
    1) National Labor Relations Act
    2) Civil Service Reform Act
    3) Taft-Hartley Act
    4) Landrum-Griffin Act

10. When engaged in concerted activity, which category of employees is not protected by the National Labor Relations Act?
    1) professional employees
    2) plant guards
    3) major-league baseball players
    4) supervisory employees

11. Which factor is used by the National Labor Relations Board to determine the appropriate bargaining unit?
    1) market constraints
    2) jurisdiction of the union
    3) the number of employees
    4) community of interests

12. During an economic strike, strikers are replaced by permanent employees. A decertification election is held within 12 months of the strike. What is the voting status of the strikers as determined by the National Labor Relations Board (NLRB)?
    The NLRB
    1) allows strikers to vote.
    2) does not allow strikers to vote.
    3) decides on a case-by-case basis.
    4) petitions the courts for a ruling.

13. Which process begins with an authorization card campaign and ends with the National Labor Relations Board's certification of the representation election?
    1) contract settlement
    2) union organizing
    3) a corporate campaign
    4) good faith bargaining

14. Under which set of conditions is management most strongly motivated to continue negotiations and settle a contract without a strike?
    1) Product demand is low, replacement workers are scarce, and substitute goods are available to customers.
    2) Product demand is low, replacement workers are available, and substitute goods are available to customers.

Sample Questions: Labor Relations

      3) Product demand is high, replacement workers are scarce, and substitute goods are available to customers.
      4) Product demand is high, replacement workers are available, and substitute goods are not available to customers.

15. Which issue is most likely to be the subject of integrative bargaining?
    1) wage rates
    2) alcoholism treatment program
    3) amount of vacation
    4) overtime pay rate

16. Which approach to collective bargaining is likely to be the most adversarial?
    1) distributive bargaining
    2) integrative bargaining
    3) intraorganizational bargaining
    4) mandatory bargaining

17. Which security clause is preferred by a labor organization?
    1) agency shop
    2) union shop
    3) open shop
    4) maintenance of membership

18. Which union security agreement requires any bargaining unit employee who is not a union member to pay a service fee to the union for its representation activities?
    1) closed shop
    2) maintenance of membership
    3) open shop
    4) agency shop

19. A union strikes a company. No unfair labor practices are filed. During the strike, the company hires permanent replacements for many of the company jobs. What are the rights of the striking employees when a settlement is reached?
Striking employees
    1) are placed in their old jobs; replacement workers are put on a preferential hiring list.
    2) are put on a preferential hiring list; replacement workers keep their new jobs.
    3) have their job status determined by the U.S. Department of Labor.
    4) have their job status determined by the company based on job qualifications.

20. What is typically used to define a grievance under a collective bargaining agreement?
    1) violation of the terms of the contract
    2) violation of labor law
    3) any complaint at the workplace
    4) violation of past practice

21. What is a union's duty of fair representation when a nonunion member of the bargaining unit files a grievance?
The union is required to
    1) take the grievance to arbitration.
    2) present the grievance without taking a position.

3) effectively use the grievance procedure at the union's expense.
4) effectively use the grievance procedure at the grievant's expense.

22. Who has the burden of proof in a discharge arbitration hearing?
    1) arbitrator
    2) employee
    3) employer
    4) union

23. Which similarity exists between New United Motor Manufacturing, Inc. (NUMMI) and Saturn (General Motors) in their joint ventures with the United Automobile Workers (UAW)?
    1) A large percentage of the workforce had never worked in a unionized environment.
    2) A large percentage of the workforce was initially laid off.
    3) The allocation of resources to employee training was increased.
    4) The number of production job classifications was increased.

24. In unionized settings, which is an appropriate activity of joint labor-management committees?
    1) discussing noncontractual problems
    2) processing grievances
    3) setting wages
    4) disciplining employees

Recommended Resources

The Holley and Jennings textbook listed below provides very good coverage of the topics on the content outline. It is essential that you study from this textbook rather than just rely on practical experience in labor relations. Bear in mind that your study of the textbook should include the exhibits and "Labor Relations in Action" features, both of which are interspersed throughout the text. In addition, the text has a companion study guide. You may find it helpful to purchase the study guide for additional review of the material covered in the text. The study guide contains key terms and approximately 20 multiple-choice questions for each of the 16 chapters in the text. The fill-in-the-blank chapter summaries may not be as useful to you.

Holley, W.H., & Jennings, K.M. (1997). *The labor relations process* (6th ed.). Fort Worth, TX: Dryden.

Additional Resources

Deshpande, S.P. (1994). *Study mate to accompany The labor relations process* (5th ed.) Fort Worth, TX: Dryden.

Fossum, J.A. (1995). *Labor relations* (6th ed.). Homewood, IL: Richard D. Irwin.

Kahn, L.G. (1994). *The primer of labor relations* (25th ed.). Washington, DC: BNA.

Study Guide
Organizational Behavior (435)

Credit Hours: 3
Credit Level: Upper
Question Type(s): Multiple-choice

The information in this study guide is valid until Summer 2001.
If you will be taking the examination after that date, be sure to check for a new edition of this guide before you complete your preparation for the exam.

General Description of the Examination

The Organizational Behavior examination measures knowledge, comprehension, application, and analysis of material typically taught in a one-semester course required of business administration majors in the junior or senior year. Examination content is drawn from that commonly included in courses taught in business or psychology programs with such titles as Organizational Behavior, Organizational Psychology, Behavior in Organizations, Psychology of Business, or Psychology for Managers. A knowledge of the principles of management is assumed. The examination tests for a knowledge of facts and terminology, an understanding of basic concepts, and the ability to apply this knowledge and understanding to typical business situations.

Content Outline

Content Area	Percent of Examination
I. The Field of Organizational Behavior	5%
II. The Individual and Workforce Diversity	30%
III. Interpersonal Processes and the Group	35%
IV. The Organization	25%
V. Integrating Individuals, Groups, and Organizations	5%
Total	**100%**

NOTE: *Additional coverage of a topic in other sections of the outline is indicated in parentheses.*

I. The Field of Organizational Behavior (5%)

A. What is organizational behavior?

B. Historical evolution of organizational behavior

C. Theories and research methods

II. The Individual and Workforce Diversity (see also IIIB3a and VB) (30%)

A. Foundations of individual behavior
 1. Biographical/demographical characteristics of diversity
 2. Ability
    a. Physical
    b. Intellectual
 3. Personality
    a. Determinants
    b. Characteristics and traits

B. Values and attitudes
 1. Types of values (for example: terminal, instrumental, and cultural)
 2. Values and ethical behavior (see also IIIF6 and VD)
 3. Components of attitudes
 4. Attitudes and consistency
 5. Cognitive dissonance
 6. Attitudes and behavior
 7. Job satisfaction, commitment, and involvement

C. Perception
 1. Models of perception
    a. Physical
    b. Social
 2. Perceptual biases and stereotypes
 3. Attributions

D. Learning
 1. Classical conditioning
 2. Operant conditioning
 3. Social learning theory

E. Motivation
 1. Definition and concept
 2. Content (endogenous)
    a. Need theories (Maslow, McClelland, Alderfer)
    b. Motivation-hygiene theory (Herzberg)
 3. Process (exogenous)
    a. Expectancy (Vroom)
    b. Equity (Adams)
    c. Goal-setting (Locke)
 4. From theory to application
    a. Theory X and Theory Y (McGregor)

       b. Cognitive evaluation
       c. Management by objectives (MBO)
       d. Behavior modification
       e. Performance-based compensation
       f. Job characteristics theory (Hackman and Oldham) (see also IVA4d)
   F. **Decision making**
       1. Types of decisions
           a. Formal/informal
           b. Programmed/nonprogrammed
       2. Process
       3. Models and applications
           a. Rational/optimizing
           b. Bounded rationality/satisficing
           c. Garbage can
           d. Intuitive
           e. Leader-participation model (Vroom-Yetton) (see also IIIE4d)

III. Interpersonal Processes and the Group (35%)

A. Communication
   1. Communication process
   2. Types and methods
       a. Formal/informal
       b. Verbal/nonverbal
       c. Electronic
   3. Effective communication
       a. Enhancing communication
       b. Overcoming barriers
   4. Communication networks

B. Foundations of group behavior
   1. Definition and theories of group formation
   2. Types of groups
   3. Characteristics
       a. Composition and diversity (see also II and VB)
       b. Status
       c. Size
   4. Norms
   5. Roles
   6. Cohesiveness

C. Group dynamics/processes
   1. Stages of group formation/development
   2. Individual vs. group decision-making
   3. Effects of groups on individuals
       a. Social loafing
       b. Loss of individuality
       c. Social facilitation
       d. Group think and conformity
       e. Polarization/groupshift
       f. Synergy

4. Decision-making tools/techniques
   a. Brainstorming
   b. Delphi technique
   c. Nominal group
   d. Devil's advocacy

D. **Work teams** (see also IVA4f)
   1. Autonomous/self-managed
   2. Cross functional/task forces
   3. Quality circles

E. **Leadership**
   1. Leaders vs. managers
   2. Trait theories
   3. Behavioral theories
      a. Ohio State studies
      b. University of Michigan studies
      c. Managerial grid (Blake and Mouton)
   4. Contingency theories
      a. Contingency (Fiedler)
      b. Situational (Hersey-Blanchard)
      c. Path-goal (House)
      d. Leader-participation model (Vroom-Yetton) (see also IIF3e)
      e. Leader-member exchange
   5. Other theories
      a. Attributional
      b. Transformational vs. transactional
      c. Substitutes for leadership

F. **Power and political behavior**
   1. Definitions and concepts (authority, power, and influence)
   2. Sources of power
      a. Individual
      b. Organizational
   3. Empowerment
   4. Organizational politics—concepts and causes
   5. Political strategies
   6. Ethical behavior (see also IIB2 and VD)

G. **Conflict**
   1. Nature and causes (for example: scarce resources, workforce diversity, and interdependence)
   2. Functional and dysfunctional conflict
   3. Managing conflict
      a. Resolution tactics
      b. Negotiation

IV. The Organization (25%)

A. Organizational design/structure
1. Classical principles (for example: division of labor, span of control)
2. Structural models and types
3. Determinants of organizational design/structure
4. Job design
   a. Job rotation/cross-training
   b. Job enlargement
   c. Job enrichment
   d. Job characteristics theory (Hackman and Oldham) (see also IIE4f)
   e. Technology and job design (see also VE)
   f. Alternative approaches to job design (for example: social information processing model, alternative work schedules and workteams) (see also IIID)

B. Organizational culture
1. Characteristics and determinants
2. Maintaining organizational culture
   a. Employee selection
   b. Socialization process
   c. Employee development
3. Behavioral implications of organizational culture

C. Organizational change and organizational development
1. Definitions and concepts
2. Forces for change
3. Resistance to change
4. Models for managing change
5. Organizational development

D. Stress
1. Definition
2. Sources
3. Individual differences
4. Consequences
5. Managing stress
   a. Individual strategies
   b. Organizational strategies

V. Integrating Individuals, Groups, and Organizations (5%)

A. Global organizational behavior

B. Workforce diversity (see also II and IIIB3a)

C. Improving organizational quality

D. Social responsibility/ethics (see also IIB2 and IIIF6)

E. Technology and human behavior (see also IVA4e)

Sample Questions: Organizational Behavior

1. A study examining the effect of job satisfaction on employee attendance determined that employees with high job satisfaction came to work during snowstorms, while employees with low job satisfaction stayed home during snowstorms. In this example, which type of variable is job satisfaction?
    1) confounding
    2) dependent
    3) independent
    4) moderating

2. An organization is about to implement a nonsmoking policy at work and expects opposition from many of its employees. In the publicity campaign, what should management share with employees to promote acceptance of the policy?
    1) only the positive aspects of the policy
    2) only the negative aspects of smoking
    3) both the positive and negative aspects of the policy
    4) both the positive and negative aspects of smoking

3. Under which circumstances should an organization be more interested in the average level of employee satisfaction rather than in the correlation between satisfaction and performance?
    1) when turnover and absenteeism are high
    2) when productivity is high
    3) when employees with higher levels of performance are leaving the organization
    4) when the majority of employees display a low level of effort

4. A supervisor makes attributions on the basis of how well an employee performs. Which form of information processing is the supervisor using to make attributions?
    1) consensus
    2) consistency
    3) distinctiveness
    4) stereotyping

5. The rural scene on an office calendar brings back fond memories for an employee who grew up on a farm. This is an example of which type of learning?
    1) classical conditioning
    2) operant conditioning
    3) social learning
    4) behavior modification

BASE YOUR ANSWERS TO QUESTIONS 6–9 ON THE FOLLOWING INFORMATION:

Williamson owns a polystyrene recycling business. She employs 10 machine operators, two material handlers, and a truck driver who transports polystyrene. Williamson knows that her business success is tied to the productivity of the machine operators.

Two months ago, Williamson made several organizational changes in an attempt to motivate the machine operators. First, she expanded the scope of their jobs by assigning them additional tasks. Second, she changed their pay system from an hourly wage to a piece-rate schedule.

Sample Questions: Organizational Behavior

Third, she implemented a performance goal system that increased the production target by 20 percent.

Two months later, the productivity of the machine operators has increased by only 5 percent. All the machine operators are upset because they feel that they are not being paid for all the work they perform. Some machine operators are angry because they are actually making less money than they did before. The truck driver and the material handlers are upset because their hourly wage system did not change. They feel they are now working harder for the same pay. Finally, Williamson is upset because productivity has not increased as planned.

6. Which component of goal-setting theory best accounts for the failure of Williamson's performance goal?
    1) goal acceptance
    2) goal difficulty
    3) goal specificity
    4) self-efficacy

7. From an equity point of view, the complaints of the truck driver and the material handlers seem to be concerned with procedural justice. Which action should Williamson take to eliminate the inequity for these three workers?
    1) Eliminate their performance goal.
    2) Increase their hourly wage by 5 percent.
    3) Develop a piece-rate system for them.
    4) Assign additional duties to the machine operators.

8. If Williamson wants to continue using the new piece-rate system, what should she do to address the complaints of those machine operators who are now making less money?
    1) Demonstrate that a pay-for-performance system does not guarantee that everyone will make more money.
    2) Increase the piece-rate amount by 5 percent to compensate for the relatively small increase in performance.
    3) Adjust the performance goal from a 20 percent increase in production to a 10 percent increase.
    4) Ensure that all operators will make at least as much money as they used to.

9. What belief regarding compensation led Williamson to implement a pay-for-performance compensation system?
Compensation systems
    1) should guarantee a consistent income.
    2) should guarantee a flexible benefits package.
    3) oriented toward individuals are generally the most effective.
    4) with a group incentive plan require that employees trust each other.

10. Which communication medium has the highest information capacity?
    1) bulletin
    2) electronic mail
    3) letter
    4) memorandum

Sample Questions: Organizational Behavior

11. Which type of communication network is most effective in ensuring group member satisfaction in small formal groups?
    1) all-channel
    2) formal chain
    3) grapevine
    4) wheel

12. Which group function is a maintenance role?
    1) taking charge and setting goals
    2) communicating information to outsiders
    3) gathering information for decisions
    4) supporting group members

13. A manager is involved in a participative decision-making process with employees. Which step could the manager take to reduce the potential for groupthink?
    1) State a position clearly before the group makes a decision.
    2) Encourage group members to reach consensus as quickly as possible.
    3) Ask group members to avoid reexamining decision alternatives.
    4) Encourage group members to voice objections about the group's course of action.

14. The executive council of a youth organization votes to invest all surplus funds in an aggressive venture involving some risk. A poll of the individual council members following the vote reveals that each member had planned to vote to invest the funds in a conservative, less risky mutual fund. The voting behavior at the council meeting illustrates which phenomenon?
    1) groupshift
    2) group cohesiveness
    3) involvement
    4) social facilitation

15. Which is an important aspect of quality circles?
    1) involving the entire organization in the change process
    2) focusing on customer satisfaction and process improvement
    3) incorporating upper management participation in the change process
    4) empowering employees to solve problems in their area of responsibility

16. What do research results indicate regarding the trait approach to explaining predictors of leadership?
    1) Physical traits distinguish leaders from followers.
    2) Some traits predict leadership and are present in all leaders.
    3) Some traits predict leadership but these predictions are not consistent.
    4) Certain traits differentiate effective leaders from ineffective leaders.

Sample Questions: Organizational Behavior

17. A supervisor is in charge of a work team whose members have considerable ability and willingness to perform their jobs. According to Hersey and Blanchard's situational theory, which leader behavior is most appropriate for the supervisor?
    1) delegating
    2) participating
    3) selling
    4) telling

18. Which leadership theory defines a leader as one who enhances follower motivation so that followers experience need gratification?
    1) Graen's leader-member exchange theory
    2) Hersey and Blanchard's situational theory
    3) Fiedler contingency theory
    4) House's path-goal theory

19. Which organizational design is characterized by standardization?
    1) adhocracy
    2) bureaucracy
    3) matrix structure
    4) simple structure

20. A corporation has a program that enables managers to present certificates to employees who achieve the highest sales record in the unit. This program exemplifies which level of culture?
    1) artifacts
    2) basic assumptions
    3) socialization
    4) latent

21. Action research is comprised of which activities?
    1) systematic study of employee behavior on a case-by-case basis
    2) executive actions needed to solve organizational problems
    3) collection and analysis of data for systematic change in the organization
    4) systematic study of opportunities and threats in the organizational environment

22. In order to reduce resistance to change, who should implement a planned organizational change?
    1) quality circle group
    2) group of employees affected by the change
    3) change agent external to the organization
    4) interdepartmental team

23. Which situation is the best example of technostress?
    1) A manager fails to provide employees with feedback on reports submitted electronically.
    2) An employee learns a new tracking system quickly and causes resentment among the rest of the office staff.

Sample Questions: Organizational Behavior

   3) A manager promises employees a new computer system but fails to provide the computer due to budget constraints.
   4) An employee makes corrections to a document more easily with a new software application, but finds the system is frequently down.

24. A customer service department manager schedules weekly staff meetings as a way to exchange pertinent information with department employees. One employee is very hesitant about disagreeing with the manager during meetings. According to Hofstede, which cultural dimension could explain the employee's behavior?
    1) individualism
    2) power distance
    3) quantity orientation
    4) uncertainty avoidance

25. Which activity is <u>not</u> consistent with a reengineering approach to work processes?
    1) identifying the organization's distinctive competencies
    2) using computers to automate outdated processes
    3) assessing the organization's core processes
    4) reorganizing horizontally by process

Recommended Resources

The examination development committee recommends that you obtain <u>both</u> of the resources listed below for your use in preparing for the examination. It is essential that you study from <u>both</u> of the recommended textbooks rather than just relying on practical experience in organizational behavior. Together, these two textbooks provide very good coverage of the topics on the content outline.

Nelson, D.L., & Quick, J.C. (1996). Organizational behavior: The essentials. *St. Paul, MN: West.*

Robbins, S.P. (1998). Organizational behavior: Concepts, controversies, applications *(8th ed.). Englewood Cliffs, NJ: Prentice Hall.*

Study Guide
Production/Operations Management (582)

Credit Hours: 3
Question Type(s): Multiple-choice
Credit Level: *

The information in this study guide is valid until Summer 2001.
If you will be taking the examination after that date, be sure to check for a new edition of this guide before you complete your preparation for the exam.

General Description of the Examination

The Regents College Examination in Production/Operations Management measures knowledge and understanding of material typically taught in a one-semester course in production/operations management at the undergraduate level. The examination corresponds to an introductory course required of business majors. The content is drawn from that commonly included in courses with such titles as Production/Operations Management, Operations Management, Production Management, Management of Operations, Production and Operations, and Production and Inventory Management. A knowledge of generally accepted production/operations management principles, principles of economics, statistics, and basic computer concepts is assumed. The examination tests for a knowledge of facts and terminology, an understanding of basic concepts, and the ability to apply this knowledge and understanding to typical production/operations decision-making problems.

* In the Regents College business programs, this examination meets a core requirement and is not awarded advanced-level status. In the Regents College liberal arts program, this examination can be applied as an upper-level elective.

Use of Calculators

You will <u>not</u> be permitted to use a calculator in answering questions on this examination. Any necessary tables (for example, statistical distributions, present values) will be provided with the examination.

Content Outline

Content Area	Percent of Examination
I. Definition and Description of Production/Operations Management	5%
II. Design of the Productive System	30%
III. Planning the Use of the Productive System	40%
IV. Control of the Productive System	25%
Total	**100%**

I. Definition and Description of Production/Operations Management (5%)

A. Scope, purpose, and characteristics of systems designed to produce goods and/or deliver services

B. Manufacturing and service strategy

C. Relationship of the production/operations function to other functions

D. Organizational structure for the production/operations function

E. Production of goods and services—distinctions and commonalities

F. Management of people, materials, technology, and information

II. Design of the Productive System (30%)

A. Product and service design
   1. Product life cycle
   2. Product development process
   3. Concepts of waiting line (no mathematical computations required)

B. Production processes
   1. Purpose of production processes
   2. Conceptual understanding of different processes
   3. Appropriateness, advantages, and disadvantages of different types

C. Facility capacity planning
   1. Purpose
   2. Conceptual understanding of different approaches
   3. Appropriateness, advantages, and disadvantages of different approaches
   4. Quantitative application of breakeven analysis, decision trees, and decision tables

D. Facility location
   1. Purpose
   2. Conceptual understanding of different approaches
   3. Appropriateness, advantages, and disadvantages of different approaches
   4. Quantitative applications of transportation model and factor rating

E. Facility layout
   1. Purpose
   2. Conceptual understanding of pure and hybrid types
   3. Appropriateness, advantages, and disadvantages of different types
   4. Quantitative application of assembly line balancing and process layout design

F. Design of work systems
   1. Purpose
   2. Conceptual understanding of job design, work methods, work measurement, learning curves, and incentive plans
   3. Appropriateness, advantages, and disadvantages of different concepts
   4. Quantitative applications of work sampling, time standards, learning curves, and incentive plans

G. Computer integrated manufacturing
    1. Purpose
    2. Conceptual understanding of different technologies: computer-aided design (CAD), robotics, flexible manufacturing, computer-aided manufacturing (CAM)

III. Planning the Use of the Productive System (40%)

A. Forecasting
    1. Purpose
    2. Conceptual understanding of different models: moving averages, exponential smoothing (first order), seasonality and trend techniques, linear regression analysis, and qualitative (i.e., judgmental or subjective) techniques
    3. Appropriateness, advantages, and disadvantages of different models
    4. Quantitative applications of the above models

B. Aggregate planning
    1. Purpose
    2. Conceptual understanding of different approaches
    3. Appropriateness, advantages, and disadvantages of different approaches
    4. Quantitative applications of the trial and error method (i.e., cut-and-try, cut-and-paste)

C. Material requirements planning (MRP)
    1. Purpose
    2. Conceptual understanding of MRP and MRP II systems
    3. Appropriateness, advantages, and disadvantages of this approach
    4. Quantitative application of MRP

D. Operations scheduling
    1. Purpose
    2. Conceptual understanding of different approaches and evaluation criteria (priority rules, Johnson's two-operations rule, and assignment method)
    3. Appropriateness, advantages, and disadvantages of approaches
    4. Quantitative applications of the above approaches

E. Project management
    1. Purpose
    2. Conceptual understanding of different methods: Gantt-Milestone charts, project evaluation and review technique (PERT)/critical path method (CPM)
    3. Appropriateness, advantages, and disadvantages of different methods
    4. Quantitative applications of the above methods

IV. Control of the Productive System (25%)

A. Inventory management
    1. Purpose
    2. Conceptual understanding of different models: basic economic order quantity (EOQ) models (instantaneous and noninstantaneous replenishment), reorder point models, price break (quantity discount) model, fixed interval ordering model, ABC method, and single-period order quantity model

3. Appropriateness, advantages, and disadvantages of the methods
4. Quantitative applications of the above models excluding fixed interval

B. Purchasing and materials management
1. Purpose
2. Conceptual understanding of different practices
3. Appropriateness, advantages, and disadvantages of the methods

C. Just-in-time production
1. Purpose
2. Conceptual understanding of this approach
3. Appropriateness, advantages, and disadvantages of this approach

D. Quality management
1. Purpose
2. Conceptual understanding of different approaches
3. Appropriateness, advantages, and disadvantages of different approaches
4. Quantitative applications of acceptance sampling and control charts

Sample Questions: Production/Operations Management

1. Which is an example of a service organization that provides both goods and services?
    1) manufacturer of packaged goods
    2) bank with 24-hour automatic teller machines
    3) fire department
    4) restaurant

2. Which statement best characterizes the effect of facility location decisions?
    1) They do not have a profound effect on a firm's competitive advantage.
    2) They only affect distribution costs.
    3) They have no effect on the management of operations at lower levels of the organization.
    4) They effectively position each element of the production-distribution system with respect to the overall system.

3. What is a critical path?
    1) the shortest path through a network
    2) the longest path through a network
    3) the path with the most slack time
    4) the path with the highest probability of delay

4. Which is a true statement regarding exponential smoothing?
    1) It requires the storage of enormous amounts of data.
    2) It allows weighting patterns to be altered.
    3) It is suitable for data that include long-term upward movements.
    4) It is suitable for data that show seasonal fluctuations.

5. A product's demand for the last six periods was 100, 110, 125, 140, 120, and 130, respectively. What is the forecasted value for the seventh period using a 3-period moving average?
    1) 127.5 units
    2) 130.0 units
    3) 135.0 units
    4) 140.0 units

6. Which is an important element of total quality control?
    1) the use of control charts to monitor all aspects of the control process
    2) the inspection of every part produced
    3) the involvement of all personnel in maintaining quality
    4) the determination of an acceptable number of defectives for all lots

7. The annual demand for an item is 10,000 units. If annual holding costs are $10 per unit and order costs are $20 per order, what is the best order quantity?
    1) 100 units
    2) 150 units
    3) 200 units
    4) 300 units

Sample Questions: Production/Operations Management

Textbooks

Chase, R. (1998). *Production and operations management: Manufacturing and services* (8th ed.). Homewood, IL: Richard D. Irwin.

Evans, J., Anderson, D., Sweeney, D., & Williams, T. (1996). *Production/operations management: Quality, performance, and value* (5th ed.). St. Paul, Minnesota: West.

Stevenson, W.J. (1996). *Production/Operations Management* (5th ed.). Homewood, IL: Richard D. Irwin.

Table

A copy of the normal distribution table as shown on page 239 of this study guide will be provided for your use during the examination. The table is taken from Stevenson's *Production/Operations Management*. You may not bring this copy of the table, or any other study materials, into the examination.

Standard Abbreviations

The following glossary will be provided for your use during the examination:

AOQ	average outgoing quality
AOQL	average outgoing quality limit
AQL	acceptable quality level
BOM	bill of materials
CAD	computer-aided design
CAM	computer-aided manufacturing
CPM	critical path method
CRP	capacity requirements planning
CRAFT	computerized relative allocation of facilities technique
EOQ	economic order quantity
FCFS	first-come, first-served
FIFO	first-in, first-out
FMS	flexible manufacturing system
JIT	just-in-time
LCL	lower control limit
LIFO	last-in, first-out
LTPD	lot tolerance percent defective
MAD	mean absolute deviation
MPS	master production schedule
MRP	material requirements planning
MRP II	manufacturing resource planning
MSE	mean squared error
NC	numerically controlled
OC	operating characteristic
OPT	optimized production technology
OSHA	Occupational Safety and Health Administration
PERT	project evaluation and review technique

Sample Questions: Production/Operations Management

RSFE   running (cumulative) sum of forecast errors
S/O   slack per operation
SPT   shortest processing time
UCL   upper control limit

Production/Operations Management

TABLE A

Areas under the Normal Curve, 0 to z

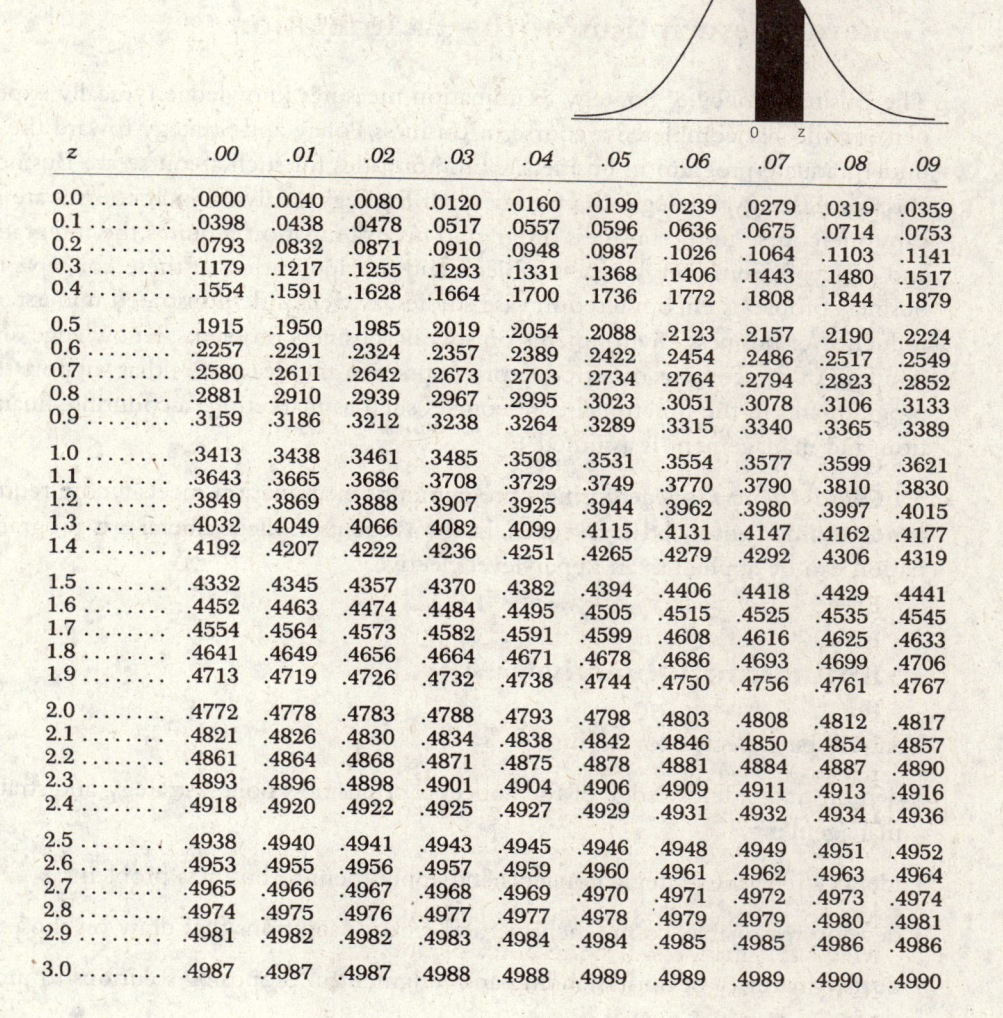

z	.00	.01	.02	.03	.04	.05	.06	.07	.08	.09
0.0	.0000	.0040	.0080	.0120	.0160	.0199	.0239	.0279	.0319	.0359
0.1	.0398	.0438	.0478	.0517	.0557	.0596	.0636	.0675	.0714	.0753
0.2	.0793	.0832	.0871	.0910	.0948	.0987	.1026	.1064	.1103	.1141
0.3	.1179	.1217	.1255	.1293	.1331	.1368	.1406	.1443	.1480	.1517
0.4	.1554	.1591	.1628	.1664	.1700	.1736	.1772	.1808	.1844	.1879
0.5	.1915	.1950	.1985	.2019	.2054	.2088	.2123	.2157	.2190	.2224
0.6	.2257	.2291	.2324	.2357	.2389	.2422	.2454	.2486	.2517	.2549
0.7	.2580	.2611	.2642	.2673	.2703	.2734	.2764	.2794	.2823	.2852
0.8	.2881	.2910	.2939	.2967	.2995	.3023	.3051	.3078	.3106	.3133
0.9	.3159	.3186	.3212	.3238	.3264	.3289	.3315	.3340	.3365	.3389
1.0	.3413	.3438	.3461	.3485	.3508	.3531	.3554	.3577	.3599	.3621
1.1	.3643	.3665	.3686	.3708	.3729	.3749	.3770	.3790	.3810	.3830
1.2	.3849	.3869	.3888	.3907	.3925	.3944	.3962	.3980	.3997	.4015
1.3	.4032	.4049	.4066	.4082	.4099	.4115	.4131	.4147	.4162	.4177
1.4	.4192	.4207	.4222	.4236	.4251	.4265	.4279	.4292	.4306	.4319
1.5	.4332	.4345	.4357	.4370	.4382	.4394	.4406	.4418	.4429	.4441
1.6	.4452	.4463	.4474	.4484	.4495	.4505	.4515	.4525	.4535	.4545
1.7	.4554	.4564	.4573	.4582	.4591	.4599	.4608	.4616	.4625	.4633
1.8	.4641	.4649	.4656	.4664	.4671	.4678	.4686	.4693	.4699	.4706
1.9	.4713	.4719	.4726	.4732	.4738	.4744	.4750	.4756	.4761	.4767
2.0	.4772	.4778	.4783	.4788	.4793	.4798	.4803	.4808	.4812	.4817
2.1	.4821	.4826	.4830	.4834	.4838	.4842	.4846	.4850	.4854	.4857
2.2	.4861	.4864	.4868	.4871	.4875	.4878	.4881	.4884	.4887	.4890
2.3	.4893	.4896	.4898	.4901	.4904	.4906	.4909	.4911	.4913	.4916
2.4	.4918	.4920	.4922	.4925	.4927	.4929	.4931	.4932	.4934	.4936
2.5	.4938	.4940	.4941	.4943	.4945	.4946	.4948	.4949	.4951	.4952
2.6	.4953	.4955	.4956	.4957	.4959	.4960	.4961	.4962	.4963	.4964
2.7	.4965	.4966	.4967	.4968	.4969	.4970	.4971	.4972	.4973	.4974
2.8	.4974	.4975	.4976	.4977	.4977	.4978	.4979	.4979	.4980	.4981
2.9	.4981	.4982	.4982	.4983	.4984	.4984	.4985	.4985	.4986	.4986
3.0	.4987	.4987	.4987	.4988	.4988	.4989	.4989	.4989	.4990	.4990

From page 812 of *Production/Operations Management* by William J. Stevenson. Copyright 1986 by Richard D. Irwin, Inc. Used by permission of the publisher.

Study Guide
Business Policy & Strategy (579)

Credit Hours: 3 **Credit Level:** ★
Question Type(s): Extended response

The information in this study guide is valid until Summer 2001.
If you will be taking the examination after that date, be sure to check for a new edition of this guide before you complete your preparation for the exam.

General Description of the Examination

The Business Policy & Strategy examination measures knowledge typically expected of a person who has completed a course in Business Policy and Strategy toward the end of an undergraduate program in business. Common titles for such a course are Business Policy, Business Strategy, Strategic Management, or Strategy Analysis. Such courses are often the capstone course in the business program. This examination requires the integration of facts and concepts from core business subjects and the application of these concepts to address business problems encountered in case studies, as well as demonstrated understanding of the influence of business environments on solving business problems. Knowledge and understanding of the content of introductory courses in the disciplines that support the business program and in the functional core courses such as marketing, accounting, finance, production, and management is assumed.

★ In the Regents College business program, this examination meets a core requirement and is not awarded advanced-level status. In the Regents College liberal arts program, this examination can be applied as an upper-level elective.

Examination Objectives

You will be expected to:

- demonstrate a knowledge of the concepts of business policy, strategy, and strategic management;
- identify relevant strategic concepts and apply them to business problems;
- develop reasonable, comprehensive, and creative solutions that draw on those concepts;
- display maturity of understanding and judgment in proposing solutions to problems.

> # Content Outline
>
> **Content Area**
>
> I. Strategy Definition
>
> II. Strategy Formulation
>
> III. Strategy Implementation
>
> IV. Strategy Evaluation

The content covered by the Business Policy & Strategy examination is divided into four categories. The first category delineates the definition of business policy, strategy, and strategic management and outlines the management tasks and responsibilities associated with these areas of business. The other three categories outline the major steps in the strategic process: formulation, implementation, and evaluation. The content categories are listed below, together with explanatory material and a listing of typical topics included in each category.

I. Strategy Definition

- **A. Strategic management tasks and responsibilities** (for example: environmental scanning, strategy formulation, implementation, evaluation, and control)
- **B. Strategic skills** (for example: problem-solving skills, analytical skills, integrating skills)
- **C. Strategic fit with internal and external environments** (for example: corporate culture, style of leadership, resource allocation)
- **D. Strategic vision** (infusing the organization with sense of purpose)
- **E. Evolution of firm** (for example: birth, growth, maturity, decline)
- **F. Emergent vs. deliberate strategy** (unplanned vs. planned)
- **G. Hierarchy of strategy (for example: corporate, business, functional)**

Policy or strategy involves both process and people in an organizational setting. Although this examination focuses specifically on policy and strategy in business organizations, strategy considerations are found in almost all organizations, public and private, small and large, profit-making and not-for-profit, etc.

Because strategy involves a process, the term strategic management is often used. Strategic management can be defined as the art and science of formulating, implementing, and evaluating cross-functional decisions that enable an organization to achieve its objectives. It focuses on integrating organizational resources, including people, physical and capital resources, and information necessary to achieve organizational success. In this definition it should be clear that strategic management integrates management, marketing, finance/accounting, production/operations, research and development, and information systems.

In addition to linking, integrating, and considering many parts of the organization, strategic management also has clear links to the internal and external environments. Issues in the internal environment, including organizational culture and structure, resource requirements and resource allocations, have an important impact on strategy. Issues in the external environment, including the social, legal, political, and competitive and industry environments must similarly be considered. In considering both the internal and external environments, the issue of strategic fit, or the congruence between the strategy and the opportunities and limitations of the environment, is important.

Strategy decisions are not restricted to decisions at the very top of an organization. A hierarchy of strategy decisions is possible, including strategies at the corporate level, at the business unit or divisional level, and even functional strategies to guide activities in areas such as marketing or financial management.

Most strategic decisions require deliberate consideration of the stakeholders, including customers, suppliers, investors, etc., in light of the firm's vision and objectives. In implementing strategies, one should be able to communicate ideas and infuse the organization with purpose. The skills required to formulate and implement strategy include problem formulation, analysis, integration, and communication.

Strategic decisions must also be examined within the evolutionary stage of the firm. For instance, entrepreneurial skills are critical for organizational "start-ups." As organizations grow and learn, different strategic capabilities are needed and different types of problems, specific to the particular business stage, come to the surface.

II. Strategy Formulation

Strategy formulation includes developing a business mission, identifying the organization's external opportunities and threats, determining internal strengths and weaknesses, establishing long-term objectives, generating alternative strategies, and choosing particular strategies to pursue.

Examples of formulation issues would include deciding what businesses or product categories to enter, what businesses to abandon and when, how to allocate resources, whether to expand operations in existing areas or diversify, whether to enter international markets, whether to merge or form a joint venture, and how to avoid a hostile takeover.

There are many useful methods for formulating and analyzing strategies, many of which focus on the importance of the competitive environment. Michael Porter's (1980) industry analysis (often called competitive analysis or the model of competitive analysis), which appears in most standard business policy and strategy texts (see reference section) is one of the most popular. Other useful models and concepts for analyzing and formulating strategy include:

- portfolio analysis
- classical economic models of perfect and imperfect competition
- models of international competition
- life-cycle analysis
- various forecasting techniques
- value chain analysis
- break-even analysis/ratio analysis
- stakeholder analysis

- SWOT/WOTS UP/ situation audit
- critical (key) success factor analysis
- benchmarking
- strategic groups
- forecasting

Several elements of strategy formulation are important and should be considered in most situations. Specific examples include:

Mission, purpose, and long-range objectives
(Business definition, market identification, analysis of the stakeholders and needs to be filled, the principal technology, the product or service offering, organizational values and philosophy, and organizational goals)

External environment
(Opportunities and threats; the social, legal, regulatory and political environments; the creditor, consumer, and labor markets; the industry structure and competitive situation; environmental complexity and dynamics; and the technological environment)

Internal situation
(Organizational strengths and weaknesses, resources, product life cycle, organizational culture, analysis of functional aspects)

Strategic choices
(Product differentiation, specialized niches, low cost, diversification, vertical integration, content divestiture, mergers and acquisitions)

III. Strategy Implementation

Strategy implementation requires the establishment of objectives and policies, leadership, the motivation of employees, and the allocation of resources so that formulated strategies can be executed. This is the action stage of strategic management. Successful implementation also includes developing a strategy-supportive culture, creating an effective organizational structure, redirecting marketing efforts, preparing budgets, developing and utilizing information systems, and motivating individuals to act.

Implementing strategy usually means managing change. One model useful for examining the implementation process is the "Seven S" framework (structure, strategy, style [culture], skills, systems, staff, superordinate goals) of Peters and Waterman (1984). Other important elements of implementation include:

- Planning processes
- Annual objectives, functional strategies, action plans, programs, and policies
- Organizational task processes and structures including divisions, strategic business units, matrix design, and types of coordination
- Leadership, communication, culture, motivation and reward systems
- Resource acquisition and allocation including capital, personnel, facilities, and information
- Control systems including budgets (sales, expenditure, capital), review cycle, and operations scheduling

IV. Strategy Evaluation

All strategies are subject to future modification because external and internal factors are constantly changing. Therefore, strategy evaluation is a critical stage in the strategic management process. Three fundamental strategy evaluation activities are the following:

Environmental monitoring and scanning
(for example: public attitudes and opinions, shifting demographics, monetary and fiscal policies, macroeconomic trends, government regulation, competitor analyses, new technologies, consumer tastes)

Monitoring and measuring performance
(for example: financial results, quality of work life, product quality, market share)

Determining appropriate response
(for example: redefining the mission or the business, redeploying assets, changing structure, or taking other corrective actions such as developing a new corporate strategy)

Several tools and techniques can be used in strategy evaluation, including:

- benchmarking
- cost benefit analysis
- value added and total value analysis
- the review of outcomes explicitly related to goals
- total quality management
- decision environment
- strategy reevaluation
- management by objectives
- cybernetics
- feedforward/feedback systems

Responding to Case Questions

Examination questions will apply to the situation described in the case and will require you to address that situation using the following problem-solving activities:

1. Defining the problem described in the case. This may include, for example:

    a. describing and defining key issues of strategic management, business strategy, or business policy that are illustrated or exemplified by the case, and identifying concepts that are relevant to a resolution of the problem described in the case.

    b. identifying important information that a manager or planner should seek in order to appreciate the implications and ramifications of the situation described in the case.

    c. identifying the roles, responsibilities, and influence of various groups and individuals, both within the organization and external to it, with respect to the situation described in the case.

2. Proposing a course of action to address the problem described in the case. This may include, for example:

   a. identifying the advantages and disadvantages of one or more potential actions described in the case.

   b. describing a viable corporate or individual strategy to address the problem, including who would originate and execute the strategy, what actions the strategy would involve, and what outcomes would be expected.

3. Justifying the recommended course of action. This may include, for example:

   a. establishing the soundness and feasibility of the recommendation, including economic, technical, and human considerations, where appropriate.

   b. describing the desired outcomes and explaining how and why the recommended action would produce these outcomes.

   c. describing any potential negative outcomes and explaining how these would be resolved.

Sample Case Study: Business Policy & Strategy

Starr Industries

Starr Industries is a multidivisional corporation with diversified product lines in the home appliance industry. Its major products include washers and dryers, stoves and ovens, refrigerators and freezers, toasters, and food mixers.

Corporate strategy defines Starr's various divisions as a portfolio of businesses, made up of four basic categories:

- Divisions that have high profitability, high market share, and long-established positions in mature markets. The major products in this category include washers and dryers, refrigerators and freezers, and stoves and ovens.

- Divisions that have good profitability, high market share, and good prospects for future growth. The major product in this category is the microwave oven.

- Divisions that have low profitability, low market share, but high long-term potential for growth and profitability. Products in this category include toasters, food mixers, trash compactors, and vacuum cleaners.

- Divisions that have low profitability, low market share, and a small potential for industry sales growth. Major products in this category include popcorn poppers and electric frying pans.

Corporate management has designated each division as an individual profit center. Each division has a high degree of autonomy in day-to-day operations. However, net earnings of all divisions are controlled at the corporate level. The net earnings are invested in opportunities that are deemed beneficial for the firm as a whole.

In the past five years, Starr has developed a variety of new products, many of which targeted markets that were entirely new for the firm. Some of the new products are popcorn poppers, vacuum cleaners, trash compactors, and electric frying pans. The product development and marketing costs for these products were financed by reallocating resources among divisions. Corporate management allocated the cash generated by divisions in mature businesses to support this penetration into new product markets. Profits were also reallocated to expand market shares of divisions having good growth opportunities.

Starr had experienced a strong demand in growing markets for the majority of its products. This year, however, a severe economic recession has caused overall earnings and sales growth to decline. All of Starr's divisions have experienced significant downturns in earnings, with losses especially severe in the new product markets.

Corporate management of Starr Industries feels a change in strategy is necessary to counteract the effects of the recession.

Sample Case Study: Business Policy & Strategy

The executive vice president of Starr Industries has been asked to identify major strategic alternatives for consideration at the next executive committee meeting. The vice president will also discuss a possible reorientation of annual planning, budgeting, and performance evaluations for the divisions and for corporate management.

(A) Starr is managing a portfolio of businesses. Use a competitive portfolio analysis matrix (i.e., BCG Growth–Share Matrix; GE Business Screen; Grand Strategy Matrix) to analyze Starr's current strategic position. (10 credits)

(B) Identify and describe three (3) key issues of business strategy formulation relevant to Starr's business portfolio. (10 credits)

(C) Based on your analysis in part (A) and part (B), identify two (2) major strategic alternatives that would be viable for Starr to pursue. (10 credits)

Recommended Resources

Any one of the following three general-purpose textbooks may be used to study the material listed in the examination content description section above. Key terms and other notations used in the examination questions were drawn from David, *Strategic Management*, 4th edition.

Primary References

David, F.R. (1999). Strategic management: Concepts and cases *(7th ed.). Upper Saddle River, NJ: Prentice Hall.*

Pearce, J.A., & Robinson, R.B. (1997). Formulation, implementation and control of competitive strategy *(6th ed.). New York: McGraw Hill.*

Thompson, A.A., Jr., & Strickland, A.J. (1999). Strategic management *(11th ed.). New York: McGraw Hill.*

Additional Resources

Andrews, K.R. (1987). The concept of corporate strategy. *Homewood, IL: Irwin.*

Galbraith, J.R., & Kazanjian, R. (1986). Strategy implementation: Structure, systems and process *(2nd ed.). St. Paul: West.*

Hill, C.W., & Jones, G.R. (1992). Strategic management: An integrated approach. *Boston: Houghton Mifflin.*

Hoffman, A.N., & O'Neill, H.M. (1993). The strategic management casebook and skill builder. *St. Paul: West.*

Hosmer, L.T. (1982, Fall). The importance of strategic leadership. *Journal of Business Strategy.*

Lorange, P. et al. (1986). Strategic control. *St. Paul: West.*

MacMillan, I.C., & Jones, P.E. (1985). Strategy formulation: Power and politics. *St. Paul: West.*

Mintzberg, H. (1975 July-August). The manager's job: Folklore and fact. *Harvard Business Review, 49–61.*

Mintzberg, H. (1987 Fall). Five P's for strategy. *California Management Review, 30 (1), 11–24.*

Sample Case Study: Business Policy & Strategy

Mintzberg, H., & Quinn, J.B. (1992). *The strategy process: Concepts and context.* Englewood Cliffs, NJ: Prentice Hall.

Oliver, A.R., & Garber, J.R. (1983 March-April). Implementing strategic planning: Ten sure-fire ways to do it wrong. *Business Horizons, 26 (2), 49–54.*

Peters, T.J. (1984 Spring). Strategy follows structure: Developing distinctive skills. *California Management Review, 26 (3), 111–125.*

Peters, T.J., & Waterman, R.H. (1984). *In search of excellence: Lessons from America's best run companies.* New York: Warner.

Porter, M.E. (1980). *Competitive strategy: Techniques for analyzing industries and competitors.* New York: Free Press.

Richards, M.D. (1986). *Setting strategic goals and objectives* (2nd ed.). St. Paul: West.

Rowe, A. et al. (1994). *Strategic management: A methological approach.* Reading, MA: Addison-Wesley.

Steiner, G.A., & Steiner, J.D. (1985). *Business, government & society* (4th ed.). New York: Random House.

Vesper, K.H. (1993). *New venture mechanics.* Englewood Cliffs, NJ: Prentice Hall.

Other Resources

For enrichment and continued study, these resources are suggested:

Journal of Business Strategy

Journal of Business Strategies

Long Range Planning

Strategic Management Journal

The Executive

Business News - Local Papers

Business Week

California Management Review

Forbes Magazine

Fortune Magazine

Harvard Business Review

INC.

New York Times

Newsweek

Time Magazine

U.S.A. Today

U.S. News and World Report

Wall Street Journal

Education Examination

Regents College currently offers just one examination in Education, the six-credit upper-level examination in Reading Instruction in the Elementary School. This examination may satisfy a certification requirement for elementary education.

Students seeking teacher certification may find many other Regents College Examinations that provide a convenient and timely means to satisfy degree requirements. New York State recognizes the Regents College Examinations as applicable for teacher certification, and under the terms of the Interstate Agreement on Qualification of Educational Personnel, New York State Teaching Certificates entitle teachers to certification in at least 26 other states. This agreement extends interstate certification to those prepared through New York State certification procedures.

Some school districts in New York State grant salary credit to faculty for the successful completion of Regents College Examinations in the same manner that salary credits are awarded for completion of college courses. Some requirements for New York City teacher in-service credits may also be met through Regents College Examinations.

Study Guide

Reading Instruction in the Elementary School (555)

Credit Hours: 6 **Credit Level:** Upper
Question Type(s): Multiple-choice

The information in this study guide is valid until Summer 2001.
If you will be taking the examination after that date, be sure to check for a new edition of this guide before you complete your preparation for the exam.

General Description of the Examination

The Regents College Examination in Reading Instruction in the Elementary School measures knowledge and understanding of material typically taught in a two-semester sequence of courses in elementary school reading instruction (or a one-semester course carrying up to six semester hours of credit). The content of the examination is drawn from that commonly included in courses with titles such as Reading in the Elementary School, Teaching of Reading in the Elementary School, Methods of Teaching Reading, and Reading and Language Arts. The examination assumes a knowledge of content that would be included in such lower-level education courses as Foundations of Education, Educational Psychology, Orientation to Teaching, and Instructional Planning. A knowledge of child development, some learning theory, and instructional planning and implementation, as well as practicum experience, would be helpful in learning the content of the examination.

The examination tests for a knowledge and understanding of the fundamental concepts and principles guiding elementary school reading instruction; for the ability to apply, synthesize, and evaluate information; and for the ability to read critically.

Applicants for elementary school teacher certification in New York State who have not completed an approved elementary teacher education program are required to show evidence of having completed six semester hours of study in the teaching of reading. One of the ways this requirement can be met is by successful completion of the Regents College Examination in Reading Instruction in the Elementary School.

Content Outline

Content Area	Percent of Examination
I. Theoretical Framework: Reading and Writing as Learning Processes	15%
II. Emergent Literacy	10%

III.	Identifying and Understanding Words	10%
IV.	Constructing Meaning: Comprehension and Response	20%
V.	Teaching and Learning Practices	20%
VI.	The Teacher as Decision Maker: Planning and Implementing a Classroom Literacy Program	15%
VII.	Assessment and Evaluation	10%
	Total	100%

I. Theoretical Framework: Reading and Writing as Learning Processes (15%)

A. **Constructivism, social constructivism, and literacy learning**

B. **Response-based theories of literacy**

C. **Schema theory**

D. **Theories of language acquisition—relations among semantic, syntactic, and morphophonemic systems**

E. **Theories of written language acquisition** (for example: print awareness, concepts about print, scribbling, invented spellings, symbolic and pictorial representations)

F. **Theories of reading**
   1. Subskill theories (bottom-up, part-to-whole, text-based, behavioral)
   2. Holistic theories (top-down, whole-to-part, reader-based, psycholinguistic)
   3. Interactive theories
   4. Transactional (transactive) theories

G. **Interrelationships among the language arts (reading, writing, listening, speaking) and literacy development**

H. **Language and cultural considerations** (for example: dialect, second language, developmental variations)

I. **The role of literature in learning to read and reading to learn**

II. Emergent Literacy (10%)

A. **Language acquisition** (for example: developmental patterns, functions of language, print awareness, scribbling, invented or temporary spellings)

B. **Concepts about print** (for example: directionality, spacing, the reading-writing connection)

C. **Sound-symbol concepts** (for example: phonemic awareness, alphabetic principle)

D. **Experiences with language** (for example: lap reading, storytelling, print-rich environment, predictable books, shared book experiences, guided reading, interactive reading)

E. **Social, affective, cognitive, and linguistic aspects of literacy**

F. **Assessment strategies and issues**

III. Identifying and Understanding Words (10%)

A. **Cuing systems**
   1. Graphic cues (including sight vocabulary and phonics generalizations and definitions)
   2. Syntactic cues (for example: contextual analysis, intratext redundancies, signal words)
   3. Semantic cues (including structural [morphemic] analysis and contextual analysis)

B. **Monitoring strategies** (for example: "Read to the end," "Reread," "Does it make sense?")

C. **Instructional activities for fostering the knowledge and use of cuing systems** (for example: word walls, word banks, word sorts, onsets and rimes, cloze procedure)

D. **Strategies for developing fluency** (for example: choral reading, repeated reading, assisted reading)

E. **Assessment strategies and issues**

IV. Constructing Meaning: Comprehension and Response (20%)

A. **Elements within the *reader/writer* that influence comprehension**
   1. Prior knowledge
   2. Motivation, attitude, interest
   3. Cognition
   4. Metacognition
   5. Reader response and stance

B. **Elements within the *text* that influence comprehension**
   1. Text structure (narrative and expository)
   2. Genre (for example: poetry, fiction, nonfiction)
   3. Language (for example: vocabulary, concepts, dialect, imagery)
   4. Text difficulty (for example: predictability, sentence/passage length, topic)
   5. Text format/features (for example: title, table of contents, graphics, illustrations)

C. **Elements of the *context* that influence comprehension**
   1. Classroom (management, atmosphere, physical environment, materials)
   2. Purpose (inquiry-based, efferent/aesthetic, teacher-centered, student-centered)
   3. Instructional frameworks (facilitating, modeling, scaffolding, guiding, questioning)

D. **Assessment strategies and issues**

V. Teaching and Learning Practices (20%)

A. **Approaches to literacy instruction**
   1. Basal reader programs
   2. Language experience approach (LEA)
   3. Phonics approaches—explicit (synthetic) and implicit (analytic)
   4. Literature-based approaches
      a. Individualized or self-selected reading
      b. Literature discussion groups (for example: literature circles, book clubs, response groups)
      c. Integrated approaches (for example: whole language, thematic units)
   5. Other approaches

B. **Instructional strategies for constructing meaning**
   1. Prereading strategies (for example: predicting, sampling)
   2. During-reading strategies (for example: monitoring, self-questioning)
   3. Postreading strategies (for example: review, retelling, summarizing)
   4. Questioning
   5. Directed reading activity (DRA) and directed reading-thinking activity (DRTA)
   6. Shared book experiences
   7. Graphic organizers (for example: semantic mapping and webbing, story maps, think sheets, story frames)
   8. Organizational tools (for example: SQ3R, QAR, K-W-L)

C. **Developing vocabulary**
   1. Vocabulary acquisition
   2. Interconnections between vocabulary and comprehension
   3. Instructional components
      a. Direct vocabulary instruction (criteria for selection, semantic features analysis, word sorts, word maps)
      b. Contextualized (wide reading, life experiences, discussions)
   4. Assessment strategies and issues

D. **Writing**
   1. Developmental patterns of writing
   2. Reading-writing connections
   3. Writing as process (for example: drafting, editing, publishing)
   4. Classroom environment (for example: centers, sharing space)
   5. Activities (for example: journals, writer's workshop, author's chair, technology)
   6. Spelling, punctuation, grammar issues
   7. Social nature of writing (audience, voice, response)
   8. Assessment strategies and issues

VI. The Teacher as Decision Maker: Planning and Implementing a Classroom Literacy Program (15%)

A. **Classroom organization and management**
   1. Grouping (for example: heterogeneous grouping, cooperative learning, peer tutoring)
   2. Learning centers
   3. Reading and writing areas (including a library)
   4. Planning (for example: scheduling, grouping, learning sequences)
   5. Time management (for example: instruction, interacting with students)

B. **Instructional planning**
   1. Teaching reading strategies (processes)
   2. Teaching content of reading selection (product)
   3. Fostering responses to reading
   4. Themes, units, lessons
   5. Meeting the needs of diverse learners

C. **Responding to all learners** (for example: culturally and linguistically diverse students, students with special needs)
   1. Intervention programs
   2. Collaboration with specialists (for example: special education teachers, bilingual/ESL teachers)

D. **Evaluating and selecting instructional resources**
   1. Literature (for example: picture books, chapter books)
   2. Textbooks
   3. Teacher-made materials
   4. Technology
   5. Other media (for example: newspapers, commercial materials, kits, games, multimedia materials)

E. **Home/school/community collaboration**

VII. Assessment and Evaluation (10%)

A. **Principles to guide assessment**

B. **Observation and assessment tools**
   1. Observation of child's behavior in a variety of settings (kidwatching, anecdotal record)
   2. Reading miscue analysis/running record
   3. Informal reading inventory (IRI)
   4. Interviews, interest inventories, and learning styles
   5. Portfolio assessment
   6. Norm-referenced, standardized achievement tests
   7. Benchmarks and rubrics

C. **Assessment issues** (for example: formal and informal assessment, authentic vs. standardized measures, national standards)

Sample Questions: Reading Instruction in the Elementary School

1. Which best defines schema?
    1) a strategy to teach comprehension
    2) a modeling process used by teachers
    3) a method of organizing a classroom assessment program
    4) a framework of acquired knowledge drawn from life experiences

2. What is the value of understanding the stages of invented spelling?
Teachers are able to
    1) assess children's emerging literacy development.
    2) participate in literacy-related classroom research.
    3) become participants in current instructional trends.
    4) focus on patterned word recognition instruction.

3. When should students who are learning English as a second language be introduced to reading and writing?
    1) as soon as they enter the classroom situation
    2) as soon as they have a survival vocabulary
    3) only after they have listening and speaking proficiency
    4) only after they have developed a 200–300 word listening/speaking vocabulary

4. According to research, how would an emergent writer be likely to first write the word "clock"?
    1) clk
    2) cluk
    3) coc
    4) cok

5. Which best defines directionality?
    1) ability to follow instructions
    2) left-right, top-bottom orientation
    3) distinguishing lowercase letters
    4) auditory sequencing

6. How are phonic generalizations useful for children learning to read?
    1) They guide students in the use of the dictionary.
    2) They provide students with tools to approximate the pronunciation of a new word.
    3) They demonstrate to students the regularity of phoneme-grapheme correspondences.
    4) Learning phonic generalizations enhances memory skills.

7. What can a teacher determine by using retellings with beginning readers?
The beginning readers'
    1) ability to decode unknown words
    2) progress in learning to construct meaning
    3) ability to break words into phonemes
    4) frequency of self-correction of miscues

Sample Questions: Reading Instruction in the Elementary School

8. A student reads the text, "The troll huddled beneath the bridge waiting for his next meal." The student sees the word *huddled* and says *jumped*. This miscue represents a reliance on which cuing system?
    1) graphic
    2) orthographic
    3) phonic
    4) syntactic

9. Which word illustrates the soft sound of *c*?
    1) centimeter
    2) chair
    3) considerate
    4) match

10. Why is semantic mapping an effective strategy to activate and develop prior knowledge? It helps students to
    1) improve word recognition.
    2) become independent readers.
    3) visualize conceptual relationships.
    4) learn the dictionary definition of words.

11. Which teaching practice would best help students to develop their vocabulary and improve their reading comprehension?
    The teacher
    1) places emphasis on the use of the dictionary.
    2) places stress on memorizing new vocabulary terms.
    3) has students write new vocabulary terms in their notebooks.
    4) works with students on using their prior knowledge.

12. Which best describes metacognitive ability?
    The ability of students to
    1) identify stated and implied main ideas
    2) think clearly in order to interpret an author's message
    3) be aware of and control their own thinking during reading and writing
    4) interpret an author's message based on their individual background and experiences

13. Which teacher behavior models a strategy for comprehension?
    The teacher
    1) posts a list of strategies.
    2) pauses after each sentence.
    3) spells new words aloud.
    4) thinks aloud after sentences are read.

14. Which best defines aesthetic reading?
    Aesthetic reading refers to reading
    1) a story to understand its narrative structure.
    2) a text for discussion in small groups.

3) to monitor one's comprehension strategies.
4) a text to experience, think, and feel during the reading.

15. Which best defines genre?
    1) classifications of stories by authors
    2) descriptions of actions by writers
    3) different types and categories of literature
    4) children's literature organized by time period

16. Which statement best describes the language experience approach?
    1) Students are given regular, fixed time periods for silently reading self-selected materials.
    2) Students retell what they have read to their teacher or to their peers either orally or in writing.
    3) Students practice reading from a script and then share their oral interpretations with selected audiences.
    4) Students' personal stories are recorded and used for reading material.

17. According to Theodore Clymer, how should phonic generalizations be taught? Teachers should
    1) teach large numbers of phonic generalizations.
    2) teach a limited number of carefully selected phonic generalizations.
    3) teach phonic generalizations at all grade levels.
    4) encourage students to point out exceptions to phonic generalizations.

18. What is a literature circle?
    1) a group of students discussing a piece of literature
    2) students performing a work of literature from beginning to end
    3) a class creating a semantic web prior to reading a piece of literature
    4) a class reading and retelling a chapter of a book

19. Which strategy would provide students with the opportunity to access background knowledge, generate questions before reading, take notes and summarize, and prepare for response to the reading?
    1) cloze procedure
    2) K-W-L
    3) retelling
    4) story grammar

20. Which is a strategy for understanding word elements?
    1) phonetic analysis
    2) semantic mapping
    3) structural analysis
    4) syntactic analysis

Sample Questions: Reading Instruction in the Elementary School

21. As students in the third grade read, the teacher wants them to engage in a writing activity to help them construct their own meanings, reflect and ask questions, and develop fluency and confidence in their writing. Which writing activity would best serve this purpose?
    1) diary
    2) free writing
    3) learning log
    4) response journal

22. Which guideline should the teacher consider when planning independent reading and writing?
    1) Wait until children demonstrate an ability to work independently before beginning the program.
    2) Wait until children gain proficiency in reading and writing before beginning the program.
    3) Require students to share their work on a regular basis.
    4) Have designated periods of time for independent reading and writing.

23. Which is the most important characteristic of guided reading?
    1) Each student silently skims the text before beginning oral reading.
    2) Students who have read the same book get together to discuss their reactions to the book.
    3) The teacher questions, prompts, or helps students to formulate questions before silent reading.
    4) The teacher masks and frames a particular word or a part of a word during repeated readings of a book.

24. Which is an advantage of using curriculum integration?
    1) It follows the linear nature of oral and written language development.
    2) It allows for breadth rather than depth in learning.
    3) It fosters the learning of related concepts.
    4) It encourages more knowledge acquisition due to extended time for activities.

25. A first-grade teacher plans to teach a lesson that would introduce children to the four seasons of the year. Which book would best serve this purpose?
    1) *In the Small, Small Pond*, by Denise Fleming
    2) *Owl Moon*, by Jane Yolen
    3) *Smokey Night*, by Eve Bunting
    4) *Tar Beach*, by Faith Ringgold

26. A teacher is designing a thematic unit that focuses on helping students understand and explore the complexities of racism and prejudice. Which book would best serve this purpose?
    1) *Dear Mr. Henshaw*, by Beverly Cleary
    2) *The Girl Who Loved Wild Horses*, by Paul Goble
    3) *The Giver*, by Lois Lowry
    4) *Maniac Magee*, by Jerry Spinelli

Sample Questions: Reading Instruction in the Elementary School

27. Which method would be best to use to gain information about a student's oral reading level?
    1) conference
    2) running record
    3) literature discussion
    4) standardized test

28. What does an informal reading inventory (IRI) contain?
    1) a number of statements that students respond to during interviews
    2) a series of text passages organized in increasing difficulty
    3) a sampling of students' work over a period of time
    4) a series of checklists to assess language qualities and traits

29. Which assessment tool compares the reading abilities of students with other students across the country?
    1) informal assessment
    2) norm-referenced assessment
    3) portfolio assessment
    4) teacher-made assessment

30. Which technique is typically associated with authentic assessment?
    1) cloze procedure
    2) informal reading inventory (IRI)
    3) portfolio
    4) standardized test

Study Materials

Note that the Book of Readings, a collection of documents assembled especially for this examination, is available only through the Regents College Bookstore.

Textbooks

Cooper, J. (1997). Literacy: Helping children construct meaning *(3rd ed.). Boston: Houghton Mifflin.*

Regents College. (1998). Reading instruction in the elementary school: A book of readings. *Acton, MA: Copley.*

Reutzel, D.R., & Cooter, R. (1996). Teaching children to read: From basals to books *(2nd ed.). Englewood Cliffs, NJ: Prentice Hall.*

Sample Questions: Reading Instruction in the Elementary School

Children's Literature

The award-winning books listed below are available in public libraries and local bookstores. They can also be purchased from the Regents College Bookstore. You will need to be familiar with all of these books. The examination will test your ability to use these books in elementary reading instruction.

Newbery Award Books
1971 *Summer of the Swans*, by Betsy Byers
1977 *Roll of Thunder, Hear My Cry*, by Mildred D. Taylor
1978 *Bridge to Terabithia*, by Katherine Paterson
1984 *Dear Mr. Henshaw*, by Beverly Cleary
1988 *Lincoln: A Photobiography*, by Russell Freedman
1990 *Number the Stars*, by Lois Lowry
1991 *Maniac Magee*, by Jerry Spinelli
1993 *Missing May*, by Cynthia Rylant
1994 *The Giver*, by Lois Lowry
1995 *Walk Two Moons*, by Sharon Creech

Caldecott Award Books and Honor Books
1971 *Frog and Toad Are Friends*, by Arnold Lobel
1978 *Castle*, by David Macaulay (Honor Book)
1979 *The Girl Who Loved Wild Horses*, by Paul Goble
Freight Train, by Donald Crew (Honor Book)
1982 *Jumanji*, by Chris Van Allsburg
1983 *When I Was Young in the Mountains*, by Cynthia Rylant, illus. Diane Goode (Honor Book)
1988 *Owl Moon*, by Jane Yolen, illus. John Schoenherr
Mufaro's Beautiful Daughters, retold by John Steptoe (Honor Book)
1989 *Song and Dance Man*, by Karen Ackerman, illus. Stephen Gammell
1990 *Lon Po Po: A Red-Riding Hood Story from China*, trans. and illus. Ed Young
1992 *Tar Beach*, by Faith Ringgold (Honor Book)
1993 *Mirette on the High Wire*, by Emily A. McCully
1994 *Grandfather's Journey*, by Allen Say
Peppe, the Lamplighter, by Elisa Bartone, illus. Ted Lewin (Honor Book)
In the Small, Small Pond, by Denise Fleming (Honor Book)
1995 *Smokey Night*, by Eve Bunting, illus. David Diaz

Other Resource
For enrichment and continued study, the following resource is suggested:

Fountas, I.C., & Pinnell, G.S. (1996). *Guided reading: Good first teaching for all children.* Portsmouth, NH: Heinemann.

Examinations for the Regents College Degree Programs in Nursing

The nursing components of the Regents College degree programs in nursing are designed to ensure that graduates possess competence in theory and performance in nursing comparable to the competence of graduates of campus-based degree programs. Most students satisfy the nursing component requirements by taking the appropriate series of written and performance examinations in the Regents College Examinations series. In addition, Regents College nursing students often use other Regents College Examinations to satisfy general education requirements in the arts and sciences or to fulfill elective requirements.

The two Regents College associate degree programs (Associate in Science [Nursing] and Associate in Applied Science [Nursing]) have identical nursing component requirements. Emphasis is placed on the integration of nursing knowledge and related sciences in the care of people who have common recurring health problems with predictable outcomes. The content of the seven written examinations (Nursing Concepts 1, 2, and 3; Differences in Nursing Care A (modified), B, and C; and Occupational Strategies) corresponds to that typically included in the curriculum of associate degree nursing programs at accredited junior and community colleges. The examinations assess essential knowledge of medical, surgical, maternity, pediatric, and psychiatric nursing as integrated with knowledge related to growth and development, nutrition and pharmacology, ethical and legal issues, and arts and sciences. The passing score for the Regents College written nursing examinations is a scaled score equivalent to a C grade. You must also successfully complete the Clinical Performance in Nursing Examination (CPNE). You will not be eligible for the performance examination until you have completed all of the written examinations.

The Regents College baccalaureate degree program (Bachelor of Science in Nursing) emphasizes the integration of nursing knowledge and related sciences in a variety of complex situations related to the nursing care of individuals, families, and communities with major health problems. The content of the six written examinations (Health Restoration: Areas I and II, Health Support: Areas A and B, Professional Strategies in Nursing, and Research in Nursing) corresponds to that typically included in the curriculum of campus-based B.S.(n) programs. You may take the examinations in any order, but the most logical sequence is that just listed. The examinations are the primary methods for documenting the required theoretical knowledge at the B.S.(n) level in the nursing component. The passing score for the Regents College written nursing examinations is a scaled score equivalent to a C grade. You must also successfully complete four performance examinations: the Clinical Performance in Nursing Examination (CPNE), Health Assessment Performance Examination (HAPE), Teaching Performance Examination (TPE), and Professional Role Performance Examination (PRPE). You will not be eligible for the performance examinations until you have completed all six of the written examinations.

Our nurse educators are available by appointment to help enrolled students with questions about the content of the written nursing examinations. Appointments are available on weekdays and one evening each month. You should prepare for your content conference by having your study guide available, listing your questions, and being prepared to take notes on your conference. At the end of the conference, try to summarize what you have learned and share it with your nurse educator to be sure that you understood her or him correctly.

NOTE: We also offer three (3) associate-level and three (3) baccalaureate-level nursing examinations that are not applicable toward the Regents College nursing degrees. These examinations—Fundamentals of Nursing, Maternal & Child Nursing (associate), Maternity Nursing, Adult Nursing, Maternal & Child Nursing (baccalaureate), and Psychiatric/Mental Health Nursing—reflect a course-specific or classical nursing curriculum design rather than the integrated design used at Regents College.

Note Concerning Wording of Nursing Diagnoses

The North American Nursing Diagnosis Association (NANDA) continually revises and updates its listing of diagnostic categories, defining characteristics, and etiological factors. For example, between 1989 and 1995 the term "potential for" was revised first to "high risk for" and then to "risk for." Questions on examinations that include nursing diagnoses are not intended to test your knowledge of current wording or phrasing. The questions are intended to test your ability to recognize nursing diagnoses that result from nursing assessments. For the purposes of the examination, all diagnoses should be considered correctly worded, even if a newer version of the diagnosis is being used by NANDA.

Suggestions for Success on the Written Nursing Examinations

1) Allow yourself enough time to study. Remember that you will receive three (3) to eight (8) semester hours of credit for successfully completing an examination. To earn these credits for a course you were taking on campus, you would be expected to spend anywhere from 135 to 360 hours attending classes and doing out-of-class assignments. You may need to spend a comparable amount of time preparing for the nursing examinations.

2) Check to make sure that the study guide you are using is the most current one available. Sometimes students acquire study guides a long time prior to using them and end up using outdated copies. Each study guide in this book has a "validity date" in the text block below the exam title. If your book is more than a year old, you will need either to obtain a new book (the best choice if you will be taking several of our exams) or call 1-888-RCEXAMS toll-free to order an updated copy of the content outline and reference list for the specific exam you will be taking.

3) Organize your study according to the content outline in the study guide rather than working your way systematically through any one textbook. You may find that textbooks vary in their presentation of material. The Content/Reference Lists found in some of the study guides will help you to locate the material for each content area.

4) Read broadly, using the textbooks and any reference articles suggested in the study guide. Reading any one textbook is likely to be insufficient preparation for the exams. For example, if you are studying cardiovascular problems, you will need to use a pediatric textbook as well as a medical-surgical text, and you may want to supplement your study using a pharmacology text, a nutrition text, and reference articles.

5) Aim for understanding rather than memorization during study. With the exception of content areas such as nursing history, most examination questions will be designed to test your understanding of the content, not your ability to recall facts. It helps to quiz yourself as you study or to take notes, rephrasing what you have read into your own words. Some students read aloud, taping as they go, so that they can listen to the material as they commute, exercise, etc.

6) Use review books, workbooks, and manuals appropriately. Most books that are designed to summarize important points do not provide the depth that is required to learn new content. They are helpful to use as a review after you have studied. State board review books that include question-and-answer areas can help you to assess your test-taking ability (i.e., how well you handle multiple-choice examinations). However, they should not be used as your primary method of study.

7) Use journal articles to help you understand content areas that are difficult for you or to help you gain a better understanding of an unfamiliar area of practice. Journal articles are often easy to read, provide lots of real-life examples, and make nursing theory "come alive." The study guides provide a list of relevant journal articles and you may find others as you browse through the journals.

8) Remember that taking an examination can be a tiring and stressful experience. Don't overextend yourself by registering for too many examination at one time. Students who try to take more than two examinations at once often fail at least one of them.

9) If you're concerned about taking your exam by computer, be sure to try out the Sylvan tutorial on the CD-ROM that came with this book. You will still benefit from taking the tutorial on the day of your test, but practicing on your own may decrease your anxiety. Remember, if you plan to take the NCLEX exam, you'll be glad you have some experience with computer-delivered tests.

10) If it has been a long time since you took a test or if you know that you have had trouble in the past with multiple-choice examinations, take some steps to prepare yourself for the experience. Although confidence that you are well prepared can help tremendously, improving your study and test-taking strategies and controlling stress can also increase the likelihood of success. The Regents College Bookstore carries several books and audiotapes that you can use.

11) Make sure you are rested and comfortably dressed the day of the examination. Anything you can do to increase your ability to concentrate during the exam will help.

12) Don't be defeated if you are unsuccessful with one of the examinations! Instead, try to determine why you had difficulty with the examination and take steps to correct the problem. Ask yourself, "Did I know the content well enough? Did I study long enough? Are there particular content areas that I omitted or didn't really understand? Did my test-taking skills or stress level interfere with my ability to document my knowledge? What can I do differently next time to help myself succeed?"

Study Guides
Associate Degree Nursing Examinations Series

This section contains study guides for the following examinations required of students in the Regents College associate degree programs Associate in Science (Nursing) and Associate in Applied Science (Nursing):

- Nursing Concepts 1
- Nursing Concepts 2
- Nursing Concepts 3
- Differences in Nursing Care: Area A (modified)
- Differences in Nursing Care: Area B
- Differences in Nursing Care: Area C
- Occupational Strategies in Nursing

Important: The examinations in Commonalities in Nursing Care: Areas A and B will be withdrawn after September 30, 2000, and the examination in Differences in Nursing Care: Area A will exist in a modified form only through September 30, 2001, after which it will be replaced with Nursing Concepts 4. Students in the Regents College AAS(n) and AS(n) degree programs who have not completed Commonalities A and B **and** Differences A by September 30, 2000, will be required to complete Nursing Concepts 1, 2, and 3 and the modified Differences A—and enroll by February 1, 2001—to use any old-series examinations toward completion of their degree. The current examination in Differences B will be replaced in October 2001 by Nursing Concepts 5, and the examinations in Differences C and Occupational Strategies will be replaced in October 2002 by Nursing Concepts 6 and 7.

Using the ADN Study Guides

These study guides have certain common features that should help you to structure your study effectively. For example, the content outlines for the Nursing Concepts and Differences exams are set up so that within each content area, theoretical framework is discussed first, followed by nursing care related to theoretical framework. Further, the nursing care section is organized using the five-part nursing process.

Recommended Textbooks: Building a Nursing Library

If you are planning to take several of the associate degree nursing examinations, you will need to begin building a library of nursing textbooks. Each of the textbooks recommended by the examination development committee provides in-depth exploration of the material in the content areas to be tested. In addition, many of them have a companion study guide. If you would like assistance in organizing your study and reviewing the material in the textbooks, the committee recommends that you consider purchasing the study guides as well. Accompanying each entry is a brief description of the materials. This may assist you in deciding which of the materials to obtain. You do not need to purchase two textbooks in the same area. You may prefer a certain author or prefer the way in which the material is presented. When two textbooks are listed, either of them will meet your study needs. If you encounter topics in the content outline that are not covered in the textbook you are using, you should supplement your study with another textbook.

Specific recommendations are made in each individual exam guide. If a text is used for more than one exam, descriptive information will appear only the first time it is listed. Your library will eventually contain at least one textbook from each of the following nursing practice areas: fundamentals, pediatrics, maternal-newborn, medical-surgical, nursing diagnosis, and pharmacology. The nursing faculty recommend that you also obtain a good medical dictionary. In addition, textbooks in anatomy and physiology, microbiology, therapeutic communication, nutrition, fluids and electrolytes, and laboratory and diagnostic procedures will supplement your study. You may want to arrange to have access to textbooks in these areas.

NOTE: You should consult a reference on laboratory and diagnostic procedures to locate material on the specific laboratory and diagnostic tests when they are listed within a content area. You should consult Carpenito (7th edition, 1997) to locate material on the nursing diagnoses for each content area.

Content/Reference List

In each study guide, you will find a section called Content/Reference List. This identifies some of the major references that cover the material in each content area. The list may help you begin to locate the topics in the content outline. The list is not intended to be comprehensive. To cover all of the material in this study guide, you may need to refer to other chapters in the reference textbooks. It is also helpful to review basic anatomy, physiology, and microbiology principles as they apply to each content area. You may not need to be familiar with every concept in each of the textbook chapters listed. You should locate the necessary information in each textbook chapter using the Content Outline. Chapter numbers and titles may differ in subsequent editions.

Additional or Other Resources

These resources are suggested to supplement your understanding of the material presented in the recommended resources. They include both textbooks and journal articles, selected because they are current and relevant to the content to be tested by a particular examination. You are encouraged to read widely. You may find other textbooks, articles, or audiovisual resources to be of interest. These additional resources are an important supplementary learning activity because they address issues that are of interest to practicing nurses and provide "real world" examples of how the theory in textbooks can be applied to actual clinical situations.

You should be able to find many of these resources at a nearby school of nursing library, college library, or hospital library. You might also find them at your state nurses' association library. In addition, your local public librarian may be able to assist you with an interlibrary loan request. It is not necessary to purchase these resources.

Journal Articles

As a professional nurse, you have a responsibility for lifelong learning. One way you can keep current is by reading journal articles. Subscribing to one or two journals, or reading them regularly in a library, is a helpful way to gain exposure to current articles in the field. Libraries may also have access to on-line search and document delivery services that supply journal articles for a fee.

Journal articles recommended for each exam are listed by the content area to which they most clearly apply. Because journal articles tend to be written in a simple, straightforward manner, you may find them useful in explaining or expanding upon difficult concepts. Many articles include case studies or post-tests to help you assess your learning. You may also find them helpful in providing an "inside view" into areas of nursing practice with which you are not familiar. You may want to review nursing journals from this year to locate more current articles.

Audiovisual Resources

Audiovisual materials such as audiocassettes, videotapes, computer-assisted instruction, and interactive videodiscs may be indicated as additional resources. They may be available for viewing at a nearby school of nursing library or a hospital library. Since such resources are costly, purchase is not recommended.

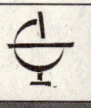

Study Guide
Nursing Concepts 1 (Associate Level)

Credit Hours: 4 **Credit Level:** Lower
Question Type(s): Multiple-choice

The information in this study guide becomes valid on October 1, 2000. See page 261 for information on the Nursing Concepts examination series.

Description of the Examination

The Nursing Concepts 1 examination measures knowledge and understanding of basic concepts of nursing care and nursing actions common to all patients throughout the life cycle, regardless of their health status. Questions concern common recurring nursing problems frequently encountered by the associate degree nurse. Questions are based on the needs of patients of various age groups and the nursing care actions properly associated with them.

The examination requires students to possess the technical vocabulary and have the knowledge of anatomy and physiology, psychosocial and physical development, and microbiology generally expected of the associate degree nurse. The examination requires students to demonstrate knowledge of the theoretical framework for each content area as well as the ability to apply this knowledge to nursing practice using the nursing process. In addition, students are required to use critical thinking skills to apply principles, concepts, and theories from the natural and social sciences, the humanities, and nursing science to the practice of nursing.

Content Outline

Content Area	Percent of Examination
I. Nursing Process	10%
II. Health, Wellness, and Illness	20%
III. Environmental Safety	15%
IV. Biological Safety	20%
V. Medication Safety	15%
VI. Psychological Safety	20%
	100%

Emphasis

    I. Theoretical Framework: Basis for Care   34%
    II. Nursing Care Related to Theoretical Framework   <u>66%</u>
                                                                                                                     100%

I. Nursing Process (10%)

The nursing process is a systematic problem-solving process directed toward the provision of nursing care for patients. It provides a framework that can be utilized in all nursing situations. This clinical decision making model consists of a series of five components: assessment, analysis, planning, implementation, and evaluation. The nursing process is carried out in conjunction with the patient and other members of the health care team.

A. Theoretical framework: basis for care
1. Characteristics of the nursing process
   a. Universally applied in a variety of settings (for example: acute care facility, extended care, home care)
   b. Cyclical and dynamic (for example: throughout the process the nurse continues to collect data, evaluate patient's response, and reassess)
   c. Patient-centered (for example: nursing diagnosis identifies the patient's health problem, nursing care plan is organized in terms of patient-centered goals)
   d. Interpersonal and collaborative (for example: the nurse involves the patient in establishing outcomes)
2. Required competencies
   a. Cognitive (for example: provide rationale for patient plan of care, use critical thinking, select appropriate nursing interventions)
   b. Technical (for example: skill performance, competency in use of technical equipment)
   c. Interpersonal (for example: use therapeutic communication techniques to relate to others, establish collaborative relationship with health care team members)
   d. Ethical and legal implications (for example: the nurse practices within the parameters of the Nursing Practice Act, functions as patient advocate, adheres to ANA code of ethics, demonstrates accountability)

B. Nursing care related to theoretical framework
1. Assessment: gather and organize data in relation to the patient's health status
   a. Establish the database (for example: patient history, physical assessment)
   b. Continually update the database (for example: add information, such as laboratory test results; identify new problems; evaluate status of identified problems; record assessment findings in a timely fashion; record significant changes)
   c. Document in a retrievable form (for example: chart data pertinent to nursing diagnosis, chart objectively without making value judgment)
2. Analysis: in conjunction with the patient and members of the health care team, synthesize data to identify the patient's actual or potential health problems (nursing diagnosis)
   a. Interpret and analyze patient data (for example: identify defining characteristics [signs and symptoms] and cluster data)

    b. Identify patient strengths (for example: knowledge, support system, compliance, individual coping strategies)
    c. Identify actual or potential health problems (for example: impaired skin integrity, altered cognitive ability)
    d. Formulate a nursing diagnosis, including diagnostic category and contributing/risk factors (for example: sensory/perceptual alterations [visual] related to the effects of aging, as evidenced by decreased visual acuity; risk for injury related to impaired cognitive functioning)
    e. Set priorities based on the patient's developmental level, based on Maslow's hierarchy of needs, based on optimal use of resources (for example: dealing with ineffective airway clearance before addressing altered growth and development)
    f. Determine clinical problems that require collaboration with other health care professionals (for example: physician, physical therapist, respiratory therapist)
3. Planning: in conjunction with the patient and members of the health care team, determine the expected outcomes (patient-centered goals) and formulate specific strategies to achieve the expected outcomes
    a. Establish expected outcomes (patient-centered goals) for care related to health promotion, health maintenance, and health restoration (for example: patient-centered, measurable behaviors, realistic, short- or long-term)
    b. Incorporate factors influencing the patient's health status (for example: sex, age, individual preferences, physical condition, cultural and spiritual/religious considerations, socioeconomic factors, environmental factors, psychological factors)
    c. Using established nursing standards and protocols, plan nursing measures to help the patient to achieve the expected outcomes (patient-centered goals) (for example: ANA Standards of Practice, state nursing practice acts)
    d. Assign patient care activities to other members of the health care team as appropriate (for example: assign nursing assistant to help patient with activities of daily living [ADLs], assign LPN/LVN to perform specific interventions)
4. Implementation: initiate and complete nursing actions/interventions designed to move the patient toward the expected outcomes (patient-centered goals) related to health promotion, health maintenance, and health restoration
    a. Use nursing measures appropriate to the patient's identified health problem
    b. Provide information and instruction related to the patient's identified health problem
    c. Use nursing measures to promote continuity of care (for example: referrals, community resources)
5. Evaluation: assess the patient's response to nursing care including progress toward the expected outcome (patient-centered goal)
    a. Record and report the patient's response to nursing actions (for example: record patient outcomes on clinical pathways, report multidisciplinary progress notes, report changes in patient's situation to primary physician)
    b. Reassess and revise the patient's plan of care as necessary (for example: determine the extent to which the goals/outcomes of care have been achieved, compare patient's response to nursing intervention with expected outcomes [patient-centered goals], revise the plan of care as needed)

c. Determine the patient's response to care provided by other members of the health care team (for example: ask questions of the nursing assistant to determine the patient's response to care)

II. Health, Wellness, and Illness (20%)

This area focuses on the concept of a health continuum from wellness to illness. It includes variations on the health continuum, stress and adaptation, health assessment, and health promotion and maintenance.

A. Theoretical framework: basis for care
   1. Models of health and illness (general overview)
      a. Health/wellness as a continuum (for example: health as a dynamic state)
      b. High-level wellness (for example: maximizing health potential of an individual, modifying high-risk behaviors, achievement of developmental tasks)
      c. Health belief model (for example: individual's perception of susceptibility to an illness, convictions and attitudes about health and illness)
      d. Agent–host–environment model (for example: dynamic relationship of agent, host, and environment)
   2. Stress and adaptation
      a. Concepts of stress (for example: stimulus based, response based, transaction based)
      b. Types of stressors (for example: physiological, psychosocial)
      c. Defining characteristics of increased stress
         1) Physiological/General Adaptation Syndrome (for example: increased heart rate, increased respiratory rate, diaphoresis, patient reports nervous stomach)
         2) Psychological (for example: inability to focus, decreased perception, patient reports feelings of anxiety)
         3) Cognitive (for example: decreased attention span, diminished problem-solving skills, reliance on daydreaming or fantasy)
      d. Adaptive mechanisms to deal with stress (for example: denial, displacement, rationalization, regression, projection)
   3. Principles related to health assessment
      a. Data
         1) Sources (for example: patient, chart, health team member, family members)
         2) Objective and subjective (for example: objective data such as laboratory results, vital signs, skin conditions; subjective data such as complaints of pain, anxiety)
      b. Health history
         1) Purpose (for example: collect subjective data to contribute to a database used to determine the health status of the patient)
         2) Present illness (for example: onset of symptoms, duration; exploration of the patient's perception of the current health problem)
         3) Past health history (for example: allergies, immunizations, prior hospitalizations)
         4) Family history: obtain data regarding immediate relatives' health status and presence of genetic illnesses (for example: mother and

grandmother have breast cancer, father died at age 46 with myocardial infarction)
        5) Environmental history (for example: worked in a subway for 25 years, exposure to pollutants and carcinogens)
        6) Review of systems (for example: respiratory, gastrointestinal, cardiac)
    c. Physical examination
        1) Assessment techniques (for example: inspection, auscultation, palpation, percussion)
        2) General survey (for example: vital signs, height and weight, general appearance, affect, skin)
        3) Head-to-toe examination of body systems
            a) Techniques (for example: neurological assessment, respiratory assessment, peripheral/vascular assessment, abdominal assessment)
            b) Normal findings (for example: bowel sounds present in all four quadrants; pupils equal, round, and reactive to light and accommodation [PERRLA])
    d. Functional assessment
        1) Activities of daily living (ADLs) (for example: bathing, dressing, toileting, eating, walking)
        2) Instrumental ADLs (for example: ability to use telephone, shopping, food preparation, housekeeping, laundry; mode of transportation; responsibility for own medications; ability to handle finances)
    e. Mental status assessment (for example: consciousness, orientation, appropriateness of responses)
4. Principles related to health promotion and maintenance
    a. Primary prevention (for example: immunizations, nutritional practices, exercise)
    b. Secondary prevention (for example: health screening, smoking cessation)
    c. Tertiary prevention (for example: referring a patient with hypertension to a stress-reduction group, teaching a patient how to prevent complications of a disease)
5. Factors influencing the patient's health, wellness, and illness
    a. Sex (for example: disease risk, differences in morbidity and mortality)
    b. Age/Developmental level: infant through older adult (for example: increased incidence of chronic illness in older adults, infants' and children's susceptibility to infection)
    c. Individual preferences and patterns (for example: lifestyle, past experiences, education level, substance abuse, stages of behavior change, personal perception of health)
    d. Physical condition (for example: presence of chronic disease, disproportional height-to-weight relationship, fatigue)
    e. Cultural and spiritual/religious considerations (for example: values, perception of health, female-male roles, language, communication patterns)
    f. Socioeconomic factors (for example: availability of health resources, health insurance, family structure, support system, employment status, peer pressure)
    g. Environmental factors (for example: temperature, housing conditions, occupational hazards, light and sound levels)

h. Psychological factors (for example: level of motivation; orientation to time, place, and person; hopelessness; helplessness)
6. Theoretical basis for interventions related to health, wellness, and illness
   a. Interventions to promote effective coping and decrease stress (for example: counseling, relaxation techniques)
   b. Alternative/complementary treatments (for example: therapeutic touch, massage, acupressure, foot reflexology, meditation)
   c. Research findings (for example: *Healthy People 2000: National Health Promotion and Disease Prevention Objectives,* Framingham heart study, Harvard Women's Health Study, Agency for Health Care Policy Research [AHCPR])
   d. Ethical and legal implications (for example: access to health care, allocation of resources, clinical practice guidelines)

B. **Nursing care related to theoretical framework**
   1. Assessment: gather and organize data in relation to the patient's health status
      a. Obtain the patient's history related to patient's health status (for example: nutrition, elimination, activity, exercise)
      b. Assess factors influencing the patient's health, wellness, and illness (see IIA5)
      c. Obtain objective patient assessment data (for example: vital signs, intake and output, weight)
      d. Review laboratory and other diagnostic data (for example: complete blood count [CBC], blood glucose, radiology reports)
   2. Analysis: in conjunction with the patient and members of the health care team, synthesize data to identify the patient's actual or potential health problem (nursing diagnosis)
      a. Identify nursing diagnoses (for example: altered health maintenance related to stress; fatigue related to excessive role demands; health-seeking behavior [breast self-examination] related to desire for high-level wellness; ineffective individual coping related to knowledge deficit regarding stress management)
      b. Set priorities (for example: based on the patient's developmental level, based on Maslow's hierarchy of needs, based on optimal use of resources)
   3. Planning: in conjunction with the patient and members of the health care team, determine the expected outcomes (patient-centered goals) and formulate specific strategies to achieve the expected outcomes
      a. Establish expected outcomes (patient-centered goals) related to health promotion, health maintenance, and health restoration (for example: patient will identify stressors and effective health maintenance behaviors, patient will report an increase in energy level, patient will correctly and regularly perform breast self-examination [BSE], patient will use adaptive coping methods to reduce anxiety)
      b. Incorporate factors influencing the patient's health, wellness, and illness in planning the patient's care (for example: consider patient's developmental level, occupation, exercise routine, smoking habits, level of anxiety, support systems, stage of wellness-illness) (see IIA5)
      c. Using established nursing standards and protocols, plan nursing measures to help the patient achieve the expected outcomes (patient-centered goals)

(for example: encourage the patient to keep a log of incidents that arouse anxiety and frustration, assist the patient to set priorities and manage time effectively, demonstrate the procedure for breast self-examination [BSE] to the patient, provide information about relaxation techniques and problem-solving skills)
- d. Assign patient care activities to other members of the health care team (for example: assign the LPN/LVN to obtain the patient's height and weight)
4. Implementation: initiate and complete nursing actions/interventions designed to move the patient toward the expected outcomes related to health promotion, health maintenance, and health restoration
    - a. Use nursing measures to structure an environment conducive to health (for example: eliminate annoying noises and odors, control temperature)
    - b. Use nursing measures to maintain psychological comfort (for example: involve the patient in decision making, respect the patient's needs, encourage the patient to express feelings)
    - c. Provide information and instruction regarding health maintenance and promotion (for example: advise the patient regarding the use of health care services and Internet resources, provide information about self-examination for early detection of disease, provide a list of community screening agencies)
    - d. Use nursing measures to promote continuity of care (for example: teaching, referrals, support groups, community resources)
5. Evaluation: assess the patient's response to nursing care including progress toward the expected outcome (patient-centered goals)
    - a. Record and report the patient's response to nursing actions (for example: patient correctly performs relaxation techniques, patient demonstrates ability to use the health care system, patient reports less anxiety)
    - b. Reassess and revise the patient's plan of care as necessary (for example: identify need for further instruction, provide written instructions to reinforce the nurse's explanation and demonstration, revise the teaching plan)
    - c. Determine the patient's response to care provided by other members of the health care team (for example: patient's response to stress-reduction group conducted by nurse practitioner, patient's response to exercise program designed by the occupational therapist)

III. Environmental Safety (15%)

This area focuses on the principles of a safe physical environment. The environment may be the health care agency, the home, or the community. A safe environment is one in which physical hazards are reduced and accidents are prevented.

A. Theoretical framework: basis for care
1. Principles (for example: scientific principles related to the effects of physical, mechanical, thermal, chemical, and radiation hazards on the body)
2. Common safety hazards in the environment
    - a. Physical/mechanical (for example: wet floors, scatter rugs, toys with small parts, poor lighting, unsecured firearms, defective equipment, improper use of restraints)
    - b. Thermal (for example: fire, electrical hazards, exposure to heat and cold)

c. Chemical (for example: medications, poisons, carbon monoxide, radon, lead paint)
d. Radiation (for example: sunburn, heat lamps, X rays)
e. Ecological (for example: air quality, noise pollution, water pollution)
3. Factors influencing the patient's environmental safety
   a. Age/developmental level: infants through older adult (for example: dangers specific to each age range, pillow in crib of newborn, toddler access to open staircase, contact sports in school-age children, danger of falls in older adults)
   b. Individual preferences and patterns (for example: lifestyle choices, occupation, previous accidents, use of medications)
   c. Physical condition (for example: level of awareness, sensory perception, mobility status, ability to communicate)
   d. Cultural and spiritual/religious considerations (for example: burning candles, burning incense, clothing choices)
   e. Socioeconomic factors (for example: crowded housing, unemployment, income level)
   f. Environmental factors (for example: proximity to nuclear plants, proximity to airports, climate, occupational hazards, ergonomics, neighborhood crime rate)
   g. Psychological factors (for example: emotional state, cognition)
4. Theoretical basis for interventions related to environmental safety
   a. Environmental modifications (for example: lighting, furniture arrangement, use of adaptive equipment, storage of toxic substances)
   b. Safety instruction (for example: use of sports equipment such as helmets for biking; need for appropriate footwear; use of infant car seat; rescue, alarm, confine, extinguish [RACE] fire procedures)
   c. Medications/Topical agents (for example: sunscreens, lotions, treatments for poisoning)
   d. Safety devices (for example: siderails for bath tub, toilet grab bars, motion sensors, smoke detectors, carbon monoxide detectors, restraints)
   e. Research findings (for example: statistics regarding incidence of accidents in relation to age and developmental level, specific risk of suffocation for infants)
   f. Ethical and legal implications (for example: nurses' duty to ensure a safe environment, Omnibus Budget Reconciliation Act [OBRA] of 1987, regulations on the use of restraints)

B. Nursing care related to theoretical framework
1. Assessment: gather and organize data in relation to the patient's health status
   a. Obtain the patient's history related to environmental safety (for example: previous falls and reports of dizziness)
   b. Assess factors influencing the patient's environmental safety (see IIIA3)
   c. Obtain objective patient assessment data (for example: confused mental state, sensory deficit, weakened physical state)
   d. Review laboratory and other diagnostic data (for example: complete blood count [CBC], blood alcohol, lead levels, cognitive assessment)
2. Analysis: in conjunction with the patient and members of the health care team, synthesize data to identify the patient's actual or potential health problem (nursing diagnosis)

a. Identify nursing diagnoses (for example: high risk for injury related to altered mobility, risk for poisoning related to unsecured cleaning products, impaired home maintenance related to disturbed cognitive function, risk for trauma related to lack of appropriate car seats)
   b. Set priorities (for example: based on patient's developmental level, based on Maslow's hierarchy of needs, based on optimal use of resources)
3. Planning: in conjunction with the patient and members of the health care team, formulate specific strategies to achieve the expected outcomes (patient-centered goals)
   a. Establish expected outcomes (patient-centered goals) for care related to health promotion, health maintenance, and health restoration (for example: patient will verbalize factors that minimize potential for injury, patient will not sustain injury, patient will use safety measures when ambulating, patient will modify home environment to eliminate hazards, patient will use car seats when transporting children)
   b. Incorporate factors influencing the patient's environmental safety in planning the patient's care (for example: establish a safe environment for a toddler, provide grab bars in the shower for an older adult, plan safety program for new mothers, reinforce motor vehicle safety for middle-aged adult) (see IIIA3)
   c. Using established nursing standards and protocols, plan nursing measures to help the patient achieve the expected outcomes (for example: inform the patient of Poison Control Center telephone number, teach the patient about risk related to exposure to the sun, identify potential hazards in the patient's environment, encourage the patient to use a hearing aid)
   d. Assign patient care activities to other members of the health care team (for example: assign nursing assistant to help the patient use a walker)
4. Implementation: initiate and complete nursing actions/interventions designed to move the patient toward the expected outcomes (patient-centered goals) related to health promotion, health maintenance, and health restoration
   a. Use nursing measures to structure an environment conducive to safety (for example: maintain availability of call bell, place furniture in an uncluttered arrangement, remove safety hazards)
   b. Use nursing measures appropriate to particular safety needs (for example: shield from radiation, adjust temperature maximum of home hot water heater, answer call bell promptly)
   c. Use adaptive and safety devices properly (for example: wheelchairs, walkers, canes, siderails, motion sensors, fire extinguishers)
   d. Provide information and instruction regarding environmental safety (for example: orient patient to the unit, explain use of mobilizing devices, provide instruction regarding proper use of restraints)
   e. Use nursing measures to promote continuity of care (for example: teaching, referrals, support groups, community resources)
5. Evaluation: assess the patient's response to nursing care including progress toward expected outcomes (patient-centered goals)
   a. Record and report the patient's response to nursing actions (for example: correct use of safety devices, incidence and prevalence of falls)

b. Reassess and revise the patient's plan of care as necessary (for example: discontinue the use of restraints, revise the teaching plan for a young adult with sunburn)

c. Determine the patient's response to care provided by other members of the health care team (for example: patient's ability to use walker or ambulate with nursing assistant)

IV. Biological Safety (20%)

This area focuses on the principles of a safe biological environment. A safe biological environment is one in which the transmission of pathogens is reduced through physical, mechanical, and chemical means and the normal defense mechanisms of the body are supported. The inflammatory process is considered a common body response to invasion by pathogens. The skin and mucous membranes are considered to be the body's first line of defense against biological hazards. Therefore, maintenance of the integument includes the care of hair, nails, and teeth.

A. Theoretical framework: basis for care
1. Principles related to biological safety
   a. Medical asepsis (for example: standard precautions, transmission-based precautions, cleaning and disinfecting)
   b. Surgical asepsis (for example: establishment and maintenance of a sterile field, methods of sterilization)
2. Chain of infection
   a. Agent (for example: bacteria, viruses, fungi, protozoa, rickettsiae)
   b. Reservoir (for example: contaminated food, water, insects, gastrointestinal tract, blood)
   c. Portal of exit from the reservoir (for example: mouth, nose, anus)
   d. Mode of transmission (for example: droplet, contact, vector)
   e. Portal of entry (for example: broken skin or mucous membrane, mouth, urinary meatus)
   f. Host (for example: person with impaired immune response)
3. Principles related to the body's ability to defend itself from infection
   a. Normal body defenses (for example: resident flora, transient flora, intact skin and mucous membranes)
   b. Nonspecific defenses
      1) Localized defining characteristics of inflammation (for example: edema, pain, erythema, increased local temperature)
      2) Systemic defining characteristics of inflammation (for example: altered vital signs, fatigue, anorexia, increased white blood cells)
      3) Stages of an inflammatory process (for example: vascular and cellular responses, exudate, reparative)
   c. Specific defenses (active and passive immunity, antibody-mediated defenses, cell-mediated defenses)
4. Stages in the infectious process (for example: incubation period, prodromal period, illness period, convalescent period)
5. Process of wound healing
   a. Phases of wound healing (for example: inflammatory phase, proliferative phase, maturation phase)
   b. Types of healing (for example: primary intention, secondary intention)

c. Types of skin lesions (for example: papules, pustules, pressure ulcers)
   d. Types of exudate (for example: serous, purulent, suppurative, sanguineous)
   e. Complications of wound healing (for example: hemorrhage, infection, dehiscence, fistulas)
6. Factors influencing the patient's biological safety
   a. Age/developmental level: infant through older adult (for example: decreased skin turgor in older adults, friable skin in infants, lack of active immunity in infants)
   b. Individual factors (for example: lifestyle, health habits, risk-taking behavior in adolescents, education level, smoking, hygiene practices)
   c. Physical condition (for example: nutritional status, presence of other illness, level of consciousness, immunosuppressive therapy, presence of invasive lines)
   d. Cultural and spiritual/religious considerations (for example: beliefs about health and illness, influence of cultural or spiritual/religious practices in infection control or hygiene practices)
   e. Socioeconomic factors (for example: income level, access to health care)
   f. Environmental factors (for example: overcrowding, unsanitary conditions, pollution, reservoirs of infection, bathing facilities)
   g. Psychological factors (for example: stress, privacy)
7. Theoretical basis for interventions to promote biological safety
   a. Medications (for example: antibiotics, anti-inflammatory agents, antipyretics)
   b. Maintenance of medical asepsis (for example: by use of standard precautions and transmission-based precautions, by cleaning and disinfecting)
   c. Maintenance of surgical asepsis (for example: establish and maintain sterile field)
   d. Wound care (for example: types of dressing, drainage systems)
   e. Application of heat and cold (for example: compresses, aquathermia pads, ice packs)
   f. Dietary modifications (for example: increase fluid intake; increase intake of protein, vitamins, and minerals)
   g. Ethical and legal implications (for example: privacy, laws regarding reporting of communicable diseases)

B. Nursing care related to theoretical framework
   1. Assessment: gather and organize data in relation to the patient's health status
      a. Obtain patient's history related to biological safety (for example: susceptibility to infection, response to infection process, condition of the patient's integument, exposure to pathogens, hygiene practices)
      b. Assess factors influencing the patient's biological safety (see IVA6)
      c. Obtain objective patient assessment data (for example: vital signs, stage of pressure ulcer, nature of drainage, condition of wounds, shape of pressure ulcer)
      d. Review laboratory and other diagnostic data (for example: white blood count [WBC] and differential, sedimentation rates, serum albumin, wound culture and sensitivity report, erythrocyte sedimentation rate)
   2. Analysis: in conjunction with the patient and members of the health care

team, synthesize data to identify the patient's actual or potential health problem (nursing diagnosis)
   a. Identify nursing diagnoses (for example: risk for infection related to presence of surgical incisions, risk for infection related to altered immune response, altered tissue perfusion related to inflammation, risk for infection related to altered nutritional status, body image disturbance related to pressure ulcer, impaired skin integrity related to circulatory impairment)
   b. Set priorities (for example: based on the patient's developmental level, based on Maslow's hierarchy of needs, based on optimal use of resources)
3. Planning: in conjunction with the patient and members of the health care team, determine the expected outcomes (patient-centered goals) and formulate specific strategies to achieve the expected outcomes
   a. Establish expected outcomes (patient-centered goals) for care related to health promotion, health maintenance, and health restoration (for example: patient's temperature, pulse, and white blood cells will remain within normal limits; patient will show no signs of infection; patient will show signs of increased tissue perfusion; patient will verbalize a positive body image; patient will maintain intact skin and mucous membranes)
   b. Incorporate factors influencing the patient's biological safety in planning the patient's care (for example: consider the patient's hygiene practices, explore the patient's previous strategies for coping with stress, adapt teaching materials to the patient's developmental level) (see IVA6)
   c. Using established nursing standards and protocols, plan nursing measures to help the patient achieve the expected outcomes (for example: monitor the patient's vital signs q4h, teach the patient appropriate aseptic practices, apply a warm soak to the site of inflammation, wash hands before and after direct patient contact, use standard precautions)
   d. Assign patient care activities to other members of the health care team as appropriate (for example: assign nursing assistant to bathe an older adult client, assign LPN/LVN to change dressing on pressure ulcer)
4. Implementation: initiate and complete nursing plans designed to move the patient toward expected outcomes (patient-centered goals) related to health promotion, health maintenance, and health restoration
   a. Maintain aseptic technique (for example: maintain sterile technique during dressing changes, use handwashing technique prior to dressing changes, use standard precautions in caring for patients)
   b. Use nursing measures to aid in the resolution of the inflammatory process (for example: elevate extremities, apply heat or cold, encourage fluid intake, cleanse wound)
   c. Use nursing measures to prevent the spread of infection (for example: isolation technique, standard protections, use of disposable equipment)
   d. Administer medications (for example: antibiotics, antipyretics, use of emollients, consider modifications related to the patient's age)
   e. Use nursing measures to provide hygienic care to patients (for example: administer bed bath, apply clean linen, wash hair, trim and clean nails, provide tissues, encourage patient participation, reduce the amount of soap used when bathing older adults)

     f. Use nursing measures to maintain skin integrity (for example: provide high-protein foods, reposition patient, use mechanical devices)
     g. Provide information and instruction regarding biological safety (for example: instruct patient regarding antibiotic therapy, instruct patient regarding mode of transmission of pathogens, emphasize preventive measures, discuss the spread of infection, refer to neighborhood health care centers)
     h. Use nursing measures to promote continuity of care (for example: teaching, referral, support groups, community resources)
  5. Evaluation: assess the patient's response to nursing care including progress toward the expected outcome (patient-centered goals)
     a. Record and report the patient's response to nursing actions (for example: changes in vital signs, condition of wound, level of discomfort, characteristics of drainage, condition of skin, stage of pressure ulcer)
     b. Reassess and revise the patient's plan of care as necessary (for example: increase fluid intake based on the patient's preferences, revise the teaching plan)
     c. Determine patient's response to care provided by other members of the health care team (for example: ask questions of nursing assistant to determine patient's response to bath, reassess the effectiveness of wound care provided by LPN/LVN)

V. Medication Safety (15%)

This area focuses on safety in the administration of medications to patients across the life span.

A. Theoretical framework: basis of care
  1. Principles related to the safe administration of medication
     a. Legal aspects of drug administration (for example: controlled substance laws, possession and handling of narcotics, federal or state legislation related to drug administration, institutional policies regarding drug administration, licensed personnel who can legally dispense medications)
     b. Components of complete medication order (for example: name of patient, date of order, name of drug, dosage, route of administration, time and frequency, physician signature)
     c. Drug names (for example: generic, brand name, trade name)
     d. Pharmacokinetics (for example: absorption, distribution, metabolism, excretion)
     e. Therapeutic drug action (for example: palliative, curative, supportive, prophylactic, diagnostic)
     f. Undesired effects (for example: side effects and adverse effects, antagonistic effects, toxic effects, idiosyncratic effects, allergic response, drug tolerance)
     g. Routes of administration (for example: oral, intramuscular, subcutaneous, intravenous, topical, installations or irrigations, nebulizers, intradermal, transdermal, metered dose inhalers)
     h. Types of preparations (for example: syrups, pills, lotions, powders, suppositories, transdermal patches)
     i. Classifications of medication (for example: antibiotics, anti-inflammatory agents, antiemetics, antipyretics)

      j. Systems of measurement (for example: metric system, apothecary system, household system, determination of drug dosage for age-specific populations)
      k. Calculation of dosage (for example: IV rates, titration, ratio and proportion, dimensional analysis)
  2. Theoretical basis for interventions to promote safe medication administration
      a. Five "rights" of medication administration: right patient, right medication, right dose, right route, right time
      b. Monitor drug action, drug interaction or allergy (for example: monitor peak-trough level, observe for skin rash following antibiotic administration, assess appearance of eye and surrounding tissue prior to administering ophthalmic instillation)
  3. Factors influencing the patient's response to medications
      a. Sex (for example: hormonal effect, distribution of body fat)
      b. Age/developmental level: infant through older adult (for example: decreased metabolism in older adults, rapid absorption in infants, intramuscular site selection in infants)
      c. Individual preferences and patterns (for example: preference of liquids over tablets, idiosyncratic responses to medications, control of medication schedule, use of over-the-counter medications)
      d. Physical condition (for example: difficulty in swallowing capsules, nutritional status, allergies, obesity, immobility)
      e. Cultural and spiritual/religious considerations (for example: prohibitions on use of certain types of drugs, imposed fasting for religious purposes, use of herbal preparations)
      f. Socioeconomic factors (for example: insurance coverage for medications, choice of generic vs. trade name medication)
      g. Environmental factors (for example: adequate space and conditions for drug storage)
      h. Psychological factors (for example: drug dependence, usage, cognitive/memory impairments, stress, placebo effect, motivation to comply, knowledge level, patient's expectations)

B. Nursing care related to theoretical framework
  1. Assessment: gather and organize data in relation to the patient's health status
      a. Obtain the patient's history relative to medications (for example: allergies, understanding of prescribed medications)
      b. Assess factors influencing medication administration (see VA3)
      c. Obtain objective patient assessment data (for example: evidence of therapeutic or adverse effects, vital signs)
      d. Review laboratory and other diagnostic data (for example, electrolytes, blood levels of drug, serum albumin, blood urea nitrogen [BUN], creatinine)
      e. Review sources of medication information (for example: American Hospital Formulary Service (AHFS) Drug Information, *Physicians' Desk Reference,* pharmacology texts, drug reference books for nurses)
  2. Analysis: in conjunction with the patient and members of the health care team, synthesize data to identify the patient's actual or potential health problem (nursing diagnosis)

a. Identify nursing diagnoses (for example: health seeking behaviors: new medications related to lack of knowledge; noncompliance related to inability to obtain medication)
   b. Set priorities (for example: based on the patient's developmental level, based on Maslow's hierarchy of needs, based on optimal use of resources)
3. Planning: in conjunction with the patient and members of the health care team, determine expected outcomes (patient-centered goals) and formulate specific strategies to achieve the expected outcomes
   a. Establish expected outcomes (patient-centered goals) for care related to health promotion, health maintenance and health restoration (for example: patient will verbalize understanding of desired effect of medication, patient will follow an established schedule for drug administration)
   b. Incorporate factors influencing medication safety in planning patient care (for example: establish a safe environment for storage of medications, provide adequate instruction for drug administration, select proper equipment for medication administration, integrate of patient's preferences) (see VA3)
   c. Using established nursing standards and protocols, plan nursing measures to help the patient achieve the expected outcomes (patient-centered goals) (for example: time of administration)
   d. Assign patient care activities to other members of the health care team as appropriate (for example: instruct LPN/LVN to report evidence of adverse drug effects, instruct nursing assistant to delay assisting the patient to ambulate until therapeutic effects of analgesic are evident)
4. Implementation: initiate and complete nursing care plans designed to move the patient toward the expected outcomes (patient-centered goals) related to health promotion, health maintenance, and health restoration
   a. Use nursing measures to enhance drug absorption (for example: selection of correct site for administration, selection of methods to enhance absorption, nursing responsibility in medication administration, administering medications with or without food as indicated)
   b. Use nursing measures to create an environment conducive to safe medication administration (for example: use five "rights" in drug administration, use medication administration devices properly, correctly calculate medication dosage)
   c. Use nursing measures to promote continuity of care (for example: teaching, referrals, support groups, community resources)
   d. Record drug administered on the medication administration record
5. Evaluation: assess the patient's response to nursing care including progress toward the expected outcome (patient-centered goals)
   a. Record and report the patient's response to the administration of medications, to patient teaching (for example: evidence of therapeutic effect of medication, evidence of rash following the administration of a new antibiotics)
   b. Reassess and revise the patient's plan of care as necessary (for example: effectiveness of medication administration, adherence to medication schedule, appropriateness of the route of administration; alter the time of the day of drug administration to accomodate work responsibilites)

c. Determine patient's response to care provided by other members of the health care team (for example: ask the night nurse if sedative was effective, ask the LPN/LVN if the inclusion of a stool softener in care plan has minimized constipation)

VI. Psychological Safety (20%)

This area focuses on a safe psychological environment. A safe psychological environment is one in which the patient understands what to expect from others. The nurse and patient exchange information and feelings by communication, therapeutic relationship, and the teaching/learning process.

A. Theoretical framework: basis for care
1. Communication
    a. Definition and goals (for example: use of interpersonal communication skills, observations of behavior; means to convey information)
    b. Types of communication
        1) Verbal (for example: written and spoken)
        2) Nonverbal (for example: body language, silence, touch)
    c. Characteristics of effective communication (for example: simplicity, clarity, brevity, appropriate vocabulary, timing, relevance, pace and intonation)
    d. Elements of the communication process
        1) Stimulus or referent (motivation for communication)
        2) Sender or encoder (initiator of message)
        3) Message (information that is sent)
        4) Channel (auditory, visual, or tactile vehicle of communication)
        5) Receiver or decoder (person to whom message is sent)
        6) Feedback (evidence that the message has been received)
2. Therapeutic communication
    a. Definition and goals (for example: planned nurse-patient interaction directed toward achievement of patient-centered outcomes/goals)
    b. Techniques that facilitate communication (for example: attending, paraphrasing, reflecting, using open-ended statements, listening, employing touch)
    c. Blocks or barriers to effective communication (for example: use of judgmental responses, offering false reassurance, stereotyped responses, probing, advising)
3. The therapeutic nurse-patient (helping) relationship: dynamic process in which the nurse and patient collaborate to promote the patient's health and solve problems
    a. Characteristics of the relationship (for example: empathy, trust and security, respect, autonomy, acceptance, genuineness)
    b. Phases of the relationship and associated activities
        1) Introductory (for example: structuring and formulating the contract, testing, building trust)
        2) Working (for example: exploring and understanding thoughts and feelings, confrontation, self-disclosure)
        3) Termination (closure) (for example: evaluation of goal achievement, separation)
    c. Roles in the relationship

        1) Roles of the nurse (for example: leader, person, caregiver, patient advocate, counselor, teacher)
        3) Roles of the patient (for example: person, health care consumer, active participant)
  4. Principles of teaching and learning
    a. Definitions
      1) Teaching (for example: interactive process, assisting the person to gain new knowledge and skill)
      2) Learning: the acquisition of new knowledge or skills
        a) Cognitive: intellectual behaviors (for example: acquiring knowledge, understanding ways to control stress, understanding effects of medications)
        b) Psychomotor: skill performance (for example: performs a finger stick to test blood glucose, administers an injection)
        c) Affective: attitudes and feelings (for example: demonstrates change in attitude regarding chronic illness, motivation to comply with prescribed regimen)
    b. Basic learning principles
      1) Motivation: the impulse or desire that causes a person to take an action (for example: patient identifies need to learn factors involved in weight control)
      2) Readiness and ability to learn: the physical, emotional, and cognitive capacity (for example: sensory acuity, presence of language skills, developmental status, physical discomfort, anxiety levels)
      3) Learning environment: setting that assists the patient to focus on the learning task (for example: setting is private, setting has adequate lighting; setting is appropriate to the size of the group)
    c. Basic teaching principles
      1) Set priorities: based on nursing diagnoses and patient's learning needs (for example: patient may need to learn about how to administer medication before learning about the actions and side effects)
      2) Timing (for example: length of session, interval between learning and use, individual preference for morning or afternoon session)
      3) Organize teaching (for example: simple to complex, logical sequence, significant content)
      4) Involve patient in planning and implementing teaching plan (for example: mutual setting of goals)
      5) Build on existing knowledge (for example: individualize teaching plan to avoid redundancy)
      6) Select teaching method (for example: role playing, demonstration, discussion, discovery)
  5. Factors influencing communication and ability to learn
    a. Sex (for example: differences in communication style and responsiveness to touch)
    b. Age/developmental level: infant through older adult (for example: use of pictures or toys with the young child)
    c. Individual preferences and patterns (for example: territoriality, personal experiences and needs, perceptions, learning styles, educational level)

d. Physical condition (for example: pain, level of consciousness, sensory deficits)
   e. Socioeconomic factors (for example: access to technology)
   f. Cultural and spiritual/religious considerations (for example: language barriers, personal space, values related to touching and expression of feelings, roles and relationships)
   g. Environmental factors (for example: noise level, physical space, furniture arrangement, distance from health care resource)
   h. Psychological factors (for example: stress, anxiety level, self-awareness, readiness to learn, presence of support system)
 6. Theoretical basis for intervention related to psychological safety
   a. Physiological considerations (for example: degree of illness, sensory deficits, stress, comfort, other factors that interfere with communication and learning)
   b. Environmental and legal implications (for example: A Patient's Bill of Rights, maintaining confidentiality)

B. Nursing care related to theoretical framework
 1. Assessment: gather and organize data in relation to the patient's health status
   a. Obtain the patient's history related to communication patterns and learning needs (for example: patient reports feeling intimidated communicating with authority figures, patient reports learning best by demonstration)
   b. Assess factors influencing the patient's communication (see VIA5)
   c. Obtain patient assessment data (for example: language development, communication skills, learning style)
 2. Analysis: in conjunction with the patient and members of the health care team, synthesize data to identify the patient's actual or potential health problem (nursing diagnosis)
   a. Identify nursing diagnoses (for example: impaired verbal communication related to language barrier, impaired social interaction related to cultural differences, altered health maintenance related to insufficient knowledge of the effects of alcohol and drug interactions)
   b. Set priorities (for example: based on the patient's developmental level, based on Maslow's hierarchy of needs, based on optimal use of resources)
 3. Planning: in conjunction with the patient and members of the health care team, determine the expected outcomes (patient-centered goals) and formulate specific strategies to achieve the expected outcomes
   a. Establish expected outcomes (patient-centered goals) for care related to health promotion, health maintenance, and health restoration (for example: patient will express basic needs clearly, patient will participate in one group activity daily, patient will verbalize two symptoms of drug interaction)
   b. Incorporate factors influencing the patient's communication in planning the patient's care (for example: locate a private room for a patient interview, plan to use closed-ended questions with a patient who has impaired verbal communication, ensure that the patient's hearing aid is functioning, use active listening with an adolescent patient, establish age-appropriate communication techniques to facilitate understanding in children and in older adults) (see VIA5)

c. Using established nursing standards and protocols, plan nursing measures to help the patient achieve the expected outcomes (patient-centered goals) (for example: teach the patient simple phrases to communicate needs, establish age-appropriate methods of communication for expressing needs, encourage the patient to express feelings)
   d. Assign patient care activities to other members of the health care team as appropriate (for example: instruct the LPN/LVN to observe patient while changing dressing, instruct nursing assistant to maintain limit setting with patient who is abusive)
4. Implementation: initiate and complete nursing actions/interventions/plans designed to move the patient toward the expected outcomes (patient-centered goals) related to health promotion, health maintenance, and health restoration
   a. Use effective communication techniques (for example: listen attentively to a patient who is anxious, inject humor into a stressful situation)
   b. Use therapeutic communication techniques to establish an effective nurse-patient relationship (for example: restatement, reflection, open-ended statements, paraphrasing, focusing)
   c. Promote a therapeutic nurse-patient relationship (for example: introduce self to patient, establish trust, be empathetic, maintain consistency)
   d. Structure the environment to promote communication and learning (for example: arrange furniture, provide privacy, reduce noise level)
   e. Provide alternate methods of communication (for example: language boards, play, interpreters, magic slates, computers for patients with special needs)
   f. Use a variety of teaching strategies (for example: audio-visual materials, role playing, demonstration)
   g. Use nursing measures to promote continuity of care (for example: referrals, support groups, community resources)
5. Evaluation: assess the patient's response to nursing care including progress toward expected outcomes (patient-centered goals)
   a. Record and report the patient's response to nursing actions (for example: increased verbalization, ability to recognize symptoms, refuses to use a hearing aid, participates in group activities, expresses feelings about illness)
   b. Determine patient's response to care provided by other members of the health care team (for example: ask for patient feedback on the teaching session provided by the nurse)
   c. Reassess and revise the patient's plan of care as necessary (for example: encourage the patient and family to teach staff some words and phrases in the patient's native language, revise the teaching plan)

Sample Questions: Nursing Concepts 1

1. Which nursing action would the nurse perform in the evaluation phase of the nursing process?
    1) Demonstrate correct procedures for wound care.
    2) Explain the preparation required prior to a diagnostic test.
    3) Ask the patient to describe pain intensity following administration of an analgesic.
    4) Discuss expected outcomes with the patient.

2. Identification of expected outcomes is made during which step of the nursing process?
    1) analysis
    2) assessment
    3) evaluation
    4) planning

3. The nursing assistant reports that a patient has a temperature of 38.0°C (100.5° F). Which action should the nurse carry out first?
    1) Assess the patient for symptoms related to temperature.
    2) Administer medication to lower the patient's temperature.
    3) Write a nursing diagnosis based on the temperature.
    4) Set a goal to lower that patient's temperature.

4. To which nursing diagnosis should the nurse give priority?
    1) ineffective breathing pattern related to upper abdominal pain
    2) fatigue related to immobility
    3) altered nutrition: less than body requirements related to nausea
    4) fluid volume deficit related to fever

5. Which is the best example of an accurately written patient goal (expected outcome)?
    1) The patient will receive a bed bath this morning.
    2) Risk for injury related to weakness.
    3) Patient will look at the incision before discharge.
    4) Get the patient out of bed three times a day.

6. The nurse is about to perform a physical examination on a patient with dyspnea. Which position would be most comfortable for this patient to assume?
    1) right sidelying
    2) supine, with the head on a pillow
    3) sitting up, leaning forward on the arms
    4) bed elevated to 35°, with the knees flexed

7. The nurse is assessing a patient on bed rest. Why should the nurse inquire about the patient's usual stress-management techniques?
    1) to provide the patient with a stress-free environment
    2) to understand how the patient is likely to deal with stress in the hospital
    3) to help the patient develop new coping mechanisms
    4) to determine whether the patient should have a private room

Sample Questions: Nursing Concepts 1

8. The nurse is teaching a patient in preparation for discharge. Which patient response indicates the need for further instruction?
   1) "I can usually figure things out easily."
   2) "I understand right now. Who can I call if I have questions later?"
   3) "You have explained this very thoroughly. I have no questions."
   4) "Now I feel comfortable doing this myself."

9. The use of restraints for the prevention of falls should be limited to which situation?
   1) Other measures have not been effective.
   2) Frequent observation of the patient is not possible.
   3) The patient is chronically confused.
   4) The family has requested application of the restraints.

10. Which measure should be included in the plan of care to promote a patient's wound healing?
    1) Provide a diet high in protein and vitamin C.
    2) Encourage a daily exercise routine.
    3) Use clean technique during dressing changes.
    4) Maintain the patient on bed rest.

11. Which sign is usually seen in a dark-skinned patient with dehydration?
    1) slowed pulse rate
    2) slowed respirations
    3) red buccal mucosa
    4) decreased skin elasticity

12. Which action should parents take when a child ingests a poisonous substance?
    1) Administer syrup of ipecac.
    2) Dilute the poison with milk.
    3) Induce vomiting with a spoon.
    4) Call the poison control center.

13. Which patient behavior should alert the nurse to the need for instruction related to safety hazards in the home?
    The patient
    1) covers a tile floor with scatter rugs.
    2) has a step stool in the kitchen.
    3) Stores cleaning solutions in the basement.
    4) Uses a gas stove to cook meals.

14. Which patient is most susceptible to infection?
    1) a 16 year old who has been in an accident
    2) a 32 year old who is recovering from surgery
    3) a 50 year old who has hypertension
    4) a 76 year old who has respiratory problems

Sample Questions: Nursing Concepts 1

15. A patient has just been admitted with a laceration of the knee. Which finding should the nurse expect to observe during the next 24 hours?
    1) swelling at the site
    2) purulent drainage from the site
    3) severe pain at the site
    4) full movement of the knee joint

16. Which sign indicates adequate wound healing?
    1) Amount of drainage increases.
    2) Wound edges are not approximated.
    3) WBC remains elevated.
    4) Edema at the wound edges subsides.

17. Which sensory deficit in an older adult should alert the nurse to the need for instruction regarding self-administration of medications?
    1) hearing
    2) taste
    3) touch
    4) vision

18. What is the purpose of using the Z-track method for specific intramuscular medications?
    1) to minimize tissue irritation
    2) to reduce pain at the injection site
    3) to facilitate the action of the drug
    4) to control the rate of absorption

19. The physician orders digoxin (Lanoxin) 0.25 mg PO. The pharmacy has 0.125 mg tablets available. How many tablets should the nurse administer?
    1) 1.0
    2) 2.0
    3) 1.5
    4) 0.5

20. A patient has just been told that a diagnostic test confirms cancer. Which response by the nurse would be most therapeutic?
    1) "I'm sure everything will turn out all right."
    2) "Perhaps you would like to talk about it."
    3) "You have the right to a second opinion."
    4) "This form of cancer is easily treated."

Sample Questions: Nursing Concepts 1

21. During a patient assessment, the nurse observes that the patient tries to articulate words but the patient's speech is not intelligible. The patient responds appropriately to questions by nodding to indicate "yes" or "no." The patient appears to be very frustrated. Which nursing diagnosis is most appropriate for this patient?
    1) altered health maintenance
    2) altered thought processes
    3) impaired verbal communication
    4) ineffective individual coping

22. A 63-year-old patient is being prepared for abdominal surgery. The patient tells the nurse, "I know my family will miss me when I'm gone." Which response by the nurse would be most therapeutic?
    1) "Your surgery has a favorable prognosis."
    2) "I'm going to give you something to help you to relax."
    3) "Your family will miss you when you're gone?"
    4) "You'll only be gone from your family for an hour."

23. During an assessment, the nurse wishes to explore a patient's feelings about his family. Which approach would be most therapeutic?
    1) "Do you have a favorite family member?"
    2) "Please tell me about your family."
    3) "What is your worst memory about growing up in your family?"
    4) "Do you have a family?"

Recommended Resources

Textbooks
Fundamentals
Kozier, B., Erb, G., Berman, A., & Burke, K. (2000). Fundamentals of nursing: Concepts, process, and practice (6th ed.). Upper Saddle River, NJ: Prentice Hall.

This textbook addresses a wide variety of contemporary fundamental nursing principles under major section headings, such as health beliefs and practices, nursing process, lifespan development, assessing health, integral components of client care and promoting both physiologic and psychological health. Special features of this textbook include a focus on critical thinking, sample nursing care plans, clinical guidelines, and critical pathways.

Study Guide:
Van Leuven, K. (2000). Study guide for Fundamentals of Nursing: Concepts, process, and practice. (6th ed.). Upper Saddle River, NJ: Prentice Hall.

Nursing Process (Diagnosis)
Wilkinson, J.M. (1996). Nursing Process: A Critical Thinking Approach. (2nd ed.). Menlo Park, CA: Addison-Wesley.

This textbook integrates each step of the nursing process, considering concepts such as professional standards of care, nursing frameworks, ethical issues and wellness. Each chapter contains objectives as well as key terms. Critical thinking exercises assist in the development of this skill. The application activities contain an answer key with a rationale provided for the wrong answers.

Pediatrics
Wong, D. (1997). Whaley and Wong's Essentials of pediatric nursing (5th ed.). St. Louis: Mosby. **Please note: The 6th edition of this text will be available in October, 2000.**

This textbook presents learning objectives for each chapter and contains many color photographs. Guidelines and emergency treatments are presented in boxes within each chapter. Hundreds of tables, boxes, and diagrams are used to highlight key concepts. Key points are summarized at the end of each chapter.

Study Guide:
Murphy, A. (1997). Study guide to accompany Whaley and Wong's Essentials of pediatric nursing (5th ed.). St. Louis: Mosby.

Pharmacology
Eisenhauer, L.A., Nichols, L.W., Spencer, R.T., & Bergan, F.W. (1999) Clinical pharmacology and nursing management (5th ed.). Philadelphia, PA: Lippincott.

This textbook incorporates essential pharmacological concepts, critical thinking activities, and clinical judgment skills so that drug therapy is as safe and appropriate as possible for patients and for nurses. Each chapter is organized beginning with an outline and review of physiology and pathophysiology as it relates to the drug class discussed. Key pharmacological content and nursing management links present the connection between drug theory and each step of the nursing process.

Student Workbook:
Eisenhauer et al. (1999). Clinical pharmacology and nursing management. (5th ed) Philadelphia: PA, Lippincott.

Additional Resources

Textbooks
The textbook below may provide further clarification in the areas of clinical nursing skill procedures and cultural assessment of patients and families. You should also use a math-for-medications textbook for reference.

Van Leuven, K. (2000). Clinical Companion for Fundamentals of nursing: Concepts, process, and practice (6th ed.). Upper Saddle River, NJ: Prentice Hall.

Journal Articles

I. Nursing Process

Nicoteri, J.A. (1998). Critical thinking skills. American Journal of Nursing, 98 *(10)* 62–65.

Oermann, M.H. (1999). Patient outcomes: A measure of nursing's value. American Journal of Nursing, 99 *(9)*, 40–47.

II. Health, Wellness, and Illness

Assessing the older patient (1998). RN, March, 46.

Falter, E.J. (1999). The health care continuum: How to make the business of nursing work for you. American Journal of Nursing, 99 *(1)*, 63–64.

Sample Questions: Nursing Concepts 1

Keegan, L. (1999). Alternative and complementary therapies, an overview for nursing students. NSNA/Imprint, February/March, *36–38.*

Leighton, C. (1998). A change of heart. American Journal of Nursing, 98 *(10), 33–37.*

Understanding the mind/body link (1998). RN, January, *28.*

III. Environmental Safety

Nine steps to effective restraint use (1998). RN, December, *23.*

Rogers, P.D. (1999). Restraint free care, is it possible? American Journal of Nursing, 99 *(10), 26–33.*

IV. Biological Safety

Thompson, J. (2000). A practical guide to wound care. RN, 63 *(1), 48–54.*

When wounds won't heal (1998). RN, January, *20.*

V. Medication Safety

Confidentially: IV error: Watch your drip. (1999). Nursing, 29(7), *32.*

Karch, A.M. (1999). Med Errors. "Like taking a vitamin." American Journal of Nursing, 99 *(11), 12.*

Karch, A.M. (2000). Practice Errors. "Cutting it close." American Journal of Nursing, 100 *(1), 23.*

VI. Psychological Safety

Hansen, M. (1998). Patient-centered teaching from theory to practice. American Journal of Nursing, 98 *(1), 56–60.*

How to deal with an angry patient (1998). RN, October, *63.*

Hubert, P. (1998). Revealing patient concerns. American Journal of Nursing, 98 *(10), 16H–6L.*

Keller, V., & Baker, L. (2000). Communicate with CARE. RN, 63 *(1), 32–33.*

Nield-Anderson, L. et al. (1999). Responding to "difficult" patients. American Journal of Nursing, 99 *(12), 26–35. CE credit available.*

Patient education: We have a better system now (1997). RN, June, *19.*

Zook, R. (1998). Learning to use positive defense mechanisms. American Journal of Nursing, 98 *(3), 16B–16H.*

Audiovisual Resources

A very good source of videocassettes is the American Journal of Nursing Company's Multimedia Catalog. To order, call 800-CALL-AJN. Other sources for computer and video programs are Concept Media, Irvine, CA (call 800-233-7078 or visit their Web site at www.Conceptmedia.com) and Insight Media, New York City (call 800-233-9910).

1. CD-ROM: Transcultural Perspectives in Nursing (Improving nurse-client effectiveness, Communication, Parts 1 and 2). *Concept Media.*
2. Video: Pediatric Medication Administration (Principles, calculations, oral and parenteral meds). *Concept Media.*
3. Whaley and Wong's Pediatric Nursing Video Series including Communication with Children and Families, Medications and Injections. *Mosby.*
4. Video: Administering Medications by Nonparenteral Routes (oral, topical, instillations, inhalants, irrigations) *Insight Media.*

Sample Questions: Nursing Concepts 1

5. *Video:* Communicating with Clients from Different Cultures. *Insight Media.*
6. *Video:* Communication in Nursing Across the Lifespan-Children, Families, and the Elderly. *Insight Media.*
7. *Video:* Patient Teaching. *Insight Media.*

Web sites for general information in nursing concepts:

http://www.nursingcenter.com
http://www.rnweb.com
http://s-witch.com: This site has a CD ROM course available on interpersonal communication and basic counseling

Content/Reference List

I. Nursing Process
Kozier et al. (6th edition, 2000)
- Chapter 16   Critical Thinking and the Nursing Process
- Chapter 17   Assessing
- Chapter 18   Diagnosing (Analysis)
- Chapter 19   Planning
- Chapter 20   Implementing and Evaluating
- Chapter 21   Documenting and Reporting (see sections on ethical and legal considerations, documenting nursing activities, guidelines for recording and reporting, only)

Wong (5th edition, 1997)
- Chapter 2   Nursing Process in Care of the Child and Family

Wilkinson (2nd edition, 1996)
- Chapter 1   Overview of the Nursing Process (see sections on defining nursing process, benefits of nursing process. and ethical considerations, only)
- Chapter 3   Assessment
- Chapter 4   Diagnostic Reasoning
- Chapter 5   Writing Diagnostic Statements
- Chapter 6   Planning
- Chapter 7   Implementation
- Chapter 8   Evaluation

PLEASE NOTE: Although this content area, **Nursing Process,** occupies 10% of Nursing Concepts 1, the material it contains is a vital part of professional nursing and the foundation for all test questions found in Nursing Concepts 1 through 6. The nursing process must be **applied,** not just memorized. In clinical practice, you will be applying the nursing process, not simply recalling facts. It will be much more helpful if you start to practice that now and focus primarily on **Section B, Nursing Care Related to Theoretical Framework,** found in each content guide for Nursing Concepts, 1 through 6 as you study.

II. Health, Wellness, and Illness
Kozier et al. (6th edition, 2000)
- Chapter 11   Health, Wellness, and Illness
- Chapter 15   Holistic Healing Modalities (see section on Alternative Medical Therapies, only)
- Chapter 28   Vital Signs
- Chapter 29   Health Assessment (see section on Physical Assessment and General Survey only)
- Chapter 39   Stress and Coping

Sample Questions: Nursing Concepts 1

Wong (5th edition, 1997)
- Chapter 5 Developmental Influences on Child Health Promotion (see section on growth and development, stop before section on physiological changes)
- Chapter 7 Physical and Developmental Assessment of the Child (see section on general approaches and physical examination, stop before section on general appearance)

Eisenhauer et al. (5th edition, 1999)
- Chapter 9 Cultural Aspects of Drug Therapy

III. Environmental Safety

Kozier et al. (6th edition, 2000)
- Chapter 31 Safety

Wong (5th edition, 1997)
- Chapter 22 Pediatric Variations of Nursing Interventions (see sections on Safety: Environmental Factors, Limit Setting, Transporting, and Restraints, only)

IV. Biological Safety

Kozier et al. (6th edition, 2000)
- Chapter 30 Asepsis
- Chapter 32 Hygiene
- Chapter 34 Skin Integrity and Wound Care

Wong (5th edition, 1997)
- Chapter 22 Pediatric Variations of Nursing Interventions (see section on Safety: Infection Control, only)
- Chapter 7 Physical and Developmental Assessment of the Child (see section on general appearance and skin, only)

Eisenhauer et al. (5th edition, 1999)
- Chapter 41 Antimicrobial Drugs That Affect Bacterial Cell Wall Synthesis

V. Medication Safety

Kozier et al. (6th edition, 2000)
- Chapter 33 Medications

Wong (5th edition, 1997)
- Chapter 22 Pediatric Variations of Nursing Interventions (see section on Administration of Medications, only)

Eisenhauer et al. (5th edition, 1999)
- Chapter 7 Principles of Medication

VI. Psychological Safety

Kozier et al. (6th edition, 2000)
- Chapter 25 Caring, Comforting, and Communicating
- Chapter 26 Teaching

Wong (5th edition, 1997)
- Chapter 6 Communication and Health Assessment of the Child and Family (see section on communication, only)

Study Guide
Nursing Concepts 2 (Associate Level)

Credit Hours: 4 **Credit Level:** Lower
Question Type(s): Multiple-choice

The information in this study guide becomes valid on October 1, 2000. See page 261 for information on the Nursing Concepts examination series.

Description of the Examination

The Nursing Concepts 2 examination measures knowledge and understanding of basic concepts of nursing care and related nursing actions common to all patients throughout the life cycle, regardless of the health status of the patient. Questions concern nursing problems frequently encountered by the associate degree nurse. Questions are based on the needs of patients of various age groups and the nursing care actions properly associated with them.

The examination requires students to possess the technical vocabulary and have the knowledge of anatomy and physiology, emotional and physical development, and microbiology generally expected of the associate degree nurse. The examination requires students to demonstrate knowledge of a nursing framework for each content area as well as the ability to apply this knowledge to nursing practice using the nursing process. In addition, students are required to use critical thinking skills to apply principles, concepts, and theories from the natural and social sciences, and the humanities to the practice of nursing.

Content Outline

Content Area	Percent of Examination
I. Nutrition	20%
II. Elimination	15%
III. Oxygenation	20%
IV. Fluid and Electrolyte Balance	25%
V. Activity and Mobility	10%
VI. Rest and Sleep	10%
Total	100%

Emphasis

    I. Theoretical Framework—Basis for Care   34%
   II. Nursing Care Related to Theoretical Framework   66%
                                                                       100%

I. Nutrition (20%)

This area focuses on the common nutritional needs of patients across the life span. Emphasis is placed on the components of normal nutrition as well as the common nutritional disturbances.

A. Theoretical framework: basis for care
1. Principles related to normal nutrition (for example: anatomy and physiology)
2. Components of normal nutrition: definitions, basic functions, common food sources, daily requirements, estimation of caloric needs (for example: from the Food Guide Pyramid, exchange lists, recommended daily allowances)
   a. Carbohydrates
   b. Proteins
   c. Lipids (fats)
   d. Vitamins
   e. Minerals
   f. Fiber
   g. Fluids
3. Factors influencing the patient's nutrition
   a. Sex (for example: effect of gender on metabolic requirements)
   b. Age/developmental level: infants through older adults (for example: effect of age on metabolic requirements, irregular eating patterns in adolescents, decreased gastric juice secretion in older adults)
   c. Individual preferences and patterns (for example: vegetarian diet, health habits, use of vitamin supplements, knowledge of basic nutrients, cooking habits, use of herbs, antioxidants, effects of excessive intake of alcohol)
   d. Physical condition (for example: dental status, metabolic rate, weight status, level of physical activity, circulatory status, status of peristalsis)
   e. Cultural and spiritual/religious considerations (for example: religious practices and restrictions, traditional ethnic foods, cultural preferences/taboos)
   f. Socioeconomic factors (for example: income level, work habits)
   g. Environmental factors (for example: means of procuring food, food storage, refrigeration, eating and cooking facilities)
   h. Psychological factors (for example: peer pressure, mental status, stress, increased dependency, loneliness, anxiety, depression)
4. Common nutritional disturbances (for example: altered ingestion; digestion, absorption, and metabolism; nutritional deficiencies)
5. Theoretical basis for interventions to promote nutrition
   a. Physiological considerations (for example: oral care, increased activity, positioning, reduction of stress, pleasant environment)
   b. Enteral nutrition: oral and tube feedings
   c. Parenteral nutrition: total parenteral nutrition (TPN), lipid emulsions, total nutrient admixture (three-in-one)
   d. Altered consistency of diets

                (1) Clear liquid
                (2) Full liquid
                (3) Soft
            e. Vitamin and mineral supplements
            f. Ethical and legal implications (for example: enteral feeding for patients who are terminally ill)
    B. **Nursing care related to theoretical framework**
        1. Assessment: gather and organize data in relation to the patient's health status
            a. Obtain the patient's history related to nutritional status (for example: daily nutritional intake, intolerance of certain foods, food preferences, food allergies, pattern of intake [24-hour food diary], anorexia, dysphagia, nausea and vomiting)
            b. Assess factors influencing the patient's nutrition (see IA3)
            c. Obtain objective patient assessment data (for example: weight changes; skin turgor; level of physical activity; condition of hair and nails; amount, type, and pattern of intake; triceps skinfold thickness)
            d. Review laboratory and other diagnostic data (for example: serum albumin, complete blood count [CBCs], blood urea nitrogen, creatinine)
        2. Analysis: in conjunction with the patient and members of the health care team, synthesize data to identify the patient's actual or potential health problem
            a. Identify nursing diagnoses (for example: altered nutrition: less than body requirements related to hectic schedule; altered nutrition: more than body requirements related to dependence on fast foods; altered health maintenance related to insufficient knowledge of nutritional needs)
            b. Set priorities (for example: based on the patient's developmental level, based on Maslow's hierarchy of needs, based on optimal use of resources)
        3. Planning: in conjunction with the patient and members of the health care team, determine the expected outcomes (patient-centered goals) and formulate specific strategies to achieve the expected outcomes
            a. Establish expected outcomes (patient-centered goals) for care related to health promotion, health maintenance, and health restoration (for example: patient will identify from the Food Guide Pyramid preferred foods that are accessible and easy to prepare, patient will select low-calorie foods from fast-food menus, patient will select a balanced daily diet from a list of basic food groups)
            b. Incorporate factors influencing the patient's nutrition in planning the patient's care (for example: plan a clear liquid diet for a patient following surgery, plan a nutritionally adequate diet based on patient's religious preferences, plan a nutritionally adequate diet for an older adult) (see IA3)
            c. Use established nursing standards and protocols, plan nursing measures to help the patient achieve the expected outcomes (for example: review nutritional requirements based on the Food Guide Pyramid, monitor the patient's weight)
            d. Assign patient care activities to other members of the health care team as appropriate (for example: assign nursing assistant to feed patient, assign nursing assistant to record patient intake)
        4. Implementation: initiate and complete nursing actions/interventions designed

to move the patient toward the expected outcomes (patient-centered goals) related to health promotion, health maintenance, and health restoration
- a. Assist in food selection (for example: for a patient with altered chewing or swallowing ability, for patients of various developmental levels, for a patient with an imbalanced diet)
- b. Use nursing measures appropriate to particular feeding methods (for example: provide nasogastric tube feedings, administer gastrostomy tube feedings, monitor total parenteral nutrition [TPN])
- c. Use nursing measures to promote nutritional intake (for example: remove noxious stimuli from the environment; make the patient comfortable; provide mouth care; administer small, frequent feedings; use assistive feeding devices such as softer, more pliable nipples for infants born prematurely; provide large-handled spoon for a patient with arthritis)
- d. Use nursing measures specific to prescribed nutritional supplements (for example: administer iron supplements with orange juice, administer vitamin supplements as ordered, check the serum albumin level for a patient who is receiving a high-protein liquid supplement)
- e. Provide information and instruction regarding nutrition (for example: instruct the patient regarding food preservation and preparation, instruct the patient to read nutritional content on food labels, instruct the patient with lactose intolerance about alternative food sources, instruct the patient about developmental modifications of nutritional requirements, instruct the patient on a vegetarian diet about plant proteins, instruct family members on administration of tube feedings)
- f. Use nursing measures to promote continuity of care (for example: teaching, referrals, support groups for weight loss, community resources)

5. Evaluation: assess the patient's response to nursing care including progress toward the expected outcomes (patient-centered goals)
- a. Record and report patient's response to nursing actions (for example: weight changes, improved skin turgor, changes in nutritional intake, noncompliance)
- b. Reassess and revise the patient's plan of care as necessary (for example: provide small, frequent feedings for a patient with anorexia; revise the teaching plan)
- c. Determine the patient's response to care provided by other members of the health care team (for example: ask questions of the nursing assistant to determine amount of food patient consumed, check patient intake recorded by nursing assistant, evaluate caregiver's ability to handle home nutrition therapy)

II. Elimination (15%)

This area focuses on the common bowel and bladder elimination patterns of patients across the life span. Emphasis is placed on the principles of normal elimination as well as on common intestinal and urinary elimination disturbances.

A. Theoretical framework: basis for care
1. Principles related to normal elimination (for example: anatomy and physiology, microbiology)
2. Factors influencing the patient's intestinal and urinary elimination

a. Sex (for example: effect of gender on risk for urinary retention, anatomic differences)
b. Age/developmental level: infants through older adult (for example: changes in peristalsis, sphincter control)
c. Individual preferences and patterns (for example: use of laxatives, health habits, fluid intake, dietary habits, activity level)
d. Physical condition (for example: immobility, decreased sphincter tone, decreased abdominal and pelvic muscle tone, colonic atony)
e. Cultural and spiritual/religious considerations (for example: cleansing, modesty)
f. Socioeconomic factors (for example: excess intake of refined carbohydrates, decreased intake of fresh fruits and vegetables)
g. Environmental factors (for example: access to sanitary facilities, privacy, time schedule demands, height of toilets)
h. Psychological factors (for example: hospitalization, loneliness, anxiety, depression, stress)
3. Common disturbances of intestinal elimination (for example: constipation, diarrhea, impaction, flatulence, incontinence)
4. Common disturbances of urinary elimination (for example: incontinence, frequency, urgency, retention, dysuria, polyuria, enuresis)
5. Theoretical basis for interventions to promote intestinal and urinary elimination
    a. Physiological considerations (for example: positioning, exercise, gastrocolic reflex)
    b. Medications (for example: stool softeners, cathartics, urinary tract antiseptics and analgesics, antidiarrheal agents)
    c. Catheterization (for example: indwelling, external, straight)
    d. Enemas (for example: cleansing, carminative, retention)
    e. Dietary modifications (for example: alter intake of fiber, establish regular eating times, alter intake of fluids)

B. Nursing care related to theoretical framework
1. Assessment: gather and organize data in relation to the patient's health status
    a. Obtain the patient's history related to elimination (for example: pattern of bowel elimination [time of day and frequency], use of laxatives and cathartics, anorexia, frequency of urination, dysuria)
    b. Assess factors influencing the patient's elimination (see IIA2)
    c. Obtain objective patient assessment data (for example: intake and output; consistency, color, and amount of urine; altered bowel sounds; bladder distention)
    d. Review laboratory and other diagnostic data (for example: specific gravity, stool for guaiac, urinalysis, culture and sensitivity, stool for ova and parasites, presence of ketones or glucose in urine)
    e. Collect specimens (for example: specimen from a retention catheter, stool for guaiac, clean catch/midstream urine specimen)
2. Analysis: in conjunction with the patient and members of the health care team, synthesize data to identify the patient's actual or potential health problem (nursing diagnosis)

a. Identify nursing diagnoses (for example: constipation related to decreased abdominal muscle tone associated with aging, constipation related to immobility, urinary retention related to loss of muscle tone, stress incontinence related to weak pelvic muscles, high risk for urinary tract infection related to improper perineal hygiene)
b. Set priorities (for example: based on the patient's developmental level, based on Maslow's hierarchy of needs, based on optimal use of resources)

3. Planning: in conjunction with the patient and members of the health care team, determine the expected outcomes (patient-centered goals) and formulate specific strategies to achieve the expected outcomes
    a. Establish expected outcomes (patient-centered goals) for care related to health promotion, health maintenance, and health restoration (for example: patient will pass a soft, formed stool at regular intervals; patient will remain free of infection; patient will verbalize understanding of perineal floor exercises; patient will wipe perineal area from front to back after urinating and defecating)
    b. Incorporate factors influencing the patient's elimination in planning the patient's care (for example: a patient with an indwelling catheter, an older adult on bed rest, a patient with increased urine specific gravity) (see IIA2)
    c. Using established nursing standards and protocols, plan nursing measures to help the patient achieve the expected outcomes (for example: discuss the problems associated with the misuse of laxatives and enemas, establish an elimination routine, encourage the patient to practice perineal floor exercises q2h while awake)
    d. Assign patient care activities to other members of the health care team as appropriate (for example: assign nursing assistant to empty Foley bag at end of shift and record amount of output)

4. Implementation: initiate and complete nursing actions/interventions designed to move the patient toward the expected outcomes (patient-centered goals) related to health promotion, health maintenance, and health restoration
    a. Ensure appropriate intake (for example: encourage adequate intake of fiber, provide daily fluid intake appropriate to the patient's developmental level)
    b. Ensure appropriate activity (for example: encourage ambulation, provide range-of-motion exercises)
    c. Establish an environment conducive to elimination (for example: decrease stress, provide proper positioning, ensure privacy)
    d. Use nursing measures appropriate to particular elimination needs (for example: perform bladder catheterizations and irrigations, insert rectal tube, administer enema, administer laxatives, administer stool softeners, provide bladder and bowel retraining, consider modifications related to the patient's age)
    e. Provide information and instruction regarding elimination (for example: assist an older adult to plan a high-fiber diet, instruct parents about toilet training for their child, instruct the patient about hygiene and asepsis, instruct the patient to perform Kegel exercises)
    f. Use nursing measures to promote continuity of care (for example: teaching, referrals, support groups, community resources)

5. Evaluation: assess the patient's response to nursing care including progress toward expected outcomes (patient-centered goals)

a. Record and report patient's response to nursing actions (for example: relief of symptoms, increased fluid intake, altered consistency of stool, increased volume of urine, adverse reactions to treatments)
b. Reassess and revise patient's plan of care as necessary (for example: change pattern of patient's fluid intake to control enuresis, use a fracture pan rather than a regular bedpan, provide a bedside commode, revise the teaching plan)
c. Determine patient's response to care provided by other members of the health care team (for example: check results of Fleet enema administered by LPN/LVN)

III. Oxygenation (20%)

This area focuses on the common oxygenation needs of patients across the life span. Emphasis is placed on the principles of normal oxygenation as well as the common disturbances of oxygenation.

A. Theoretical framework: basis for care

1. Principles related to normal oxygenation (for example: anatomy and physiology, intrapulmonary pressure, diffusion)
2. Factors influencing the patient's oxygenation
   a. Sex (for example: predominance of abdominal breathing in males)
   b. Age/developmental level (for example: oxygen variations through older adults, vital capacity)
   c. Individual preferences and patterns (for example: physical activity, diet, smoking, sedentary lifestyle, occupation)
   d. Physical condition (for example: breathing patterns, body weight, body temperature, hemoglobin, exercise patterns, pain, airway obstruction)
   e. Cultural and spiritual/religious practices (for example: unwillingness to accept blood transfusion, use of incense in cultural practices)
   f. Environmental factors (for example: air pollution, altitude, room ventilation, air temperature and humidity, overcrowded conditions, occupation)
   g. Psychological factors (for example: stress, emotional status, anxiety)
   h. Alternative/complementary treatments (for example: relaxation breathing, acupuncture for smoking cessation, hypnosis)
3. Common disturbances of oxygenation (for example: altered oxygen intake and supply, altered oxygen diffusion and transportation, altered cellular demand for oxygen)
4. Theoretical basis for interventions to promote oxygenation
   a. Positioning (for example: elevation of the extremities, high-Fowler's position)
   b. Activity and rest patterns (for example: passive and active exercises, stress reduction)
   c. Dietary modifications (for example: sodium restriction, increased fluids, caloric restriction, modifications to promote erythrogenesis)
   d. Administration of oxygen (for example: nasal cannula, masks, humidification, mechanical ventilation)
   e. Administration of blood and blood products (for example: packed cells, clotting factors, blood typing)

f. Airway maintenance (for example: coughing and deep breathing, cupping and clapping, incentive spirometry, nasopharyngeal suctioning, pursed-lip breathing, postural drainage)
   g. Ethical and legal implications (for example: use of ventilators, protocols for blood administration, institution of life support measures)

B. Nursing care related to theoretical framework
   1. Assessment: gather and organize data in relation to the patient's health care status
      a. Obtain patient's history related to oxygenation (for example: altered breathing patterns, dyspnea, fatigue, altered sensation, occupation, health habits)
      b. Assess factors influencing the patient's oxygenation (see IIIA2)
      c. Obtain objective patient assessment data (for example: clinical signs of hypoxia, dyspnea, fatigue, respiratory rate and rhythm, peripheral pulses, skin color, breath sounds, restlessness, tachycardia, apnea, tachypnea, cyanosis, confusion, hypoventilation, hyperventilation, airway patency, capillary refill)
      d. Review laboratory and other diagnostic data (for example: arterial blood gases, hemoglobin, hematocrit, sputum cultures, chest X ray, pulmonary function studies, pulse oximetry)
      e. Collect specimens (for example: sputum, stool for guaiac)
   2. Analysis: in conjunction with the patient and members of the health care team, synthesize data to identify the patient's actual or potential health problem (nursing diagnosis)
      a. Identify nursing diagnoses (for example: ineffective airway clearance related to immobility, noncompliance with smoking cessation related to physiological addiction, activity intolerance related to shortness of breath)
      b. Set priorities (for example: based on the patient's developmental level, based on Maslow's hierarchy of needs, based on optimal use of resources)
   3. Planning: in conjunction with the patient and members of the health care team, determine expected outcomes (patient-centered goals) and formulate specific strategies to achieve the expected outcomes
      a. Establish expected outcomes (patient-centered goals) for care related to health promotion, health maintenance, and health restoration (for example: patient's breath sounds will be clear over entire lung field, patient will enroll in a behavior modification program for smoking cessation, patient will ambulate 200 feet without shortness of breath)
      b. In planning the patient's care, incorporate factors influencing the patient's oxygenation (for example: plan for humidification, ensure adequate ventilation, discuss with parents the effects of secondary smoke, plan activities to allow for periods of rest) (see IIIA2)
      c. Using established nursing standards and protocols, plan nursing measures on the basis of established priorities to help the patient achieve the expected outcomes (patient centered goals) (for example: establish physical activity program, plan coughing and deep-breathing regimen with the patient, plan for frequent position changes, refer the patient to smoking cessation programs)

d. Assign patient care activities to other members of the health care team as appropriate (for example: instruct nursing assistant to maintain patient in high-Fowler's position, assign LPN/LVN to maintain prescribed oxygen flow rate.)
4. Implementation: initiate and complete nursing plans designed to move the patient toward the expected outcomes (patient-centered goals) related to health promotion, health maintenance, and health restoration
   a. Maintain oxygen intake and supply (for example: assist with turning, positioning, and repositioning; assist with deep breathing and coughing; perform oralpharyngeal, nasopharyngeal, and tracheostomy suctioning; provide percussion, vibration, and postural drainage; administer oxygen via face mask, tent, and cannula; maintain a patent airway; perform Heimlich maneuver; encourage use of an incentive spirometer; CPR)
   b. Administer medications as ordered (for example: bronchodilators, expectorants, antitussives)
   c. Promote oxygen diffusion and transport (for example: encourage increased intake of dietary protein, iron, and vitamin C; encourage increase in exercise; promote good peripheral circulation by avoiding constricting positions, clothing, dressings)
   d. Reduce cell demand for oxygen (for example: promote rest, reduce anxiety, encourage weight loss, prevent shivering, teach controlled breathing and relaxation techniques)
   e. Use safety measures related to oxygen therapy (for example: enforce no-smoking regulations, check electrical outlets, use only electrical devices that are grounded and in good working order)
   f. Provide information and instruction to the patient and family regarding oxygenation (for example: instruct the patient about the benefits of aerobic conditioning, teach patient abdominal and pursed-lip breathing, provide instruction regarding occupational exposure to pollutants, teach patient to use selected inhalation therapy devices and practices, teach the use of metered dose inhalers, adjunctive therapy, percussion, postural drainage or supportive equipment)
   g. Use nursing measures to promote continuity of care (for example: teaching, referrals, support groups, community resources)
5. Evaluation: assess the patient's response to nursing care including progress toward the expected outcomes (patient-centered goals)
   a. Record and report patient's response to nursing actions (for example: changes in vital signs, alteration in skin color, improvement in blood gas values, increased or decreased alertness, improved tolerance for activities, alterations in level of consciousness, signs of blood reaction)
   b. Reassess and revise the patient's plan of care as necessary (for example: provide additional pillows for the patient who is experiencing orthopnea, revise the teaching plan)
   c. Determine patient's response to care provided by other members of the health care team (for example: monitor vital signs as recorded by nursing assistant, ask patient to demonstrate deep breathing and coughing exercises taught by LPN/LVN)

IV. Fluid and Electrolyte Balance (25%)

This area focuses on the common fluid and electrolyte needs of patients across the life span. Emphasis is placed on the principles of normal fluid and electrolyte balance as well as the common disturbances of fluid and electrolyte balance. (It may be especially helpful to refer to a fluid and electrolyte textbook or an anatomy and physiology textbook when preparing for this section.)

A. Theoretical framework: basis for care
1. Principles related to normal fluid and electrolyte balance (for example: anatomical, physical, and chemical principles relating to intracellular and extracellular fluid compartments; the movement of substances across semipermeable membranes by osmosis, diffusion, filtration, and active transport; the role of specific electrolytes in normal body function; homeostatic mechanisms controlling the levels of fluids and electrolytes in the body)
2. Factors influencing the patient's fluid and electrolyte balance
   a. Sex (for example: percentage of body fluid)
   b. Age/developmental level: infants through older adult (for example: ability to concentrate urine, higher metabolic rate in children causes fluid loss, blunted thirst response in older adults)
   c. Individual preferences and patterns (for example: excessive salt intake, NPO status, aerobic exercise)
   d. Physical condition (for example: general adaptation syndrome, altered level of consciousness, vomiting, diarrhea, increased body temperature, renal and cardiac status, medications, dehydration, surgery)
   e. Cultural and spiritual/religious practices (for example: dietary or religious restrictions)
   f. Socioeconomic factors (for example: income level)
   g. Environmental factors (for example: temperature and humidity, potable water supply)
   h. Psychological factors (for example: stress)
3. Common disturbances of fluid balance (for example: dehydration, hypovolemia, hypervolemia, edema, ascites, fluid shifts)
4. Common disturbances of electrolyte balance (for example: acid-base imbalances, hypernatremia, hyponatremia, hypokalemia, hyperkalemia, hypercalcemia, hypocalcemia, hypomagnesemia, hypermagnesemia, respiratory acidosis, respiratory alkalosis, metabolic acidosis, metabolic alkalosis)
5. Theoretical basis for interventions to promote fluid and electrolyte balance
   a. Dietary modifications (for example: encourage fluid intake, maintain dietary restrictions)
   b. Intravenous fluid therapy (for example: hypotonic, hypertonic, isotonic, electrolyte replacement solutions)
   c. Medications (for example: diuretics, electrolyte supplements)
   d. Ethical and legal implications (for example: maintenance of hydration)

B. Nursing care related to theoretical framework
1. Assessment: gather and organize data in relation to the patient's health status
   a. Obtain the patient's history relative to fluid and electrolyte balance (for example: urinary elimination patterns; dietary habits; symptoms of

imbalance such as lethargy, thirst, and muscle weakness; therapies that create potential fluid and electrolyte imbalances)
    b. Assess factors influencing the patient's fluid and electrolyte balance (see IVA2)
    c. Obtain objective patient assessment data (for example: skin turgor, intake and output, weight changes, twitching, fatigue, vital signs, increased abdominal girth, edema, dehydration, Trousseau's sign, Chvostek's sign, breath sounds, neck veins distension)
    d. Review laboratory and other diagnostic data (for example: hematocrit, serum electrolyte levels, urine specific gravity and pH, blood urea nitrogen [BUN], arterial blood gases)
2. Analysis: in conjunction with the patient and members of the health care team, synthesize data to identify the patient's actual or potential health problem (nursing diagnoses)
    a. Identify nursing diagnoses (for example: fluid volume excess related to high sodium intake, fluid volume deficit related to diarrhea, activity intolerance related to potassium loss from diuretic therapy, fluid volume deficit related to alterations in renal function associated with aging)
    b. Set priorities (for example: based on the patient's developmental level, based on Maslow's hierarchy of needs, based on optimal use of resources)
3. Planning: in conjunction with the patient and members of the health care team, determine expected outcomes (patient-centered goals) and formulate specific strategies to achieve the expected outcomes
    a. Establish expected outcomes (patient-centered goals) for care related to health promotion, health maintenance, and health restoration (for example: patient will decrease intake of foods that are high in sodium, infant's fontanelle will regain normal contours, patient's serum potassium level will be within normal limits, patient will drink four to six 8-oz. glasses of water a day)
    b. Incorporate factors influencing the patient's fluid and electrolyte status in planning the patient's care (for example: establish a pattern of fluid intake based on an older adult's preferences and physical needs, replace fluid and electrolytes for a patient with gastrointestinal fluid loss) (see IVA2)
    c. Using established nursing standards and protocols, plan nursing measures on the basis of established priorities to help the patient achieve the expected outcomes (for example: plan instruction regarding the sodium content of prepared foods, monitor the administration of oral rehydration solutions, administer prescribed potassium as ordered, plan instruction regarding the need for additional fluids)
    d. Assign patient care activities to other members of the health care team as appropriate (for example: assign nursing assistant to encourage patient to increase fluid intake)
4. Implementation: initiate and complete nursing plans designed to move the patient toward the expected outcomes (patient-centered goals) related to health promotion, health maintenance, and health restoration
    a. Promote fluid and electrolyte balance (for example: assist with food and fluid selection, adapt measures to patient's developmental level)
    b. Use nursing measures appropriate to fluid and electrolyte deficits
        (1) Natural replacement of fluids (for example: establish daily fluid regimen with patient)

(2) Artificial replacement of fluids (for example: assist with parenteral administration of fluids, which includes calculating flow rate, monitoring flow rate, adding a new IV solution, monitoring infusion site, administration of volume expanders)

(3) Natural replacement of electrolytes (for example: modify dietary intake)

(4) Artificial replacement of electrolytes (for example: administer parenteral or oral potassium chloride)

(5) Prevention of excessive fluid and electrolyte loss (for example: administer antiemetics, antipyretics, antidiarrheal agents; alter room temperature as needed)

c. Use nursing measures appropriate to fluid and electrolyte excesses
  (1) Dietary restriction (for example: limit PO intake to 1,000 mL/day, limit sodium intake)
  (2) Medications (for example: administer diuretics, administer sodium polystyrene sulfonate [Kayexalate])
  (3) Parenteral therapy (for example: monitor for signs of fluid excess)

d. Provide information and instruction regarding fluid and electrolyte requirements (for example: instruct the patient receiving a loop diuretic to increase dietary intake of potassium, provide instruction regarding increased intake of salt prior to strenuous exercise in hot weather, consider modifications related to the patient's age)

e. Use nursing measures to promote continuity of care (for example: teaching, referrals, support groups, community resources)

5. Evaluation: assess the patient's response to nursing care including progress toward the expected outcomes (patient-centered goals)

  a. Record and report patient's response to nursing actions (for example: weight changes, altered hematocrit levels, altered urine specific gravity, alterations in output, increased energy level, adverse effects, signs or symptoms of untoward reactions; 24-hour Intake and Output record [I & O], skin turgor, vital signs)

  b. Reassess and revise patient's plan of care as necessary (for example: recommend that the patient further increase intake of foods high in potassium, revise the teaching plan)

  c. Determine patient's response to care provided by other members of the health care team (for example: ask the nursing assistant to report fluid intake if less than 500 mL per shift)

V. Activity/Mobility (10%)

This area focuses on principles related to mobility and factors affecting activity/mobility, and common disturbances related to immobility.

A. Theoretical framework: basis for care

1. Principles related to mobility (for example: normal body alignment, posture, body mechanics, balance, range of motion, positioning, transfer, effect of regular exercise on body systems, effects of bedrest)

2. Factors influencing the patient's activity/mobility
   a. Sex (for example: the development of osteoporosis in women)
   b. Age/developmental level: infants through older adult (for example: muscle

mass in adolescent boys, loss of joint mobility and muscle tone in older adults)
   c. Individual preferences and patterns (for example: sedentary lifestyle, smoking, energy levels, exercise patterns)
   d. Physical condition (for example: nutritional status, muscle atrophy, presence of other illness or disability, congenital or acquired postural anomalies)
   e. Cultural and spiritual/religious considerations (for example: value of physical activity, compliance with treatment)
   f. Socioeconomic factors (for example: finances, housing)
   g. Environmental factors (for example: climate, altitude, occupation)
   h. Psychological factors (for example: compliance, hopelessness, helplessness)
3. Common disturbances related to immobility
   a. Physiological responses (for example: decreased lung expansion, diminished cardiac reserve, decreased metabolic rate, pooling of respiratory secretions, orthostatic hypotension, pressure ulcer, constipation, contractures, renal calculi, thrombophlebitis)
   b. Psychological responses (for example: hopelessness, sensory deprivation, changes in sleep patterns, attention-seeking behaviors, feelings of powerlessness)
   c. Developmental responses (for example: regression in children, increased dependence in the older adult)
4. Theoretical basis for interventions related to activity/mobility
   a. Interventions to promote activity/mobility
      (1) Exercises (for example: quadriceps-setting, active and passive range-of-motion, use of weights for older adults)
      (2) Positioning (for example: supine, prone, Sims', Fowler's)
      (3) Supportive devices (for example: footboard, splints, trochanter rolls, handrails, restraints)
      (4) Transfer techniques (for example: lying to sitting, bed to chair)
      (5) Use of assistive devices (for example: walkers, canes, crutches)
      (6) Prevention programs (for example: walking, use of weights)
      (7) Alternative/complementary treatments (for example: chiropractics, acupuncture, therapeutic touch, massage)
   b. Interventions to prevent complications of immobility
      (1) Maintain nutrition
      (2) Maintain fluid balance
      (3) Prevent stasis of pulmonary secretions
      (4) Promote venous return
      (5) Maintain skin integrity
      (6) Maintain normal elimination patterns
      (7) Prevent contractures
      (8) Provide psychosocial stimulation
      (9) Foster independence

B. Nursing care related to theoretical framework
   1. Assessment: gather and organize data in relation to the patient's health status
      a. Obtain the patient's history related to activity/mobility patterns (for example: activity tolerance, pattern of regular exercise, ability to perform activities of daily living [ADLs], endurance)

b. Assess factors influencing the patient's activity/mobility (see VA2)
   c. Obtain objective patient assessment data (for example: range of motion, gait, body alignment, muscle strength and symmetry, ambulation, joint movement, endurance)
   d. Review laboratory and other diagnostic data (for example: X rays, bone scans, serum calcium levels, bone density studies)
2. Analysis: in conjunction with the patient and members of the health care team, synthesize data to identify the patient's actual or potential health problem (nursing diagnosis)
   a. Identify nursing diagnoses (for example: impaired physical mobility related to prolonged bedrest, activity intolerance related to sedentary lifestyle, impaired skin integrity related to increased pressure over bony prominences, high risk for injury related to unsteady gait)
   b. Set priorities (for example: based on the patient's developmental level, based on Maslow's hierarchy of needs, based on optimal use of resources)
3. Planning: in conjunction with the patient and members of the health care team, determine expected outcomes (patient-centered goals) and formulate specific strategies to achieve the expected outcomes
   a. Establish expected outcomes (patient-centered goals) for care related to health promotion, health maintenance, and health restoration (for example: patient will demonstrate active range of motion in all body joints; patient will verbalize the need to incorporate exercise into daily activities; patient's skin will be clean, intact, and well-hydrated; patient will not experience injury)
   b. Using established nursing standards and protocols, plan nursing measures to help the patient achieve the expected outcomes (patient-centered goals) (for example: instruct the patient to perform range-of-motion exercises, explore the patient's activity preferences, turn and position the patient q2h, provide a safe environment for the patient)
   c. Incorporate factors influencing the patient's activity/mobility in planning the patient's care (for example: establish an age-appropriate exercise program, plan activities based on the patient's age and physical findings, administer prn pain medication prior to exercise)
   d. Assign patient care activities to other members of the health care team as appropriate (for example: ask the nursing assistant to perform range-of-motion exercises with patient)
4. Implementation: carry out nursing plans designed to move the patient toward the expected outcomes (patient-centered goals) related to health promotion, health maintenance, and health restoration
   a. Use nursing measures to establish a collaborative relationship with the patient (for example: use therapeutic communication skills, respect cultural and individual differences, establish expectations with the patient)
   b. Use nursing measures to maintain the patient's activity/mobility (for example: turning, positioning, active and passive range-of-motion exercises)
   c. Promote use of assistive equipment (for example: walkers, canes, crutches, bedside rails, trapeze bar)
   d. Administer medications before beginning exercise programs (for example: muscle relaxants, pain medication)

    e. Provide information and instruction regarding activity/mobility (for example: instruct the patient in crutch walking, instruct the patient regarding transfer activities, instruct the patient about body mechanics and range-of-motion exercises, instruct parent and child on importance of regular exercise, teach the avoidance of hazards to mobility in the home)
    f. Use nursing measures to promote continuity of care (for example: teaching; referrals; community resources such as fitness centers, sports programs)
 5. Evaluation: assess the patient's response to nursing care including progress toward the expected outcome (patient-centered goal)
    a. Record and report the patient's response to nursing actions (for example: color and condition of the skin, development of pressure areas, range-of-motion exercises performed, ambulates independently, participates in regular exercise routine)
    b. Reassess and revise the patient's plan of care as necessary (for example: turn and reposition the patient more frequently, select a device to minimize pressure for a patient to keep weight off pressure areas, revise the teaching plan)
    c. Determine patient's response to care provided by other members of the health care team (for example: ask LPN/LVN to report any patient mobility problems, ask nursing assistant to describe changes in skin conditions due to restricted mobility)

VI. Rest and Sleep (10%)

This area focuses on principles related to rest and sleep; as well as common disturbances and factors affecting rest and sleep.

A. Theoretical framework: basis for care
 1. Principles related to rest and sleep (for example: stages of sleep, sleep cycles, sleep requirements and patterns, circadian rhythms)
 2. Factors influencing the patient's rest and sleep
    a. Age/developmental level: infants through older adult (for example: patterns and needs)
    b. Individual preferences and patterns (for example: sleep patterns, lifestyle, changes in work schedule, use of caffeine and alcohol, smoking)
    c. Physical condition (for example: illness, health status, activity level, obesity, nocturia)
    d. Cultural and spiritual/religious practices (for example: co-sleeping)
    e. Socioeconomic (for example: living conditions)
    f. Environmental factors (for example: temperature extremes, ventilation, noise)
    g. Psychological factors (for example: security, anxiety, stress)
    h. Medications (for example: impact of sedatives, narcotics, and diuretics on REM sleep)
 3. Common disturbances in rest and sleep (for example: insomnia, sleep apnea, narcolepsy, sleep deprivation, sleep pattern disturbances)
 4. Theoretical basis for interventions to promote rest and sleep
    a. Medications (for example: sedatives, hypnotics)
    b. Environmental modifications (for example: room temperature, ventilation)

c. Physical modifications (for example: positioning, backrubs, warm milk, elevate head of bed, use of pillows, call light, time scheduled for uninterrupted sleep, noise reduction)
   d. Psychological modifications (for example: distraction, imagery, soft music)
   e. Ethical and legal implications (for example: avoidance of medication for chemical restraints)
   f. Alternative/complementary treatments (for example: therapeutic touch, massage, white noise, music therapy)

B. **Nursing care related to theoretical framework**
   1. Assessment: gather and organize data in relation to the patient's needs for rest and sleep
      a. Obtain patient's history related to rest and sleep (for example: sleep history, sleep diary)
      b. Assess factors influencing the patient's rest and sleep (see VIA2)
      c. Obtain objective data (for example: alteration in vital signs, body position, facial appearance)
      d. Review laboratory and other diagnostic data (for example: electroencephalogram [EEG], electromyogram [EMG], electro-olfactogram [EOG], pulse oximetry)
   2. Analysis: in conjunction with the patient and members of the health care team, synthesize data to identify the patient's actual or potential health problem (nursing diagnosis)
      a. Identify nursing diagnoses (for example: sleep pattern disturbance related to change in environment, fatigue related to altered sleep patterns)
      b. Set priorities (for example: based on the patient's developmental level, based on Maslow's hierarchy of needs, based on optimal use of resources)
   3. Planning: in conjunction with the patient and members of the health care team, formulate specific strategies to achieve the expected outcomes (patient-centered goals)
      a. Establish expected outcomes (patient-centered goals) related to health promotion, health maintenance, and health restoration (for example: patient will demonstrate decreased signs of sleep deprivation, patient will verbalize feeling refreshed after awakening)
      b. Using established nursing standards and protocols, plan nursing measures to help the patient achieve the expected outcomes (patient-centered goals) (for example: reduce environmental distractions such as noise and lighting, position the patient to aid muscle relaxation, provide sleep medications as needed)
      c. Incorporate factors influencing the patient's rest and sleep in planning the patient's care (for example: discourage the use of caffeine prior to bedtime, adhere to a child's usual bedtime routine, apply principles for promoting sleep in older adults) (see VIA2)
      d. Assign patient care activities to other members of the health care team as appropriate (for example: assign nursing assistant to administer backrub to patient before sleep)
   4. Implementation: initiate and complete nursing plans to move the patient toward the expected outcomes (patient-centered goals) related to health promotion, health maintenance, and health restoration

a. Use nursing measures to promote rest and sleep (for example: promote bedtime rituals, encourage voiding before bedtime, administer a backrub, positioning)
b. Administer prescribed medications (for example: schedule administration of medications to avoid nocturnal awakenings)
c. Use nursing measures to modify the environment (for example: eliminate noises, provide soft music, decrease lighting)
d. Provide information and instruction regarding rest and sleep (for example: instruct patient about relaxation techniques, instruct patient about the effects of daily exercise)
e. Use nursing measures to promote continuity of care (for example: teaching, referrals to sleep clinics, community resources)
5. Evaluation: assess the patient's response to nursing care including progress toward the expected outcomes (patient-centered goals)
    a. Record and report the patient's response to nursing actions (for example: changes in sleep patterns, response to medications)
    b. Reassess and revise the patient's plan of care as necessary (for example: modify the outcome, revise the teaching plan)
    c. Determine patient's response to care provided by other members of the health care team (for example: ask the night nurse to describe patient's sleep pattern)

Sample Questions: Nursing Concepts 2

1. Which factor will decrease a patient's blood urea nitrogen (BUN) value?
    1) severe dehydration
    2) urinary obstruction
    3) insufficient protein intake
    4) prolonged immobility

2. Which is a function of vitamin C?
    1) enhancement of calcium metabolism
    2) stimulation of prostaglandin production
    3) promotion of iron absorption
    4) augmentation of the clotting mechanism

3. A patient is receiving an oral iron preparation. What is the most common side effect of this therapy?
    1) fatigue
    2) fever
    3) impairment of fat absorption
    4) indigestion

4. Which meal should the nurse recommend to a 35-year-old patient who has been instructed to consume foods that are high in iron?
    1) tuna sandwich, chocolate pudding, fruit salad, and tea
    2) grilled cheese sandwich, tossed salad, raw apple, and skim milk
    3) omelet, dried apricots, spinach salad, and coffee
    4) hamburger, french fries, fruit cup, and cola

5. Which type of laxative is preferred for the preservation of normal bowel function?
    1) bulk-forming
    2) emollient
    3) saline
    4) stimulant

6. To facilitate the natural flow of fluid during an enema administration, the nurse should place the patient in which position?
    1) dorsal recumbent
    2) left lateral
    3) right sidelying
    4) prone

7. Which clinical manifestation is an early indicator of hypoxia?
    1) bradycardia
    2) cyanosis
    3) hypotension
    4) tachypnea

Sample Questions: Nursing Concepts 2

8. The nurse plans to teach a patient with stress incontinence about the use of absorbent pads. Which goal is appropriate?
   The patient will experience
   1) increased bladder control.
   2) relief from dysuria.
   3) decreased skin irritation.
   4) longer periods between voiding.

9. Which data supports the diagnostic category of activity intolerance?
   1) Patient reports dyspnea on exertion.
   2) Nurse observes flaccid muscles.
   3) Patient's history indicates a lack of exercise.
   4) Family reports that the patient sleeps for long periods.

10. Which nursing measure best decreases the viscosity of a patient's sputum?
    1) Assist the patient to cough productively.
    2) Provide the patient with humidified air.
    3) Provide oral hygiene frequently.
    4) Maintain the patient on bed rest.

11. The physician orders 35% oxygen for a patient. Which device should the nurse use to administer the oxygen?
    1) nasal cannula
    2) non-rebreather mask
    3) simple mask
    4) Venturi mask

12. Which evidence best indicates improved gas exchange in a patient with a respiratory disorder?
    1) Patient is free of infection.
    2) Nail bed color is normal.
    3) Breath sounds are clear.
    4) Blood gas values have stabilized.

13. Which is a major role of sodium in normal body function?
    1) controlling fluid balance
    2) maintaining acid-base balance
    3) metabolizing carbohydrates
    4) regulating enzyme activity

14. Which physiological factor places an infant at higher risk for fluid volume deficit than an adult?
    Infants have a relatively
    1) smaller amount of insensible fluid loss.
    2) lower metabolic rate.
    3) higher serum potassium level.
    4) larger body surface area.

Sample Questions: Nursing Concepts 2

15. Which physiological change that commonly occurs with aging places older adults at risk for fluid imbalances?
    1) decreased percentage of body fluid
    2) increased fluid filtration rate
    3) increased volume of extracellular fluid
    4) decreased viscosity of body fluid

16. Which is a common side effect of loop diuretic therapy?
    1) increased appetite
    2) blurred vision
    3) postural hypotension
    4) interstitial edema

17. When a patient's intravascular fluid volume decreases, the nurse should initially assess for which physiological adaptation?
    1) hypertension
    2) hypoventilation
    3) pyrexia
    4) tachycardia

18. A patient has the following laboratory results: elevated hematocrit and blood urea nitrogen, elevated serum sodium and chloride, and high urine specific gravity. The nurse should further assess the patient for which sign?
    1) crackles in the lung bases
    2) dry, furrowed tongue
    3) high blood pressure
    4) slow, bounding pulse

19. The physician orders 1,000 cc of 5% dextrose in 0.45% sodium chloride every 12 hours. The IV administration set delivers 15 gtt/cc. The intravenous drip rate should be regulated at the rate of how many gtt/min?
    1) 14–15
    2) 20–21
    3) 26–27
    4) 30–31

20. Which observation indicates that the condition of a patient with persistent diarrhea is improving?
    1) increase in bowel sounds
    2) increase in muscle strength
    3) decrease in urinary output
    4) decrease in tissue turgor

21. Which guideline should the nurse follow when carrying a heavy object?
    1) The object should be carried below the center of gravity.
    2) The object should be supported on one shoulder.
    3) The object should weigh no more than 50 percent of body weight.
    4) The object should be held as close to the nurse's body as possible.

Sample Questions: Nursing Concepts 2

22. An increase in fluid intake is essential to decrease the risk of which problem in a patient who is immobile?
    1) atelectasis
    2) orthostatic hypotension
    3) proteinuria
    4) renal calculi

23. Which goal should be included in the plan of care for a patient with a nursing diagnosis of high risk for impaired skin integrity related to immobility?
    The patient will
    1) change position frequently.
    2) drink adequate amounts of fluid.
    3) experience no skin breakdown.
    4) be alert for patches of warm, dry skin.

24. The nurse is discussing the care plan with a patient who has right-sided weakness. The patient asks the nurse why passive range-of-motion exercises will be necessary following discharge. The nurse's response should be based upon which knowledge about passive range-of-motion exercises?
    1) They prevent muscle contractures.
    2) They minimize muscle pain.
    3) They restore joint function to previous levels.
    4) They prevent joint weakness from recurring.

25. Which nursing intervention will help prevent orthostatic hypotension?
    1) Encourage increased dietary intake of calcium and protein.
    2) Perform passive range-of-motion exercises regularly.
    3) Instruct the patient to rise gradually to a standing position.
    4) Elevate the patient's legs when the patient is in bed.

26. What is the theoretical basis for giving a patient a bedtime snack that includes a dairy product, such as warm milk?
    1) to supply the amino acid tryptophan
    2) to promote hormone secretion
    3) to increase body temperature
    4) to decrease the duration of REM sleep

27. Which nursing action should be included in the plan of care for a patient who complains of difficulty sleeping at night?
    1) Encourage the patient to take a warm shower at bedtime.
    2) Provide the patient with a bedtime snack of tea and toast.
    3) Schedule the patient to ambulate just prior to bedtime.
    4) Suggest that the patient try to nap during the day.

Sample Questions: Nursing Concepts 2

28. The nurse has provided care for a patient who has a sleep pattern disturbance. Which patient statement indicates the need to revise the plan of care?
    1) "I sleep long hours on days that I am off from work."
    2) "I fall asleep within thirty minutes of going to bed."
    3) "I use relaxation techniques every night before bedtime."
    4) "I feel less irritable and depressed when I wake up."

Recommended Textbooks

The textbooks you used to prepare for Nursing Concepts 1 should be used for this exam as well. For complete descriptions of these texts, see page 289.

Fundamentals
Kozier, B., Erb, G., Berman, A.J., & Burke, K. (2000). Fundamentals of nursing: Concepts, process and practice *(6th ed.). Upper Saddle River, NJ: Prentice Hall.*

Medical-Surgical Nursing
Smeltzer, S,. & Bare, B. (2000). Brunner and Suddarth's Textbook of medical-surgical nursing *(9th ed.). Philadelphia: Lippincott.*

This textbook makes extensive use of diagrams, charts, tables, colored photographs, and nursing care plans to present information. Each chapter begins with a series of learning objectives and a glossary of terms, then proceeds with a review of the physiology and pathology, clinical manifestations, and nursing management. Each chapter concludes with a critical thinking exercise related to the content presented. Interspersed throughout each chapter are discussions about important considerations on gerontological issues and community-based care. The use of color in chapter readings and tables makes this a very usable reference. Included with the text is a self-study disk that offers several different ways to evaluate your learning.

OR

Monahan, F.D., & Neighbors, M. (1998). Medical-surgical nursing: Foundations for clinical practice *(2nd ed.). Philadelphia: W.B. Saunders*

This textbook presents content in logically paired chapters. The chapters related to nursing's knowledge base begin with a review of the anatomy and physiology of the system affected, then present the clinical manifestations of the various problems. A separate chapter on the nursing care of patients with these conditions is presented. The text uses color to highlight important headings and includes colored diagrams and charts. Tables listing common procedures and patient education highlights are included. Clinical pathways and clinical thinking exercises are also included. A series of questions for review appears at the end of each chapter. A companion guide entitled A practical guide to medical-surgical nursing in the home is available.

Maternal-Newborn Nursing
Dickason, E., Silverman, B.L., & Kaplan, J. (1998). Maternal-infant nursing care *(3rd ed.). St. Louis: Mosby.*

OR
Olds, S., London, M.L., & Ladewig, P (2000). Maternal newborn nursing: A family-centered approach *(6th ed.). Upper Saddle River, NJ: Prentice Hall.*

Nursing Diagnosis
Wilkinson, J.M. (1996). Nursing process: A critical thinking approach *(2nd ed.). Menlo Park, CA: Addison-Wesley.*

Nutrition
Williams, S.R. (1999). Essentials of nutrition and diet therapy *(7th ed.). St. Louis: Mosby.*

> This textbook uses of color in tables, figures and photographs. It is easily readable and presents content in a sound and organized manner. Chapter openers help students focus on the topic covered. Chapter outlines, key terms, and chapter summaries help students identify important content. Each chapter includes questions to focus review of content. An interactive nutrient analysis CD-ROM accompanies the text.

Pediatrics
Wong, D. (1997). Whaley and Wong's Essentials of pediatric nursing *(5th ed.). St. Louis: Mosby.*

Pharmacology
Eisenhauer, L.A., Nichols, L.W., Spencer, R.T., & Bergan, F.W. (1999). Clinical pharmacology & nursing management *(5th ed.). Philadelphia: Lippincott.*

Additional Resources
Metheney, N.M. (1996). Fluid and electrolyte balance: Nursing considerations *(3rd ed.). Philadelphia: Lippincott.*

> This text takes a clear, organized approach to the understanding of fluid and electrolyte balance, placing emphasis on the nursing considerations in assessing and maintaining fluid and electrolyte balance.

Journal Articles

I. Nutrition
Boucher, M.A. (1998). Delegation alert. American Journal of Nursing, 98*(2), 26–32.*

Gants, R. (1997). Detection and correction of underweight problems in nursing home residents. Journal of Gerontological Nursing, 23*(12), 26–31.*

Jones, S.A., & Guenter, P (1997). Automatic flush feeding pumps: A move forward in enteral nutrition. Nursing 97, 27*(2), 56–68.*

Kohn-Keeth, C. (2000). How to keep feeding tubes flowing freely. Nursing 2000, 30*(3), 58–59.*

Loan, T., Magnuson, B., & Williams, S. (1998). Debunking six myths about enteral feeding. Nursing 98, 28*(8), 43–48.*

II. Elimination

<u>Fecal</u>

Benton, J.M., O'Hara, P.A., Chen, H., Harper, D.W., & Johnston, S.F. (1997). Changing bowel hygiene practice successfully: A program to reduce laxative use in chronic care hospitals. Geriatric Nursing, 18*(1), 12–17.*

Dammel, T. (1997). Fecal occult blood testing. Nursing 97. 27*(7), 44–45.*

Dossey, B., & Dossey, L. (1998). Body-mind-spirit: Attending to holistic care. American Journal of Nursing, 98*(8), 35–38.*

Wald, A. (1997). Fecal incontinence: Three steps to successful management. Geriatrics, 52*(7), 44–52.*

Sample Questions: Nursing Concepts 2

<u>Urinary</u>

Catanzaro, J. (1996). Managing incontinence: An update. RN, 59(10), 38–39, 41–45, 47.

Marchiondo, K. (1998). A new look at urinary tract infection. American Journal of Nursing. 98(3), 34–39.

Schakenbach, L. (1997). Consult stat. The proper way to manage a distended bladder. RN, 60(7), 63.

III. Oxygenation

Keegan, L. (1999). Alternative and complementary therapies. Imprint. February/March, 36–38.

Galvin, W.F. and Cusano, A.L. (1998). Making a clean sweep: Using a closed tracheal suction system. Nursing 98, 28(6), 50–51.

Goldy, D. (1998). Circulatory overload secondary to blood transfusion. American Journal of Nursing, 98(7) 33.

IV. Fluid and Electrolytes

Cook, L. (1999). The value of lab values. American Journal of Nursing. 99(5), 66–72.

White, V.M. (1997). Hyperkalemia. American Journal of Nursing. 97(6), 35.

Young, J. (1998). A closer look at IV fluids: Learn how to avoid complications by choosing the right fluid for your patient's condition. Nursing 98, 28(10), 52–55.

V. Activity/Mobility

Jones, J.M., & Jones, K.D. (1997). Healthy people 2000. Promoting physical activity in the senior years. Journal of Gerontological Nursing, 23(7), 41–48.

Schuldenfrei, P. (1998). No heavy lifting. American Journal of Nursing, 98(9), 46–48.

Sobezak, J. (1998). Exercising for better health and mobility. Community Nurse, 4(1), 20–22.

VI. Rest and Sleep

Ancoli-Israel, S. (1997). Sleep problems in older adults: Putting myths to bed. Geriatrics, 52(1), 20–22, 25–26, 28.

Wardell, D., & Mentgen, J. (1999). Healing touch: An energy-based approach to healing. Imprint, February/March, 34–35.

Content/Reference List

I. Nutrition

Kozier et al. (6th edition, 2000)
- Chapter 44 Nutrition
- Chapter 32 Hygiene—section on mouth care
- Chapter 29 Health Assessment (sections on assessing the mouth and oropharynx)

Eisenhauer et al (5th edition, 1998)
- Chapter 49 Oral Nutritional Supplements
- Chapter 48 Parenteral Supplements (sections on total parenteral nutrition and clear solutions only)

Williams (7th edition, 1999)
- Part I Introduction to Human Nutrition (Chap. 1–8)
- Chapter 15 Nutritional Assessment and Therapy in Patient Care
- Chapter 17 Feeding Methods: Enteral and Parenteral Nutrition

Smeltzer & Bare (9th edition, 2000)
- Chapter 5 Health Assessment (section on nutritional assessment only)

Sample Questions: Nursing Concepts 2

Wong (5th edition, 1997)
- Chapter 10   Health Promotion of the Infant and Family (section on promoting optimum health during infancy related to nutrition)
- Chapter 11   Health Problems in Infants (section on nutritional disturbances and feeding difficulties)

II. Elimination

Kosier et al. (6th edition, 2000)
- Chapter 45   Fecal Elimination
- Chapter 46   Urinary Elimination
- Chapter 29   Health Assessment (section on assessing the abdomen only)

Eisenhauer et al (5th edition, 1998)
- Chapter 29   Drugs That Affect the Lower Gastrointestinal Tract
- Chapter 43   Other Antimicrobial Drugs (section on urinary tract anti-infectives)

Smeltzer & Bare (9th edition, 2000)
- Chapter 10   Principles and Practices of Rehabilitation (section on the nursing process with altered elimination patterns)
- Chapter 11   Health Care of the Older Adult (section on genitourinary and gastrointestinal systems)

III. Oxygenation

Kozier et al. (6th edition, 2000)
- Chapter 47   Oxygenation
- Chapter 29   Health Assessment (section on assessing the thorax and lungs)
- Chapter 48   Fluid, Electrolyte and Acid-Base Balance (section on blood transfusions)
- Chapter 33   Medications (section on respiratory inhalation—using metered dose inhaler)

Smeltzer & Bare (9th edition, 2000)
- Chapter 19   Assessment of Respiratory Function
- Chapter 11   Health Care of the Older Adult (section on body system changes—cardiovascular system, respiratory system)

IV. Fluid and Electrolyte Balance

Kozier et al. (6th edition, 2000)
- Chapter 48   Fluid and Electrolyte and Acid-Base Balance

Eisenhauer et al (5th edition, 1998)
- Chapter 48   Parenteral Fluids
- Chapter 49   Oral Nutritional Supplements (minerals only)

Williams (7th edition, 1999)
- Chapter 8   Minerals

Smeltzer & Bare (9th edition, 2000)
- Chapter 13   Fluids and Electrolytes: Balance and Disturbances

Monahan and Neighbors (2nd edition, 1998)
- Chapter 5   Knowledge Base for Patients with Fluids, Electrolyte, and Acid-Base Imbalances

V. Activity/Mobility

Kozier et al. (6th edition, 2000)
- Chapter 41   Activity and Exercise
- Chapter 29   Health Assessment (section on assessing the musculoskeletal system)

Sample Questions: Nursing Concepts 2

Eisenhauer et al. (5th edition, 1998)
    Chapter 38   Drugs that Affect the Musculoskeletal System (sections on drugs that relax skeletal muscles and treat spasticity

Monahan & Neighbors (2nd edition, 1998)
    Chapter 19   Knowledge Base for Patients with Musculoskeletal Dysfunction (section on assessment of musculoskeletal system only)

Smeltzer & Bare (9th edition, 2000)
    Chapter 10   Principles and Practices of Rehabilitation (section on patient with impaired physical mobility)
    Chapter 11   Health Care of the Older Adult (section on body system changes and health promotion activities related to musculoskeletal system)

Williams (7th edition, 1999)
    Chapter 13   Nutrition for Adults: Early, Middle and Later Years (section on aging process and nutritional needs of elderly persons).

VI. Rest and Sleep

Kozier et al. (6th edition, 2000)
    Chapter 42   Rest and Sleep
    Chapter 15   Holistic Healing Modalities

Eisenhauer et al. (5th edition, 1998)
    Chapter 18   Drugs that Depress the Central Nervous System (section on sedative-hypnotic drugs only)

Monahan and Neighbors (2nd edition, 1998)
    Chapter 4   Special Considerations for Nursing Care of Elderly Patients (section on sleep patterns)

Smeltzer & Bare (9th edition, 2000)
    Chapter 10   Principles and Practices of Rehabilitation (section on coping with fatigue)

Study Guide
Nursing Concepts 3 (Associate Level)

Credit Hours: 4 **Credit Level:** Lower
Question Type(s): Multiple-choice

The information in this study guide becomes valid on October 1, 2000. See page 261 for information on the Nursing Concepts examination series.

Description of the Examination

This examination measures knowledge and understanding of concepts of nursing care and related nursing actions common to all patients throughout the life cycle, regardless of the health status of the patient. Questions concern nursing problems frequently encountered by the associate degree nurse. Questions are based on the needs of the patient of various age groups and the nursing care actions properly associated with them.

The examination requires students to possess the technical vocabulary and have the knowledge of anatomy and physiology, psychosocial and physical development, and microbiology generally expected of the associate degree nurse. The examination requires students to demonstrate knowledge of the nursing theoretical framework for each content area as well as the ability to apply this knowledge to nursing practice using the nursing process. In addition, students are required to use critical thinking skills to apply principles, concepts, and theories from the natural and social sciences and the humanities to the practice of nursing.

Content Outline

Content Area	Percent of Examination
I. Comfort and Pain	10%
II. Human Sexuality	10%
III. Cultural Diversity	10%
IV. Chronic Illness	10%
V. Community-Based Nursing	15%
VI. Needs of the Childbearing Family	25%
VII. Sensory Impairments	10%
VIII. Reproductive Disorders	10%
Total	**100%**

Emphasis
>   I. Theoretical Framework—Basis for Care   34%
>   II. Nursing Care Related to Theoretical Framework   66%
>   100%

I. Comfort and Pain (10%)

This area focuses on principles related to management of patients' comfort and pain across the life span. Emphasis is placed on the various components of comfort and pain management including pharmacological and nonpharmacological techniques.

A. Theoretical framework: basis for care
1. Types of pain (for example: acute vs. chronic, procedural, postoperative) Characteristics (for example: duration, intensity, onset, location)
2. Physiology of pain: Gate control theory, pain threshold, neuromodulators of pain (for example: endorphins, enkephalins)
3. Psychology of pain
    a. Cognitive factors (for example: time-limited pain)
    b. Emotional factors (for example: anxiety increases pain, pain threshold, pain tolerance)
    c. Myths about pain (for example: pain is part of aging, pain is part of a hysterical personality, people with chronic pain have hypochondriasis, infants don't feel pain, lack of complaint means pain free)
4. Suffering (for example: intractable pain, persistent pain)
5. Principles related to the management of comfort and pain (for example: treat before pain becomes severe, use a combination of non-pharmacological and pharmacological approaches, anticipate the need for pain management, administer analgesics around the clock rather than as needed)
6. Factors influencing patient's comfort and pain
    a. Sex (for example: differences in ways of expressing pain)
    b. Age/Developmental level: neonate through older adults (for example: use age-appropriate pain scales, age-related neurological and cognitive changes, age-related approaches to pain management; recognize patient's inability to verbalize pain)
    c. Individual preferences and patterns (for example: pain relief practices, self-management of pain, past pain experiences)
    d. Physical condition (for example: length of illness, ability to self-manage pain, debilitation, fatigue)
    e. Cultural and spiritual/religious beliefs (for example: stoicism, ceremonies, rituals, meaning of pain, prayer and meditation)
    f. Socioeconomic factors (for example: lack of transportation, costs of medication and equipment, lack of health insurance)
    g. Environmental factors (for example: presence of stairs, seasonal changes, time of day, temperature)
    h. Psychological factors (for example: depression, isolation, powerlessness, anxiety, fear of addiction)
    i. Alternative/complementary treatments (for example: acupuncture, massage, hydrotherapy, aromatherapy, therapeutic touch, humor)
7. Theoretical basis for interventions to promote comfort and relieve pain
    a. Physical modifications (for example: massage, pressure, positioning,

backrubs, warm milk, heat or cold, exercise, elevate head of bed, use of pillows, transcutaneous electric nerve stimulation [TENS], time for uninterrupted sleep)
- b. Environmental modifications (for example: assistive devices, room temperature, ventilation, noise reduction)
- c. Psychological modifications (for example: distraction, relaxation techniques, guided imagery, cognitive behavioral therapies, biofeedback, meditation)
- d. Medications (for example: narcotic and non-narcotic analgesics, sedatives, hypnotics, antidepressants, topicals, World Health Organization [WHO] 3-step ladder approach, nonsteroidal anti-inflammatory medications)
- e. Research findings (for example: music therapy, nurse's bias related to use of pain medications, distraction, postoperative analgesia administration)
- f. Ethical and legal implications (for example: marijuana use, terminal illness and use of narcotics, use of placebos, withholding medications during surgical procedures in neonates)

B. Nursing care related to theoretical framework
1. Roles of the nurse in pain management (for example: provider of care, manager of care, teacher, patient advocate)
2. Assessment: gather and organize data in relation to the patient's comfort and pain
   a. Obtain information about the patient's history related to comfort and pain (for example: verbalization of pain level, pain relief measures, the effects of pain on daily living, past experiences with pain)
   b. Assess factors influencing the patient's comfort and pain (see IA1, IA3, IA4, IA5, IA6, and IA7)
   c. Obtain physical data (for example: vital signs; body position; facial expressions; onset, intensity, duration and location of pain; rate pain on pain scale)
3. Analysis: in conjunction with the patient and members of the health care team, synthesize data to identify the patient's actual or potential health problem (nursing diagnosis)
   a. Identify nursing diagnoses (for example: chronic pain related to reduced blood supply to tissues, potential for injury related to the side effects of medication, knowledge deficit related to lack of information on pain relief measures, acute pain related to physical injury, sleep pattern disturbance related to change in environment, fatigue related to sleep disturbances)
   b. Set priorities (for example: based on the patient's developmental level, based on sociocultural considerations, based on Maslow's hierarchy of needs, based on individual preference, based on optimal use of resources)
4. Planning: in conjunction with the patient and members of the health care team, determine expected outcomes (patient-centered goals) and formulate specific strategies to achieve the expected outcomes
   a. Establish expected outcomes (patient-centered goals) related to health promotion, health maintenance, and health restoration (for example: patient reports pain level has been decreased to a 3 on a 10-point scale, patient describes positive effects of guided imagery as evidenced by decreased need for medication, patient sleeps 7 hours each night)

b. Plan nursing measures on the basis of established standards and priorities to help the patient achieve the expected outcomes (patient-centered goals) (for example: use measures to relieve pain such as backrub, distraction, and repositioning; administer analgesics as ordered; reduce environmental distractions such as noise and lighting; apply World Health Organization [WHO] 3-step ladder approach to promote pain relief; comply with the patient's pain bill of rights; comply with the Agency for Health Care Policy and Research [AHCPR] management of pain guidelines)
   c. Incorporate factors influencing the patient's comfort and pain in planning the patient's care (for example: consider the patient's usual pain relief measures, consider the patient's cultural and spiritual/religious response to pain) (see IA3, IA5, IA6, and IA7)
   d. Assign patient care activities to other members of the health care team as appropriate (for example: assign nursing assistant to distract patient who is in pain, assign nursing assistant to assist other team members to reposition the patient with acute pain)
5. Implementation: initiate and complete nursing plans designed to move the patient toward the expected outcomes (patient-centered goals) related to health promotion, health maintenance, and health restoration
   a. Use nursing measures to promote comfort and reduce pain (for example: administering a backrub, use of heat or cold, positioning, active listening, following standard protocols, distraction techniques, guided imagery)
   b. Administer prescribed medications (for example: administer pain medication before the pain becomes severe, schedule administration of medications to avoid nocturnal awakenings, schedule pain medication prior to ambulation, consider dosage modifications and drug selection related to the patient's age)
   c. Use technology to moderate pain (for example: transcutaneous electrical nerve stimulation [TENS], nebulizers, patient-controlled analgesia [PCA] pumps, continuous subcutaneous infusion, peripherally inserted central catheter [PIC] lines)
   d. Use nursing measures to modify the environment (for example: eliminate noises, provide music, decrease lighting, eliminate odors, control temperature, provide the appropriate assistive devices)
   e. Use nursing measures to promote safety (for example: use side rails when patient is sedated, teach patient not to operate machinery while on pain medication, position patient to maintain airway)
   f. Provide information and instruction regarding comfort and pain relief to patient and significant others (for example: instruct patient about relaxation techniques, instruct patient regarding use of patient-controlled analgesia [PCA], instruct patient in use of transcutaneous electrical nerve stimulation [TENS], modify lifestyle to accommodate pain relief measures)
   g. Use nursing resources to promote continuity of care (for example: teaching, referrals, support groups, community resources, pain clinics, American Chronic Pain Association, the American Pain Society)
   h. Provide information on patient's pain and ability to manage to physicians and other members of the health care team (for example: patient's need for adjustment in medication, method used to manage pain)

6. Evaluation: assess the patient's response to nursing care including progress toward the expected outcomes (patient-centered goals)
   a. Document assessment findings in response to interventions (for example: chart effectiveness of pain intervention, use of pain flow sheets, changes in vital signs, record patient's rating on pain scale)
   b. Assess and report the patient's response to actions taken to reduce pain (for example: increased activity after application of heat or cold, statements of pain relief after analgesic administration)
   c. Reassess and revise the patient's plan of care as necessary (for example: encourage the patient to request a change in pain medication, revise the teaching plan to include guided imagery when patient does not want to use medications, collaborate with physician on analgesic prescription and administration protocol)
   d. Determine the patient's response to care provided by other members of the health care team (for example: ask nursing assistant to report if ambulation has improved after pain interventions)

II. Human Sexuality (10%)

This area focuses on the understanding of human sexuality as an aspect of holistic health care. Emphasis is placed on the various components of human sexuality as they effect and are affected by illness.

A. Theoretical framework: basis for care
1. Sexuality (definition)—The physical, emotional, and sociocultural factors that affect sexual response.
   a. Developmental factors (for example: fale genitalia, breasts, menstrual cycle, menopause; male genitalia, ejaculation, and male menopause; age-related changes such as slower sexual arousal, enlarged prostate, decreased fertility, side effects of medications and illness)
   b. Learning of gender roles (for example: female may stay at home to rear children and care for household, male may be the provider of money to support family. In the U.S., role reversal is more common today.)
   c. Sociocultural factors (for example: women are taught to tolerate sex, women are encouraged to participate in sex, sexual modesty is valued, incest is taboo, women work in nontraditional jobs)
   d. Preferences (for example: contraception; reproductive choice; sex only after marriage; sexual orientation including heterosexual, homosexual, bisexual, and transsexual)
   e. Sexual activity (for example: masturbation; sexual intercourse; oral-genital stimulation; fantasy; stimulation of erogenous zones including lips, ears, skin, thighs, and breasts; celibacy)
   f. Cultural/Religious beliefs (for example: contraception, termination of pregnancy, monogamous relationship, only female-male coitus is acceptable, no premarital intercourse, modesty, privacy, clothing choices, patterns of touching)
   g. Sexual response cycle
      1) Excitement (for example: increased heart rate and blood pressure, flushed skin, increased blood flow to the genitals)

2) Plateau (for example: "sex flush," vasocongestion of the vagina, secretion from Cowper's glands in the male, increase in length and diameter of the penis)
3) Orgasm (for example: involuntary spasmodic contractions of the genitals, decreased muscular control of arms and legs, altered level of consciousness)
4) Resolution (for example: relaxation, fatigue, fulfillment)
2. Sexual dysfunction
   a. Gender-specific problems (for example: women—orgasmic dysfunction, dyspareunia, vaginismus, dryness and decreased elasticity of tissues with menopause; men—impotence, slower arousal, fewer spontaneous erections, premature ejaculation, lessened orgasmic intensity)
   b. Age-related changes (for example: chronic diseases, decreased mobility, body image, medications)
3. Sexually transmitted diseases
   a. Prevention of sexually transmitted diseases (for example: use of condom, abstinence, testing for HIV infection)
   b. Impact of sexually transmitted diseases on sexuality (for example: infertility, cervical carcinoma)
4. Theoretical basis for interventions related to human sexuality
   a. Physical manifestations (for example: sexual ambiguity, sexual changes in aging, genetics)
   b. Environmental modifications (for example: need for privacy in discussion of sexual concerns)
   c. Alternative/complimentary therapy (for example: use of massage for sexual stimulation)
   d. Psychological manifestions (for example: sexual orientation, comfort with touch)
   e. Safety (for example: following safe sex practices, use of birth control measures, methods to minimize rape/sexual assault)
   f. Medications (for example: effects of antianxiety agents, antihypertensives, and anti-arrhythmics on sexual response; Viagra; vaginal lubricants)
   g. Research findings (for example: research on the patient's preference for nurse to initiate discussion on sexual concerns, patient preference for birth control methods, effective teaching of safe sex practices)
   h. Ethical and legal implications (for example: teenage access to birth control measures, sex education in schools, access to rape counseling)
   i. Contraception (for example: types of birth control, rationale for use, complications of various methods)

B. **Nursing care related to theoretical framework**
   1. Roles of the nurse in human sexuality (for example: provider of care, manager of care, teacher, patient advocate)
   2. Assessment is the process of gathering and organizing data in relation to the patient's health status.
      a. Obtain the patient's history
         1) Health history (for example: acute or chronic illness, medications, frequency of physical exams, urinary function, lumps, discharge)

2) Conduct an interview on sexual activity (for example: reproductive history, sexual role performance and functioning, sexual identity, birth control practices, family planning measures)
   3) Identify sexual self-care behaviors (for example: breast self-examination [BSE], testicular self-examination [TSE], Pap smear, mammogram)
  b. Assess factors influencing the patient's sexual history (for example: age of onset of sexual maturity, religion, culture, educational level, socioeconomic status)
  c. Obtain objective data (for example: results of Pap smear, mammogram, hormone levels, cultures of discharge, blood tests for sexually transmitted diseases, PSA levels)
  d. Identify inappropriate sexual behaviors
   1) Sexual harassment (for example: unwanted verbal or physical advance, or sexually explicit language)
   2) Sexual abuse (for example: incest, sexual assault or rape of a child or adult)
   3) Sexually acting out (for example: in residential settings)
  e. Review laboratory and other diagnostic data (for example: cultures; blood tests for Venereal Disease Research Laboratory [VDRL], human immunodeficiency virus [HIV], hepatitis B)
3. Analysis: in conjunction with the patient and members of the health care team, synthesize data to identify the patient's actual or potential health problem (nursing diagnosis)
  a. Identify nursing diagnoses (for example: altered sexuality pattern related to fear of pregnancy, anxiety related to loss of sexual functioning, fear related to history of sexual abuse, knowledge deficit related to self-care behaviors, pain related to dyspareunia)
  b. Set priorities (for example: based on the patient's developmental level, based on sociocultural needs, based on Maslow's hierarchy of needs, based on optimal use of resources)
  c. Establish expected outcomes (patient-centered goals) related to health promotion, health maintenance, and health restoration (for example: patient's anxiety will decrease after learning alternative sexual activities, patient will be less fearful after receiving psychological and sexual counseling, patient will demonstrate correct breast self-examination [BSE] and health restoration (for example: patient's anxiety will decrease after learning alternative sexual activities, patient will be less fearful after receiving psychological and sexual counseling, patient will demonstrate correct breast self-examination [BSE] procedures, patient will increase comfort level by using different positions during sexual activity)
4. Planning is the process of determining the expected outcomes (patient-centered goals) and formulating specific strategies to achieve the expected outcomes.
  a. Using established nursing standards and protocols, plan nursing measures to help the patient (for example: open patterns of communication with patient, Rape Protocols, safe-sex practices, sex education in schools)
  b. Consider factors influencing the patient's willingness to work with the health care team (for example: lifestyle, culture, religion, mobility)

c. Incorporate factors influencing the patient's willingness to work with the health care team (for example: encourage participation of the significant other, identify resources for the patient such as free or low-cost clinics, maintain privacy of the hospitalized patient, ask health care provider to decrease dose or change medications which may influence sexual response)
   d. Assign patient care activities to other members of the health care team as appropriate (for example: assign patient translator, assign nursing care assistant to report nursing home resident's inappropriate behavior)
5. Implementation: initiate and complete nursing plans designed to move the patient toward the expected outcomes (patient-centered goals) related to health promotion, health maintenance, and health restoration
   a. Use nursing measures to establish a collaborative relationship with the patient (for example: use therapeutic communication skills, identify cultural and individual differences, establish expectations with the patient)
   b. Provide information and instructions regarding self-care behaviors (for example: breast self-examination [BSE], testicular self-examination [TSE], hygiene, provide information and instruction on family planning)
   c. Provide information to correct sexual myths (for example: each person is born with a certain amount of sexual desire, sexual abstinence is necessary for sports training, excessive sexual activity can lead to mental illness, and women should not enjoy sexual activity as much as men)
   d. Use nursing measures to promote continuity of care (for example: teach about American Association of Sex Educators, Women's Health Watch, National Child Abuse Hotline, National Coalition Against Sexual Assault)
6. Evaluation: assess the patient's response to nursing care, including progress toward the expected outcomes (patient-centered goals)
   a. Document and report the patient's response to nursing actions (for example: decreased anxiety, improved level of comfort, understanding of self-care behaviors)
   b. Reassess and revise the patient's plan of care (for example: need to change dose of antihypertensive medication, need for additional counseling, patient's response to post-rape care)
   c. Determine the patient's response to care provided by other members of the health care team (for example: patient understands written information provided by the translator, nursing assistant reports that resident demonstrates less inappropriate sexual behavior)

III. Cultural Diversity (10%)

This area focuses on understanding the impact of the patient's culture on the patient's response to health, illness, care, and the caregivers. This section will focus primarily on the five largest cultural groups in the U.S. today: European Americans, African Americans, Hispanic Americans (Latinas/Latinos), Asian Americans, and Native Americans. Examples of cultural beliefs and practices listed reflect traditional values of the culture. The nurse is responsible for ascertaining the importance of these values to individual patients and their families.

A. Theoretical framework: basis for care
   1. Cultural definitions: culture, cultural diversity, and cultural competency
      a. Culture is the way people of a group see the world based on a set of

values, beliefs, patterns of behavior, customs, traditions, and language. It is learned and passed from generation to generation.
  b. Cultural diversity is the differences among people of different population groups.
  c. Cultural competency is the ability to recognize and respect cultural differences. It includes an understanding of how culturally based beliefs, values, and attitudes influence one's perception of wellness, illness, and health care. The nurse demonstrates cultural competence by incorporating these cultural beliefs and practices into treatment plans and patient care.
2. Cultural considerations
  a. Ethnicity based on common heritage (for example: same religious practices, political interests, folklore, language and dialect, and employment patterns)
  b. Race based on specific physical characteristics (for example: skin pigmentation, facial features, and hair texture)
3. Cultural diversity concerns
  a. Stereotyping (for example: all older adults are senile, men never cry, Germans are stoic)
  b. Gender-specific issues (for example: many African Americans and European Americans identify the female as the main decision maker and dominant figure in the family, many Arab Americans identify the male as the dominant figure in the family)
  c. Language and communication (for example: patients who do not speak English, avoiding eye contact or direct eye contact, need for an interpreter)
  d. Socioeconomic factors (for example: poverty, lack of health care, homelessness, poor nutrition, immigration)
  e. Age-related perspectives (for example: Asian Americans and Native Americans respect older adults and view them as symbolic leaders, Hawaiians have a hierarchical family structure, the increasing incidence of elder abuse in the United States)
  f. Time orientation (for example: for many Native Americans, time is present oriented; for many African Americans, time orientation is not strict)
  g. Personal space (for example: many African Americans stand and sit close when communicating, many Asian Americans and European Americans place distance between self and others when communicating)
  h. Food and nutrition (for example: rice and vegetables are staples of Asian American diets; many Native Americans and Hispanic Americans eat two meals a day; Jews, Muslims, and Seventh Day Adventists do not eat pork)
  i. Health care (for example: many European American cultures believe that illness has a known cause that can be treated or cured; many other cultures believe that illness has a supernatural cause, illness is a punishment, and that illness occurs when the body's equilibrium is disturbed; many cultures have greater reliance on folk or faith healers, folk remedies)
4. Theoretical basis for intervention related to cultural diversity
  a. Physical manifestations (for example: common physical characteristics, language and ancestry; use of charms and amulets to protect against evil spirits, wearing religious articles such as medals by Hispanic Americans; use of meditation, exercise to maintain balance by Asian Americans; use of medicine man or woman by Native Americans)

    b. Environmental (for example: the patient, family, and community are part of the healing model for some African Americans; use of traditional healing practices such as voodoo practitioners; Native Americans' perception of time may be different)
    c. Psychological (for example: illness may be seen as a state of disharmony that results from natural causes by African Americans; wellness may be viewed as a reward for good behavior by Hispanic Americans; maintenance of balance between hot and cold is characteristic of the naturalistic belief system of some Hispanic Americans; illness is thought to be caused by an imbalance between yin and yang by many Asian Americans; Native Americans may believe that health depends on maintenance of equilibrium among the body, mind, and environment)
    d. Research (for example: Leininger's theory "Culture Case Diversity and Universality"; personal space requirements of various cultural groups; perceived resistance due to cultural differences; response of native peoples from oral traditions to written materials)
    e. Healthy practices (for example: use of traditional herbal remedies only; combined use of ritual and prayer and herbal remedies; Asians may require lower doses of certain drugs to achieve therapeutic serum blood levels)
    f. Food preferences (for example: Hispanic American classification of hot and cold foods; use of herbs, religious dietary practices)

B. Nursing care related to theoretical framework
  1. Roles of the nurse in cultural diversity (for example: provider of care, manager of care, teacher, patient advocate)
  2. Assessment: gather and organize data in relation to the patient's health status
    a. Obtain the patient's health history including a cultural assessment (for example: patient's beliefs about the cause of illness—germ theory, spirits, curses, and punishments)
    b. Assess cultural factors influencing the patient's health status (for example: nutrition including ethnic foods, key family members are involved in health care decisions, healing systems, health habits, lifestyle risks, religious rites, talisman, religious restrictions)
    c. Obtain objective data (for example: cultural preferences during physical assessment including female-male relationships, limiting body exposure; patient who wears amulet, patient with cupping marks)
    d. Review laboratory and other diagnostic data (for example: sickle-cell anemia and hypertension in African Americans, lactose enzyme deficiency and diabetes mellitus in Hispanic Americans, alcoholism and communicable diseases in Native Americans, and cardiovascular and gastrointestinal diseases in European Americans)
  3. Analysis: in conjunction with the patient and members of the health care team, synthesize data to identify the patient's actual or potential health problems (nursing diagnosis)
    a. Identify nursing diagnoses (for example: impaired verbal communication related to shyness about cultural differences, spiritual distress related to inability to participate in culturally based rituals, ineffective management of therapeutic regime related to mistrust of health care providers, powerlessness related to health care provider's inability to understand

significance of dietary and religious beliefs)
- b. Set priorities (for example: based on cultural, social, and religious needs, optimal use of resources, developmental level, and Maslow's hierarchy of needs)
4. Planning: in conjunction with the patient and members of the health care team, determine the expected outcomes (patient-centered goals) and formulate specific strategies to achieve the expected outcomes
   - a. Establish expected outcomes (patient-centered goals) related to health promotion, health maintenance, and health restoration (for example: the patient will communicate effectively with the health care team with the use of an interpreter, patient will report enhanced spiritual well-being when use of a spiritual counselor is incorporated into patient care, the patient will identify traditional folk remedies that may be incorporated into the plan of care, the patient will explain important religious and dietary needs to the health care team)
   - b. Use established nursing standards and protocols, plan nursing measures to help the patient (for example: cultural assessment, holistic health care, health risk appraisal)
   - c. Consider cultural factors influencing the patient's plan of care (for example: dietary needs, rituals, spiritual advisors, birth attendants, death attendants)
   - d. Assign patient care activities to other members of the health care team, as appropriate (for example: encourage spiritual advisors to participate in health care decisions, provide privacy for practice of rituals and prayer, involve the dietitian in meeting special needs)
5. Implementation: initiate and complete nursing plans designed to move the patient toward the expected outcomes (patient-centered goals) related to health promotion, health maintenance, and health restoration
   - a. Use nursing measures to establish a collaborative relationship with the patient (for example: respect cultural and individual differences, define expectations with the patient, use an interpreter to facilitate communication)
   - b. Use nursing measures to enhance patient compliance with the health care team (for example: introduce patient and family to hospital staff and volunteers who are from the same culture, ethnic group, religion; incorporate cultural practices into care as appropriate)
   - c. Provide information and instruction regarding health promotion, maintenance, and restoration (for example: impact of dietary practices on healing; interaction of herbal remedies and prescribed medications, develop plan for medication administration that does not interfere with religious practices)
   - d. Use nursing measures to promote continuity of care (for example: referrals of patient and staff to the World Health Organization [WHO], International Council of Nurses, community support groups, and resources such as sources for ethnic foods)
6. Evaluation: assess the patient's response to nursing care including progress toward the expected outcomes (patient-centered goals)
   - a. Document and report the patient's response to nursing actions (for example: the patient communicates understanding of treatment plan, the

patient and family are compliant with the treatment plan, the patient has improved nutritional intake)
   b. Reassess and revise the patient's plan of care (for example: use visiting nurse for follow-up care, encourage family to bring food from home)
   c. Determine the patient's response to care provided by other members of the health care team (for example: patient's nutritional status improved, patient's spiritual needs are met)

IV. Chronic Illness (10%)

This area focuses on the concept of chronicity and the impact of chronic illness on the patient, family, and community. Chronic illness affects patients across the life span and is characterized by periods of exacerbations and remissions.

A. Theoretical framework: basis for care
   1. Principles related to chronic illness
      a. Chronic illness trajectory (for example: duration, direction and movement, predictability, shape)
      b. Comparison of acute/chronic illness (for example: incidence, prevalence, duration, exacerbations and remissions)
      c. Adjustment patterns in chronic illness (for example: acceptance of illness, stigma, socialization, use of coping skills and resources)
      d. Disability issues (for example: access to health care, discrimination, environmental barriers, correct use of terminology such as person with a disability rather than disabled person)
   2. Common problems associated with chronic illness
      a. Decreased self-care capacity (for example: patient with hemiplegia, patient with physical limitations, patient experiencing fatigue)
      b. Deterioration and decline of health (for example: patient with progressive oxygenation deficit, patient with progressive neurological disorders)
      c. Issues of quality of life (for example: sexual activity, inability to enjoy life, financial inability to maintain adequate self care)
      d. Family/caregiver dimensions of chronic illness (for example: caregiver fatigue, lack of caregiver)
   3. Factors influencing the patient's adjustment to chronic illness
      a. Sex (for example: caregiver expectations and gender roles)
      b. Age/Developmental level: infants through older adults (for example: child with a disability adapts to limitations of the disability easier than an adult who experiences a loss of ability)
      c. Individual preferences and patterns (for example: family response patterns, relationship with health care providers, marriage and family planning)
      d. Physical condition (for example: pain, fatigue, decreased self-care ability, deconditioning)
      e. Cultural and spiritual/religious beliefs (for example: use of religious ritual healing as a belief pattern; cultural interpretation of quality of life; cultural expectation of family members; cultural responses to chronic illness)
      f. Socioeconomic factors (for example: unemployment, low income level, cost of equipment and supplies, family resources, availability of health insurance)

g. Environmental factors (for example: timing as a care factor, environmental barriers, transportation, occupational hazards, the home setting, availability of respite care)
h. Psychological factors (for example: emotional balance, denial, anger, depression, regression, stigma, normalization, dissociation, overcompensation, learned helplessness)
i. Alternative/complementary treatments (for example: massage, stress reduction via biofeedback, herbal medications such as gingko for cognitive loss)
4. Theoretical basis for interventions related to chronic illness
   a. Environmental modifications (for example: durable medical equipment, housing modifications, access ramps)
   b. Safety instruction (for example: functional alterations in activities of daily living, instrumental activities for daily living)
   c. Medications/topical agents (for example: use of chronic pain medications, complex medication routines and issues of compliance, polypharmacy)
   d. Safety devices (for example: electronic openers, light clappers, upper mobility braces, automatic lifts, use of call systems)
   e. Ethical and legal implications (for example: impact of American with Disabilities Act, caregiver legitimacy, medical fraud, guardianship, Developmental Disabilities Act, advanced directives, do-not-resuscitate [DNR] orders)

B. **Nursing care related to theoretical framework**
   1. Role of nurse in caring for the patient who is chronically ill (for example: provider of care, manager of care, teacher, patient advocate)
   2. Assessment: gather and organize data in relation to the patient's chronic illness
      a. Determine the presence of functional ability related to activities of daily living, instrumental activities of daily living, and cognitive ability (for example: cognitive loss as determined by mental status testing, limited upper mobility function as determined by ADL assessment)
      b. Identify patients at risk for physical injury (for example: confused mental state, sensory deficit, weakened physical state)
      c. Determine the patient's position on the chronic illness trajectory (for example: adjustment to chronic illness, body image, self-care, emotional balance, uncertain future)
      d. Assess environmental factors that influence the patient's chronic illness (for example: home and community access, adaptive equipment access, support systems, family response patterns, caregiver and patient's response to health care workers, health care system access, caregiver strain)
   3. Analysis: in conjunction with the patient and members of the health care team, synthesize data to identify the patient's actual or potential health problems (nursing diagnosis)
      a. Identify nursing diagnoses (for example: caregiver role strain related to 24-hour care responsibility, feeding self-care deficit related to confusion, health maintenance impaired related to decreased mobility, home maintenance management impaired related to lack of motivation)
      b. Set priorities (for example: based on the patient's self-care capacity, based on quality of life, based on access to health care and use of resources)

4. Planning: in conjunction with the patient and members of the health care team, formulate specific strategies to achieve the expected outcomes
    a. Establish expected outcomes (patient-centered goals) for care related to health promotion, health maintenance, and health restoration (for example: patient will verbalize factors that alter chronic pain, caregiver will state plan for respite, patient will identify environmental modifications that will allow for home maintenance behaviors)
    b. Using established nursing standards and protocols, plan nursing measures to help the patient achieve the expected outcomes (patient-centered goals) (for example: monitor patient's rest and activity pattern, refer patient with cognitive impairments to day care, help patient develop a realistic plan for daily activities)
    c. Incorporate factors influencing the patient's environmental safety in planning the patient's care (for example: check equipment for correct function, monitor the patient for cognitive loss, install safety equipment such as handrails on tubs)
    d. Assign patient care activities to other members of the health care team, as appropriate (for example: instruct the home health aide to report changes in the patient's ability to meet activities of daily living)
5. Implementation: carry out nursing plans designed to move the patient toward the expected outcomes related to health promotion, health maintenance, and health restoration
    a. Use nursing measures to establish a collaborative relationship with the patient (for example: use therapeutic communication to discuss patient's attitudes towards receiving help, identify with the patient goals for dealing with presenting symptom)
    b. Use nursing measures to structure an environment conducive to safety (for example: suggest the placement of furniture in an uncluttered arrangement, assist family in organizing care routines and obtaining equipment, discuss patient's plan for prioritizing self-care needs)
    c. Use nursing measures to promote the resolution of the patient's chronic illness (for example: suggest caregiver support group, guide caregiver through a process of anticipating unpredictable situations)
    d. Use nursing measures appropriate to particular safety needs (for example: check caregiver for correct use of turning schedule, assess patient for deconditioning after exacerbation, monitor patient for depression and potential for self-violence)
    e. Use safety devices properly (for example: use mobilizing devices correctly, assess caregiver ability to set ventilator settings)
    f. Use measures to safely administer medications (for example: assess patient for polypharmacy, set-up weekly medication administration system, teach caregiver to give g-tube medications correctly)
    g. Provide information and instruction regarding chronic illness (for example: encourage patient to attend self-help classes, encourage caregiver to allow patient to perform self-care)
    h. Use nursing measures to promote continuity of care (for example: teaching, referrals, support groups, community resources, obtain listings of subacute facilities in patient's location, refer to self-help groups, advocate for the rights of patients with disabilities)

6. Evaluation: appraise the effectiveness of the nursing interventions relative to the nursing diagnosis and the expected outcomes
   a. Record and report the patient and caregiver's response to nursing actions (for example: patient maintains organized system of care, patient and caregiver stay connected to health care system, patient has less frequent self-reported distressing life events, patient reports increased control over life events)
   b. Reassess and revise the patient's plan of care as necessary (for example: caregiver assumes more decision making as patient's cognitive loss increases, patient revises rest/activity cycle during acute exacerbation)
   c. Determine the patient's response to care provided by other members of the health care team (for example: observe the caregiver perform g-tube flush, determine the caregiver's understanding of medication protocol)

V. Community-based Nursing (15%)

This area focuses on community-based nursing practice. The community is a group, population, or cluster of people with at least one common characteristic (for example: geographic location, occupation, ethnicity, housing condition, shared interests, or work toward common goals.) Community-based nursing focuses on the care of individuals, families, or groups and is designed to increase patient self-care ability and enhance patient decision making. Community-based nursing care is provided in the setting where the patient lives, works, plays, or studies.

A. Theoretical framework: basis for care
   1. Defining community, community based care, home care, nurse's role in community settings
      a. Patient focus (for example: individuals, groups, families, populations at risk)
      b. Levels of prevention (for example: primary, secondary, tertiary)
      c. Practice settings (for example: home, ambulatory care, schools, correctional facilities, residential settings, occupational work sites, shelters, the street)
      d. Dimensions of community (for example: location, population, social system)
      e. Healthy community (for example: definition, characteristics)
   2. Community care systems, policy, and legislation
      a. Global (for example: World Health Organization, American Red Cross)
      b. National/Federal Legislation (for example: Medicare, Social Security, Supplemental Security Income, *Healthy People 2000,* Department of Health and Human Services)
      c. State (for example: Medicaid, state Health Department)
      d. Local health department service (for example: level of care, point of service, eligibility of service)
   3. Epidemiologic principles that impact on understanding of community-based practice (for example: primary, secondary, tertiary, endemic, epidemic, pandemic, frequency rates, morbidity and mortality rates)
   4. Communicable diseases (for example: role in prevention, responsibility when confronted with reportable diseases such as tuberculosis and hepatitis)
   5. Factors influencing community-based care
      a. Sex (for example: female and male populations who are at risk)

      b. Age/Developmental level: infants through older adults (for example: infant immunizations, toddlers and lead poisoning, school-age children and drugs, adolescent pregnancy, middle-aged adults and hypertension screening, older adults and elder abuse, developmental disabilities)
      c. Family (for example: family violence, divorce, disrupted family, ineffective parenting skills)
      d. Individual factors (for example: educational level, gay and lesbian rights, lifestyle, health habits)
      e. Physical condition (for example: family nutritional status, presence of chronic diseases, substance abuse patterns, maternal–infant health)
      f. Cultural and spiritual/religious beliefs (for example: beliefs about community, expectations of health and illness, spiritual and religious practices)
      g. Socioeconomic factors (for example: income level, access to health care, poverty, legal and illegal immigration patterns)
      h. Environmental factors (for example: overcrowding, unsanitary conditions, pollution, reservoirs of infection, homelessness, home settings, contaminated food, waste disposal, disaster plans)
      i. Psychological factors (for example: chronic mental illness, post-traumatic stress disorder)
      j. Alternative/complementary treatments (for example: use of community-based ethnic healers, lay midwives)
  6. Theoretical basis for interventions to promote community-based health care
      a. Medications (for example: direct observation, compliance, teaching)
      b. Maintenance of asepsis (for example: communicable disease control measures, adaptations for home care)
      c. Treatments and procedures (for example: environmental modifications for safe home care, disease reporting, screening)
      d. Dietary modifications (for example: safe handling and preparation of family food, safe water)
      e. Maintenance of environment (for example: unsafe housing, stray animals)
      f. Ethical and legal implications (for example: issues of legitimate caregiver roles, undocumented residents and access to health care, the home health visit)

B. Nursing care related to theoretical framework
  1. Role of the nurse in the community (for example: provider of care, manager of care, teacher, patient advocate)
  2. Assessment: gather and organize data in relation to the family and patient's health status
      a. Determine the family and patient's ability to promote functional health patterns (for example: observe home environment for hazards, assess families ability to access community resources)
      b. Gather home health or community health assessment data (for example: assess handwashing behavior of children in the first grade classroom, assess availability of services for patients with Alzheimer's disease in a given geographic area)
      c. Determine the patient's response to the ongoing home care or community need (for example: observations that indicate patient continues to reside in an unsafe home environment, observations that indicate a group of

schoolchildren need more instruction on hygienic practices)
   d. Review laboratory and other diagnostic data (for example: sexually transmitted disease frequency rate, immunization rates, violence rates)
3. Analysis: in conjunction with the patient and members of the health care team, synthesize data to identify the patient's actual or potential health problem (nursing diagnosis)
   a. Identify nursing diagnoses (for example: post-traumatic response to house fire, risk for violence related to sudden loss of income, health-seeking behaviors related to concern about environmental condition)
   b. Set priorities (for example: based on the patient's developmental level, based on the access to health care, based on use of resources, based on reimbursement procedures, based on acuity)
4. Planning: in conjunction with the patient and members of the health care team, determine expected outcomes (patient-centered goals) and formulate specific strategies to achieve the expected outcomes (patient-centered goals)
   a. Establish expected outcomes (patient-centered goals) for care related to health promotion, health maintenance, and health restoration (for example: patient will integrate the experience of a house fire in a meaningful way and pursue life goals; family will report involvement in domestic violence support group, group will demonstrate ways to modify the environment)
   b. Using established nursing standards and protocols, plan nursing measures to help the patient achieve the expected outcomes (patient-centered goals) (for example: Standards of Home Health Nursing Practice, family follows immunization schedule for infant follow-up)
   c. Incorporate factors influencing the patient home and community health (for example: family establishes safe hygiene routine to care for a child who has been injured, family reports use of day care center for member with Alzheimer's disease)
   d. Plan for anticipated health care needs based on populations at risk (for example: offer prenatal classes to pregnant adolescents at the local YWCA, teach older adults at the community center about the risk of falls)
   e. Assign patient activities to other members of the health care team as appropriate (for example: send the homemaker to do the shopping, assign the home health aide to bathe the patient)
5. Implementation: initiate and complete nursing plans designed to move the patient toward expected outcomes (patient-centered goals)
   a. Use nursing measures to obtain needed supplies, equipment, and services in the home or community (for example: assist family in selecting durable medical equipment needed for patient care, inform family of services available for child with disabilities, advocate for increased services for people who are homeless)
   b. Maintain aseptic technique (for example: teach caregiver to maintain sterile/clean technique during dressing changes, modify handwashing technique in homes)
   c. Use nursing measures to aid in the resolution of patient needs in home or community (for example: assist family in selecting adult day care for the patient with cognitive loss, ensure safe mobility pattern of patient with sensory deficits who is homebound, inform family of patient who has active tuberculosis to arrange for a follow-up chest x-ray)

d. Administer medications (for example: teach home medication routine to caregiver of toddler with pneumonia, administer immunizations at community sites, consider modifications related to the patient's age)
   e. Provide information and instruction regarding biological safety (for example: instruct family regarding hazards of stray animals, emphasize preventive measures, discuss the spread of infection, refer person who has been abused to domestic violence shelter)
   f. Use nursing measures to promote continuity of care (for example: teaching, referrals, support groups, community resources, teach safe-sex practices to sexually active groups, refer new mother to Special Supplemental Food Program for Women, Infants, and Children [WIC])
6. Evaluation: assess the patient's response to nursing care including progress toward the expected outcomes (patient-centered goals)
   a. Record and report the patient's response to nursing actions (for example: first grade class wash hands correctly after instruction, family misses immunization appointment for newborn, older adult class visits school for socialization activities)
   b. Reassess and revise the patient's plan of care as necessary (for example: reinforce correct sterile dressing technique, revise the teaching plan, follow up with family who missed immunization appointment and plan for future date)
   c. Determine the patient's response to care provided by other members of the health care team (for example: home caregiver is reported for leaving a toddler at home unattended, patient who is ventilator dependent and homebound indicates the homemaker cleans the house weekly)

VI. Needs of the Childbearing Family (25%)

This area focuses on the nursing care of the childbearing family. Health care needs and problems that occur during the antepartal, intrapartal, postpartal, and neonatal periods are included.

A. Theoretical framework: basis for care of the family
1. The childbearing family
   a. Antepartal period
      1) Signs and symptoms of pregnancy
      2) Physiological changes (for example: uterine growth, cardiovascular changes, respiratory, gastrointestinal/genitourinary [GI/GU] changes, hormonal alterations)
      3) Discomforts of pregnancy (for example: morning sickness, urinary frequency, nasal stuffiness, heartburn, backache)
      4) Psychosocial changes in the expectant family (for example: emotional responses, role transition, alterations in sexuality, differences based on age and culture, couvade syndrome, emotional responses of extended family)
      5) Health maintenance
         a) Mother (for example: calculate estimated date of confinement [EDC]; conception; obstetrical history; lab tests such as serology for syphilis, smear for gonorrhea, tests for chlamydia, HIV, Beta Strep, herpes, Pap smear; patient education regarding nutrition, breast

                    self-examination [BSE], activities of daily living [ADLs], symptoms to be reported, amniocentesis, nonstress test, sonogram)
                b) Fetus (for example: fetal heart rate, fundal height, chorionic villi sampling)
            6) Childbirth education (for example: birthing options, childbirth exercises, sibling participation)
            7) Complications of pregnancy
                a) Pregnancy-induced complications (for example: gestational diabetes, spontaneous abortion, ectopic pregnancy, pregnancy-induced hypertension [PIH], incompetent cervix, placenta previa, abruptio placenta, preterm labor)
                b) Coexisting medical conditions (for example: diabetes mellitus, anemia, cardiac disease, hypertension, obesity, malnutrition)
                c) Coexisting psychosocial problems (for example: substance abuse, adolescent pregnancy, advanced maternal age, poverty-level income)
            8) Medications (for example: prenatal vitamins, magnesium sulfate, ritodrine, terbutaline sulfate [Brethine], iron preparation and docusate sodium [Colace], betamethasone sodium phosphate [Celestone])
            9) Medical interventions (for example: fetal monitoring, terbutaline sulfate pumps, blood pressure monitoring)
        b. Intrapartal period
            1) Process of labor
                a) true vs. false labor
                b) onset—lightening, increased show, increased urinary frequency, nesting instinct
                c) stages and phases of labor, fetal presentation and positions
            2) Complications of labor (for example: fetal malpresentation; pattern of early, late, and variable decelerations; primary and secondary inertia; premature rupture of membranes; prolapsed cord)
            3) Medical interventions (for example: amniotomy, episiotomy, induction of labor, forceps, vacuum extraction, cesarean section)
            4) Medications (for example: oxytocics, prostaglandins, anesthesia, analgesics)
        c. Postpartal period
            1) Anatomical and physiological changes (for example: uterine involution, breast changes, body system changes)
            2) Psychosocial adaptation (for example: differentiate between postpartum blues and depression)
            3) Role adaptation (for example: mother who works inside the home, single mother)
            4) Family planning (for example: adaptations in the postpartum period) (see content area II)
            5) Postpartal complications (for example: hemorrhage, puerperal infections, lacerations, mastitis, cardiac decompensation)
            6) Medications (for example: Rho[D] immune globulin [RhoGAM)] methylergonovine maleate [Methergine], oxytocin [Pitocin], acetaminophen)
            7) Teaching (for example: breast-feeding and bottle feeding)

8) Maternal nutrition considerations (for example: lactation, postpartum diet)
9) Self-care activities (for example: lochia, fundal massage, breast care, alterations to exercise, incisional care)
2. Theoretical basis for interventions to promote nursing care for women and newborns (for example: National Association of American Colleges of Obstetricians and Gynecologists [NAACOG], standards for the nursing care of women and the newborn, scope of practice, maternal fetal conflicts, termination of pregnancy issues, advanced maternal age)

B. Nursing care related to theoretical framework: the childbearing family
1. Roles of the nurse in childbearing families (for example: provider of care, manager of care, teacher, patient advocate)
2. Assessment: gather and organize data in relation to the antepartal, intrapartal, and postpartal childbearing family
    a. Obtain the patient's health history (for example: obstetric-gynecologic history, expected date of delivery, risk factors, substance abuse [recreational use], fetal movement patterns, current and previous medical-surgical history, medication use)
    b. Risk assessment (for example: age, socioeconomic factors, previous birth history, genetic factors, smoking, and drug history)
    c. Assess factors influencing the family's response to childbearing (for example: preparation for childbirth, cultural factors, socioeconomic status, age, lifestyle, psychological factors, nutrition, bonding)
    d. Obtain physical data (for example: fetal heart rate, fetal movement, weight gain, amount and color of lochia, color of amniotic fluid, location and contraction of the fundus, baseline vital signs, dip stick urine specimen)
    e. Review laboratory and other diagnostic data (for example: sonogram, fetal heart monitor, nonstress test, stress test, hemoglobin, hematocrit, white blood cells [WBCs])
3. Analysis: in conjunction with the patient and members of the health care team, synthesize data to identify the patient's actual or potential health problem (nursing diagnosis)
    a. Synthesize assessment data (see VIB1)
    b. Identify actual or potential nursing diagnoses (for example: fluid volume deficit related to inadequate fluid intake during labor, risk for infection related to episiotomy, urinary retention related to urethral trauma, knowledge deficit related to care of the perineum, altered comfort related to sore nipples, risk for injury related to compromised circulation secondary to pregnancy)
    c. Set priorities (for example: based on optimal use of resources, based on patient's development level, based on cultural considerations, based on Maslow's hierarchy of needs)
4. Planning: in conjunction with the patient and members of the health care team, determine expected outcomes (patient-centered goals) and formulate specific strategies to achieve the expected outcomes (patient-centered goals)
    a. Establish expected outcomes (patient-centered goals) for care related to health promotion, health maintenance, and health restoration (for example: patient will correctly demonstrate childbearing exercises, patient will

perform care of perineum correctly, patient will demonstrate safe care of infant)
- b. Consider factors influencing the patient's response to childbearing (see VIB1) and involve the patient's family in planning patient care (for example: plan sibling and grandparent visits; consider socioeconomic status in relation to health maintenance; consider ethnicity, age, health care insurance, Medicaid, WIC)
- c. Plan nursing measures on the basis of established standards and priorities to help the family achieve the expected outcomes (for example: referrals, pain protocols, critical pathways, care plans)

5. Implementation: initiate and complete nursing plans designed to move the patient toward the expected outcomes (patient-centered goals) related to health promotion, health maintenance, and health restoration
   - a. Use nursing measures to enhance positive outcomes for the childbearing family (for example: provide instruction regarding the effects of nutrition, lifestyle, drugs, medications, and infections; manipulate the environment to foster rest, nutrition, and reduction of stress)
   - b. Use nursing measures to promote optimal fetoplacental blood flow (for example: position to prevent vena caval syndrome, provide oxygen and intravenous fluids)
   - c. Use nursing measures to ensure a safe environment (for example: safety measures for the patient with preeclampsia, safety measures with use of analgesics)
   - d. Use nursing measures to facilitate the progress of labor (for example: positioning, coaching, encourage ambulation, encourage voiding)
   - e. Use nursing measures to facilitate involution and healing (for example: episiotomy care, nipple care, fundal massage, breast-feeding)
   - f. Use nursing measures to provide emotional support (for example: assist with role transition, foster bonding)
   - g. Use nursing measures to ensure optimal nutrition (for example: provide instruction regarding antepartal weight gain, provide postpartal dietary instruction)
   - h. Use nursing measures to maintain patient comfort (for example: instruction in breathing patterns, application of heat or cold, small frequent meals, good body mechanics)
   - i. Use nursing measures specific to prescribed medications during the childbearing cycle (for example: monitor uterine contractions for a patient receiving oxytocin [Pitocin]; keep calcium gluconate available for a patient receiving magnesium sulfate; check the blood pressure of a patient receiving ergonovine maleate [Ergotrate]; monitor the blood pressure of a patient receiving anesthesia; consider modifications related to the patient's age)
   - j. Use nursing measures to assist the patient in making educated choices throughout the childbearing cycle (for example: birthing options, family planning)
   - k. Provide information and instruction (for example: signs and symptoms of impaired involution, self-care needs, infant care, follow-up care)
   - l. Use nursing measure to establish a collaborative relationship with the patient (for example: respect cultural differences or differences in child rearing practices; define parenting expectations with patient)

m. Use nursing resources to promote continuity of care (for example: referrals, support groups, community resources)
 6. Evaluation: assess the patient's response to nursing care, including progress toward the expected outcome
    a. Document assessment findings (for example: chart color and amount of lochia, condition of nipples, condition of episiotomy)
    b. Assess and report the patient's response to nursing actions (for example: applications of heat or cold, signs and symptoms of infection, response to pain management, patient's understanding of teaching)
    c. Revise the plan of care based on reassessment of patient (for example: change the outcome for a patient who has experienced hemorrhage; administer medication to avoid preterm labor for a patient with placenta previa)
    d. Determine family's response to care provided by other members of the health care team (for example: ask questions of the care provider to determine patient's hygienic status)

C. Theoretical framework: basis of care for the neonate
  1. The fetus and neonate
     a. Conception and implantation
     b. Embryonic/fetal development
        1) Patterns of development (for example: cephalocaudal, proximodistal)
        2) Fetal circulation
     c. Diagnostic tests: biophysical profile, amniotic fluid index, amniocentesis, L/S (Lecithin/sphingomyelin) ratio, phenylketonuria (PKU), and Dextrastix
     d. Umbilical cord and placenta
        1) Anatomy and physiology (for example: three vessels, Wharton's jelly, cord length)
        2) Functions (for example: nutrition, waste elimination, oxygen exchange, endocrine system)
     e. Factors influencing fetal growth and well-being (for example: genetic makeup, nutrition, oxygen supply, medications, teratogens, maternal diabetes, maternal substance abuse, condition of placenta)
     f. Physiology of the neonate: normal transition to extrauterine life (for example: respiratory changes, circulatory changes, temperature regulation, newborn reflexes, gastrointestinal/genitourinary [GI/GU] function, effect of vaginal delivery vs. cesarean section)
     g. Fluid and nutritional needs of the neonate (for example: iron supplements, solid foods, calorie and fluid requirements, breast feeding vs. bottle feeding, infant feeding behaviors, cultural variations of infant feeding, vitamin K)
     h. Complications of the neonate (for example: prematurity, postmaturity, large or small for gestational age, respiratory distress syndrome, hemolytic disease, infection, fetal alcohol syndrome, hypoglycemia, cold stress)
     i. Immunizations and medications (for example: vitamin K, hepatitis B, erythromycin eyedrops)

D. Nursing care related to theoretical framework: the fetus and neonate
   1. Roles of the nurse in relation to neonates (for example: provider of care, manager of care, patient advocate)
   2. Assessment: gather and organize data in relation to the health status of the fetus and neonate
      a. Obtain the fetus/neonate's health history (for example: history of prenatal care, length of gestation, length of labor, type of delivery, maternal history of substance abuse, response to analgesia and anesthesia, knowledge of congenital anomaly, stage of activity, and normal physical findings)
      b. Obtain physical data related to the fetus/neonate's health status (for example: Apgar score, head-to-toe physical assessment, maturity rating)
      c. Review laboratory and other diagnostic data (for example: dextrose heel stick, bilirubin, hematocrit, hemoglobin, white blood cell count [WBCs])
   3. Analysis: in conjunction with the patient and members of the health care team, synthesize data to identify the patient's actual or potential health problem (nursing diagnosis)
      a. Synthesize assessment data (see VIC1)
      b. Identify actual or potential nursing diagnoses (for example: ineffective thermoregulation related to newborn transition to the extrauterine environment, ineffective airway clearance related to retained secretions, ineffective infant feeding pattern related to poor sucking reflex)
      c. Set priorities (for example: based on optimal use of resources, patient's development level, Maslow's hierarchy of needs, cultural considerations such as ritual circumcision, use of amulets)
   4. Planning: in conjunction with the patient and members of the health care team, determine expected outcomes (patient-centered goals) and formulate specific strategies to achieve the expected outcomes (patient-centered goals)
      a. Establish expected outcomes (patient-centered goals) for care related to health promotion, health maintenance, and health restoration (for example: axillary temperature of neonate will be stable, mother will use the rooting mechanism to initiate feeding, circumcision will show no signs of infection, neonate will demonstrate effective sucking mechanism)
      b. Plan for anticipated needs of the fetus/neonate on the basis of established priorities (for example: plan to facilitate bonding, plan to meet nutritional needs)
      c. Plan nursing measures on the basis of established standards and priorities to help the family achieve the expected outcomes (patient-centered goals) (for example: match baby identification bands with mother's band, swaddle the neonate to promote security and maintain body temperature, increase fluid volume for a neonate who is undergoing phototherapy)
   5. Implementation: initiate and complete nursing plans designed to move the patient toward the expected outcome related to health promotion, health maintenance, and health restoration
      a. Use nursing measures to promote a safe environment (for example: provide warmth for the neonate, cover the eyes of a neonate undergoing phototherapy, complete newborn identification procedure, teach use of car seat and safe crib)

b. Use nursing measures to increase the fetus/neonate's oxygen supply (for example: suction the neonate's airway, administer oxygen at no more than 60%, position neonate on back or side)

c. Use nursing measures to ensure optimal nutrition (for example: assist with neonate feeding, facilitate breast-feeding, use correct formula)

d. Use nursing measures to relieve neonatal discomfort (for example: care of circumcision site, comfort crying baby)

e. Use nursing measures to provide emotional support (for example: foster bonding, swaddle, encourage skin-to-skin contact)

f. Use nursing measures specific to prescribed medications (for example: administer prophylactic eyedrops, administer phytonadione [AquaMEPHYTON])

g. Use nursing measures to facilitate healing (for example: cord care, circumcision care)

h. Use nursing measures to maintain physiological stability (for example: care during phototherapy, positioning, maintain cord clamp, maintain thermoregulation)

6. Evaluation: assess the patient's response to nursing care, including progress toward the expected outcome (patient-centered goal)

a. Document assessment findings (for example: daily weight, color and consistency of stool, elevated bilirubin levels)

b. Assesses neonates response to nursing actions (for example: response to feeding, bonding, phototherapy)

c. Revise the plan of care (for example: provide fluid in response to temperature elevation, refer mother to the appropriate agency for follow-up care if the neonate's weight gain is poor, revise the teaching plan)

VII. Sensory Impairments (10%)

This area focuses on the nursing care of patients with sensory dysfunction. Areas include visual, auditory, olfactory, gustatory, tactile, proprioception.

A. Theoretical framework: basis for care

1. Types of sensory alterations
   a. Hearing (for example: otitis media, cerumen impaction, presbycusis, Meniere's disease, labyrinthitis, otosclerosis)
   b. Vision (for example: macular degeneration, cataracts, retinopathy, glaucoma, conjunctivitis, corneal abrasions, retinal detachment, presbyopia, hyperopia, myopia)
   c. Proprioception (for example: gait imbalance, falls)

2. Clinical manifestations of sensory dysfunction
   a. Impaired sensory function (for example: neurovascular deficits, paresthesia, visual impairments, hearing impairments, deafness)
   b. Alterations in comfort (for example: acute and chronic pain)
   c. Alterations in mental status (for example: confusion, slowed thought processes, disorientation)

3. Factors influencing the patient's response to sensory dysfunction
   a. Sex (for example: color blindness)
   b. Age (for example: otitis media in younger child, macular degeneration in older adult, strabismus in younger child, otosclerosis in young adult

women, genetic abnormalities of vision and hearing in older adults)
- c. Psychological factors (for example: stress, sensory deprivation, sensory overload, social isolation, paranoia)
- d. Socioeconomic factors (for example: access to health care, access to assistive devices)
- e. Environmental factors (for example: sensory overload, sensory deprivation, loud noises, exposure to fumes and toxic substances, improper lighting)
- f. Impact of other illness (for example: diabetes mellitus on vision, peripheral vascular disease on proprioception, arthritis on proprioception)
- g. Impact of medications (for example: photophobia, ototoxicity, altered taste, altered smell)

4. Theoretical basis for interventions to identify, promote, restore, or maintain sensory function
   - a. Diagnostic testing (for example: assessment of visual acuity, eye movement, visual fields, opthalmoscopy, tomometry, refraction and accommodations; assessment of auditory acuity; otoscopic examination, Weber test, Rinne test, audiometry, functional hearing and vision assessment)
   - b. Medications (for example: topical eye analgesics, anti-inflammatory agents, antibiotics, steroids, myotics, mydriatics, osmotic diuretics, decongestants, cerumenolytics, lubricants)
   - c. Environmental modifications (for example: assistive devices for people with hearing impairments, assistive devices for people with visual impairments, safety devices in the home, use of animals and guides)
   - d. Preoperative and postoperative care (for example: cataract removal, lens implantation, iridectomy, myringotomy, cochlear implants)

B. **Nursing care related to theoretical framework**
   1. Nurse's role with patients with sensory impairments (for example: provider of care, manager of care, teacher, patient advocate)
   2. Assessment: gather and organize data in relation to the patient's sensory impairment
      - a. Gather assessment data
      - b. Obtain the patient's health history (for example: subjective symptoms, medications, history of trauma, history of infection, allergies, familial and genetic history, onset and duration of symptoms, medical illness, occupation)
      - c. Assess factors influencing the patient's response to sensory dysfunction (see VIIA3)
      - d. Obtain physical data related to the patient's sensory dysfunction (for example: pupils equal, round, reactive to light and accommodation [PERRLA], visual fields test; peripheral challenge test; color correctness test; Weber and Rinne tests; otoscopic exams; touch sensation for sharp and dull; gait and balance tests; Snellen test)
      - e. Review laboratory and other diagnostic data (for example: audiometry, white blood cells [WBCs], ultrasound of the eye, measurement of intraocular pressure, ophthalmologist exam)
   3. Analysis: in conjunction with the patient and members of the health care team, synthesize data to identify the patient's actual or potential sensory impairment (nursing diagnosis)

a. Synthesize assessment data (see VIIB1)
   b. Identify actual or potential nursing diagnoses (for example: activity intolerance related to impaired balance and coordination, high risk for injury related to decreased or impaired sensation, risk for trauma related to not using safety glasses, social isolation related to auditory impairment)
   c. Set priorities (for example: based on Maslow's hierarchy of needs, based on the patient's developmental level, based on optimal use of resources)
4. Planning: in conjunction with the patient and members of the health care team, determine expected outcomes (patient-centered goals) and formulate specific strategies to achieve the expected outcomes (patient-centered goals)
   a. Establish expected outcomes (patient-centered goals) for care related to health promotion, health maintenance, and health restoration (for example: a patient will modify environment to avoid injury, the patient will demonstrate self-care behaviors following postoperative cataract surgery, the patient will initiate conversation, patient will use hearing aids daily)
   b. Consider factors influencing the patient's response to sensory dysfunction in planning patient care (see VIIA3)
   c. Plan nursing measures on the basis of established priorities to help the patient achieve the expected outcomes (patient-centered goals) (for example: patient washes hands prior to administering eye medications, patient learns to lip read)
   d. Assign patient activities to other members of the health care team as appropriate (for example: assign nursing assistant to help a patient whose vision is impaired, assign LPN/LVN to assist patient to insert hearing aids)
5. Implementation: process of initiating and completing nursing actions/interventions designed to move the patient toward expected outcomes (patient-centered goals) related to health promotion, health maintenance, health restoration
   a. Use nursing measures to protect the patient (for example: teach a patient who is visually impaired to ambulate safely, keep the environment clutter free, assist the patient who is hearing impaired in obtaining assistive devices, assist patient with vertigo with ambulation)
   b. Use nursing measures to promote, maintain, or restore the patient's sensory functioning and/or prevent complications (for example: administer prescribed eyedrops to a patient with glaucoma, position patient to facilitate postmyringotomy drainage, irrigate ears for cerumen impaction)
   c. Use nursing measures to minimize patient discomfort (for example: administer decongestant, lubricants, administer pain medications following surgery, teach patient to correctly apply contact lenses)
   d. Use nursing measures specific to prescribed medications (for example: administer antibiotics for otitis media and conjunctivitis, observe for change in pupil size after administering myotics, administer anti-glaucoma medications, gently pull down on lower lid and have patient look up when administering eyedrops)
   e. Use nursing measures to enhance communication (for example: enhance spoken voice, directly face the patient when communicating, make sure assistive devices are in place, encourage use of assistive devices)
   f. Provide information and instruction (for example: instruct the patient in the use of safety glasses, instruct the caregiver on pre- and postoperative

care, instruct the patient about the medication regimen; instruct the patient regarding the use of community resources; instruct the patient regarding the use of assistive devices; emphasize the need for follow-up care; reinforce rehabilitation instruction)
      g. Use nursing measures to promote continuity of care (for example: teaching, referrals, support groups, community resources, guide dog foundation for the blind, AT&T National Relay Service, Lions Club)
   6. Evaluation: assess the patient's response to nursing care including progress toward the expected outcomes (patient-centered goals)
      a. Document assessment findings (for example: the patient is more alert and initiates conversation, self-care behaviors, patient cannot respond to spoken word, color selection not appropriate)
      b. Assess and report the patient's response to nursing actions relative to the expected outcomes (patient-centered goals) (for example: patient is free from pain, patient verbalizes the need for follow-up care, patient verbalizes the need to take medication at the prescribed time, patient reports hearing improved after cerumen disimpaction)
      c. Revise the patient's plan of care as necessary (for example: following unsuccessful ear irrigation, request cerumenolytics; revise care plan to provide social activities for the patient who is hearing impaired)
      d. Determine the patient's response to care provided by other members of the health care team (for example: observe husband administering eyedrops to wife after cataract surgery, ask the patient who is visually impaired to demonstrate how the physical therapy assistant taught the use of a cane)

VIII. Reproductive Disorders (10%)

This area focuses on the impact of female and male reproductive disorders on the patient's health. Emphasis is placed on the management of the disorder including surgical, pharmacological, and nonpharmacological techniques.

A. Theoretical framework: basis for care
   1. Normal female reproductive function (for example: female hormones, menarche, menstrual cycle, menopause)
   2. Normal male reproductive function (for example: male hormones, spermatogenesis, male climacteric, male menopause)
   3. Hormonal and structural alterations (for example: hysterectomy, hormone replacement therapy [HRT], atropic vaginitis, endometriosis, benign prostatic hypertrophy)
   4. Clinical manifestations of hormonal and structural alterations (for example: abnormal bleeding, changes in urination, recurrent infections, pruritus, menstrual abnormalities, prolapses, urinary retention, stress incontinence, pelvic pain)
   5. Factors influencing the patient's response to hormonal and structural alterations
      a. Age (for example: postmenopausal atrophic vaginitis, pre- vs. postmenopausal hysterectomy)
      b. Individual preferences or patterns (for example: hormone replacement therapy, selection of hygiene products, use of alcohol and tobacco)
      c. Physical condition (for example: diabetes, atrophic vaginitis, cancer

treatment, genetic predisposition)
- d. Cultural, spiritual, religious beliefs (for example: female or male circumcision, sterilization, contraception)
- e. Socioeconomic factors (for example: access to health care, nutrition, access to bathing facilities)
- f. Environmental factors (for example: exposure to heat, chemicals, radiation)
- g. Psychological factors (for example: domestic violence and abuse, mood changes with decreased hormone production)
- h. Alternative therapies (for example: use of dong quai for menopause, use of soy, relaxation therapy, massage therapy)

6. Theoretical basis for interventions to promote, restore, or maintain hormonal and structural integrity
   - a. Medications (for example: antihypertensives, steroids, chemotherapeutics, hypoglycemics, hormones)
   - b. Activity and positioning (for example: Kegel exercises, limiting activity postoperatively, early ambulation)
   - c. Assistive devices (for example: penile implants and pumps, pessaries, scrotal supports)
   - d. Patient monitoring (for example: monitoring sanitary pad counts, incision inspection, intake and output, laboratory values)
   - e. Preoperative and postoperative care (for example: transurethral resection of the prostate, hysterectomy, dilatation and curettage, anterior-posterior colporrhaphy, hydrocelectomy, orchiopexy)

B. Nursing care related to theoretical framework
1. Nurse's role in caring for patients with reproductive disorders (for example: provider of care, manager of care, teacher, patient advocate)
2. Assessment is the process of gathering and organizing data in relation to the patient's health status
   - a. Obtain the patient's health history (for example: childhood diseases, allergies, major illnesses, medications, menstrual cycles, past surgical procedures)
   - b. Obtain the patient's sexual history (for example: self-perception, voiding disturbances, fertility management, sexually transmitted diseases, changes in libido, impotence, abortion, gynecological and obstetrical history)
   - c. Assist with physical examination and diagnostic testing (for example: pelvic examination, laparoscopy, digital rectal examination, testicular examination)
   - d. Assess factors influencing the patient's reproductive disorder
     1) stress and activity
     2) physical disease processes (for example: diabetes mellitus, hypertension)
     3) use of medication (for example: antihypertensives, steroids, chemotherapeutics, hypoglycemics)
     4) occupation and environment (for example: exposure to chemicals, heat, hormones, radiation)
     5) habits (for example: use of alcohol, tobacco, and illicit drugs; multiple partners)
     6) history of domestic violence and abuse
   - e. Obtain objective data (for example: clinical manifestations, vital signs)
   - f. Review laboratory and other diagnostic data (for example:

ultrasonography, magnetic resonance imaging [MRI], cultures, biopsy, mammography, prostate specific antigen [PSA], complete blood cell count [CBC], hormone studies)
3. Analysis: in conjunction with the patient and members of the health care team, synthesize data to identify the patient's actual or potential health problems (nursing diagnosis)
   a. Identify nursing diagnoses (for example: fear related to alterations in sexual functioning, acute pain related to tissue trauma secondary to surgery, knowledge deficit related to medical treatment, ineffective individual coping related to effects of PMS, body image disturbance related to altered sexual relations with partner)
   b. Set priorities (for example: based on the patient's developmental level, based on individual preference, based on Maslow's hierarchy of needs, based on optimum use of resources)
4. Planning: in conjunction with the patient and members of the health care team, determine expected outcomes (patient-centered goals) formulating specific strategies to achieve the expected outcomes (patient-centered goals)
   a. Establish expected outcomes (patient-centered goals) related to health promotion, health maintenance, and health restoration (for example: patient will state that pain has been relieved; patient will be able to discuss fears and concerns; patient will understand disease, manifestations, and medical treatment as evidenced by patient comments; patient will cope effectively with PMS and its manifestations as evidenced by patient comments; patient will verbalize and demonstrate acceptance of self after hysterectomy)
   b. Plan nursing measures to help the patient achieve the expected outcomes (for example: monitor the patient's vital signs, allow the patient to talk about feelings and experiences, teach the patient about medications and assistive devices)
   c. Incorporate factors influencing the patient's psychosocial aspects in planning the patient's care (for example: consider the patient's spiritual, religious, and cultural responses; allow patient to express concerns regarding role performance and self-esteem)
   d. Assign patient care activities to other members of the health care team as appropriate (for example: have nursing assistant report sanitary pad count, ask home health care aid to assess urinary drainage of patient following prostate surgery)
5. Implementation: initiate and complete nursing plans designed to move the patient toward expected outcomes (patient-centered goals) related to health promotion, health maintenance, and health restoration
   a. Use nursing measures to promote comfort (for example: use bland skin cream and lotions to prevent dryness of skin, administer analgesics for pain, use active listening and provide support during the grieving process, monitor continuous bladder irrigation, monitor for urinary retention after catheter removal, use water soluble vaginal lubricants, maintain perineal hygiene, conduct daily bathing, clean after each voiding and defecation)
   b. Administer prescribed medications (for example: administer pain medications before pain becomes severe, schedule administration of medications to prevent nocturnal awakenings, administer hormone

replacement therapy according to regimen, administer oral contraceptives the same time every day, teach the patient or caregiver to administer pain medications, teach the patient the therapeutic effects and side effects of medications)
   c. Use nursing measures to modify the environment (for example: provide privacy to allow open expression of feelings, provide room deodorizers to control odors)
   d. Provide information and instruction regarding health maintenance (for example: instruct patient about breast-self examination [BSE] techniques; instruct patient about testicular self-examination [TSE] techniques; instruct patient in perineal exercises; instruct patient about yearly gynecological examinations; instruct patient in lifestyle factors that affect health maintenance, such as smoking, diet, exercise; avoid straining during defecation; teach patient about drugs that alter sexuality)
   e. Use nursing measures to promote continuity of care (for example: referral to counseling or support groups such as RESOLVE)
6. Evaluation: assess the patient's response to nursing care including progress toward the expected outcomes (patient-centered goals)
   a. Document assessment findings and response to interventions (for example: patient demonstrates adequate coping mechanisms; patient verbalizes the need for psychological follow-up care; patient demonstrates no signs of inflammation; patient verbalizes dietary restrictions; patient asks questions about diagnoses and treatment available; patient verbalizes activities that produce the Valsalva effects; patient produces clear urinary output in relation to intake; condition of wound; patient reports reduced level of stress)
   b. Revise the plan of care as necessary (for example: encourage increased fluid intake for urine that is concentrated and bloody; patient selects alternative measures such as diet, vitamins, and exercise to control postmenopausal symptoms in place of hormone replacement therapy; patient reports an increase in pain and discomfort; patient develops an elevated temperature and pulse; patient demonstrates dysfunctional grieving)
   c. Determine the patient's response to care provided by other members of the health care team (for example: ask patient if nursing assistant provided perineal care, determine patient's understanding of use of penile pumps as directed by physician)

Sample Questions: Nursing Concepts 3

1. The nurse charts "complains of continuous abdominal pain in incisional area, rates pain as an 8 on 1 to 10 scale." Which characteristic of pain is omitted from this note?
    1) duration
    2) intensity
    3) location
    4) onset

2. By which mechanism do noradrenergic drug agonists relieve pain?
    1) interruption of the pain signal at the peripheral level
    2) inhibition of pain signal relay across the neuronal synapses
    3) blockage of ion channels in the neurolemma
    4) modulation of the ascending pain signal from the dorsal horn

3. Which observation indicates that the analgesic administered postoperatively to a seven-year-old child is effective?
    The child
    1) talks with a visitor and smiles.
    2) plays a video game on the television.
    3) tells his parent that he feels better.
    4) sips on clear fluids and ice pops.

4. A patient reports difficulty achieving and sustaining erections. It is important for the nurse to ask the patient which question?
    1) "Have you been getting too much exercise?"
    2) "How high is your cholesterol level?"
    3) "Have you been checked for diseases such as diabetes?"
    4) "Do you understand the normal sexual response cycle?"

5. Which diagnostic test provides a definitive diagnosis for a female patient who presents with symptoms of gonorrhea?
    1) rapid plasma reagin (RPR)
    2) darkfield examination of exudate
    3) Pap smear
    4) culture of cervical discharge

6. Which is a nursing priority for a patient in the acute phase of the rape trauma syndrome?
    The nurse
    1) provides effective counseling.
    2) collects appropriate evidence.
    3) establishes a safe environment.
    4) creates a trusting relationship.

7. Which nursing action demonstrates cultural competence in patient care?
    The nurse
    1) treats older patients in a similar manner.
    2) maintains direct eye contact with patients.
    3) provides an interpreter for patients who do not speak English.
    4) accepts health care decisions from the patient.

Sample Questions: Nursing Concepts 3

8. A Native American patient is admitted to the hospital with a rash, cough, and fever. Which is the most important information for the nurse to gather from the nursing assessment? The patient's
    1) use of alcohol
    2) employment status
    3) food preferences
    4) immunization history

9. As the patient advocate, the nurse should make which of the following a priority action in the care of a chronically ill patient?
    1) Support the patient's family in their decisions about how they will care for the patient.
    2) Ensure the patient's access to knowledge and respectful treatment.
    3) Provide the patient with information about advance directives.
    4) Educate the family and the patient about how to meet the patient's care needs.

10. Which action should the nurse include in the plan of care to enable patients with a chronic illness to develop a realistic plan for daily living?
    1) Refer patients to the closest agency providing home health care.
    2) Assist patients in setting priorities for important self-care activities.
    3) Assign family members responsibility for assisting with specific needs.
    4) Explain to patients that they will not be able to live life as they did previously.

11. Which is a goal of Healthy People 2000 National Health Promotion and Disease Prevention Objectives?
    In the United States,
    1) a list of community resource referrals will be developed.
    2) health care for populations will be equalized.
    3) accidental injuries will be eliminated.
    4) the use of computerized diagnostic tools will be improved.

12. Which resource best provides for the immediate safety of battered women?
    1) halfway houses
    2) shelters
    3) missions
    4) respite centers

13. What is the priority diagnostic category for a home care hospice patient?
    1) altered bowel elimination
    2) altered nutritional status
    3) self-care deficit
    4) anticipatory grieving

14. Which is a positive sign of pregnancy?
    1) auscultation of fetal heart tones
    2) elevation of basal body temperature
    3) maternal perception of fetal movement
    4) absence of menses for two consecutive months

Sample Questions: Nursing Concepts 3

15. Why should a patient who is trying to get pregnant be advised to stop smoking before conceiving?
    1) Smoking causes thinning of the bronchial walls.
    2) Smoking increases perinatal loss.
    3) Smoking decreases mucus production.
    4) Smoking is associated with uterine fibroid formation.

16. Which observation of a patient during the second stage of labor indicates that delivery is imminent?
    1) The patient pushes with each contraction.
    2) The fundus rises above the umbilicus.
    3) The fetal head is crowning.
    4) The contractions become shorter.

17. A postpartum patient whose breasts are engorged is having difficulty breast-feeding her neonate. Which nursing action should facilitate the feedings?
    1) Teach the patient to express some milk manually before each feeding.
    2) Allow the patient to substitute formula until the engorgement subsides.
    3) Provide the patient with a nipple shield and instructions for its use.
    4) Instruct the patient to roll each nipple between her thumb and forefinger.

18. Which normal physiological change occurs during the antepartal period of pregnancy?
    1) decreased tidal volume
    2) decreased heart rate
    3) increased blood volume
    4) increased urinary output

19. Which neonatal system is affected when kernicterus results from untreated hyperbilirubinemia?
    1) cardiovascular
    2) gastrointestinal
    3) nervous
    4) respiratory

20. Which factor can cause a neonate to develop hemorrhagic disease?
    1) genetic predisposition
    2) immune system disorder
    3) hemolysis of red blood cells
    4) absence of intestinal flora

21. Which clinical manifestation should the nurse expect when assessing a patient with a retinal detachment?
    1) flashing lights
    2) periorbital edema
    3) purulent discharge
    4) profuse tearing

Sample Questions: Nursing Concepts 3

22. Which is a clinical manifestation of a bulging tympanic membrane?
    1) drainage
    2) pain
    3) tinnitus
    4) vertigo

23. An older adult patient who takes a multivitamin and aspirin daily is experiencing tinnitus. What should the nurse suspect as the cause of this condition?
    1) niacin toxicity
    2) hypotension
    3) salicylate toxicity
    4) middle-ear infection

24. A woman has been diagnosed as having endometriosis. What is the pathological process that occurs with this disease?
    1) The uterine endometrium and underlying muscle tissue are infected.
    2) The uterine lining, the fallopian tubes, and the ovaries are atrophied.
    3) Multiple fibrotic tumors develop in the uterus and around the cervix.
    4) Endometrial tissue proliferates on abdominal organs and support structures.

25. A woman who is postmenopausal is considering estrogen replacement therapy. An increase in which serum laboratory data contraindicates therapy?
    1) blood urea nitrogen
    2) cholesterol
    3) creatinine
    4) bilirubin

26. The nurse assesses a woman following a total abdominal hysterectomy. The nurse notes the following patient data: 45 years old, 195 lb, height 5'3", stopped taking oral contraceptives two weeks ago, smokes three to four cigarettes per day. Based upon the data, which intervention is a priority for this patient?
    1) Put the ordered compression stockings on the patient as soon as possible.
    2) Encourage the patient to begin drinking at least 2,000 mL of water a day.
    3) Allow the patient to rest for as long as possible.
    4) Monitor the patient's vital signs more frequently than the stated standard protocol.

Recommended Textbooks

The following are the textbooks being used to develop the Nursing Concepts examination series.

Community-Based Nursing

Ayers, M., Bruno, A.A., & Langford, R.W. (1999). Community-based Nursing Care: Making the transition. St. Louis: Mosby.

This text presents an introduction to community-based nursing and the competencies and tools of community-based nursing. It also presents the care of special populations in the community. The text includes learning objectives for each chapter, critical thinking exercises, and application exercises. Ten cards to guide assessment in the clinical area are included in the textbook.

Fundamentals
Kozier, B., Erb, G., Berman, A.J., & Burke, K. (2000). Fundamentals of nursing: Concepts, process and practice *(6th ed.). Upper Saddle River, NJ: Prentice Hall.*

Medical-Surgical Nursing
Smeltzer, S., & Bare, B. (2000). Brunner and Suddarth's Textbook of medical-surgical nursing *(9th ed.). Philadelphia: Lippincott Williams & Wilkins.*

OR
Monahan, F.D., & Neighbors, M. (1998). Medical-surgical nursing: Foundations for clinical practice *(2nd ed.). Philadelphia: W.B. Saunders.*

Maternal-Newborn Nursing
Dickason, E., Silverman, B.L., & Kaplan, J. (1998). Maternal-infant nursing care *(3rd ed.). St. Louis: Mosby.*

OR
Olds, S., London, M.L., & Ladewig, P (2000). Maternal newborn nursing: A family-centered approach *(6th ed.). Upper Saddle River, NJ: Prentice Hall.*

Nursing Diagnosis
Wilkinson, J.M. (1996). Nursing process: A critical thinking approach *(2nd ed.). Menlo Park, CA: Addison-Wesley.*

Nutrition
Williams, S.R. (1997). Essentials of nutrition and diet therapy *(8th ed.). St. Louis: Mosby.*

Pediatrics
Wong, D. (1997). Whaley and Wong's Essentials of pediatric nursing *(5th ed.). St. Louis: Mosby.*

Pharmacology
Eisenhauer, L.A., Nichols, L.W., Spencer, R.T., & Bergan, F.W. (1999). Clinical pharmacology & nursing management *(5th ed.). Philadelphia: Lippincott.*

Additional Resources
Spector, R.E. (1996). Cultural diversity in health and illness. *(4th edition). Stanford, CT: Appleton & Lange*

This textbook is an excellent reference on cultural issues in nursing practice. In addition to a discussion on the needs of a multicultural society and the issues involved in the delivery of culturally sensitive nursing care, the text provides in-depth information on the traditional views of specific cultural groups with regard to health and illness.

Web Sites
American Pain Management Society: http://www.ampainsoc.org
American Sleep Disorders Association: http://www.asda.org
Chronic net: http://www.chronicnet.org/chronnet/project.htm
National Sleep Foundation Home Page: http://www.sleepfoundation.org

Journal Articles

I. Comfort and Pain
Acello, B. (2000). Meeting JCAHO standards for pain control. Nursing 2000, *30(3), 52–54.*

Loeb, J.L. (1999). Pain management in long-term care. American Journal of Nursing, *99(2), 48–52.*

Sample Questions: Nursing Concepts 3

Pasero, C. (1998). *How aging affects pain management*. American Journal of Nursing, 98(6), 12–13.

Pasero, C., & McCaffery, M. (1999). *Pain Control: Opiods by the rectal route*. American Journal of Nursing, 99(11), 20.

Rhiner, M., & Kadziera, P. (1999). *Managing breakthrough pain: A new approach*. American Journal of Nursing, Supplement, 99(3), 3–14.

II. Human Sexuality

Moore, A.S. (1999). *Emergency contraceptual options*. RN, 62(12), 43–45.

Muscani, M.E. (1999) *Adolescent health: The first gynecologic exam*. American Journal of Nursing, 99(1), 66–67.

Nwoga, I. (2000). *African American mothers and stories for family sexuality education*. The Journal of Maternal/Child Nursing, 25(1), 31–36.

Ventura, M. (1999). *Where women stand on abortion*. RN, 62(3), 44–48.

III. Cultural Diversity

Harris Sumner, C. (1998). *Recognizing and responding to spiritual distress*. American Journal of Nursing, 98(1), 26–30.

Lester, N. (1998). *Cultural Competence: A nursing dialogue*. American Journal of Nursing, 98(8), 26–33.

Lindsay, J., Narayan, M.C., & Rea, K. (1998) *The Vietnamese client*. Home Healthcare Nurse, 16(10), 693–700.

IV. Chronic Illness

Michael, S.R. (1996). *Integrating chronic illness into one's life: a phenomenological inquiry*. Journal of Holistic Nursing, 14(31), 251–267.

Smith-Stoner, M. (1999). *How to build your 'hope skills'*. Nursing 99, 29(9), 49–51.

Sterling-Fisher, C. (1998). *Spiritual care and chronically ill clients*. Home Healthcare Nurse, 16(4), 243–250.

V. Community Based Nursing

Allan, M.A. (1998). *Elder abuse: A challenge for home care nurses*. Home Healthcare Nurse, 16(2), 103–110.

Baldwin, M.E., & Stephenson, L.C. (1998). *Notes: A system for defending patient education through effective documentation*. Home Healthcare Nurse, 16(4), 253–255.

Hunt, R. (1998). *Community-based nursing*. American Journal of Nursing, 98(10), 45–48.

Rokosky, J.M. (1997). *Misuse of metered dose inhalers: Helping patients get it right*. Home Healthcare Nurse, 15(1), 13–21.

VI. Needs of the Child bearing Family

Lindrea, K.B., & Stainton, M.C. (2000). *A case study of infant massage outcomes*. American Journal of Maternal/Child Nursing, 25(2), 95–99

McVeigh, C.A. (2000). *Investigating the relationship between satisfaction with social support and functional status after childbirth*. American Journal of Maternal/Child Nursing, 25(1), 25–30.

VII. Sensory Impairments

Blair, C. (1999). *The dizzy patient*. American Journal of Nursing, 99(9), 61+.

Boyd-Monk, H. (1999). *Action state: Retinal detachment*. Nursing 99, 29(9), 33.

Cavendish, R. (1998). *Adult hearing loss*. American Journal of Nursing, 98(8), 50–51.

Sheehan, J. (2000), *Caring for the deaf: Do we do enough?* RN 63(3), 69.

Tupper, S.Z. (1999), When the inner ear is out of balance. RN, 62(11), 36–39.

VIII. Reproductive Disorders

Andrist, L. (1997). Genital Herpes: Overcoming barriers to diagnoses and treatment. American Journal of Nursing, 97(10), 16AAA–16DDD.

Scura, K., & Whipple, B. (1997). How to provide better care for the post-menopausal woman. American Journal of Nursing, 97(4), 36–43.

Smith, A., & Hughes, P. (1998). The estrogen dilemma. American Journal of Nursing, 98(4), 17-20.

Content/Reference List

I. Comfort and Pain
Eisenhauer et al. (5th edition, 1998)
- Chapter 18 Drugs that Depress the Central Nervous System
- Chapter 36 Drugs that treat Inflammation (specifically the section on drugs used to reduce inflammation and pain)

Kozier et al (6th edition, 2000)
- Chapter 43 Pain Management

Wong, D. (5th edition, 1997)
- Chapter 6 Communication and Health Assessment of the Health History of the Child and Family (specifically the section on performing a health history and analyzing a symptom: pain)
- Chapter 21 Family Centered Care of the Child during Illness and Hospitalization (specifically section on pain assessment and management)

II. Human Sexuality
Dickason (3rd edition, 1998)
- Chapter 3 Human Reproduction and Sexuality
- Chapter 5 Fertility Care
- Chapter 6 Infertility Care

Eisenhauer et al (5th edition, 1998)
- Chapter 31 Drugs that Affect Sexual Behavior and Reproduction (specifically sections on drugs that affect sexuality and drugs that prevent conception)

Kozier et al. (6th edition, 2000)
- Chapter 23 Development from Conception Through Adolescence (specifically the section on adolescence)
- Chapter 24 Development from Young through Older Adulthood

Olds et al (6th edition, 2000)
- Part III Human Reproduction (Chapter 6–8)

III. Cultural Diversity
Ayers et al (1999)
- Chapter 11 Special Populations in The Community

Dickason et al (3rd edition, 1998)
- Chapter 2 The Family in a Multicultural Society

Eisenhauer et al (5th edition, 1998)
- Chapter 9 Cultural Aspects of Drug Therapy

Sample Questions: Nursing Concepts 3

Kozier et al (6th edition, 2000)
        Chapter 13   Culture and Ethnicity
        Chapter 14   Spirituality

Smeltzer & Bare (9th edition, 2000)
        Chapter 8   Perspectives in Transcultural Nursing

Wong, (5th edition, 1997)
        Chapter 3   Social, Cultural and Religious Influences on Child Health Promotion.

IV. Chronic Illness

Eisenhauer et al (5th edition, 1998)
        Chapter 12   Drug Therapy in Gerontological Nursing

Smeltzer & Bare (9th edition, 2000)
        Chapter 9   Chronic Illness

Williams (7th edition 1999)
        Chapter 25   Nutritional Support in Disabling Disease and Rehabilitation

Wong (5th edition, 1997)
        Chapter 18   Impact of Chronic Illness, Disability or Death on the Child and Family

V. Community-Based Nursing

Ayers et al (1999)
        Part I   Introduction to Community-Based Nursing (Chapters 1–3)
        Part II   Competencies and Tools for Community-Based Nursing (Chapters 4 and 5)
        Part IV   Issues and Trends in Community-Based Nursing (Chapters 12-13)

Eisenhauer et al (5th edition, 1998)
        Chapter 13   Drug Therapy in the Home and Community

Kozier et al (6th edition, 2000)
        Chapter 7   Community-Based Nursing and Care Continuity

Monahan & Neighbors (2nd edition, 2000)
        Chapter 2   Medical–Surgical Nursing in Multiple Settings

Olds et al (6th edition)
        Chapter 2   Community-Based Teaching for Childbearing Families

Smeltzer & Bare (9th edition, 2000)
        Chapter 2   Community-Based Nursing

Wong (5th edition, 1997)
        Chapter 18   Impact of Chronic Illness, Disability or Death on the Child and Family (section on Helping Family Cope)

VI. Needs of the Childbearing Family

Ayers et al (1999)
        Chapter 6   Maternal-Infant Clients in the Community

Dickason et al (3rd edition, 1998)
        Unit Two   Pregnancy (Chapters 8–12)
        Unit Three   Labor, Birth and Recovery (Chapter 13–17)
        Unit Four   Newborn Care (Chapters 18-20)
        Unit Five   Pregnancy at Risk (Chapter 21)

Eisenhauer et al (5th edition, 1998)
        Chapter 10   Drug Therapy in Maternal Care

Sample Questions: Nursing Concepts 3

Olds et al (6th edition, 2000)
- Part Four — Pregnancy (Chapters 9–17)
- Part Five — Birth (Chapters 18–23)
- Part Six — The Newborn (Chapters 24–28)
- Part Seven — Postpartum (Chapters 30–33)

Williams (7th edition 1999)
- Chapter 11 — Nutrition During Pregnancy and Lactation
- Chapter 12 — Nutrition for Growth and Development

VII. Sensory Impairments

Monahan & Neighbors (2nd edition, 2000)
- Chapter 44 — Knowledge Base for Patients with Eye Dysfunction
- Chapter 45 — Nursing Care of Patients with Eye Disorders
- Chapter 46 — Knowledge Base for Patients with Ear Dysfunction
- Chapter 47 — Nursing Care of Patients with Ear Disorders

Smeltzer & Bare (9th edition, 2000)
- Chapter 54 — Assessment and Management of Patients with Eye and Vision Disorders
- Chapter 55 — Assessment and Management of Patients with Hearing and Balance Disorders

Wong (5th edition, 1997)
- Chapter 7 — Physical and Developmental Assessment of the Child (Section on auditory testing, and visual testing)
- Chapter 19 — Impact of Cognitive or Sensory Impairment on the Child and Family (specifically the section on sensory impairment)
- Chapter 23 — The Child with Respiratory Dysfunction (section on Otitis Media)

VIII. Reproductive Disorders

Dickason (3rd edition, 1998)
- Chapter 4 — Women's Health Care (specifically the section from physical concerns to climacteric)

Eisenhauer et al (5th edition, 1998)
- Chapter 31 — Drugs that Affect Sexual Behavior and Reproduction

Monahan & Neighbors (2nd edition, 1998)
- Chapter 38 — Knowledge Base for Men with Reproductive Dysfunction
- Chapter 39 — Nursing Care of Men with Reproductive Disorders
- Chapter 40 — Knowledge Base for Women with Reproductive Dysfunction
- Chapter 41 — Nursing Care of Women with Reproductive Disorders
- Chapter 42 — Nursing Care of Patients with Breast Disorders (up to the section on cancer)
- Chapter 43 — Nursing Care of Patients with Sexually Transmitted Diseases

Olds et al (6th edition, 2000)
- Chapter 3 — Women's Health Care

Smeltzer & Bare (9th edition, 2000)
- Chapter 42 — Assessment and Management: Problems Related to Female Physiologic Processes
- Chapter 43 — Management of Patients with Female Reproductive Disorders
- Chapter 44 — Assessment and Management of Patients with Breast Disorders (omit section on malignant conditions)
- Chapter 45 — Assessment and Management: Problems Related to Male Reproductive Processes

Study Guide

Differences in Nursing Care: Area A (modified) (468) (Associate Level)

Credit Hours: 4
Question Type(s): Multiple-choice
Credit Level: Lower

The information in this study guide is valid from October 1, 2000, through September 30, 2001.
If you will be taking the examination after that date, be sure to check for a new edition of this guide before you complete your preparation for the exam.

General Description of the Examination

The Differences in Nursing Care: Area A (modified) examination measures knowledge and understanding of the various health care needs and problems encountered by the associate degree nurse. Questions are based on the common and specific manifestations of these needs and problems and the nursing care actions properly associated with them. Questions pertain to patients of various age groups in the proportion that members of these groups use health care services. Questions concern both acute and long-term needs and problems of medical, surgical, obstetric, and pediatric patients.

The examination requires you to possess the technical vocabulary and knowledge of anatomy and physiology, microbiology, emotional and physical development, and nutrition generally expected of the associate degree nurse. The examination requires you to demonstrate knowledge of the theoretical framework for each content area as well as the ability to apply this knowledge to nursing practice using the nursing process.

Examination Objectives

You will be expected to demonstrate the ability to:
1. identify the typical patterns of deviation from wellness associated with each content area
2. identify the differences in nursing care that result from:
   a. manifestations of the specific health problems
   b. the influence of culture on the patient's perception of illness and health care
   c. the individualized response of the patient to illness
3. apply knowledge of the theoretical framework for each content area when using the nursing process to provide direct care to patients

Content Outline

Content Area	Percent of Examination
I. Cardiovascular/Pulmonary Problems	50%
II. Abnormal Cellular Growth	50%
	Total 100%

I. Cardiovascular/Pulmonary Problems (50%)

This area focuses on the nursing care of patients with problems such as respiratory failure, croup, asthma, smoke inhalation, chronic obstructive pulmonary disease (COPD), atelectasis, pneumonia, pulmonary edema, peripheral vascular disease, hypertension, myocardial infarction (MI), congestive heart failure (CHF), shock, anemias.

A. Theoretical framework—basis for care
  1. Types of cardiovascular/pulmonary problems
     a. Problems of intake and supply
        1) Depression of respiratory center (for example: drugs, pH imbalances, respiratory failure)
        2) Blocked airway (for example: croup, foreign body, laryngeal edema, mucoid secretions, asthma)
        3) Altered expansion (for example: fractured rib, paralysis of diaphragm, aging process, surgery)
        4) Alteration in supply of oxygen (for example: smoke inhalation)
     b. Problems of absorption
        1) Blocked alveoli (for example: COPD, atelectasis)
        2) Decreased absorbing surface (for example: pneumonia, pneumothorax, lung surgery, pulmonary edema, adult respiratory distress syndrome [ARDS])
     c. Problems of transportation
        1) Impairment of blood vessels (for example: hypertension, peripheral vascular disease, pulmonary embolus, arteriosclerotic heart disease, angina pectoris, gangrene, abdominal aortic aneurysm)
        2) Pump problems (for example: dysrhythmia, MI, CHF, valvular disease, cardiac infections)
        3) Disturbance in volume (for example: hemorrhagic diseases, shock)
        4) Alteration in oxygen-carrying factors (for example: iron deficiency anemia, pernicious anemia, sickle cell anemia, polycythemia)
        5) Alteration in coagulation (for example: disseminated intravascular coagulation, thrombocytopenia purpura)

Differences in Nursing Care A

2. Clinical manifestations of cardiovascular/pulmonary problems
   a. Altered vital signs
   b. Altered breathing patterns
   c. Altered breath sounds
   d. Altered skin and body temperature
   e. Altered skin color
   f. Altered physical appearance (for example: clubbing of the fingers, barrel chest, jugular vein distention, chest retraction, flaring nostrils, trophic changes)
   g. Alterations in behavior (for example: restlessness, confusion, lethargy, altered mentation)
   h. Alteration in comfort (for example: pain, fatigue)
   i. Altered sensory perception (for example: tingling, numbness, blurred vision)
3. Factors influencing the patient's susceptibility and response to cardiovascular/pulmonary problems
   a. Age and physiological factors
   b. Psychological factors (for example: stress)
   c. Socioeconomic and cultural factors (for example: dietary patterns, smoking, occupation, sedentary lifestyle, family history, health practices)
   d. Nutritional status
   e. Presence of other illnesses
   f. Site of problem (for example: CHF, peripheral vascular disease)
   g. Degree of involvement (for example: acute vs. chronic, pneumonia/COPD, MI/CHF)
4. Theoretical basis for interventions related to cardiovascular/pulmonary problems
   a. Medications (for example: coronary and peripheral vasodilator, anticoagulants, calcium channel blockers, beta blockers, diuretics, antihypertensives, antiarrhythmic agents, cardiac glycosides, drugs used to treat anemias and hyperlipidemia; antihistamines, decongestants, expectorants, antitussive drugs, bronchodilators, mucolytic agents)
   b. Dietary modifications (for example: sodium, fat, cholesterol, calorie and fluid restriction)
   c. Therapeutic devices (for example: chest tubes, Doppler device, mechanical ventilators, pulse oximeters, central venous pressure monitors, cardiac monitors, cardiac pacemakers)
   d. Preoperative and postoperative care (for example: thoracic surgery, angioplasty, coronary artery bypass graft, peripheral vascular surgery, abdominal aneurysm)
   e. Health instruction (for example: rationale for breathing exercises, stress management, instruction relative to diagnostic and laboratory tests, preventive measures for health maintenance, perioperative instruction)

B. Nursing care related to theoretical framework
1. Assessment—gather and synthesize data about the patient's health status in relation to the patient's functional health patterns
   a. Gather assessment data
      1) Obtain the patient's health history (for example: subjective symptoms, diet, medications, past illnesses, health habits, family history, allergies, occupation)

2) Assess factors influencing the patient's response to cardiovascular/pulmonary problems (for example: stress in patient's daily life, dietary patterns [see IA3])
3) Obtain objective data related to the patient's cardiovascular/pulmonary problems (for example: determine clinical manifestation, altered vital signs, capillary refill, peripheral pulses, breath sounds)
4) Review laboratory and other diagnostic data (for example: blood gases, electrolyte levels, stress tests, pulse oximetry, complete blood count [CBC], cardiac enzymes, pulmonary function test, bronchoscopy, thoracentesis, cardiac catheterization, electrocardiogram, theophylline levels)

   b. Synthesize assessment data (see IB1a [1-4])

2. Analysis—identify the nursing diagnosis (patient problem) and determine the expected outcomes (goals) of patient care
   a. Identify actual or potential nursing diagnoses (for example: acute pain [chest] related to coronary spasm, noncompliance related to negative side effects of antihypertensive drug therapy, ineffective airway clearance related to bronchial edema)
   b. Set priorities (for example: based on Maslow's hierarchy of needs, based on the patient's developmental level)
   c. Establish expected outcomes (patient-centered goals) for care (for example: patient will state that discomfort is relieved, patient's blood pressure will be within designated limits, patient will verbalize that respirations are less labored)

3. Planning—formulate specific strategies to achieve the expected outcomes
   a. Consider factors influencing the patient's response to cardiovascular/pulmonary problems in planning patient care (see IA3) (for example: plan care of patient post-MI to include ethnic dietary patterns, plan to discuss resumption of patient's sexual activities)
   b. Plan nursing measures on the basis of established priorities to help the patient achieve the expected outcomes (for example: monitor breath sounds, encourage fluid intake to loosen secretions, provide rest to decrease myocardial oxygen demand)

4. Implementation—carry out nursing plans designed to move the patient toward the expected outcomes
   a. Use nursing measures to maintain a patent airway (for example: provide suctioning, provide tracheotomy care, encourage coughing and deep breathing)
   b. Use nursing measures to increase oxygen supply (for example: positioning, administration of oxygen, instruction in breathing exercises and use of an inhaler, administration of blood, management of mechanical ventilation, management of chest drainage apparatus, position for postural drainage, provide a humidified croupette for a child with croup)
   c. Use nursing measures to reduce cell demand for oxygen (for example: promote rest and comfort, manipulate the environment to reduce anxiety)
   d. Use nursing measures to prevent complications of cardiovascular/pulmonary problems (for example: encourage coughing and deep breathing, apply antiembolic stockings, administer humidified oxygen, encourage ambulation, position chest drainage tubes, apply intermittent compression devices)

e. Use nursing measures specific to prescribed medications (see IA4a) (for example: take blood pressure prior to the administration of an antihypertensive agent, check prothrombin times prior to the administration of a long-acting anticoagulant, administer intramuscular iron preparations via Z-track, determine the pulse rate prior to the administration of cardiac glycosides)
   f. Use measures to assist the patient and/or significant others to cope with the health problem (for example: refer the patient to a local support group, discuss lifestyle changes to reduce stress)
   g. Provide information and instruction (for example: instruct the patient regarding breathing techniques, instruct the patient about the use and side effects of medications, instruct the patient about risk factors for cardiovascular/pulmonary problems, discuss the avoidance of allergens for a child with asthma)
5. Evaluation—appraise the effectiveness of the nursing interventions relative to the nursing diagnosis and the expected outcomes
   a. Assess and report the patient's response to nursing actions (for example: chart changes in color and amount of sputum, chart changes in breath sounds, chart absence of redness and swelling in a light-skinned patient with thrombophlebitis, report that patient verbalizes lack of pain relief following the administration of nitroglycerin)
   b. Revise the patient's plan of care as necessary (for example: encourage additional fluid intake to increase production of sputum, provide diversional activity for the patient with an MI who is experiencing boredom and restlessness)

II. Abnormal Cellular Growth (50%)

This area focuses on the nursing care of patients with problems such as fibroids; pyloric stenosis; cancer of the liver, prostate, breast, lung, and uterus; Wilms' tumor; leukemias; sarcomas; and lymphomas.

A. **Theoretical framework—basis for care**
   1. Types of abnormal cellular growth
      a. Problems resulting from benign abnormal cellular growth (for example: fibroids, gestational trophoblastic disease [hydatidiform mole], fibrocystic disease of the breast)
      b. Problems resulting from hypertrophy (for example: pyloric stenosis, prostatic hypertrophy)
      c. Problems resulting from malignant abnormal cellular growth (for example: cancer of the skin, stomach, intestines, liver, prostate, breast, uterus, lungs, bladder; Wilms' tumor; neuroblastoma; leukemia; sarcomas; lymphomas)
   2. Clinical manifestations of abnormal cellular growth
      a. Alteration in size
      b. Alteration in rate of growth
      c. Altered function of involved cells
      d. Local and systemic effects resulting from altered size, altered rate of growth, and altered function of involved cells (for example: metastasis, pressure on vital organs, pain)
      e. Behavioral changes (for example: confusion, slurred speech, altered mentation)

3. Factors influencing the patient's response to abnormal cellular growth
   a. Age and physiological factors (for example: genetic predisposition)
   b. Psychological factors
   c. Socioeconomic and cultural factors (for example: lifestyle, family history, occupation, health practices)
   d. Nutritional status
   e. Presence of other illness
   f. Site of abnormal cell growth (for example: local vs. distant)
   g. Degree of involvement (for example: benign vs. malignant, acute vs. chronic)
4. Theoretical basis for interventions related to abnormal cellular growth
   a. Medications (for example: antineoplastic agents, steroids, analgesics, hormonal therapy)
   b. Other treatment modalities (for example: chemotherapy, radiation therapy, surgical intervention, immunotherapy, bone marrow transplant)
   c. Preoperative and postoperative care (for example: laryngectomy, mastectomy, intestinal resection, prostatectomy, colostomy, ileal conduit)
   d. Health instruction (for example: risk factors, warning signs, prevention, breast self-examination [BSE], testicular self-examination [TSE])

B. Nursing care related to theoretical framework
1. Assessment—gather and synthesize data about the patient's health status in relation to the patient's functional health patterns
   a. Gather assessment data
      1) Obtain the patient's health history (for example: subjective symptoms, diet, medications, health habits, family history, allergies, occupation)
      2) Assess factors influencing the patient's response to abnormal cell growth (for example: weight loss, occupation) (see IIA3)
      3) Obtain objective data related to the patient's abnormal cellular growth (for example: determine clinical manifestations, weight changes, presence of mass, abdominal distention)
      4) Review laboratory and other diagnostic data (for example: biopsy, scan, blood studies, vital signs, complete blood count [CBC], uric acid, calcium, acid phosphatase, prostate-specific antigen [PSA], magnetic resonance imaging [MRI])
   b. Synthesize assessment data (see IIB1a [1-4])
2. Analysis—identify the nursing diagnosis (patient problem) and determine the expected outcomes (goals) of patient care
   a. Identify the psychological and physiological ramifications of treatment modalities on the patient and family (for example: consider the effects of alopecia, stomatitis, osteoporosis, erythema, bone marrow depression, pancytopenia, nausea and vomiting, bone marrow transplant, depressed mood, body image)
   b. Identify actual or potential nursing diagnoses (for example: impaired oral mucous membranes related to immunosuppression secondary to chemotherapy; altered nutrition: less than body requirements related to difficulty swallowing; ineffective individual coping related to denial secondary to diagnosis of cancer)

c. Set priorities (for example: based on Maslow's hierarchy of needs, based on the patient's developmental level)
  d. Establish expected outcomes (patient-centered goals) of nursing care (for example: patient will state coping mechanisms to be utilized, patient's mouth will be free of ulcers)
3. Planning—formulate specific strategies to achieve the expected outcomes
  a. Consider factors influencing the patient's response to abnormal cell growth and involve the patient's family in planning individualized patient care (for example: consider role changes, sexuality, changes in body image, changes in lifestyle)
  b. Plan nursing measures on the basis of established priorities to help the patient achieve the expected outcomes (for example: provide a low-residue diet for a patient receiving radiation therapy, provide a mechanically soft diet for the patient with stomatitis, provide play therapy for a child with leukemia)
4. Implementation—carry out nursing plans designed to move the patient toward the expected outcomes
  a. Provide instruction in the prevention and detection of abnormal cellular growth (for example: instruct patients concerning breast self-examination [BSE] or testicular self-examination [TSE], the seven danger signals of cancer, carcinogenic factors, screening and diagnostic testing, preventive dietary measures)
  b. Use nursing measures to provide patient comfort (for example: imaging, meditation, medications, patient-controlled analgesia [PCA], intraspinal analgesia, positioning, mouth care, skin care)
  c. Use nursing measures to promote optimal nutrition (for example: offer small frequent feedings, continuous enteral feedings, total parenteral nutrition [TPN])
  d. Use nursing measures to promote elimination (for example: manage altered elimination routes such as ileo-conduit or colostomy, instruct the patient regarding self-care, monitor urinary drainage in a patient following a transurethral prostatectomy)
  e. Use nursing measures to promote safety (for example: prevention of infection and hemorrhage; minimize side effects of treatment modalities by providing skin care, mouth care, and protective isolation)
  f. Use nursing measures to provide spiritual and emotional support
  g. Use nursing measures specific to prescribed medications (for example: monitor platelet count with antineoplastic agents, monitor fluid balance for a patient receiving steroids, monitor for side effects of medications)
  h. Use nursing measures to provide information and instruction (for example: provide referrals to self-help groups, reinforce patient's knowledge about prosthetic devices, emphasize conception control for a patient following removal of a gestational trophoblastic neoplasm [hydatidiform mole])
5. Evaluation—appraise the effectiveness of the nursing interventions relative to the nursing diagnosis and the expected outcomes
  a. Assess and report the patient's response to nursing actions (for example: record daily weight for a patient on total parenteral nutrition, report skin breakdown for a patient undergoing radiation therapy, chart intake and output for an infant with pyloric stenosis)
  b. Revise the plan of care (for example: increase fluid intake when hematuria is noted in a patient on chemotherapy)

Sample Questions: Differences in Nursing Care: Area A

1. Which data support a nursing diagnosis of activity intolerance related to insufficient oxygen secondary to chronic obstructive pulmonary disease?
   1) respiratory rate of 26, pulse of 120, and weakness with exercise
   2) orthopnea, bradypnea, and guarded respirations
   3) pursed-lip breathing, fatigue, and PCO_2 of 40
   4) nasal flaring, ineffective cough, and dyspnea

2. A patient has a permanent demand pacemaker. Which finding should the nurse report immediately?
   The heart rate
   1) increases gradually.
   2) increases with activity.
   3) slows with rest.
   4) slows suddenly.

3. Which observation should be included in the nurse's report on a patient who is receiving digitalis therapy?
   1) weight
   2) heart rate
   3) blood pressure
   4) urinary output

4. A patient is receiving furosemide (Lasix) 80 mg bid IV. Upon noting that the patient's morning serum potassium level is 2.8, the nurse should take which action?
   1) Administer the Lasix as ordered and offer the patient potassium-rich foods throughout the day.
   2) Administer the ordered dose and notify the physician.
   3) Withhold the medication and repeat the laboratory test.
   4) Withhold the medication and notify the physician.

5. A patient with pneumonia has a nursing diagnosis of ineffective airway clearance related to thick tracheobronchial secretions. Which nursing action will help decrease the viscosity of the secretions?
   1) Administer humidified oxygen at 4 L/min.
   2) Encourage the liberal intake of clear liquids.
   3) Implement postural drainage.
   4) Request an order for intravenous fluids.

6. Which treatment should most effectively improve tissue oxygenation for a patient with anemia?
   1) administration of vitamin B_{12}
   2) administration of vitamin C
   3) infusion of packed red blood cells
   4) infusion of plasma

Sample Questions: Differences in Nursing Care: Area A

7. Which action should the nurse include in the plan of care for a patient with anemia?
   1) Encourage PO fluids.
   2) Encourage frequent ambulation.
   3) Provide frequent rest periods.
   4) Provide a high-protein diet.

8. Why should the nurse plan to maintain a preschooler who is in sickle cell crisis on bed rest?
   1) to minimize oxygen consumption
   2) to prevent bacterial infection
   3) to reduce oxygen tension
   4) to correct respiratory acidosis

9. Which statement by a patient with angina best indicates that the patient is following an appropriate self-care regimen?
   1) "I do mild isometric exercises daily."
   2) "I take a short walk right after breakfast daily."
   3) "I avoid bending and lifting."
   4) "I take a nitroglycerin tablet prior to sexual intercourse."

10. A patient who exhibits ventricular asystole on the cardiac monitor will usually be given which medication?
    1) atropine sulfate
    2) lidocaine hydrochloride (Xylocaine)
    3) morphine sulfate
    4) propranolol hydrochloride (Inderal)

11. Which assessment data is indicative of pernicious anemia?
    1) spoon-shaped fingernails
    2) smooth, sore, red tongue
    3) inflamed, swollen joints
    4) petechiae on the face and neck

12. The nurse is assessing a patient with a tension pneumothorax. Which clinical manifestation indicates the need for emergency measures?
    1) bounding pulse
    2) labile hypertension
    3) peripheral edema
    4) profuse diaphoresis

13. Which information regarding alternative methods of communication should the nurse include in the preoperative teaching for a patient who is scheduled for a laryngectomy?
    1) "You will begin esophageal speech lessons once you have learned to belch."
    2) "You will be provided with paper and pencil for communication in the immediate postoperative period."
    3) "Tracheoesophageal puncture can be created at the same time as your laryngectomy."
    4) "You should learn sign language now, so you can communicate your needs in the postoperative period."

Sample Questions: Differences in Nursing Care: Area A

14. Which potential side effect of treatment with an antineoplastic agent makes the patient vulnerable to infection?
    1) nausea and vomiting
    2) pulmonary fibrosis
    3) bone marrow suppression
    4) cardiotoxicity

15. A patient receiving chemotherapy is experiencing stomatitis. The nurse's plan of care for this patient should include which action?
    1) Encourage a regular diet and good oral hygiene.
    2) Provide snacks of liquids, hard candy, and ice chips prn.
    3) Keep the patient NPO and promote hygiene with sterile water mouth rinses q2h.
    4) Provide a soft-bristled toothbrush and normal saline mouth rinse q2h.

16. Which clinical manifestation indicates that a six-week-old infant has pyloric stenosis?
    1) poor sucking reflex
    2) absence of bowel movements
    3) nonprojectile vomiting containing bile
    4) visible gastric peristaltic waves

17. Which is an indicator of an untreated basal cell carcinoma?
    1) invasion and erosion of adjoining tissue
    2) mutation of the cells to a malignant melanoma
    3) inflammation of the tumor and underlying tissue
    4) metastasis to the lymph nodes and surrounding tissue

18. Regular intake of which foods would place a patient at risk for the development of colon cancer?
    Foods that are
    1) high in fat
    2) high in fiber
    3) low in protein
    4) low in iron

19. Which clinical manifestations indicate that cancer of the pancreas may be present?
    1) fat intolerance, belching, and flatulence
    2) hyperglycemia, mid-abdominal pain, and profound weight loss
    3) vomiting, burning epigastric pain, and diarrhea
    4) weight gain, lower abdominal pain, and polycythemia

20. When planning care for a patient with advanced cancer, the nurse should be especially concerned with increasing the patient's intake of which nutrient?
    1) calcium
    2) fiber
    3) iron
    4) protein

Sample Questions: Differences in Nursing Care: Area A

21. Which information in a patient's sexual history is a risk factor for cancer of the cervix?
    1) first pregnancy after age 30
    2) late menopause
    3) multiple partners
    4) multiple pregnancies

22. A decrease in which laboratory value indicates that a patient with prostate cancer is responding positively to the treatment regimen?
    1) alpha-fetoprotein level (AFP)
    2) carcinoembryonic antigen (CEA)
    3) erythrocyte sedimentation rate (ESR)
    4) prostate-specific antigen (PSA)

Recommended Resources

For this examination, you will need to acquire textbooks in medical-surgical nursing for your library, in addition to your chosen texts in nursing diagnosis, pediatrics, and pharmacology. Remember, you do not need to purchase two textbooks in an area. You may prefer a certain author or prefer the way in which the material is presented.

Medical-Surgical Nursing
Smeltzer, S., & Bare, B. (2000). Brunner and Suddarth's Textbook of medical-surgical nursing *(9th ed.). Philadelphia: Lippincott Williams & Wilkins.*

OR
Phipps, W. et al. (1999). Medical-surgical nursing: Concepts and clinical practice *(6th ed.). St. Louis: Mosby.*

Each chapter begins with learning objectives and key terms and concludes with a chapter summary, questions for the learner to consider, and critical-thinking activities. Examples of nursing care plans and critical pathways are included. This textbook relies more on written material to explore the content. It contains fewer pictures, diagrams, tables, and charts than the Smeltzer text provides.

Study Guide:
Phipps, W. et al. (1999). Student learning guide to accompany Medical-surgical nursing *(6th ed.) St. Louis: Mosby.*

Nursing Diagnosis
Carpenito, L.J. (1997). Nursing diagnosis: Application to clinical practice *(7th ed.). Philadelphia: J.B. Lippincott.*

OR
Wilkinson, J.M. (1996). Nursing process: A critical thinking approach *(2nd ed.). St. Louis: Mosby.*

Pediatrics
Wong, D. (1997). Whaley and Wong's Essentials of pediatric nursing *(5th ed.). St. Louis: Mosby.*

Murphy, A. (1997). Study Guide to accompany Whaley and Wong's Essentials of pediatric nursing *(5th ed.). St. Louis: Mosby.*

Pharmacology
McKenry, L., & Salerno, E. (1995). Mosby's Pharmacology in nursing *(19th ed.). St. Louis: Mosby-Year Book, Inc.*

McKenry, L., & Salerno, E. (1995). Student learning guide for Mosby's Pharmacology in nursing *(19th ed.). St. Louis: Mosby-Year Book, Inc.*

OR

Shlafer, M. (1993). *The nurse, pharmacology and drug therapy: A prototype approach* (2nd ed.). Menlo Park, CA: Addison-Wesley.

Additional Resources

These textbooks may provide further clarification or enrichment in the areas of aging and nutrition.

Eliopoulos, C. (1993). *Gerontological nursing* (3rd ed.). Philadelphia: J.B. Lippincott.

> This textbook presents in-depth content on older adults, including their role in the family and the common changes that occur with aging. The changing needs of older adults are addressed in depth, as well as specific health problems and appropriate modifications in care. Assessment data and nursing diagnoses are highlighted in boxes within each chapter.

Williams, S.R. (1997). *Essentials of nutrition and diet therapy* (8th ed.). St. Louis: Mosby.

> This textbook uses chapter outlines to introduce the learner to the topics. Each chapter opens with an illustration and brief opening paragraph. Chapter summaries and review questions are included. A special feature in each chapter is a brief article on a nutrition-related issue. The textbook includes color photographs, tables, and charts.

Journal Articles

I. Cardiovascular/Pulmonary Problems

Boisvert, J.T. et al. (1995). *Overview of pediatric arrhythmias.* Nursing Clinics of North America, 30(2), 365–379.

Borkgren, M.W., & Gronkiewicz, C.A. (1995). *Update your asthma care from hospital to home.* American Journal of Nursing, 95(1), 26–35.

Bove, L.A. (1995). *Now! Surgery for heart failure.* RN 1995, 58(5), 26–31.

Byers, J.F., & Goshorn, J. (1995). *How to manage diuretic therapy.* American Journal of Nursing, 95(2), 38–44.

Dennison, R.D. (1995). *Making sense of hemodynamic monitoring.* American Journal of Nursing, 94(8), 24–32.

Dracup, K. et al. (1995). *Rethinking heart failure.* American Journal of Nursing, 95(7), 22–28.

Fellows, E. (1995). *Abdominal aortic aneurysm: Warning flags to watch for.* American Journal of Nursing, 95(5), 26–33.

Laskowski-Jones, L. (1995). *Meeting the challenge of chest trauma.* American Journal of Nursing, 95(9), 23–30.

Lavell, D.R. (1995). *Lung surgery: When less is more.* RN 1995, 58(7), 40–46.

Mays, D.A. (1995). *Turn ABGs into child's play.* RN 1995, 58(1), 36–40.

Owen, A. (1995). *Tracking the rise and fall of cardiac enzymes.* Nursing 1995, 25(5), 34–38.

Perez, A. (1995). *Electrolytes: Restoring the balance—hyperkalemia.* RN 1995, 58(11), 32–37.

Raimer, F., & Thomas, M. (1995). *Clot stoppers: Using anticoagulants safely and effectively.* Nursing 1995, 25(3), 34–45.

Redeker, N.S., & Sadowski, A.V. (1995). *Update on cardiovascular drugs and elders.* American Journal of Nursing, 95(9), 34–41.

Sample Questions: Differences in Nursing Care: Area A

Snowberger, P. (1995). Arrhythmia review: Wide-complex tachycardia. RN 1995, 58(10), 37–39.

Wallace, C.J. (1995). When digoxin harms instead of helps. RN 1995, 58(9), 26–29.

Yacone-Morton, L.A. (1995). Cardiovascular drugs: Antiarrhythmics. RN 1995, 58(4), 26–36.

Yacone-Morton, L.A. (1995). Cardiovascular drugs: First-line therapy for CHF. RN 1995, 58(2), 38–44.

Yacone-Morton, L.A. (1995). Cardiovascular drugs: Inotropic agents and nitrates. RN 1995, 58(3), 22–29.

II. Abnormal Cellular Growth

Baron, R.H., & Walsh, A. (1995). Nine facts everyone should know about breast cancer. American Journal of Nursing, 95(7), 29–33.

Brenner Z.R., & Krenzer M.E. (1995). Update on cryosurgical ablation for prostate cancer. American Journal of Nursing, 95(4), 44–49.

Greifzu, S., & Tiedemann, D. (1995). Prostate cancer: The pros and cons of treatment. RN 1995, 58(6), 22–27.

Janowski, M.J. (1995). Managing cancer pain. RN 1995, 58(9), 30–33.

McCarron, E.G. (1995). Supporting the families of cancer patients. Nursing 1995, 25(6), 48–51.

Audiovisual Resources

A very good source of videocassettes is the American Journal of Nursing Company's Multimedia Catalog. To order, call 800-CALL-AJN.

Good sources for computer-assisted instruction are Lippincott Williams & Wilkins, A Walters-Kluwer Company (To order, call 800-638-3030 or visit their Web site at www.lww.com) and Inter Act Computer Systems (3200 Kinlock Ct., Plano, TX 75074, 972-881-7781 or www.nursinc.com). Their resources are quite costly, but if you have access to a media center at a school of nursing or hospital library, look for offerings by these companies.

The following interactive videodiscs are specifically recommended by the examination development committee.

1. *Auscultation of normal breath sounds.*
   Reviews the standard procedure for auscultating the posterior and anterior chest.
2. *Nursing care of elderly patients with acute cardiac disorders* (1988).
   Designed for nurses who work with older adults who have cardiac disorders.
3. *Nursing care of the elderly patient with chronic obstructive pulmonary disease* (1988).
   Presents information about a 73-year-old patient with COPD and pneumonia and requires the viewer to manage the patient's care.
4. *Nursing care of the cancer patient with compromised immunity: concepts and care.*
   O'Neill, P., Welsh, S., Volker, D., Adsit, K., Wood, P., & Moore, L. (1990).
5. *Managing the experience of labor and delivery.*
   Gilman, B., Werner, E., & Gordon, J. (1989).

Content/Reference List

I. Cardiovascular/Pulmonary Problems
McKenry & Salerno (19th ed., 1995)
    Chapter 30   Anticoagulants, Thrombolytics, and Blood Components
    Chapter 37   Mucokinetic and Bronchodilator Drugs

Sample Questions: Differences in Nursing Care: Area A

Phipps (6th ed., 1999)
- Chapter 24   Assessment of the Cardiovascular System
- Chapter 25   Management of Persons with Coronary Artery Disease and Dysrhythmias
- Chapter 26   Management of Persons with Inflammatory Heart Disease, Heart Failure, and Persons Undergoing Cardiac Surgery
- Chapter 27   Management of Persons with Vascular Problems
- Chapter 28   Assessment of the Hematological System
- Chapter 29   Management of Persons with Hematological Problems
- Chapter 30   Assessment of the Respiratory System
- Chapter 31   Management of Persons with Problems of the Upper Airway
- Chapter 32   Management of Persons with Problems of the Lower Airway

Shlafer (2nd ed., 1993)
- Chapter 35   Anticoagulant, Antiplatelet, and Thrombolytic Drugs
- Chapter 36   Drugs for Regulating Blood Lipid Levels
- Chapter 37   Structure and Function of the Respiratory System
- Chapter 38   Drugs for Managing Asthma

Smeltzer & Bare (9th ed., 2000)
- Chapter 19   Assessment of Respiratory Function
- Chapter 20   Management of Patients with Upper Respiratory Tract Disorders
- Chapter 21   Management of Patients with Chest and Lower Respiratory Tract Disorders
- Chapter 22   Respiratory Care Modalities
- Chapter 23   Assessment of Cardiovascular Function
- Chapter 24   Management of Patients with Dysrhythmias and Conduction Problems
- Chapter 26   Management of Patients with Structural, Infectious, or Inflammatory Cardiac Disorders
- Chapter 27   Management of Patients with Complications from Heart Disease
- Chapter 28   Assessment and Management of Patients with Vascular Disorders and Problems of Peripheral Circulation
- Chapter 30   Assessment and Management of Patients with Hematologic Disorders

Wong (5th ed., 1997)
- Chapter 23   The Child with Respiratory Dysfunction
- Chapter 25   The Child with Cardiovascular Dysfunction

II. Abnormal Cellular Growth

McKenry & Salerno (19th ed., 1995)
- Chapter 56   Antineoplastic Chemotherapy
- Chapter 57   Antineoplastic Agents

Phipps (6th ed., 1999)
- Chapter 11   Cancer
  See also specific diagnoses under the related system (for example: malignant conditions of the breast in Chapter 48, Management of Persons with Problems of the Breast)

Shlafer (2nd ed., 1993)
- Chapter 59   Antineoplastic Drugs

Smeltzer & Bare (9th ed., 2000)
- Chapter 15   Oncology: Nursing Management in Cancer Care
  See also specific diagnoses under the related system (for example: carcinoma of the breast under reproductive function)

Wong (5th ed., 1997)
- Chapter 26   The Child with Hematologic or Immunologic Dysfunction

Study Guide

Differences in Nursing Care: Area B (531) (Associate Level)

Credit Hours: 5
Question Type(s): Multiple-choice
Credit Level: Lower

The information in this study guide is valid until Summer 2001.
If you will be taking the examination after that date, be sure to check for a new edition of this guide before you complete your preparation for the exam.

General Description of the Examination

The Differences in Nursing Care: Area B examination measures knowledge and understanding of the various health care needs and problems encountered by the associate degree nurse. Questions are based on the common and specific manifestations of these needs and problems and the nursing care actions properly associated with them. Questions pertain to patients of various age groups in the proportion that members of these groups use health care services. Questions concern both acute and long-term needs and problems of medical, surgical, psychiatric, and pediatric patients.

The examination requires you to possess the technical vocabulary and knowledge of anatomy and physiology, microbiology, and emotional and physical development generally expected of the associate degree nurse. The examination requires you to demonstrate knowledge of the theoretical framework for each content area as well as the ability to apply this knowledge to nursing practice using the nursing process.

Content Outline

Content Area	Percent of Examination
I. Behavioral Responses	40%
II. Regulatory Mechanisms	25%
III. Metabolic Mechanisms	25%
IV. Congenital Anomalies, Genetic Disorders, and Developmental Problems	10%
Total	**100%**

I. Behavioral Responses—Observable Responses of the Individual to Life Stressors (40%)

A. **Theoretical framework—basis for care**
   1. Types of behavioral responses
      a. Affective responses
         1) Persons who exhibit loss/grief responses, including denial, anger, and bargaining (for example: families that have experienced sudden infant death syndrome [SIDS], a patient recently diagnosed with chronic renal failure)
         2) Persons who exhibit elated behavior, including psychomotor hyperactivity, euphoria, and flight of ideas
         3) Persons who exhibit depressed behavior, including psychomotor retardation, disruption in sleeping and eating patterns, social isolation, and disturbance in self-esteem
         4) Persons who exhibit elation/depression behaviors indicative of bipolar moods
      b. Anxiety responses
         1) Persons who exhibit anxiety responses (for example: persons with generalized anxiety disorder, post-traumatic stress disorder, panic disorder, obsessive-compulsive disorder, specific phobia, and social phobia)
         2) Persons who express anxiety through dissociative disorders (for example: amnesia, fugue, dissociative identity disorder)
      c. Somatoform psychophysiological responses (for example: ulcerative colitis, impotence, conversion disorder, hypochondriasis)
      d. Withdrawal responses—psychogenic withdrawal from reality, including delusions, hallucinations, paranoid behavior, and autistic behavior (for example: schizophrenia and other psychotic disorders)
      e. Aggressive responses
         1) Persons who demonstrate self-destructive behavior, including suicide, substance abuse, and eating disorders
         2) Persons who demonstrate antisocial behavior (for example: those who abuse or neglect adults and children, those with personality disorders)
      f. Disruptive responses (for example: attention-deficit hyperactivity disorder, conduct disorder)
      g. Dysfunctional coping behaviors in response to situational crises, including anger, withdrawal, denial, and dissociation (for example: as manifested by victims of rape, child abuse, spouse abuse, and elder abuse)
      h. Alterations in behavior related to organic mental disorders, including delirium, memory impairment, loss of impulse control, and wandering (for example: dementia of the Alzheimer's type, vascular dementia, dementia due to HIV disease, Wernicke-Korsakoff syndrome, Huntington's chorea)
   2. Factors influencing an individual's behavioral responses
      a. Personality characteristics (for example: introverted, suspicious, rigid, passive, aggressive)
      b. Developmental level (for example: trust vs. mistrust; oral stage)
      c. Use of defense mechanisms (for example: denial, projection, regression)
      d. Interpersonal experiences (for example: family roles and relationships, peer

relationships)
  e. Socioeconomic and cultural factors (for example: race, religion, nationality, lifestyle, environmental factors, occupation, education)
  f. Precipitating event (for example: rape, divorce, illness, situational and maturational crises)
  g. Genetic background (for example: bipolar disorders, alcoholism, Alzheimer's disease)
  h. Substance abuse (for example: food, alcohol, chemical agents)
  i. Nutritional status (for example: potassium imbalance)
3. Theoretical concepts that help explain variations in behavioral responses. (This area includes general concepts developed by the individuals listed, but not specific quotations from these individuals.)
  a. Biological theories
    1) Genes
    2) Hormones
    3) Neurotransmitters
  b. Psychosocial theories
    1) Intrapsychic theory (Sigmund Freud)
    2) Developmental stages and tasks (Erik Erikson)
    3) Hierarchy of needs (Abraham Maslow)
    4) Social-interpersonal relationships (Harry Stack Sullivan)
    5) Crisis theory (Gerald Caplan)
4. Therapeutic modalities
  a. Therapeutic nurse–patient relationship
  b. Therapeutic milieu
  c. Crisis intervention
  d. Community mental health programs (for example: Overeaters Anonymous, Alcoholics Anonymous)
  e. Behavior modification therapy
  f. Individual psychotherapy
  g. Group psychotherapy
  h. Family therapy
  i. Occupational/recreational therapy
  j. Reminiscing therapy
  k. Relaxation therapy
  l. Cognitive therapy
  m. Detoxification programs
  n. Somatic therapies
    1) Psychopharmacology
      (a) Antipsychotic drugs
      (b) Antianxiety/antihistamines
      (c) Antidepressant drugs
      (d) Antimanic drugs (lithium)
      (e) Antiparkinsonian drugs
      (f) Central nervous system stimulants
      (g) Anticonvulsant drugs
    2) Electroconvulsive therapy
    3) Phototherapy

B. Nursing care related to theoretical framework
   1. Assessment—gather and synthesize data about the patient's health status in relation to the patient's functional health patterns
      a. Gather assessment data
         1) Obtain the patient's health history (for example: subjective symptoms, medications, diet, past illnesses, health habits, family history, usual coping mechanisms)
         2) Assess factors influencing the patient's behavioral responses (see IA2)
         3) Obtain objective data related to the patient's behavioral responses (for example: body language, affect, personal appearance, psychomotor activity, ritualistic behaviors, communication patterns, mental status)
         4) Review laboratory and other diagnostic data (for example: dexamethasone levels, lithium levels, electroencephalogram [EEG])
      b. Synthesize assessment data (see IB1a[1-4])
   2. Analysis—identify the nursing diagnosis (patient problem) and determine the expected outcomes (goals) of patient care
      a. Identify actual or potential nursing diagnoses (for example: disturbance in self-concept related to biochemical imbalance; ineffective individual coping related to maturational crisis; altered thought processes related to delusion and/or hallucinations; risk for violence related to impaired ability to control aggression; altered nutrition: less than body requirements related to reluctance to eat)
      b. Set priorities (for example: based on Maslow's hierarchy of needs, based on the patient's developmental level)
      c. Establish expected outcomes (patient-centered goals) for care (for example: patient will verbalize perception of body image that is congruent with reality, patient will verbalize feelings of anger and loss, patient will seek assistance when delusions become threatening, patient will not harm self or others, patient will gain one pound in three days)
   3. Planning—formulate specific strategies to achieve the expected outcomes
      a. Consider factors influencing the patient's behavioral responses in planning patient care (see IA2)
      b. Plan nursing measures on the basis of established priorities to help the patient achieve the expected outcomes (for example: help the patient explore negative self-perceptions, provide a nonthreatening environment for the patient to practice risk-taking, do not reinforce the patient's delusions through discussion or validation, reduce environmental stimulation)
   4. Implementation—carry out nursing plans designed to move the patient toward the expected outcomes
      a. Use nursing measures to provide for the patient's physiological needs (for example: monitor vital signs, provide dietary instruction for patients with stress-related gastrointestinal problems, monitor elimination patterns of the depressed patient)
      b. Use therapeutic communication skills (for example: to clarify the patient's thinking, to encourage a higher level of functioning)
      c. Use nursing measures to provide for patient safety (for example: provide a structured milieu, observe suicide precautions, apply restraints, decrease or increase environmental stimuli, provide for patient safety before and after

electroconvulsive therapy [ECT], prevent destructive activity through use of de-escalation techniques)
   d. Use nursing measures to increase the patient's level of functioning (for example: encourage participation in patient government, encourage involvement in reality orientation groups, use music therapy, use group therapy, use reminiscing therapy, encourage activities of daily living [ADLs] for the patient with Alzheimer's disease)
   e. Use nursing measures to provide the patient with alternate methods of dealing with stressors (for example: encourage patient's interests in hobbies, encourage verbalization of thoughts and feelings, encourage the patient with depression to externalize anger, assist the patient to develop or strengthen support systems, provide age-appropriate diversionary activities)
   f. Use nursing measures to assist the patient to maintain optimal function (for example: refer patient to Alcoholics Anonymous, Overeaters Anonymous; encourage participation in supportive psychotherapy or family therapy)
   g. Use nursing measures specific to prescribed medications (for example: monitor compliance with monoamine oxidase [MAO] diet, monitor the intake and output of the patient receiving lithium, monitor for side effect of medications)
   h. Provide information and instruction (for example: instruct the patient regarding relaxation techniques, provide information about problem-solving techniques, provide instruction regarding the need for compliance with lithium therapy)
5. Evaluation—appraise the effectiveness of the nursing interventions relative to the nursing diagnosis and the expected outcomes
   a. Assess and report the patient's response to nursing actions (for example: verbalized freely, anxiety decreased from +3 to +1, gained weight, assumed responsibility for personal hygiene, increased acting out in group)
   b. Revise the patient's plan of care as necessary (for example: encourage the patient to take more responsibility in patient government as self-esteem increases, recommend an increase in the patient's privileges, introduce the patient to social interaction in groups, renegotiate no-suicide contract)

II. Regulatory Mechanisms (25%)

This area includes the adrenal gland, thyroid gland, pituitary gland, parathyroid gland, and kidney. This area focuses on the nursing care of patients with health problems such as myxedema, Graves' disease, Cushing's syndrome, Addison's disease, pheochromocytoma, diabetes insipidus, acromegaly, nephrotic syndrome, renal calculi, and renal failure.

A. Theoretical framework—basis for care
1. Types of regulatory disorders
   a. Disorders related to excess production of hormones (for example: pheochromocytoma, Graves' disease, Cushing's syndrome, acromegaly)
   b. Disorders related to deficient production of hormones (for example: myxedema, Addison's disease, diabetes insipidus, hypoparathyroidism)
   c. Disorders related to impaired renal function (for example: acute and chronic renal failure, renal calculi, glomerulonephritis, nephrosis, nephrotic syndrome)

2. Clinical manifestations of regulatory disorders
   a. Altered respiratory functioning (for example: dyspnea, crackles, wheezes, hypoventilation)
   b. Altered circulatory functioning (for example: tachycardia, hypertension, bradycardia, hypotension)
   c. Altered nutrition (for example: weight loss, weight gain)
   d. Altered elimination (for example: constipation, diarrhea, hematuria, oliguria, anuria, dysuria, polyuria)
   e. Altered activity (for example: hyperactivity, hypoactivity)
   f. Altered comfort (for example: fatigue, pain)
   g. Altered appearance (for example: buffalo hump, moon face, exophthalmos, goiter)
   h. Altered mental status (for example: mood swings, lethargy, coma)
   i. Altered integument (for example: dry skin, pruritus, edema, friability, changes in turgor, changes in color)
   j. Altered fluid and electrolyte balance (for example: hypernatremia, metabolic acidosis, hypercalcemia, hyper/hypokalemia, hyper/hypovolemia)
   k. Altered sensory perception (for example: auditory and visual changes)
3. Factors influencing the patient's response to regulatory disorders
   a. Age and physiological factors (for example: allergies, body surface area, immobility, age-related circulatory changes)
   b. Psychological factors (for example: stress, cognitive ability, body image, coping mechanisms)
   c. Nutritional status (for example: obesity, malnutrition)
   d. Presence of other illness (for example: infection, hypertension, diabetes mellitus, other chronic illnesses)
   e. Socioeconomic and cultural factors (for example: health practices, lifestyle, occupation, education, environmental factors)
   f. Availability of support systems (for example: family, friends, community resources)
4. Theoretical basis for interventions related to regulatory disorders
   a. Medications (for example: analgesics, hormones, electrolytes, antithyroid agents, immunosuppressive agents)
   b. Preoperative and postoperative care (for example: thyroidectomy, adrenalectomy, hypophysectomy, nephrectomy, renal transplant)
   c. Treatment modalities (for example: dietary modifications, hemodialysis, peritoneal dialysis, lithotripsy)
   d. Health instruction (for example: rationale for lifestyle changes, risk factors, preventive measures)

B. **Nursing care related to theoretical framework**
   1. Assessment—gather and synthesize data about the patient's health status in relation to the patient's functional health patterns
      a. Gather assessment data
         1) Obtain the patient's health history (for example: subjective symptoms, diet, medications, past illnesses, family history, impact of illness on family/occupational roles and self-image)
         2) Assess factors influencing the patient's response to regulatory disorders (see IIA3)

3) Obtain objective data related to the patient's regulatory disorder (for example: alterations in the vital signs, integument, sleep patterns, intake and output)
4) Review laboratory and other diagnostic data (for example: urine tests, hormone levels, blood chemistry, scans, biopsies)
   b. Synthesize assessment data (see IIB1a[1-4])
2. Analysis—identify the nursing diagnosis (patient problem) and determine the expected outcomes (goals) of patient care
   a. Identify actual or potential nursing diagnoses (for example: disturbance in body image related to change in appearance, activity intolerance related to fatigue, ineffective individual coping related to inability to manage stressors, impaired gas exchange related to fluid overload)
   b. Set priorities (for example: based on Maslow's hierarchy of needs, based on the patient's developmental level)
   c. Establish expected outcomes (patient-centered goals) for patient care (for example: patient will participate in grooming, patient will increase participation in activities, patient will identify one significant stressor, patient's arterial blood gas values will be within normal limits)
3. Planning—formulate specific strategies to achieve the expected outcomes
   a. Consider factors influencing the patient's response to regulatory disorders (see IIA3)
   b. Plan nursing measures on the basis of established priorities to help the patient achieve the expected outcomes (for example: plan time for the patient to verbalize feelings about changed appearance, schedule rest periods, select relaxation techniques that are appropriate for the patient, plan a fluid restriction schedule)
4. Implementation—carry out nursing plans designed to move the patient toward the expected outcomes
   a. Use nursing measures to provide a safe environment (for example: provide suction apparatus for the patient following a thyroidectomy, regulate environmental temperature for the patient with myxedema, provide instruction about implications of corticosteroid regimen)
   b. Use nursing measures to promote comfort (for example: provide temperature control for a patient with Graves' disease, provide skin care for a patient with pruritus)
   c. Use nursing measures specific to prescribed medications (for example: monitor blood glucose in a patient who is receiving corticosteroid medications, monitor cardiac function in a patient who is receiving a thyroid medication, monitor calcium levels in a patient who is receiving parathyroid hormone)
   d. Use nursing measures to prevent/minimize complications due to regulatory disorders (for example: closely observe the patient following a thyroidectomy, monitor bowel elimination for the patient with myxedema)
   e. Use nursing measures to enhance utilization of coping mechanisms and support systems (for example: encourage verbalization of feelings about changed body image; provide information about home health agencies, social services)

f. Provide information and instruction (for example: provide the patient's family with information regarding condition and treatment to enhance patient compliance, provide instruction about dietary management for the patient with impaired renal function)
5. Evaluation—appraise the effectiveness of the nursing interventions relative to the nursing diagnosis and the expected outcomes
   a. Assess and report the patient's response to nursing actions relative to the expected outcomes (for example: increased activity levels in the patient with hypothyroidism, weight loss or gain for a child with nephrotic syndrome, decreased pain in the patient with renal calculi)
   b. Revise the patient's plan of care as necessary (for example: increase observation of the patient showing signs of impending thyroid crisis, raise the room temperature for the patient with myxedema, explore the patient's reasons for noncompliance with dietary regimen)

III. Metabolic Mechanisms (25%)

This area includes the liver, gallbladder, and pancreas. This area focuses on the nursing care of patients with health problems such as cirrhosis, cholecystitis, insulin-dependent diabetes mellitus (type I), noninsulin-dependent diabetes mellitus (type II), pancreatitis, and cholelithiasis.

A. Theoretical framework—basis for care

1. Types of metabolic disorders
   a. Responses to obstruction (for example: cholelithiasis, pancreatitis, cholecystitis)
   b. Responses to toxic substances (for example: chronic pancreatitis, cirrhosis, hepatic coma)
   c. Responses to inadequate production or utilization of secretions (for example: insulin-dependent diabetes mellitus [type I], noninsulin-dependent diabetes mellitus [type II])
2. Clinical manifestations of metabolic disorders
   a. Altered fluid and electrolyte balance (for example: polyuria, polydipsia, muscle weakness, bradycardia, shallow respirations, diarrhea, hypotension, edema, cardiac dysrhythmia)
   b. Altered nutrition (for example: anorexia, nausea, vomiting, polyphagia, dyspepsia)
   c. Altered elimination (for example: clay-colored stool, frothy urine)
   d. Altered appearance (for example: edema, ascites, jaundice, spider nevi)
   e. Altered neurological function (for example: lethargy, memory loss, behavioral changes, decreased sensory perception, changes in fine motor control)
   f. Altered comfort (for example: pain, fatigue)
   g. Altered activity (for example: changes in sleep patterns, fatigue)
   h. Altered respiratory function (for example: Kussmaul's respiration, dyspnea)
   i. Altered circulatory functioning (for example: hypotension, tachycardia)
   j. Altered integument (for example: pruritus, poor wound healing)
3. Factors influencing the patient's response to metabolic disorders
   a. Age and physiological factors (for example: allergies)
   b. Psychological factors (for example: stress, cognitive ability, body image, coping mechanisms)
   c. Nutritional status (for example: obesity, malnutrition)

d. Presence of other illness (for example: infection, chronic illnesses)
e. Socioeconomic and cultural factors (for example: health practices, lifestyle, occupation, education, environmental factors)
f. Availability of support systems (for example: family, friends, community resources)
4. Theoretical basis for interventions related to metabolic disorders
   a. Medications (for example: insulin, oral hypoglycemic agents, diuretics, vitamins, analgesics, antispasmodic agents, lactulose, propranolol)
   b. Preoperative and postoperative care (for example: cholecystectomy [abdominal and laparoscopic], choledochostomy)
   c. Treatment modalities (for example: diabetic exchange diet, low-protein diet, double-balloon tamponade)
   d. Health instruction (for example: rationale for preventive measures, lifestyle changes, risk factors)

B. Nursing care related to theoretical framework
1. Assessment—gather and synthesize data about the patient's health status in relation to the patient's functional health patterns
   a. Gather assessment data
      1) Obtain the patient's health history (for example: subjective symptoms, diet, medications, drug and alcohol use, past illnesses, family history, allergies, impact of illness on family/occupational roles)
      2) Assess factors influencing the patient's response to metabolic disorders (see IIIA3)
      3) Obtain objective data related to the patient's metabolic disorder (for example: alterations in vital signs, integument, weight, abdominal girth, psychomotor function)
      4) Review laboratory and diagnostic data (for example: blood chemistry, serum enzyme levels, liver function studies, biopsy, scans, glycosylated hemoglobin)
   b. Synthesize assessment data (see IIIB1a[1-4])
2. Analysis—identify the nursing diagnosis (patient problem) and determine the expected outcomes (goals) of patient care
   a. Identify actual or potential nursing diagnoses (for example: risk for injury: bleeding related to vitamin K deficiency; ineffective breathing pattern related to incisional pain; altered nutrition: less than body requirements related to vomiting and anorexia; noncompliance related to denial of illness; knowledge deficit: administration of insulin related to lack of information; risk for injury related to confusion)
   b. Set priorities (for example: based on Maslow's hierarchy of needs, based on the patient's developmental level)
   c. Establish expected outcomes (patient-centered goals) for care (for example: patient will not experience bleeding, patient will list foods high in sodium, patient will increase caloric intake to 2,000 calories, patient will demonstrate correct administration of insulin, patient will remain free of injury)
3. Planning—formulate specific strategies to achieve the expected outcomes
   a. Consider factors influencing the patient's response to metabolic disorders (see IIIA3)
   b. Plan nursing measures on the basis of established priorities to help the patient achieve the expected outcomes (for example: plan to instruct the

patient about safe oral hygiene practices, plan to provide the patient with a list of high-sodium foods, plan to provide oral care frequently, plan to show the patient a videotape regarding the administration of insulin, plan protective measures)
 4. Implementation—carry out nursing plans designed to move the patient toward the expected outcomes
    a. Use nursing measures to provide a safe environment (for example: provide the patient with a soft toothbrush, pad the siderails for a patient who is confused, eliminate obstacles from the ambulatory path of a patient with neuropathy)
    b. Use nursing measures to promote comfort (for example: place the patient with ascites in position of comfort, administer medications for pain relief, control the environmental temperature for the patient with pruritus, provide mouth care for a patient with a double-balloon tamponade)
    c. Use nursing measures specific to prescribed medications (for example: monitor serum glucose for a patient who is receiving insulin, monitor electrolytes for a patient who is receiving diuretics, monitor serum prothrombin times for a patient who is receiving vitamin K, monitor pulse for a patient who is receiving propranolol)
    d. Use nursing measures to prevent/minimize complications due to metabolic disorders (for example: provide skin and nail care for the patient with diabetes mellitus, rotate insulin sites for the patient with diabetes mellitus, use small-gauge needles for injections for the patient with bleeding tendencies, apply pressure to injection sites for 5–10 minutes to minimize bleeding tendencies, test the stool of a patient with a bleeding disorder for occult blood, monitor bleeding following biopsies)
    e. Use nursing measures to enhance utilization of coping mechanisms and support systems (for example: provide information about available age-appropriate support services, such as camps for children with diabetes mellitus; encourage the patient and family to participate in decision making; encourage verbalization of feelings related to the grief process and loss of function)
    f. Use nursing measures to provide information and instruction (for example: review predisposing factors with the patient with noninsulin-dependent diabetes mellitus [type II], instruct the patient with cirrhosis to read labels when shopping for food, encourage the patient with diabetes mellitus to schedule an annual eye examination, instruct the patient with diabetes mellitus about foot care)
 5. Evaluation—appraise the effectiveness of the nursing interventions relative to the nursing diagnosis and the expected outcomes
    a. Assess and report the patient's response to nursing actions (for example: appetite has changed, nausea and vomiting is relieved, patient reports relief from pain, bleeding is minimized, skin is intact, weight is stable)
    b. Revise the patient's plan of care as necessary (for example: consider alternate methods of pain relief to enhance medication effectiveness, increase observation of a patient with an increased serum amylase level, reevaluate fluid and nutritional intake when a patient with cirrhosis continues to gain weight, review the diet and exercise program of a patient with diabetes mellitus whose glycosylated hemoglobin level remains elevated)

IV. Congenital Anomalies, Genetic Disorders, and Developmental Problems (10%)

This area includes congenital anomalies, which are those acquired during fetal development in utero; genetic disorders, which are hereditary in nature; and developmental problems, which interfere with normal growth and development. This area focuses on the nursing care of patients with health problems such as cardiac anomalies, cystic fibrosis, hemophilia, hydrocephalus, Down syndrome, phenylketonuria (PKU), meningomyelocele (spina bifida), muscular dystrophy, cerebral palsy, clubfoot, developmental dysplasia of the hip, Hirschsprung's disease, tracheoesophageal fistula, imperforate anus, congenital heart disease, biliary atresia, and mental retardation.

A. Theoretical framework—basis for care

1. Types of congenital anomalies, genetic disorders, and developmental problems
   a. Problems affecting oxygenation (for example: tetralogy of Fallot, patent ductus arteriosus, cystic fibrosis, hemophilia, sickle cell anemia)
   b. Problems affecting alimentation (for example: Hirschsprung's disease, tracheoesophageal fistula, imperforate anus, cleft palate)
   c. Problems affecting mobility (for example: meningomyelocele, muscular dystrophy, cerebral palsy, clubfoot, developmental dysplasia of the hip)
   d. Problems affecting mental function (for example: PKU, Down syndrome, hydrocephalus)

2. Clinical manifestations of congenital anomalies, genetic disorders, and developmental problems
   a. Altered respiratory functioning (for example: increased amount and viscosity of secretions, tachypnea, crackles, cough)
   b. Altered gastrointestinal functioning (for example: vomiting, inability to suck, abdominal distention, constipation, obstipation, fatty stools, indigestion)
   c. Altered mobility (for example: paralysis, weakness, spastic gait, choreiform movements, retarded physical development)
   d. Altered neurological status (for example: retarded mental development, seizures, increased intracranial pressure, impulsive behaviors)
   e. Altered urinary elimination (for example: incontinence, abnormal opening)
   f. Altered fluid and electrolyte balance (for example: hypovolemia)
   g. Altered appearance (for example: clubbed fingers, frontal enlargement, bulging fontanelle)
   h. Altered comfort (for example: pain, fatigue)
   i. Altered circulatory function (for example: dysrhythmias, tachycardia)
   j. Altered integument (for example: skin breakdown, abnormal opening)

3. Factors influencing the patient's response to congenital anomalies, genetic disorders, and developmental problems
   a. Age and physiological factors (for example: allergies)
   b. Psychological factors (for example: awareness of problem, behavioral manifestations, impulse control, parental and family responses)
   c. Nutritional status (for example: malnutrition, obesity)
   d. Presence of other illness (for example: infection)
   e. Site of congenital anomaly or genetic problem (for example: facial, genital, musculoskeletal, systemic)
   f. Socioeconomic and cultural factors (for example: access to health care, religious and cultural beliefs, lifestyle, occupation, education)

g. Extent or severity of involvement (for example: operable vs. incurable or progressively deteriorating)
  h. Availability of support systems (for example: family, friends, community resources)
4. Theoretical basis for interventions related to congenital anomalies, genetic disorders, and developmental problems
  a. Medications (for example: enzymes, diuretics, cardiac glycosides)
  b. Preoperative and postoperative care (for example: repair of clubfoot, imperforate anus, tetralogy of Fallot)
  c. Genetic counseling (for example: Tay-Sachs disease, cystic fibrosis)
  d. Treatment modalities (for example: dietary modifications, pulmonary therapy, mobility devices)
  e. Health instruction (for example: rationale for preventive measures, risk factors)

B. Nursing care related to theoretical framework
1. Assessment—gather and synthesize data about the patient's health status in relation to the patient's functional health patterns
  a. Gather assessment data
    1) Obtain the patient's health history (for example: subjective symptoms, diet, medications, past illnesses, family history, developmental task achievement, sleeping patterns, immunizations, growth and developmental data)
    2) Assess factors influencing the patient's response to congenital anomalies and genetic problems (see IVA3)
    3) Obtain objective data related to the patient's health problem (for example: breath sounds, altered integument, gait, developmental task achievement, growth rate, sensory-motor ability, physical abnormalities, altered vital signs, general appearance, head size, energy level)
    4) Review laboratory and other diagnostic data (for example: chest X ray, skeletal X ray, sweat test, complete blood count [CBC], arterial blood gases [ABG], electrocardiogram [EKG], barium enema, ultrasound, magnetic resonance imaging [MRI])
  b. Synthesize assessment data (see IVB1a [1-4])
2. Analysis—identify the nursing diagnosis (patient problem) and determine the expected outcomes (goals) of patient care
  a. Identify actual or potential nursing diagnoses (for example: altered family process related to situational crisis; activity intolerance related to imbalance between oxygen supply and demand; risk for infection related to pulmonary congestion; impaired mobility related to neuromuscular problems; altered cerebral tissue perfusion related to increased intracranial pressure; altered nutrition: less than body requirements related to inadequate pancreatic enzymes)
  b. Set priorities (for example: based on Maslow's hierarchy of needs, based on the patient's developmental level)
  c. Establish expected outcomes (patient-centered goals) for care (for example: family will demonstrate understanding of child's abilities, child will be free of cyanosis during morning care, patient will move independently with the aid of assistive devices, head circumference will remain stable, child will be free of irritability and headaches and will have vital signs within normal limits, patient will be free of abdominal distention, stools will be brown

and of medium consistency and size)
3. Planning—formulate specific strategies to achieve the expected outcomes
    a. Consider factors influencing the patient's response to congenital anomalies and genetic problems (for example: site of anomaly, severity of problem, patient's access to health care [see IVA3])
    b. Plan nursing measures on the basis of established priorities to help the patient achieve the expected outcomes (for example: plan to change the child's position frequently, schedule rest periods, establish a schedule for chest physiotherapy, plan instruction regarding assistive devices)
4. Implementation—carry out nursing interventions designed to move the patient toward the expected outcomes
    a. Use nursing measures to assist the patient and family to cope with the disability (for example: use therapeutic communication, make referrals to support groups)
    b. Use nursing measures to promote, maintain, or restore physiological functioning (for example: establish a rest schedule for the patient with a cardiac anomaly, provide chest physiotherapy for a patient with cystic fibrosis, elevate the head of the bed for a patient with hydrocephalus, position the child with a meningomyelocele on the abdomen)
    c. Use nursing measures to stimulate and encourage psychosocial development (for example: use appropriate verbal communication, provide assistance and encouragement for the child to perform developmental tasks, encourage age-appropriate play activities)
    d. Use nursing measures to prevent/minimize complications (for example: monitor vital signs, use sterile technique during dressing changes, position the child to prevent contamination from urine and stool)
    e. Use nursing measures to provide comfort, rest, and sleep (for example: maintain bedtime routines; provide a quiet, calm environment; position for comfort; relieve abdominal distention)
    f. Use nursing measures specific to prescribed medications (for example: take the pulse prior to administering digitalis, check for response to pain-relieving medications, check for allergies prior to administering antibiotics, administer pancreatic enzymes with meals)
    g. Use nursing measures to provide information and instruction (for example: instruct the family about low-phenylalanine diet, provide skin care instruction for a patient who is wearing a brace, instruct the family in positioning techniques for the child with hydrocephalus, instruct the family in postural drainage techniques)
5. Evaluation—appraise the effectiveness of the nursing interventions relative to the nursing diagnosis and the expected outcomes
    a. Assess and report the patient's response to nursing actions relative to the expected outcomes (for example: changes in elimination patterns, head circumference, ability to ingest food; achievement of bowel and bladder function; achievement of developmental tasks)
    b. Revise the patient's plan of care as necessary (for example: consider addition of percussion to postural drainage program for a child with cystic fibrosis, obtain self-help devices for the patient with a progressive coordination disability)

Sample Questions: Differences in Nursing Care: Area B

1. Which finding is common in patients during the manic phase of bipolar disorder?
    1) delusional thought patterns
    2) psychomotor retardation
    3) excessive sleepiness
    4) passive communication style

2. Which affective state is typically observed in patients with schizophrenia?
    1) anger
    2) apathy
    3) euphoria
    4) sadness

3. Which is a characteristic of a patient with a passive-aggressive personality disorder? The patient
    1) suspects the motives of others.
    2) displays a high degree of insight.
    3) shows insensitivity to the feelings of others.
    4) displays manipulative behaviors.

4. Which side effects are associated with the use of lithium carbonate (Eskalith)?
    1) blurred vision, tremors, and diarrhea
    2) neutropenia, palpitations, and drowsiness
    3) psychological dependence, ataxia, and depression
    4) akathisia, tardive dyskinesia, and delusions

5. A female patient is admitted to the emergency department after having been abducted and raped. Which patient behavior illustrates use of the defense mechanism of dissociation?
    1) The patient states that she is fine and does not need to be hospitalized.
    2) The patient states that she does not have any recollection of the incident.
    3) The patient discusses the incident in a matter-of-fact manner.
    4) The patient states that she knows she needs follow-up care but does not want to talk about it.

6. Which diagnosis should receive priority for a hospitalized patient who demonstrates suspicious behavior?
    1) anxiety related to lack of trust in new environment and caregivers
    2) impaired verbal communication related to argumentative speech patterns
    3) self-esteem disturbance related to inaccurate self-perception
    4) social isolation related to withdrawal from interactions with others

7. Which goal should the nurse include in the plan of care for a patient with a diagnostic category of high risk for self-directed violence?
    1) The patient's use of tranquilizers will decrease.
    2) The patient will seek out mutual relationships.
    3) The patient will demonstrate an increased ability to concentrate.
    4) The patient will seek out staff when suicidal ideation occurs.

Sample Questions: Differences in Nursing Care: Area B

8. Which goal should be included in the plan of care for a patient who is a victim of spouse abuse?
   The patient will
   1) articulate a safety plan for use in abusive situations.
   2) understand the psychodynamics of the abusive behavior.
   3) identify ways in which the abuse could have been avoided.
   4) verbalize the reasons for the abuse.

9. When a patient with schizophrenia begins to hallucinate, the nurse should take which action?
   1) Provide the patient with privacy.
   2) Administer the ordered antianxiety medication.
   3) Redirect the patient to activities focused on the here and now.
   4) Convince the patient that the hallucination is not real.

10. A patient with obsessive behavior spends so much time at ritual handwashing that he misses the scheduled breakfast time each morning. Which action should the nurse take?
    1) Insist that the patient stop the handwashing when it is time for breakfast.
    2) Restrict the patient's access to the sink until after breakfast.
    3) Awaken the patient early, so that the handwashing can be completed before breakfast.
    4) Ask the patient to postpone the handwashing until after breakfast.

11. Which action should the nurse take when a patient who is receiving an antipsychotic medication exhibits muscle rigidity and tremors?
    1) Administer the ordered antiparkinsonian medication.
    2) Withhold the medication and continue to observe the patient.
    3) Inform the patient that these are expected side effects of the medication.
    4) Request the physician to increase the dosage of medication.

12. Which alteration in the integument is a clinical manifestation of diabetes insipidus?
    1) cool, clammy skin
    2) edema
    3) poor skin turgor
    4) pruritus

13. A patient with Addison's disease who is on corticosteroid therapy may be at risk for the development of which health problem?
    1) fine hand tremors
    2) hyperkalemia
    3) infection
    4) weight loss

14. How should the nurse assess a patient for hemorrhage following a thyroidectomy?
    1) Loosen one edge of the dressing to examine the incisional line.
    2) Gently lift the patient to check the bed linens for bloody drainage.
    3) Roll the patient to the side to examine the sides and back of the neck.
    4) Examine the posterior pharynx for evidence of bleeding.

Sample Questions: Differences in Nursing Care: Area B

15. Which laboratory finding supports a diagnostic category of activity intolerance in a patient with chronic renal failure?
    1) decreased hemoglobin
    2) decreased serum magnesium
    3) increased serum bicarbonate
    4) increased serum phosphate

16. A patient is in the diuretic phase of acute renal failure. Which action by the nurse demonstrates awareness of the physiological changes that are occurring?
    1) Check for a positive Chvostek's sign.
    2) Observe the neck for distended veins.
    3) Attempt to elicit Trousseau's sign.
    4) Assess the apical pulse for irregularities.

17. Which discharge instruction should the nurse give to a patient who is receiving hormone therapy for hypothyroidism?
    1) Decrease the dosage when symptoms subside.
    2) Expect palpitations and diaphoresis to occur.
    3) Take the medication at the same time each day.
    4) Take the medication with meals.

18. Which serum elevation may contribute to the development of hepatic encephalopathy?
    1) hyperglycemia
    2) hyperkalemia
    3) hypernatremia
    4) hyperproteinemia

19. Which nursing assessment should receive priority for a patient with cirrhosis who has esophageal varices?
    1) bilirubin levels
    2) skin color
    3) urinary output
    4) vital signs

20. A patient with hepatic dysfunction complains of itching. The nurse should associate the itching with which other assessment finding?
    1) anorexia
    2) ascites
    3) jaundice
    4) malnutrition

21. Which nursing diagnosis would be appropriate for a patient with chronic pancreatitis?
    1) colonic constipation related to immobility
    2) impaired tissue integrity related to mechanical destruction
    3) ineffective breathing pattern related to pain
    4) risk for injury related to sensory deficits

Sample Questions: Differences in Nursing Care: Area B

22. Which measure should the nurse include in the plan of care for a patient who has a liver dysfunction?
    1) Use small-gauge needles for injections, to minimize bleeding tendencies.
    2) Bathe the patient frequently, to remove oil and salts from the skin.
    3) Monitor the vital signs closely, to detect hypotension.
    4) Use physical restraints as necessary, to control excessive motor activity.

23. Which nursing intervention should receive priority for a patient with acute pancreatitis?
    1) monitoring the patient's intake and output
    2) relieving the patient's pain
    3) changing the patient's position frequently
    4) monitoring the patient's lab values

24. The nurse should instruct a patient with cirrhosis of the liver who has ascites to adhere to which type of diet?
    1) high-fat
    2) high-fiber
    3) low-carbohydrate
    4) low-sodium

25. Which statement by a patient with insulin-dependent diabetes mellitus (type I) indicates that the patient understands the symptoms of hypoglycemia that should be reported?
    1) "I will watch for increased urination and nausea."
    2) "I will watch for sweating and shakiness."
    3) "I will watch for unusual thirst and rapid breathing."
    4) "I will watch for dry skin and fruity breath odor."

26. Why do children with tetralogy of Fallot frequently assume a squatting position?
    1) to decrease postural hypotension
    2) to increase peripheral circulation
    3) to maximize peripheral resistance
    4) to relieve chronic hypoxia

27. Which information in an infant's health history is most consistent with a diagnosis of Hirschsprung's disease?
    1) greasy stools
    2) chronic constipation
    3) projectile vomiting
    4) frequent respiratory infections

28. The nurse's assessment of a neonate with a meningomyelocele should focus on which area?
    1) the extent of the neurological deficit
    2) the degree of respiratory paralysis
    3) the amount of pain associated with movement
    4) the strength of the pharyngeal, laryngeal, and oral muscles

Sample Questions: Differences in Nursing Care: Area B

29. Which lunch choice by the parents of a two-year-old child indicates that they are maintaining their child on a low-phenylalanine diet?
    1) chicken salad
    2) fruit salad
    3) egg salad sandwich
    4) peanut butter and jelly sandwich

Recommended Resources

For this examination, you will need to acquire a textbook in psychiatric nursing for your library, in addition to your chosen texts in medical-surgical nursing, nursing diagnosis, pediatrics, and pharmacology. Remember, you do not need to purchase two textbooks in an area. You may prefer a certain author or prefer the way in which the material is presented.

Psychiatric Nursing
Varcarolis, E. (1998). Foundations of psychiatric mental health nursing *(3rd ed). Philadelphia: W.B. Saunders.*

This textbook uses anxiety and the mental health continuum as the organizing framework. Each chapter begins with an outline, a list of key terms and concepts, and objectives. Chapters discussing psychiatric disorders are written in a nursing process framework with sample care plans and case studies included. Figures and tables highlight key concepts. Each chapter ends with a variety of self-study exercises.

There is no study guide to accompany this text.

OR
Townsend, M. (1996). Psychiatric mental health nursing: Concepts of care *(2nd ed.). Philadelphia: F.A. Davis.*

This textbook uses stress-adaptation as its conceptual framework. It has incorporated changes reflective of the DSM-IV. Each chapter begins with a chapter outline, key terms, and objectives. Case studies, critical pathways, and care plans are included. Figures and tables highlight key concepts. Each chapter ends with review questions.

There is no study guide to accompany this text.

Maternal-Newborn Nursing
Dickason, E. et al. (1998). Maternal-infant nursing care *(3rd ed.). St. Louis: Mosby.*

Dickason, E. (1998). Student learning guide to accompany Maternal-infant nursing care *(3rd ed.). St. Louis: Mosby.*

OR
Gorrie, T. et al. (1994). Foundations of maternal newborn nursing. *Philadelphia: W.B. Saunders.*

Medical-Surgical Nursing
Smeltzer, S., & Bare, B. (2000). Brunner and Suddarth's Textbook of medical-surgical nursing *(9th ed.). Philadelphia: Lippincott Williams & Wilkins.*

Sample Questions: Differences in Nursing Care: Area B

OR

Phipps, W. et al. (1999). Medical-surgical nursing: Concepts and clinical practice (6th ed.). St. Louis: Mosby.

Phipps, W. et al. (1999). Student learning guide to accompany Medical-surgical nursing (6th ed.). St. Louis: Mosby.

Nursing Diagnosis
Carpenito, L.J. (1997). Nursing diagnosis: Application to clinical practice (7th ed.). Philadelphia: J.B. Lippincott.

OR

Wilkinson, J.M. (1996). Nursing process: A critical thinking approach (2nd ed.). St. Louis: Mosby.

Pediatrics
Wong, D. (1997). Whaley and Wong's Essentials of pediatric nursing (5th ed.). St. Louis: Mosby.

Murphy, A. (1997). Study guide to accompany Whaley and Wong's Essentials of pediatric nursing (5th ed.). St. Louis: Mosby.

Pharmacology
McKenry, L., & Salerno, E. (1995). Mosby's Pharmacology in nursing (19th ed.). St. Louis: Mosby.

McKenry, L., & Salerno, E. (1995). Student learning guide for Mosby's Pharmacology in nursing (19th ed.). St. Louis: Mosby.

OR

Shlafer, M. (1993). The nurse, pharmacology, and drug therapy: A prototype approach (2nd ed.). Menlo Park, CA: Addison-Wesley.

Additional Resources

Journal Articles
I. Behavioral Responses—Observable Responses of the Individual to Life Stressors

Amora, A., & Cerrato, P. (1996). Eating disorders—still a threat. RN, 59(6), 30–35.

Antai-Otong, D. (1995). Helping the alcoholic patient recover. American Journal of Nursing, 95(8), 22–30.

Badger, J. (1995). Reaching out to the suicidal patient. American Journal of Nursing, 95(3), 24–32.

Barstow, D. (1995). Self-injury and self-mutilation. Journal of Psychosocial Nursing and Mental Health Services, 33(2), 19–22.

Burgess, A., Burgess, A., & Douglas, J. (1994). Examining violence in the workplace: A look at work related fatalities. Journal of Psychosocial Nursing and Mental Health Services, 32(7), 11–18, 53.

Chez, N. (1994). Helping the victim of domestic violence. American Journal of Nursing, 94(7), 33–37.

D'Arrigo, T. (1994). Depression and recovery in home care patients. Caring, 13(6), 42–46.

Fitzsimmons, L. (1995). Electroconvulsive therapy: What nurses need to know. Journal of Psychosocial Nursing and Mental Health Services, 33(12), 14–17.

Hall, G. (1996). Managing acute confusion in the elderly. Nursing '96, 26(7), 33–37.

Henderson, A., & Ericksen J. (1994). Enhancing nurses' effectiveness with abused women: Awareness, reframing, support, education. Journal of Psychosocial Nursing and Mental Health Services, 32(6), 11–15.

Lynch, S. (1997). Elder abuse: What to look for, how to intervene. American Journal of Nursing, 97(1), 27–32.

Sample Questions: Differences in Nursing Care: Area B

Navaria, T. (1995). Enabling behavior: The tender trap. American Journal of Nursing, 95(1), 50–52.

Spear, H. (1996). Anxiety—when to worry, what to do. RN, 59(7), 40–46.

Stolley, J.M. (1994). When your patient has Alzheimer's disease. American Journal of Nursing, 94(8), 34–41.

Valente, S. (1994). Recognizing depression in elderly patients. American Journal of Nursing, 94(12), 18–25.

II. Regulatory Mechanisms

Angelucci, P. (1995). Caring for patients with hypothyroidism. Nursing '95, 25(5), 60–61.

Howser, R. (1995). What you need to know about corticosteroid therapy. American Journal of Nursing, 95(8), 44–49.

Jankowski, C. (1996). Irradiating the thyroid: How to protect yourself and others. American Journal of Nursing, 96(10), 51–54.

Stark, J. (1994). Interpreting BUN/creatinine levels, it's not as simple as you think. Nursing '94, 24(9), 58–61.

III. Metabolic Mechanisms

Ambrose, M., & Dreher, H. (1996). Pancreatitis, managing a flare-up. Nursing '96, 26(4), 33–39.

Deakins, D. (1994). Teaching elderly patients about diabetes. American Journal of Nursing, 94(4), 38–43.

Dorgan, M.B. et al. (1995). Performing food screening for diabetic patients. American Journal of Nursing, 94(11), 32–37.

Hoyson, P.M. (1995). Diabetes 2000: Oral medications. RN, 58(5), 34–40.

Norton, R. (1995). Diabetes 2000: The right mix of diet and exercise. RN, 58(4), 20–25.

Peragallo-Dittko, V. (1995). Diabetes 2000: Acute complications. RN, 58(8), 36–42.

Robertson, C. (1995). Diabetes 2000: Chronic complications. RN, 58(9), 34–41.

Shapero, M., & Stegall, M. (1995). Diabetes 2000: When insulin isn't enough. 58(7), 34–37.

Strowig, S. (1995). Diabetes 2000: Insulin therapy. 58(6), 30–37.

Tomky, D. (1995). Diabetes 2000: Advances in monitoring. RN, 58(3), 38–45.

IV. Congenital Anomalies, Genetic Disorders, and Developmental Problems

Gutteridge, C., & Kuhn, R.J. (1994). Pulmozyme (Dornase alpha). Pediatric Nursing, 20(3), 278–279.

Harns, M.D. (1995). Caring for individuals in the community who are mentally retarded/developmentally disabled. Home Health Care Nurse, 13(6), 27–38.

Hays, M.A.B. (1995). Traction at home for infants with developmental dysplasia of the hip. Orthopedic Nursing, 14(1), 33–40.

Higgins, S.S., & Reid, A. (1994). Common congenital heart defects: Long-term followup. Nursing Clinics of North America, 29(2), 233–248.

Audiovisual Resources
Videocassettes

1. *Fanlight Productions, 47 Halifax Street, Boston, MA 02130*
   Four lives
2. *Insight Media, 2162 Broadway, New York, NY 10024, Phone: 212-721-6316*
   Communication with clients with mental disorders or emotional problems
   Controlling violence in health care
   Domestic violence: Behind closed doors
   Treating borderline personality disorders
3. *Concept Media, P.O. Box 19542, Irvine, CA 92623-9542, Phone: 800-233-7078*
   Techniques of therapeutic communication
   Blocks to therapeutic communication
   Interactions for study

Sample Questions: Differences in Nursing Care: Area B

Interactive Videodiscs

FITNE, 5 Depot Street, Athens, OH 45701, Phone: 614-592-2511
  Therapeutic communication

Computer-Assisted Instruction

1. *Lippincott Williams & Wilkins, P.O. Box 1600, Hagerstown MD 21741, Phone 800-638-3030*
    Clinical simulations in nursing I, Psychiatric nursing series
    Clinical simulations in nursing II, Psychiatric nursing series
    Clinical simulations in mental health nursing III
    Critical care nursing simulations: Endocrine system series
    Clinical simulations in nursing, Pediatric nursing simulations I
    Clinical simulations in nursing, Pediatric nursing simulations II
    Nursing care of patients with anxiety disorders
2. *Lippincott-Raven Publishers, Audiovisual Department, 227 East Washington Square, Philadelphia, PA 19106, Phone: 800-523-2945*
    Nurs-comps: Clients with bipolar disorder, manic episode
    Nurs-comps: Nursing interventions for an adolescent with anorexia nervosa
    Nurs-comps: Nursing interventions for the client with anxiety
    Nursing: Mr. Drew, an adult who abuses alcohol
    Nursing: Ms. Alt, a young adult with depression
3. *Computerized Educational Systems, 307 Park Lake Circle, P.O. Box 536905, Orlando, FL 32853-6905, Phone: 800-275-1474*
    Care of the client with borderline personality disorder
    Therapeutic communication with the chemically dependent client
    Therapeutic counseling session

Content/Reference List

I. Behavioral Responses

McKenry & Salerno (19th ed., 1995)

Chapter 14	Antianxiety, Sedative, and Hypnotic Drugs
Chapter 17	Psychotherapeutic Drugs
Chapter 18	Drugs for Specific CNS-Peripheral Dysfunctions

Shlafer (2nd ed., 1993)

Chapter 22	Sedatives, Hypnotics, Anxiolytics
Chapter 23	Antipsychotic Drugs
Chapter 24	Drugs for Treatment of Depression and Mania

Townsend (2nd ed., 1996)

Chapter 1	An Introduction to the Concept of Stress
Chapter 2	Mental Health and Mental Illness
Chapter 3	Theories of Personality Development
Chapter 5	Relationship Development
Chapter 6	Therapeutic Communication
Chapter 7	The Nursing Process in Psychiatric/Mental Health Nursing
Chapter 8	Therapeutic Groups
Chapter 9	Intervention with Families
Chapter 10	Milieu Therapy—The Therapeutic Community
Chapter 11	Crisis Intervention
Chapter 12	Relaxation Therapy
Chapter 15	Anger/Aggression Management
Chapter 16	The Suicidal Client
Chapter 17	Behavior Therapy

Sample Questions: Differences in Nursing Care: Area B

    Chapter 18   Psychopharmacology
    Chapter 19   Electroconvulsive Therapy
    Chapter 20   Disorders Usually First Diagnosed in Infancy, Childhood, or Adolescence
    Chapter 21   Delirium, Dementia, and Amnestic Disorders
    Chapter 22   Substance-Related Disorders
    Chapter 23   Schizophrenia and Other Psychotic Disorders
    Chapter 24   Mood Disorders
    Chapter 25   Anxiety Disorders
    Chapter 26   Somatoform and Sleep Disorders
    Chapter 27   Dissociative Disorders
    Chapter 29   Eating Disorders
    Chapter 31   Psychological Factors Affecting Medical Conditions
    Chapter 32   Personality Disorders
    Chapter 33   The Aging Individual
    Chapter 35   Problems Related to Abuse or Neglect
    Chapter 37   Cultural Concepts Relevant to Psychiatric/Mental Health Nursing

Varcarolis (3rd ed., 1998)
    Chapter 2   Mental Health: Theories and Therapies
    Chapter 5   Framework for Culturally Relevant Psychiatric Nursing
    Chapter 6   The Nurse-Client Relationship
    Chapter 7   Communication and the Clinical Interview
    Chapter 8   Psychiatric Nursing in the Acute Psychiatric Hospital
    Chapter 10   Communication within Groups
    Chapter 13   Reducing Stress and Anxiety
    Chapter 14   Crisis and Crisis Intervention
    Chapter 15   Families in Crisis: Family Violence
    Chapter 16   Rape
    Chapter 17   Anxiety Disorders
    Chapter 18   Somatoform and Dissociative Disorders
    Chapter 19   Personality Disorders
    Chapter 20   Alterations in Mood: Grief and Depression
    Chapter 21   Alterations in Mood: Elation in Bipolar Disorders
    Chapter 22   Schizophrenic Disorders
    Chapter 23   Cognitive Disorders
    Chapter 24   People Who Contemplate Suicide
    Chapter 25   People Who Depend Upon Substances of Abuse
    Chapter 26   People with Eating Disorders
    Chapter 29   Children and Adolescents

II. Regulatory Mechanisms

McKenry & Salerno (19th ed., 1995)
    Chapter 32   Overview of the Urinary System
    Chapter 33   Diuretics
    Chapter 35   Drug Therapy for Renal System Dysfunction
    Chapter 46   Overview of the Endocrine System
    Chapter 47   Drugs Affecting the Pituitary
    Chapter 48   Drugs Affecting the Parathyroid and Thyroid
    Chapter 49   Drugs Affecting the Adrenal Cortex

Phipps (6th ed., 1999)
    Chapter 33   Assessment of the Endocrine System
    Chapter 34   Management of Persons with Problems of the Pituitary, Thyroid, Parathyroid, and Adrenal Glands
    Chapter 43   Assessment of the Renal System
    Chapter 44   Management of Persons with Problems of the Kidney and Urinary Tract
    Chapter 45   Management of Persons with Renal Failure

Sample Questions: Differences in Nursing Care: Area B

Shlafer (2nd ed., 1993)
- Chapter 43   Structure and Function of the Endocrine System
- Chapter 44   Pituitary-Hypothalamic Relationships
- Chapter 45   Adrenocorticosteroids
- Chapter 47   Thyroid and Parathyroid Hormones and Antithyroid Drugs

Smeltzer (9th ed., 2000)
- Chapter 38   Assessment and Management of Patients with Endocrine Disorders
- Chapter 39   Assessment of Urinary and Renal Function
- Chapter 40   Management of Patients with Urinary and Renal Dysfunction
- Chapter 41   Management of Patients with Urinary and Renal Disorders

Wong (5th ed., 1996)
- Chapter 27   The Child with Genitourinary Dysfunction
- Chapter 29   The Child with Endocrine Dysfunction

III. Metabolic Mechanisms

McKenry & Salerno (19th ed., 1995)
- Chapter 50   Drugs Affecting the Pancreas

Phipps (6th ed., 1999)
- Chapter 35   Management of Persons with Diabetes Mellitus and Hypoglycemia
- Chapter 36   Assessment of the Hepatic System
- Chapter 37   Management of Persons with Problems of the Hepatic System
- Chapter 38   Assessment of the Gastrointestinal, Biliary, and Exocrine Pancreatic Systems
- Chapter 42   Management of Persons with Problems of the Gallbladder and Exocrine Pancreas

Shlafer (2nd ed., 1993)
- Chapter 46   Drugs for Managing Diabetes Mellitus and Hypoglycemia

Smeltzer (9th ed., 2000)
- Chapter 36   Assessment and Management of Patients with Hepatic and Biliary Disorders
- Chapter 37   Assessment and Management of Patients with Diabetes Mellitus

Wong (5th ed., 1996)
- Chapter 24   The Child with Gastrointestinal Dysfunction

IV. Congenital Anomalies, Genetic Disorders, and Developmental Problems

McKenry & Salerno (19th ed., 1995)
- Chapter 40   Drugs Affecting the Upper Gastrointestinal Tract (Section on Digestants)

Wong (5th ed., 1997)
- Chapter 9   Health Problems of Newborns
- Chapter 23   The Child with Respiratory Dysfunction
- Chapter 24   The Child with Gastrointestinal Dysfunction
- Chapter 25   The Child with Cardiovascular Dysfunction
- Chapter 28   The Child with Cerebral Dysfunction
- Chapter 31   The Child with Musculoskeletal or Articular Dysfunction
- Chapter 32   The Child with Neuromuscular or Muscular Dysfunction

Study Guide

Differences in Nursing Care: Area C (Associate Level) (509)

Credit Hours: 5
Credit Level: Lower
Question Type(s): Multiple-choice

The information in this study guide is valid until Summer 2001.
If you will be taking the examination after that date, be sure to check for a new edition of this guide before you complete your preparation for the exam.

General Description of the Examination

The Differences in Nursing Care: Area C examination measures knowledge and understanding of the various health care needs and problems encountered by the associate degree nurse. Questions are based on the common and specific manifestations of these needs and problems and the nursing care actions properly associated with them. Questions pertain to patients of various age groups in the proportion that members of these groups use health care services. Questions concern both acute and long-term needs and problems of medical, surgical, and pediatric patients.

The examination requires you to possess the technical vocabulary and knowledge of anatomy and physiology, microbiology, and emotional and physical development generally expected of the associate degree nurse. The examination requires you to demonstrate knowledge of the theoretical framework for each content area as well as the ability to apply this knowledge to nursing practice using the nursing process.

Content Outline

Content Area	Percent of Examination
I. Infectious and Communicable Disease Problems	35%
II. Tissue Trauma	30%
III. Neurological, Sensory, and Musculoskeletal Dysfunctions	35%
Total	**100%**

I. Infectious and Communicable Disease Problems (35%)

This area focuses on the nursing care of patients with infections of body systems such as acquired immunodeficiency syndrome (AIDS), cytomegalic inclusion disease, encephalitis, epiglottitis, gram-negative sepsis, hepatitis, herpes viruses (including varicella), human immunodeficiency virus (HIV), infectious gastroenteritis, Legionnaires' disease, Lyme disease, meningitis, mononucleosis, mumps, otitis media, pertussis (whooping cough), rabies, rheumatic fever, rubella, rubeola (measles), salmonella, sexually transmitted diseases (STDs), shigellosis, urinary tract infection, and tuberculosis.

A. Theoretical framework—basis for care

1. Types of infectious and communicable diseases
   a. Diseases transmitted via blood and body fluids (for example: AIDS, hepatitis type B)
   b. Diseases transmitted via respiratory secretions (for example: tuberculosis, mononucleosis, streptococcal infections, rubeola [measles], varicella, Haemophilus influenza)
   c. Diseases transmitted via body drainage and secretions (for example: conjunctivitis, nosocomial infections, staphylococcal infections, herpes simplex, STDs)
   d. Diseases transmitted via the gastrointestinal tract (for example: infectious diarrhea, salmonella, shigellosis, hepatitis type A, helminthic diseases)
2. Clinical manifestations of infectious and communicable diseases
   a. Altered respiratory functioning (for example: increased secretions, presence of abnormal breath sounds, cough, dyspnea, tachypnea)
   b. Altered gastrointestinal functioning (for example: anorexia, nausea, vomiting, diarrhea, melena)
   c. Altered genitourinary functioning (for example: frequency, urgency, flank pain, hematuria, pyuria, dysuria, vaginal or penile discharge)
   d. Altered integument (for example: rash, vesicles, macules, swelling, pruritus, erythema)
   e. Altered vital signs (for example: fever, tachycardia)
   f. Alterations in comfort (for example: pain, fatigue, anorexia, insomnia)
   g. Alterations in mental status (for example: confusion, slowed thought processes)
3. Factors influencing the patient's response to infectious and communicable diseases
   a. Age and physiological factors (for example: active and passive immunity)
   b. Psychological factors (for example: stress, cognitive ability)
   c. Socioeconomic and cultural factors (for example: health practices, lifestyle, nutritional status, environmental factors, substance abuse)
   d. Presence of other illness (for example: patient with diabetes, patient with leukemia, patients receiving immunosuppressive drugs, patient receiving antibiotic therapy, patient with an opportunistic infection)
   e. Causative agent (for example: bacteria, viruses, other pathogens)
   f. Site of infectious or communicable disease
   g. Extent or severity of involvement (for example: local vs. systemic infection)

4. Theoretical basis for interventions related to infectious and communicable diseases
    a. Medications (for example: antibiotics, antifungal agents, anti-inflammatory agents, antipyretics, antiviral agents, antidiarrheal agents)
    b. Immunizations (for example: mumps, measles, rubella [MMR]; diphtheria, tetanus, pertussis, [DTP]; Haemophilus b [Hib], polio, hepatitis B vaccine)
    c. Preventive measures (for example: tuberculosis screening, health teaching, sex education, proper nutrition, universal precautions, body substance isolation)

B. **Nursing care related to theoretical framework**
    1. Assessment—gather and synthesize data about the patient's health status in relation to the patient's functional health patterns
        a. Gather assessment data
            1) Obtain the patient's health history (for example: subjective symptoms, nutritional status, medications, past illnesses, health habits, family history, allergies, occupation, social habits, previous exposure to causative agents)
            2) Assess factors influencing the patient's response to infectious and communicable diseases (see IA3)
            3) Obtain objective data related to the patient's infectious and communicable disease problem (for example: determine clinical manifestations, altered vital signs, alterations in the integument)
            4) Review laboratory and other diagnostic data (for example: complete blood count [CBC], rubella titers, VDRL, sputum for acid-fast bacilli, culture and sensitivity reports, Mantoux test, sedimentation rate, diagnostic radiology and imaging modalities, serum screening for hepatitis viruses, human immunodeficiency virus [HIV])
        b. Synthesize assessment data (see IB1a [1-4])
    2. Analysis—identify the nursing diagnosis (patient problem) and determine the expected outcomes (goals) of patient care
        a. Identify actual or potential nursing diagnoses (for example: risk for infection related to decreased immune response; risk for infection related to presence of indwelling catheter; risk for social isolation related to reduced environmental stimuli; impaired skin integrity related to pruritus; knowledge deficit: unprotected sexual practices)
        b. Set priorities (for example: based on Maslow's hierarchy of needs, based on the patient's developmental level)
        c. Establish expected outcomes (patient-centered goals) for care (for example: patient will be afebrile, patient will verbalize preventive measures, patient's skin will remain intact)
    3. Planning—formulate specific strategies to achieve the expected outcomes
        a. Consider factors influencing the patient's response to the health problem in planning patient care (for example: stress reduction measures, age-related factors, immune status [see IA3])
        b. Plan nursing measures on the basis of established priorities to achieve the expected outcomes (for example: monitor hydration status, alleviate skin discomfort, provide protective isolation)

4. Implementation—carry out nursing plans designed to move the patient toward the expected outcomes
   a. Use nursing measures to control the spread of the causative organism (for example: universal precautions, isolation techniques, personal protective equipment, protective barrier techniques, body substance isolation, environmental considerations)
   b. Use nursing measures to promote, maintain, or restore physiological functioning (for example: provide adequate fluids for a patient with infectious gastroenteritis, provide skin care for a patient with varicella, establish a rest schedule for a patient with mononucleosis, make dietary adjustments for altered elimination patterns)
   c. Use nursing measures to minimize patient discomfort (for example: provide a sitz bath for a patient with vaginitis; provide skin care for a patient with pruritus; provide a cool, nonstimulating environment for a patient with meningitis)
   d. Use nursing measures specific to prescribed medications (for example: assess vital signs prior to the administration of analgesics, monitor temperature following the administration of antipyretics, assess for allergies prior to the administration of antibiotics, administer urinary analgesics to relieve dysuria, apply skin preparations to relieve itching, administer antiviral agents to inhibit infection, monitor for adverse reactions)
   e. Use nursing measures to assist the patient and/or significant others to cope with the health problem (for example: use therapeutic communication techniques with the patient and/or family, refer the patient with AIDS to a support group, make referrals to community health agencies for patients with tuberculosis)
   f. Provide information and instruction (for example: emphasize the need for protective asepsis, instruct the patient about the need for proper nutrition, instruct the patient with an STD about prophylactic measures, provide instruction about hygienic practices, instruct parents about the need for their child to complete the course of antibiotic therapy, advise the patient with hepatitis type B to refrain from donating blood)
5. Evaluation—appraise the effectiveness of the nursing interventions relative to the nursing diagnosis and the expected outcomes
   a. Assess and report the patient's response to nursing actions relative to the expected outcomes (for example: decrease in wound drainage, decrease in pain due to otitis media, effects of antipyretic medication, condition of the skin, alterations in the patient's condition, patient verbalizes the intention to practice safe sex, patient verbalizes knowledge of the route of transmission, patient with tuberculosis adheres to medication regimen)
   b. Revise the patient's plan of care as necessary (for example: increase observation of the patient with an infection who is febrile, provide additional diversional activities for the child with varicella who is experiencing increasing pruritus)

II. Tissue Trauma (30%)

This area focuses on the nursing care of patients with all types of tissue trauma. Tissue trauma includes such problems as burns, accidents, ulcers, inflammatory diseases, and accidental poisoning, as well as surgical intervention.

A. Theoretical framework—basis for care

1. Types of tissue trauma
   a. Physical/mechanical/degenerative (for example: soft tissue trauma, accidents, falls, hiatal hernia, pressure ulcers, traumatic amputation, bee stings, animal bites)
   b. Thermal (for example: burns, frostbite)
   c. Chemical (for example: medications, poisons, toxins, burns)
   d. Inflammatory (for example: appendicitis, inflammatory bowel disease [Crohn's disease, ulcerative colitis], diverticulitis, cholecystitis, gastritis, gastric ulcers, lupus erythematosus)
   e. Surgical intervention (for example: appendectomy, tonsillectomy, hernia repair, reconstructive surgery, exploratory laparotomy, gastrectomy, ileostomy, cholecystectomy, laparoscopic surgery)

2. Clinical manifestations of tissue trauma
   a. Altered vital signs (for example: elevated pulse, temperature alteration)
   b. Altered neurological status (for example: confusion, lethargy)
   c. Altered neurovascular status (for example: diminished peripheral pulses)
   d. Altered digestive and elimination patterns (for example: urinary frequency, absence of bowel sounds, constipation)
   e. Alterations in mobility (for example: gait disturbance, weakness)
   f. Alterations in comfort (for example: pruritus)
   g. Alterations in integument and mucous membrane (for example: edema, erythema, ulceration, hematoma)
   h. Altered fluid and electrolyte balance (for example: metabolic alkalosis, metabolic acidosis, fluid volume deficit)

3. Factors influencing the patient's response to tissue trauma
   a. Age and physiological factors (for example: physical activity patterns)
   b. Psychological factors (for example: stress, body image)
   c. Socioeconomic and cultural factors (for example: lifestyle, health practices, occupation, environmental conditions, substance abuse)
   d. Nutritional status (for example: obesity, malnutrition)
   e. Presence of other illness (for example: diabetes mellitus, cardiac disease, long-term steroid therapy)
   f. Site of tissue trauma
   g. Extent or severity of tissue involvement

4. Theoretical basis for interventions related to tissue trauma
   a. Medications (for example: analgesics, antibiotics, chelating agents, nonsteroidal anti-inflammatory agents, corticosteroids, antidotes, narcotic antagonists, antacids, antihistamines, beta inhibitors, anticholinergics, antiflatulents, debriding agents, histamine blockers)
   b. Preoperative care (for example: types of anesthesia, preoperative teaching, premedications)

c. Intraoperative care (for example: anesthesia, blood and fluid replacement, positioning)
   d. Postoperative care (for example: comfort management, immediate assessment of the patient postoperatively, routine care, wound care, physical activity, diet)
   e. Emergency interventions (for example: first aid measures, antidotes, splints)
   f. Treatment modalities (for example: burn treatments, pressure dressings, wet-to-dry dressings)

B. **Nursing care related to theoretical framework**
   1. Assessment—gather and synthesize data about the patient's health status in relation to the patient's functional health patterns
      a. Gather assessment data
         1) Obtain the patient's health history (for example: subjective symptoms, nutritional status, medications, recent injuries, past illnesses, health habits, family history, occupation)
         2) Assess factors influencing the patient's response to tissue trauma (see IIA3)
         3) Obtain objective data related to the patient's tissue trauma problem (for example: clinical manifestations, activity tolerance, altered vital signs, cardiopulmonary assessment, behavioral responses, extent of tissue trauma)
         4) Review laboratory and other diagnostic data (for example: central venous pressure readings, vital signs, endoscopic procedures, diagnostic imaging modalities, serum electrolytes, serum albumin, CBC, liver enzymes)
      b. Synthesize assessment data (see IIB1a [1-4])
   2. Analysis—identify the nursing diagnosis (patient problem) and determine the expected outcomes (goals) of patient care
      a. Identify actual or potential nursing diagnoses (for example: risk for infection related to break in skin integrity; altered peripheral tissue perfusion related to thrombus formation)
      b. Set priorities (for example: based on Maslow's hierarchy of needs, based on the patient's developmental level)
      c. Establish expected outcomes (patient-centered goals) for care (for example: patient will verbalize diminished pain, patient will comply with diet and fluid regimen)
   3. Planning—formulate specific strategies to achieve the expected outcomes
      a. Consider factors influencing the patient's response to tissue trauma (see IIA3) in planning patient care (for example: consider cultural dietary restrictions for the patient with Crohn's disease, plan pain management for the patient with a history of substance abuse)
      b. Plan nursing measures on the basis of established priorities to help the patient achieve the expected outcomes (for example: monitor fluid and electrolyte balance for a patient with burns)
   4. Implementation—carry out nursing plans designed to move the patient toward the expected outcomes
      a. Use nursing measures to control the extent of tissue trauma (for example: provide skin care for the patient with an ileostomy, use surgical asepsis when changing a burn dressing)
      b. Use nursing measures to minimize patient discomfort (for example: provide skin care to T-tube drainage site, provide diversional activities for the patient postoperatively)

c. Use nursing measures to promote fluid, electrolyte, and nutritional balance (for example: offer small, frequent feedings for the patient following a gastrectomy; monitor intake and output for the patient with burns; report alterations in the patient's condition)
   d. Use nursing measures to assist the patient and/or significant others to cope (for example: refer the patient with an ileostomy to a self-help group, use therapeutic communication to encourage patient to verbalize feelings regarding changes in body image)
   e. Use nursing measures specific to prescribed medications (for example: monitor the electrolyte status of the patient receiving potassium supplements, monitor vital signs prior to the administration of analgesics, monitor the elimination pattern of a patient receiving lactulose [Cephulac])
   f. Use nursing measures to provide information and instruction (for example: reinforce crutch walking for a patient with an amputation, provide preoperative and postoperative instruction, provide instruction regarding endoscopic procedures)
5. Evaluation—appraise the effectiveness of the nursing interventions relative to the nursing diagnosis and the expected outcomes
   a. Assess and report the patient's response to nursing actions relative to the expected outcomes (for example: condition of the skin around a surgically created opening, patient verbalizes relief of pain following the administration of a narcotic analgesic, record body weight and urinary output for the patient with burns, report alterations in the patient's condition)
   b. Revise the patient's plan of care as necessary (for example: assess the effectiveness of the ostomy device, increase frequency of coughing and deep-breathing exercises for the patient postoperatively)

III. Neurological, Sensory, and Musculoskeletal Dysfunctions (35%)

This area focuses on the nursing care of patients with problems affecting the neurological system, such as cerebrovascular accidents, multiple sclerosis, Parkinson's disease, myasthenia gravis, brain tumors, spinal cord injuries, seizure disorders, and head trauma. Sensory dysfunction includes such problems as glaucoma, Meniere's disease, otosclerosis, and cataracts. Musculoskeletal dysfunction includes such problems as rheumatoid arthritis, joint replacement, degenerative joint disease, contractures, fractures, scoliosis, gout, slipped femoral epiphysis, and lumbar disc disease.

A. Theoretical framework—basis for care
   1. Types of neurological, sensory, and musculoskeletal dysfunctions
      a. Age-related conditions (for example: scoliosis, osteoporosis, juvenile rheumatoid arthritis, Legg-Calvé-Perthes disease, cataracts, presbyopia, presbycusis)
      b. Degenerative conditions (for example: multiple sclerosis, degenerative joint disease, Parkinson's disease, myasthenia gravis, Huntington's chorea, disc problems)
      c. Conditions of altered neurological pathways (for example: seizure disorders, head injuries, spinal cord injuries, cerebrovascular accidents)
      d. Conditions of musculoskeletal dysfunction (for example: fractures, joint replacement, slipped femoral epiphysis)

e. Conditions of altered sensation (for example: glaucoma, cataracts, detached retina, loss of hearing, paresthesia)
2. Clinical manifestations of neurological, sensory, and musculoskeletal dysfunction
   a. Impaired motor function (for example: paralysis, immobility, muscular weakness, ataxia)
   b. Impaired sensory function (for example: neurovascular deficits, paresthesia, visual and hearing impairment)
   c. Altered neurological status (for example: seizure activity, change in level of consciousness, coma)
   d. Altered vital signs (for example: indicators of increased intracranial pressure)
   e. Alterations in behavior (for example: flat affect, scanning speech, masked facies, emotional lability)
   f. Alterations in comfort (for example: acute and chronic pain)
   g. Alterations in mental status (for example: confusion, slowed thought processes, disorientation)
3. Factors influencing the patient's response to neurological, sensory and musculoskeletal dysfunction
   a. Age and physiological factors (for example: women who are postmenopausal)
   b. Psychological factors (for example: stress)
   c. Socioeconomic and cultural factors (for example: lifestyle, environmental factors, nutritional status)
   d. Presence of other illness (for example: diabetes mellitus)
   e. Site of dysfunction (for example: level of spinal cord injury)
   f. Extent or severity of involvement (for example: exacerbations or remission, local or systemic involvement)
4. Theoretical basis for interventions to promote, restore, or maintain neurological, sensory, and musculoskeletal function
   a. Medications (for example: analgesics, anti-inflammatory agents, hormone replacement therapy, antibiotics, anticholinergics, antimetabolites, steroids, myotics, mydriatics, osmotic diuretic, antiseizure medications)
   b. Activity and positioning (for example: exercises, assistive devices, logrolling)
   c. Immobilizing devices (for example: traction, casts, external fixation devices)
   d. Patient monitoring (for example: neurological assessment, vital signs, neurovascular assessment)
   e. Preoperative and postoperative care (for example: craniotomy, open reduction with internal fixation of the fracture, cataract removal, iridectomy, lens implantation, laminectomy)

B. Nursing care related to theoretical framework
1. Assessment—gather and synthesize data about the patient's health status in relation to the patient's functional health patterns
   a. Gather assessment data
      1) Obtain the patient's health history (for example: subjective symptoms, nutritional status, medications, history of trauma, family history, onset of symptoms, occupation)
      2) Assess factors influencing the patient's response to neurological, sensory, and musculoskeletal dysfunction (see IIIA3)

3) Obtain objective data related to the patient's neurological, sensory, and musculoskeletal dysfunction (for example: clinical manifestations, altered vital signs, Glasgow coma scale, reflexes, behavioral responses, range of motion)
4) Review laboratory and other diagnostic data (for example: cerebrospinal fluid results, diagnostic imaging modalities, hemoglobin and hematocrit in the patient postoperatively, sedimentation rate)
   b. Synthesize assessment data (see IIIB1a [1-4])
2. Analysis—identify the nursing diagnosis (patient problem) and determine the expected outcomes (goals) of patient care
   a. Identify actual or potential nursing diagnoses (for example: impaired physical mobility related to muscular weakness; impaired verbal communication related to altered speech patterns; activity intolerance related to weakness; diversional activity deficit related to prolonged bed rest; ineffective individual coping related to mood swings)
   b. Set priorities (for example: based on Maslow's hierarchy of needs, based on the patient's developmental level)
   c. Establish expected outcomes (patient-centered goals) for care (for example: patient's skin will remain intact, patient will be able to communicate needs, patient will be free of injury)
3. Planning—formulate specific strategies to achieve the expected outcomes
   a. Consider factors influencing the patient's response to neuromuscular, sensory, and musculoskeletal dysfunction in planning patient care (see IIIA3)
   b. Plan nursing measures on the basis of established priorities to help the patient achieve the expected outcomes (for example: monitor traction devices, reinforce crutch-walking instruction)
4. Implementation—carry out nursing plans designed to move the patient toward the expected outcomes
   a. Use nursing measures to protect the patient (for example: assist a patient who is visually impaired to ambulate, provide abductor devices for a patient following hip replacement, prevent fluid overload in a patient who is on fluid restriction, provide safety measures for a patient with seizures)
   b. Use nursing measures to promote, maintain, or restore the patient's neurological, sensory, or musculoskeletal functioning and/or prevent complications (for example: perform passive range-of-motion exercises for a patient with paralysis, maintain skeletal traction for a patient with a fractured femur, elevate the casted extremity, administer prescribed eyedrops to a patient with glaucoma)
   c. Use nursing measures to minimize patient discomfort (for example: assist with mechanical devices, administer anti-inflammatory medications to the patient with arthritis, promote or limit activity, apply heat and cold treatments)
   d. Use nursing measures specific to prescribed medications (for example: administer antiseizure medications on a regular schedule to control seizure activity, monitor the bowel movements of a patient receiving stool softeners, emphasize the need to adhere to steroid therapy, monitor body weight for a patient who is receiving corticosteriods)

e. Use nursing measures to assist the patient and/or significant others to cope with the health problem (for example: refer a patient with multiple sclerosis to a support group, suggest that the significant others of a patient with myasthenia gravis learn cardiopulmonary resuscitation techniques)
f. Provide information and instruction (for example: provide information to patients undergoing diagnostic tests such as angiograms, EEGs, CAT scans, magnetic resonance imaging [MRI], and lumbar punctures; instruct the patient about the medication regimen; instruct the patient regarding the use of community resources; instruct the patient regarding the use of assistive devices; emphasize the need for follow-up care; reinforce rehabilitation instruction)

5. Evaluation—appraise the effectiveness of the nursing interventions relative to the nursing diagnosis and the expected outcomes
    a. Assess and report the patient's response to nursing actions relative to the expected outcomes (for example: patient is free from pain, patient verbalizes the need for follow-up care, patient verbalizes the need to take medication at the prescribed time, alterations in the patient's condition)
    b. Revise the patient's plan of care as necessary (for example: increase observation to q15min for a patient with increasing intracranial pressure, revise the exercise schedule for a patient in traction)

Sample Questions: Differences in Nursing Care: Area C

1. Which behavior is frequently observed in adolescents who have acquired sexually transmitted diseases (STDs)?
   1) Adolescents deny having the disease.
   2) Adolescents seek medical attention early.
   3) Adolescents openly discuss the symptoms of the disease.
   4) Adolescents accept health care recommendations willingly.

2. A patient develops diarrhea several days after being treated for a severe respiratory infection. Which information is needed by the nurse to assess the cause of the diarrhea?
   1) the patient's activity tolerance
   2) the medications used for treatment of the infection
   3) the amount of fluid consumed by the patient during the last 24 hours
   4) the presence or absence of bowel sounds

3. Which discharge instruction should the nurse include in the plan of care for a patient with a urinary tract infection?
   1) Take warm tub baths as needed.
   2) Drink 2 to 3 liters of fluid daily.
   3) Refrain from sexual intercourse.
   4) Increase intake of vitamin C.

4. Which pathophysiological factor accounts for the increased incidence of opportunistic infections and tumors among patients with acquired immunodeficiency syndrome (AIDS)?
   1) a defect in the B lymphocyte population
   2) an increased number of T lymphocytes
   3) a decreased number of T-helper cells
   4) hyperactivity of the humoral response

5. The nurse is evaluating a patient who is on warfarin sodium (Coumadin) therapy. Which patient behavior indicates the need for further instruction regarding the medication? The patient reports
   1) taking the medicine at the same time each day.
   2) returning to the clinic for a prothrombin level check.
   3) taking ibuprofen for a headache.
   4) swimming three times a week for exercise.

6. Why should tetanus toxoid be administered to a patient who has a puncture wound?
   1) to provide passive immunity
   2) to decrease the number of resident microorganisms
   3) to stimulate antibody production
   4) to neutralize the bacterial toxins

7. The parents of a four-year-old child who has varicella express concern about scarring and ask how to best discourage their child from scratching. Which suggestion by the nurse would be most appropriate?
   1) Gently remove the crusts as they come loose.
   2) Tell the child that scratching can lead to scarring.
   3) Teach the child to apply pressure to pruritic areas.
   4) Apply medicated powder to the pruritic areas.

Sample Questions: Differences in Nursing Care: Area C

8. What is the rationale for using the multiple-puncture skin test for tuberculosis?
    1) to screen large groups
    2) to establish a diagnosis
    3) to determine drug sensitivity
    4) to determine the treatment modality

9. When administering the initial parenteral dose of amphotericin B to a patient with severe histoplasmosis, the nurse should monitor the patient for which side effect?
    1) emotional lability
    2) pulmonary edema
    3) hyperkalemia
    4) shaking chills

10. Which assessment of a patient with severe frostbite should receive priority?
    1) abdominal
    2) cardiac
    3) neurovascular
    4) respiratory

11. Immediately following an above-the-knee amputation, a patient has a rigid cast dressing applied. Which observation indicates the desired outcome of this treatment?
    1) moderate wound drainage
    2) uniform compression of the stump
    3) absence of phantom limb pain
    4) constricted circulation

12. Which assessment indicates that a wound is healing by secondary intention?
    1) The sutures are intact in the epithelium.
    2) The wound edges are well approximated.
    3) The wound is dry with no drainage.
    4) The wound base contains granulation tissue.

13. Which assessment data should lead the nurse to suspect that a toddler may have recently ingested a caustic substance?
    1) constant drooling
    2) frequent swallowing
    3) tinnitus
    4) white, swollen oral mucosa

14. Which nursing measure is appropriate when providing immediate care to a patient with a thermal burn?
    1) Soak the burned area briefly in cold water.
    2) Apply antibacterial ointment to the burned area.
    3) Leave the burned area exposed to air and light.
    4) Rinse the burned area with tepid tap water.

Sample Questions: Differences in Nursing Care: Area C

15. When assessing a patient following a tonsillectomy, the nurse notices the patient swallowing frequently. Which nursing diagnosis should receive priority for this patient?
    1) impaired swallowing related to inflammation
    2) risk for injury related to hemorrhage
    3) acute pain related to surgical procedure
    4) anxiety related to altered comfort

16. Which action should the nurse take when caring for an older adult who has suffered heatstroke?
    1) Administer a cool sponge bath.
    2) Assess for hyperkalemia.
    3) Take a rectal temperature q4h.
    4) Maintain a warm environment.

17. What is the expected effect of an antacid such as aluminum hydroxide (Amphojel) on the stomach?
    1) It decreases gastric acidity.
    2) It reduces gastric motility.
    3) It blocks the action of histamine.
    4) It inhibits the production of gastric acid.

18. Which is the first sign of altered neurological status related to brain injury?
    1) seizure activity
    2) poor pupillary response
    3) widening pulse pressure
    4) change in the level of consciousness

19. The nurse is taking the history of a patient who is scheduled for magnetic resonance imaging (MRI). Which data should the nurse consider significant when preparing the patient for the MRI?
    1) claustrophobia
    2) hypertension
    3) iodine allergy
    4) impaired vision

20. The nurse performs a neurovascular assessment on a seven-year-old child who had a cast applied for a fractured tibia. Which evidence indicates possible neurovascular compromise?
    1) capillary refill time of less than five seconds
    2) complaint of pain on movement of the toes
    3) palpable dorsalis pedis pulse
    4) toes that are warm to the touch

21. A patient with a spinal cord injury has been taught to perform intermittent self-catheterization. Which observation indicates that the patient is performing the procedure correctly?
    1) The post-voiding measurement of residual urine is less than 100 cc.
    2) At least 500 cc of urine is obtained with each catheterization.
    3) The patient experiences no dribbling between catheterizations.
    4) The patient does not develop urinary tract infections.

Sample Questions: Differences in Nursing Care: Area C

22. Which class of medications is generally administered to reduce cerebral edema?
    1) antihypertensives
    2) calcium channel blockers
    3) corticosteroids
    4) vasodilators

23. The nurse is caring for a patient who has a history of multiple sclerosis with numerous exacerbations of the condition. Which instruction should the nurse give to this patient?
    1) Limit intake of carbonated beverages.
    2) Avoid emotionally stressful situations.
    3) Limit exposure to persons with viral infections.
    4) Increase the number of hours of sleep at night.

24. Which assessment confirms the presence of gout?
    1) accumulation of crystals in the urine
    2) palpation of tophi in the joint cavity
    3) biopsy of tissue around the joint cavity
    4) presence of urate crystals in joint cavity aspirate

25. Which statement best describes decerebrate posture?
    1) The arms are flexed and adducted, with the spine fixated.
    2) The legs are in extension, with the neck hyperextended.
    3) The arms and legs are extended, with pronation of the hands and feet.
    4) The arms are extended and abducted, with the legs in knee-chest position.

Recommended Resources

You will need your textbooks in medical-surgical nursing, nursing diagnosis, pediatrics, and pharmacology as you study for the Differences in Nursing Care: Area C examination. Remember that you can find textbook descriptions on page 315 (medical-surgical) and pages 289 and 290 (nursing diagnosis, pediatrics, pharmacology).

Medical-Surgical Nursing
Smeltzer, S., & Bare, B. (2000). Brunner and Suddarth's Textbook of medical-surgical nursing *(9th ed.). Philadelphia: Lippincott Williams & Wilkins.*

OR
Phipps, W. et al. (1999). Medical-surgical nursing: Concepts and clinical practice *(6th ed.). St. Louis: Mosby.*

Phipps, W. et al. (1999). Student learning guide to accompany Medical-surgical nursing *(6th ed.) St. Louis: Mosby.*

Nursing Diagnosis
Carpenito, L.J. (1997). Nursing diagnosis: Application to clinical practice *(7th ed.). Philadelphia: J.B. Lippincott.*

OR
Wilkinson, J.M. (1996). Nursing process: A critical thinking approach (2nd ed.). St. Louis: Mosby.

Sample Questions: Differences in Nursing Care: Area C

Pediatrics
Wong, D. (1997). Whaley and Wong's Essentials of pediatric nursing (5th ed.). St. Louis: Mosby.

Murphy, A. (1997). Study Guide to accompany Whaley and Wong's Essentials of pediatric nursing (5th ed.). St. Louis: Mosby.

Pharmacology
McKenry, L., & Salerno, E. (1995). Mosby's Pharmacology in nursing (19th ed.). St. Louis: Mosby.

McKenry, L., & Salerno, E. (1995). Student learning guide for Mosby's Pharmacology in nursing (19th ed.). St. Louis: Mosby.

OR
Shlafer, M. (1993). The nurse, pharmacology, and drug therapy: A prototype approach (2nd ed.). Menlo Park, CA: Addison-Wesley.

Additional Resources

Journal Articles

I. Infectious and Communicable Disease Problems
Gordon, S.L. (1994). Lyme disease in children. Pediatric Nursing, 20*(4), 415–418.*

Grimes, D.E., & Grimes, R.M. (1995). Tuberculosis: What nurses need to know to help control the epidemic. Nursing Outlook, 43*(4), 164–173.*

McKinney, B.C. (1995). Cut your patients' risk of nosocomial UTI. RN, 58*(11), 20–24.*

McMillan, M.J., & Rymer, T.E. (1994). Viral hepatitis: Anatomy of a diagnosis. American Journal of Nursing, 94*(1), 43–48.*

Meissner, J.E. (1995). Caring for patients with meningitis. Nursing 1995, 25*(7), 50–51.*

Munroe-Metcalf, J.A. (1995). Managing neurologic infections. American Journal of Nursing, 95*(5), 24A–24D.*

New guidelines for preventing opportunistic infections. (1995). Nursing 1995, 25*(11), 32I–32O. (HIV/AIDS)*

Newland, J.A. (1995). Hepatitis B prophylaxis. American Journal of Nursing, 95*(5), 16B, 16D.*

Repasky, T. (1995). Epiglottitis. American Journal of Nursing, 95*(9), 52.*

Russell, S. (1994). Septic shock: Can you recognize the clues? Nursing 1994, 24*(4), 40–48.*

Schmidt, J., & Crespo-Fierro, M. (1995). Who says there's nothing we can do? RN, 58*(10), 30–36. (HIV/AIDS)*

Self-test: Caring for AIDS patients. (1995). Nursing 1995, 25*(4), 76–78.*

Self-test: Understanding antibacterials and antivirals. Nursing 1995, 25*(11), 28–29.*

Stewart, K.B. (1994). Tetanus. Nursing 1994, 24*(5), 51.*

II. Tissue Trauma
Campbell, J. (1995). Making sense of clinical features of inflammation. Nursing Times, 91*(14), 32–33.*

Howser, R. (1995). What you need to know about corticosteroid therapy. American Journal of Nursing, 95*(8), 44–49.*

Jackson, L. (1995). Quick response to hypothermia and frostbite. American Journal of Nursing, 95*(3), 52.*

Kuper, B.C., & Failla, S. (1994). Shedding new light on lupus. American Journal of Nursing, 94*(11), 26–33.*

Maklebust, J. (1995). Pressure ulcers: What works. RN, 58*(9), 46–51.*

Sample Questions: Differences in Nursing Care: Area C

Marchiondo, K. (1994). When the diagnosis is diverticular disease. RN, 57(2), 42–47.

Meissner, J. (1994). Caring for patients with ulcerative colitis. Nursing 1994, 24(7), 54–55.

Somerson, S.J. et al. (1995). Insights into conscious sedation. American Journal of Nursing, 95(6), 26–33.

Stein, R.H. (1995). The perioperative nurse's role in anesthesia management. Journal of the Association of Operating Room Nurses, 62(5), 794–804.

Taking a close look at laparoscopy. (1995). Nursing 1995, 25(6), 32M.

III. Neurological, Sensory, and Musculoskeletal Dysfunctions
Easing your patients' joint replacement. (1995). Nursing 1995, 25(5), 32C–32D, 32F.

Fecht-Gramley, M.E. (1995). Pediatric head trauma. American Journal of Nursing, 95(5), 54.

Hardy, E.M., & Rittenberry, K. (1994). Myasthenia gravis: An overview. Orthopaedic Nursing, 13(6), 37–42.

How to help someone with Alzheimer's disease. (1995). Nursing 1995, 25(5), 32R, 32T, 32V.

Meissner, J.E. (1995). Caring for patients with glaucoma. Nursing 1995, 25(1), 56–57.

Meissner, J.E. (1994). Caring for patients with multiple sclerosis. Nursing 1994, 24(8), 60–61.

Moore, K. (1994). Stroke: The long road back. RN, 57(3), 50–55.

Moore, K., & Trifiletti, E. (1994). Stroke: The first critical days. RN, 57(2), 22–28.

Pellino, T. (1994). How to manage hip fractures. American Journal of Nursing, 94(4), 46–50.

Professional Development: Unit 22: Trauma. Part I: Knowledge for practice. Nursing Times, 91(44), 1–4; *Part II: Role of the nurse.* Nursing Times, 91(45), 5–8; *Part III: Revision notes.* Nursing Times, 91(46), 9–14. *(Three-part series on musculoskeletal trauma.)*

Self-test: Managing musculoskeletal conditions. (1995). Nursing 1995, 25(3), 68–70.

Spoltore, T., & O'Brien, A.M. (1995). Rehabilitation of the spinal cord injured patient. Orthopaedic Nursing, 14,(3), 7–15.

Stratton, M., & Gregory, R. (1995). What happens after a traumatic brain injury? Four case studies. Rehabilitation Nursing, 20(6), 323–327.

Zavotsky, K.E., & Banavage, A. (1995). Management of the patient with complex orthopaedic fractures. Orthopaedic Nursing, 14(5), 53–57.

Ziemba, S.K. (1995). Seizures. American Journal of Nursing, 95(2), 32–33.

Content/Reference List

I. Infectious and Communicable Disease Problems
McKenry & Salerno (19th ed., 1995)
- Chapter 34 Antimicrobials for Urinary Tract Infections
- Chapter 58 Overview of Infection, Inflammation, and Fever
- Chapter 59 Antibiotics
- Chapter 60 Antifungal and Antiviral Drugs
- Chapter 61 Other Antimicrobial Drugs and Antiparasitic Drugs
- Chapter 65 Serums, Vaccines, and Other Immunizing Agents

Phipps et al. (6th ed., 1999)
- Chapter 10 Inflammation and Infection
- Chapter 31 Management of Persons with Problems of the Upper Airway

Sample Questions: Differences in Nursing Care: Area C

        Chapter 32   Management of Persons with Problems of the Lower Airway
        Chapter 37   Management of Persons with Problems of the Hepatic System
        Chapter 44   Management of Persons with Problems of the Kidney and Urinary Tract
        Chapter 47   Management of Women with Reproductive Problems
        Chapter 50   Management of Persons with Sexually Transmitted Diseases
        Chapter 67   Management of Persons with HIV Infection and AIDS

Shlafer (2nd ed., 1993)
        Chapter 52   Anti-inflammatory and Analgesic/Antipyretic Drugs
        Chapter 54   Immunostimulant and Immunosuppressant Drugs
        Chapter 55   Principles of Antimicrobial Therapy
        Chapter 56   Antibiotics
        Chapter 57   Miscellaneous Anti-infective Agents

Smeltzer & Bare (9th ed., 2000)
        Chapter 20   Management of Patients with Upper Respiratory Tract Disorders
        Chapter 21   Management of Patients with Chest and Lower Respiratory Tract Disorders
        Chapter 36   Assessment and Management of Patients with Hepatic and Biliary Disorders
        Chapter 41   Management of Patients with Urinary and Renal Disorders
        Chapter 43   Management of Patients with Female Reproductive Disorders
        Chapter 46   Management of Patients with HIV Infection and AIDS
        Chapter 64   Management of Patients with Infectious Diseases

Wong (4th ed., 1993)
        Chapter 14   Health Problems of Early Childhood
        Chapter 22   The Child with Respiratory Dysfunction
        Chapter 23   The Child with Gastrointestinal Dysfunction
        Chapter 25   The Child with Hematologic or Immunologic Dysfunction
        Chapter 26   The Child with Genitourinary Dysfunction
        Chapter 29   The Child with Integumentary Dysfunction

II. Tissue Trauma

McKenry & Salerno (19th ed., 1995)
        Chapter 12   Analgesics and Antagonists
        Chapter 13   Anesthetics
        Chapter 22   Skeletal Muscle Relaxants
        Chapter 40   Drugs Affecting the Upper Gastrointestinal Tract
        Chapter 41   Drugs Affecting the Lower Gastrointestinal Tract
        Chapter 62   Nonsteroidal Anti-inflammatory Drugs
        Chapter 64   Overview of the Immunologic System
        Chapter 66   Immunosuppressants and Immunomodulators
        Chapter 68   Dermatologic Drugs
        Chapter 69   Debriding Agents

Phipps et al. (6th ed., 1999)
        Chapter 10   Inflammation and Infection
        Chapter 12   Pain and Pain Control
        Chapter 18   Preoperative Nursing
        Chapter 19   Intraoperative Nursing
        Chapter 20   Postoperative Nursing
        Chapter 39   Management of Persons with Problems of the Mouth and Esophagus
        Chapter 40   Management of Persons with Problems of the Stomach and Duodenum
        Chapter 41   Management of Persons with Problems of the Intestines
        Chapter 42   Management of Persons with Problems of the Gallbladder and Exocrine Pancreas
        Chapter 60   Management of Persons with Trauma to the Musculoskeletal System
        Chapter 63   Management of Persons with Problems of the Skin

Sample Questions: Differences in Nursing Care: Area C

    Chapter 64   Management of Persons with Burns
    Chapter 66   Management of Persons with Problems of the Immune System

Shlafer (2nd ed., 1993)
    Chapter 19   Local Anesthetic Agents
    Chapter 20   General Anesthetic Agents
    Chapter 21   Narcotic Analgesics and Their Antagonists
    Chapter 22   Sedatives, Hypnotics, and Anxiolytics
    Chapter 39   Structure and Function of the Gastrointestinal Tract
    Chapter 40   Pharmacological Management of Peptic Ulcer Disease
    Chapter 41   Laxatives, Cathartics, and Antidiarrheal Medications
    Chapter 45   Adrenocorticosteroids
    Chapter 50   Structure and Function of the Immune System
    Chapter 51   Histamine Receptor Agonists and Antagonists

Smeltzer & Bare (9th ed., 2000)
    Chapter 12   Pain Management
    Chapter 16   Preoperative Nursing Management
    Chapter 17   Intraoperative Nursing Management
    Chapter 18   Postoperative Nursing Management
    Chapter 32   Management of Patients with Oral and Esophageal Disorders
    Chapter 34   Management of Patients with Gastric and Duodenal Disorders
    Chapter 35   Management of Patients with Intestinal and Rectal Disorders
    Chapter 49   Assessment and Management of Patients with Allergic Disorders
    Chapter 50   Assessment and Management of Patients with Rheumatic Disorders
    Chapter 53   Management of Patients with Burn Injury
    Chapter 65   Emergency Nursing

Wong (4th ed., 1993)
    Chapter 14   Health Problems of Early Childhood
    Chapter 23   The Child with Gastrointestinal Dysfunction
    Chapter 29   The Child with Integumentary Dysfunction

III. Neurological, Sensory, and Musculoskeletal Dysfunctions
McKenry & Salerno (19th ed., 1995)
    Chapter 11   Overview of the Central Nervous System
    Chapter 15   Anticonvulsants
    Chapter 18   Drugs for Specific CNS-Peripheral Dysfunction
    Chapter 22   Skeletal Muscle Relaxants
    Chapter 42   Overview of the Eye
    Chapter 43   Ophthalmic Drugs
    Chapter 44   Overview of the Ear
    Chapter 45   Drugs Affecting the Ear

Phipps et al. (6th ed., 1999)
    Chapter 51   Assessment of the Nervous System
    Chapter 52   Management of Persons with Traumatic, Neoplastic, and Related Problems of the Brain
    Chapter 53   Management of Persons with Vascular, Degenerative, and Autoimmune Problems of the Brain
    Chapter 54   Management of Persons with Problems of the Spinal Cord and Peripheral Nerves
    Chapter 55   Assessment of the Visual System
    Chapter 56   Management of Persons with Problems of the Eye
    Chapter 57   Assessment of the Auditory and Vestibular System
    Chapter 58   Management of Persons with Problems of the Ear

Sample Questions: Differences in Nursing Care: Area C

    Chapter 59   Assessment of the Musculoskeletal System
    Chapter 60   Management of Persons with Trauma to the Musculoskeletal System
    Chapter 61   Management of Persons with Inflammatory and Degenerative Disorders of the Musculoskeletal System

Shlafer (2nd ed., 1993)
    Chapter 12   Acetylcholinesterase Inhibitors
    Chapter 17   Neuromuscular Blockers and Miscellaneous Skeletal Muscle Relaxants
    Chapter 18   Structure and Function of the Central Nervous System
    Chapter 25   Antiparkinson Agents
    Chapter 26   Anticonvulsant Drugs
    Chapter 53   Drugs for Gout and Other Hyperuricemic States

Smeltzer & Bare (8th ed., 1996)
    Chapter 52   Management of Patients with Rheumatic Disorders
    Chapter 56   Assessment and Management of Patients with Vision Problems and Eye Disorders
    Chapter 57   Assessment and Management of Patients with Hearing Problems and Ear Disorders
    Chapter 58   Assessment of Neurologic Function
    Chapter 59   Management of Patients with Neurologic Dysfunction
    Chapter 60   Management of Patients with Neurologic Problems
    Chapter 61   Assessment of Musculoskeletal Function
    Chapter 62   Management Modalities for Patients with Musculoskeletal Dysfunction
    Chapter 63   Management of Patients with Musculoskeletal Disorders
    Chapter 64   Management of Patients with Musculoskeletal Trauma

Wong (4th ed., 1993)
    Chapter 19   Impact of Cognitive or Sensory Impairment on the Child and Family
    Chapter 27   The Child with Cerebral Dysfunction
    Chapter 30   The Child with Musculoskeletal or Articular Dysfunction
    Chapter 31   The Child with Neuromuscular or Muscular Dysfunction

Study Guide

Occupational Strategies in Nursing (532) (Associate Level)

Credit Hours: 3 **Credit Level: Lower**
Question Type(s): Multiple-choice

The information in this study guide is valid until Summer 2001.
If you will be taking the examination after that date, be sure to check for a new edition of this guide before you complete your preparation for the exam.

General Description of the Examination

The Occupational Strategies in Nursing examination measures knowledge and understanding of the roles and functions of the associate degree nurse within the occupation of nursing. Content includes the health care delivery system; the interdisciplinary health team; and the legal, ethical, and educational aspects of current nursing practice. The influences of nursing history, nursing organizations, and licensure on the associate degree nurse's function in the delivery of care are considered.

Examination Objectives

You will be expected to demonstrate the ability to:
1. evaluate historical and current trends and issues for their relevance to current and future nursing practice;
2. evaluate the impact of social, cultural, legislative, economic, and educational factors on the health care delivery system;
3. describe current practices and trends in the delivery of health care services;
4. apply ethical and legal concepts to nursing practice;
5. apply a continuous quality improvement model to nursing practice;
6. describe the roles and responsibilities of the associate degree nurse in relation to the client and to other providers to the health care delivery system;
7. use identified strategies to improve effectiveness in nursing practice.

Content Outline

Content Area	Percent of Examination
I. Forces Influencing the Development of Nursing Practice	10%
II. The Health Care Delivery System	15%
III. Framework for Nursing Practice	50%
IV. Delivery of Nursing Care by the Associate Degree Graduate	25%
Total	100%

I. Forces Influencing the Development of Nursing Practice (10%)

A. World events and trends
1. Religion and religious orders (for example: the Reformation, deaconesses, Sisters of Mercy, Sisters of Charity, Benedictine order)
2. Wars (for example: Crimean War, American Civil War, World War I, World War II)
3. Socioeconomic factors (for example: the Industrial Revolution, immigration, women's movement, labor movements)
4. Changes in nursing education (for example: Nurse Cadet Corps, Nurse Training Act)

B. Major contributions of significant leaders in nursing (Clara Barton, Dorothea Dix, Virginia Henderson, Mary Mahoney, Mildred Montag, Florence Nightingale, Melinda Ann [Linda] Richards, Isabel Hampton Robb, Lillian Wald)

C. Significant studies
1. *Nursing and Nursing Education in the United States* (Goldmark Report 1923)
2. *Nursing for the Future* (Brown Report 1948)
3. *Community College Education for Nursing* (1959)
4. *Study of Credentialing in Nursing: A New Approach* (1979)
5. National Commission on Nursing study (1983)
6. *Health Professions Education for the Future: Schools in Service to the Nation* (1993)

D. Nursing organizations—origin, membership, purposes and functions, publications, impact on nursing
1. American Nurses Association (ANA)
2. International Council of Nurses (ICN)
3. National League for Nursing (NLN)

4. American Academy of Nursing (AAN)
5. National Council of State Boards of Nursing
6. National Student Nurses Association (NSNA)
7. National Organization for the Advancement of Associate Degree Nursing (NOAADN)
8. Organizations representing members of historically underrepresented groups
9. Clinical specialty organizations (for example: operating room nurses, industrial nurses)

II. The Health Care Delivery System (15%)

A. Factors influencing the current system
1. Social
   a. Changing roles (for example: family roles, single-parent family, working parents, adolescent parents, female-male roles)
   b. Changing demographic patterns (for example: increase in the aging population, shift from rural to suburban to urban, shift in immigrant populations, increase in low-income groups)
   c. Health problems related to changing lifestyles (for example: substance abuse, violence, acquired immunodeficiency syndrome [AIDS], sexually transmitted diseases [STDs], persons who are homeless or displaced)
2. Cultural/Spiritual
   a. Communication processes (for example: language barriers, body language)
   b. Health practices (for example: perception of illness, cultural healers, use of traditional remedies, religious sanctions and restrictions, nutritional restrictions)
   c. Valued behaviors (for example: territoriality, privacy, stoicism)
3. Economic
   a. Cost containment (for example: preventive services, rationing of health care, prospective payment systems, community-based care, diagnosis-related groups [DRGs], managed care)
   b. Health care financing
      1) Personal payment or fee for service
      2) Workers' compensation
      3) Medicare
      4) Medicaid
      5) Capitation funding (capitated payment) (for example: HMOs, preferred provider organizations [PPOs])
4. Legislative
   a. Legislation—local, state, federal
   b. Strategies to affect the legislative process (for example: political awareness, negotiating, lobbying, letter writing, testifying, networking)
      1) By the individual nurse
      2) By professional organizations (for example: ANA-PAC, NLN, state nursing associations)
      3) By special interest groups (for example: tobacco industry, labor unions, insurance companies)
5. Educational
   a. Consumer awareness (for example: participation in self-care, health promotion, expectations for accountability)

        b. Diversity in the educational background of the consumer (for example: persons who are illiterate, persons who are highly educated)
    6. Technological (for example: computerization, lasers, imaging, diagnostic techniques)
B. **Current practices and trends in delivery of services**
    1. Organization and administration
        a. Levels of health care delivery
            1) Primary care
            2) Secondary care
            3) Tertiary care
        b. Regulatory agencies
            1) Joint Commission on Accreditation of Healthcare Organizations (JCAHO)
            2) Health Care Financing Administration (HCFA)
            3) Community Health Accreditation Program (CHAP)
            4) State health departments
    2. Types of facilities
        a. Ambulatory care facilities (for example: community health centers, wellness centers, health maintenance organizations [HMOs], clinics)
        b. Hospitals (for example: government, nonprofit, proprietary)
        c. Long-term care facilities
        d. Home health care agencies
        e. Other types of facilities/services (for example: hospice, rehabilitation centers, respite, day care)
    3. The interdisciplinary health team
        a. Composition
        b. Functions and responsibilities of each member
        c. Interdependence and collaboration among members

III. Framework for Nursing Practice (50%)

A. **Total quality management/continuous quality improvement**
    1. Standards of nursing practice
        a. ANA *Standards of Clinical Nursing Practice*
        b. Specialty organization practice standards
        c. Other standards (for example: health care agencies, professional literature)
    2. Mechanisms for total quality management/continuous quality improvement
        a. Outcome achievement (critical pathways)
        b. Peer review
        c. Record audit
        d. Certification of nurses
        e. Documentation
        f. Utilization review
        g. Risk management
        h. Research utilization
        i. Consumer involvement

B. **Ethical aspects of nursing practice**
  1. Values clarification
     a. Personal values
     b. Codes of ethics
        1) ANA *Code for Nurses*
        2) ICN *Code for Nurses* (1973)
     c. *Nursing: A Social Policy Statement* (ANA) 1980
  2. Rights and responsibilities in health care
     a. Consumers' rights (for example: the American Hospital Association's [AHA] *A Patient's Bill of Rights*, informed consent, living wills, autonomy/right to self-determination)
     b. Nurse's responsibilities (for example: personal, professional, patient advocacy)
  3. Process of making ethical decisions
  4. Ethical theories (for example: utilitarianism, deontology, caring)
  5. Ethical principles (for example: justice, beneficence, autonomy, nonmaleficence, obligations, veracity, fidelity, confidentiality)
  6. Ethical issues in nursing practice (for example: informed consent, code/no code decisions, abortion, organ transplants, privacy and confidentiality, gene therapy, euthanasia, right to die, nutrition/hydration, diagnostic tests, reporting illegal and unethical conduct)
  7. Personal and professional accountability
     a. Ethical committees
     b. Application of the ANA *Code for Nurses* in practice

C. **Legal liability affecting nursing practice**
  1. Types of laws
     a. Civil vs. criminal
     b. Statutory vs. common and case law
  2. Civil law
     a. Torts (intentional and unintentional)
        1) Negligence
        2) Malpractice
        3) Assault and battery
        4) Invasion of privacy (confidentiality)
        5) Privileged communication
        6) Fraud
        7) Defamation of character (slander, libel)
        8) False imprisonment (for example: restraining)
        9) Abandonment
        10) Breach of duty
     b. Contracts
        1) Elements of a valid contract
        2) Rights and responsibilities of the nurse in a contractual situation
        3) *Respondeat superior*
     c. Legal documents (for example: wills, consent forms, health care records, advance directives)
     d. Patient Self-Determination Act

       3. Criminal law
          a. Criminal negligence
          b. Patient abuse (for example: physical and psychological abuse)
          c. Assisted suicide
       4. Statutory law
          a. Licensure
             1) Purpose
             2) Legal source—nurse practice acts
             3) Implementation
                 a) Current requirements
                 b) Licensure by endorsement
                 c) Grounds for revocation
                 d) Role of state boards of nursing
             4) Developments affecting licensure legislation
                 a) Entry into practice issues
                 b) Mandatory continuing education as a condition for continuing licensure
                 c) Sunset laws
                 d) Institutional licensure
          b. Federal statutes (for example: controlled substance acts, Freedom of Information Acts, Omnibus Budget Reconciliation Act [OBRA] of 1987)
          c. Nurse's responsibility
             1) Good Samaritan laws
             2) Reporting requirements related to the abuse of children and adults
             3) Expert witness

D. Educational aspects of nursing practice
    1. Outcomes of academic nursing education programs
       a. Practical/vocational
       b. Diploma
       c. Associate degree
       d. Baccalaureate degree (generic and RN programs)
       e. Master's degree (for example: advanced practice nursing)
       f. Doctoral degree
    2. Alternative educational programs (for example: assessment programs, RN to BSN programs, articulation programs)
    3. Credentialing (for example: ANA certification, other specialty groups)
    4. Continuing education
    5. Accreditation of academic programs (regional, NLN)

IV. Delivery of Nursing Care by the Associate Degree Graduate (25%)

A. Characteristics of a profession (for example: unique body of knowledge, specialized expertise, autonomy, service, education)

B. Foundations for associate degree practice
    1. *The Education of Nursing Technicians* (1951)
    2. *Educational Outcomes of Associate Degree Nursing Programs: Roles and Competencies* (1990)

C. **Roles and functions of the associate degree nurse** (as identified in the document in IVB2)
    1. Provider of care
    2. Manager of care
    3. Member within the discipline

D. **Organizational patterns for the delivery of nursing care**
    1. Case method
    2. Primary nursing
    3. Team nursing
    4. Functional nursing
    5. Case management
    6. Differentiated practice
    7. Shared governance

E. **Strategies employed by the associate degree nurse in practice**
    1. Critical thinking/decision making
    2. Nursing process
    3. Group process
    4. Communication techniques (for example: assertiveness, management information systems)
    5. Conflict management
    6. Time management
    7. Collective bargaining
    8. Delegation (for example: to LPN/LVN, to unlicensed staff, to members of other disciplines)
    9. Cost containment
    10. Change process
    11. Leadership styles
    12. Independent/dependent/collaborative interventions

Sample Questions: Occupational Strategies in Nursing

1. Continuing assessment of a patient's postoperative status causes the nurse to be increasingly concerned about the patient's well-being. After several telephone calls, the physician continues to instruct the nurse to monitor the patient's status. After documenting the physician's response, the nurse should take which action?
   1) Continue to monitor the patient's status as directed by the physician.
   2) Ask another physician who is in the area to examine the patient.
   3) Report the breach of medical duty to the hospital's medical board.
   4) Inform the nursing administration of the patient's status and the physician's response.

2. What is the primary purpose of the Patient Self-Determination Act?
   1) to allow patients to make informed decisions about lifesaving or life-prolonging actions
   2) to inform patients about what types of care are available if they become incapacitated
   3) to educate older adults about choices available if they become critically ill
   4) to ensure that family members agree on the treatments given for a family member who is terminally ill

3. After receiving treatment for a hip injury, an older adult patient is recommended for transfer to a long-term care facility. The patient refuses to be transferred. Which action by the nurse best illustrates the use of ethical decision-making skills?
   The nurse
   1) persuades the patient to agree to the transfer, since the patient has demonstrated an inability to care for herself at times.
   2) gathers additional information about the patient's situation, reviews possible alternatives, and discusses these options with the physician.
   3) discusses the situation with the physician and asks the physician to rescind the decision about the transfer.
   4) discusses the physician's decision with the patient's family and asks them to talk to the physician further.

4. What is the primary goal of the ANA Political Action Committee (ANA-PAC)?
   1) to demonstrate partisan support of a political party
   2) to influence legislation pertaining to health care
   3) to encourage nurses to take part in governmental affairs
   4) to provide financial support for political candidates

5. Which action by the nurse is an appropriate example of cost containment?
   1) removing unnecessary furniture from a patient's room
   2) instructing a patient to reuse a safety razor
   3) ordering large quantities of a new medication
   4) minimizing the use of disposable equipment

Sample Questions: Occupational Strategies in Nursing

6. Which entry in a patient's chart provides the most factual information?
    The patient is
    1) cheerful.
    2) frustrated.
    3) lonely.
    4) tearful.

7. How did Mildred Montag's 1951 report, *The Education of Nursing Technicians,* change the prevailing system of nursing education?
    1) Baccalaureate education became the minimum requirement for entry into professional practice.
    2) Nursing research was added as a competency required of registered nurses.
    3) Nursing education moved from being predominantly an apprenticeship model to a collegiate model.
    4) Admission criteria to schools of nursing became more selective.

8. What impact has continuing education had on nursing?
    1) Nurses are more accountable for clinical competence.
    2) Fewer nurses are maintaining their licensure.
    3) More inactive nurses have returned to active employment.
    4) The incidence of burnout in nurses has decreased.

9. Which assignment pattern is an example of primary nursing?
    1) The nursing assistant bathes the assigned patients and the RN provides all treatments.
    2) The LPN/LVN administers medications to the assigned patients while the RN makes assessments and attends physicians' rounds.
    3) The RN gives complete care to the assigned patients and directs their care for their entire hospitalization.
    4) The RN works with the LPN/LVN to provide care to the assigned patients.

10. Which patient would be best suited to use the services of a day-care center?
    1) a six-year-old patient who is undergoing an appendectomy
    2) a 35-year-old patient who is being screened for tuberculosis
    3) a 40-year-old patient who has diabetes mellitus
    4) an 80-year-old patient who has Alzheimer's disease

11. At the request of the family of a 78-year-old patient, the physician does not inform the patient about the medical diagnosis. Which action by the nurse would be appropriate?
    1) Ensure that the request of the patient's family is honored.
    2) Refer any questions the patient may have about the diagnosis to the physician.
    3) Discuss the patient's right to know about the diagnosis with the physician.
    4) If the patient requests information, then inform the patient about the diagnosis.

Sample Questions: Occupational Strategies in Nursing

12. Which function is a graduate of an associate degree nursing program prepared to assume?
    1) managing a nursing unit in an acute care setting
    2) leading a team composed of RNs and LPN/LVNs
    3) caring for a caseload of patients who require respirator care in their homes
    4) providing care in a primary care setting for a group of patients who have had strokes

13. Which historical event focused attention on the need for hospitals, surgeons, and nurses in the United States?
    1) Civil War
    2) Depression
    3) Industrial Revolution
    4) Revolutionary War

14. What is the purpose of the ANA *Standards of Clinical Nursing Practice*?
    1) to provide guidelines for nursing education
    2) to establish requirements for nursing licensure
    3) to improve the practice of nursing
    4) to promote unity within the nursing profession

15. Why should nurses participate in letter-writing campaigns to inform legislators about health care issues?
    1) Nurses have exclusive knowledge of matters relating to nursing care.
    2) Nurses' opinions are highly regarded by legislators.
    3) Nurses have valuable expertise in a specific aspect of health care.
    4) Nursing licensure is dependent upon active communication between nurses and elected representatives.

16. Which organization provides voluntary accreditation for nursing education programs?
    1) American Hospital Association
    2) American Nurses Association
    3) National League for Nursing
    4) National Council of State Boards of Nursing

17. A staff nurse is confronting the issue of euthanasia and seeks the nurse manager's guidance. Through discussion, the manager allows the staff nurse to decide on the course of action. The manager is using which process to foster ethical nursing practice?
    1) appeal to conscience
    2) modeling
    3) reflecting
    4) values clarification

18. Which action will help protect the nurse from allegations of professional liability?
    1) following physicians' orders explicitly
    2) adhering to institutional standards of practice
    3) acting consistently according to personal values
    4) accepting responsibility as a patient advocate

Sample Questions: Occupational Strategies in Nursing

19. Mildred Montag is recognized for having made which important contribution to nursing education?
    1) She developed a uniform educational model for professional nursing.
    2) She provided the framework for the establishment of associate degree programs.
    3) She clearly identified the distinctions between professional and technical education.
    4) She succeeded in securing major federal funding for nursing education projects.

20. A patient is hospitalized with severe hypertension. During the hospitalization, a registered nurse monitors care for the patient and consults with the attending physician and appropriate staff to arrange for home care services for the patient upon discharge. The nurse also visits the patient after discharge to ensure that all needs are being met. This situation is an example of which method of nursing care delivery?
    1) managed care
    2) case management
    3) primary nursing
    4) team nursing

21. Which example illustrates application of the differentiated practice pattern of nursing care delivery?
    1) employing graduates of different types of nursing programs for the same type of work
    2) assuring that practice competencies in the workplace are consistent with expected competencies of different nursing programs
    3) providing opportunity for graduates from different types of nursing programs to care for patients in both the hospital and home care setting
    4) providing financial support to associate degree nursing graduates who are pursuing advanced education

22. The registered nurses on a medical unit develop and implement a new flow sheet to improve the charting system on the unit. Another registered nurse who was on vacation when the new flow sheet was developed refuses to use it. Which is the most likely reason for this nurse's resistance to change?
    1) lack of involvement in the decision-making process
    2) lack of research to indicate the need for the change
    3) increase in the amount of paperwork to be completed
    4) lack of familiarity with the new forms being used

23. The nurse forgets to remove a heat lamp used in the treatment of a patient's pressure ulcer. As a result, the patient receives a minor burn. What is the nurse liable for?
    1) assault
    2) battery
    3) criminal negligence
    4) malpractice

Sample Questions: Occupational Strategies in Nursing

24. What is the nurse's responsibility when serving as a witness to a patient's will?
    1) to ensure that the patient is of sound mind before signing the will
    2) to record the names of those present when the will is signed
    3) to chart the patient's mental and physical condition when the will is signed
    4) to confirm that the will has been drawn up by an attorney

25. What is the purpose of nursing certification?
    1) to confirm that nurses have skills in a specialty area
    2) to ensure safe nursing care for the public
    3) to license nurses to practice nursing
    4) to identify minimum standards for nursing practice

Recommended Resources

Textbooks

The examination development committee recommends that you obtain the Kelly textbook listed below for use in preparing for the examination. You will also want to refer to your fundamentals of nursing textbook. For your convenience, the recommended Fundamentals textbooks and accompanying study guides are listed here as well. NOTE: If you will be taking the Nursing Concepts exam series, you should choose the Kozier text for your Fundamentals reference.

Professional Nursing Issues
Kelly, L.Y., & Joel, L.A. (1999). *Dimensions of professional nursing (8th ed.). New York: McGraw Hill.*

This textbook is a classic reference for professional issues in nursing. The content is very readable, and diagrams and exhibits are used where appropriate. Headings and subheadings help students locate content easily.

Fundamentals of Nursing
Kozier, B., Erb, G., Blais, K.C., & Wilkinson, J. (2000). *Fundamentals of nursing: Concepts, process, and practice (6th ed.). Upper Saddle River, NJ: Prentice Hall.*

This textbook makes extensive use of tables and charts. Key concepts are highlighted in boxes. Clinical problems are presented in critical-thinking boxes. Many full-color pictures are presented throughout the text, making it appealing and easy to read. Each chapter begins with learning objectives and ends with a table of chapter highlights and a suggested reading and reference list.

Study Guide:
Van Leuven, K. (2000). *Study guide for Fundamentals of nursing: Concepts, process, and practice (6th ed.). Upper Saddle River, NJ: Prentice Hall.*

This study guide accompanies the textbook by Kozier et al. It consists of a series of review exercises arranged by chapters as identified in the textbook. It presents a useful way to validate your understanding of the material in the textbook.

Sample Questions: Occupational Strategies in Nursing

OR

Potter, P., & Perry, A. (1997). Fundamentals of nursing: Concepts, process, and practice *(4th ed.).* St. Louis: Mosby.

This text features a clear, engaging writing style. The text carefully integrates full-color photos with the material presented. Bold headings make the text easy to follow. The nursing process is used as the organizing framework for clinical content. Each chapter begins with learning objectives and ends with tables of key concepts, key terms, and critical-thinking exercises.

Study Guide:

Ochs, G. (1997). Study guide to accompany Fundamentals of nursing: Concepts, process, and practice *(4th ed.).* St. Louis: Mosby.

Additional Resources

Textbooks

Aiken, T., with Cataldo, J. (1994). Legal, ethical, and political issues in nursing. *Philadelphia: F.A. Davis.*

This textbook presents in-depth content on legal, ethical, and political issues that affect nursing. Every chapter contains case studies, points to remember, and important information highlighted in boxes.

Ellis, J., & Hartley, C. (1995). Nursing in today's world. *(5th ed.). Philadelphia: J.B. Lippincott.*

This textbook presents a comprehensive overview of nursing education, legal and ethical issues, the health care delivery system, and nursing organizations. Each chapter includes critical-thinking activities and key concepts.

Hanston, R., & Washburn, M. (1994). Clinical delegation skills. *Gaithersburg, MD: Aspen.*

This textbook presents in-depth content on the art of delegation. Included is content related to skills required for effective delegation, personal barriers to effective delegation, and communication skills necessary for effective delegation. Evaluation, feedback, and conflict resolution are also addressed.

Harrington, N., Smith, N., & Spratt, W. (1996). LPN to RN transitions. *Philadelphia: J.B. Lippincott.*

This textbook builds nicely on the content learned in licensed practical/vocational nursing programs, and it points out the similarities and differences in nursing practice. The book is designed for use with individual students in an independent study format. All chapters include learning objectives and key terms. Critical-thinking exercises are presented at the end of each chapter to challenge students to evaluate their learning. Topics covered include critical thinking, managing client systems, managing client care, legal and ethical issues, and professional responsibilities.

Tappen, R. (1995). Nursing leadership and management: Concepts and practice *(3rd ed.). Philadelphia: F.A. Davis.*

This textbook presents in-depth content on leadership and management. Strategies such as time management, change, communication, and conflict resolution are well presented.

Sample Questions: Occupational Strategies in Nursing

Journal Articles

Because knowledge in nursing and health care is changing at a remarkable rate, textbooks are unable to keep pace with these rapid changes. Journal articles provide the most current information on nursing practice issues. Thus, keeping up with professional journals is especially important as you prepare for this examination. You may want to review nursing journals from this year to locate more current articles.

I. Forces Influencing the Development of Nursing Practice

Backer, B. (1993). Lillian Wald: Connecting caring with activism. Nursing & Health Care, 14(3), 122–129.

Calhoun, J. (1993). The Nightingale pledge: A commitment that survives the passage of time. Nursing and Health Care, 14(3), 130–136.

Cook, P.R. (1995). Isabel Stewart, nursing education leader. Nursing and Health Care, 16(1), 20–23.

Keeling, A.W., & Ramos, M.C. (1995). The role of nursing history in preparing nursing for the future. Nursing & Health Care, 16(1), 24–29.

Macrea, J. (1995). Nightingale's spiritual philosophy and its significance for modern nursing. Image, 27, 8–14.

Minkowski, W.L. (1992). Women healers of the Middle Ages: Selected aspects of their history. American Journal of Public Health, 82(2), 288–295.

Montag, M. (1991). Nursing: Then and now. Advanced Clinical Care, 6(4), 12–18.

Pitts Mosley, M.O. (1995). Mabel K. Staupers: A pioneer in professional nursing. Nursing and Health Care: Perspectives on Community, 16(1), 12–17.

II. The Health Care Delivery System

Aiken, L. (1995). Transformation of the nursing workforce. Nursing Outlook, 43(5), 201–209.

Anderson, A. (1996). Nursing clinics in urban settings. Home Healthcare Nurse, 14(7), 543–546.

Burgel, B. (1994). Occupational health: Nursing in the workforce. Nursing Clinics of North America, 29(3), 293.

Calfee, B. (1996, February). Labor laws: Working to protect you. Nursing 96, 34–39.

Carter, J. (1996). Can hospice care be provided to people who live alone? Home Healthcare Nurse, 14(9), 711–716.

Chafey, K. (1996). Caring is not enough. Ethical paradigm for community-based care. Nursing and Health Care, 17(1), 11–15.

Dracup, K. (1996, February) Clinical practice guidelines. Nursing 96, 41–47.

Dunham-Taylor, J., Marquette, R.P., & Pinczak, J. (1996). Surveying capitation. American Journal of Nursing, 96(3), 26–29.

El-Sherif, C. (1996, January). How to collaborate with nurse practitioners. Nursing 96, 64.

Fondiller, S., & Nerone, B.J. (1996). Preparing for nursing's future. American Journal of Nursing, 96(9).

Gerber, D., & McGuire, S. (1995). Understanding contemporary health and welfare services. The Social Security Act of 1935 and the Public Health Service Act of 1994. Nursing Outlook, 43(6), 266–272.

Grossman, D. (1996). Cultural dimensions in home health nursing. American Journal of Nursing, 96(7), 33–36.

Hadley, E. (1996). Nursing in the political and economic marketplace: Challenges for the 21st century. Nursing Outlook, 44(1) 6–10.

Hall-Long, B. (1995). Nursing's past, present and future political experiences. Nursing and Healthcare: Perspectives on Community, 16(1), 24–28.

Sample Questions: Occupational Strategies in Nursing

Malone-Rising, D. (1994). The changing face of long term care. Nursing Clinics of North America, 29(3), 417–429.

Mandell, M. (1995). What to expect of your malpractice attorney. American Journal of Nursing, 95(11), 29–31.

Shindul-Rothschild, J., Berry, D., & Long-Middleton, E. (1996). Where have all the nurses gone? Final results of our patient care survey. American Journal of Nursing, 96(11), 25–39.

III. Framework for Practice

Berrio, M.W., & Levesque, M.E. (1996). Advance directives: Most patients don't have one. Do yours? American Journal of Nursing, 96(8), 25–29.

Brooten, D. (1995). Nurses' effect on changing patient outcomes. Image, 27(2), 95–99.

Davis, A. et al. (1995). Nurses' attitudes toward active euthanasia. Nursing Outlook, 43(5), 174–179.

Fiesta, J. (1995). Home care liability. Nursing Management, 26(11), 24–26.

Greer, A., Crismon, C., Waddell, L., & Fitzpatrick, O. (1995). Are you at risk for disciplinary action? American Journal of Nursing, 95(7), 36–42.

Lang, N.M. (1995). Quality assurance: The foundation of professional care. The Journal of the American Nurses Association, 26(1), 48–50.

Mohr, W. (1996). Ethics, nursing and health care in the age of reform. Nursing and Healthcare, 96(1), 16–21.

Ott, B. (1995). The human genome project: An overview of ethical issues and public policy concerns. Nursing Outlook, 43(5), 228–231.

Richman, D., & Valentini, S.M. (1995). Legally speaking: If you're asked to be a health care proxy. RN, 58(11), 51–55.

Simpson, R. (1995). Ethics in the information age. Nursing Management, 26(11), 20–21.

Vergara, M., & Lynn-McHale, D. (1995). Withdrawing life support: Who decides? American Journal of Nursing, 95(11), 47–49.

Weinstein, L. (1995). The right to refuse treatment. American Journal of Nursing, 95(8), 52–53.

Zonsus, M., & Murphy, M. (1995). Use of total quality management sparks staff nurse participation in continuous quality improvement. Nursing Clinics of North America, 30(11), 1–12.

IV. Delivery of Nursing Care by the Associate Degree Graduate

Badger, J. (1995). Tips for managing stress on the job. American Journal of Nursing, 95(9), 31–33.

Boynton, D. (1995). Start managing change: Supporting new patient care models. Nursing Economics, 13(3), 166–173.

Cullen, A. (1995). Burnout: Why do we blame the nurse? American Journal of Nursing, 95(11), 23–27.

Gorden, S., & Grady, E. (1995). What's in a name? American Journal of Nursing, 95(8), 31–33.

Grensing-Pophal, L. (1995, November). Dealing with co-worker conflicts. Nursing 95, 78–81.

Huston, C. (1996). Unlicensed assistive personnel: A solution to dwindling health care resources or a precursor to the apocalypse of Registered Nursing? Nursing Outlook, 44(2), 67.

Kersbergen, A. (1996). Case management: A rich history of coordinating care to control costs. Nursing Outlook, 4(4), 169–172.

King, M., & Weston, L. (1995, August). How to organize a nursing portfolio. Nursing 95, 79–81.

Laino-Curren, D. (1995, July). Choosing your mentor. Nursing 96, 78–79.

Manion, J. (1995). Understanding the seven stages of change. American Journal of Nursing, 95(4), 41–43.

Sample Questions: Occupational Strategies in Nursing

Parkman, C. (1996). *Delegation: Are you doing it right?* American Journal of Nursing, 96(9), 43–47.

Stark, J. (1995, November). *Critical thinking: Taking the road less traveled.* Nursing 95, 53–56.

Zimmerman, P. (1995, September). *10 tips for a top interview.* Nursing 95, 83–85.

Content/Reference List

I. Forces Influencing the Development of Nursing Practice
Kelly & Joel (8th ed., 1999)
- Chapter 1 Care of the Sick: A Historical Overview
- Chapter 2 The Influence of Florence Nightingale
- Chapter 3 The Evolution of the Trained Nurse, 1873–1903
- Chapter 4 The Emergence of the Modern Nurse, after 1904
- Chapter 5 Major Studies of the Nursing Profession
- Chapter 23 Organizational Procedures and Issues
- Chapter 24 National Student Nurses' Association
- Chapter 25 American Nurses Association
- Chapter 26 The Tri-Council for Nursing
- Chapter 27 Other Nursing and Related Organizations in the United States
- Chapter 28 Major International Organizations

Kozier et al. (6th ed., 2000)
- Chapter 1 Historical and Contemporary Nursing Practice

Potter & Perry (4th ed., 1997)
- Chapter 13 Profession of Nursing

II. The Health Care Delivery System
Kelly & Joel (8th ed., 1999)
- Chapter 4 The Emergence of the Modern Nurse, after 1904
- Chapter 6 The Impact of Social and Scientific Changes
- Chapter 7 Health Care Delivery: Where?
- Chapter 8 Health Care Delivery: Who?
- Chapter 18 The Legislative Process
- Chapter 19 Major Legislation Affecting Nursing

Kozier et al. (6th ed., 2000)
- Chapter 2 Nursing Education and Research
- Chapter 6 Health Care Delivery Systems
- Chapter 13 Culture and Ethnicity
- Chapter 14 Spirituality

Potter & Perry (4th ed., 1997)
- Chapter 2 The Health Care Delivery System
- Chapter 21 Cultural Diversity
- Chapter 25 Spiritual Health

III. Framework for Nursing Practice
Kelly & Joel (8th ed., 1999)
- Chapter 9 Nursing as a Profession
- Chapter 10 Professional Ethics and the Nurse
- Chapter 12 Major Issues and Trends in Nursing Education
- Chapter 13 Programs in Nursing Education
- Chapter 14 Nursing Research: Status, Problems, Issues
  (read section on Research into Practice)

Sample Questions: Occupational Strategies in Nursing

    Chapter 17 An Introduction to Law
    Chapter 20 Licensure and Health Care Credentialing
    Chapter 21 Nursing Practice and the Law
    Chapter 22 Health Care and the Rights of Patients

Kozier et al. (6th ed., 2000)
    Chapter 4 Legal Aspects of Nursing
    Chapter 5 Values, Ethics, and Advocacy
    Chapter 20 Implementing and Evaluating

Potter & Perry (4th ed., 1997)
    Chapter 16 Research
    Chapter 18 Values
    Chapter 19 Ethics
    Chapter 20 Legal Issues

IV. Delivery of Nursing Care by the Associate Degree Graduate

Kelly & Joel (8th ed., 1999)
    Chapter 9 Nursing as a Profession
    Chapter 15 Opportunities in Modern Nursing
    Chapter 16 Leadership for an Era of Change

Kozier et al. (6th ed., 2000)
    Chapter 6 Health Care Delivery Systems
    Chapter 16 Critical Thinking and the Nursing Process
    Chapter 27 Leading, Managing, and Influencing Change

Potter & Perry (4th ed., 1997)
    Chapter 17 Leadership and Management

Study Guide
Baccalaureate Degree Nursing Examinations Series

This section contains study guides for the following examinations required of students in the Regents College baccalaureate degree program Bachelor of Science in Nursing:

- Health Restoration: Area I
- Health Restoration: Area II
- Health Support A: Health Promotion & Health Protection
- Health Support B: Community Health Nursing
- Professional Strategies in Nursing
- Research in Nursing

Using the BSN Study Guides

These study guides have certain common features that should help you to structure your study effectively. For example, the content outlines for the two Health Restoration exams have an identical structure based on the five-part nursing process. Further common features are described below.

Recommended Textbooks: Building a Nursing Library

If you are planning to take several of the baccalaureate degree nursing examinations, you will need to begin building a library of nursing textbooks. Each of the textbooks recommended by the examination development committee provides in-depth exploration of the material in the content areas to be tested. In addition, many of them have a companion study guide. If you would like assistance in organizing your study and reviewing the material in the textbooks, the committee recommends that you consider purchasing the study guides as well. In general, you do not need to purchase two textbooks in the same area unless the introductory paragraph specifically recommends this. If you encounter topics in the content outline that are not covered in the textbook you are using, you should supplement your study with another textbook.

Additional or Other Resources

These resources are suggested to supplement your understanding of the material presented in the recommended resources. They include both textbooks and journal articles, selected because they are current and relevant to the content to be tested by a particular examination. You are encouraged to read widely. You may find other textbooks, articles, or audiovisual resources to be of interest. These additional resources are an important supplementary learning activity because they address issues that are of interest to practicing nurses and provide "real world" examples of how the theory in textbooks can be applied to actual clinical situations.

You should be able to find many of these resources at a nearby school of nursing library, college library, or hospital library. You might also find them at your state nurses' association library. In addition, your local public librarian may be able to assist you with an interlibrary loan request. It is not necessary to purchase these resources.

Journal Articles

As a professional nurse, you have a responsibility to continue your education. One way you can keep current is by reading journal articles. Subscribing to one or two journals, or reading them regularly in a library, is a helpful way to gain exposure to current articles in the field. Libraries may also have access to on-line search and document delivery services that supply journal articles for a fee.

The articles listed for each examination are arranged according to the content area to which they most apply. Because journal articles tend to be written in a simple, straightforward manner, you may find them useful in explaining or expanding upon difficult concepts. You may also find them helpful in providing an "inside view" into unfamiliar areas of nursing practice.

Definitions

For purposes of the BSN examinations, the following definitions are used in the content outline.

1. **Client System**
   A. An **individual** is a single human being as contrasted with a family or community.
   B. A **family** is "two or more individuals, belonging to the same or different kinship groups, who are involved in a continuous living arrangement, usually residing in the same household, experiencing common emotional bonds, and sharing certain obligations toward each other and toward others."

   Stanhope, M., & Lancaster, J. (1996). Community health nursing: Promoting health of aggregates, families, and individuals *(4th ed.). St. Louis: Mosby, p. 453.*

   C. A **community** is a "locality-based entity, composed of systems of formal organizations reflecting societal institutions, informal groups, and aggregates. These components are interdependent and their function is to meet a wide variety of collective needs."

   Stanhope, M., & Lancaster, J. (1996). Community health nursing: Promoting health of aggregates, families, and individuals *(4th ed.). St. Louis: Mosby, p. 290.*

2. **Nursing Process**
   A. **Assessment** is the process of gathering and synthesizing data about the client's health status.
   B. **Analysis** is the identification of the client problem (nursing diagnosis) and the determination of the expected outcomes (goals) of client care.
   C. **Planning** is the formulation of specific strategies to achieve the expected outcomes.
   D. **Implementation** is the carrying out of nursing plans designed to move the client toward the expected outcomes.
   E. **Evaluation** is the appraisal of the effectiveness of the nursing interventions relative to the nursing diagnosis and the expected outcomes.

Study Guide

Health Restoration: Area I (425) (Baccalaureate Level)

Credit Hours: 4 **Credit Level:** Upper
Question Type(s): Multiple-choice

The information in this study guide is valid until Summer 2001.
If you will be taking the examination after that date, be sure to check for a new edition of this guide before you complete your preparation for the exam.

General Description of the Examination

Health Restoration: Area I is part of a two-examination series. Health Restoration: Area I and Health Restoration: Area II test your ability to apply the nursing process in caring for clients with major health problems. While the client may be the individual, the family, or the community, emphasis for this examination is placed on the individual at all stages of the life cycle. The examination tests the ability to utilize critical thinking for clinical decisions in the application of the nursing process.

The concepts that support health restoration are included in the first content area of Health Restoration: Area I. These concepts serve as a foundation for the content covered in content areas II–VII of Health Restoration: Area I and in all content areas of Health Restoration: Area II.

A variety of theories from nursing and related disciplines can be identified that will give the professional nurse a strong base of knowledge on which to practice. The major nursing theorists most applicable to the Health Restoration: Area I examination are Sister Callista Roy, Dorothea Orem, and Virginia Henderson. The organizing framework underlying all of their theories includes the concepts of client, health, nursing, and environment.

Examination Objectives for the Health Restoration Series

You will be expected to demonstrate the ability to:
1. utilize the nursing process to assist the client in managing major health problems by:
   a. assessing the client's health status;
   b. analyzing assessment data to identify the client's health care needs/problems and to determine expected client outcomes
   c. formulating a plan to achieve the expected outcomes;
   d. implementing the appropriate plan;
   e. evaluating the effectiveness of an intervention in terms of outcome achievement;
2. synthesize knowledge from the humanities, social sciences, natural sciences, and nursing science in the practice of professional nursing;
3. apply knowledge of culture and recognition of the client's value system.

Content Outline

Content Area	Percent of Examination
I. Concepts that Support Health Restoration	5%
II. Cardiovascular and Hematologic Problems	20%
III. Respiratory Problems	15%
IV. Neoplasms and Hematologic Malignancies	20%
V. Traumatic Injuries and Multisystem Failure	10%
VI. Endocrine and Metabolic Problems	15%
VII. Immune System Problems	15%
Total	**100%**

The content areas dimension of the examination must be considered in the context of a multicultural society in which responses of the client (individual, family, and community) to health problems are influenced by widely varying social norms, cultural values, religious beliefs, age- and gender-related attitudes, and socioeconomic circumstances. Nursing care decisions are made in consideration of all these complex factors.

I. Concepts that Support Health Restoration (5%)

A. Chronic Illness

B. Rehabilitation

C. Pain and symptom management

D. Inflammation and infection

E. Self-care and self-monitoring

F. Fluids and electrolytes and acid-base balance

G. Tissue perfusion and oxygenation

II. Cardiovascular and Hematologic Problems (20%)

This area focuses on conditions such as aneurysm, dysrhythmias, cardiogenic shock, congenital heart anomalies, congestive heart failure, coronary artery disease, acquired valvular disease, hemophilia, hypertension, myocardial infarction, peripheral vascular disease, pernicious anemia, sickle cell disease, tetralogy of Fallot, thalassemia, arteriosclerosis, atherosclerosis, and stasis ulcers.

A. The Individual: nursing care of the individual with a cardiovascular or hematologic problem
1. Assessment (for example: discussing sexual attitudes and practices with a client who has coronary artery disease; assessing for signs of reduced cardiac output

in a client with cardiogenic shock or congestive heart failure; monitoring continuously for rate, rhythm, and changes in PR, QRS, and QT intervals in a client with conduction defect; observing for characteristics of myocardial pain in a client with reduced coronary blood flow; assessing the impact of cultural and environmental factors in a client with myocardial pain; assessing the spiritual significance of cardiac illness to a client; assessing for signs of allograft rejection in a client with a cardiac transplant; monitoring for hypercyanotic spells in an infant with tetralogy of Fallot; assessing circulation following cardiac catheterization; assessing use of over-the-counter drugs or herbal preparations for a client on anticoagulants)

2. Analysis (for example: analyzing for signs of noncompliance in a client with congestive heart failure, clarifying attitudes and emotional reactions toward the treatment regimen in a client receiving antihypertensive medications, analyzing response to the dietary and antilipemic drug regimen in a client with coronary artery disease, formulating a nursing diagnosis of pain related to vaso-occlusive crisis in a child with sickle cell disease, identifying individuals at high risk for cardiovascular disease)

3. Planning (for example: preparing a teaching plan about signs and symptoms of digoxin toxicity for a child with congestive heart failure, developing pharmacologic and nonpharmacologic strategies to prevent constipation in a client after myocardial infarction, developing strategies to reduce sleep-pattern disturbance in a client following cardiac surgery, anticipating the need to use morphine sulfate in a client experiencing anxiety related to pulmonary edema, planning strategies to provide adequate rest periods and to decrease oxygen consumption in a client experiencing activity intolerance related to anemia, preparing a teaching plan about post-cardiac catheterization recovery, discharge planning for cardiac rehabilitation program)

4. Implementation (for example: instituting therapeutic interventions to relieve pain in a client with chronic peripheral vascular disease; teaching methods to minimize adverse reactions of medications to a client with a cardiac disorder; advising about how to use herbs and nonirritating spices to flavor foods and improve appetite in a client on a controlled sodium diet due to congestive heart failure; teaching strategies to reduce identified risk factors of atherosclerosis in a client with coronary artery disease; encouraging client involvement in decision making to reduce feelings of powerlessness in a client recovering from cardiac surgery; teaching the client with hypertension the importance of maintaining the medical regimen; encouraging alternative ways of expressing intimacy in a client with concerns about sexuality due to chronic congestive heart failure; providing information about the effects of medication, disease process, and/or surgery on sexual functioning to a client scheduled for abdominal aortic aneurysm repair; arranging for pastoral services for a client with advanced cardiac disease; administering antiarrhythmics, inotropic agents, vasodilators, diuretics, anticoagulants, or other cardiac-related drugs to a client with a cardiac disorder; teaching about the reason for the muddy yellow complexion to a child with thalassemia; administering blood to a client with pernicious anemia)

5. Evaluation (for example: evaluating the response to the medication regimen aimed at relieving pain in a client with angina pectoris, determining the effectiveness of nonpharmacologic therapeutic interventions in a client with

peripheral vascular disease, evaluating the effectiveness of care given to the client with congestive heart failure)

B. **The Family: nursing care of the family with a member who has a cardiovascular or hematologic problem**
   1. Assessment (for example: assessing feelings of anger and powerlessness in a family with a member on a life-support system, eliciting feelings about a do-not-resuscitate decision in a family with a member who has cardiomyopathy, assessing risk for cardiac anomalies in a family)
   2. Analysis (for example: identifying the need for social support services for a family with a member who has advanced congestive heart failure, formulating a nursing diagnosis of powerlessness for the family of a neonate who has transposition of the great vessels and is being maintained on life support)
   3. Planning (for example: planning strategies to encourage recreational and diversional activities for a family with a member who has severe peripheral vascular disease)
   4. Implementation/monitoring (for example: teaching about expected psychological responses to a family with a child recovering from corrective cardiac surgery; teaching about discharge precautions to a family with a member who has had a permanent pacemaker or defibrillator implanted; providing orientation to the coronary care unit environment for a family member who has myocardial infarction; promoting effective coping skills in a family with a child who has hemophilia; teaching a family with a history of hypertensive disease the appropriate preventive and screening measures)
   5. Evaluation (for example: evaluating the effectiveness of teaching about the use of medical equipment in a family with a child who has a congenital heart anomaly, evaluating the family's ability to care for a family member with end-stage cardiac disease)

C. **The Community: nursing care in the community with individuals who have cardiovascular or hematologic problems**
   1. Assessment (for example: identifying community resources to provide cardiopulmonary resuscitation classes, identifying availability of heart-healthy nutrition programs)
   2. Analysis (for example: identifying the need for community support groups such as Mended Hearts, analyzing the fat content of a meal plan in a senior citizen center)
   3. Planning (for example: promoting community programs for a culturally diverse population of individuals with cardiac problems; identifying community resources to provide information, support, and counseling for individuals with sickle cell disease; planning a cardiac screening program for a group of older adults)
   4. Implementation (for example: teaching a community about the need for organ procurement to support cardiac transplant programs)
   5. Evaluation (for example: evaluating the allocation of community resources for older adults who have cardiac problems, evaluating community response to a blood drive.)

III. Respiratory Problems (15%)

This area focuses on conditions affecting the respiratory system, such as adult respiratory distress syndrome, bronchiolitis, bronchopulmonary dysplasia, chronic obstructive pulmonary disease, cystic fibrosis, laryngotracheobronchitis, tuberculosis, *Pneumocystis carinii* pneumonia, pneumonia, pulmonary embolus, sudden infant death syndrome, lung abscesses, atelectasis, and tracheoesophageal fistula.

A. The Individual: nursing care of the individual with a respiratory problem

1. Assessment (for example: assessing for evidence of impending airway obstruction in a child with laryngotracheobronchitis, identifying alterations of normal respiratory patterns in an older adult client with chronic obstructive pulmonary disease, observing for mediastinal shift in a client with pneumothorax, observing physiologic parameters in a client following a lobectomy, assessing for alterations in body temperature in a child with bronchiolitis, determining the extent of activity tolerance in a client with chronic obstructive pulmonary disease, monitoring for evidence of increasing respiratory distress in an adolescent with cystic fibrosis)

2. Analysis (for example: categorizing behaviors that indicate unresolved conflict over dependency in a client who has emphysema and who is unable to work, anticipating complications in a client with drug-resistant pneumonia, identifying indicators of powerlessness in a client who has adult respiratory distress syndrome and is ventilator dependent, formulating a nursing diagnosis of impaired gas exchange related to increased mucus production for a child with cystic fibrosis, analyzing laboratory data for a client with impaired gas exchange related to pulmonary embolus, correlating clinical data with laboratory data to ascertain the status of a toddler with epiglottitis, analyzing the response to dietary and corticosteroid drug therapy in a client with chronic obstructive pulmonary disease, formulating a nursing diagnosis of altered sexuality patterns related to infertility for a male client with cystic fibrosis)

3. Planning (for example: planning strategies to prevent hypostatic pneumonia in a client on prolonged bed rest, planning strategies to promote adequate fluid balance in an infant with bronchiolitis, planning measures to reduce the drying effect of oxygen therapy on mucous membranes in a client with a tracheotomy, prioritizing interventions for a client with pneumothorax due to a ruptured emphysematous bleb, collaborating with the client to determine long-term outcomes related to managing home maintenance for a client with chronic obstructive pulmonary disease, developing a teaching plan about the therapeutic use of oxygen for a client with chronic obstructive pulmonary disease)

4. Implementation (for example: administering care to a client with acute pulmonary edema following lung surgery; intervening immediately to minimize physical injury in a client with a pulmonary embolus; undertaking measures to restore fluid balance in a child with bronchiolitis; teaching about exercises to reduce dyspnea in a client with chronic obstructive pulmonary disease; supporting efforts to achieve positive body image in a client with chronic obstructive pulmonary disease; minimizing the potential for nutritional deficits in an adolescent with fever and vomiting related to bronchitis; supporting the grief process in a client who is in the terminal phases of *Pneumocystis carinii* pneumonia; intervening promptly in the event of an impaired airway for a client with stasis of secretions secondary to

atelectasis; providing comfort measures for a client after pneumonectomy; promoting rest for a client following the insertion of chest tubes; administering bronchodilators, corticosteroids, and mucolytic expectorants to a client with chronic obstructive pulmonary disease; administering expectorants and antibiotics to a child with cystic fibrosis)
   5. Evaluation (for example: evaluating the effectiveness of exercises to improve respiratory function in a client with chronic obstructive pulmonary disease; evaluating the effectiveness of teaching about alternative ways of expressing intimacy in a client with weakness and fatigue related to chronic dyspnea; evaluating the effectiveness of bronchodilators, corticosteroids, and mucolytic expectorants in a client with chronic obstructive pulmonary disease; comparing the effectiveness of planned interventions with intended outcomes for a client with bronchopulmonary dysplasia)

B. **The Family: nursing care of the family with a member who has a respiratory problem**
   1. Assessment (for example: assessing understanding of infection transmission in a family with a member who has tuberculosis, assessing coping in a family with a member who has end-stage respiratory disease)
   2. Analysis (for example: identifying a family's strengths in coping with the needs of a child who is ventilator dependent following an aborted episode of sudden infant death syndrome, formulating a nursing diagnosis of altered parenting related to the presence of life-threatening chronic illness for the parents of a child with cystic fibrosis)
   3. Planning (for example: developing a teaching plan for a family who is caring for a member with a tracheostomy, developing a therapy plan for a client with chronic obstructive pulmonary disease [COPD])
   4. Implementation (for example: teaching methods of home care to a family with a child who has bronchopulmonary dysplasia and is on mechanical ventilation, referring a family to a support group for caretakers of persons with chronic pulmonary disease, collaborating with a family to minimize the social isolation of a member who has end-stage respiratory disease, teaching the family of a client with tuberculosis the importance of screening)
   5. Evaluation (for example: evaluating a spouse's satisfaction with the alterations in sexual patterns of a client with chronic obstructive pulmonary disease, evaluating a family's effectiveness in caring for a child on mechanical ventilation)

C. **The Community: nursing care in the community with individuals who have respiratory problems**
   1. Assessment (for example: assessing a community's resources related to the needs of individuals requiring assistance with home oxygen therapy, assessing level of environmental pollutants in a community with high rates of respiratory illness)
   2. Analysis (for example: identifying the cultural and economic factors that contribute to a community's response to the needs of individuals with *Pneumocystis carinii* pneumonia)
   3. Planning (for example: developing a plan to provide information about environmental hazards to individuals with severe respiratory problems)
   4. Implementation (for example: conducting educational programs regarding pertussis immunization for groups of individuals with chronic respiratory disease)

5. Evaluation (for example: evaluating the effectiveness of educational programs in raising community awareness about the health maintenance needs of individuals with respiratory conditions)

IV. Neoplasms and Hematologic Malignancies (20%)

This area focuses on conditions such as bladder cancer, brain cancer, breast cancer, cervical cancer, colorectal cancer, Ewing's sarcoma, head and neck cancer, Hodgkin's disease, leukemias, lung cancer, lymphomas, malignant melanoma, neuroblastoma, osteogenic sarcoma, ovarian cancer, prostate cancer, retinoblastoma, rhabdomyosarcoma, skin cancer, testicular cancer, uterine cancer, and Wilms' tumor.

A. The Individual: nursing care of the individual with a neoplasm or hematologic malignancy
1. Assessment (for example: assessing the psychosocial response to a diagnosis of cancer in a child with Wilms' tumor, exploring alternative communication patterns for an older adult client with a laryngectomy, determining the level of activity tolerance in a child receiving chemotherapy, assessing for complications from the treatment regimen in a client with testicular cancer, identifying indications of lymphedema in a client recovering from surgery for breast cancer, identifying medications that mask the signs and symptoms of infection in a client receiving treatment for cancer)
2. Analysis (for example: identifying factors related to self-esteem disturbance in a male client with a recent ostomy, determining the impact of impaired thought processes in a middle-aged client who has lung cancer and is unable to return to work, analyzing diagnostic laboratory data for a client with advanced cancer who is confused and is vomiting, analyzing sleep-pattern disturbance in an adolescent with osteogenic sarcoma, identifying altered elimination patterns in a client recovering from a prostatectomy)
3. Planning (for example: planning measures to reduce the risk of infection in a client receiving chemotherapy for treatment of ovarian cancer, planning interventions to promote nutrition in a client receiving chemotherapy for treatment of cancer, developing strategies to minimize bleeding in a client who has leukemia and a reduced platelet count, developing strategies to reduce the risk of pathological fractures in a client with multiple myeloma)
4. Implementation (for example: providing instruction about how to perform breast self-examination to a client who has had surgery for breast cancer, providing instruction about how to perform ostomy care to a client following abdominal surgery for cancer, providing instruction about skin care to a client receiving radiation therapy to the chest wall for treatment of breast cancer, teaching adolescent males the importance of testicular self-examination, suggesting dietary interventions to a client with stomatitis related to chemotherapy, monitoring for a transfusion reaction in a client who has undergone a bone marrow transplant and who is receiving a platelet transfusion, monitoring the response to narcotic pain medication in a client with metastatic colon cancer, teaching measures to reduce fatigue to a client with Hodgkin's disease, providing information on support groups such as Reach to Recovery and the Look Good...Feel Better program to a client with breast cancer, providing information about how to cope with alopecia to a client with cancer, inspecting the IV site in a child receiving chemotherapy for treatment of retinoblastoma)

5. Evaluation (for example: evaluating the degree of constipation in a client who has cancer and who is receiving morphine, evaluating lymphedema in a client who had breast surgery five years ago and has been wearing a compression sleeve, evaluating the understanding of measures to reduce infection by a client recovering from a bone marrow transplant, evaluating exertional dyspnea and pulse oximetry findings in a client with lung cancer, evaluating the ability to perform self-care in a client who has had a urinary diversion, evaluating for evidence of bone marrow suppression in a child receiving chemotherapy for treatment of Wilms' tumor)

B. **The Family: nursing care of the family with a member who has a neoplasm or hematologic malignancy**
   1. Assessment (for example: exploring resources available to assist a family in providing home care for a client with advanced cancer, assessing a family's ability to cope with a recent diagnosis of retinoblastoma in their toddler, determining a family's willingness to utilize support groups following the death of a parent)
   2. Analysis (for example: analyzing a family's ability to make decisions regarding advance directives, analyzing the adjustment of a single parent family with a child undergoing treatment for leukemia)
   3. Planning (for example: planning instruction for families regarding long-term effects of chemotherapy on children, planning counseling to discuss the impact of chemotherapy on childbearing for a couple in which the husband is undergoing chemotherapy, planning measures to assist children in understanding how a diagnosis of neuroblastoma in a sibling will affect them, planning instruction about home care for the spouse of a client who is receiving feedings via a percutaneous endoscopic gastrostomy, planning counseling to assist a family in adjusting to a member's bone marrow transplant)
   4. Implementation (for example: providing instruction about ostomy care to a couple with one partner who has colorectal cancer, monitoring a family's ability to minimize the potential for infection in a child receiving chemotherapy)
   5. Evaluation (for example: evaluating a family's ability to assess and utilize resources and bereavement support groups following the death of their child)

C. **The Community: nursing care in the community with individuals who have neoplasms or hematologic malignancies**
   1. Assessment (for example: assessing the availability of cancer information and cancer support groups such as the National Coalition for Cancer Survivorship, the American Cancer Society, and the Leukemia Society of America in a community, assessing cancer rates and types in a community)
   2. Analysis (for example: determining the availability of image resources in a community for individuals with cancer, determining the availability of hospice resources in a community to assist families in caring for individuals with cancer)
   3. Planning (for example: planning cancer rehabilitation services and support in a community, collaborating with community leaders to provide high-technological services for individuals with cancer who live in rural settings)
   4. Implementation (for example: providing information to the community about

the National Cancer Institute toll-free hot line, providing community counseling and support programs for individuals and families with cancer in conjunction with organizations such as the United Ostomy Association, implementing a cancer awareness program in the community)
5. Evaluation (for example: evaluating the utilization of community support groups and resources by individuals with cancer)

V. Traumatic Injuries and Multisystem Failure (10%)

This area focuses on conditions such as burns, disseminated intravascular coagulation, drug overdose, fat emboli, foreign body aspiration, frostbite, motor vehicle accidents, near-drowning, poisoning, septic shock, hemorrhagic shock, traumatic amputations, and wounds of violence.

A. The Individual: nursing care of the individual with a traumatic injury or multisystem failure

1. Assessment (for example: assessing for indications of hypovolemic shock in a client with massive injuries following a motor vehicle accident, investigating the health history of a client who has a history of insulin-dependent diabetes mellitus [type I] and has 45% deep partial-thickness [second-degree] and full-thickness [third-degree] burns, assessing for suspected poisoning in a toddler, determining indicators of inhalation injury in a client with burns resulting from a fire, assessing neurovascular function of the involved limb in a client with a gunshot wound of the thigh, assessing for complications of acid-base imbalance in a client with dehydration and starvation, assessing for signs and symptoms of gastrointestinal hemorrhage in a client recovering from major burns)
2. Analysis (for example: formulating nursing diagnoses for a client with 25% full-thickness [third-degree] burns; analyzing the results of radiographic examinations, laboratory tests, or special procedures for a client with blunt abdominal trauma; anticipating respiratory complications in a client with burns due to a blast injury; correlating laboratory and clinical data for a client with a drug overdose; identifying relevant laboratory data related to acid-base imbalance in a client with chemical burns; interpreting the arterial blood gas results of a client with near-drowning; analyzing urinalysis data to determine urinary tract involvement in a client with a stab wound of the lower abdomen)
3. Planning (for example: determining outcomes for the nutritional needs of a client with 60% deep partial-thickness [second-degree] and full-thickness [third-degree] burns, identifying nursing interventions to assist a client in adjusting to disfiguring wounds, developing outcomes related to ambulation for a client with a traumatic above-the-knee amputation, planning for the protection from injury of a client with seizures related to a drug overdose, collaborating with the respiratory therapist to meet the oxygenation needs of a client with near-drowning, anticipating the need for asepsis in performing procedures on a client with 80% body surface areas burns)
4. Implementation (for example: implementing nonpharmacologic pain control measures to assist a client with severe burns in coping with pain, monitoring for gastrointestinal complications in a client with blunt abdominal trauma, providing for fluid replacement in a client with major burns, teaching about potential complications to a client with frostbite, explaining the need to promptly report any symptoms of impaired respiration to a client with foreign body aspiration, monitoring for evidence of hemorrhage in a client at risk for developing disseminated intravascular coagulation, administering

histamine H2 receptor antagonists as prophylaxis against Curling's stress ulcer in a client with burns over 40% of the body surface area, monitoring for indicators of septic shock in a client with massive infection following major trauma, caring for donor sites in a client undergoing skin grafting procedures)

5. Evaluation (for example: determining the effectiveness of interventions to prevent contractures in a client with major burns, evaluating the effectiveness of teaching about possible sources of hemorrhage in a client at risk for disseminated intravascular coagulation, evaluating the effectiveness of proteolytic enzymes in the debridement of wounds in a client with burns of the hands, ascertaining the effectiveness of interventions for a client with a drug overdose)

B. The Family: nursing care of the family with a member who has a traumatic injury or multisystem failure

1. Assessment (for example: interviewing a family about precipitating factors related to the fall of an older adult member, performing a home safety assessment)
2. Analysis (for example: formulating nursing diagnoses for the family of a child who sustained an accidental drug overdose, identifying unsafe behaviors in a family)
3. Planning (for example: involving the family as well as the client in developing a care plan for a client who has been involved in a motor vehicle accident when driving while intoxicated, developing a discharge teaching plan for the family with a member who has inhalation burns)
4. Implementation (for example: providing support to the family of a severely injured child to aid them in coping with feelings of powerlessness, implementing a teaching plan for a family with a member who has major burns, including the family when intervening in a consistent manner to reduce excessively controlling behavior of a family member in long-term traction, referring a family for counseling following a child's attempted suicide)
5. Evaluation (for example: evaluating the ability to cope in a family with a member who has been disfigured by severe burns, evaluating a family's response to the diagnosis of multisystem failure in a family member)

C. The Community: nursing care in the community with individuals who have traumatic injuries or multisystem failures

1. Assessment (for example: assessing community needs for instruction about the emergency care of individuals with traumatic injuries)
2. Analysis (for example: analyzing plans for prehospital care of employees who sustain chemical injuries in the workplace)
3. Planning (for example: collaborating with community leaders to develop a plan for individuals being transported by emergency medical services)
4. Implementation (for example: conducting community education programs about the care of individuals with suspected poisoning)
5. Evaluation (for example: evaluating the effectiveness of community teaching programs about the care of traumatically amputated body parts to allow for later replantation)

VI. Endocrine and Metabolic Problems (15%)

This area focuses on conditions such as acromegaly, Addison's disease, adrenal insufficiency, biliary atresia, cirrhosis, Cushing's syndrome, diabetes mellitus, hypothyroidism, hyperthyroidism, hypoparathyroidism, inborn errors of metabolism, pancreatitis, premenstrual syndrome, phenylketonuria, and syndrome of inappropriate antidiuretic hormone.

A. The Individual: nursing care of the individual with an endocrine or metabolic problem

1. Assessment (for example: assessing for compliance with the prescribed insulin regimen in an adolescent client with insulin-dependent diabetes mellitus [type I], identifying signs and symptoms of anabolic steroids use in an adolescent athlete, assessing for factors that precipitate uncomfortable symptoms in a client with premenstrual syndrome, monitoring for signs of complications in a client who has had a thyroidectomy, identifying subjective evidence of body image changes in a client with Cushing's syndrome, collecting assessment data indicating complications in a client with hypothyroidism, assessing for signs of complications of immunosuppression in a client who has had a liver transplant, monitoring for hyponatremia in a client with syndrome of inappropriate antidiuretic hormone)

2. Analysis (for example: formulating a nursing diagnosis for a client with fluid imbalance related to diabetic ketoacidosis, analyzing signs of Addisonian crisis in a client who is dependent on steroids, analyzing evidence of sexual dysfunction in a client with diabetes mellitus, differentiating between hypoglycemia and hyperglycemia in a symptomatic client with insulin-dependent diabetes mellitus [type I])

3. Planning (for example: specifying outcomes for the nutritional management of a client with cirrhosis, developing a teaching plan about the use of an insulin pump for a client with insulin-dependent diabetes mellitus [type I], developing a teaching plan about hormone therapy for a client who is postmenopausal, collaborating with a client and a nutritionist to develop a plan for compliance with the American Dietetic Association diabetic diet, planning nutritional support for a client who has acute pancreatitis, planning for protection from injury in a client with osteoporosis secondary to hyperparathyroidism)

4. Implementation (for example: teaching about the importance of fluid replacement to a client with adrenal insufficiency, promoting foot care for a client with noninsulin-dependent diabetes mellitus [type II], instructing about methods to prevent constipation in a client with hypothyroidism, intervening to reduce the risk of impaired skin integrity in a client on long-term corticosteroid therapy, facilitating diet modification in a client with end-stage liver disease, managing fluid and blood replacement therapy for a client with bleeding esophageal varices, teaching management of insulin therapy to a client with an islet cell transplant, supporting efforts to acquire effective methods of coping with stress by a client with adrenal insufficiency, assisting a child with phenylketonuria to live a normal lifestyle within dietary restrictions, intervening to relieve abdominal pain in a client with acute pancreatitis, teaching injury prevention to a client experiencing sensory loss related to advanced diabetes mellitus, teaching about the effects of oral hypoglycemic agents to a client with noninsulin-dependent diabetes mellitus

[type II], teaching clients regarding blood levels of glycosylated hemoglobin)
    5. Evaluation (for example: collecting data to determine the effectiveness of self-monitoring in a client with insulin-dependent diabetes mellitus [type I], evaluating the effectiveness of nutritional and fluid support in a client with acute pancreatitis, evaluating client satisfaction with lifestyle changes related to a diagnosis of cirrhosis, evaluating the effectiveness of glucagon administered to a client with profound hypoglycemia, evaluating the effectiveness of an insulin pump used in treatment of an adolescent with insulin-dependent diabetes mellitus [type I])

B. **The Family: nursing care of the family with a member who has an endocrine or metabolic problem**
    1. Assessment (for example: gathering data related to environmental stressors in a family with a member who has an adrenal disorder, evaluating the effectiveness of an insulin pump used in treatment of an adolescent with insulin-dependent diabetes mellitus [type I])
    2. Analysis (for example: analyzing the support system in a family with a member who has end-stage liver disease)
    3. Planning (for example: supporting family efforts to promote normal growth and development in an infant with an inborn error of metabolism)
    4. Implementation (for example: teaching about early signs of physiologic stress to a family with a member who has Addison's disease; teaching the balancing of activity, diet, and insulin therapy for the family with a child who has insulin-dependent diabetes mellitus [type I])
    5. Evaluation (for example: reassessing the needs of a family with a member who has chronic pancreatitis)

C. **The Community: nursing care in the community with individuals who have endocrine or metabolic problems**
    1. Assessment (for example: identifying community resources available to provide support to individuals with diabetes mellitus)
    2. Analysis (for example: identifying a community's need to be taught about the recognition and use of medical identification bracelets for individuals with endocrine disorders)
    3. Planning (for example: facilitating goal setting in a community with children who have special needs related to endocrine disorders)
    4. Implementation (for example: teaching groups of individuals with diabetes mellitus more about the disorder, adapting American Dietetic Association guidelines to the cultural and ethnic needs of a community)
    5. Evaluation (for example: evaluating the allocation of community resources for older adults with sensory deficits related to diabetes mellitus)

VII. Immune System Problems (15%)

This area focuses on conditions such as acquired immunodeficiency syndrome (AIDS), allergies, asthma, glomerulonephritis, human immunodeficiency virus, idiopathic thrombocytopenia purpura (ITP), mucocutaneous lymph node syndrome, polyarteritis nodosa, polymyositis, reactive airway disease, rheumatoid arthritis, scleroderma, and systemic lupus erythematosus.

A. **The Individual: nursing care of the individual with an immune system problem**
    1. Assessment (for example: assessing for functional deficits in a client with scleroderma; assessing for fluid volume excess in a child with acute

glomerulonephritis; collecting subjective and objective data to identify impaired swallowing in a client with systemic lupus erythematosus; observing for altered skin integrity in a client with systemic lupus erythematosus; observing for fluid volume deficit in a child with mucocutaneous lymph node syndrome; assessing for potential injury related to thrombocytopenia in a client with idiopathic thrombocytopenia purpura; assessing for impaired gas exchange in a client with asthma; assessing the risk for injury related to extreme muscle dysfunction and atrophy in a client with polymyositis; assessing for renal dysfunction related to renal vascular ischemia in a client with polyarteritis nodosa; assessing for evidence of increasing bronchospasm in a child with asthma)

2. Analysis (for example: formulating nursing diagnoses for a client with rheumatoid arthritis, anticipating a knowledge deficit in a client recently diagnosed with polyarteritis nodosa, identifying threats to self-concept in an adolescent client with rheumatoid arthritis, analyzing the physiologic response to beta adrenergic agents in a client with asthma, identifying impaired social interaction in an older adult client with rheumatoid arthritis, identifying feelings of powerlessness in a client with AIDS, identifying signs and symptoms related to leukopenia and steroid therapy in a client with systemic lupus erythematosus, anticipating altered sexual patterns related to chronic fatigue and pain in a client with systemic lupus erythematosus)

3. Planning (for example: planning nursing interventions for a client with polyarteritis nodosa, planning strategies to minimize impaired skin integrity in a client with AIDS-related complex, planning strategies related to anticipatory grieving for a client with AIDS, preparing a teaching plan about the side effects of corticosteroids for the client with rheumatoid arthritis, developing a teaching plan about the use of inhalers for a client with asthma, specifying outcomes for nutritional management of a client with acute glomerulonephritis, developing outcomes for management of fatigue and chronic pain for a client with rheumatoid arthritis)

4. Implementation (for example: providing emotional support during periods of reactive depression associated with corticosteroids for a client with an immune disorder; administering immune system modifiers to a client with human immunodeficiency virus or to a client following a transplant; intervening to resolve dependence/independence issues in an adolescent client with rheumatoid arthritis; facilitating the grieving process in a client with AIDS; promoting comfort in a client with scleroderma; teaching about environmental factors that may worsen the pulmonary condition in a client with allergies; assisting in the detection of altered oral mucous membranes related to Sjögren's syndrome in a client with systemic lupus erythematosus; assisting with activities of daily living for a client who is experiencing altered mobility related to scleroderma; teaching about the use of a metered dose inhaler that delivers a beta-adrenergic agonist such as albuterol or metaproterenol to a child with asthma; monitoring oxygen saturation level with an oximeter and, when less than 95%, administering oxygen for a child with asthma; providing parenteral nutritional support for an infant with AIDS; providing supportive devices for an individual with severe rheumatoid arthritis)

5. Evaluation (for example: evaluating the effectiveness of coping mechanisms related to social isolation in a client with AIDS, determining the effectiveness

of racemic epinephrine in a client experiencing acute episodes of reactive airway disease, evaluating the effectiveness of immune system modifiers in a client with polyarteritis nodosa, evaluating the effectiveness of plasmapheresis in a client with an immune disorder, evaluating satisfaction with lifestyle changes in a client with newly diagnosed scleroderma, evaluating interventions to assist with self-concept related to altered role performance in a client with systemic lupus erythematosus, evaluating the effectiveness of Cox-2 inhibitors in a client with rheumatoid arthritis)

B. The Family: nursing care of the family with a member who has an immune system problem
1. Assessment (for example: assessing feelings of anger and powerlessness in a family with a member who has AIDS, assessing for a knowledge deficit related to the risk for opportunistic infection in a family with a member who has AIDS, assessing understanding of infection transmission in a family with a member who has *Pneumocystis carinii* pneumonia)
2. Analysis (for example: formulating a nursing diagnosis related to coping in a family with a member who has newly diagnosed reactive airway disease)
3. Planning (for example: planning strategies related to anticipatory grieving in a family with a member who has AIDS, developing a teaching plan about the medication regimen for the family of a child who has asthma)
4. Implementation (for example: implementing a teaching plan for a family with an infant born with severe combined immunodeficiencies, supporting a family who is providing home care for a member with severe rheumatoid arthritis, assisting a family in obtaining financial aid to meet health care needs for a member with AIDS)
5. Evaluation (for example: evaluating the effectiveness of a teaching plan about the medication regimen for a family with a member who has rheumatoid arthritis)

C. The Community: nursing care in the community with individuals who have immune system problems
1. Assessment (for example: assessing the availability of community-based programs for individuals with immune disorders)
2. Analysis (for example: analyzing the adjustment of a community with a growing population of individuals with AIDS)
3. Planning (for example: planning with community leaders to enhance accessibility of public buildings for individuals with physical disabilities related to immune disorders)
4. Implementation (for example: fostering community-based support groups for individuals with human immunodeficiency virus, teaching clients to access technological resources)
5. Evaluation (for example: evaluating the effectiveness of community strategies to ensure adequate housing for individuals with AIDS, evaluating the accessibility of public buildings for individuals with mobility impairments)

Sample Questions: Health Restoration: Area I

1. When evaluating a client's response to treatment for metabolic alkalosis, the nurse notes slow shallow respirations. The nurse should understand that this finding is due to which compensatory effort by the pulmonary system?
    1) decreasing carbonic acid
    2) decreasing oxygen needs
    3) increasing bicarbonate levels
    4) conserving carbon dioxide

2. Which outcome indicates that therapy for a client with a fluid volume deficit has been effective?
The client
    1) has a urine specific gravity of 1.040.
    2) exhibits hemoconcentration.
    3) exhibits normal skin turgor.
    4) maintains low blood pressure.

3. A client is receiving epidural analgesia postoperatively. Which nursing intervention is most important?
    1) Assess for constipation.
    2) Observe for depressed respirations.
    3) Check for increased blood pressure.
    4) Monitor for bradycardia.

4. Which dysrhythmia is represented in the following six-second rhythm strip?

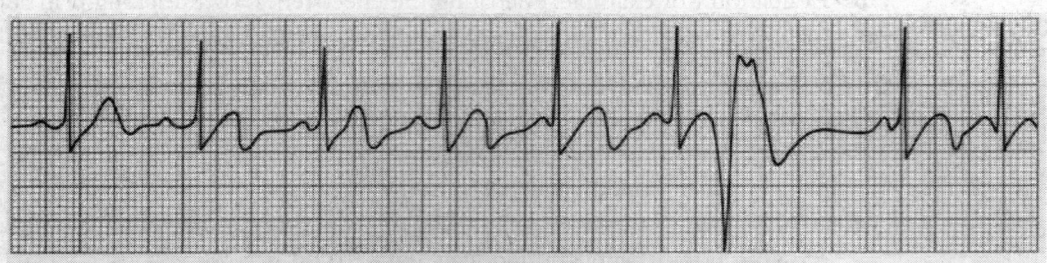

Reprinted with permission from EKG CARDS. Copyright 1987, Springhouse Corporation. All rights reserved.

    1) asystole
    2) atrial fibrillation
    3) premature ventricular contraction
    4) sinus tachycardia

5. When preparing a care plan for a client admitted with a diagnosis of congestive heart failure, the nurse should give priority to which nursing diagnosis?
    1) decreased cardiac output related to ventricular damage
    2) ineffective breathing pattern related to fatigue
    3) high risk for impaired skin integrity related to immobility secondary to bed rest
    4) altered family processes related to hospitalization of parent

Sample Questions: Health Restoration: Area I

6. A six-month-old infant has been taking digoxin elixir since birth. Which finding indicates that the infant may be developing toxicity to the ordered dosage?
   1) resting apical heart rate of 90 bpm
   2) vomiting with feedings
   3) tetany
   4) hypertension

7. The nurse is auscultating the chest of a client following a right upper lobectomy for bronchogenic carcinoma. Which sign should alert the nurse to a potential problem?
   1) bronchial breath sounds over the tracheal area
   2) bilateral decreased breath sounds in the lung bases
   3) absence of adventitious breath sounds
   4) vesicular breath sounds bilaterally in the lung bases

8. Which is the most appropriate nursing intervention for an older adult client who develops a pulmonary embolism postoperatively?
   Teach the client that
   1) heparin therapy is used to prevent formation of new clots.
   2) anticoagulant therapy is used to dissolve the pulmonary embolus.
   3) it is important to remain in a supine position to prevent emboli movement.
   4) blood is infused to increase hemoglobin and hematocrit levels.

9. Which early sign should the nurse expect to assess in a client experiencing hypoxia?
   1) confusion
   2) constricted pupils
   3) cyanosis
   4) enlarged liver

10. An adult client is admitted with bacterial pneumonia. Which dietary intervention should the nurse implement?
    1) Restrict fluids to no more than 1,500 cc per day.
    2) Institute a low-sodium, low-fat diet.
    3) Encourage at least 2 liters of fluid per day.
    4) Provide a mechanically soft diet high in vitamin A.

11. A client is receiving a standard chemotherapy regimen for treatment of leukemia. Following the treatment, the nurse should anticipate that the client will also require which intervention?
    1) Administer allopurinol (Zyloprim) for the treatment of hyperuricemia.
    2) Administer furosemide (Lasix) for the management of fluid retention.
    3) Administer phenytoin (Dilantin) for the management of drug-induced seizures.
    4) Administer heparin (Liquaemin Sodium) for the treatment of thrombocytopenia.

Sample Questions: Health Restoration: Area I

12. The nurse teaches a client and the client's wife about side effects of the radiation and chemotherapy used to treat the client's Hodgkin's disease. Which statement by the wife indicates that additional teaching is needed?
    1) "The nausea and vomiting will stop after therapy is completed."
    2) "We're planning to start a family as soon as the chemotherapy is finished."
    3) "I'll make certain that my husband wears loose clothes until the radiation therapy is finished."
    4) "We don't mind that the treatment may cause baldness. The hair will grow back quickly."

13. The nurse is collecting data from an adolescent client with suspected lymphoma. The nurse should assess the client for the presence of which symptoms?
    1) thirst, hepatomegaly, and diuresis
    2) weight loss, fever, and night sweats
    3) food hypersensitivity, tachypnea, and rash
    4) headache, constipation, and footdrop

14. The nurse is evaluating the effectiveness of fluid resuscitation for a client who sustained a burn injury 16 hours ago. Which finding indicates that fluid resuscitation efforts were effective?
    1) PaO_2 of 60 mm Hg
    2) blood pressure of 80/60
    3) urinary output of 35 cc/hr
    4) urine specific gravity of 1.450

15. Which nursing intervention is appropriate for the administration of continuous IV dopamine to a client who is in hypovolemic shock?
    1) Protect the drug container from light.
    2) Observe the client for tachydysrhythmias.
    3) Discontinue the IV when optimum blood pressure is attained.
    4) Select a small peripheral vein as the best infusion site.

16. Which nursing intervention should receive priority in the plan of care for a newly admitted client with head trauma?
    1) Elevate the head of the bed to decrease intracranial pressure.
    2) Start an intravenous line and begin D_5W.
    3) Maintain an open airway.
    4) Monitor for cerebrospinal fluid loss.

Sample Questions: Health Restoration: Area I

17. The nurse teaches a client about the health management of the early stage of cirrhosis. Which client statement indicates that the teaching was effective?
    1) "I have the lists of foods to eat, and I will take a small drink of wine before each meal to stimulate my appetite."
    2) "I know how to take the water pills at night, and limit my intake of meat, bananas, and eggs."
    3) "I realize that over-the-counter medications are not good for me, and I will take my diuretic according to your written guidelines."
    4) "I read the list of high-sodium foods, and I know that I should eat chicken baked and eggs poached."

18. A client has myxedema. Which client statement indicates an understanding of the nurse's teaching about levothyroxine (Synthroid) therapy?
    1) "I will take the medication until my symptoms are gone."
    2) "I know occasional chest pain will be normal while I'm taking the medication."
    3) "I should take my medication early in the morning."
    4) "I may need to increase my sleeping pill dose while I'm taking the medication."

19. When taking a health history from a client diagnosed as having hypothyroidism, the nurse should expect the client to report which of the following?
    1) extreme fatigue
    2) diarrhea
    3) heat intolerance
    4) muscle tremors

20. Which findings should alert the nurse to potential hypoglycemia in a client who is being treated with insulin for diabetes mellitus?
    1) nausea and vomiting
    2) sweating and tremors
    3) tachypnea and dehydration
    4) ketonuria and malaise

21. Which client response should alert the nurse to a potential problem in a client who is taking diphenhydramine hydrochloride (Benadryl) for allergies?
    1) dizziness
    2) dry mouth
    3) difficulty falling asleep
    4) increased alertness

22. When caring for a child who has newly diagnosed juvenile rheumatoid arthritis, the nurse should give priority to which goal?
    1) Enhance self-concept.
    2) Promote socialization.
    3) Reduce discomfort.
    4) Encourage self-care.

Sample Questions: Health Restoration: Area I

23. When assessing a client who has progressive systemic sclerosis with the CREST syndrome, the nurse should be most concerned about which finding?
    1) diarrhea
    2) dysphagia
    3) malaise
    4) pain

Recommended Resources—Textbooks

Black, J.M., & Matassarin-Jacobs, E. (1997). Medical-surgical nursing: Clinical management for continuity of care (5th ed.). Philadelphia: W.B. Saunders.

Ignatavicius, D. et al. (1999). Medical-surgical nursing across the health care continuum (3rd ed.). Philadelphia: W.B. Saunders.

Smeltzer, S., & Bare, B. (1996). Brunner and Suddarth's Textbook of medical-surgical nursing (8th ed.). Philadelphia: J.B. Lippincott.

Eisenhauer, L. et al. (1998). Clinical pharmacology and nursing management (5th ed.). Philadelphia: J.B. Lippincott.

Wong, D. (1999). Whaley & Wong's Nursing care of infants and children (6th ed.). St. Louis: Mosby.

Additional Resources—Textbooks

Bastable, S. (1997). Nurse as educator: Principles of teaching and learning. Sudbury, MA: Jones & Bartlett.

Carpenito, L. (1999). Nursing diagnosis: Application to clinical practice (8th ed.). Philadelphia: J.B. Lippincott.

Chenitz, W., Stone, J., & Salisbury, S. (1991). Clinical gerontological nursing: A guide to advanced practice. Philadelphia: W.B. Saunders.

Clark, M.J. (1999). Nursing in the community (3rd ed.). Stamford, CT: Appleton & Lange.

Friedman, M. (1992). Family nursing: Theory and practice (3rd ed.). Norwalk, CT: Appleton & Lange.

Haber, J. et al. (1997). Comprehensive psychiatric nursing (6th ed.). St. Louis: Mosby.

Purnell, L., & Paulanka, B. (1998). Transcultural health care. Philadelphia: F.A. Davis.

Williams, S.R. (1997). Nutrition and diet therapy (8th ed.). St. Louis: Mosby.

Additional Resources—Articles

I. Concepts that Support Health Restoration

Robinson, C.A. (1994). Nursing intervention with families. Journal of Advanced Nursing, 19(5), 897–904.

Snelling, J. (1994). The effect of chronic pain on the family unit. Journal of Advanced Nursing, 19(3), 543–551.

Tasota, F.T. et al. (1994). Assessing ABG's: Maintaining the delicate balance. Nursing 94, 24(5), 34–46.

II. Cardiovascular and Hematologic Problems

Alleyne, J. et al. (1994). *The management of sickle cell crisis pain as experienced by patients and their carers.* Journal of Advanced Nursing, 19(4), 725–732.

Baker, A. (1994). *Acquired heart diseases in infants and children.* Critical Care Nursing Clinics in North America, 6(10) 175–186.

Funk, M. et al. (1994). *Predicting hospital mortality in patients with acute M.I.* American Journal of Critical Care, 3(3), 168–176.

Hagenhoff, B.D. et al. (1994). *Patient education needs as reported by CHF patients and their nurses.* Journal of Advanced Nursing, 19(4), 685–690.

Josker, J. et al. (1994). *Advance case studies in hemodynamic monitoring: Postoperative cardiovascular patients.* Critical Care Nursing Clinics in North America, 6(1), 187–197.

O'Neal, P.V. (1994). *How to spot early signs of cardiogenic shock.* American Journal of Nursing, 94(5), 36–41.

Tong, E. et al. (1994). *Special management issues for adolescents and young adults with congenital heart disease.* Critical Care Nursing Clinics in North America, 6(1), 199–214.

III. Respiratory Problems

Esler, R. et al. (1994). *Patient-centered pneumonia care: A case management success story.* American Journal of Nursing, 94(11), 34–38.

Hedrick, L.E. (1993). *Pneumocystis carinii pneumonia: A look at treatment and prophylaxis.* Journal of Home Health Care Practice, 6(1), 53–59.

Kuhn, M.A. (1994). *Multiple trauma with respiratory distress.* Critical Care Nurse, 14(2), 68–72, 77–80.

McKinney, B. (1994). *Myths and facts...about pneumonia.* Nursing 94, 24(5), 25.

Robinson, K.S. (1993). *Emergency! Resolving pulmonary edema.* American Journal of Nursing, 93(12), 45.

Whyte, D.A. (1992). *The experience of families caring for a child with cystic fibrosis: A nursing response.* Journal of Clinical Nursing, 1(3), 170.

IV. Neoplasms and Hematologic Malignancies

DeLaney, T.F. (1994). *Radiation therapy for the treatment of skin cancer of the head and neck.* Dermatologic Nursing, 6(2), 104–111.

Dest, V.M. et al. (1994). *Breast cancer: Dreaded diagnosis, complicated care.* RN, 57(6), 48–55.

Dillon, P. (1994). *Ovarian cancer.* Nursing 94, 24(5), 66–69.

Hagan, C., & Penrose-White, J. (1999). *Common but curable: Responding to symptoms of testicular cancer.* Advance for Nurse Practitioners, April, 25–30.

Newton, C. et al. (1994). *Uncertainty: Strategies for patients with brain tumors and their families.* Cancer Nursing, 17(2), 137–140.

Ruble, K. (1999). *Long-term effects of childhood cancer.* Advance for Nurse Practitioners, September, 49–56.

Walker, R. (1993). *Modeling and guided practice as components within a comprehensive testicular self-examination educational program for high school males.* Journal of Health Education, 24(3), 162–168.

V. Traumatic Injuries and Multisystem Failure

Hopkins, A.G. (1994). *The trauma nurse's role with families in crisis.* Critical Care Nurse, 14(2), 35–43.

Reilly, E. et al. (1994). *Multiple organ failure syndrome.* Critical Care Nurse, 14(2), 25–26, 28–33.

Russell, S. (1994). *Septic shock: Can you recognize the clues?* Nursing 94, 24(4), 40–46, 48.

Sommers, M.S. (1994). *The near death experience following multiple trauma.* Critical Care Nurse, 14(2), 62–67.

Sample Questions: Health Restoration: Area I

VI. Endocrine and Metabolic Problems

Andrews, G. (1994). Constructive advice for a poorly understood problem: Treatment and management of premenstrual syndrome, Professional Nurse, 9*(6), 364–370.*

Corsetti, A., & Buhl, B. (1994). Managing thyroid storm. Nursing 94, 24*(11), 39.*

Czenis, A.L. (1999). Thyroid disease in the elderly. Advance for Nurse Practitioners, *September, 38–45.*

Duffield, P. (1994). Pediatric management problems…case of delayed puberty. Pediatric Nursing, 20*(1), 54–55.*

Gusek, A. (1994). 10 commonly asked questions about diabetes. American Journal of Nursing, 94*(2), 19–20.*

Schaller, J. (1994). …about diabetic hypoglycemia. Nursing 94, 24*(6), 67.*

VII. Immune System Problems

Henry, S.B. et al. (1994). The relationship between type of care planning system and patient outcomes in hospitalized AIDS patients. Journal of Advanced Nursing, 19*(4), 691–698.*

Kuper, B., & Failla, S. (1994). Shedding new light on lupus. American Journal of Nursing, 94*(11), 26–33.*

Peterson, K. et al. (1994). Interpreting lab values in chronic renal insufficiency. American Journal of Nursing, 94*(5), 56B–56H.*

Smith, J.P. (1994). Care of asthma patients. Journal of Advanced Nursing, 19*(4), 613.*

Weber, M. (1994). Thrombocytopenia. American Journal of Nursing, 94*(11), 46.*

Study Guide

Health Restoration: Area II (477) (Baccalaureate Level)

Credit Hours: 4 **Credit Level:** Upper
Question Type(s): Multiple-choice

The information in this study guide is valid until Summer 2001.
If you will be taking the examination after that date, be sure to check for a new edition of this guide before you complete your preparation for the exam.

General Description of the Examination

Health Restoration: Area II is part of a two-examination series. Health Restoration: Area I and Health Restoration: Area II test your ability to apply the nursing process in caring for clients with major health problems. While the client may be the individual, the family, or the community, emphasis for this examination is placed on the individual at all stages of the life cycle.

The concepts that support health restoration are included in content area I of Health Restoration: Area I. These concepts serve as a foundation for the content covered in content areas II–VII of Health Restoration: Area I and in all content areas of Health Restoration: Area II.

A variety of theories from nursing and related disciplines can be identified that will give the professional nurse a strong base of knowledge on which to practice. The major nursing theorists most applicable to the Health Restoration: Area II examination are Sister Callista Roy, Dorothea Orem, and Virginia Henderson. The organizing framework underlying all of their theories includes the concepts of client, health, nursing, and environment. Some questions on the examination will test an understanding of nursing and other related theories.

Examination Objectives for the Health Restoration Series

You will be expected to demonstrate the ability to:
1. utilize the nursing process to assist the client in managing major health problems by:
   a. assessing the client's health status;
   b. analyzing assessment data to identify the client's health care needs/problems and to determine expected client outcomes;
   c. formulating a plan to achieve the expected outcomes;
   d. implementing the appropriate plan;
   e. evaluating the effectiveness of an intervention in terms of outcome achievement;
2. synthesize knowledge from the humanities, social sciences, natural sciences, and nursing science in the practice of professional nursing;
3. apply knowledge of culture and recognition of the client's value system.

Content Outline

Content Area	Percent of Examination
I. Emotional and Behavioral Problems	25%
II. Neurological and Sensory Health Problems	20%
III. Gastrointestinal, Genitourinary, and Reproductive Health Problems	10%
IV. Infections and Communicable Diseases	20%
V. Complications of Pregnancy, Problems of the High-Risk Mother, and Problems of the High-Risk Neonate	15%
VI. Musculoskeletal Health Problems	10%
Total	**100%**

I. Emotional and Behavioral Problems (25%) (based on the categories of the *Diagnostic and Statistical Manual of Mental Disorders*, 4th edition [DSM IV, 1994])

This area focuses on conditions such as disorders usually first diagnosed in infancy, childhood, or adolescence (including disorders related to learning, motor skills, attention-deficit and disruptive behavior, communication, feeding and eating, tic, elimination, and mental retardation); delirium, dementia, amnesia, and other cognitive disorders; substance-related disorders (including disorders related to alcohol ingestion, amphetamine use, cocaine use, and hallucinogen use); schizophrenia and other psychotic disorders; mood disorders; anxiety disorders; somatoform disorders; factitious disorders; dissociative disorders; sexual and gender identity disorders (including disorders related to sexual dysfunction and paraphilias); eating disorders; sleep disorders; impulse control disorders; adjustment disorders; personality disorders; trisomy 18 and trisomy 21.

A. The Individual: nursing care of the individual with an emotional or behavioral problem

1. Assessment (for example: identifying noncompliance with the medication regimen in a client with a bipolar disorder, observing for electrolyte imbalance in a client receiving lithium carbonate, gathering data on the altered thought processes of a client with schizophrenia, assessing altered growth and development related to impaired cognitive function in a child with Down syndrome)
2. Analysis (for example: determining short-term outcomes for sleep pattern disturbance in a client with manic behavior, formulating nursing diagnoses for a client who has Alzheimer's disease and who is experiencing an alteration in orientation, defining long-term outcomes for a client with learning difficulties secondary to fetal alcohol syndrome)

3. Planning (for example: planning interventions to alleviate constipation in a client with depression, developing strategies to deal with health management problems in a client with chronic mental illness, collaborating on a "no suicide" contract with a client experiencing depression, determining priorities for nursing interventions for a client with a dual diagnosis of mental retardation and psychotic disorder, eliciting information from appropriate health team members in planning interventions for a client who has alcoholism and who is homeless)
4. Implementation (for example: promoting a safe environment for a client with self-destructive or assaultive behavior, enlisting the help of support groups for a client with memory deficits, facilitating compliance with the therapeutic regimen for a client with a somatoform disorder, explaining lithium carbonate to a client with a bipolar disorder, teaching nutrition to a client with alcoholism)
5. Evaluation (for example: revising the care plan for a client who is no longer delusional, determining outcome attainment for a client with an adjustment disorder, identifying alterations in the treatment regimen for a client with attention-deficit hyperactivity disorder, comparing actual outcomes to expected outcomes in a client who is manipulative, determining the degree of compliance with the medication regimen in a client with mania)

B. The Family: nursing care of the family with a member who has an emotional or behavioral problem
1. Assessment (for example: identifying deficits in role relationships between a family and a member who has an emotional disorder, observing for impaired adjustment in a family with a member who has Alzheimer's disease, assessing a family's grief behaviors related to the impending death of a neonate with trisomy 18)
2. Analysis (for example: determining short- and long-term outcomes for impaired communication patterns in a family with abusive behavior, formulating nursing diagnoses for a family with a child who has learning disabilities due to fetal alcohol syndrome)
3. Planning (for example: developing strategies to assist a family in coping with a member who has a substance abuse disorder, determining priorities for interventions for a family with a history of violence, planning interventions for a family with a member who has an eating disorder)
4. Implementation (for example: facilitating family use of community resources for rehabilitation of a member who has an emotional disorder, supporting a family's capacity to cope with a child who becomes suicidal, teaching a family about the side effects of psychotropic medications)
5. Evaluation (for example: revising the care plan for a family with abusive behavior; following the death of one parent; reassessing the needs of a family with an adult child who is chronically mentally ill; comparing actual outcomes to expected outcomes in family adjustment in a family with a member who has autism)

C. **The Community: nursing care in the community with individuals who have emotional or behavioral problems**
   1. Assessment (for example: identifying a knowledge deficit in a community related to the support required by individuals who have emotional problems)
   2. Analysis (for example: determining short- and long-term outcomes in a community for parents of adolescents who have committed suicide)
   3. Planning (for example: deciding on intervention for a community with a large population of individuals who have chronic mental illness and are homeless; collaborating with the neighborhood on expected behaviors of individuals who have organic mental disorders and are living in group homes)
   4. Implementation (for example: promoting health planning and development of long-term resources in a community experiencing an increase in group homes due to deinstitutionalization; facilitating acceptance of individuals with chronic mental illness through workshops, meetings, and the media)
   5. Evaluation (for example: determining the degree of community acceptance of individuals with mental retardation, evaluating strategies to foster values clarification in a community with individuals who have chronic mental illness and who are homeless)

II. Neurological and Sensory Health Problems (20%)

This area focuses on conditions affecting the central nervous system, such as amyotrophic lateral sclerosis, cerebral palsy, cerebrovascular accident, head injury, hydrocephaly, meningitis, meningomyelocele, migraine headache, multiple sclerosis, Parkinson's disease, seizure disorders, and spinal cord lesions or injuries; conditions affecting the peripheral nervous system, such as Guillain-Barré syndrome, myasthenia gravis, and trigeminal neuralgia; conditions affecting the sensory system, such as blindness, cataracts, deafness, detached retina, glaucoma, macular degeneration, and otitis media.

A. **The Individual: nursing care of the individual with a neurological or sensory health problem**
   1. Assessment (for example: using objective data to determine nutritional status in a client recovering from a stroke; eliciting subjective data to identify depression in a client with Parkinson's disease; observing for early signs of increased intracranial pressure in a client with a head injury; monitoring for respiratory deterioration in a client with Guillain-Barré syndrome; identifying the symptoms of cataract development in an older adult client; using health assessment data to determine the impact of meningomyelocele on the sensory function of a child; interviewing a client to determine the situational factors related to the onset of migraine; testing for the effects of chronic otitis media on hearing in a child; using physiological monitoring data to assess the adequacy of cerebral oxygenation following aneurysm clipping)
   2. Analysis (for example: anticipating the risk of injury in a client with a seizure disorder; identifying a health management deficit in a client adjusting to the onset of a degenerative neurological condition; identifying the etiological factors of body image disturbance in a child with a neurological deficit; using appropriate defining characteristics to diagnose ineffective coping in a client with retinal detachment; using a combination of subjective data, physiological monitoring, and laboratory data to formulate nursing diagnoses for a client

with amyotrophic lateral sclerosis; formulating a nursing diagnosis of fluid volume excess related to the placement of a ventriculoatrial shunt in an infant with hydrocephaly)
3. Planning (for example: identifying appropriate long-term outcomes for a child with impaired physical mobility related to cerebral palsy, developing short-term outcomes for a child with meningomyelocele, planning priorities for a client with self-care deficits related to a visual disorder, planning outcomes for a client with spinal cord injury, involving a client in planning for the long-term impact of a cerebrovascular accident)
4. Implementation (for example: teaching preventive strategies to a client prone to migraine headaches, intervening to prevent falls in a client with visual impairment, administering fluid replacement in a child with bacterial meningitis, ensuring a nonstimulating environment for a client with the potential for increased intracranial pressure following a head injury, referring a client with sexual dysfunction related to multiple sclerosis for sexual counseling, intervening immediately to treat manifestations of autonomic dysreflexia in a client with spinal cord injury, providing a safe environment for a child during a seizure, instructing a client with a seizure disorder about the long-term management of anticonvulsant therapy, monitoring for signs and symptoms of infection in a neonate with meningomyelocele)
5. Evaluation (for example: determining the effectiveness of an osmotic diuretic in decreasing intracranial pressure in a client with head injury, identifying the side effects of antiparkinsonian agents in a client with head injury, evaluating teaching about the medication regimen in a client with glaucoma, evaluating the effectiveness of an exercise regimen for a client with immobility related to multiple sclerosis)

B. **The Family: nursing care of the family with a member who has a neurological or sensory health problem**
1. Assessment (for example: using interview data to determine health management skills in a family with a child who needs developmental stimulation due to a congenital neurological condition, identifying symptoms of ineffective coping in a family with a member who has had a cerebrovascular accident, determining the level of family knowledge about providing a safe environment for a client with visual or hearing impairment)
2. Analysis (for example: anticipating the risk for social isolation in a family with a member who is developmentally delayed, using family behaviors to identify a role performance disturbance in a family with a member who has multiple sclerosis, identifying the etiological factors producing health management deficits in a family with a member with amyotrophic lateral sclerosis, using appropriate defining characteristics to diagnose impaired communication in a family with a member who has aphasia)
3. Planning (for example: identifying appropriate long-term outcomes for a family with a member who has Parkinson's disease, developing short-term outcomes for a family with an infant who has meningitis, developing a teaching plan for a family with a child who has meningomyelocele, planning priorities for a family with an infant newly diagnosed with a profound hearing loss)

4. Implementation (for example: teaching strategies for managing cognitive impairment to a family with a member who has a head injury, supporting effective coping in a family with a member who has neurological deficits due to a ruptured cerebral aneurysm, referring a family for counseling when independence-dependence issues arise in an adolescent member with hearing or visual impairment, teaching strategies to promote a safe home environment to a family with a member who has visual impairment)
5. Evaluation (for example: determining the effectiveness of teaching about a supervised exercise program in a family with a member who has multiple sclerosis, evaluating the effectiveness of nursing actions to promote growth in a family coping with a member who has idiopathic epilepsy)

C. **The Community: nursing care in the community with individuals who have neurological or sensory health problems**
1. Assessment (for example: assessing the effectiveness of health management in a multicultural community attempting to address the needs of individuals with neurological and sensory health problems, assessing community response to individuals requiring assistance with visual and hearing deficits)
2. Analysis (for example: identifying ineffective outcomes in a community addressing the needs of children with developmental disabilities, identifying the cultural and economic factors contributing to values conflict in a community responding to the needs of individuals with neurological deficits)
3. Planning (for example: identifying long-term outcomes for a community developing a plan to allow access for individuals with physical disabilities related to neurological deficits, planning priorities for a community with a large number of older adult clients who have visual and hearing impairments)
4. Implementation (for example: developing a hospice program that is congruent with community values for individuals with terminal neurological conditions, providing a community education program to promote an understanding of epilepsy)
5. Evaluation (for example: determining the effectiveness of community services for individuals with sensory deficits, evaluating support services for families of children with degenerative neurological diseases)

III. Gastrointestinal, Genitourinary, and Reproductive Health Problems (10%)

This area focuses on conditions affecting the gastrointestinal system, such as appendicitis, biliary atresia, bowel obstruction, cholelithiasis, cleft lip, cleft palate, diverticulosis, familial polyposis, hernias, imperforate anus, inflammatory bowel diseases, megacolon, peptic ulcer, peritonitis, and tracheoesophageal fistula; conditions affecting the genitourinary system, such as acute and chronic renal failure, benign prostatic hypertrophy, bladder injuries, congenital bladder anomalies, epispadias, exstrophy of the bladder, hydrocele, hypospadias, nephrotic syndrome, and renal calculi; conditions affecting the reproductive system, such as endometriosis, fibrocystic breast disease, impotence, infertility, Klinefelter's syndrome, ovarian cyst, and pelvic inflammatory disease.

A. **The Individual: nursing care of the individual with a gastrointestinal, genitourinary, or reproductive health problem**
   1. Assessment (for example: identifying noncompliance with the treatment regimen in an adolescent client with Crohn's disease, observing for nutritional deficits in a client with bowel obstruction, determining fluid volume imbalance in a client on hemodialysis, identifying body image disturbance in a client requiring urinary diversion, examining the ineffective individual coping of a client with irritable bowel syndrome, assessing for self-esteem disturbance in an adolescent with Klinefelter's syndrome)
   2. Analysis (for example: identifying a health management deficit in a client adjusting to treatment with continuous ambulatory peritoneal dialysis, determining fluid volume excess in a client with acute renal failure, identifying altered nutrition related to ineffective sucking in an infant with cleft palate)
   3. Planning (for example: alleviating altered urinary elimination patterns in an older adult client with benign prostatic hypertrophy, minimizing ineffective breathing patterns in a client recovering from a cholecystectomy, discussing decisional conflicts in a client with infertility, reducing powerlessness in a client on long-term hemodialysis, developing a teaching plan on breast self-examination for a client with fibrocystic breast disease, establishing strategies to avoid ear and respiratory infections in an infant with cleft lip)
   4. Implementation (for example: preventing impaired skin integrity in a child with nephrotic syndrome, monitoring for diarrhea in a client receiving continuous tube feedings, teaching management strategies to a client with pelvic inflammatory disease, referring a client with chronic renal failure for infertility counseling, counseling a client who has peptic ulcer disease and a pain self-management deficit, minimizing self-esteem disturbance in an adolescent client with an ileostomy, supporting the adjustment of a child with hydrocele, explaining the surgical procedure and the need for an indwelling catheter postoperatively to a child with hypospadias)
   5. Evaluation (for example: exploring the effectiveness of diversional activities with a client who has inflammatory bowel disease, evaluating measures to enhance sexual function with a transurethral prostatectomy, evaluating medication management with antacids or histamine receptor antagonists in a client with peptic ulcer disease, determining the client's response to immunosuppressive therapy following a renal transplant)

B. **The Family: nursing care of the family with a member who has a gastrointestinal, genitourinary, or reproductive health problem**
   1. Assessment (for example: identifying health management skills in a family with a member who has chronic inflammatory bowel disease, determining disturbance in role performance in a family with a child who has a congenital bladder anomaly)
   2. Analysis (for example: formulating nursing diagnoses for a family with a child who has short bowel syndrome, analyzing coping strategies in a family with a member who is rejecting a recently transplanted kidney)
   3. Planning (for example: developing a care plan to reduce fear in a family with a member who has acute bowel infarction and who is critically ill; establishing outcomes related to home care with a family who has a child recovering from a kidney transplant; planning strategies to limit impaired

adjustment in a family with an adolescent member who has newly diagnosed pelvic inflammatory disease; preparing a teaching plan about home care, medications, and signs of fluid and electrolyte imbalance for parents of an infant with biliary atresia)
   4. Implementation (for example: supporting the adjustment of a family with a member who has newly diagnosed polycystic kidney disease, fostering coping in a family with a member who has impotence, teaching a family with a member who has familial polyposis, encouraging the expression of feelings in a nonjudgmental manner when interacting with parents of an infant with Hirschsprung's disease)
   5. Evaluation (for example: evaluating the effectiveness of strategies to resolve independence-dependence issues in a family with an adolescent member who requires intermittent peritoneal dialysis; evaluating the ability to perform ostomy care by a family with a member who is unable to manage self-care; evaluating understanding of the defect, plans for its repair, and long-term follow-up care in parents with an infant who has tracheoesophageal fistula; evaluating a return demonstration of feeding and burping techniques by parents of an infant with cleft lip)

C. **The Community: nursing care in the community with individuals who have gastrointestinal, genitourinary, or reproductive health problems**
   1. Assessment (for example: assessing the need for instruction in a community with increasing numbers of children and adults requiring long-term home parenteral nutrition)
   2. Analysis (for example: identifying health management outcomes in a multicultural community with a growing number of individuals with infertility)
   3. Planning (for example: collaborating with community agencies to develop a plan to meet the needs of a growing population of clients requiring home dialysis services)
   4. Implementation (for example: minimizing impaired adjustment in a multicultural community with a growing population requiring home care for chronic renal failure, exploring values conflicts in a community trying to establish criteria for choosing recipients of kidney transplants)
   5. Evaluation (for example: evaluating the effectiveness of community resources for families with children who have congenital anomalies)

IV. Infections and Communicable Diseases (20%)

This area focuses on infections and communicable diseases such as encephalitis, gastritis, genital herpes, helminthic infestations, hepatitis A and B, herpes zoster, influenza, Lyme disease, measles, mumps, nosocomial infections, osteomyelitis, pediculosis, pertussis, pyelonephritis, sexually transmitted diseases, staphylococcal and streptococcal infections, tuberculosis, and varicella.

A. **The Individual: nursing care of the individual with an infection or communicable disease**
   1. Assessment (for example: identifying health management needs in a client with acute pyelonephritis, assessing for ineffective airway clearance in a client with streptococcal pharyngitis, identifying hyperthermia in a client with an infection or a communicable disease, assessing for signs and symptoms of altered nutrition in a client with a helminthic infestation)

2. Analysis (for example: determining compliance with drug therapy in a client with tuberculosis, identifying outcomes related to impaired physical mobility in a child with acute osteomyelitis, determining activity intolerance in a client with a long-term infectious process)
3. Planning (for example: planning strategies to prevent social isolation in a client with varicella, developing a teaching plan to enhance social skill development in a client with chronic pyelonephritis, determining priorities to facilitate adjustment in a client with osteomyelitis)
4. Implementation (for example: counseling a client with altered sexuality patterns related to a sexually transmitted disease, alleviating pain in a client with genital herpes, teaching about the medication regimen to a client with tuberculosis, establishing priorities in caring for a client with hepatitis)
5. Evaluation (for example: evaluating the effectiveness of antimicrobial therapy for a client with a nosocomial infection, evaluating strategies to enhance self-esteem in a client with a sexually transmitted disease, evaluating strategies to enhance self-worth in a client following confirmation of sterility resulting from mumps, revising plans to reestablish fluid balance in a client with gastroenteritis)

B. The Family: nursing care of the family with a member who has an infection or communicable disease
1. Assessment (for example: identifying health management alterations in a family with a member who has Lyme disease, assessing for health management deficits in a family with a child who has sequelae to an infectious process, formulating a nursing diagnosis of compromised family coping related to the lengthy hospitalization of an adolescent with osteomyelitis)
2. Analysis (for example: analyzing the potential for family infections when a member develops a communicable disease)
3. Planning (for example: developing a teaching plan about communicability for a family with a client who has measles, planning strategies to deal with dependence-independence issues in a family with an adolescent member who has mononucleosis)
4. Implementation (for example: minimizing role strain in a family with a member whose energy is depleted due to a long-term infection, dealing with social isolation in a family with a member who has a communicable disease)
5. Evaluation (for example: evaluating compliance with disease control measures in a family with a member who has tuberculosis, evaluating outcomes related to coping in a family with a member who has a sexually transmitted disease)

C. The Community: nursing care in the community with individuals who have infections or communicable diseases
1. Assessment (for example: assessing health management behaviors in a community with an outbreak of food poisoning)
2. Analysis (for example: analyzing knowledge of prevention in a community with a growing population of individuals who have tuberculosis)
3. Planning (for example: identifying outcomes in a community with a growing population of children who have pertussis)
4. Implementation (for example: strengthening health management in a multicultural community attempting to address the needs of a population

during an epidemic; promoting health maintenance behaviors in a community with an increase in cases of encephalitis following a measles epidemic)
5. Evaluation (for example: evaluating strategies to resolve values conflict in a community with a growing population of individuals with sexually transmitted diseases)

V. Complications of Pregnancy, Problems of the High-Risk Mother, and Problems of the High-Risk Neonate (15%)

This area focuses on complications of pregnancy such as abruptio placentae, cephalopelvic disproportion, dysfunctional labor, gestational diabetes, placenta previa, postpartum depression, pregnancy-induced hypertension, and stillborn neonate; problems of the high-risk mother such as adolescent pregnancy and pregnant client with a preexisting disorder; problems of the high-risk neonate such as fetal alcohol syndrome, hyperbilirubinemia, low birth weight, narcotic abstinence syndrome, and prematurity.

A. The Individual: nursing care of the individual with a complication of pregnancy, problem of the high-risk mother, or problem of the high-risk neonate

1. Assessment (for example: monitoring for toxic effects of elevated bilirubin in a neonate, identifying a health management deficit in a pregnant client with gestational diabetes, assessing the level of compliance with the therapeutic regimen in a pregnant adolescent client, identifying a deficit in sensory and social stimulation in a high-risk neonate)
2. Analysis (for example: analyzing nutritional deficits in the neonate of a client with diabetes mellitus, formulating a nursing diagnosis of fluid volume deficit in a pregnant client with dystocia, determining ineffective thermal regulation in a neonate, analyzing nutritional deficits in a neonate with necrotizing enterocolitis)
3. Planning (for example: planning strategies to monitor for ineffective breathing pattern in a neonate with meconium aspiration syndrome, establishing priorities to maintain tissue perfusion in a pregnant client with pregnancy-induced hypertension, planning strategies to minimize hyperactivity in a neonate with narcotic abstinence syndrome secondary to maternal use of crack cocaine)
4. Implementation (for example: teaching about the signs and symptoms of congestive heart failure to a pregnant client with heart disease, teaching a pregnant client about the impact of high-risk pregnancy on sexual activity, managing fluid volume deficit related to blood loss in a pregnant client with a pregnancy-related bleeding disorder, intervening to promote coping in a high-risk pregnant client during labor and delivery)
5. Evaluation (for example: evaluating the effectiveness of medication use in a pregnant client experiencing preterm labor, evaluating strategies to enhance role performance in the high-risk pregnant client, determining the effectiveness of measures to enhance self-image in a client with postpartum depression, evaluating the effectiveness of medication therapy in a compromised neonate)

B. **The Family: nursing care of the family with a member who has a complication of pregnancy, or is a high-risk mother, or a high-risk neonate**
   1. Assessment (for example: assessing health management skills in a family with a neonate who has fetal alcohol syndrome)
   2. Analysis (for example: determining delayed parent-infant attachment in a family with a neonate who is preterm or sick)
   3. Planning (for example: preparing a teaching plan about infant growth and development for a family with a neonate who is compromised)
   4. Implementation (for example: facilitating parenting related to prolonged hospitalization of a neonate who is compromised; counseling a family about roles, relationships, and lifestyles during a high-risk pregnancy; supporting grieving related to fetal or neonatal death)
   5. Evaluation (for example: evaluating strategies to foster coping in a family with a preterm or compromised neonate)

C. **The Community: nursing care in the community with individuals who have complications of pregnancy, or are high-risk mothers, or high-risk neonates**
   1. Assessment (for example: identifying health management resources in a community with high-risk neonates who require long-term care)
   2. Analysis (for example: analyzing health management resources for families with neonates who are developmentally delayed)
   3. Planning (for example: planning outcomes in a community with a high incidence of low-birth-weight neonates)
   4. Implementation (for example: organizing support systems in a community with a large number of adolescent pregnancies)
   5. Evaluation (for example: evaluating the effectiveness of community strategies to improve the outcomes of pregnancy in a high-risk multicultural population of women)

VI. Musculoskeletal Health Problems (10%)

This area focuses on conditions such as clubfoot, degenerative joint disease, disc problems, hip dysplasia, fractures, muscular dystrophy, osteoarthritis, osteomalacia, osteoporosis, and scoliosis.

A. **The Individual: nursing care of the individual with a musculoskeletal health problem**
   1. Assessment (for example: using objective data to determine circulatory status in a client with compartment syndrome following a fracture, eliciting subjective data to identify body image disturbance in a client following amputation, observing for early signs and symptoms of fat embolism syndrome in a client following pelvic fracture, identifying symptoms of osteoarthritis in a client)
   2. Analysis (for example: anticipating the risk of complications in an older adult client after joint replacement surgery; identifying health management deficits in a client with disc problems; identifying the etiological factors in a client with chronic pain from carpal tunnel syndrome; using a combination of subjective and objective data to formulate a nursing diagnosis for a child with muscular dystrophy; formulating a nursing diagnosis of ineffective coping related to developmental stage, altered body image, chronicity, and complex treatment protocols for an adolescent client with scoliosis; formulating a nursing diagnosis of impaired skin integrity related to a casted body part)

3. Planning (for example: identifying short-term outcomes for an infant with clubfoot; prioritizing strategies for a client with osteoporosis; planning realistic outcomes for a client with degenerative joint disease; formulating strategies for log rolling, breathing exercises, and avoidance of pulmonary complications following insertion of a Harrington rod in an adolescent client with scoliosis; developing strategies to assist a client who is having difficulty adapting to a wheelchair)
4. Implementation (for example: teaching an exercise program to a client with osteoarthritis, intervening to prevent edema in a client with a fracture treated with casting, intervening immediately to correct problems with traction in a child with musculoskeletal abnormalities, providing pain control for a client with osteomalacia)
5. Evaluation (for example: evaluating the effectiveness of strategies for maintaining mobility in a child with muscular dystrophy, determining the effectiveness of teaching about crutch walking to a client with a fractured tibia, determining the effectiveness of interventions for correcting hip dysplasia in a child)

B. **The Family: nursing care of the family with a member who has a musculoskeletal health problem**
   1. Assessment (for example: interviewing a family to determine the effectiveness of coping following the birth of a child with clubfoot, observing family response to a member with above-the-knee amputation, assessing the knowledge level of a family with a member who has scoliosis)
   2. Analysis (for example: formulating a nursing diagnosis related to home management for a family with a member who has an external fixator, determining long-term outcomes for a family with a member who has degenerative joint disease)
   3. Planning (for example: developing a teaching plan for a family with an infant who has clubfoot, planning strategies for a family who must modify the home environment for a member with muscular dystrophy, determining priorities for a family with a member who is in chronic pain due to a musculoskeletal condition)
   4. Implementation (for example: referring a family with an adolescent who has scoliosis for counseling when independence-dependence issues arise, teaching a family positioning and exercise strategies for treating an infant with hip dysplasia, supporting family coping when a client requires an amputation)
   5. Evaluation (for example: determining the effectiveness of teaching in a family with a member who requires surgery for degenerative disease, evaluating outcomes for a family with a member who has a musculoskeletal condition)

C. **The Community: nursing care in the community with individuals who have musculoskeletal health problems**
   1. Assessment (for example: assessing access limitations in a community with a large population of individuals with limited mobility related to musculoskeletal conditions)
   2. Analysis (for example: analyzing community support services available for individuals with chronic pain related to musculoskeletal conditions)

3. Planning (for example: planning outcomes in a community with children who have special needs related to musculoskeletal conditions)
4. Implementation (for example: organizing community counseling resources for individuals with body image changes and emotional responses related to chronic musculoskeletal conditions)
5. Evaluation (for example: evaluating strategies in a community to promote supervised exercise programs for individuals with special needs related to musculoskeletal conditions)

Sample Questions: Health Restoration: Area II

1. During his regular monthly appointment with the nurse at the clinic of a mental health center, a client with chronic schizophrenia says that he sometimes forgets to take his daily medication. Which alternative medication would be indicated for this client?
    1) fluphenazine decanoate (Prolixin)
    2) loxapine succinate (Loxitane)
    3) thioridazine hydrochloride (Mellaril)
    4) trifluoperazine hydrochloride (Stelazine)

2. Which client behavior best indicates that trust has been established between a primary nurse and a client who is socially withdrawn?
   The client
    1) takes a walk with the nurse.
    2) attends unit activities with the nurse.
    3) sits with the nurse in the day area.
    4) discusses past life experiences with the nurse.

3. A client with a panic disorder reports that her heart is racing, she has difficulty breathing, and she feels as if she is about to die. The nurse observes that the client is trembling, is restless, and has difficulty staying focused when questioned about her symptoms. Which is the best immediate nursing intervention for this client?
    1) Arrange for the client to be transported to the emergency department for medical evaluation.
    2) Lead the client in using relaxation and visual imagery techniques to reduce her anxiety.
    3) Attempt to distract the client from her anxiety by suggesting that she work on her needlework project.
    4) Use a calm but firm manner and have the client follow a deep-breathing exercise.

4. Which nursing measure will best decrease the danger of malnutrition as a complication of acute mania in a client?
    1) Encourage small frequent feedings.
    2) Provide three substantial meals daily.
    3) Allow frequent finger foods.
    4) Administer nutritional supplements.

5. Which information should be included in the discharge teaching plan for a client with epilepsy who experiences generalized tonic-clonic seizures?
    1) Prescribed medications should be taken regularly, but should be withheld during acute illness.
    2) Precipitating factors for seizure activity include increased stress, insomnia, and alcohol use.
    3) Increasing lethargy and decreasing level of consciousness will occur up to 48 hours following a seizure.
    4) If an aura is experienced, lie down to prevent the airway from occluding.

Sample Questions: Health Restoration: Area II

6. Which statement by a family member indicates that discharge teaching about nutritional intake for a client with amyotrophic lateral sclerosis has been effective?
    1) "We'll give him plenty of fluids to wash down his food."
    2) "We'll serve him dry foods that are easy to swallow."
    3) "We'll feed him after placing him in an upright position with his neck slightly extended."
    4) "We'll leave him in an upright position for 15 to 30 minutes after he eats."

7. Which nursing action is most appropriate for a client who has expressive aphasia following a left hemisphere cerebrovascular accident?
    1) Encourage the client to speak clearly.
    2) Obtain a picture board and show the client how to use it.
    3) Allow the client time to speak, and then correct any errors.
    4) Teach the client facial muscle exercises.

8. Which long-term outcome is appropriate for a client with early Parkinson's disease? The client will
    1) continue to participate in usual activities.
    2) institute measures to prevent diarrhea.
    3) begin looking at alternative living arrangements.
    4) maintain a regular diet with protein supplements.

9. Which is the most appropriate preoperative nursing diagnosis for a six-week-old infant with pyloric stenosis?
    1) impaired adjustment related to a congenital anomaly
    2) impaired tissue integrity related to age
    3) fluid volume deficit related to vomiting
    4) pain related to peristalsis

10. A client with end-stage renal disease is receiving intermittent peritoneal dialysis. Which intervention should the nurse carry out to prevent peritonitis?
    1) Use strict aseptic technique when adding exchanges or emptying drainage containers.
    2) Carefully monitor the client's lung sounds and apical pulse after each exchange.
    3) Move the client from side to side during drainage to prevent stagnation of dialysate.
    4) Calculate the status of the client's fluid balance at the end of each exchange.

11. In formulating a plan of care for the family of an 80-year-old client who is cognitively impaired and who has functional incontinence, the nurse should include which instruction?
    1) Limit the client's fluids to 500 cc per day and give fluids only with meals.
    2) Remind the client to go to the bathroom every two hours, after meals, and before bedtime.
    3) Keep a portable commode or bedpan near the client's bed.
    4) Encourage the family to use adult undergarments rather than diapers to deal with the client's incontinence.

Sample Questions: Health Restoration: Area II

12. The nurse teaches the family of a child with pinworms how to prevent transmission to other family members. Which behavior indicates that the teaching was effective?
    1) The bathroom is disinfected daily.
    2) Dishes are sterilized with boiling water after use.
    3) Bed linen is washed frequently and carefully.
    4) Disinfectant soap is used for showers daily.

13. A child with varicella returns to day camp two days after the initial rash appears, with a note from the parent stating that the rash is not bothering the child. How should the camp nurse intervene?
    1) Keep the child in the nurse's office for the day to evaluate the characteristics of the rash.
    2) Allow the child to return to the camp group because primary transmission occurs before the vesicles appear.
    3) Return the child to the camp group only after determining if the counselor is immune to the disease.
    4) Call the parent to discuss the period of communicability of the disease and have the child taken home.

14. The nurse is evaluating a four-year-old child who has been on continuous IV antibiotic therapy for one week for treatment of osteomyelitis of the left tibia. Which finding indicates that the child is still in the acute phase of the illness?
    The child
    1) requires a leg splint while he sleeps.
    2) needs to use a wheelchair to go to the activity room.
    3) complains of a pain in his leg when he turns in bed.
    4) allows passive range-of-motion exercise but resists active range-of-motion exercise.

15. Which intervention should be included in the teaching plan for a pregnant woman who has Class II heart disease and who is in the third trimester?
    1) Promote Lamaze breathing in preparation for delivery without anesthesia.
    2) Provide the rationale for the significance of penicillin prophylaxis during labor.
    3) Explain that bed rest for much of each day will be necessary for one month following delivery.
    4) Tell the client that breast-feeding is contraindicated.

16. The nurse is caring for a client who is in labor at 39 weeks of gestation. Baseline vital signs on admission were FHR 140, BP 110/50, P 70. The client has a confirmed placenta previa and a history of one bleeding episode 10 days prior to admission. Which outcome criteria indicate that the care plan for this client has been effective?
    1) urinary output 25 ml per hour
    2) no visible vaginal bleeding
    3) FHR 130, BP 120/70, P 80
    4) FHR 180, BP 80/50, P 100

Sample Questions: Health Restoration: Area II

17. The nurse is providing supportive care to a couple who have been told that their neonate has trisomy 21. The mother says that they are shocked and they cannot believe it. Based on the client's remarks, which conclusion should the nurse draw?
    1) Nursing interventions have been inadequate.
    2) The couple are in a normal phase of grieving.
    3) Further referrals are necessary.
    4) The mother is not bonding with the neonate.

18. Which finding should alert the nurse to a potential neurological problem in a child who is in skeletal traction for treatment of a fractured femur?
    1) itching around the pin site
    2) numbness and tingling of the toes
    3) weak femoral pulse
    4) warm, puffy toes

19. To prevent dislocation in a client recovering from a total hip replacement, how should the nurse position the client's legs?
    1) adducted with hip flexion less than 90°
    2) adducted with hip flexion greater than 90°
    3) slightly abducted with hip flexion less than 90°
    4) slightly abducted with hip flexion greater than 90°

20. The nurse teaches a client how to control swelling after surgery for carpal tunnel syndrome. Which action by the client indicates that the teaching was effective? The client
    1) places a heating pad on the incision area.
    2) wraps the area involved with an elastic bandage.
    3) minimizes movement of the affected wrist and fingers.
    4) applies intermittent ice packs to the surgical area.

Recommended Resources—Textbooks

For the Health Restoration: Area II examination, you should add textbooks in the areas of maternity, pediatric, and psychiatric nursing to your nursing library.

Black, J.M., & Matassarin-Jacobs, E. (1997). Medical-surgical nursing: Clinical management for continuity of care *(5th ed.). Philadelphia: W.B. Saunders.*

Haber, J. et al. (1997). Comprehensive psychiatric nursing *(5th ed.). St. Louis: Mosby.*

Ignatavicius, D. et al. (1999). Medical-surgical nursing across the health care continuum *(3rd ed.). Philadelphia: W.B. Saunders.*

Lowdermilk, D., Perry, S., & Bobak, I. (2000). Maternity and women's health care *(7th ed.). St. Louis: Mosby.*

Olds, S., London, M., & Ladewig, P. (2000). Maternal newborn nursing: A family and community-based approach *(6th ed.). Menlo Park, CA: Addison-Wesley.*

Smeltzer, S., & Bare, B. (1996). Brunner and Suddarth's Textbook of medical-surgical nursing *(8th ed.). Philadelphia: J.B. Lippincott.*

Wilson, H., & Kneisl, C. (1996). *Psychiatric nursing (5th ed.).* Menlo Park, CA: Addison-Wesley.

Wong, D. (1999). *Whaley & Wong's Nursing care of infants and children (6th ed.).* St. Louis: Mosby.

Additional Resources—Textbooks

Carpenito, L. (1997). *Nursing diagnosis: Application to clinical practice (7th ed.).* Philadelphia: J.B. Lippincott.

Chenitz, W., Stone, J., & Salisbury, S. (1991). *Clinical gerontological nursing: A guide to advanced practice.* Philadelphia: W.B. Saunders.

Friedman, M. (1992). *Family nursing: Theory and practice (3rd ed.).* Norwalk, CT: Appleton & Lange.

George, J. (1995). *Nursing theories: The base for professional nursing practice (4th ed.).* Norwalk, CT: Appleton & Lange.

Giger, J., & Davidhizar, R. (1995). *Transcultural nursing: Assessment and intervention (2nd ed.).* St. Louis: Mosby.

Kuhn, M.A. (1998). *Pharmacotherapeutics: A nursing process approach (4th ed.).* Philadelphia: J.B. Lippincott.

Stanhope, M., & Lancaster, J. (1996). *Community health nursing: Promoting health of aggregates, families, and individuals (4th ed.).* St. Louis: Mosby.

Additional Resources—Articles

I. Emotional and Behavioral Problems

Badger, J.M. (1994). *Calming the anxious patient.* American Journal of Nursing, 94(5), 46–50.

Basolo-Kunzer, M. (1994). *Caring for families of psychiatric patients.* Nursing Clinics in North America, 29(1), 73–79.

Beck, C.K. et al. (1994). *Interventions in treating disruptive behavior in demented elderly people.* Nursing Clinics in North America, 29(1), 143–155.

Hancock, C.K. et al. (1994). *Altered thought processes and sensory perceptual alterations: A critique.* Nursing Diagnosis, 5(1), 26–30.

Manss, V.C. (1994). *Effective communication: Gender issues.* Nursing Management, 25(6), 79–80.

Sommers, M.S. (1994). *Alcohol and trauma: The critical link.* Critical Care Nurse, 14(2), 82–93.

Staples, P. et al. (1994). *Empowering the angry patient.* Canadian Nurse, 90(4), 28–30.

II. Neurological and Sensory Health Problems

Cochran, I. et al. (1994). *Stroke care: Piecing together the long-term picture.* Nursing 94, 24(6), 34–42.

Held, J.L. (1994). *Identifying spinal cord compression.* Nursing 94, 24(5) 28.

Kelley, C. et al. (1994). *Betaseron: The new MS treatment.* Journal of Neuroscience Nursing, 26(1), 52–56.

Prendergast, V. (1994). *Current trends in research and treatment of intracranial hypertension.* Critical Care Nursing Quarterly, 17(1), 1–8.

Robertson, M.T. (1994). *Michael's scrapbook...how one nurse gave her husband's caregivers a sense of the man inside the patient...Amyotrophic Lateral Sclerosis.* Nursing 94, 24(5), 64.

Roccograndi, J.F. et al. (1993). *Managing AIDS-related meningitis.* RN, 56(11), 36–39.

Sample Questions: Health Restoration: Area II

III. Gastrointestinal, Genitourinary, and Reproductive Health Problems
Keltz, M.D. et al. (1993). *Diagnostic and therapeutic options in endometriosis.* Hospital Practice, 28(10A), 15–22.

Murphy, D. et al. (1994). *Mechanical lithotripsy.* Gastroenterological Nursing, 16(5), 204–209.

Strohschein, B.L. et al. (1994). *Continuous venovenous hemodialysis.* American Journal of Critical Care, 3(2), 92–101.

IV. Infections and Communicable Diseases
Boutotte, J. (1994). *What to do if you've been exposed to TB.* Nursing 94, 24(6), 26.

Erickson, M.J. (1994). *Chlamydial infections: Combating the silent threat.* American Journal of Nursing, 94(6), 16B–16F.

Margolis, H.S. (1993). *Prevention of acute and chronic liver disease through immunization: Hepatitis B and beyond.* Journal of Infectious Diseases, 168(1), 9–14.

Mertz, G.J. (1993). *Epidemiology of genital herpes infection.* Infectious Diseases Clinics in North America, 7(4), 825–839.

V. Complications of Pregnancy, Problems of the High-Risk Mother, and Problems of the High-Risk Neonate
Barnes, L.P. (1994). *Gestational diabetes: Teaching aspects of self-care.* American Journal of Maternal/Child Nursing, 19(3), 175.

McFarlin, B.C. (1994). *Intrauterine growth retardation: Etiology, diagnosis and management.* Journal of Nurse Midwifery, 39(2), Suppl, 525–655, 35–85.

Redding, B.A. et al. (1993). *Perinatal substance abuse: Assessment and management of the pregnant woman and her children.* Nurse Practice Forum, 4(4), 216–225.

Roberts, J. (1994). *Current perspectives on preeclampsia.* Journal of Nurse Midwifery, 39(2), 70–90.

VI. Musculoskeletal Health Problems
Carr, B.R. et al. (1993). *A real-world approach to osteoporosis.* Patient Care, 27(8), 31–38.

Lester, V.S. et al. (1993). *Total knee arthroplasty: Indications, preparation, procedure.* Association of OR Nurses Journal, 58(4), 731–746.

Meadows, L.L. (1994). *Pediatric management problems.* Pediatric Nursing, 20(2), 168–169.

Study Guide

Health Support A: Health Promotion & Health Protection (540) (Baccalaureate Level)

Credit Hours: 4
Credit Level: Upper
Question Type(s): Multiple-choice

The information in this study guide is valid until Summer 2001.
If you will be taking the examination after that date, be sure to check for a new edition of this guide before you complete your preparation for the exam.

General Description of the Examination

The Health Support A: Health Promotion & Health Protection examination measures knowledge and understanding of nursing roles and appropriate nursing action related to health promotion and health protection. Major emphasis is placed on the individual and family as client. The examination measures knowledge and understanding expected of students at the end of a baccalaureate nursing program.

The examination tests the use of the nursing process to support the health of the individual and the family. Emphasis is placed on health promotion interventions and primary prevention interventions. As applied to the individual or family, nursing activities include assessment, health education, health promotion and protection strategies, and risk appraisal and risk reduction strategies. Health promotion and protection is applied to the developmental periods: prenatal; infancy; toddler and preschool age; school age; adolescent; and young, middle, and older adult.

Selected models that can be applied to health promotion and protection give the professional nurse a base of knowledge on which to practice. The models most applicable to the Health Support A examination are Pender's model for health promotion, Becker's Health Belief Model, and Bandura's Self-Efficacy Model. Growth and development is viewed across the life span, based on the theories of Piaget, Erikson, Kohlberg, and Duvall.

The Health Support Examination Series

Health Support A: Health Promotion & Health Protection is part of a two-examination series. The Health Support A examination covers foundations for health promotion and protection, growth and development across the life span, strategies to promote and protect health, and health promotion and protection applied to the prenatal period; the infant; the toddler and preschooler; the school-age child; the adolescent; and the young, middle, and older adult. The Health Support B examination covers foundations of community health nursing, community as client, the social/cultural environment, epidemiology, environmental health, vulnerable population groups/populations at risk, community health nursing in specialized settings, and common community health problems.

Definitions

For purposes of this examination, the following definitions are used in the content outline:

1. Health Promotion and Health Protection

    Health promotion is "the science and art of helping people change their lifestyle to move toward a state of optimal health." (O'Donnell [1987])

    Health protection is "activity directed toward decreasing the probability of experiencing health problems by active protection against pathogens or detection of health problems in the asymptomatic stage." Health protection focuses on avoidance of disease.

    Primary prevention includes generalized health promotion as well as specific protection against disease.

    Secondary prevention emphasizes early diagnoses and prompt treatment to halt the pathological process, thereby shortening its duration and severity and enabling the individual to return to a state of health at the earliest possible time.

    Tertiary prevention stops a disease process and prevents complete disability. It focuses on rehabilitation to obtain optimal level of functioning.

    Health risk appraisal is "both a method and tool that describes a person's chances of becoming ill or dying from a specific disease. It generates a probability, not a diagnosis."

    Edelman, C., & Mandle, C. (1998). Health promotion throughout the lifespan *(4th ed.). St. Louis: Mosby, pp. 14, 231.*

    Pender, N. (1996). Health promotion in nursing practice *(3rd ed.). Stamford, CT: Appleton & Lange, p. 34.*

2. Nursing Process

    The content of many items in this examination is related to a specific stage of the nursing process. The nursing process is perceived as a problem-solving process that is cyclical in nature. Refer to p. 389 for definitions.

3. Client

    The examination tests the use of the nursing process to support the health of the individual and family. For the purposes of the examination, these terms are defined as follows:

    1) An individual is a single human being as contrasted with a family or community.
    2) A family is "a social system composed of two or more people living together who may be related by blood, marriage, or adoption, or who stay together by mutual agreement. Family members usually share living arrangements, obligations, goals, the continuity of generations, and a sense of belonging and affection."

    Clark, M.J. (1999). Nursing in the community *(3rd ed.). Stamford, CT: Appleton & Lange, p. 392.*

Content Outline

Content Area	Percent of Examination
I. Foundations for Health Promotion and Protection	5%
II. Growth and Development Across the Life Span	5%
III. Strategies to Promote and Protect Health	10%
IV. Health Promotion and Protection Applied to the Prenatal Period (pregnant client, fetus, stages of labor, postpartum client)	10%
V. Health Promotion and Protection Applied to the Infant (neonate to 18 months)	10%
VI. Health Promotion and Protection Applied to the Toddler and Preschooler	10%
VII. Health Promotion and Protection Applied to the School-Age Child	10%
VIII. Health Promotion and Protection Applied to the Adolescent	10%
IX. Health Promotion and Protection Applied to the Young Adult	10%
X. Health Promotion and Protection Applied to the Middle Adult	10%
XI. Health Promotion and Protection Applied to the Older Adult	10%
Total	**100%**

I. Foundations for Health Promotion and Protection

A. Theoretical foundations
   1. Emerging views of health: actualization, adaptation, high-level wellness, systems, holism
   2. Definitions
      a. Health
         (1) World Health Organization definition
         (2) Pender's definition
      b. Health promotion
      c. Health protection
         (1) Primary prevention
         (2) Secondary prevention
         (3) Tertiary prevention

3. Context of health (for example: culture, environment, socioeconomic status)
4. Selected models applied to health promotion and protection
    a. Pender's model for health promotion
    b. Becker's Health Belief Model
    c. Bandura's self-efficacy model
5. Selected theories applied to the family as client
    a. Developmental theory (Duvall)
    b. Systems theory
    c. Family theories

B. **Nurse-client relationship**
   1. Values clarification
   2. Therapeutic use of self
   3. The helping relationship

C. **Relevant ethical issues (for example: confidentiality, promoting individual autonomy, respect for culture)**

II. Growth and Development Across the Life Span

A. **Concepts and principles of growth and development**
   1. Critical periods
   2. Developmental milestones
   3. Areas of competency

B. **Physical development**
   1. Physical growth (for example: cephalocaudal; proximodistal; head, trunk, and limb development; neuronal maturation; organ development)
   2. Developmental tasks (for example: age-appropriate behavior)

C. **Cognitive development (Piaget)**

D. **Psychosocial development (Erikson)**

E. **Moral development (Kohlberg)**

III. Strategies to Promote and Protect Health

A. **Assessment for health promotion and protection** (based on the functional health patterns framework)
   1. Individual assessment
       a. Developmental patterns across the life span (for example: physical patterns; psychosocial patterns; cognitive patterns; pediatric, adult, and geriatric patterns)
       b. Health perception–health management patterns (for example: individual's assessment of own health, health practices, use of health care providers, economic adequacy, financial limitations, access to care)
       c. Nutritional-metabolic patterns (for example: eating patterns, importance of food, fluid and electrolyte balance, physiological measures such as height and weight)
       d. Elimination patterns (for example: bowel and bladder habits)
       e. Activity-exercise patterns (for example: mobility, physical activity, work/leisure, energy/vitality levels)

       f. Sleep-rest patterns (for example: chronobiology, timing of sleep, characteristics of sleep, daily rhythms)
       g. Cognitive-perceptual patterns (for example: ability to learn, memory, problem-solving, visual and hearing acuity)
       h. Self-perception-self-concept patterns (for example: self-worth, self-esteem, body language)
       i. Role-relationship patterns (for example: verbal and nonverbal communication, distancing, closeness, interaction with significant others, satisfaction with work and/or parenting, perception of role performance)
       j. Value-belief patterns (for example: religious beliefs, cultural values, recognition of diversity, importance of education)
       k. Sexuality-reproductive patterns (for example: sexual practices, sexual identification, personal satisfaction, sexual knowledge and attitudes)
       l. Coping–stress tolerance patterns (for example: level of stress; sources of emotional support; coping with developmental crises; level of dependence on alcohol, caffeine, tobacco, and drugs; personal management of stress)
  2. Family assessment
       a. Cross-generational (vertical) transmission patterns (for example: genogram)
       b. Health-perception–health management patterns (for example: financial status, preference for health care services, health practices)
       c. Nutritional-metabolic patterns (for example: dietary knowledge, beliefs, and practices; cultural influences; impact of limited income)
       d. Role-relationship patterns (for example: occupation, level of education, family dynamics, boundaries, family structure, communication patterns, decision making, power and authority, division of labor, relationship with society)
       e. Value-belief patterns (for example: religious beliefs, cultural values, recognition of diversity, importance of education)
       f. Sexuality-reproductive patterns (for example: family beliefs about sex education, intimacy, and sexual practices)
       g. Coping–stress tolerance patterns (for example: grieving, loss, situational crises, relationship between income and perceived needs)

B. Health education: Teaching and learning (developmental stage, cultural context)
  1. Domains of learning
       a. Cognitive learning
       b. Affective learning
       c. Psychomotor learning
  2. Assumptions about learning
       a. Client readiness: developmental stage
       b. Client perceptions
       c. Educational environment
       d. Client participation
       e. Content relevance
       f. Client satisfaction
       g. Client application
  3. The teaching process
       a. Interaction
       b. Assessment and diagnosis
       c. Outcomes

        d. Planning
        e. Teaching
        f. Evaluation
    4. Teaching methods and tools (for example: lecture, discussion, demonstration, tutorials, roleplaying, audio/visual aids, computer-assisted instruction, open forum, mass media, public campaigns)

C. **Health promotion and protection strategies for the individual and family** (for example: therapeutic touch, imagery, massage, self-care, values clarification, relaxation techniques, meditation, cognitive therapies, stress management, exercise, weight control, personality development, anticipatory guidance, interpersonal skills, lifestyle behaviors, hygiene practices, immunizations; recommendations of *Healthy People 2000: National Health Promotion and Disease Prevention Objectives*)

D. **Risk appraisal strategies for the individual and family** (for example: appraisal of health hazards, activities of daily living, psychological factors, abuse, nutrition, exercise, heredity and genetic factors)

E. **Risk reduction strategies for the individual and family** (for example: contracting, self-monitoring, self-reevaluation, cognitive restructuring, reinforcement management, modeling, counterconditioning, stimulus control)

IV. Health Promotion and Protection Applied to the Prenatal Period (pregnant client, fetus, stages of labor, postpartum client)

A. **Health promotion**
    1. Nutritional needs (for example: nutritional needs of the pregnant woman, maternal body weight, vitamin and mineral supplements, sociocultural and financial influences on diet)
    2. Anticipatory guidance/education for the client and family (for example: preconception counseling; birthing alternatives; bonding; childbirth and parenting education [for example: stages of labor, fetal development]; physiological changes of pregnancy [for example: increase in urination, musculoskeletal changes]; psychosocial changes of pregnancy [for example: body image and self-concept changes, role changes, fantasies and fears about the child, attitudes toward breast-feeding]; sibling preparation; counseling to prevent constipation and urinary tract infections; exercise; body mechanics; need for rest and sleep; work patterns; Women, Infants, and Children [WIC] program; cultural beliefs about birth and childrearing; identification of support systems)

B. **Health protection**
    1. Risk appraisal: screening techniques (for example: amniocentesis, ultrasound, glucose monitoring, weight, blood pressure, postpartum depression, exposure to environmental hazards, substance use, role/relationship changes, potential for domestic violence)
    2. Common health problems (for example: depression, iron deficiency anemia, circulatory problems)

V. Health Promotion and Protection Applied to the Infant (neonate to 18 months)

A. Health promotion
1. Nutritional needs (for example: recommended daily allowances, weaning, introduction of solid foods and new foods, fluoride supplements, sociocultural and financial influences on diet)
2. Anticipatory guidance/education for the individual and family (for example: bonding and attachment; nursing and weaning; anticipating needs; opportunities for stimulation, play, and exploration; developmental tasks; safety counseling [accidents, falls, poisoning, aspiration, abuse]; changing sleep and rest patterns; teething; prevention of nursing caries; encouraging speech development; sun protection; selection of day care)

B. Health protection
1. Risk appraisal: screening techniques (for example: phenylketonuria testing [PKU], Denver Developmental Screening Test [DDST], tuberculin skin testing, HIV screening, appraisal for abuse)
2. Immunizations (for example: recommended schedule and guidelines, precautions, contraindications)
3. Common health problems (for example: ear infections, iron deficiency anemia, colic, fever, diarrhea, food intolerances, allergies, eczema, diaper rash)

VI. Health Promotion and Protection Applied to the Toddler and Preschooler

A. Health promotion
1. Nutritional needs (for example: recommended daily allowances, self-feeding, serving size, finger foods, ritualistic food behaviors)
2. Anticipatory guidance/education for the individual and family (for example: counseling on physiologic anorexia; dental care; play; discipline and limit setting; counseling on safety, including automobile safety [airbags and car seats]; protective gear; childproofing; lead poisoning; toilet training; speech development; sibling rivalry; masturbation [preschooler]; bedtime rituals; sex education; childhood fears)

B. Health protection
1. Risk appraisal: screening techniques (for example: screening for lead levels and anemias, vision and hearing screening, developmental screening, screening for abuse)
2. Immunizations (for example: recommended schedule and guidelines, precautions, contraindications)
3. Common health problems (for example: anemia, upper respiratory infections, ear infections, parasitic infections, poisoning, sleep disturbances, strabismus, communicable diseases, speech problems, temper tantrums)

VII. Health Promotion and Protection Applied to the School-Age Child

A. Health promotion
1. Nutritional needs (for example: recommended daily allowances, nutritional habits)
2. Anticipatory guidance/education for the individual and family (for example: nutrition; self-care [personal hygiene; dental health; exercise and physical fitness; drug, tobacco, and alcohol use]; discipline and limit setting; accident prevention [bicycles, water, firearms, recreational vehicles]; sexuality and sexual development; AIDS education; risk-taking behaviors; peer influences; monitoring activities [including television]; building self-esteem; impact of loss through death or separation; labeling/taunting; children who care for themselves after school)

B. Health protection
1. Risk appraisal: screening techniques (for example: vision and hearing screening; screening for learning disabilities, high blood pressure, lipid profile, scoliosis)
2. Immunizations (for example: recommended schedule and guidelines, precautions, contraindications)
3. Common health problems (for example: obesity, attention-deficit hyperactivity disorder [ADHD], sports injuries, enuresis, stress, school phobia, pediculosis)

VIII. Health Promotion and Protection Applied to the Adolescent

A. Health promotion
1. Nutritional needs (for example: recommended daily allowances, increased calories related to growth and activity, increased calcium intake)
2. Anticipatory guidance/education for the individual and family (for example: physical and emotional changes; erratic eating habits, including snacking and irregular mealtimes, low calcium intake, and high-fat foods; hearing protection; sun protection; motor vehicle safety; risk-taking behaviors; peer pressure; responsible decision making; sex education; sexual identification; maintaining good parental relationships; implications of parenthood)

B. Health protection
1. Risk appraisal: screening techniques (for example: hearing screening, screening for hepatitis, breast self-examination and testicular self-examination, Pap smears for sexually active females, tuberculosis screening, screening for depression and suicidal ideation)
2. Immunizations (according to recommended guidelines)
3. Common health problems (for example: eating disorders [anorexia, bulimia]; sexually transmitted diseases [STDs]; abusive relationships; substance abuse [drugs, alcohol, tobacco]; accidents; sports injuries; stress; acne)

IX. Health Promotion and Protection Applied to the Young Adult

A. Health promotion
1. Nutritional needs (for example: recommended daily allowances)
2. Anticipatory guidance/education for the individual and family (for example: relaxation techniques; establishing healthy lifestyle patterns, healthy interpersonal and role relationships, and independence from family of origin; career direction; readiness for parenting; occupational health hazards such as repetitive motion disorders; implications of technology; body mechanics)

B. Health protection
1. Risk appraisal: screening techniques (for example: breast self-examination and testicular self-examination; screening for hypertension, tuberculosis, lipid profile, and cervical cancer; establishing baseline Pap smears)
2. Immunizations (for example: recommended schedule and guidelines, precautions, contraindications)
3. Common health problems (for example: high-risk behaviors, substance abuse [drugs, alcohol, tobacco], reckless driving, sexually transmitted diseases [STDs], partner abuse, impaired fertility)

X. Health Promotion and Protection Applied to the Middle Adult

A. Health promotion
1. Nutritional needs (for example: recommended daily allowances, decreased sodium intake, decrease in saturated fats)
2. Anticipatory guidance/education for the individual and family (for example: exercise, stress reduction techniques, satisfying social relationships, preventive health screening, dietary counseling, menopause, osteoporosis, hormone replacement therapy, grief and grieving counseling, preparation for retirement, acceptance of aging)

B. Health protection
1. Risk appraisal: screening techniques (for example: Pap smears; mammograms; screening for hypertension, lipid profile, hyperglycemia, ovarian cancer, uterine cancer, prostate cancer, colorectal cancer, and skin cancer; establishing baseline EKG; tuberculosis screening)
2. Immunizations (for example: recommended schedule and guidelines, precautions, contraindications)
3. Common health problems (for example: obesity, presbyopia, gingivitis, stress incontinence, delayed parenting and impaired fertility, sexually transmitted diseases [STDs], problems resulting from multigenerational caregiving responsibilities)

XI. Health Promotion and Protection Applied to the Older Adult

A. Health promotion
1. Nutritional needs (for example: recommended daily allowances, increase in complex carbohydrates, reduced fats and refined sugars, decreased intake of highly processed foods)
2. Anticipatory guidance for the individual and family (for example: available community resources, physiological and psychological changes related to aging, exercise counseling, need for continued mental stimulation, accident prevention, counseling on over-the-counter and prescribed medications, loss, sources of social support, counseling on advance directives [living will, durable power of attorney])

B. Health Protection
1. Risk appraisal: screening techniques (for example: need for continued cancer screening [for example: skin, prostate, colon], vision and hearing screening, screening for malnutrition, screening for depression)
2. Immunizations (for example: recommended schedule and guidelines, precautions, contraindications)
3. Common health problems (for example: reduced mobility, decreased activities of daily living, glaucoma, sensory loss, presbycusis, poor nutrition, noncompliance with medications, incontinence, constipation, social isolation, depression, alcoholism)

Sample Questions: Health Support A

1. A client reports episodes of binge drinking to the nurse. The client refuses to share this information with the doctor. Which ethical belief reflecting individualism is consistent with the client's behavior?
   The client
   1) is concerned about confidentiality.
   2) equates binge drinking to active euthanasia.
   3) values quality of life over quantity of life.
   4) values lifestyle, personal freedom, and independence.

2. At Kohlberg's preconventional level of moral development, a child can be expected to obey on what basis?
   1) loyalty to family
   2) fear of punishment
   3) the need to be a good child
   4) the desire to follow the "golden rule"

3. The nurse is planning additional teaching for a parent who complains that her toddler urinates in his diaper after she takes him off the toilet. Which information is most important for the nurse to include in the teaching?
   1) Practice sessions limited to 15 minutes are helpful.
   2) It is important to tell the toddler that his behavior is unacceptable.
   3) The toddler's demonstrated ambivalence is a predictor of future behavioral problems.
   4) The average age of successful completion of toilet training is between two and three years of age.

4. Which is the best strategy for the nurse to use when a pregnant client says that some of the childbearing ideas of her culture are old-fashioned?
   1) Encourage the client to abide by the cultural practices to avoid conflict.
   2) Follow the client's need and agree with her.
   3) Assess how the client's family feels about maintaining cultural rituals.
   4) Allow the client to express her annoyance about cultural restrictions.

5. Which instruction is most important for the nurse to include when providing anticipatory guidance to a pregnant client who complains of leg cramps?
   1) Restrict milk intake to 8 ounces per day.
   2) Practice dorsiflexion.
   3) Practice toe pointing when exercising.
   4) Avoid the use of aluminum hydroxide antacids.

6. A mother brings her four-year-old child to the clinic for routine immunizations. The mother tells the nurse that her 12-year-old child is taking immunosuppressants and asks the nurse which vaccine would be safe to give the four year old at this time. The nurse should tell the mother that the four year old will be given which immunization?
   1) DTP
   2) HBV
   3) MMR
   4) TOPV

Sample Questions: Health Support A

7. During a home visit, the nurse observes a neonate crying for five minutes. Which response should the nurse give to the parent's inquiry about why the infant is crying?
   1) Crying is the infant's first means of verbal communication.
   2) In the first few weeks of life, crying is mostly related to expanding lung development.
   3) Unexplained fussiness and crying is the first sign of a problem.
   4) Periods of infant crying usually peak at one month of age.

8. The nurse is teaching the parent of a two-year-old child about dental health. Which comment by the parent indicates that additional teaching is needed?
   1) "I put my child to bed with a bottle filled with plain water."
   2) "Our water is adequately fluoridated, so I do not give my child oral fluoride supplements."
   3) "My child brushes her own teeth independently every day, morning and night."
   4) "I give my child one cookie a day after she has her lunch."

9. During a meeting with parents of school-age children, a parent asks the nurse about selecting an appropriate activity for an 11-year-old child. The nurse's response should be based upon which developmental understanding?
   1) Games with rules allow children to develop proficiency and power over their play.
   2) Team play provides exercise and muscle development without the concern for competition.
   3) Children at this age become easily bored with hobbies or activities that are complex.
   4) Creative activities and organizing elaborate collections are becoming less interesting at this time.

10. The camp nurse is assessing a light-skinned eight-year-old child. Which finding on the child's skin should lead the nurse to suspect that the child may have Lyme disease?
    1) several red ring-shaped lesions on the thigh
    2) isolated skin-colored vesicles on the forearm and ankles
    3) raised track-like burrowing lesions on the lower legs
    4) multiple scattered pink papules on the palms and soles

11. Which nursing intervention should be given priority in the plan of care for an adolescent experiencing tension due to strict family rules?
    1) Tell the parents to explain the rules to the adolescent, but to remain firm in limit setting.
    2) Encourage the adolescent to spend some time each day exercising to reduce stress.
    3) Tell the adolescent to demonstrate responsibility by obtaining employment.
    4) Discuss stressors with the family and work out how power struggles can be negotiated.

Sample Questions: Health Support A

12. During a behavioral health history, a young adult client reports that seat belts only need to be worn on trips greater than five miles. Which initial nursing strategy is consistent with Pender's Health Promotion Model?
    1) Collect information about the client's perceptions of the benefits and the barriers to seat belt use.
    2) Explain that better use of automobile restraint systems has contributed to a 40 percent decline in the fatality rate for persons 15 to 24 years old.
    3) Emphasize that failure to wear a seat belt may result in a traffic citation in 48 states.
    4) Discuss with the client the fact that people are most likely to have an accident within five miles of their home.

13. Which nursing strategy for a young adult female client is aimed at preventing the development of osteoporosis later in life?
    1) Instruct the client to obtain daily calcium requirements from dairy products.
    2) Recommend that a baseline bone density test be performed while the client is a young adult.
    3) Advise the client to maintain a daily calcium intake of at least 1,200 mg.
    4) Recommend daily consumption of green leafy vegetables and citrus fruits.

14. Which outcome indicates that the nurse's teaching about prostate cancer to a 45-year-old client has been successful?
    The client
    1) agrees to have a prostate-specific antigen (PSA) test.
    2) agrees to begin annual digital rectal examinations (DREs).
    3) says he has had a negative transrectal ultrasound (TRUS) and is now safe.
    4) says he will see his doctor should symptoms of prostate cancer appear.

15. In performing an initial assessment of a middle-aged couple experiencing a lifestyle crisis, the nurse should recognize that this couple are probably in which of Erikson's developmental stages?
    1) ego integrity vs. despair
    2) generativity vs. stagnation
    3) identity vs. role confusion
    4) intimacy vs. isolation

16. A 72-year-old woman confides to the nurse that she is still sexually active. Which information is most important for the nurse to obtain?
    1) frequency of the client's sexual contact
    2) client's use of proper precautions against STDs
    3) problems the client may have with physiological changes
    4) how many sexual partners the client has

Sample Questions: Health Support A

17. Which information reported by an older adult client indicates that the nurse's teaching about decreased sensation to temperature has been successful?
    1) "I bathe or shower only when other family members are at home."
    2) "I use oven mitts instead of a dish towel for removing hot items from the oven."
    3) "I apply skin lotion to my hands and arms at least three times each day."
    4) "I have my water heater set at 130° F."

18. An older adult client whose spouse has just died says, "I've no reason to go on living." Which nursing intervention is most appropriate?
    1) Offer to call the client's family.
    2) Plan specific activities to keep the client busy.
    3) Assist the client to see a mental health professional.
    4) Reminisce about the client's accomplishments.

Recommended Resources

Clark, M.J. (1999). Nursing in the community *(3rd ed.). Stamford, CT: Appleton & Lange.*

This text provides a thorough introduction to community health nursing and aspects of this practice specialty. This book also provides a summary listing of the national health objectives that have been specified for the year 2000. A computer disk is provided as a study aid.

Edelman, C., & Mandle, C. (1998). Health promotion throughout the lifespan *(4th ed.) St. Louis: Mosby.*

This text is based on the *Healthy People 2000* goals, objectives, and strategies. It provides a developmental approach to health data and includes nursing interventions at the primary (health promotion and specific protection) and secondary levels of prevention. This text is also used for the Regents College Examination in Health Support B: Community Health Nursing and for the Health Assessment and Teaching Performance Examination (HATPE).

Haber, J. et al. (1997). Comprehensive psychiatric nursing *(5th ed.). St. Louis: Mosby.*

This text covers theoretical and therapeutic foundations and the psychiatric client, and has a limited mental health focus. It provides adequate coverage of family and group and has a limited community focus. DSM-IV is integrated throughout the clinical chapters. Study aids include objectives and key terms at the beginning of chapters, key terms italicized, and key points highlighted at the end of chapters.

Olds, S., London, M., & Ladewig, P. (1996). Maternal newborn nursing: A family-centered approach *(5th ed.). Menlo Park, CA: Addison-Wesley.*

This textbook covers theoretical and therapeutic nursing foundations in the care of the childbearing woman and her family. It provides broad coverage of family needs within the context of normal as well as abnormal adaptation. Critical-thinking scenarios provide practice with decision-making criteria in commonly occurring practice situations. Key terms and points are highlighted throughout the text. A workbook that provides review exercises is available.

Sample Questions: Health Support A

Pender, N. (1996). Health promotion in nursing practice (3rd ed.). Norwalk, CT: Appleton & Lange.

This textbook discusses the various definitions and models of health, along with related research findings. Strategies for developing health promotion plans for individuals and families are discussed, including interventions promoting healthy behaviors. Approaches for developing and maintaining a healthy society are also analyzed.

Smeltzer, S., & Bare, B. (1996). Brunner and Suddarth's Textbook of medical-surgical nursing (8th ed.). Philadelphia: J.B. Lippincott.

This textbook makes extensive use of diagrams, tables, photographs, charts, and nursing care plans to present information. Each chapter begins with learning objectives and ends with critical-thinking activities and a bibliography. Many color photographs are included. The textbook includes a free self-study disk that contains sample test questions along with rationales for the correct answer.

Wong, D. (1999). Whaley & Wong's Nursing care of infants and children (6th ed.). St. Louis: Mosby.

This textbook covers theoretical and therapeutic interventions for the child within the context of normal growth and development and family interaction, as well as deviations from normal system functioning. The text provides broad coverage of individual, family, and community influences on health/illness states. Key terms are highlighted throughout the text. A study guide is available.

Journal Articles

I. Strategies to Promote and Protect Health

Breslow, L. (1996). *Social ecological strategies for promoting healthy lifestyles.* American Journal of Health Promotion, 10(4), 253–257.

Sharp, P.C. (1998). *Working with lay health educators in a rural cancer prevention program.* American Journal of Health Behavior, 22(1), 28–36.

II. Health Promotion and Protection: Prenatal Period

Barnett, E. (1995). *Race differences in the proportion of low birth weight attributable to maternal cigarette smoking in a low-income population.* American Journal of Health Promotion, 10(2), 105–110.

Frede, D.J., & Strohbach, M.E. (1992). *The state of preconceptional health education.* Journal of Perinatal Education, 1(2), 19–26.

III. Health Promotion and Protection: The Infant

Biester, D.J. (1994). *Bright futures...recommendations by Bright futures: Guidelines for health supervision of infants, children and adolescents.* Journal of Pediatric Nursing, 10(4), 264–265.

IV. Health Promotion and Protection: The Toddler and Preschooler

Cagle, C.S., & Keen-Payne, R. (1996). *Health promotion teaching in preschools.* American Journal of Maternal-Child Nursing, 21(2), 96–99.

Finan, S.L. (1997). *Promoting healthy sexuality: Guidelines for infancy through preschool.* Nurse Practitioner: American Journal of Primary Health Care, 22(10), 79–80, 83–84, 86.

Ulione, M.S., & Donovan, E. (1996). *Nursing in Project Head Start: Improving health.* Issues in Comprehensive Pediatric Nursing, 19(4), 227–237.

Sample Questions: Health Support A

V. Health Promotion and Protection: The School-Age Child

Coppens, N.M., & McCabe, B.M. (1995). *Promoting children's use of bicycle helmets.* Journal of Pediatric Health Care, 9(2), 51–58.

Davis, S.M., Lambert, L.C., Gomez, Y., & Skipper, B. (1995). *Southwest cardiovascular curriculum project: Study findings for American Indian elementary students.* Journal of Health Education, 26(2), Supplement S72–81.

Finan, S.L. (1997). *Promoting healthy sexuality: Guidelines for the school-age child and adolescent.* Nurse Practitioner: American Journal of Primary Health Care, 22(11), 62, 65–67, 71–72.

Stewart, K.J. (1995). *Heart healthy knowledge, food patterns, fatness, and cardiac risk factors in children receiving nutrition education.* Journal of Health Education, 26(6).

VI. Health Promotion and Protection: The Adolescent

Allensworth, D.D., & Bradley, B. (1996). *Guidelines for adolescent preventive services: A role for the school nurse.* Journal of School Health, 66(8), 281–285.

CDC's guidelines for school and community programs; promoting lifelong physical activity. (1997) United States Department of Health and Human Services Publications (6 p.).

Ervin, M.H. (1998). *Teaching self-care to delinquent adolescents.* Journal of Pediatric Health Care, 12(1), 20–26.

Levenburg, P.B. (1998). *GAPS: An opportunity for nurse practitioners to promote the health of adolescents through clinical preventive services.* Journal of Pediatric Health Care, 12(1), 2–9.

Story, M., & Alton, I. (1996). *Adolescent nutrition: Current trends and critical issues.* Topics in Clinical Nutrition, 11(3), 56–69.

VII. Health Promotion and Protection: The Young Adult

Beitz, J.M. (1998). *Sexual health promotion in adolescents and young adults: Primary prevention strategies.* Holistic Nursing Practice, 12(2), 27–37.

Grace, T.W. (1998). *Health problems of late adolescence.* Primary Care: Clinics in Office Practice, 25(1), 237–252.

Standards for adult immunization practice. (1993). American Journal of Infection Control, 21(6), 331–332.

VIII. Health Promotion and Protection: The Middle Adult

Browder, S.E. (1998). *Attention, women over 50! The 3 health problems you have most to fear...and what to do now.* New Choices: Living Even Better After 50, 38(1), 20–21, 25–26.

Flowers, J.S., & McLean, J.E. (1996). *Psychometric studies of the Flowers Midlife Health Questionnaire [sic] (FMHQ) for women.* Journal of Nursing Science, 1(3/4), 115–126.

IX. Health Promotion and Protection: The Older Adult

Barry, R., & Burggraf, V. (1996). *Healthy people: Objectives look at the elderly.* Journal of Gerontological Nursing, 22(10), 9–11.

Chen, Y.D. (1996). *Conformity with nature: A theory of Chinese American elders' health promotion and illness prevention processes.* Advances in Nursing Science, 19(2), 17–26.

Pizzi, E.R., & Wolf, Z.R. (1998). *Health risks and health promotion for older women: Utility of a health promotion diary.* Holistic Nursing Practice, 12(2), 62–72.

Rubenstein, L.Z., & Nahas, R. (1998). *Primary and secondary prevention strategies in the older adult.* Geriatric Nursing: American Journal of Care for the Aging, 19(1), 11–18, 28.

Williams, M.P. (1996). *Increasing participation in health promotion among older African-Americans.* American Journal of Health Behavior, 20(6), 389–399, 440–441.

Zhan, L., Cloutterbuck, J., Keshian, J., & Lombardi, L. (1998). *Promoting health: Perspectives from ethnic elderly women.* Journal of Community Health Nursing, 15(1), 31–44.

Study Guide

Health Support B: Community Health Nursing (541) (Baccalaureate Level)

Credit Hours: 4
Question Type(s): Multiple-choice
Credit Level: Upper

The information in this study guide is valid until Summer 2001.
If you will be taking the examination after that date, be sure to check for a new edition of this guide before you complete your preparation for the exam.

General Description of the Examination

The Health Support B: Community Health Nursing examination measures knowledge and understanding of community health nursing practice. The goal of community health nursing is to improve the health of the community. The nurse accomplishes this goal by working with individuals, families, and population groups within the community.

The examination tests the knowledge base that is essential for community health nursing practice at the baccalaureate level. The nursing process serves as the framework for the provision of nursing care to clients with commonly encountered health problems. Emphasis is placed on the secondary and tertiary prevention aspects of health promotion. Nursing activities include advocacy, counseling, case finding, health teaching, screening, and discharge planning.

The Health Support Examination Series

Health Support B: Community Health Nursing is part of a two-examination series. The Health Support A examination covers foundations for health promotion and protection, growth and development across the life span, strategies to promote and protect health, and health promotion and protection applied to the prenatal period; the infant; the toddler and preschooler; the school-age child; the adolescent; and the young, middle, and older adult. The Health Support B examination covers foundations of community health nursing, community as client, the social/cultural environment, epidemiology, environmental health, vulnerable population groups/populations at risk, community health nursing in specialized settings, and common community health problems.

Content Outline

Content Area	Percent of Examination
I. Foundations of Community Health Nursing	15%
II. Community as Client	20%
III. The Social/Cultural Environment	10%
IV. Epidemiology	15%
V. Environmental Health	10%
VI. Community Health Nursing in Specialized Settings	10%
VII. Common Community Health Problems/Populations at Risk	20%
Total	100%

I. Foundations of Community Health Nursing

A. Theoretical foundations for community health nursing
1. Definitions
    a. Community—compare and contrast with aggregates
    b. Community health nursing—health promotion, health of the general public, autonomy, continuity, collaboration, public accountability
    c. Public health nursing—provides care to individuals, families with community focus
    d. Home health nursing—primary focus is illness, care of individuals or aggregates
    e. Health promotion—activities designed to improve or maintain the health status of individuals, families, and communities (for example: school health programs, older adult programs, day-care programs, parenting programs, substance abuse education)
    f. Levels of prevention
        (1) Primary prevention—actions taken to prevent the occurrence of health problems: health promotion, risk identification, and specific protection
        (2) Secondary prevention—the early identification and treatment of specific health problems, early diagnosis, screening, prompt treatment, disability limitation
        (3) Tertiary prevention—activities aimed at returning the client to the highest level of function possible following the correction of a health problem: rehabilitation, prevention of recurrences
    g. Epidemiology—study of health and illness patterns and determinants in populations
2. Attributes of community health nursing (for example: population focus, family as a unit of care, community as client, orientation to health, interactivity, autonomy, collaboration, advocacy, accountability, continuity, sphere of intimacy)

3. ANA *Standards of Community Health Nursing Practice*: principles of nursing applied to community health nursing that were developed by the profession and are used to evaluate the quality of care

B. **Historical foundations for community health nursing**
   1. Historical roots (for example: Code of Hammurabi, early Greece and Rome)
   2. Influences of religious groups (for example: Hebrew Mosaic law, early Christianity through the Renaissance, religious orders)
   3. Revolution—wars, Industrial Revolution
   4. Development and evolution of community health nursing in the United States (for example: organizations, public health movement, legislation)
   5. Leaders (for example: Florence Nightingale, Lillian Wald, Margaret Sanger)

C. **The nurse-client relationship**
   1. Values clarification
      a. Clarification of the nurse's personal values: method to seek awareness of one's own principles, standards which guide life
      b. Clarification of the client's values (for example: understanding of client's meaning of health and illness care)
      c. Identification of the potential for conflicting values (for example: how particular value affects health, self-awareness, openness to others, acceptance of differences)
   2. Therapeutic use of self (for example: negotiating, promoting community autonomy)
   3. The helping relationship (for example: caregiver, educator, advocate)
   4. Cultural competence—includes awareness of own values, knowledge and understanding of client's culture, acceptance and respect of cultural differences, and adapting care to be congruent with client's culture

D. **Nursing roles and practice strategies in community health nursing**
   1. Roles and functions of the community health nurse
      a. Client-oriented roles (caregiver, educator, counselor, referral resource, role model, advocate, primary care provider, case manager)
      b. Delivery-oriented roles (coordinator, collaborator, liaison, discharge planner)
      c. Group-oriented roles (case finder, leader, change agent, community care agent, researcher)
   2. The home visit
      a. Assessment of the client and environmental parameters (preparatory assessment prior to visit; client factors of biology; physical, psychological, and social environments; lifestyle)
      b. Analysis (diagnosis)—generation of positive, health promotive, or problem-focused diagnoses
      c. Planning (for example: preparing for the visit, collaborating with the client to prioritize needs, reviewing previous interventions, prioritizing client needs, developing goals and objectives, acceptance and timing, selecting interventions, gathering materials, planning for evaluation)
      d. Implementation (for example: teaching, validation of assessment and diagnoses, implementing interventions, dealing with distracting factors)
      e. Evaluation (review for possible modifications in subsequent home visits)

  f. Documentation and reimbursement (documentation of client's status, nursing interventions, and their effectiveness that is usually necessary for reimbursement)
 3. Discharge planning (purposes and advantages)
  a. Assessment (determine need for routine vs. detailed discharge plans based on potential risk for complications)
  b. Analysis (diagnosis)—develop problem-focused and wellness-oriented nursing diagnoses
  c. Planning—prioritize needs with client and develop plans to meet them
  d. Implementation—communicate with other health care providers
  e. Evaluation (for modification depending on success of meeting client goals and objectives)
 4. The referral process (purposes and advantages)
  a. Assessment (determine which client needs cannot be met by community health nurse, assess for client acceptability, eligibility, situational restraints, availability)
  b. Analysis (diagnosis)—develop diagnoses
  c. Planning (for example: using community resources, identifying goals and objectives, using results of assessment data)
  d. Implementation—provide client with all relevant data, assist client to initiate referral, provide resource information to referral agency
  e. Evaluation (follow up on client's use of and benefit from referral)

E. Ethical issues relevant to community health nursing (for example: social justice, access, individual vs. societal good, resource allocation)

F. The organization of community health care
 1. National (for example: U.S. Public Health Service, Department of Health and Human Services, Medicare, Medicaid, Tax Equity and Fiscal Responsibility Act, American Public Health Association)
 2. State (for example: state health departments, bureaus of vital statistics)
 3. Local (for example: city and county health departments, direct-care community agencies [for example: visiting nurses, voluntary agencies])

G. Global issues relevant to community health nursing (for example: World Health Organization [WHO], free enterprise vs. welfare systems, pandemics, epidemics, famines, environmental issues, international travel, food distribution, water safety)

II. Community as Client

A. Community assessment
1. Definition of community assessment: process by which data is collected about the health status of a community and health problems are identified
2. Types of communities (for example: geopolitical communities, communities of solution, communities of problem ecology, communities of interest-orientation)
3. Sources of information (for example: census information, mortality rates, morbidity rates, key informants, voluntary agencies)
4. Factors that influence community health: biology, environment, lifestyle, the health care system
5. Methods of community assessment (for example: windshield survey, use of statistics, interviewing key informants, participant observation)

B. Analysis (diagnosis) (for example: violence, adolescent pregnancy, infant mortality, environmental hazards, mental health problems, older adults in the community)

C. Planning (general principles, types, process)
1. Identifying populations at risk (for example: violence, adolescent pregnancy, infant mortality, environmental hazards, mental health problems, older adults in the community)
2. Collaboration among agencies (for example: access to health services, acceptability)
3. Setting priorities (that is, need-service mismatch, severity of problem, concern of community, resources)

D. Implementation
1. Acceptance of the plan (by policy makers, by implementers, by target group)
2. Tasks (that is, determination of tasks and sequencing, skills needed to implement plan, task allocation)
3. Strategies (for example: assigning responsibility, coordination, keeping group informed of progress)

E. Evaluation
1. Outcomes—evaluation process that documents effects of program and justifies whether to continue program
2. Process—examines program performance in terms of efficiency, effort

III. The Social/Cultural Environment

A. Relationship between culture and health (for example: health care beliefs, dietary practices, life events, health care practitioners, cultural beliefs and practices related to diagnosis and treatment of illness)

B. Nursing responses to clients from other cultures
1. Positive responses (for example: cultural sensitivity, cultural competence)
2. Negative responses (for example: ethnocentrism, racism)

C. Nursing process
1. Assessment (for example: communication, family roles and organization, biocultural ecology, nutrition, death rituals, health care practices)
2. Analysis (diagnosis) (for example: decreased clinic attendance related to need to involve folk healers in health care)
3. Planning (for example: mutual goal setting involving decision makers in family)
4. Implementation (for example: use of folk healers, folk practices)
5. Evaluation (for example: determination of acceptability and use of health care)

IV. Epidemiology

A. **Basic concepts of epidemiology**
   1. Causality (for example: theories of disease causation, criteria for causality)
   2. Risk (for example: susceptibility, exposure potential, relative risk ratio, target groups)
   3. Rates—mortality (such as crude death rate and age-specific death rates); morbidity (such as incidence and prevalence)

B. **Epidemiological models**
   1. Epidemiologic triad model (that is: host/agent/environment)
   2. The web of causation (that is: interplay of multiple factors on development of a health problem)
   3. Dever's model (that is: human biology, environment, lifestyle, health care system)

C. **The epidemiological process**
   1. Natural history of disease—preexposure, preclinical, clinical, and resolution stages
   2. Levels of prevention—primary, secondary, tertiary
   3. Screening—methods that detect abnormal findings to be confirmed by further diagnostic work (for example: vision, hearing, scoliosis)

D. **Types of epidemiological investigation**
   1. Descriptive—distribution by person, place, and time
   2. Analytic—factors contributing to health status to identify cause
      a. Hypothesis generating—ecological and correlational studies
      b. Hypothesis testing
         (1) Observational—retrospective, prospective, cross-sectional
         (2) Experimental—application of an intervention in prophylactic or therapeutic trials

V. Environmental Health

A. **Environmental influences on health**
   1. Physical hazards (for example: radiation; lead and other heavy metals; noise; safety issues such as need for seat belts, bicycle helmets; monitoring for pollutants)
   2. Biological hazards (for example: infectious agents, insects, plants, animals, solid waste)
   3. Chemical and gaseous hazards (for example: poisons, air pollution, water pollution, industrial pollution, asbestos)
   4. Social, political, and economic influences (for example: crowded environments, poverty, violence, limited access to health care, allocation of resources, in- and out-migration, availability of public housing and shelters, racial/ethnic mix, age and gender distribution, employment/unemployment, crime, violence)

B. **Nursing process**
   1. Assessment—identification of hazards and their effect on the health of a community

2. Analysis (diagnosis)—potential and actual diagnoses (for example: risk for lead poisoning related to old housing)
3. Planning—development of interventions at primary, secondary, and tertiary levels
4. Implementation—creating community support for programs to reduce environmental hazards (for example: legislation for clean air, environmental monitoring for pollutants)
5. Evaluation—determining effectiveness of interventions (for example: effectiveness of teaching regarding food sanitation)

VI. Community Health Nursing in Specialized Settings

A. School health nursing
1. Roles and responsibilities of the school health nurse (for example: screening for vision, hearing, scoliosis; providing health education; collaborating with teachers; anticipatory guidance; immunization surveillance; developmental tests; nutritional appraisal; physical fitness appraisal; family assessment)
2. Assessment in the school setting
3. Common health problems (for example: eating disorders, substance abuse, communicable diseases, seizure disorders, asthma, head lice, attention-deficit hyperactivity disorder, developmental delays, children with special needs)
4. Levels of prevention
   a. Primary prevention (for example: immunization, school safety, nutrition)
   b. Secondary prevention (for example: scoliosis screening, counseling, and treatment)
   c. Tertiary prevention (for example: rehabilitative programs for children with chronic illness)

B. Occupational health nursing
1. Roles and responsibilities of the occupational health nurse (for example: screening for hypertension, hearing, respiratory problems; identifying hazards; making referrals; counseling; providing health education; wellness inventories)
2. Assessment in the work setting—use of epidemiologic model to examine potential risk factors
3. Common health problems (for example: lung diseases, musculoskeletal problems, noise-induced hearing loss, cardiovascular problems, trauma, skin conditions)
4. Levels of prevention
   a. Primary prevention (for example: nutrition, exercise, or stress management programs; influenza or hepatitis B immunization programs; safety education)
   b. Secondary prevention (for example: preemployment and periodic screening for respiratory or blood problems, employee assistance programs, treatment of existing health problems)
   c. Tertiary prevention (for example: preventing recurrence of health problems such as musculoskeletal injury, preventing spread of communicable diseases)

C. Rural health nursing
1. Roles and responsibilities of the rural health nurse (for example: identifying hazards, screening for skin cancer, involvement of resources in rural community, triaging for emergency care)

2. Settings for rural health nurses (for example: working with clients who are migrant workers, clients who live on farms, clients who live in Appalachia)
3. Assessment in the rural setting (for example: populations at risk [young and old], occupational hazards, stress, isolation, substance abuse, health care system)
4. Common health problems (for example: accidents, sun exposure, lung disease, hearing loss, adolescent pregnancy, sexually transmitted diseases [STDs], stroke, diabetes, obesity, smoking, alcoholism, limited access to health care, communicable diseases, hepatitis, pesticide exposure, interrupted immunization schedules, limited access to health care)
5. Levels of prevention
    a. Primary prevention (for example: accident prevention, family planning, sex education for children, health teaching)
    b. Secondary prevention (for example: screening for health problems, environmental health screening, advocacy for rural health programs)
    c. Tertiary prevention (for example: case management of clients with chronic conditions, involvement of family in care and rehabilitation)

D. Disaster nursing
1. Roles and responsibilities of the community health nurse (for example: providing triage, providing immediate care, providing supportive care, providing crisis intervention)
2. Stages of disaster response
    a. Pre-event response—activities that occur prior to a disaster (for example: planning, warning, preimpact mobilization)
    b. Post-event response—response during and immediately following disaster such as rescue and care of victims
    c. Recovery response—responses needed to return to normal (for example: restoration, reconstitution, mitigation)
3. Principles of disaster planning
4. Assessment in the disaster setting (for example: examining preparation for disasters, potential for disaster, and effectiveness of plan)
5. Preparedness and the prevention of disasters (for example: preparedness checklist, WHO)
6. Levels of prevention
    a. Primary prevention—preimpact mobilization to prevent or limit consequences of disaster risk factors
    b. Secondary prevention—measures at individual level (for example: triage, treatment of victims) and community level (for example: shelter and food)
    c. Tertiary prevention—counseling with effect after immediate disaster and work to prevent future disasters

VII. Common Community Health Problems and Populations at Risk

A. Substance abuse
1. Scope of the problem (for example: commonly abused substances, risk factors, street drug addiction, medically prescribed addiction, alcoholism)

2. Effects of substance abuse (for example: personal, family, and societal effects; escape patterns such as suicide; divorce; dependency patterns such as welfare and adolescent pregnancy)
   3. Levels of prevention
      a. Primary prevention (for example: Parent Effectiveness Training, Big Brothers/Big Sisters, support groups, teaching coping skills, public awareness campaigns)
      b. Secondary prevention—case finding, early referral for treatment, educating public on signs of abuse
      c. Tertiary prevention—refer to support groups, vocational rehabilitation
   4. National health objectives related to substance abuse (for example: reduce drug-related deaths to less than three per 100,000 population, decrease cigarette smoking)

B. **Communicable diseases**
   1. Common communicable diseases (for example: childhood diseases, STDs, encephalitis, influenza, Lyme disease, hepatitis, HIV, tuberculosis, waterborne infections, foodborne infections, chickenpox/herpes zoster)
   2. Epidemiology of communicable diseases
      a. General concepts
         (1) Causation
         (2) Chain of infection—series of events leading to development of communicable disease
         (3) Modes of transmission—the means by which disease is spread
            (a) Airborne transmission (for example: measles and chickenpox)
            (b) Fecal-oral transmission (for example: salmonella, hepatitis A)
            (c) Direct contact (for example: lice, impetigo)
            (d) Sexual transmission (for example: gonorrhea, HIV/AIDS)
            (e) Transmission by direct inoculation (for example: HIV/AIDS, hepatitis B & C)
            (f) Transmission by other means (for example: malaria, tetanus)
         (4) Portals of entry and exit
         (5) Incubation and prodromal periods
         (6) Active and passive immunity (for example: polio vaccine or gamma globulin)
      b. Principles of communicable disease control
         (1) Prevent spread of infection (for example: use of adequate ventilation)
         (2) Decrease exposure (for example: isolation principles)
         (3) Increase host resistance (for example: immunization, measures to improve health)
   3. Roles and responsibilities of the community health nurse (for example: screening, controlling communicable diseases)
   4. Levels of prevention
      a. Primary prevention (for example: school-based clinics, Planned Parenthood, home visits, school health education, child development programs, immunization, water treatment, vector control, health department food inspection)
      b. Secondary prevention (for example: STD, HIV, and tuberculosis screening at the local level; high-risk clinics; prompt treatment; long-term public treatment for tuberculosis)

c. Tertiary prevention—curtailing spread of infection and long-term sequelae
5. National health objectives related to communicable diseases (for example: reduce number of cases of tetanus and diptheria in persons under 25 to zero, immunize 90% of children)

C. Violence
1. Theories of assaultive violence (for example: biological, psychological, sociological, multifactorial)
2. Scope of the problem (for example: child abuse, spouse abuse, elder abuse, homicide, suicide, sexual abuse/assault, criminal activity)
3. Roles and responsibilities of the community health nurse (for example: assessing for violence, education, support, referral, legal responses)
4. Nursing Process
    a. Assessment (for example: assessing for risk factors; evidence of child, elder, or spousal abuse)
    b. Analysis (diagnosis) (for example: at individual or community level)
    c. Planning and implementing care
        (1) Primary prevention (for example: gun control, parenting classes, treating substance abuse, providing emotional support, improving coping skills)
        (2) Secondary prevention (for example: protecting victim, reporting suspected abuse, treating abuser)
        (3) Tertiary prevention (for example: parenting classes for abusive individuals, support groups, respite services for elder care)
    d. Evaluation—individual, community and national
5. National health objectives related to violence (for example: reduce homicide to no more than 7.2 per 100,000 population, reduce physical abuse of women to no more than 27 per 1,000 couples)

D. Chronic health problems
1. Scope of the problem (for example: risk, economic concerns, morbidity, early mortality)
2. Common chronic health problems (for example: asthma, arthritis, COPD, peripheral vascular disease, cardiovascular disease, cerebrovascular disease, cancer, diabetes mellitus, mental health problems, depression)
3. Epidemiology of chronic health problems
    a. General concepts
        (1) Natural history of chronic disease—body's response from time of exposure to agent to development of clinical signs and symptoms
            (a) Latency—the time during which the disease is developing at cellular level, but person has no symptoms
            (b) Onset—appearance of recognizable symptoms of chronic illness
        (2) Levels of prevention
            (a) Primary prevention (for example: weight control, prevention of smoking, exercise, stress reduction programs)
            (b) Secondary prevention (for example: screening for early symptoms, early diagnosis)
            (c) Tertiary prevention (for example: support groups, rehabilitation programs, vocational rehabilitation)
    b. Strategies for chronic disease control (for example: risk identification and reduction, development of health promotion programs)

4. Effects of chronic health problems (that is, personal, family, and societal effects)
5. Roles and responsibilities of the community health nurse in controlling chronic health problems (for example: advocacy, referral to support groups, education, case management, caregiver role)
6. National health objectives related to chronic health problems (for example: increase percentage of people engaged in regular exercise, reduce smoking, increase seat belt and helmet use)

E. Maternal/child health problems
1. Common community health problems related to maternal/child health (for example: low-birth-weight infants, lead poisoning, congenital anomalies, adolescent pregnancy, delayed parenting, impaired fertility, abortion)
2. Scope of the problem (for example: risk factors, problems of poverty, access to care, sexually transmitted diseases)
3. Effects (that is, personal, family, and societal effects)
4. Roles and responsibilities of the community health nurse (for example: providing screening, education; acting as caregiver, advocate, case-finder)
5. Levels of prevention
    a. Primary prevention (for example: WIC program, sex education and pregnancy prevention programs in high school, fertility control)
    b. Secondary prevention (for example: screening for breast cancer, cervical cancer, sexually transmitted diseases)
    c. Tertiary prevention (for example: rehabilitation, referral, prevention of additional unplanned pregnancies)
6. National health objectives related to maternal/child health problems (for example: reduce teenage pregnancy to less that 50 per 1,000 girls, reduce smoking in women to less than 15%)

F. Homelessness
1. Definition of population group—individual who lacks fixed regular and adequate residence, and who uses a nighttime shelter or place not intended for sleeping or is forced to live with family or friends
2. Scope of the problem—not a homogenous group but one that includes people with chronic mental illness who live on the streets, individuals with substance abuse, and people who are situationally homeless
3. Assessing the health needs of clients who are homeless (for example: effects on young and old, chronic health problems, inadequate housing)
4. Common health problems of clients who are homeless (for example: skin diseases, depression, mental illness, lead poisoning, nutritional problems, accidents, violence, lice, tuberculosis)
5. Adapting nursing care to meet the health care needs of clients who are homeless (for example: access to health services, acceptability of services, food supplement programs, availability of shelters, rhythm of street activities, child health care services)

G. Poverty
1. Definition of population group—federal definitions of poverty levels
2. Scope of the problem (for example: women, children, rural poor, migrants, in retirement)

3. Assessing the health needs of clients who are living in poverty (for example: the uninsured, access to health care, continuity, advocacy)
4. Common health problems of clients who are living in poverty (for example: malnutrition, communicable diseases, hepatitis, inadequate immunizations, infant mortality, foodborne diseases)
5. Adapting nursing care to meet the health care needs of clients who are living in poverty (for example: access to health services, acceptability of services, food supplement programs, availability of public housing, employment/unemployment patterns)

H. End-of-life care
1. Ethical issues (for example: client autonomy, advance directives, termination of support)
2. Scope of the problem
3. Philosophy of hospice (for example: quality of life, pain control, volunteers)
4. Effects (that is, personal, family, and societal effects)
5. Roles and responsibilities of the community health nurse—caregiver, case manager, counselor

Sample Questions: Health Support B

1. Which statement most accurately describes the ANA *Standards of Community Health Nursing Practice*?
   The standards
   1) provide specific guidelines for physical care of clients in the home setting.
   2) provide criteria for evaluating the quality of care delivered.
   3) are distinct from general principles of nursing.
   4) delineate the specific legal practice of nursing in the community health setting.

2. The community health nurse has just received a referral on a 76-year-old client who was recently discharged to home after suffering a stroke. The client's spouse is frail but capable of self-care. Which activity is typical of the community health nurse in the role of case manager, as differentiated from that of coordinator?
   1) contacting the speech pathologist and the occupational and physical therapist to establish a schedule of visits for the client
   2) identifying needs and arranging for the client to have a shower chair, a home health aide, and homemaker services
   3) scheduling a case conference involving the client, the physician, a speech pathologist, and occupational and physical therapists
   4) discussing with the physical therapist the client's hesitation about using the walker when the therapist is not present

3. Which statement best illustrates client advocacy at the national level for universal health care access?
   1) joining a professional nursing organization that lobbies for health care for all
   2) writing a letter to the editor of a local newspaper encouraging employer provision of health insurance
   3) picketing an employer who does not provide health benefits to employees
   4) encouraging a client to apply for the Women, Infants, and Children (WIC) program

4. Measuring the appropriateness of the use of resources is an example of what aspect of process evaluation?
   1) effectiveness
   2) efficiency
   3) effort
   4) impact

5. While conducting a community assessment, the nurse learns that 90 percent of the physicians would not take Medicaid clients because of the paperwork involved and the length of time between service and payment. What is the best community diagnosis?
   1) decreased risk of fraud as shown by a low number of Medicaid clients
   2) increased risk of health problems attributable to physicians' refusal to see Medicaid clients
   3) need-service match because of the number of physicians for non-Medicaid clients
   4) need-service mismatch related to bureaucratic barriers

Sample Questions: Health Support B

6. When a nurse is developing clinical protocols for older adult women with a history of fractures, which nursing activity focuses on secondary prevention?
   1) assessing the home environment
   2) teaching dietary modification
   3) referring for bone-density examination
   4) counseling clients about sensory changes

7. While conducting a windshield survey of River City, the nurse notes that several police cars are visible cruising around town, numerous downtown stores have closed, 25 to 30 young people are waiting for the soup kitchen to open, and the streets contain many potholes. Which community diagnosis should be given highest priority by the nurse?
   1) high potential for crime as shown by the number of police cars cruising the streets
   2) high potential for motor vehicle accidents because of poorly maintained streets
   3) increased risk of health problems because of unemployment and a poor economy
   4) increased risk of violence as shown by the number of young people whose basic needs are unmet

8. While analyzing the data from a community assessment, the nurse notes that the segment of the population with the greatest growth is the group age 65 and over. What is the primary implication related to this data?
   There likely will be an increased need for
   1) health services.
   2) leisure-time programs.
   3) educational opportunities.
   4) retirement planning services.

9. Which action best demonstrates cultural accommodation?
   1) A client consistently comes on time for clinic appointments as a result of the nurse's teaching.
   2) The nurse assists clients in integrating folk remedies into their health care regimens.
   3) The nurse refers client who is an immigrant to an English as a Second Language (ESL) class.
   4) Prenatal classes are planned at a time convenient for fathers to attend.

10. A Chinese American client who follows traditional culture has been prescribed an anti-depressive medication for a severe depressive illness. After a period of time, the family brings the client to the clinic. In evaluating the intervention, why would the nurse ask the client if the prescribed dosage is relieving the symptoms?
    1) Larger doses of psychotropic medications may be necessary in clients of Asian background.
    2) The client may refuse to take the drugs because of religious beliefs.
    3) Evaluation of a therapeutic regimen is a key component of the nursing process.
    4) Asian clients may experience extrapyramidal effects at lower doses.

Sample Questions: Health Support B

11. Which assessment action on the part of the community health nurse could make use of Dever's epidemiologic model as an organizing framework, but could not be addressed using the epidemiologic triad model?
    1) assessing biological risk factors of a client with a family history of coronary heart disease and diabetes
    2) assessing factors that place a family at economic risk after a change in employment status of the major provider
    3) assessing the risk factors and associated health outcomes of families who are homeless and lack access to health care
    4) assessing the impact of sidestream smoke on the health of families with members who are heavy smokers

12. Which important factor contributes to the development of Lyme disease?
    1) season of the year
    2) immunization status of the population
    3) population density
    4) maturation and aging

13. After analyzing assessment data, the nurse develops a program to improve the health of a community and to meet national health objectives related to environmental health. Which action best reflects these goals?
    1) attending town council meetings to solicit monetary support for community-wide blood glucose screenings for undiagnosed diabetes
    2) collecting soil samples from each square mile in the community to test for contamination resulting from improper waste disposal
    3) organizing community support to lobby state legislators to require posting of information related to presence of lead-based paint in all buildings offered for sale
    4) scheduling health fairs at religious and service organizations throughout the community to check blood pressures and provide educational information on hypertension

14. Community members have been experiencing nausea and diarrhea because of using and drinking groundwater contaminated by sewage. Which initial action should the nurse take to resolve this problem?
    1) Alert community members to boil water for 15 minutes before using it.
    2) Collaborate with the town engineer to eliminate the contamination.
    3) Lobby legislators to pass legislation requiring sewage treatment.
    4) Provide supplies of Compazine and Lomotil to control nausea and diarrhea.

15. Which statement about natural radiation is accurate?
    1) Ionizing radiation derives from sources several miles above the earth.
    2) Natural radiation is harmless to human beings.
    3) Radon accounts for most human exposure to ionizing radiation.
    4) Diagnosis of illness induced by natural radiation shows a direct causal relationship.

Sample Questions: Health Support B

16. The occupational health nurse determines that there is an increased incidence of hypertension among workers in an industry. Which initial action should the nurse take?
    1) Set up a blood pressure screening clinic for all the workers to determine the extent of the problem.
    2) Investigate whether a factor in the setting is responsible for the problem.
    3) Make sure the workers who have hypertension have access to care and then monitor compliance.
    4) Provide all employees with information about the dangers of hypertension.

17. The rural health nurse has determined that the community has inadequate emergency care. Which action would be most appropriate for the nurse to take?
    1) Inform the community that their emergency health care system is inadequate.
    2) Wait for an emergency situation before taking action.
    3) Lobby the community to build a hospital in their immediate area.
    4) Develop protocols to assist other nurses in emergency care situations.

18. Which is considered a primary preventive measure in school health nursing?
    1) making referrals to child protective agencies
    2) providing immunizations if necessary
    3) screening for existing health problems
    4) preventing recurrence of acute problems

19. Which group of health assessment areas should receive priority in a client with a history of long-term use of cocaine?
    1) nutrition, sleep and rest, mental status
    2) sexuality, gastrointestinal, vision and hearing
    3) cardiovascular, respiratory, memory
    4) musculoskeletal, neurological, oral cavity

20. The visiting nurse has been caring for a child with neuroblastoma who is now entering the terminal stages of the disease process. What is the most appropriate action for the nurse to take at this time?
    1) Discuss referral to hospice services with the child's family.
    2) Encourage the parents to sign a do-not-resuscitate order.
    3) Suggest that the child's family become involved in a cancer support group.
    4) Teach the family a variety of options for pain control.

21. Which national health objective from *Healthy People 2000* is related to poverty?
    1) improvement of local health department services nationwide
    2) compliance with nutritional guidelines by food services for school-age children
    3) provision of a guaranteed annual income for all citizens
    4) access to preschool programs for all children who are economically disadvantaged

22. The child protective agency asks for services for a family whose two-year-old child fell off the balcony of a second-story apartment. The child suffered only a broken collarbone. The parents are very concerned and say that they had asked the property owner to fix the balcony, but got no help. How would this incident be classified?
    1) child neglect
    2) physical abuse
    3) child maltreatment
    4) medical neglect

Recommended Resources

Primary Textbook
Clark, M.J. (1999). Nursing in the community (3rd ed.). Stamford, CT: Appleton & Lange.

This text provides a thorough introduction to community health nursing and aspects of this practice specialty. This book also provides a summary listing of the national health objectives that have been specified for the year 2000. A computer disk is provided as a study aid.

Supplemental Textbooks
Benenson, A. (1995). Control of communicable disease in man (16th ed.). New York: American Public Health Association.

This manual provides specific information about communicable diseases. Organized alphabetically, the manual presents each disease with a standardized format. Content includes identification of the disease, principal clinical features, laboratory diagnostic procedures, occurrence, reservoir, mode of transmission, incubation period, period of communicability, and methods of control.

Edelman, C., & Mandle, C. (1998). Health promotion throughout the lifespan (4th ed.). St. Louis: Mosby.

This text is based on the *Healthy People 2000* goals, objectives, and strategies. It provides a developmental approach to health data and includes nursing interventions at the primary (health promotion and specific protection) and secondary levels of prevention. This text is also used for the Regents College Examination in Health Support A: Health Promotion & Health Protection and for the Health Assessment and Teaching Performance Examination (HATPE).

Giger, J., & Davidhizar, R. (1995). Transcultural nursing: Assessment and intervention (2nd ed.). St. Louis: Mosby.

This book was written for nurses and nursing students who are interested in developing a knowledge of transcultural concepts to apply to client-centered care. During the last three decades, nurses have begun to develop an appreciation for the need to incorporate culturally appropriate clinical approaches into the daily routine of client care. This book provides a systematic approach to this aspect of client care. This text will be useful in preparing for Content Area III, The Social/Cultural Environment.

Sample Questions: Health Support B

Purnell, L.D., & Paulanka, B.J. (1998). Transcultural health care: A culturally competent approach. *Philadelphia: F.A. Davis.*

This text presents Purnell's model for cultural competence to aid the nurse in learning about cultural groups and avoiding stereotyping. It presents selected characteristics of various cultural groups. This book is also used for the Health Assessment and Teaching Performance Examination (HATPE).

Smeltzer, S., & Bare, B. (1996). Brunner and Suddarth's Textbook of medical-surgical nursing *(8th ed.). Philadelphia: J.B. Lippincott.*

This textbook makes extensive use of diagrams, tables, photographs, charts, and nursing care plans to present information. Each chapter begins with learning objectives and ends with critical-thinking activities and a bibliography. Many color photographs are included. The textbook includes a free self-study disk that contains sample test questions along with rationales for the correct answer.

Valanis, B. (1992). Epidemiology in nursing and health care *(2nd ed.). Norwalk, CT: Appleton & Lange.*

Epidemiology provides ways of thinking about health and disease and tools for critical appraisal of the medical, nursing, and public health literature. This text provides an introduction to the concepts and methods of epidemiology and to issues in the application of epidemiology to clinical practice, public health, and health administration. This text will be useful in studying for Content Area IV, Epidemiology.

Wong, D. (1999). Whaley & Wong's Nursing care of infants and children *(6th ed.). St. Louis: Mosby.*

This textbook covers theoretical and therapeutic interventions for the child within the context of normal growth and development and family interaction, as well as deviations from normal system functioning. The text provides broad coverage of individual, family, and community influences on health/illness states. Key terms are highlighted throughout the text. A study guide is available.

Journal Articles

I. Foundations of Community Health Nursing

Ammerman, A., & Parks, C. (1998). *Preparing students for more effective community interventions: Assets assessment.* Family and Community Health, 21(1), 32–45.

Kang, R. (1995). *Building community capacity for health promotion: A challenge for public health nurses.* Public Health Nursing, 12(5), 312–318.

II. Community as Client

Lindell, D.F. (1997). *Community assessment for the home healthcare nurse.* Home Healthcare Nurse, 15(9), 618–628.

Stevens, P.E. (1996). *Focus groups: Collecting aggregate-level data to understand community health phenomena.* Public Health Nursing, 13(3), 170–176.

III. The Social/Cultural Environment

Chen, Y.D. (1996). *Conformity with nature: A theory of Chinese American elders' health promotion and illness prevention processes.* Advances in Nursing Science, 19(2), 17–26.

Duffy, S.A., Bonino, K., Gallup, L., & Pontseele, R. (1994). *Community baby shower as a transcultural nursing intervention.* Journal of Transcultural Nursing, 5(2), 38–41.

Harvey, A.R., & Rauch, J.B. (1997). *A comprehensive Afrocentric rites of passage program for black male adolescents.* Health and Social Work, 22(1), 30–37.

Sworts, V.D., & Riccitelli, C.N. (1997). *Health education lessons learned: The H.A.P.I. Kids Program...Healthy Asian and Pacific Islander Kids Program.* Journal of School Health, 67(7), 283–285.

IV. Epidemiology

Needleman, C. (1997). *Applied epidemiology and environmental health: Emerging controversies.* American Journal of Infection Control, 25(3), 262–274.

Pastides, H. (1994). *Managing measurable and perceived risk in the occupational setting.* Journal of Ambulatory Care Management, 17(2), 44–52.

Susser, M., & Susser, E. (1996). *Choosing a future for epidemiology: I. Eras and paradigms...including commentary by Koopman, J.S.* American Journal of Public Health, 86(5), 668–673, 630–632.

Susser, M., & Susser, E. (1996). *Choosing a future for epidemiology: II. From black box to Chinese boxes and eco-epidemiology...including commentary by Koopman, J.S.* American Journal of Public Health 86(5), 674–677, 630–632.

V. Environmental Health

Carruth, A.K., Gilbert, K., & Lewis, B. (1997). *Environmental health hazards: The impact on a southern community.* Public Health Nursing, 14(5), 259–267.

King, C., & Harber, P. (1998). *Community environmental health concerns and the nursing process: Four environmental health nursing care plans.* AAOHN Journal, 46(1), 20–27.

Kotchian, S.B. (1995). *Environmental health services are prerequisites to health care.* Family and Community Health, 18(3), 45–53.

Neufer, L. (1994). *The role of the community health nurse in environmental health.* Public Health Nursing, 11(3), 155–162.

Sattler, B. (1996). *Occupational and environmental health: From the back roads to the highways...including commentary by Love, C.* AAOHN Journal, 44(5), 233–237.

VI. Vulnerable Population Groups

Clark, L., Marsh, G.W., Davis, M., Igoe, J., & Stember, M. (1996). *Adolescent health promotion in a low-income, urban environment.* Family and Community Health, 19(1), 1–13.

Duffy, M.E., Bissonnette, A.M., O'Brien, E., & Townsend, D. (1996). *Ending elder homelessness: One city's solution.* Journal of Long Term Home Health Care, 15(4), 38–47.

VII. Community Health Nursing in Specialized Settings

Craig, C. (1994). *Community determinants of health for rural elderly.* Public Health Nursing, 11(4), 242–246.

Dahl, S., Gustafson, C., & McCullagh, M. (1993). *Collaborating to develop a community-based health service for rural homeless persons.* Journal of Nursing Administration, 23(4), 41–45.

Larned, C. (1997). *Crash survivors experiences.* A Journal of Prevention Assessment and Rehabilitation, 8(3), 267–270.

Slagle, M.W., Sun, S.M., & Mathis, M.G. (1998). *A conceptual model of occupational health nursing: The resource model.* AAOHN Journal, 46(3), 121–126.

Worley, N.K. & Sloop, T. (1996). *Psychiatric nursing in a rural outreach program.* Perspectives in Psychiatric Care, 32(2), 10–14.

Yoder, R.E., Preson, D.B., & Forti, E.M. (1997). *Rural school nurses' attitudes about AIDS and homosexuality.* Journal of School Health, 67(8), 341–347.

VIII. Common Community Health Problems

Baldwin, J.A., Rolf, J.E., Johnson, J., Bowers, J., Benally, C., & Trotter, R.T. (1996). *Developing culturally sensitive HIV/AIDS and substance abuse prevention curricula for Native American youth.* Journal of School Health, 66(9), 322–327.

Benson, S. (1997). *The older adult and fear of crime.* Journal of Gerontological Nursing, 23(10), 24–31.

Carrington, B.W., Loftman, P.O., Jones, K., Williams, D., & Witchell, J.L. (1998). *Point of view. The Special Prenatal Clinic: One approach to women and substance abuse.* Journal of Women's Health, 7(2), 189–193.

Gilson, S.F. (1997). *The YMCA Women's Advocacy Program: A case study of domestic violence and sexual assault services.* Journal of Community Practice, 4(4), 1–25.

Kaufman, M.A. (1997). *Wellness for people 65 years and better.* Journal of Gerontological Nursing, 23(6), 7–9.

Paine-Andrews, A., Harris, K.J., Fawcett, S.B., Richter, K.P., Lewis, R.K., Francisco, V.T., Johnston, J., & Coen, S. (1997). *Evaluating a statewide partnership for reducing risks for chronic diseases.* Journal of Community Health, 22(5), 343–359.

Talsma, A., & Abraham, I.L. (1997). *Nursing and health care for an aging society: The case of the Netherlands.* Journal of Gerontological Nursing, 23(9), 37–44.

Williams, M.P. (1996). *Increasing participation in health promotion among older African-Americans.* American Journal of Health Behavior, 20(6), 389-399.

Study Guide

Professional Strategies in Nursing (426) (Baccalaureate Level)

Credit Hours: 4
Question Type(s): Multiple-choice
Credit Level: Upper

The information in this study guide is valid until Summer 2001.
If you will be taking the examination after that date, be sure to check for a new edition of this guide before you complete your preparation for the exam.

General Description of the Examination

The Professional Strategies examination measures knowledge and understanding of the professional role within the occupation of nursing. The examination focuses on the development of the profession, professional practice, and the health care delivery system.

Examination Objectives

You will be expected to demonstrate the ability to:
1. evaluate historical and current trends and issues for their relevance to current and future nursing practice;
2. integrate knowledge of ethical and legal aspects of health care and professional values into nursing practice;
3. use the research process to study problems and use research findings to improve outcomes of nursing practice;
4. comprehend the roles and responsibilities of the professional nurse in relation to the nursing profession and to the health care of society;
5. synthesize knowledge from the humanities, social sciences, natural sciences, and nursing science in making decisions in the practice of professional nursing.

Content Outline

Content Area	Percent of Examination
I. Trends and Events That Have Influenced the Development of the Profession of Nursing (1860–Present)	10%
II. Accountability for Professional Practice	35%
III. Design and Management of Professional Practice	40%
IV. The Health Care Delivery System	15%
Total	**100%**

I. Trends and Events That Have Influenced the Development of the Profession of Nursing (1860–Present) (10%)

A. **Influence of world events and trends**
   1. Religion and religious orders
   2. Wars
   3. Economic factors
   4. Social factors (for example: the role of women in the workforce and society; *Nursing: A Social Policy Statement* [ANA] 1980)
   5. Scientific and technological advances
   6. Unionization movement

B. **Significant studies**
   1. *Nursing and Nursing Education in the United States* (Goldmark Report) 1923
   2. *A Curriculum Guide for Schools of Nursing* (National League for Nursing Education) 1937
   3. *Nursing for the Future* (Brown Report) 1948
   4. *Community College Education for Nursing* (Mildred Montag) 1959
   5. *An Abstract for Action* (Lysaught Report) 1970
   6. *Nursing and Nursing Education: Public Policies and Private Actions* (Institute of Medicine study) 1983
   7. National Commission on Nursing Implementation Project (NCNIP) (ANA; Kellogg) 1985
   8. Pew Health Professions Commission Reports

C. **Nursing organizations** (membership; purposes; functions; impact on nursing, health care, and politics)
   1. International Council of Nurses (ICN)
   2. American Nurses Association (ANA)
   3. American Association of Colleges of Nursing (AACN)
   4. National Council of State Boards of Nursing
   5. National League for Nursing (NLN)
   6. Sigma Theta Tau
   7. National Student Nurses Association (NSNA)
   8. American Academy of Nursing (AAN)
   9. Clinical specialty organizations

D. **Significant leaders** (Florence Nightingale, Mary Mahoney, Isabel Hampton Robb, Lillian Wald, Mary Adelaide Nutting, Isabel M. Stewart, Mildred Montag, Loretta Ford, Abdallah Faye)

E. **Changing patterns in community-based education**
   1. Nightingale model
   2. Diploma programs
   3. Associate degree programs
   4. Baccalaureate degree programs (generic and RN programs)
   5. Masters and doctoral programs
   6. Certificate and practitioner programs
   7. Practical nurse programs
   8. Continuing education

9. Regulatory influences
   a. State and federal government
   b. Nursing organizations (for example: 1965 ANA position paper)

II. Accountability for Professional Practice (35%)

A. Quality management/quality assurance
1. Standards of nursing practice
   a. Purpose
   b. Types
      1) Structure
      2) Process
      3) Outcome
   c. Standards
      1) Generic standards
      2) ANA standards
      3) Specialty organization practice standards
2. Mechanisms for quality assurance
   a. Peer review
   b. Certification
   c. Outcome criteria
   d. Nursing audit
   e. ANA guidelines and model
   f. Utilization review
   g. Risk management
   h. Consumer involvement
3. Regulatory agencies (for example: Joint Commission on Accreditation of Healthcare Organizations [JCAHO], state health departments, federal agencies, Community Health Accreditation Program [CHAP])

B. Legal aspects
1. Statutory regulations
   a. Licensure
      1) Purpose and legal definition
      2) Requirements for licensure
      3) Licensure by endorsement
      4) Grounds for revocation (for example: professional misconduct)
   b. Nurse practice acts
   c. Issues (for example: sunset laws, appropriate roles for the state board of nursing, entry into practice, regulation of changing practice, expanded practice, unlicensed assistive personnel)
2. State boards of nursing
   a. Purpose
   b. Function
3. Civil law
   a. Torts
      1) Negligence (common acts)
      2) Malpractice, including Good Samaritan Act

             3) Slander and libel
          b. Contracts
          c. Legal documents (for example: informed consent, health care records, incident reports, advance directives)
          d. Liability
       4. Criminal and penal law
          a. Assault and battery
          b. Federal drug control legislation
          c. Physical and psychological abuse of others (for example: chemical and physical restraints)

   C. **Ethical aspects**
       1. Values clarification
       2. Rights and obligations in health care
          a. Of consumers—*A Patient's Bill of Rights*
          b. Of providers—personal and professional
       3. Ethical issues in nursing (as they relate to such situations as abortion, clients with HIV, genetic engineering, euthanasia, organ transplants, do-not-resuscitate orders [DNRs], withdrawal of nutrition and hydration)
          a. Self-determination (for example: Patient Self-Determination Act of 1990, advance directives)
          b. Privacy and confidentiality
          c. Reporting illegal and unethical conduct (whistle-blowing)
          d. Allocation of scarce resources
          e. Advocacy
       4. Process of making ethical decisions
       5. Ethical theories (for example: utilitarian, deontological, teleological)
       6. Ethical principles (for example: justice, beneficence, autonomy, nonmaleficence, fidelity)
       7. Personal and professional accountability
          a. Ethics committees
          b. Implementation of the ANA *Code for Nurses* and the ICN *Code for Nurses*

III. Design and Management of Professional Practice (40%)

   A. **Nursing as a profession**
       1. Characteristics of a profession (for example: unique body of knowledge, specialized expertise, autonomy, service, education)
       2. Professional socialization (for example: preceptorships, mentoring, Patricia Benner's model, resocialization of the RN)

   B. **Theoretical basis for professional nursing practice**
       1. Concepts of nursing theory (person [client], nurse, health, environment)
       2. Major nursing theorists (Virginia Henderson, Betty Neuman, Dorothea Orem, Hildegard Peplau, Martha Rogers, Sister Callista Roy, Jean Watson, Madeleine Leininger, Nola Pender)
       3. Application of major nursing theorists to nursing practice (for example: establishing priorities, strategy selection, evaluation of outcomes)

C. **Nursing care delivery**
   1. Types of nursing care delivery
      a. Functional nursing
      b. Team nursing
      c. Primary nursing
      d. Managed care/case management
      e. Differentiated practice
      f. Clinical/critical pathways
   2. Roles of the nurse (for example: provider of care, advocate, collaborator, educator, independent practitioner, member of interdisciplinary health care team)

D. **Strategies employed in the professional role**
   1. Change theory and the process of change
   2. Obtaining and using power
   3. Leadership theory and styles
      a. Styles (for example: democratic, autocratic, laissez-faire)
      b. Theory (for example: path-goal, life cycle)
   4. Management theory (for example: scientific management, human relations, systems)
   5. Management techniques
      a. Time management
      b. Personnel management
      c. Financial management
      d. Planning (for example: strategic, contingency)
      e. Nursing informatics
      f. Nursing classification systems (for example: nursing intervention classification [NIC], nursing outcome criteria [NOC])
   6. Human resource management
      a. Delegation
      b. Conflict management
      c. Communication techniques (for example: assertiveness, management information services)
      d. Managing groups
      e. Decision making (for example: problem solving, critical thinking)
      f. Motivating staff (for example: career mobility opportunities)
      g. Managing staff with special needs (for example: reality shock, burnout, substance abuse)
      h. Collective bargaining
      i. Sexual harassment
      j. Americans with Disabilities Act (ADA)

IV. The Health Care Delivery System (15%)

A. **Development of health care policy and legislation**
   1. Legislative process—development of local, state, and federal legislation
   2. Strategies to affect the political process (for example: negotiating, lobbying, letter writing, testifying, networking)
      a. By the individual nurse

  b. By professional organizations (for example: ANA-PAC, state nursing associations)
  c. By special interest groups
 3. Legislative issues (for example: public policy, universal and equitable access, emphasis on preventive services, cost control, rationing of health care)

B. Planning and organizing health care delivery
 1. Types, functions, and purposes of facilities
  a. Governmental (for example: Veterans Administration, U.S. Public Health Service, state health departments)
  b. Private, for profit (for example: Humana, Hospital Corporation of America, proprietary home health agencies)
  c. Voluntary, nonprofit (for example: community hospitals, hospice)
  d. Managed care (preferred provider organizations [PPOs], independent practice associations [IPAs], health maintenance organizations [HMOs], managed care organizations [MCOs])
 2. Impact of health status indicators
  a. Epidemiological trends
  b. Demographic trends
 3. Impact of societal challenges (for example: deinstitutionalization, state and federal health department regulations, changing focus of health care, disenfranchised populations, cultural diversity, accessibility and availability of services, maldistribution of health care providers)

C. Current issues in financing health care
 1. Reimbursement methods
  a. Personal payment or fee for service
  b. Workers' compensation
  c. Medicare
  d. Medicaid
  e. Private insurance (traditional, health maintenance organizations [HMOs], preferred provider organizations [PPOs])
 2. Cost containment measures (for example: diagnosis-related groups [DRGs], managed care, professional review organizations, Health Care Financing Administration)
 3. Economics of nursing care (for example: patient classification systems, maldistribution of providers, direct reimbursement for nursing service)
 4. Health care reform and national health insurance

Sample Questions: Professional Strategies in Nursing

1. Which was the major effect of the Civil War on the development of nursing in the United States?
    1) The army built multiple small field hospitals and oriented a corps to care for the sick and wounded.
    2) Religious nursing orders that had supplied most of the nurses for the war effort expanded greatly.
    3) The public learned of the need for trained nurses to care for the wounded soldiers.
    4) The American Red Cross trained a reserve corps of volunteer nurses who could be called as necessary.

2. Which was a direct result of the service given by the nurses who served in the Spanish-American War?
    1) recognition of the need for education about cultural differences in nursing schools
    2) development of nursing theory about how to care for persons with communicable diseases
    3) establishment of the role of the nurse as a researcher because nurses helped in the study of typhoid fever
    4) establishment of a permanent Army Nurse Corps comprised of hospital-trained female nurses

3. What was the purpose of the 1970 study *An Abstract for Action*?
    1) to survey nurses' attitudes towards their work roles and job satisfactions
    2) to improve the delivery of health care by improving the nursing profession
    3) to study nursing programs for their potential to ease the nursing shortage
    4) to assess the extent to which the nursing process was being utilized by nurses

4. What is the primary purpose of using retrospective chart audits in a nursing quality assurance program?
    1) to acquire data about the process of client care
    2) to evaluate the performance of individual nurses, teams of nurses, and nursing units
    3) to identify deficiencies in the documentation of client care
    4) to collect data about client outcomes for the purpose of evaluating nursing care

5. A nurse would like to find out if adding an anesthetic agent to the epidural line of a client in labor is within the scope of nursing practice. Which action would give the nurse the most reliable information?
    1) Ask an obstetrician.
    2) Write to the state board of nursing.
    3) Research the question through review of current journal articles.
    4) Ask the agency's nurse administrator for a ruling.

Sample Questions: Professional Strategies in Nursing

6. In most states, if a client signs a consent form for a procedure but the procedure has not been fully explained, the client can bring which charges to court?
    1) assault
    2) battery
    3) fraud
    4) negligence

7. What should the nurse do if asked to witness a will for a client?
   The nurse should
    1) agree, and ask to review the document before signing it.
    2) agree, and note on the chart the client's apparent mental condition at the time of the signing.
    3) decline, as it is against professional standards for nurses to witness wills.
    4) decline, as it is generally against hospital standards for nurses to witness wills.

8. How are the AHA *Patient's Bill of Rights* and the ANA *Code for Nurses* similar?
    1) Both address incompetent practice.
    2) Both focus on the client.
    3) Both place importance on respect for clients.
    4) Both emphasize the client's right to information.

9. After arranging his schedule to visit six clients today, a community health nurse receives a referral for an emergency visit to a new client. Using the principle of distributive justice, how would the nurse respond to this situation?
    1) Reschedule the least needy of the six clients to another day and include the new client today.
    2) Tell the referring physician that today's schedule has already been set and the new client cannot be added.
    3) Choose randomly to reschedule one of the six clients to another day and add the new client today.
    4) Reduce visiting time with each of the six clients and use the remaining time to visit the new client.

10. What is the major ethical function of an institutional review board in a health care facility?
    1) to evaluate the merits of research protocols intended for use with clients
    2) to protect clients from being deprived of personal rights and dignity
    3) to determine whether research projects are potentially beneficial to the institution
    4) to solve ethical dilemmas that arise with clients in the institution

11. Which nursing behavior reflects autonomy in nursing practice?
    1) cultivating a professional attitude
    2) demonstrating accountability in practice
    3) learning how to become a change agent
    4) developing fee-for-service mechanisms

Sample Questions: Professional Strategies in Nursing

12. Which statement best describes Patricia Benner's novice to expert model of professional socialization?
    1) Thorough knowledge and understanding of the nursing process is basic to entry into nursing.
    2) Application of theory to practice is reflected in the professionally mature nurse.
    3) Excellence in the application of technical tools and procedures is essential to success in nursing.
    4) Experience is absolutely necessary for the development of professional expertise.

13. What should be accomplished during the social integration stage of resolving reality shock, according to the Kramer model of socialization?
    1) executing skills and routines proficiently
    2) implementing conflict resolution
    3) maintaining professional standards while fitting into the work group
    4) managing priorities within the organization of the workplace

14. Which nursing action is an example of tertiary prevention as described by Betty Neuman?
    1) Give the client who has recently achieved a weight-loss goal the meeting place and time for a weight-loss maintenance group.
    2) Provide a client who is four weeks postpartum with information on diet and exercise to attain a desired weight loss.
    3) Make an appointment for a client with obesity to meet with the dietician to initiate discussion of meal planning.
    4) Validate with the client the value of current diet and exercise habits for the retention of health.

15. Using Martha Rogers's nursing model, how would nurses view their professional role?
    1) Nurses use intellectual judgment and scientific knowledge in interacting in creative, innovative ways to promote patterns of living that are in harmony with the environment.
    2) Nurses deliberately select and perform actions that assist individuals with self-care in a way that contributes to maintenance and promotion of structural integrity, functioning, and development.
    3) Nurses perceive clients as biopsychosocial beings who may be experiencing unusual stressors, and promote clients' effective coping and progress toward integration.
    4) Nurses in a complementary role assist clients who are sick or well, and work toward the goal of helping clients gain independence as rapidly as possible.

Sample Questions: Professional Strategies in Nursing

16. What is the purpose of the case management approach to nursing care delivery?
    1) to ensure that clients are discharged from the hospital within the guidelines for diagnosis-related groups (DRGs)
    2) to make client assignments based on care providers' level of education and experience
    3) to ensure that clients receive the services they need in an efficient and cost-effective manner
    4) to provide each client with a single nurse who will be responsible for the delivery of consistent and comprehensive care

17. Which role is the nurse fulfilling when the nurse includes the client and family members in the development of a plan of care for the client?
    1) client advocate
    2) collaborator
    3) educator
    4) independent practitioner

18. How can the nurse manager best utilize the services of the clinical nurse specialist assigned to the unit?
    1) Ask the specialist to develop unit policies and procedures.
    2) Seek the specialist's knowledge in the staff's care of the client who is most difficult.
    3) Have the specialist evaluate the staff's nursing care.
    4) Give the specialist responsibility for updating all nursing care plans written by the staff.

19. A staff nurse decides to study for a master's degree in nursing administration. How will this activity assist the nurse in achieving power in the workplace?
    1) by earning the nurse the respect of physicians
    2) by serving as a role model to other staff nurses who wish to pursue master's degrees
    3) by enhancing the nurse's qualifications as an applicant for a line authority position
    4) by increasing the nurse's knowledge of direct client care

20. Which would be the most effective way for nurses to improve the delivery of health care?
    1) Increase their awareness of public needs.
    2) Understand and become involved in public policy formation.
    3) Standardize educational requirements for nursing.
    4) Write grants for individual projects to study health care.

21. Which was an underlying factor that influenced the development of health maintenance organizations (HMOs)?
    1) balancing the loss of inpatient revenues
    2) facilitating reimbursement for physician claims
    3) reducing the cost of health care by providing preventive treatment
    4) increasing the opportunities for access to health care

Sample Questions: Professional Strategies in Nursing

22. Which nursing action would be most characteristic of the nurse practitioner in a health maintenance organization (HMO)?
    1) providing primary care for a specific group of clients
    2) assuming responsibility for individual client education rather than for group education
    3) screening all telephone calls and, based on client needs, referring clients to particular physicians
    4) obtaining hospital admitting privileges for routine client workups

23. What was the primary purpose of the development of health maintenance organizations (HMOs)?
    1) to emphasize health promotion and maintenance
    2) to offer comprehensive health care
    3) to provide a cost-effective alternative to traditional fee-for-service care
    4) to utilize nonphysician health care providers efficiently

Recommended Resources

The examination development committee recommends that you obtain all of the textbooks listed below for your use in preparing for the examination. The group of textbooks as a whole provides very good coverage of the topics on the content outline.

Aiken, T. (with Catalano, J.) (1994). Legal, ethical, and political issues in nursing. *Philadelphia: F.A. Davis.*

Huber, D. (1996). Leadership and nursing care management. *Philadelphia: W.B. Saunders.*

Kelly, L., & Joel, L. (1999). Dimensions of professional nursing *(8th ed.). New York: McGraw-Hill.*

Leddy, S., & Pepper, J. (1998). Conceptual bases of professional nursing *(4th ed.). Philadelphia: Lippincott-Raven.*

Schwirian, P.M. (1998). Professionalization of nursing: Current issues and trends *(3rd ed.). Philadelphia: Lippincott-Raven.*

Ellis, J.R., & Hartley, C.L. (1998). Nursing in today's world: challenges, issues, and trends. *Philadelphia: Lippincott-Raven.*

McCloskey, J.C., & Grace, H.K. (1997). Current issues in nursing *(5th ed.). Philadelphia: Mosby.*

Additional Resources

Textbooks

Catalame, J.T. (1996) Contemporary professional nursing. *Philadelphia: F.A. Davis.*

Chitty, K. (1993). Professional nursing: Concepts and challenges. *Philadelphia: W.B. Saunders (Content Areas IA, IC, ID, IE, IIB, IIC, IIIA, IIIB, IIIC, IVB, IVC)*

George, J. (1995). Nursing theories: The base of professional nursing practice *(4th ed.). Norwalk, CT: Appleton & Lange (Content Areas IIIA, IIIB)*

Harrington, C., & Estes, C. (1993). Health policy and nursing: Crisis and reform in the U.S. health care delivery system. *Boston: Jones and Bartlett. (Content Areas IVB, IVC)*

Sample Questions: Professional Strategies in Nursing

Kozier, B., Erb, G., & Blais, K. (1992). *Concepts and issues in nursing practice* (2nd ed.). Menlo Park, CA: Addison-Wesley. (Content Areas IA, IC, IE, IIB, IIC, IIIA, IIIB, IIIC, IVB)

Marquis, B., & Huston, C. (1992). *Leadership roles and management functions in nursing: Theory and application.* Philadelphia: J.B. Lippincott. (Content Areas IIB, IIIC, IIID)

Mitchell, P., & Grippando, G. (1993). *Nursing perspectives and issues* (5th ed.). Albany, NY: Delmar. (Content Areas IA, IB, IC, ID, IE, IIA, IIB, IIIB, IIIC, IVA, IVB)

Oermann, M. (1991) *Professional nursing practice: A conceptual approach.* Philadelphia: J.B. Lippincott. (Content Areas IIB, IIIA, IIIB)

Stanhope, M., & Lancaster, J. (1996). *Community health nursing: Promoting health of aggregates, families, and individuals* (4th ed.). St. Louise: Mosby. (Content Areas IA, IIA, IVB, IVC)

Sullivan, E., & Decker, P. (1992). *Effective management in nursing* (3rd ed.). Menlo Park, CA: Addison-Wesley. (Content Areas IIA, IIIC, IIID)

Tappen, R. (1995) *Nursing leadership and management: Concepts and practice* (3rd ed.). Philadelphia: F.A. Davis.

Zerwekh, J., & Claborn, J. (1994). *Nursing today: Transition and trends.* Philadelphia: W.B. Saunders. (Content Areas IA, IC, ID, IE, IIB, IIC, IIID, IVA)

Articles

I. Trends and Events That Have Influenced the Development of the Profession of Nursing (1860–Present)

Backer, B. (1993). *Lillian Wald: Connecting caring with activism.* Nursing and Health Care, 14(3), 122–129.

Christy, T.E. (1969). *Portrait of a leader: Isabel H. Robb.* Nursing Outlook, 17(3), 26+.

Christy, T.E. (1969). *Portrait of a leader: Isabel Maitland Stewart.* Nursing Outlook, 17(3), 44+.

Christy, T.E. (1969). *Portrait of a leader: M. Adelaide Nutting.* Nursing Outlook, 17(3), 46+.

Christy, T.E. (1970). *Portrait of a leader: Lillian D. Wald.* Nursing Outlook, 18(3), 50+.

Christy, T.E. (1975). *The fateful decade.* American Journal of Nursing, 23(7), 1163+ (Isabel Robb, Lavinia Dock, M. Adelaide Nutting).

Cook, P.R. (1995). *Isabel Stewart, nursing education leader.* Nursing and Health Care, 16(1), 20–23.

Gropper, E.I. (1990). *Said another way: Florence Nightingale: Nursing's first environmental theorist.* Nursing Forum, 25(3), 30–33.

Keeling, A.W., & Ramos, M.C. (1995). *The role of nursing history in preparing nursing for the future.* Nursing and Health Care, 16(1), 24–29.

Kippembrook, T. (1991). *Wish I'd been there: A sense of nursing's history.* Nursing and Health Care, 12(4), 208–212.

Larsen, E. (1995). *Twenty years: The American Academy of Nursing and the Institute of Medicine in perspective.* Nursing Outlook, 43(3), 105–111.

Macrae, J. (1995). *Nightingale's spiritual philosophy and its significance for modern nursing.* Image, 27, 8–14.

Maraldo, P.J. (1992). *NLN's first century.* Nursing and Health Care, 13(5), 227–228.

McBurney, B.H., & Filoromo, T. (1994). *The Nightingale pledge: 100 years later.* Nursing Management, 25(2), 72–74.

Olson, T. (1995). *Recreating past separations and the employment patterns of nurses 1900–1940.* Nursing Outlook, 43(5), 210–214.

Parker, J. (1994). *Development of the American board of nursing specialties.* Nursing Management, 25(1), 33–35.

Stratton, T. et al. (1995). *Redefining the nursing shortage: A rural perspective.* Nursing Outlook, 43(2), 71–77.

II. Accountability for Professional Practice

Ammon-Gaberson, K.B., & Piantanida, M. (1988). *Generating results from qualitative data.* Image, 20(3), 159–161.

Cohen, M.Z. et al. (1994). *Knowledge and presence: Accountability as described by nurses and surgical patients.* Journal of Professional Nursing, 10(3), 177–185.

Fiesta, J. (1995). *Home care liability.* Nursing Management, 26(11), 24–26.

Fox, A.E. (1994). *Ethical issues: Confronting the use of placebos for pain.* American Journal of Nursing, 94(9), 42–45.

Fry-Revere, S. (1994). *Ethics consultation: An update on accountability issues.* Pediatric Nursing, 20(1), 95–98.

Haddad, A. (1995). *Acute care decisions: Ethics in action.* RN, 58(11), 17–18.

Henkelman, W. (1994). *Inadequate pain management: Ethical considerations.* Nursing Management, 25(1), 48A–48D.

Hughes, T.L., & Smith, L.L. (1994). *Is your colleague chemically impaired?* American Journal of Nursing, 94(9), 31–35.

Jones, L.C. (1994). *A right to die?* Intensive and Critical Care Nursing, 10(4), 278–288.

Lang, N.M. (1995). *Quality assurance: The foundation of professional care.* The Journal of the American Nurses Association, 26(1), 48–50.

Liaschenko, J. (1995). *Ethics in the work of acting for patients.* Advances in Nursing Science, 18(2), 1–12.

Martin, P.A. (1994). *The utility of the research problem statement.* Applied Nursing Research, 7(1), 47–49.

Martin, P.A. (1994). *Responsibilities when the patient is a research subject.* Applied Nursing Research, 7(3), 158–161.

Martin, P.A. (1995). *Recruitment of research subjects.* Applied Nursing Research, 8(1), 50–54.

Michel, Y., & Sneed, N.V. (1995). *Dissemination and use of research findings in nursing practice.* Journal of Professional Nursing, 11(5), 306–311.

Ott, B. (1995). *The human genome project: An overview of ethical issues and public policy concerns.* Nursing Outlook, 43(5), 228–231.

Pieper, B. (1994). *A research primer.* Journal of Wound, Ostomy, and Continence Nursing, 21(1), 26–33.

Pieranunzi, V.R. (1992). *Informed consent with children and adolescents.* Journal of Child and Adolescent Psychiatric Mental Health Nursing, 5(2), 21–27.

Polit, D.F., & Sherman, R.E. (1990). *Statistical power in nursing research.* Nursing Research, 39(6), 355–368.

Rafael, A.R. (1995). *Advocacy and empowerment: Dichotomous or synchronous concepts?* Advances in Nursing Science, 18(2), 25–32.

Richman, D., & Valentini, S.M. (1995). *Legally speaking: If you're asked to be a health care proxy.* RN, 58(11), 51–55.

Rushton, C.H., & Infante, M.C. (1995). *Keeping secrets.* The Ethical and Legal Challenges, 21(5), 479–481.

Simpson, R. (1995). *Ethics in the information age.* Nursing Management, 26(11), 20–21.

Vergara, M., & Lynn-McHale, D. (1995). *Withdrawing life support: Who decides?* AJN, 95(11), 47–49.

III. Design and Management of Professional Practice

American Organization of Nurse Executives. (1994). *Differentiated competencies for nursing practice.* Nursing Management, 25(9), 34–35.

Boynton, D. (1995). *State managing change: Supporting new patient care models.* Nursing Economics, 13(3), 166–173.

Brooks, B., & Rosenberg, S. (1995). *Incorporating nursing theory into a nursing department's strategic plan.* Nursing Management, 26(11), 81–86.

Capriano, T. (1995). *Clinical pathways: Practical approaches, positive outcomes.* Nursing Management, 26(1), 34–37.

Davis, P.D. (1995). *Enhancing multicultural harmony: Ten actions for nurse managers.* Nursing Management, 26(7), 32A–32H.

Forsey, L.M., Cleland, V.S., & Miller, R. (1993). *Job descriptions for differentiated nursing practice and differentiated pay.* Journal of Nursing Administration, 23(5), 33–40.

Garon, M. (1992). *Contributions of Martha Rogers to the development of nursing knowledge.* Nursing Outlook, 40(2), 67–72.

Green, A. et al. (1995). *Are you at risk for disciplinary action?* AJN, 95(7), 36–42.

Gudmunsen, A.M. (1995). *Personal reflections on Martha Rogers.* Nursing and Health Care, 16(1), 36–37.

Havens, D.S. (1994). *Is governance being shared?* Journal of Nursing Administration, 24(6), 59–64.

Hernandez, C.A. et al. (1995). *Increasing the validity of a quality monitoring methodology.* Nursing Management, 26(10), 41–45.

Herrick, K. et al. (1994). *My license is not on the line: The art of delegation.* Nursing Management, 25(2), 48–50.

Hines, P. (1994). *Work restructuring: The process of redefining roles of patient caregivers.* Nursing Economics, 12(6), 346–350.

Koester, J. et al. (1995). *A nursing career leadership program.* Nursing Management, 26(9), 84–88.

Manion, J. (1995). *Understanding the seven stages of change.* AJN, 95(4), 41–43.

Pophal, L.G. (1995). *Dealing with co-worker conflicts.* Nursing 95, 25(11), 78–81.

Porter-O'Grady, T. (1995). *Managing along the continuum: A new paradigm for the clinical manager.* Nursing Administration Quarterly, 19(3), 1–12.

Queen, V. (1995). *Performance evaluation.* Nursing Management, 26(9), 52–55.

Vena, C., & Oldaker, S. (1994). *Differentiated practice: The new paradigm using a theoretical approach.* Nursing Administration Quarterly, 19(1), 66–73.

Wendle, P.E., & Houston, S. (1995). *Continuous outcome measurement technique improving patient outcomes.* Nursing Management, 26(9), 64DD, 64FF–64II.

IV. The Health Care Delivery System

Aiken, L. (1995). *Transformation of the nursing workforce.* Nursing Outlook, 43(5), 201–209.

Biordi, D. (1995). *Accounting for nursing costs by DRG... Selected authors from 1985 update their articles.* Journal of Nursing Administration, 25(1), 6–8.

Blouin, A. (1994). *Revisiting collective bargaining.* Journal of Nursing Administration, 24(9), 9–10.

Buerhaus, P. (1994). *Price controls, health care reform, and new RN shortages.* Nursing Economics, 12(6), 309–317.

Sample Questions: Professional Strategies in Nursing

Buerhaus, P. (1995). Economic pressures building in the hospital employed RN labor market. Nursing Economics, 13*(3)*, 137–141.

Brooten, D. (1995). Nurses' effect on changing patient outcomes. Image, 27*(2)*, 95–99.

Chamberlain, P. et al. (1995). Innovative cultural shock prescribed for health care. Nursing Outlook, 43*(5)*, 232–234.

Dickerson, S. (1994). Interpreting political agendas from a critical social theory perspective. Nursing Outlook, 42*(6)*, 265–271.

Haas, S.A. et al. (1995). Dimensions of the staff nurse role in ambulatory care: Part II: Comparison of role dimensions in four ambulatory settings. Nursing Economics, 13*(3)*, 152–165.

Hutchens, G.C. (1994). Differentiated interdisciplinary practice. Journal of Nursing Administration, 24*(6)*, 52–58.

Koerner, J. (1992). Differentiated practice: The evolution of professional nursing. Journal of Professional Nursing, 8*(6)*, 335–341.

Moss, M. (1994). Service integration in a reform era. Nursing Economics, 12*(5)*, 256–260.

Sharp, N. (1995). Legislative effects: What's next? Medicare: What's happening? Nursing Management, 26*(11)*, 58–59.

Study Guide

Research in Nursing (537) (Baccalaureate Level)

Credit Hours: 3   **Credit Level:** Upper
Question Type(s): Multiple-choice and Free Response

The information in this study guide is valid until Summer 2001.
If you will be taking the examination after that date, be sure to check for a new edition of this guide before you complete your preparation for the exam.

General Description of the Examination

The Research in Nursing examination measures knowledge and understanding of material typically taught in a one-semester, upper-level course in a baccalaureate program. The examination tests for a knowledge and understanding of the research process and the ability to apply this information to critiquing a research study. The content covered on the examination consists of four major categories: foundations of research, quantitative research, qualitative research, and critique of a research study. A knowledge and understanding of statistics is assumed.

You may prepare for this examination by following an independent program of study based on the study materials listed in this guide. This program of study is fully outlined in the Regents College *Course Guide for the Research in Nursing Examination*. The course guide is described on page xx, immediately following the content outline.

Examination Objectives

You will be expected to demonstrate the ability to:
1. comprehend ethical issues related to research;
2. apply knowledge of concepts fundamental to quantitative and qualitative research;
3. comprehend the roles and responsibilities of the professional nurse in relation to participation in research and implementation of research findings;
4. evaluate research studies for applicability to nursing practice.

Content Outline

The major content areas on the examination and the number of questions devoted to each content area are listed below.

Content Area	Questions on Examination
I. Foundations of Research—multiple-choice	25
II. Quantitative Research—multiple-choice	25
III. Qualitative Research—multiple-choice	10
IV. Critique of a Research Study—free response	1

NOTE: *The chapter numbers and titles provided within the content outline below refer to specific chapters in the recommended textbook for this examination (see page 540, Recommended Resources). Chapter numbers and titles may differ in subsequent editions.*

I. Foundations of Research (25 questions)
LoBiondo-Wood & Haber (1998):
    Chapter 1, The Role of Research in Nursing
    Chapter 2, Overview of the Research Process
    Chapter 3, Research Problems and Hypotheses
    Chapter 4, Literature Review
    Chapter 5, Theoretical Framework
    Chapter 11, Legal and Ethical Issues
    Chapter 19, Use of Research in Practice

A. Ethical considerations (Chapter 11)
1. Protection of human subjects
   a. Informed consent
      1) Elements of informed consent (for example: confidentiality, anonymity, may refuse to participate without penalty)
      2) Written, oral, or implied consent
   b. Institutional review boards (for example: at hospitals, at universities)
   c. Vulnerable subjects (for example: children, people who are terminally ill)
   d. Recruitment of subjects
   e. Concealment
2. Historical background
   a. Nazi medical experiments
   b. Tuskegee syphilis study
3. Researcher misconduct (for example: unauthorized research, scientific fraud, deception)
4. Professional ethics research guidelines
   a. *Nuremberg code*
   b. *Belmont Report*
   c. *Human Rights Guidelines for Nurses in Clinical and Other Research* (ANA, 1975)

B. Overview of the research process (Chapters 1 and 2)
1. Importance of nursing research to professional nursing practice (for example: explosion of knowledge, professional accountability)
2. Role of the nurse in research based on the nurse's educational preparation (for example: at the baccalaureate level, to read research critically and to use existing standards to determine readiness of research for utilization in clinical practice)
3. Evolution of nursing research
   a. Past, present, and future trends (for example: shift from research on nursing education to research on nursing practice)
   b. Research priorities within the nursing profession
4. Characteristics of the scientific approach
5. Inductive vs. deductive reasoning (Chapter 5, pp. 136–138)
6. Basic vs. applied research
7. Quantitative vs. qualitative research—research beliefs, activities, and questions (Chapter 3)
8. Content and organization of research reports

C. Research utilization (Chapter 19)
1. Barriers to using research in clinical practice
2. Strategies to overcome barriers
3. Responsibility for using valid research findings in clinical practice (responsibility of the researcher, the clinical practitioner, and the nurse administrator)
4. Research utilization process
5. Criteria for research utilization
   a. Clinical relevance
   b. Scientific merit
   c. Implementation potential (for example: feasibility for use in practice, risk/benefit ratio)
   d. Replication
6. Landmarks of research utilization
   a. Agency for Health Care Policy and Research (AHCPR)
   b. Conduct and Use of Research in Nursing (CURN) project
   c. National Child Assessment Satellite Training (NCAST)
   d. National Institute of Nursing Research (NINR)
   e. Stetler utilization model
   f. Western Interstate Commission for Higher Education (WICHE) project

D. Review of the literature (Chapters 4 and 5)
1. Conducting a literature search
   a. Library activities (for example: use of computer databases, such as Cumulative Index to Nursing and Allied Health Literature [CINAHL])
   b. Primary vs. secondary sources
2. Purposes of a literature review (for example: as a basis for every stage of the research process, such as specifying the problem, evaluating the problem, identifying the variables, and developing the methodology)
3. Theoretical/conceptual framework for study (for example: purpose of the theoretical/conceptual framework; difference among concepts, constructs, and theories; differences between conceptual and operational definitions)
4. Characteristics of a well-written literature review

E. **The research problem** (Chapter 3)
    1. Sources of research problems (for example: nursing practice, prior research)
    2. Development and refinement of a research problem
    3. Criteria for evaluation of a research problem
        a. Significance to nursing
        b. Testability
        c. Feasibility
    4. Statement of a research problem
        a. Forms of the statement—interrogative and declarative
        b. Characteristics of a well-written problem statement
    5. The research problem in quantitative research vs. in qualitative research

II. Quantitative Research (25 questions)
LoBiondo-Wood & Haber (1998):
    Chapter 3, Research Problems and Hypotheses
    Chapter 6, Introduction to Design
    Chapter 7, Experimental and Quasiexperimental Designs
    Chapter 8, Nonexperimental Designs
    Chapter 10, Sampling
    Chapter 12, Data Collection Methods
    Chapter 13, Reliability and Validity
    Chapter 14, Decriptive Data Analysis
    Chapter 15, Inferential Data Analysis
    Chapter 16, Analysis of the Findings

A. **Hypothesis** (Chapter 3)
    1. Relationship among research problem, theory, and hypothesis
    2. Appropriate use of hypothesis and appropriate use of research question
    3. Characteristics of a research hypothesis
        a. Independent variable
        b. Dependent variable
        c. Population
        d. Relationship statement
        e. Testability
    4. Types of hypotheses
        a. Statistical (null) and research
        b. Directional and nondirectional
    5. Testing the null hypothesis (Chapter 15, pp. 370–376)
        a. Level of significance
        b. Type I error
        c. Type II error
    6. Statistical vs. practical significance

B. **Research design** (Chapters 6, 7, and 8)
    1. Experimental designs
        a. Purposes
        b. Characteristics
            1) Manipulation of independent variable(s)
            2) Control

3) Random assignment
   c. Types
      1) True or classic experiment
      2) Solomon four-group design
      3) After-only experimental design
   d. Advantages and disadvantages
2. Quasi-experimental designs
   a. Purposes
   b. Characteristics (for example: nonrandom assignment)
   c. Types
      1) Nonequivalent control group design
      2) After-only nonequivalent control group design
      3) Time series design
   d. Advantages and disadvantages
3. Nonexperimental designs
   a. Purposes
   b. Characteristics (for example: naturally occurring groups, no investigator manipulation)
   c. Types
      1) Descriptive/exploratory survey studies
      2) Interrelationship studies
         (a) Correlational
         (b) Ex post facto
         (c) Cross-sectional and longitudinal
         (d) Retrospective and prospective
   d. Advantages and disadvantages
4. Design validity
   a. Internal validity
   b. External validity
   c. Threats to validity (for example: Hawthorne effect, attrition/mortality, maturation, history, selection)
5. Strategies to control for extraneous variables

C. **Sampling** (Chapter 10)
   1. Types of populations
      a. Target
      b. Accessible
   2. Types of samples
      a. Probability
         1) Simple random
         2) Stratified random
         3) Cluster
         4) Systematic
      b. Nonprobability
         1) Convenience
         2) Quota
         3) Purposive
   3. Determination of sample size (for example: power analysis, accessibility of subjects, cost)
   4. Strategies for randomization (for example: use of table of random numbers)

5. Random sampling from a population vs. random assignment to a group
6. Criteria for evaluating the sample (for example: representativeness, selection bias)

D. **Data collection** (Chapters 12 and 13)
1. Appropriate use of data collection methods in relation to problem statement and design
2. Data collection methods
   a. Physiological or biological
   b. Observation
   c. Interviews and questionnaires (for example: open-ended; closed-ended, such as Likert scales)
   d. Records or available data
3. Instrument reliability and validity
   a. Reliability
      1) Stability (for example: test-retest reliability, parallel or alternate forms)
      2) Homogeneity (for example: item-total correlation, split-half reliability, Kuder-Richardson coefficient, Cronbach's alpha)
      3) Equivalence (for example: parallel or alternate forms, interrater reliability)
   b. Validity
      1) Content
      2) Criterion-related
      3) Construct
4. Advantages and disadvantages of data collection methods

E. **Data analysis/interpretation** (Chapters 14, 15, and 16)
1. Levels of measurement
   a. Nominal
   b. Ordinal
   c. Interval
   d. Ratio
2. Descriptive statistics—situationally describing variables
   a. Frequency distributions (normal, skewed, bimodal)
   b. Measures of central tendency (mean, median, mode)
   c. Measures of variability (percentages, range, standard deviation)
3. Correlational statistics—measuring strength of a relationship
   a. Pearson r
   b. Multiple regression
   c. Factor analysis
4. Inferential statistics—testing differences between variables
   a. Parametric (for example: t tests, analysis of variance [ANOVA])
   b. Nonparametric (for example: chi-square)
5. Relationship among variable, its level of measurement, and choice of statistics

III. Qualitative Research (10 questions)
LoBiondo-Wood & Haber (1998):
      Chapter 9, Qualitative Approaches to Research

A. Topics appropriate for study

B. Types of qualitative research
1. Ethnography
2. Phenomenology
3. Historical method
4. Grounded theory

C. Data gathering and data analysis
1. Coding
2. Search for themes (for example: central meanings, domains)
3. Constant comparative method
4. External and internal criticism of historical documents
5. Data saturation
6. Bracketing

D. Criteria for establishing rigor

IV. Critique of a Research Study (1 free response question)

The material in content areas I–III serves as a foundation for the content covered in area IV. The student is expected to apply appropriate material in content areas I–III in critiquing an abbreviated research study. For content area IV, the student will respond to one (1) four-part free response question, worth a maximum of 20 points. The question will involve reading an abbreviated version of a research study and using a set of directives to guide the response. The research study is presented on the computer screen. The response will be written in a separate answer booklet especially designed for the Research in Nursing–BSN examination.

In addition to the directives for each part of the response, the student will be given criteria for critiquing a research study and instructed to use them as a guide for the analysis and evaluation of the research study. The **Instructions to Guide the Student's Response to the Free Response Question** section below will be provided on a separate reference card at the testing center.

The report presented will be a quantitative research study dealing with a common clinical nursing topic and will include all of the major sections that would be included in a research report published in a nursing research journal. An example of a research study is included in the Sample Questions section of this guide. The student is to assume that the rights of the subjects have been ensured and that informed consent has been obtained, that the statistical test(s) is(are) appropriate, and that the statistical data are calculated correctly.

Instructions to Guide the Student's Response to the Free Response Question:
Critically appraise the quantitative research study [see example on page 538]. The report is an abbreviated version of a fictitious research study. It includes all of the major sections that would be included in a research report published in a nursing research journal.

Use the twelve (12) criteria for critiquing a research study that follow to guide your analysis and evaluation. Fully address each of the four (4) directives found [below], using the special answer booklet that has been provided. Include details from the study to support your response.

Assume that the rights of subjects have been ensured and that informed consent has been obtained. Also assume that the statistical test(s) is(are) appropriate and that the statistical data are calculated correctly. However, do <u>not</u> assume that the researcher's interpretation of the findings is accurate.

Directives:
1. Identify the two (2) variables being studied and label them as independent or dependent. Indicate the type of quantitative design used (i.e., experimental, quasi-experimental, or nonexperimental). (2 points)
2. Identify three (3) distinct strengths of the research study. Each strength must relate to a different critiquing criterion. Explain why they are strengths, using your knowledge of the research process and details from the research study to support your reasoning. (6 points)
3. Identify three (3) distinct weaknesses of the research study. Each weakness must relate to a different critiquing criterion. Explain why they are weaknesses, using your knowledge of the research process and details from the research study to support your reasoning. (6 points)

NOTE: Several of the criteria have multiple parts. You may use part of a single criterion as a strength and another part of the same criterion as a weakness. However, you may not use the same criterion for more than one strength or more than one weakness.

4. Apply research utilization concepts by doing the following: (Total: 6 points)
   A. Present a logical conclusion about whether or not the strengths outweigh the weaknesses in importance. Provide a rationale to support your conclusion. Your rationale must identify which strengths or weaknesses you determine to be most significant. Consider the strengths and weaknesses of the entire study, not just those cited in your response to Directives 2 and 3. (2 points)
   B. Based on your critique of this study, discuss whether or not you would utilize the findings of the study to either support or change nursing practice. Provide a rationale supporting your decision. (2 points)
   C. Independent of the findings of the study, discuss the importance of this research problem to nursing practice. Provide a rationale supporting your position. (2 points)

Criteria for Critiquing a Research Study

1. The problem statement or purpose clearly identifies the variables, expresses the relationship between the variables, specifies the population, implies the possibility of empirical study, and indicates significance for nursing.
2. The review of the literature consists mainly of current sources, mainly of primary sources, addresses the relevant variables, and describes gaps in information pertaining to the problem.
3. The theoretical/conceptual connection between the variables is evident.
4. The hypothesis or research question is properly stated and is consistent with the problem statement.
5. The sample size is sufficient, the sample is representative of the target population, and selection biases are controlled.

6. The type of research design is appropriate for solving the problem.
7. Threats to internal validity are minimized.
8. The method of data collection is appropriate for the research problem, the sample, and the research design.
9. The instruments chosen to collect data are appropriate to measure the variables and show evidence of reliability and validity.
10. The interpretation of the data analysis is consistent with the results presented.
11. The discussion of the results is in the context of the theoretical/conceptual framework and/or the literature review.
12. The conclusions are within the scope of the findings.

Course Guide for the Research in Nursing Examination

The examination development committee strongly recommends that you order the Regents College *Course Guide for the Research in Nursing Examination* for additional guidance in preparing for this exam.

The course guide will help you structure your own examination preparation. It is designed to help you learn the content of this examination. The guide is part of an integrated guided learning package. It includes study suggestions and approaches for learning the content of the examination and for critiquing a research study. It will direct you on how to best use the recommended resources. (See the Recommended Resources section, page 540.) The course guide can be purchased only from the Regents College Bookstore.

Preparing for the Examination

Achieving success on the free response portion of the Research in Nursing examination requires more than just learning content. You must also be able to convey your understanding of that content through the writing of effective critiques of research studies. The free response portion of this examination requires you to identify and describe the parts of research designs, differentiate among strengths and weaknesses, justify your descriptions with supporting detail from the study, and evaluate the worth of the study. The course guide prepared by Regents College to accompany the required textbook includes suggestions on how to approach responding to a free response question in the field of research in nursing.

Computer-Delivered Testing: Specific Information for the Research in Nursing (BSN) Examination

You will enter your answers to the multiple-choice portion of your examination on the computer using either the keyboard or the mouse. For the free response portion, the research study will be presented on a series of labeled screens. You will handwrite your answers in a special answer booklet. You will also receive a paper copy of the critiquing criteria and question directives that you can refer to as you complete the free response portion.

To prepare yourself for critiquing a research study that is presented to you on a computer screen, you should practice taking notes on separate scrap paper. You may want to develop a system for indicating what part of the text your note applies to without being able to annotate the text itself. To help you, every screen of the research study will be numbered and will have other features designed to help you find your way around. If possible, spend some time reading from a computer workstation if this is not something you are accustomed to doing.

Sample Questions: Research in Nursing

1. Which statement reflects an accepted guideline for informed consent?
   1) The consent form should describe potential risks or discomforts to the subject.
   2) The primary researcher should obtain written consent from the research subjects.
   3) All subjects should be financially compensated for participation in a study.
   4) The researcher should not be expected to answer subjects' questions about the study.

2. A nurse systematically observes that infants in the neonatal intensive care unit tend to cry more at the change of shift. The nurse begins to formulate a theory relating sensory overload to central nervous system immaturity of infants. Which type of reasoning does the nurse's thinking illustrate?
   1) deductive
   2) inductive
   3) intuitive
   4) trial-and-error

3. Why was the conversion of the National Center for Nursing Research (NCNR) to the National Institute of Nursing Research (NINR) in 1993 such an important event in promoting research in nursing?
   1) Nursing was recognized as a profession equal to medicine.
   2) The agency was given the status of other national health institutes.
   3) Large studies not requiring replication were able to be funded.
   4) Funds were available for addressing local health problems.

4. Which best describes a well-written literature review?
   1) It consists of exact quotations of relevant content.
   2) It contains an equal number of primary and secondary sources.
   3) It concludes with the author's opinion.
   4) It identifies gaps and inconsistencies in information.

5. Which reference is most likely to be a primary source?
   1) critical evaluation of a theory
   2) monograph on educational perspectives
   3) doctoral dissertation
   4) textbook on clinical skills

6. Which activity is a component of research problem development and refinement?
   1) data collection
   2) instrument selection
   3) literature review
   4) qualitative data analysis

Sample Questions: Research in Nursing

7. Which type of hypothesis is the following statement: "Clients who receive preoperative instruction perceive their hospitalization more positively than do clients who do not receive preoperative instruction"?
   1) complex
   2) directional
   3) nondirectional
   4) statistical

8. While a researcher is conducting a study comparing shift structure and job satisfaction, a new nurse manager is hired on one of the units participating in the study. Which threat to internal validity may influence the findings of this study?
   1) history
   2) mortality
   3) selection bias
   4) testing

9. A researcher is interested in studying the attitudes of ICU nurses toward removing life support from clients who are terminally ill. To obtain the sample, the researcher chooses every third nurse employed in all of the ICUs in the hospital. Which sampling method is the researcher using?
   1) cluster
   2) quota
   3) simple
   4) systematic

10. What should the researcher consider when determining how large a sample should be?
    1) sites from which the sample will be selected
    2) number of individuals collecting data from the sample subjects
    3) convenience of the sampling
    4) the study design and power analysis

11. What is an advantage of using questionnaires as compared to using interviews? For the same cost, with questionnaires the researcher can
    1) achieve a greater depth of information.
    2) seek clarification of subjects' answers.
    3) obtain a higher number of responses.
    4) control the order in which subjects respond.

12. The Celsius temperature scale represents which level of measurement?
    1) interval
    2) nominal
    3) ordinal
    4) ratio

Sample Questions: Research in Nursing

13. Which research topic is appropriate for a qualitative study?
    1) the relationship of prenatal care to Apgar scores of newborns
    2) the experience of delivering a stillborn infant at term
    3) the number of clients with contraceptive failures who attend a prenatal clinic in one year
    4) the relationship of self-esteem to maternal attachment in adolescents

14. Which qualitative research method would be most appropriate for a study of the health behavior patterns of older African American adults living in rural areas?
    1) ethnography
    2) phenomenology
    3) grounded theory
    4) historical method

15. What is the purpose of establishing scientific rigor in qualitative research?
    1) to maintain external validity
    2) to provide instrument reliability
    3) to allow creative design
    4) to determine accuracy of interpretations

On the following pages is an example of the kind of abbreviated research study that examinees will be asked to critique.

A Randomized Clinical Trial of the Effect of Noise on the Anxiety of Anesthetized Surgical Clients
(Date of first publication: 1996)

Introduction and Literature Review[1]

High levels of noise have been linked to psychological distress such as sleeplessness, anxiety, nervousness, and nightmares in hospitalized clients (1-3). Falk found that sound levels over 80 decibels (dB) cause cochlea damage and hearing loss in adults (4). Anesthetized surgical clients are especially at risk from noise exposure up to 108 dB from conversations, intercoms, monitoring devices, and suctioning equipment (1,5). Although the goal of anesthesia is to provide amnesia and pain control (3,6), the auditory system may still register harmful input (1–3,6–8).

Surgical anxiety, stemming from unfamiliar environments, can disrupt clients' recovery by reducing their psychological well-being and their ability to cooperate with self-care activities. Nursing care of surgical clients requires interventions that address physiological and psychological needs (9). Music or white noise (for example, repetitive sounds such as ocean surf) can block annoying sounds and enhance sleep and relaxation for intensive care unit clients (10), and decrease anxiety (11,12) and blood pressure (13) for surgical clients. Introducing white noise to anesthetized clients could help clients assimilate the environment and strengthen their defenses against stressors (9,10). The purpose of this study was to examine the effect of white noise on the postoperative anxiety of anesthetized clients exposed to typical noise encountered in operating rooms.

Methods

All males between 18 and 60 years old who were scheduled to have elective hernia repair were invited to participate. Clients were excluded from the study if they could not speak English; had hearing impairment; or had cerebrovascular disease, drug addiction, or psychiatric disorders. Eligible subjects were randomly assigned to either the experimental group who heard white noise throughout the surgery or the control group who did not. Anxiety was measured presurgery and again two days following discharge using Spielberger's State-Trait Anxiety Inventory (STAI). The STAI, a forty-item self-report instrument used to measure anxiety in general (trait) and at a particular point in time (state), is reported to be reliable and valid (11,14,15). Internal consistency has been reported to range from .83 to .92 (15). Analysis of presurgery STAI scores determined baseline equality between groups. Earphones were placed on all subjects prior to administration of anesthesia. Subjects were blinded to their treatment with white noise. The control group's earphones were removed immediately after anesthetization. The experimental group listened to comfortable volumes of tape recordings of ocean surf. All clients were asked to return the STAI two days following surgery. A t test was used to test the hypothesis that anesthetized surgical clients exposed to white noise via earphones would report less postoperative anxiety, as measured by STAI, than clients exposed to surgical noise with no external interference.

---

[1]Numbers in parentheses refer to the numbered list of references found at the end of the study.

Sample Research Study: Research in Nursing

Results

Ten white males who were between 45 and 57 years old, were undergoing elective hernia repair surgery, and met selection criteria agreed to participate and were equally randomized to each group. All clients were treated as outpatients, averaging two hours in surgery and four hours in recovery. The average level of operating room noise was 95 dB, with ranges from 66 to 117 dB. There was no difference in preoperative anxiety level between the experimental and control groups. No statistically significant differences were found between group postoperative STAI scores ($p > .05$). Both groups reported experiencing high levels of anxiety during the surgical period (see Table 1).

Discussion

Anxiety can disrupt recovery of surgical clients since it interferes with participation in self-care activities necessary for healing. Although adverse effects of noise levels are well documented (1-3,6,7) and music is known to interfere with the interpretation of noise (10-13), results from this study indicate that white noise used to interfere with auditory stimuli in the operating room does not affect anxiety levels of anesthetized clients. Anesthetized clients are completely dependent on the operating room nurse to intervene with appropriate measures to decrease the effect of stressors (9). Owing to the many ramifications of noise on potential postoperative anxiety, it is in the best interest of all surgical clients for nurses to continue to use other preventive measures, because white noise is an ineffective intervention.

Table 1: Means and Standard Deviations for State-Trait Anxiety Inventory (STAI) Scores: Baseline and Two Days Following Surgery (N=10)

	Experimental Group n=5	Control Group n=5
Baseline STAI		
State-Anxiety		
Mean	46.37	45.00
SD	9.34	11.23
Trait-Anxiety		
Mean	44.39	43.69
SD	10.81	11.59
Two-day STAI		
State-Anxiety		
Mean	40.03	42.07
SD	9.22	9.34
Trait-Anxiety		
Mean	44.02	43.63
SD	8.49	10.06

Sample Research Study: Research in Nursing

**References for
A Randomized Clinical Trial of the Effect of
Noise on the Anxiety of Anesthetized Surgical Clients
(Date of first publication: 1996)**

1. Cobcraft, M., & Forsdick, C. (1993). *Awareness under anesthesia: The patient's point of view.* Anesthesia Intensive Care, 21, *837–843.*
2. Murphy, E.K. (1993). *OR nursing law: Patients deserve a respectful surgical environment.* AORN Journal, 57, *1179–1180.*
3. Kole, T.E. (1993). *Assessing the potential for awareness and learning under anesthesia.* Journal of the American Association of Nurse Anesthetists, 61, *571–577.*
4. Falk, S.A. (1972). *Combined effects of noise and otoxic drugs.* Environmental Health Perspectives, 2, *5–22.*
5. Hodge, B., & Thompson, J.F. (1990). *Noise pollution in the operating theatre.* Lancet, 335, *891–894.*
6. Andrade, J., & Braddeley, A. (1993). *Depth of anesthesia: Human memory and anesthesia.* International Anesthesiology Clinics, 4, *39–51.*
7. Westmoreland, C., Sebel, P., Winograd, E., & Goldman, W. (1993). *Indirect memory during anesthesia: The effect of Midazolam.* Anesthesiology, 78, *237–241.*
8. Ghoneim, M., & Block, R. (1993). *Learning during anesthesia.* International Anesthesiology Clinics, 4, *39–51.*
9. George, J. (1990). *Nursing theories: The base for professional nursing practice (3rd ed.).* Englewood, NJ: Appleton & Lange.
10. Williamson, J. (1991). *The effects of ocean sounds on sleep after coronary artery bypass graft surgery.* American Journal of Critical Care, 1(1), *91–97.*
11. Evans, M.M., & Rubio, P. (1994). *Music: A diversionary therapy.* Today's OR Nurse, 16(4), *17–22.*
12. Cirina, C. (1994). *Effects of sedative music on patient preoperative anxiety.* Today's OR Nurse, 16(3), *15–18.*
13. Stevens, K. (1990). *Patient's perceptions of music during surgery.* Journal of Advanced Nursing, 15, *1045–1051.*
14. Palakanis, K., DeNobile, J., Sweeney, B., & Blakenship, C. (1994). *Effect of music therapy on state anxiety in patients undergoing flexible sigmoidoscopy.* Diseases of the Colon and Rectum, 37(5), *478–481.*
15. Spielberger, C. (1970). *Manual for state-trait anxiety inventory. Palo Alto, CA: Consulting Psychologists Press, Inc.*

Recommended Resources

Textbooks

The examination development committee used the LoBiondo-Wood & Haber textbook below as the basis for developing the examination. Students are encouraged to use this text in conjunction with its study guide and computerized learning resource and the Regents College course guide to prepare for the examination.

LoBiondo-Wood, G., & Haber, J. (1998). Nursing research: Methods, critical appraisal, and utilization *(4th ed.). St. Louis: Mosby.*

Rose-Grippa, K., & Gorney-Moreno, M.J. (1998). Study guide and computerized learning resource to accompany Nursing research: Methods, critical appraisal, and utilization *(4th ed.). St. Louis: Mosby.*

Regents College. (1999). Course guide for the Research in Nursing examination.

Sample Questions: Research in Nursing

Journal Articles

As a professional, you have a responsibility to continue your education. One way to keep current is by reading journal articles. You can gain exposure to current articles in the field by subscribing to one or two journals or using the journals found in college or public libraries. Journal articles are an especially important supplementary resource as you prepare to take the Research in Nursing (BSN) examination, because they will provide practice in reading and understanding nursing research studies.

The articles listed below are arranged according to the content area to which they most apply. You are encouraged to read widely and review other articles of interest.

I. Foundations of Research

Alt-White, A.C. (1995). *Issues in clinical nursing research: Obtaining informed consent from the elderly.* Western Journal of Nursing Research, 17(6), 700–705.

Behe, R. (1995). *The individual's right to informed consent.* Nurse Researcher, 3(1), 14–23.

Berry, D.L. et al. (1996). *Ethical issues: Informed consent: Process and clinical issues.* Oncology Nursing Forum, 23(3), 507–512.

Bruette, V., & Fitzig, C. (1993). *The literature review.* Journal of the New York State Nurses Association, 24(1), 14–15.

Demi, A.S., & Warren, N.A. (1995). *Issues in conducting research with vulnerable families.* Western Journal of Nursing Research, 17(2), 188–202.

Funk, S.G. et al. (1995). *Administrators' views on barriers to research utilization.* Applied Nursing Research, 8(1), 44–49.

Hallaway, I., & Wheeler, S. (1995). *Ethical issues in qualitative nursing research.* Nursing Ethics: An International Journal for Health Care Professionals, 2(3), 223–232.

Hutchinson, S.A. et al. (1994). *Benefits of participating in research interviews.* Image: Journal of Nursing Scholarship, 26(2), 161–164.

Kachajeanos, M.K. (1995). *Keys to research: Ethical perspectives on research involving healthy children.* American Journal of Maternal Health Nursing, 20(5), 285.

Larsen, E. (1994). *Exclusion of certain clinical groups from clinical research.* Image: Journal of Nursing Scholarship, 26(3), 185–190.

Madjar, I., & Higgins, I. (1996). *Of ethics committees and protocols, behaving ethically in the field: A case study of research with elderly residents in a nursing home.* Nursing Inquiry, 3(3), 130–137.

Martin, P.A. (1994). *The utility of the research problem statement.* Applied Nursing Research, 7(1), 47–49.

Martin, P.A. (1994). *Responsibilities when a patient is a subject in a research study.* Applied Nursing Research, 7(3), 158–161.

Martin, P.A. (1995). *Finding time for research.* Applied Nursing Research, 8(3), 151–153.

Martin, P.A. (1995). *Recruitment of research subjects.* Applied Nursing Research, 8(1), 50–54.

Robley, L.R. (1995). *The ethics of qualitative nursing research.* Journal of Professional Nursing, 11(1), 45–48.

Tierney, A. (1995). *The role of research ethics committees.* Nurse Researcher, 3(1), 43–52.

II. Quantitative Research

Abrams, K.R., & Scragg, A.M. (1996). *Quantitative methods in nursing research.* Journal of Advanced Nursing, 23(5), 1008–1015.

Sample Questions: Research in Nursing

Barriball, K.L. et al. (1996). *The telephone survey method: A discussion paper.* Journal of Advanced Nursing, 24(1), 115–121.

Blacktop, J. (1996). *A discussion of different types of sampling techniques.* Nurse Researcher, 3(4), 5–15.

Coates, V.E. (1995). *Measuring constructs accurately: A prerequisite to theory testing.* Journal of Psychiatric and Mental Health Nursing, 2(5), 287–293.

Fielding, N. (1994). *Varieties of research interviews.* Nurse Researcher, 1(3), 4–13.

Kirchoff, K.T., & Dille, C.A. (1994). *Issues in intervention research: Maintaining integrity.* Applied Nursing Research, 7(1), 32–46.

Newel, R. (1996). *The reliability and validity of samples.* Nurse Researcher, 3(4), 16–26.

Newel, R. (1994). *The structured interview.* Nurse Researcher, 1(3), 14–23.

Rose, K. (1994). *Unstructured and semi-structured interviews.* Nurse Researcher, 1(3), 23–32.

Rudy, E.B., & Keir, M. (1991). *Unraveling the mystique of power analysis.* Heart & Lung: Journal of Critical Care, 20(5), 517–522.

Stokes, S.A. (1994). *Selection of a research instrument: Revisiting issues.* Journal of Professional Nursing, 10(6), 334.

Yarandi, H.N. (1996). *Hypothesis testing.* Clinical Nurse Specialist, 10(4), 186–188.

III. Qualitative Research

Bailey, P.H. (1996). *Assuring quality in narrative analysis.* Western Journal of Nursing Research, 18(2), 186–194.

Beck, C.T. (1996). *Grounded theory: Overview and application in pediatric nursing.* Issues in Comprehensive Pediatric Nursing, 19(1), 1–15.

Begley, C.M. (1996). *Using triangulation in nursing research.* Journal of Advanced Nursing, 24(1), 122–128.

Crowder, E.L.M. (1995). *What it means to be a nurse historian.* Reflections, 21(1), 13.

Gallo, K. et al. (1996). *Search and research: Qualitative research: The search for meaning.* Journal of the American Academy of Nurse Practitioners, 8(4), 167–173.

Hamilton, D.B. (1993). *The idea of history and the history of ideas.* Image: Journal of Nursing Scholarship, 25(1), 45–48.

Parse, R.R. (1996). *Building knowledge through qualitative research: The road less traveled.* Nursing Science Quarterly, 9(1), 10–16.

Sandelowski, A. (1995). *Focus on qualitative methods: Sample size in qualitative research.* Research in Nursing and Health, 18(2), 179–183.

IV. Critique of a Research Study

Albes, L.L., & Murphy, P.A. (1993). *Evaluation of research studies: Statistical significance testing.* Journal of Nurse Midwifery, 38(1), 51–53.

Beck, C.T. (1994). *Statistical power analysis in pediatric nursing research.* Issues in Comprehensive Pediatric Nursing, 17(2), 73–80.

Firly, A. (1995). *Critiquing the ethical aspects of a study.* Nurse Researcher, 3(1), 35–42.

Giuggre, M. (1995). *Reading research critically: Assessing the validity and reliability of research instrumentation.* Journal of Post Anesthesia Nursing, 10(2), 107–112.

Haughey, B.B. (1994). *Evaluating quantitative research designs.* Critical Care Nurse, 14(6), 69–72.

Classical Curriculum Nursing Examinations

The examinations in this section do <u>not</u> apply toward the Regents College nursing degrees. If you are enrolled in a Regents College nursing program or are planning to enroll, you should use the study guides beginning on page 264 (associate degree) or page 432 (baccalaureate degree). However, these subject-specific exams may be appropriate if you are in a classical curriculum program, that is, a program organized around the traditional (medical model) nursing content areas. Other institutions may recognize these exams for credit. User faculty at each institution must determine which examinations are most appropriate for their curriculum.

Definitions

For purposes of these examinations, the following definitions are used in the content outlines.

1. An <u>individual</u> is a single human being as contrasted with a family, group, or community.
2. A <u>family</u> is "represented by two or more individuals, belonging to the same or different kinship groups, who are involved in a continuous living arrangement, usually residing in the same household, experiencing common emotional bonds, and sharing certain obligations toward each other and toward others."

    Stanhope, M., & Lancaster, J. (1996). Community health nursing: Promoting health of aggregates, families, and individuals *(4th ed.). St. Louis: Mosby, p. 453.*

3. A <u>group</u> is an "interdependent association of two or more persons, interacting in such a way that each person influences and is influenced by other group members."

    Haber, J. et al. (1992). Comprehensive psychiatric nursing *(4th ed.). St. Louis: Mosby, p. 324.*

4. A <u>community</u> is a "locality-based entity, composed of systems of formal organizations reflecting societal institutions, informal groups, and aggregates. These components are interdependent and their function is to meet a wide variety of collective needs."

    Stanhope, M., & Lancaster, J. (1996). Community health nursing: Promoting health of aggregates, families, and individuals *(4th ed.). St. Louis: Mosby, p. 290.*

Study Guide
Fundamentals of Nursing (403)

Credit Hours: 8   **Credit Level:** Lower
Question Type(s): Multiple-choice

The information in this study guide is valid until Summer 2001.
If you will be taking the examination after that date, be sure to check for a new edition of this guide before you complete your preparation for the exam.

General Description of the Examination

The Fundamentals of Nursing examination measures knowledge and understanding of the material usually taught in a course in fundamentals of nursing in an associate degree nursing program. The examination assumes a basic knowledge of anatomy and physiology, chemistry, and mathematics. Questions on the examination focus on the health problems of adult patients that are commonly encountered by associate degree nurses in health care settings.

The examination requires you to demonstrate knowledge and understanding of the theoretical framework for each content area as well as the ability to apply this knowledge through use of the nursing process.

Content Outline

Content Area	Percent of Examination
I. The Profession of Nursing	8%
II. Communication and Interpersonal Relations	10%
III. Protection and Promotion of Safety	25%
IV. Comfort, Rest, and Activity	15%
V. Nutrition	10%
VI. Elimination	11%
VII. Oxygenation	10%
VIII. Fluid and Electrolyte Balance	11%
Total	**100%**

I. The Profession of Nursing (8%)

A. **Legal issues in nursing**
   1. General legal concepts: statutory, common, civil, and criminal laws
   2. Nurse practice acts
      a. Definition and purposes of nurse practice acts
      b. Impact on the practice of nursing
      c. ANA Standards of Care
      d. Licensure: legal requirements, grounds for revocation, grounds for suspension
   3. Legal liability in nursing
      a. Types of crimes: felonies, misdemeanors
      b. Areas of liability: torts, negligence, invasion of privacy, defamation of character, assault and battery, false imprisonment, abandonment
      c. Good Samaritan Laws
      d. Informed consent
      e. A Patient's Bill of Rights

B. **Roles and functions of the nurse**
   1. Caregiver
   2. Decision maker
   3. Communicator
   4. Manager of care
   5. Advocate
   6. Teacher

C. **Ethics and values in nursing**
   1. ANA Code of Ethics
   2. Resolution of ethical problems
   3. Nature and function of values

D. **Basic nursing concepts**
   1. The health continuum
      a. Wellness-illness continuum
      b. Factors influencing health
         1) Individual factors (for example: genetics, age)
         2) Environmental factors (for example: occupational hazards, stress)
         3) Socioeconomic and cultural factors (for example: lifestyle, single-parent households, fast foods, health practices)
      c. Effects of hospitalizations and/or illness (for example: loss of income, change in self-image, disruption of family)
   2. The health care delivery system
   3. Maslow's hierarchy of needs
      a. Structure of hierarchy
      b. Implication for nursing care
   4. Homeostasis and adaptation to stress
      a. General concepts of homeostasis and regulatory mechanisms
      b. General concept and nature of stress based on Selye's theory
      c. Factors influencing adaptation (for example: age, lifestyle, occupation, coping strategies)

d. Psychophysiological signs of increased stress (for example: changes in vital signs, memory or perceptual changes)
   5. Psychophysiological adaptations to stress (for example: fight or flight response, rest and activity changes, defense mechanisms)

E. **Nursing process methodology**
   1. Purposes
   2. Steps
      a. Assessment: establishing a database concerning patient needs, including gathering subjective and objective data and assessing individual factors related to health
      b. Diagnosis: identification of the patient's actual or potential nursing diagnoses after analyzing and interpreting data
      c. Planning: setting priorities, identifying patient-centered outcomes and selecting nursing interventions to achieve those outcomes using clinical pathways
      d. Implementation: using nursing interventions to help the patient achieve outcomes
      e. Evaluation: determining the extent to which outcomes have been achieved
   3. Elements of a nursing diagnosis statement according to North American Nursing Diagnosis Association Taxonomy, 1997
   4. Characteristics of a goal: measurable, patient-oriented, attainable with a specified time period

F. **Recording and reporting**
   1. Concepts and principles
      a. Purposes of recording: charting, documentation (for example: providing a record of care given, charting patient's response to care, evaluation and revision of the nursing care plan)
      b. Purposes of reporting: intermittent, change-of-shift (for example: promoting continuity of patient care, evaluation of effectiveness of nursing interventions)
      c. Principles of written communication (for example: accuracy, legibility, legality, abbreviations)
      d. Principles of oral communication (for example: objectivity, clarity, timeliness)
   2. Inclusion of appropriate information when recording and reporting (for example: when using narrative method, when using SOAP method; on a medication administration record, on a nursing care plan, in a team conference, at change-of-shift)

II. Communication and Interpersonal Relations (10%)

A. **Theoretical framework**
   1. Therapeutic communication
      a. Definition and outcomes
      b. Types of communication: verbal, nonverbal
      c. Principles of therapeutic communication
         1) Techniques that facilitate communication
         2) Techniques that block communication

2. The nurse-patient relationship
    a. Definition and outcomes of the nurse-patient relationship
    b. Components of the nurse-patient relationship
    c. Phases of the nurse-patient relationship
3. Factors influencing the communication process (for example: cultural, sensory losses, language barriers, perception of the relationship, personal experiences and needs, attitudes)
4. Patient instruction: principles of teaching/learning

B. Nursing care
1. Assessment: establish a database concerning communication
    a. Gather objective and subjective data (for example: primary language, use of sign language, unable to read, hearing ability)
    b. Assess factors influencing communication and the nurse-patient relationship (see IIA3)
2. Diagnosis: identify the patient's actual or potential nursing diagnoses related to communication
    a. Analyze and interpret data (for example: patterns of communication, readiness for learning)
    b. Identify nursing diagnoses (for example: impaired verbal communication related to oral surgery; knowledge deficit: low-calorie diet related to recently ordered therapy)
3. Planning: set priorities, identify patient-centered outcomes and select interventions related to communication
    a. Set priorities and establish (for example: patient will communicate needs using an alternate means of communication [chalkboard]; patient will make appropriate meal selections)
    b. Incorporate factors influencing communication in planning patient care (see IIA3)
    c. Select nursing interventions to facilitate communication (for example: provide the patient with a "magic slate"; select materials appropriate to the patient's educational level)
4. Implementation: use nursing interventions to achieve outcomes related to communication and the nurse-patient relationship
    a. Use facilitative communication techniques (see IIA1c)
    b. Establish a therapeutic nurse-patient relationship (see IIA2)
5. Evaluation: determine the extent to which outcomes have been achieved
    a. Evaluate, record, and report the patient's response to nursing actions (for example: due to sedation, patient is not able to use the magic slate; patient selects foods appropriate to a low-calorie diet)
    b. Modify the plan of care if necessary

III. Protection and Promotion of Safety (25%)

A. Asepsis
1. Theoretical framework
    a. Chain of infection
    b. Principles of medical and surgical asepsis
    c. Methods of transmission (for example: direct contact, vehicles, airborne)

d. Standard (universal) precautions
e. Factors influencing an individual's susceptibility to infection (for example: stress, nutritional status, physical status, medications, heredity, lifestyle, socioeconomic status, occupation)
2. Nursing care
   a. Assessment: establish a database concerning asepsis
      1) Gather objective and subjective data (for example: WBC count [normal values], history of exposure to pathogens, fever, thirst)
      2) Assess factors influencing susceptibility to infection (see IIIA1e)
   b. Diagnosis: identify the patient's actual or potential nursing diagnoses related to asepsis
      1) Analyze and interpret data (for example: identify pathogen and possible method of transmission)
      2) Identify nursing diagnoses (for example: risk for infection related to poor nutritional status and exposure to pathogens)
   c. Planning: set priorities, identify patient-centered outcomes and select appropriate interventions related to asepsis
      1) Set priorities and establish outcomes (for example: patient will wash hands after using the toilet)
      2) Incorporate factors influencing the individual's susceptibility to infection (see IIIA1e)
      3) Select nursing interventions to help the patient achieve outcomes (for example: utilize appropriate aseptic measures, determine appropriate barriers)
   d. Implementation: use nursing interventions to achieve the outcomes related to asepsis
      1) Use nursing measures to contain organisms (for example: use medical asepsis)
      2) Use nursing measures to exclude organisms (for example: use surgical asepsis when providing wound care)
      3) Instruct the patient regarding prevention of infection (for example: handwashing)
   e. Evaluation: determine the extent to which outcomes have been achieved
      1) Evaluate, record, and report the patient's response to nursing actions (for example: wound is approximated and free of drainage)
      2) Continually reassess the physical environment (for example: dressings are disposed of in a closed container)
      3) Modify the plan of care if necessary

B. **The body's defenses (includes the body systems, the immune system, and the inflammatory response)**
   1. Theoretical framework
      a. Physiological responses (for example: antigen-antibody response, leukocytosis, signs of inflammation, secretion of mucus, movement of cilia, removal of waste products, wound healing, fever)
      b. Factors influencing the body's defenses
         1) Individual factors (for example: age, nutritional status, skin integrity, hygienic practices, physical activity, health status, cigarette smoking)

2) Environmental factors (for example: climate, occupational hazards, exposure to communicable diseases, cigarette smoke, radiation)
    c. Techniques commonly used to promote the body's defenses (for example: application of heat and cold, tetanus booster, flu vaccine)
  2. Nursing care
    a. Assessment: establish a database concerning defenses
      1) Gather objective and subjective data (for example: condition of the patient's skin and mucous membrane, vital signs, redness, pain, swelling, WBC count, history of immunizations)
      2) Assess factors influencing the body's defenses (see IIIB1b)
    b. Diagnosis: identify the patient's actual or potential nursing diagnoses related to defenses
      1) Analyze and interpret data (for example: culture reports, identify impairment of the skin, WBC count [normal values], characteristics of drainage)
      2) Identify nursing diagnoses (for example: risk for infection related to altered skin integrity)
    c. Planning: set priorities, identify patient-centered outcomes and select interventions related to defenses
      1) Set priorities and establish outcomes (for example: patient will remain afebrile)
      2) Incorporate factors influencing the body's defenses (see IIIB1b)
      3) Select nursing interventions to help the patient achieve outcomes (for example: monitor vital signs q4h)
    d. Implementation: use nursing interventions to achieve outcomes related to the body's defenses
      1) Use nursing measures to promote the body's defenses (for example: provide adequate nutrition, apply heat and cold treatments, provide wound care, collect specimens for culture)
      2) Instruct the patient to support and/or restore the body's defenses (for example: emphasize the need to avoid exposure to infectious agents)
    e. Evaluation: determine the extent to which outcomes have been achieved
      1) Evaluate, record, and report the patient's response to nursing actions (for example: patient's temperature remains within normal limits)
      2) Modify the plan of care if necessary

C. **Medication administration**
  1. Theoretical framework
    a. Pharmacokinetics: absorption, distribution, metabolism, excretion
    b. Principles of administration: calculations (including equivalents), routes and sites, safety measures, controlled substances, use of nasogastric and gastrostomy tubes, transcribing medication orders
    c. Factors influencing medication action and effectiveness (for example: age, sex, weight, psychological factors, time of administration, environment)
  2. Nursing care
    a. Assessment: establish a database concerning the patient's medication regimen
      1) Gather objective and subjective data (for example: history of allergies, vital signs, duration of pain)
      2) Assess factors influencing medication action and effectiveness (see IIIC1c)

b. Diagnosis: identify the patient's actual or potential nursing diagnoses related to medications
   1) Analyze and interpret data (for example: changes in vital signs, recognize side effects)
   2) Identify nursing diagnoses (for example: noncompliance related to fear of side effects)
c. Planning: set priorities, identify patient-centered outcomes and select interventions related to the patient's medication regimen
   1) Set priorities and establish outcomes (for example: patient will adhere to regimen as agreed)
   2) Incorporate factors influencing medication action and effectiveness (see IIIC1c)
   3) Select nursing interventions to help the patient meet outcomes (for example: instruct the patient to take the medication with food)
d. Implementation: use nursing interventions to achieve outcomes related to the medication regimen
   1) Use nursing measures to safely administer medications (for example: calculation and measurement, patient identification, transcription, accurate recording, selection of correct site, administration of controlled substances)
   2) Provide information and instruction regarding the medication regimen (for example: self-administration, storage, reporting side effects)
e. Evaluation: determine the extent to which outcomes have been achieved
   1) Evaluate, record, and report the patient's response to nursing actions (for example: patient adheres to the medication regimen)
   2) Modify the plan of care if necessary

D. Safety
1. Theoretical framework
   a. Factors influencing an individual's safety
      1) Individual factors (for example: age, medications, level of awareness, sensory perception, emotional state)
      2) Environmental factors (for example: occupation, presence of lead paint)
      3) Socioeconomic and cultural factors (for example: ability to communicate, unemployment)
      4) Psychological factors (for example: stress, anxiety)
   b. Identification of environmental hazards (for example: physical and mechanical, thermal, chemical, radiation, ecological)
   c. Devices commonly used to promote safety (for example: restraints, walkers, siderails)
2. Nursing care
   a. Assessment: establish a database concerning the patient's safety needs
      1) Gather objective and subjective data (for example: confusion, visual acuity)
      2) Determine presence of environmental hazards (see IIID1b)
      3) Assess factors influencing the patient's safety (for example: age, hearing impairment) (see IIID1a)
   b. Diagnosis: identify the patient's actual or potential nursing diagnoses related to safety

          1) Analyze and interpret data (for example: recognize loss of equilibrium)
          2) Identify nursing diagnoses (for example: risk for injury related to sensory deficit)
       c. Planning: set priorities, identify patient-centered outcomes and select interventions related to safety
          1) Set priorities and establish outcomes (for example: patient will request assistance with ambulation)
          2) Incorporate factors influencing safety in planning for individualized patient care (for example: consider age, lifestyle, level of consciousness, mobility)
          3) Select nursing interventions for alleviating or minimizing safety hazards (for example: modify the environment)
          4) Select the appropriate safety device based on the individual's needs (for example: walkers, restraints)
       d. Implementation: use nursing interventions to achieve outcomes related to safety
          1) Use nursing measures to provide a safe environment (for example: elevate siderails, use restraining jacket)
          2) Use equipment and devices safely (for example: walkers, ice packs, heat applications)
          3) Instruct the patient regarding safety (for example: orient to environment, explain use of wheelchair)
       e. Evaluation: determine the extent to which outcomes have been achieved
          1) Evaluate, record, and report the patient's response to nursing actions (for example: patient ambulates with the nurse's assistance)
          2) Modify the plan of care if necessary

IV. Comfort, Rest, and Activity (15%)

A. Hygiene
   1. Theoretical framework
      a. Components of hygiene
      b. Factors influencing hygiene (for example: cultural factors, age, physical status, body image, self-esteem)
      c. Agents commonly used on the skin and mucous membrane (for example: soaps, lotions, emollients, mouthwashes)
   2. Nursing care
      a. Assessment: establish a database concerning hygiene
         1) Gather objective and subjective data (for example: cleanliness of the skin, condition of the nails, complaints of dryness)
         2) Assess factors influencing the patient's hygiene (see IVA1b)
      b. Diagnosis: identify the patient's actual or potential nursing diagnoses related to hygiene
         1) Analyze and interpret data
         2) Identify nursing diagnoses (for example: altered oral mucous membrane related to mouth breathing)
      c. Planning: set priorities, identify patient-centered outcomes and select interventions related to hygiene

1) Set priorities and establish outcomes (for example: patient's oral mucous membrane will be pink and moist)
2) Incorporate factors influencing hygiene in planning patient care (see IVA1b)
3) Select nursing interventions to achieve outcomes (for example: provide mouth care q2h)

d. Implementation: use nursing interventions to achieve outcomes related to hygiene
1) Use nursing measures to provide comprehensive hygienic care (for example: bathing, hair care, nail care, skin care, perineal care)
2) Use nursing measures to promote psychological comfort (for example: provide privacy during bathing)
3) Provide information and instruction (for example: instruct the patient on the use of dental floss, discuss indications for use of skin lotions rather than alcohol-base skin products)

e. Evaluation: determine the extent to which outcomes have been achieved
1) Evaluate, record, and report the patient's response to nursing actions (for example: the patient's lips remain dry and cracked)
2) Modify the plan of care if necessary

B. Rest and sleep
1. Theoretical framework
    a. Principles related to rest and sleep (for example: sleep stages, circadian rhythm)
    b. Factors influencing rest and sleep (for example: age, noise level, fatigue, use of caffeine, use of alcohol, hospitalization, sensory deprivation)
    c. Agents commonly used to promote rest and sleep (sedatives, hypnotic)
2. Nursing care
    a. Assessment: establish a database concerning rest and sleep
        1) Gather objective and subjective data (for example: usual sleep habits, use of over-the-counter medications, bedtime routines)
        2) Assess factors influencing the patient's rest and sleep (see IVB1b)
    b. Diagnosis: identify the patient's actual or potential nursing diagnoses related to rest and sleep
        1) Analyze and interpret data (see IVB2a)
        2) Identify nursing diagnoses (for example: sleep pattern disturbance related to unfamiliar surroundings)
    c. Planning: set priorities, identify patient-centered outcomes and select interventions
        1) Set priorities and establish outcomes (for example: patient will get six hours of uninterrupted sleep per night)
        2) Incorporate factors influencing rest and sleep (see IVB1b)
        3) Select nursing interventions to help the patient achieve outcomes (for example: reorient the patient to the surroundings)
    d. Implementation: use nursing interventions to achieve outcomes related to rest and sleep
        1) Use nursing measures to induce rest and sleep (for example: administer a backrub, provide a bedtime snack, provide a quiet environment)
        2) Use nursing measures specific to drug classifications for prescribed

medications (for example: raise the siderails after administering a sleep medication)
            3) Use nursing measures to modify the environment (for example: provide sensory stimulation, prevent sensory overload)
            4) Provide information and instruction (for example: discuss relaxation techniques with the patient)
        e. Evaluation: determine the extent to which outcomes have been achieved
            1) Evaluate, record, and report the patient's response to nursing actions (for example: patient states that he feels well rested)
            2) Modify the plan of care if necessary

C. Mobility and immobility
    1. Theoretical framework
        a. Principles of body mechanics, transfer, ambulation, range-of-motion, exercise
        b. Responses of body systems to mobility (for example: improved circulation, peristalsis)
        c. Complications resulting from immobility (for example: muscle weakness, contractures, retained secretions, decubitus ulcers, hypostatic pneumonia, constipation)
    2. Nursing care
        a. Assessment: establish a database concerning mobility and immobility
            1) Gather objective and subjective data (for example: range-of-motion, skin integrity, elimination patterns, activity level, joint mobility)
            2) Assess the patient's responses to mobility and immobility (see IVC1b–c)
        b. Diagnosis: identify the patient's actual or potential nursing diagnoses related to mobility or immobility
            1) Analyze and interpret data
            2) Identify nursing diagnoses (for example: risk for impaired physical mobility related to bed rest)
        c. Planning: set priorities, identify patient-centered outcomes, and select appropriate interventions related to mobility or immobility
            1) Set priorities and establish outcomes (for example: patient will maintain usual range of motion in all joints)
            2) Consider the responses of the body to mobility and immobility (see IVC1b–c)
            3) Select nursing interventions to help the patient achieve outcomes (for example: supervise the patient in active range-of-motion exercises t.i.d.)
        d. Implementation: use nursing interventions to achieve outcomes related to mobility or immobility
            1) Use appropriate devices to maintain normal body alignment (for example: footboard, pillows, trochanter roll)
            2) Use nursing measures to promote mobility and maintain muscle tone (for example: range of motion, ambulation, positioning)
            3) Use nursing measures to prevent tissue breakdown (for example: massage, pressure-relieving devices, turning)
            4) Use nursing measures to prevent complications related to immobility (for example: leg exercises, antiembolism stockings, deep breathing and coughing)

5) Instruct the patient regarding activity needs
e. Evaluation: determine the extent to which outcomes have been achieved
1) Evaluate, record, and report the patient's response to nursing actions (for example: patient's joints are freely movable within normal range of motion)
2) Modify the plan of care if necessary

D. The pain experience
1. Theoretical framework
   a. Concepts related to pain (for example: gate control theory, acute vs. chronic pain, pain threshold, endorphins)
   b. Factors influencing pain (for example: etiology of pain, duration of pain, sensory overload, cultural factors)
   c. Agents and techniques commonly used to control pain (for example: guided imagery, relaxation, administration of nonnarcotic analgesics, narcotic analgesics, patient-controlled analgesia, placebos, cutaneous stimulation)
2. Nursing care
   a. Assessment: establish a database concerning pain
      1) Gather objective and subjective data (for example: changes in vital signs, facial expression, body language, verbalization by the patient)
      2) Assess factors influencing the patient's pain (see IVD1b)
   b. Diagnosis: identify the patient's actual or potential nursing diagnoses related to pain
      1) Analyze and interpret data
      2) Identify nursing diagnoses (for example: pain related to recent abdominal surgery)
   c. Planning: set priorities, identify patient-centered outcomes and select interventions related to pain
      1) Set priorities and establish outcomes (for example: patient will report decrease in pain)
      2) Incorporate factors influencing pain (see IVD1b)
      3) Select nursing interventions to help the patient achieve outcomes (for example: position the patient to minimize stress on the incision; administer pain medication on a regular schedule)
   d. Implementation: use nursing interventions to achieve outcomes related to pain
      1) Use nursing measures to reduce the patient's pain (for example: positioning, cutaneous stimulation, assess the operative site, promote relaxation)
      2) Use nursing measures specific to drug classifications for prescribed medications (for example: monitor vital signs for a patient receiving a narcotic analgesic, schedule administration of medications to maximize effectiveness)
      3) Instruct the patient regarding pain (for example: use of relaxation techniques, use of guided imagery)
   e. Evaluation: determine the extent to which outcomes have been achieved
      1) Evaluate, record, and report the patient's response to nursing interventions (for example: patient states that pain has been relieved)
      2) Modify the plan of care if necessary

V. Nutrition (10%)

A. Theoretical framework
1. Processes of ingestion, digestion, and absorption of nutrients
2. Normal nutritional requirements
    a. Food Guide Pyramid
    b. Basic functions and common food sources of carbohydrates, proteins, fats, vitamins, minerals
    c. Caloric values
3. Common nutritional disturbances (for example: vomiting, heartburn, obesity, anorexia, malnutrition)
4. Factors influencing nutrition
    a. Individual factors (for example: age, sedentary lifestyle, vegetarian diet, dental status, physical condition, need for assistance with feeding)
    b. Socioeconomic and cultural factors (for example: income, religion)
    c. Psychological factors (for example: fad diets, anorexia)
5. Adaptations of normal diet: definitions, foods allowed, and indications for use
    a. Clear liquid
    b. Full liquid
    c. Soft
6. Alternative feeding methods (for example: gavage, gastrostomy)
7. Agents commonly used to promote nutrition (for example: vitamins and minerals)

B. Nursing care
1. Assessment: establish a database concerning nutritional status
    a. Gather objective and subjective data (for example: weight, height, anorexia)
    b. Assess factors influencing nutrition (see VA4)
2. Diagnosis: identify the patient's actual or potential nursing diagnoses related to nutrition
    a. Analyze and interpret data (for example: serum albumin, body weight)
    b. Identify nursing diagnoses (for example: altered nutrition: less than body requirements related to anorexia)
3. Planning: set priorities, identify patient-centered outcomes and select interventions related to nutrition
    a. Set priorities and establish outcomes (for example: patient will gain one pound per week until ideal body weight is achieved)
    b. Incorporate factors influencing nutrition in planning for patient's dietary needs (for example: plan nutritionally adequate diet based on patient's cultural preferences) (see VA4)
    c. Select nursing interventions to help the patient achieve outcomes related to nutrition
4. Implementation: use nursing interventions to achieve outcomes related to nutrition
    a. Use nursing measures to increase nutritional intake (for example: assist in food selection, assist in feeding, modify the environment, place the patient in the most appropriate position)
    b. Use nursing measures appropriate to particular feeding methods (for example: nasogastric tube feedings, gastrostomy tube feedings)

  c. Use nursing measures specific to drug classifications for prescribed medications (for example: administer liquid iron through a straw)

  d. Instruct the patient regarding nutrition

 5. Evaluation: determine the extent to which outcomes have been achieved

  a. Evaluate, record, and report the patient's response to nursing interventions (for example: the patient has gained two pounds this week)

  b. Modify the plan of care if necessary

VI. Elimination (11%)

A. Theoretical framework

1. Urinary elimination
   a. Anatomy and physiology of urinary tract
   b. Common disturbances (for example: incontinence, frequency, retention)
2. Intestinal elimination
   a. Anatomy and physiology of intestinal tract
   b. Common disturbances (for example: constipation, diarrhea, impaction, flatulence, incontinence)
3. Factors influencing elimination
   a. Individual factors (for example: age, activity level, dietary habits)
   b. Environmental factors (for example: privacy)
   c. Psychological factors (for example: stress)
4. Agents commonly used to promote elimination (for example: laxatives, stool softeners, antidiarrheal agents)

B. Nursing care

1. Assessment: establish a database concerning elimination
   a. Gather objective and subjective data (for example: changes in normal elimination patterns; color, odor, and consistency of urine and feces)
   b. Assess factors influencing elimination (see VIA3)
2. Diagnosis: identify the patient's actual or potential nursing diagnoses related to elimination
   a. Analyze and interpret data (for example: urinalysis, [normal values], frequency of elimination, intake and output, presence of occult blood)
   b. Identify nursing diagnoses (for example: constipation related to insufficient intake of dietary fiber)
3. Planning: set priorities, identify patient-centered outcomes and select interventions related to elimination
   a. Set priorities and establish outcomes (for example: patient will have one soft brown stool daily)
   b. Incorporate factors influencing elimination in planning patient care (for example: the patient is on bed rest) (see VIA3)
   c. Select nursing interventions to help the patient achieve outcomes (for example: consult with the dietician about increasing fiber in the patient's diet)
4. Implementation: use nursing interventions to achieve outcomes related to elimination
   a. Use nursing measures to facilitate elimination (for example: perform catheterization, administer enema, administer laxatives and stool softeners,

provide appropriate intake, collect specimens, ensure appropriate activity, decrease stress, provide proper positioning, ensure privacy)
    b. Use nursing measures specific to drug classifications for prescribed medications (for example: administer a laxative at the time that evacuation is desired, encourage the patient to retain the suppository for 15 minutes)
    c. Instruct the patient regarding elimination (for example: assist patient to plan an exercise program and to increase intake of fluids)
 5. Evaluation: determine the extent to which outcomes have been achieved
    a. Evaluate, record, and report the patient's response to nursing actions (for example: patient reports passing a hard, dry stool)
    b. Modify the plan of care if necessary

VII. Oxygenation (10%)

A. Theoretical framework
 1. Normal respiratory functions
    a. Anatomy and physiology
    b. Ventilation, diffusion, and transport
 2. Common respiratory disturbances (for example: dyspnea, tachypnea, orthopnea, hypoxia)
 3. Factors influencing oxygenation
    a. Individual factors (for example: fever, activity level, excess secretions)
    b. Environmental factors (for example: smoking, room ventilation)
    c. Psychological factors (for example: stress, anxiety)
 4. Techniques commonly used to promote oxygenation (for example: administration of oxygen via nasal cannula and face mask, incentive spirometry, chest physiotherapy)

B. Nursing care
 1. Assessment: establish a database concerning oxygenation status
    a. Gather objective and subjective data (for example: skin color, tolerance for activity, vital signs, respiratory status, shortness of breath, confusion, restlessness)
    b. Assess factors influencing oxygenation (see VIIA3)
 2. Diagnosis: identify the patient's actual or potential nursing diagnoses related to oxygenation
    a. Analyze and interpret data (for example: vital signs, hemoglobin, hematocrit [normal values])
    b. Identify nursing diagnoses (for example: ineffective breathing pattern related to abdominal pain)
 3. Planning: set priorities, identify patient-centered outcomes and select interventions related to oxygenation
    a. Set priorities and establish outcomes (for example: patient will demonstrate increased depth of respiration)
    b. Incorporate factors influencing oxygenation in planning patient care (for example: pain assessment, anxiety, positioning)
    c. Select nursing interventions to help the patient achieve outcomes (for example: provide comfort measures, reposition the patient, administer the prescribed analgesic)

4. Implementation: use nursing interventions to achieve outcomes related to oxygenation
   a. Use nursing measures to promote oxygenation (for example: turning, deep breathing, and coughing; administering oxygen; nasopharyngeal suctioning; monitoring vital signs; reducing anxiety)
   b. Use nursing measures appropriate to the method of oxygen administration (humidifiers, oxygen masks, cannula)
   c. Instruct the patient regarding oxygenation (for example: demonstrate coughing and deep- breathing exercises)
5. Evaluation: determine the extent to which outcomes have been achieved
   a. Evaluate, record, and report the patient's response to nursing actions (for example: patient's respirations are 12–14/minute, deep, and rhythmic)
   b. Modify the plan of care if necessary

VIII. Fluid and Electrolyte Balance (11%)

A. Concepts and principles
1. Principles related to fluid and electrolyte balance (for example: composition, regulation, and movement of fluid and electrolytes)
2. Common disturbances of fluid and electrolyte balance
   a. Hypercalcemia, hypocalcemia
   b. Hyperkalemia, hypokalemia
   c. Hypernatremia, hyponatremia
   d. Hypermagnesemia, hypomagnesemia
   e. Hypervolemia, hypovolemia
3. Common intravenous fluids
   a. Lactated Ringer's
   b. 5% dextrose and water
   c. Normal saline
   d. Half saline
4. Factors influencing fluid and electrolyte balance
   a. Physical status (for example: vomiting, fever, diarrhea, use of diuretics, exercise)
   b. Environmental factors (for example: temperature, humidity)
5. Agents commonly used to promote fluid and electrolyte balance (for example: administration of IV fluids, electrolyte supplements)

B. Nursing care
1. Assessment: establish a database concerning fluid and electrolyte status
   a. Gather objective and subjective data (for example: skin turgor, pulse quality, condition of oral mucous membranes, output, weight, edema, muscle weakness, thirst)
   b. Assess factors influencing fluid and electrolyte status (see VIIIA4)
2. Diagnosis: identify the patient's actual or potential nursing diagnoses related to fluids and electrolytes
   a. Analyze and interpret data (for example: serum electrolyte level, hematocrit [normal values] specific gravity of urine [normal values])
   b. Identify nursing diagnoses (for example: fluid volume deficit related to insufficient intake)

c. Planning: set priorities, identify patient-centered outcomes and select appropriate interventions related to fluids and electrolytes
   d. Set priorities and establish outcomes (for example: patient's total fluid intake will be 2,500 cc/day)
   e. Incorporate factors influencing fluid and electrolyte status (for example: establish a pattern of fluid intake based on individual patient preferences) (see VIIIA4)
   f. Select nursing interventions to help the patient achieve outcomes (for example: monitor IV therapy, provide oral fluids)
3. Implementation: use nursing interventions to achieve outcomes related to fluid and electrolyte balance
   a. Promote fluid and electrolyte balance (for example: assist with food and fluid selection, measure and record intake and output)
   b. Use nursing measures appropriate to oral and parenteral replacement (for example: establish daily fluid regimen with patient, assist with parenteral administration of fluids [gravity flow and IV infusion pumps], identify signs and symptoms of untoward reactions)
   c. Instruct the patient regarding fluid and electrolyte requirements (for example: discuss dietary sources of potassium)
4. Evaluation: determine the extent to which outcomes have been achieved
   a. Evaluate, record, and report the patient's response to nursing actions (for example: patient's 24-hour fluid intake is 2,500 cc)
   b. Modify the plan of care if necessary

Sample Questions: Fundamentals of Nursing

1. A mentally competent patient refuses an injection. The nurse administers the injection despite the patient's refusal. In this situation, the nurse can be held liable for which offense?
    1) assault
    2) battery
    3) invasion of privacy
    4) a misdemeanor

2. Which term describes the rules or principles that govern professional conduct?
    1) beliefs
    2) ethics
    3) morals
    4) values

3. A patient is being admitted to the hospital. The nurse notes that the patient's pulse and blood pressure are higher than they were on previous routine office visits. How should the nurse interpret these findings initially?
   The findings are indicative of
    1) the resistance stage of stress.
    2) an autonomic nervous system response.
    3) an inflammatory response.
    4) the local adaptation syndrome.

4. Which observation is most indicative of a localized infection?
    1) diaphoresis
    2) fatigue
    3) fever
    4) swelling

5. Which information in a patient's health history indicates that the patient is at risk for infection?
    1) The patient had mumps three years ago.
    2) The patient had rubella one year ago.
    3) The patient had a tetanus booster 12 years ago.
    4) The patient was a year late receiving the polio vaccine.

6. A patient is being discharged with an indwelling urinary catheter. Which instruction should the nurse give to the patient to help prevent a urinary tract infection?
    1) Allow the collection bag to fill completely before emptying it.
    2) Separate the catheter from the tubing when emptying the collection bag.
    3) Clamp the tubing before exercising or ambulating.
    4) Position the tubing so the urine flows into the collection bag.

7. Which assessment finding indicates that a hospitalized patient is at risk for physical injury?
    1) diminished lung sounds
    2) hyperactive bowel sounds
    3) weak right hand grasp
    4) bilateral +1 ankle edema

Sample Questions: Fundamentals of Nursing

8. When administering a medication via the Z-track method, the nurse should include which action?
    1) Massage the site following the injection.
    2) Give the injection into subcutaneous tissue.
    3) Change the needle prior to the injection.
    4) Administer the medication rapidly.

9. When administering a medication to a patient with decreased liver function, the nurse should be most concerned with which mechanism of the drug's action?
    1) absorption
    2) distribution
    3) excretion
    4) metabolism

10. Which instruction should the nurse give to a patient who uses a bath oil?
    1) Be certain to remove all oil residue from the skin.
    2) Take precautions to prevent falls in the bathtub.
    3) Alternate the use of bath oil with a skin lotion.
    4) Use a washcloth to apply the bath oil.

11. To which stage of sleep will a patient return after being awakened for a treatment?
    1) the stage from which she was awakened
    2) the first stage of sleep
    3) the rapid eye movement stage
    4) the second stage of sleep

12. A patient is on bed rest. To avoid a complication of immobility, the nurse should give priority to which assessment?
    1) activity tolerance
    2) bowel sounds
    3) lung sounds
    4) urinary output

13. Which analgesic is most commonly associated with an increased incidence of gastric bleeding in older adults?
    1) acetaminophen (Tylenol)
    2) codeine
    3) indomethacin (Indocin)
    4) meperidine hydrochloride (Demerol)

14. Which measure should the nurse include in the plan of care for a patient who is experiencing pain?
    1) Implement pain relief measures before the pain becomes severe.
    2) Use the same pain relief measure for each pain experience.
    3) Administer pain medications on a predetermined schedule.
    4) Encourage the patient to increase the intervals between pain medication requests.

Sample Questions: Fundamentals of Nursing

15. Which food is highest in saturated fat?
    1) butter
    2) margarine
    3) olive oil
    4) peanut oil

16. Which observation indicates that a patient is responding positively to oxygen therapy?
    1) dyspnea
    2) eupnea
    3) hyperpnea
    4) orthopnea

17. Which assessment data should alert the nurse to the likelihood that a patient may be experiencing fluid volume deficit?
    1) increased hematocrit
    2) leukocytosis
    3) distended neck veins
    4) peripheral edema

18. When a patient's serum sodium level is 129 mEq/L, the nurse should anticipate an order for which IV fluid?
    1) 5% dextrose in water
    2) 5% dextrose in 0.45% NaCl
    3) 5% dextrose in 0.9% NaCl
    4) lactated Ringer's solution

19. The physician orders an IV infusion of 1,000 cc 0.9% NaCl to run over 10 hours. The IV administration set delivers 10 drops per cc. The nurse should regulate the flow rate at how many drops per minute?
    1) 6 to 7
    2) 16 to 17
    3) 25 to 26
    4) 31 to 32

20. Which instructional technique should maximize independence for a patient who needs to limit sodium in the diet?
    1) Calculate the actual volume of salt in the patient's usual diet.
    2) Provide the patient with a list of foods that must be avoided.
    3) Give the patient a set of written, preplanned, low-sodium menus.
    4) Explain to the patient how to read and interpret food labels.

Sample Questions: Fundamentals of Nursing

Recommended Textbooks

The examination development committee recommends that you obtain one of the textbooks listed below. Each of these textbooks has a companion study guide. If you would like assistance in organizing your study and review of the material in the textbooks, the committee recommends that you consider purchasing the study guide as well.

Kozier, B., Erb, G., Blais, K., & Wilkinson, J. (1998). Fundamentals of nursing: Concepts, process, and practice *(Updated 5th ed.). Menlo Park, CA: Addison-Wesley.*

Study Guide:
Van Leuven, K. (1998). Study guide for Fundamentals of nursing: Concepts, process, and practice *(Updated 5th ed.). Menlo Park, CA: Addison-Wesley.*

OR
Taylor, C., Lillis, C., & Lemone, P. (1997). Fundamentals of nursing: The art and science of nursing care *(3rd ed.). Philadelphia: J.B. Lippincott.*

Study Guide:
Taylor, C., Lillis, C., & Lemone, P. (1997). Study guide to accompany Fundamentals of nursing: The art and science of nursing care *(3rd ed.). Philadelphia: J.B. Lippincott.*

Additional Textbooks
Cataldo, C., DeBruyne, L., & Whitney, E. (1996). Nutrition and diet therapy: Principles and practices *(4th ed.). St. Paul, MN: West.*

Kozier, B. et al. (1993). Techniques in clinical nursing: A nursing process approach *(4th ed.). Menlo Park, CA: Addison-Wesley.*

McKenry, L., & Salerno, E. (1995). Mosby's Pharmacology in nursing *(19th ed.). St. Louis: Mosby.*

Wilkinson, J. (1995). Nursing diagnosis and intervention pocket guide *(6th ed.). Redwood City, CA: Addison-Wesley.*

Study Guide
Maternal & Child Nursing (associate) (453)

Credit Hours: 6
Credit Level: Lower
Question Type(s): Multiple-choice

The information in this study guide is valid until Summer 2001.
If you will be taking the examination after that date, be sure to check for a new edition of this guide before you complete your preparation for the exam.

General Description of the Examination

The Maternal & Child Nursing (associate) examination measures knowledge and understanding of maternity nursing and care of both well and ill children from birth through adolescence. It is based on material normally taught in a course in maternal and child nursing at the associate degree level.

The examination requires you to possess knowledge and understanding of the theoretical framework related to each content area. The examination further requires you to apply this knowledge by using the nursing process (assessment, diagnosis, planning, implementation, and evaluation) to provide nursing care to the family during the childbearing and childrearing cycles.

Content Outline

Content Area	Percent of Examination
I. Antepartal Care	15%
II. Intrapartal Care	10%
III. Postpartal Care	15%
IV. The Newborn	10%
V. The Infant	10%
VI. The Toddler	10%
VII. The Preschooler	10%
VIII. The School-Age Child	10%
IX. The Adolescent	10%
Total	**100%**

I. Antepartal Care (15%)

A. Theoretical framework
1. Anatomy and physiology (for example: lab values [Rh factor, alpha-fetoprotein, rubella titer, blood type], age of parents, placental growth and function, vital signs, common discomforts, signs and symptoms, body system changes, fetal growth patterns, engagement)
2. Common health problems (pathophysiology and clinical manifestations)
   a. Acute health problems
      1) Maternal
         (a) Third trimester bleeding
         (b) Ectopic pregnancy
         (c) Abortion
         (d) Hyperemesis gravidarum
         (e) Multiple births
         (f) Gestational diabetes
         (g) Preterm labor
         (h) Pregnancy-induced hypertension
         (i) Hydatidiform mole
      2) Fetal
         (a) Intrauterine growth retardation
         (b) Malformation
         (c) Blood incompatibilities
         (d) Teratogenic/environmental effects
   b. Chronic health problems
      1) Diabetes
      2) Cardiovascular disorders
      3) Renal disorders
      4) Infectious diseases (for example: STDs, AIDS, tuberculosis, pyelonephritis, TORCH infections)
      5) Substance abuse
3. Factors influencing health care
   a. Individual factors (for example: nutrition [adolescent, cultural preferences, effects on fetus], lifestyle, cultural patterns, adolescent pregnancy, educational level, smoking, parity, family history, obstetric history, occupation, environmental factors, language barriers, childbirth preparation, family participation in birth)
   b. Safety (for example: educational deficits, bed rest, knowledge of warning signs, regular prenatal care, environmental factors, potential for child abuse, choice of appropriate birthing options, genetic counseling)
   c. Psychosocial factors (for example: emotional changes, parent ages, accessibility of health care, childbirth preparation, cultural practices and myths, developmental tasks, support systems [family, spiritual, psychological, social] parenting behaviors, birthing options)

B. Nursing care
1. Assessment: establish a database
   a. Gather objective and subjective data (for example: stress and nonstress tests, ultrasound, amniocentesis, urine analysis, biophysical profile, chorionic villi

sampling, placental function testing, previous obstetric history, coexisting health problems, height and weight, fundal height, calculation of estimated date of birth using Nägele's rule)
   b. Assess factors influencing the patient's health (for example: maternal and family history [genetic disorders], use of drugs and alcohol, nutritional status, prenatal care, medications being taken, educational level, financial constraints) (see IA3)
2. Diagnosis: identify the patient's actual or potential nursing diagnoses
   a. Analyze and interpret data (see IB1)
   b. Identify nursing diagnoses (for example: activity intolerance related to fatigue of late pregnancy; powerlessness related to limited resources; altered nutrition: risk for more than body requirements related to imbalance between intake and available insulin; risk for fetal injury related to presence of maternal high-risk behaviors or exposure to teratogens; altered comfort related to common discomforts of pregnancy; knowledge deficit: signs and symptoms of impending labor)
3. Planning: set priorities, identify patient-centered goals (expected outcomes) and select appropriate interventions
   a. Set priorities and establish goals (for example: patient will establish a schedule of regular rest periods, patient will experience an increased sense of control, patient will understand and follow prescribed diet, patient will enter a smoking cessation program, patient will identify specific measures that provide relief from discomforts, patient will recognize and act upon signs and symptoms of labor)
   b. Incorporate individual, safety, and psychosocial factors (for example: identify the patient's educational level, identify patient's level of motivation to stop smoking, identify dietary choices that are appropriate to cultural and individual preferences) (see IA3)
   c. Select nursing interventions to help the patient meet goals (for example: instruct the patient about health needs during late pregnancy, provide opportunities for decision making to enhance self-esteem, emphasize the importance of strict dietary control and maintaining a daily intake record, provide information regarding the effects of teratogens, instruct the patient to wear a supportive bra, instruct the patient to increase carbohydrate intake upon arising, instruct the patient about the signs and symptoms of labor)
4. Implementation: use nursing interventions to achieve goals
   a. Use nursing measures to promote normal growth and development (for example: encourage verbalization of feelings regarding the diagnosis of pregnancy, assist the adolescent patient in identifying realistic choices regarding the pregnancy)
   b. Use nursing measures to promote safety (for example: palpate the patient's ankles to assess the degree of edema, instruct the patient about the hazards of changing a cat litter box, emphasize the use of home glucose monitoring devices, explain the need to use safer sex practices to minimize the transmission of infection)
   c. Use nursing measures to promote oxygenation (for example: administer oxygen to the patient with abruptio placenta, encourage frequent rest periods as pregnancy progresses, emphasize the importance of continuing

iron supplements throughout pregnancy, position the mother on the left side if signs of preterm labor occur)
- d. Use nursing measures to promote nutrition (for example: encourage increased intake of iron and calcium, provide written information about prenatal diet, identify variations in dietary patterns)
- e. Use nursing measures to prevent complications (for example: increase fluid intake to prevent urinary tract infections, encourage the patient to wear cotton underwear, emphasize the importance of regular exercise, teach the patient with gestational diabetes to recognize the signs and symptoms of hyper- and hypoglycemia)
- f. Use nursing measures to relieve discomfort (for example: instruct the patient to increase intake of carbohydrates prior to arising to minimize nausea and vomiting, provide the patient with a supportive bra, encourage the patient with constipation to increase intake of fluid and fiber)
- g. Use nursing measures specific to prescribed medications (for example: emphasize need to take prenatal vitamins throughout pregnancy, suggest that the patient take iron supplements with orange juice, monitor respiratory rate prior to the administration of magnesium sulfate, instruct the patient who is receiving a tocolytic agent to report palpitations and elevated pulse rate)
- h. Provide information and instruction (for example: refer the patient to community resources [shelters, clinics, nutritional supplement programs, transportation]; provide information about childbirth classes; provide instructional materials related to the symptoms of preterm labor, hypertension, common discomforts, fetal growth and development, birthing options, anesthesia and analgesia)
5. Evaluation: determine the extent to which goals have been achieved
    - a. Evaluate, record, and report the patient's response to nursing interventions (for example: whether the patient continues to smoke during pregnancy, morning sickness interferes less with the patient's daily routine, patient's blood glucose level remains above normal, patient reports increased intake of foods rich in calcium and iron)
    - b. Modify the plan of care if necessary (for example: encourage the patient to identify stressors that lead to smoking, arrange for a consultation with a nutritionist)

II. Intrapartal Care (10%)

A. Theoretical framework
1. Anatomy and physiology (for example: maternal and fetal monitoring, reaction of fetus to contractions, presentation, station, cervical changes, vital signs, laboratory values)
2. Common health problems (pathophysiology and clinical manifestations)
    - a. Acute health problems
        1) Failure to progress (for example: cephalopelvic disproportion, hypotonic labor patterns)
        2) Bleeding disorders (for example: abruptio placenta, placenta previa, disseminated intravascular coagulation)
        3) Malpresentation (for example: breech, transverse lie)
        4) Fetal distress (for example: prolapsed cord, cord compression)

            5) Multiple birth
            6) Induction and augmentation
            7) Operative delivery (for example: cesarean, forceps)
            8) Episiotomy
            9) Perineal lacerations
        b. Chronic health problems
            1) Cardiovascular disorders
            2) Renal disorders
            3) Hypertension
            4) Substance abuse
    3. Factors influencing health care
        a. Individual factors (for example: parity, educational level, prenatal care, voiding status, preparation for labor, coping styles, cultural variations, choice of birthing option)
        b. Safety (for example: membrane status, pattern of prenatal care, use of medications during labor, maternal position, fetal heart rate pattern, emergency delivery)
        c. Psychosocial factors (for example: support systems [family, spiritual, psychological], participation in labor and delivery by significant other)

B. **Nursing care**
    1. Assessment: establish a database
        a. Gather objective and subjective data (for example: obstetric history; intake and output; frequency, duration, and intensity of contractions; fetal heart monitor; effacement and dilation; lab values [CBC, hemoglobin, blood type, hematocrit]; time of last meal)
        b. Assess factors influencing the patient's health (for example: medications being taken, coexisting health problems, anesthesia and analgesia) (see IIA3)
    2. Diagnosis: identify the patient's actual or potential nursing diagnoses
        a. Analyze and interpret data (see IIB1)
        b. Identify nursing diagnoses (for example: fear related to process of labor; fear related to unfamiliar environment; risk for fluid volume deficit related to NPO status and nausea and vomiting; knowledge deficit: effect of regional anesthesia; altered tissue perfusion related to excessive blood loss)
    3. Planning: set priorities, identify patient-centered goals (expected outcomes) and select appropriate interventions
        a. Set priorities and establish goals (for example: patient will identify effective coping styles, patient's urinary output will be 30–50 cc/hour, patient will make appropriate decision related to anesthesia, patient will maintain adequate tissue perfusion as evidenced by blood pressure within normal parameters)
        b. Incorporate individual, safety, and psychosocial factors (for example: identify cultural variations in coping styles, educational level, language barriers) (see IIA3)
        c. Select nursing interventions to help the patient meet goals (for example: demonstrate breathing patterns and distraction and relaxation techniques to relieve pain and manage stress, orient the patient to the environment and explain procedures, monitor intake and output, instruct the patient about the advantages and disadvantages of anesthesia, compare present blood pressure with the patient's baseline blood pressure)

4. Implementation: use nursing interventions to achieve goals
   a. Use nursing measures to promote the normal progression of labor (for example: position the patient to facilitate the effect of gravity, ambulate the patient prior to rupture of membranes)
   b. Use nursing measures to promote safety (for example: maintain asepsis during procedures, change the patient's position hourly, teach effective breathing techniques, support the patient's extremities, recognize emergency situations and intervene accordingly)
   c. Use nursing measures to promote oxygenation (for example: position the patient to facilitate tissue perfusion, provide oxygen via mask during the expulsion phase of labor, discontinue oxytocin infusion in the presence of tetanic contractions)
   d. Use nursing measures to promote psychological equilibrium (for example: respect personal space, use touch as tolerated, encourage expression of feelings, offer self as appropriate, provide support for the patient's significant other)
   e. Use nursing measures to prevent complications (for example: monitor vital signs frequently, monitor fetal heart rate, assess the amount and characteristics of drainage)
   f. Use nursing measures to relieve discomfort (for example: encourage use of breathing techniques, massage bony prominences, use effleurage and massage as tolerated)
   g. Use nursing measures specific to prescribed medications (for example: administer medications at the appropriate times, monitor blood pressure during epidural anesthesia, recognize the effects of medication on the fetus, have antidotes available for the patient receiving magnesium sulfate)
   h. Provide information and instruction (for example: provide information regarding the progress of labor, reinforce the patient's use of correct breathing techniques)
5. Evaluation: determine the extent to which goals have been achieved
   a. Evaluate, record, and report the patient's response to nursing interventions (for example: patient's breathing techniques are effective in reducing pain, patient's blood pressure remains within normal limits, fetal heart rate shows long-term variability, urinary output remains above 30 cc/hour, presence of meconium-stained amniotic fluid)
   b. Modify the plan of care if necessary (for example: administer analgesics as ordered to relieve pain, notify the physician)

III. Postpartal Care (15%)

A. **Theoretical framework**
   1. Anatomy and physiology (for example: involution, common discomforts, breast changes, vital signs, lab values)
   2. Common health problems (pathophysiology and clinical manifestations)
      a. Acute health problems
         1) Postpartum bleeding disorders
         2) Disseminated intravascular coagulation
         3) Pregnancy-induced hypertension
         4) Infection, inflammation, urinary retention

                5) Subinvolution
            b. Chronic health problems
                1) Cardiovascular disorders
                2) Renal disorders
                3) Diabetes
                4) Substance abuse
        3. Factors influencing health care
            a. Individual factors (for example: nutrition, maternal age, educational level, cultural variations, family history, prolonged or difficult labor, premature infant, newborn with health problem, history of depression, neonatal death, coping skills, working mother, financial considerations)
            b. Safety (for example: pain and fatigue, type of delivery, discharge instructions related to self-care, activity tolerance)
            c. Psychosocial factors (for example: role change; parenting; sibling relationships; acceptance of pregnancy; visitation; emotional needs; bonding, family relationships; changes in marital relationships; taking in, taking hold, and letting go)

B. Nursing care
    1. Assessment: establish a database
        a. Gather objective and subjective data (for example: vital signs, elimination patterns, hydration status, lochia, fatigue, laboratory data, CBC, status of incision, presence of hemorrhoids, engorgement, afterbirth pains, episiotomy, Homans' sign, fundal height, attachment behaviors, facial expression, posture)
        b. Assess factors influencing the patient's health (for example: presence of significant other, cultural variations, support systems) (see IIIA3)
    2. Diagnosis: identify the patient's actual or potential nursing diagnoses
        a. Analyze and interpret data (see IIIB1)
        b. Identify nursing diagnoses (for example: social isolation related to adolescent pregnancy and rejection by peers and parents, altered bowel elimination, constipation related to intrapartal analgesia and hemorrhoids, risk for injury related to prolonged bed rest during labor, risk for altered parenting related to delayed parent-infant attachment, anxiety related to the unmet expectation of vaginal delivery)
    3. Planning: set priorities, identify patient-centered goals (expected outcomes) and select interventions
        a. Set priorities and establish goals (for example: patient will discuss ways to increase meaningful relationships, patient's normal elimination patterns will resume, patient will not develop postpartal complications, parents will bond with the newborn, parents will verbalize acceptance of the reality)
        b. Incorporate individual, safety, and psychosocial factors (for example: cultural variations, type of delivery, family structure, role relationships) (see IIIA3)
        c. Select nursing interventions to help the patient meet goals (for example: assist the patient to identify possible support persons, increase the patient's intake of fluids and fiber and encourage activity, ambulate the patient as soon as possible following delivery, provide opportunities for the parents to see and hold the infant, provide opportunities for the patient to discuss the labor and delivery experience, assist the parent[s] to cope with loss)

4. Implementation: use nursing interventions to achieve goals
   a. Use nursing measures to promote normal growth and development (for example: reinforce parenting skills, provide information regarding postpartal emotional changes, reinforce the patient's attempts at feeding and infant care, encourage the parents to hold the infant as soon as possible following delivery)
   b. Use nursing measures to promote safety and prevent complications (for example: apply cold packs to the perineum during the first 24 hours postdelivery, assist the patient who is getting out of bed for the first time, maintain medical asepsis during procedures, place a patient with a positive Homans' sign on bed rest, massage a patient's boggy fundus)
   c. Use nursing measures to promote oxygenation (for example: provide frequent rest periods, determine amount of blood loss by assessing lochia, encourage the patient to perform incentive spirometry in the postoperative period)
   d. Use nursing measures to promote nutrition (for example: encourage intake of fluids and high-fiber foods, instruct patient to continue prenatal vitamins, increase caloric and fluid intake for the patient who is breast-feeding)
   e. Use nursing measures to promote healing (for example: apply heat to the perineum after the first 24 hours postdelivery, encourage the patient to allow sore nipples to air dry, demonstrate perineal care)
   f. Use nursing measures to relieve physiological and psychological discomfort (for example: apply ice packs to the breasts of the mother who plans to bottle-feed her newborn to reduce engorgement, encourage the mother who is breast-feeding to nurse her newborn frequently, provide local anesthetic agents for perineal discomfort, encourage expression of feelings by parent[s])
   g. Use nursing measures specific to prescribed medications (for example: assess blood pressure frequently when administering ergonovine maleate [Ergotrate], provide contraception instruction to the patient who is receiving bromocriptine mesylate [Parlodel])
   h. Provide information and instruction (for example: regarding contraception, standard psychological and physiological changes, infant safety, self-care, infant care, breast- and bottle-feeding; referrals to community agencies for follow-up care)
5. Evaluation: determine the extent to which goals have been achieved
   a. Evaluate, record, and report the patient's response to nursing interventions (for example: patient exhibits a positive Homans' sign, parents admire their infant and call the child by name, mother makes disparaging remarks about the newborn and ignores the child's crying, firm fundus located 1 cm below the umbilicus on the first day postpartum)
   b. Modify the plan of care if necessary (for example: elevate the affected leg and maintain bed rest, consult with social services for follow-up home care)

IV. The Newborn (0–1 month) (10%)

A. **Theoretical framework**
   1. Anatomy and physiology (for example: vital signs, skin color, reflexes, cry, elimination patterns, presence of mucus, laboratory and diagnostic data [PKU, bilirubin, Dextrostix, Coombs])

2. Common health problems (pathophysiology and clinical manifestations)
    a. Acute health problems
        1) Birth injuries
        2) Necrotizing enterocolitis (NEC)
        3) Respiratory distress
        4) Thermoregulation
        5) Cleft lip
        6) Tracheoesophageal defects
        7) Meconium ileus
        8) Hypoglycemia
        9) Hemolytic disease
        10) Meconium aspiration
        11) Neural tube defects
    b. Chronic health problems
        1) Clubfoot
        2) Drug dependence
        3) Venereal disease
        4) Fetal alcohol syndrome
        5) Effects of fetal hypoxia
3. Factors influencing health care
    a. Individual factors (for example: nutrition [breast-fed, bottle-fed], GI/GU function, gestational age, maternal history [smoking, drinking, diet], anesthesia, family history, weight and length, head circumference, cultural variations)
    b. Safety (for example: positioning, feeding, provision for warmth, identification procedures, Apgar scoring, eye care, administration of vitamin K)
    c. Psychosocial factors (for example: bonding, development of trust [Erikson])

B. Nursing care
1. Assessment: establish a database
    a. Gather objective and subjective data (for example: vital signs, Apgar score, PKU, Dextrostix, bilirubin, reflexes, GI/GU function, elimination pattern, color, cry, cord bloods, activity level, Ortolani's sign)
    b. Assess factors influencing the newborn's health (for example: temperature regulation, bonding, nutritional needs, maternal history, gestational age, cultural differences, interaction with significant others, parenting) (see IVA3)
2. Diagnosis: identify the patient's actual or potential nursing diagnoses
    a. Analyze and interpret data (see IVB1)
    b. Identify nursing diagnoses (for example: altered tissue perfusion, peripheral, related to environmental cold; ineffective breathing pattern related to immature respiratory center; altered growth and development related to musculoskeletal impairment; fluid volume deficit related to NPO status; altered comfort related to NPO status)
3. Planning: set priorities, identify patient-centered goals (expected outcomes) and select interventions
    a. Set priorities and establish goals (for example: the newborn's axillary temperature will be 97–98° F, the newborn's respiratory rate will be within normal limits, the newborn will gain optimal use of the affected extremity, the newborn will maintain adequate hydration status, the newborn will suck and sleep at intervals)

b. Incorporate individual, safety, and psychosocial factors (for example: plan for heat in isolette, positioning to open airway, use of suction) (see IVA3)
c. Select nursing interventions to help the patient meet goals (for example: dry the newborn immediately after birth and place in a warm environment, suction the airway as needed, immobilize the affected extremity, administer IV fluids as ordered and according to body weight, encourage use of pacifier, hold and stroke the newborn frequently)

4. Implementation: use nursing interventions to achieve goals
    a. Use nursing measures to promote normal growth and development (for example: encourage the parent[s] to hold and stroke the infant, instruct the parent[s] about newborn care, meet the newborn's needs immediately)
    b. Use nursing measures to promote safety (for example: place a protective covering over the eyes of a newborn who is under bilirubin lights, instruct patients not to leave the newborn unattended while out of the crib, position the newborn to facilitate drainage of secretions, assess the gag reflex prior to feeding, compare formula label to the physician's order prior to administration)
    c. Use nursing measures to promote oxygenation (for example: use a bulb syringe to remove excess secretions, position the newborn to promote maximum ventilation, assess vital signs following the administration of oxygen at birth)
    d. Use nursing measures to promote nutrition (for example: instruct the mother about breast- and bottle-feeding, provide adequate fluid intake for the breast-feeding mother, feed the newborn at frequent intervals)
    e. Use nursing measures to promote thermoregulation (for example: wrap the newborn snugly, dry the newborn promptly after delivery, assess the axillary temperature, apply a head covering to the newborn after delivery)
    f. Use nursing measures to provide psychological support (for example: give positive reinforcement to the mother's attempts at newborn care, provide the infant with a consistent caregiver, provide an opportunity for the parents to hold and comfort the infant after painful procedures)
    g. Use nursing measures specific to prescribed medications (for example: administer IM phytonadione [Vitamin K] in the vastus lateralis, administer calculated dose based on infant's weight)
    h. Provide information and instruction (for example: instruct the parents about newborn care, appropriate clothing, baby bath, car seat requirements, patterns of feeding and sleeping; discuss circumcision care and cord care with the parents; discuss cast care; discuss care of the suture line for the newborn with cleft lip repair)

5. Evaluation: determine the extent to which goals have been achieved
    a. Evaluate, record, and report the patient's response to nursing interventions (for example: newborn's axillary temperature remains below 97° F, newborn's bilirubin remains elevated, newborn passes meconium within 24 hours of delivery, newborn's Apgar score at one minute is 8, newborn sucks well after aspiration of mucus following delivery, blood glucose remains low)
    b. Modify the plan of care if necessary (for example: double wrap the newborn and place under warming lights, place the newborn under ultraviolet light and increase fluid intake, administer a 5–10% glucose formula orally)

V. The Infant (2-12 months) (10%)

A. Theoretical framework
1. Anatomy and physiology (for example: normal growth patterns, vital signs, developmental milestones, lab values, normal reflexes, immune system, neurological and other systems)
2. Common health problems (pathophysiology and clinical manifestations)
    a. Acute health problems
        1) Tracheoesophageal fistula
        2) Pneumonia—aspiration, infectious
        3) Sudden infant death syndrome (SIDS)
        4) Congenital heart defects
        5) Anemias
        6) Vomiting
        7) Diarrhea
        8) Dehydration
        9) Cleft lip
        10) Intestinal obstruction
        11) Pyloric stenosis
        12) Clubfoot
        13) Congenital dislocation of the hip
        14) Neural tube defects
        15) Seizures
        16) Neuroblastoma
        17) Viral meningitis
        18) Sepsis
        19) Bronchiolitis
        20) Accidental ingestion
    b. Chronic health problems
        1) Cleft palate
        2) Down syndrome
        3) Failure to thrive
        4) Fetal alcohol syndrome
3. Factors influencing health care
    a. Individual factors (for example: heredity, maternal and paternal behaviors, growth and development, language, socialization, nutrition [caloric needs, weaning, introduction of solids, etc.], sleep patterns, immunizations, age-appropriate play)
    b. Safety (for example: aspiration, ingestion of foreign substances, administration of medications, household environment)
    c. Psychosocial factors (for example: development of trust [Erikson], bonding, parenting behaviors, separation anxiety, hospitalization of the infant)

B. Nursing care
1. Assessment: establish a database
    a. Gather objective and subjective data (for example: weight; head circumference; vital signs; hydration status [fontanelles]; neurological indicators [reflexes, cry, nuchal rigidity, epicanthal folds]; respiratory effort and pattern [retractions]; laboratory and diagnostic data [specific gravity,

electrolytes, arterial blood gases, hemoglobin]; elimination patterns; sleep patterns; drooling; Ortolani's sign; skin rashes; activity level)
   b. Assess factors influencing the infant's health (for example: overcrowding, siblings, type of shelter, interaction with mother or significant others, parenting, effect of separation, language, sanitation, cultural differences) (see VA3)
2. Diagnosis: identify the patient's actual or potential nursing diagnoses
   a. Analyze and interpret data (see VB1a)
   b. Identify nursing diagnoses (for example: altered nutrition: less than body requirements related to vomiting; risk for injury related to maturational age of the child; altered parental role related to illness and/or hospitalization of a child; ineffective airway clearance related to retention of secretions)
3. Planning: set priorities, identify patient-centered goals (expected outcomes) and select interventions
   a. Set priorities and establish goals (for example: infant will be free from injury from potentially hazardous factors in the hospital environment, family will demonstrate safe practices in the hospital, infant will not lose more than 20% of body weight during hospitalization)
   b. Incorporate individual, safety, and psychosocial factors in planning patient care (for example: plan to meet the infant's needs immediately, include age-appropriate play activities, select method of medication administration appropriate for the infant's age) (see VA3)
   c. Select nursing interventions to help the patient meet goals (for example: weigh all diapers, raise the crib siderails)
4. Implementation: use nursing interventions to achieve goals
   a. Use nursing measures to promote normal growth and development (for example: ask the parents to bring toys from home, provide a mobile for sensory stimulation, hold the child frequently to develop a sense of trust)
   b. Use nursing measures to promote safety (for example: assure that there is an opening on an infant's mist tent, compare the formula label to the physician's order before administering)
   c. Use nursing measures to promote oxygenation (for example: position the infant to facilitate drainage of secretions)
   d. Use nursing measures to promote nutrition (for example: offer the infant age-appropriate foods, utilize age-appropriate feeding methods)
   e. Use nursing measures to promote healing (for example: prevent crying in an infant with a cleft lip or palate, maintain moist sterile dressings on meningomyelocele sac)
   f. Use nursing measures to relieve discomfort (for example: provide opportunities for the parents to hold and comfort the infant, administer analgesics appropriate to age and weight)
   g. Use nursing measures specific to prescribed medications (for example: administer calculated dose based on infant's weight, provide mouth care to the infant receiving an anticonvulsant medication, assess vital signs following the administration of bronchodilators)
   h. Provide information and instruction to parents (for example: explain methods to maintain cleanliness of cast, refer the parents to support groups in the community, demonstrate postural drainage to the parents, instruct the parents about the introduction of solid foods)

5. Evaluation: determine the extent to which goals have been achieved
   a. Evaluate, record, and report the patient's response to nursing interventions (for example: infant feedings taken and retained, infant's O_2 saturation is at 96% while in the mist tent, infant's breathing remains labored, parents give correct return demonstration of postural drainage)
   b. Modify the plan of care if necessary (for example: reposition the infant to maximize lung expansion, obtain an order for half-strength formula)

VI. The Toddler (13 months–35 months) (10%)

A. Theoretical framework
1. Anatomy and physiology (for example: normal growth patterns, vital signs, developmental milestones, laboratory values, normal reflexes, gross and fine motor development, immune system, elimination)
2. Common health problems (pathophysiology and clinical manifestations)
   a. Acute health problems
      1) Croup and epiglottitis
      2) Otitis media
      3) Urinary tract infections
      4) Helminthic infections
      5) Parasitic infections
      6) Fungal infections
      7) Burns
      8) Poisonings
      9) Cardiac surgery
      10) Amblyopia
      11) Bacterial meningitis
      12) Hernia repair
   b. Chronic health problems
      1) Lead poisoning
      2) Vitamin deficiencies and anemias
      3) Wilms' tumor
      4) Nephrosis
      5) Celiac disease
      6) Hemophilia
      7) Hypospadias or epispadias
      8) Maltreatment, abuse, and neglect
3. Factors influencing health care
   a. Individual factors (for example: growth and development, nutrition [finger foods, food jags, basic food groups], parallel play, toilet training, language development, immunizations, preparation for procedures)
   b. Safety (for example: active and curious, falls, accidents, drowning, poisoning, child abuse/neglect, aspiration, asphyxiation, administration of medications)
   c. Psychosocial factors (for example: autonomy vs. shame and doubt [Erikson], discipline, separation anxiety, rituals, tantrums, negativism, discipline, sibling rivalry, preparation for hospitalization, therapeutic play)

B. Nursing care
  1. Assessment: establish a database
     a. Gather objective and subjective data (for example: vital signs, weight, hydration status, neurological indicators [PERRLA, nuchal rigidity], respiratory effort and pattern [stridor, drooling, barking cough], laboratory and diagnostic data [lead levels, hemoglobin, specific gravity, electrolytes, arterial blood gases], pulling on the ears, protest, despair and denial, elimination patterns, skin rashes, activity level, signs of abuse and neglect)
     b. Assess factors influencing the toddler's health (for example: presence of lead, effect of separation, cultural differences, interaction with significant others, parenting, need for autonomy, ritualistic behavior, curiosity, activity patterns) (see VIA3)
  2. Diagnosis: identify the patient's actual or potential nursing diagnoses
     a. Analyze and interpret data (see VIB1)
     b. Identify nursing diagnoses (for example: ineffective breathing pattern related to inflammatory process/tracheobronchial obstruction; risk for infection, actual, related to short, wide eustachian tube; altered comfort related to the inflammatory process; fluid volume deficit related to increased permeability of blood vessels and fluid shift; anxiety related to separation from parent)
  3. Planning: set priorities, identify patient-centered goals (expected outcomes) and select interventions
     a. Set priorities and establish goals (for example: the toddler will exhibit no sign of respiratory distress, the toddler's behavior will indicate reduced pain, the toddler will maintain normal fluid status during hospitalization, the toddler will exhibit no signs of apprehension)
     b. Incorporate individual, safety, and psychosocial factors (for example: offer the toddler a choice of beverage following administration of a medication, encourage the child to use the playroom, use diversional activities during procedures) (see VIA3)
     c. Select nursing interventions to help the patient meet goals (for example: provide a high-humidity environment, administer analgesics as ordered, discourage chewing by offering liquids and soft foods, plan to weigh the toddler at the same time daily, encourage the parents to stay with the hospitalized toddler)
  4. Implementation: use nursing interventions to achieve goals
     a. Use nursing measures to promote normal growth and development (for example: allow the toddler to explore; provide choices when appropriate; encourage a parent to stay with the toddler; encourage the parents to bring a familiar object from home, such as a blanket or stuffed animal; ignore tantrums; provide for time out)
     b. Use nursing measures to promote safety (for example: do not palpate the abdomen of a toddler with Wilms' tumor, provide a tracheostomy set at the toddler's bedside, keep all medications in a secure location, use a soft toothbrush for the toddler with hemophilia, avoid friction toys in an oxygen mist tent, instruct and counsel the parents about normal toddler behaviors and activities)

c. Use nursing measures to promote oxygenation (for example: organize activities to decrease the toddler's oxygen needs and promote rest, maintain the toddler with epiglottitis in an upright position, avoid examining the throat of a toddler with epiglottitis, provide a high-humidity environment for a toddler with croup)
   d. Use nursing measures to promote nutrition (for example: observe for signs of dehydration, offer the toddler finger foods and choices within food groups, avoid foods with gluten for the toddler with celiac disease)
   e. Use nursing measures to promote healing (for example: provide a diet that is high in iron-rich foods, protein, and vitamin C for a toddler following cardiac surgery; encourage foods that are rich in vitamin C and protein for a toddler with burns; encourage activity to promote circulation to burned areas)
   f. Use nursing measures to relieve discomfort (for example: encourage the parents to stay with the toddler during painful procedures, administer analgesics as ordered, apply ointment to skin rash)
   g. Use nursing measures specific to prescribed medications (for example: administer calculated dosage based on toddler's weight, provide mouth care to the toddler receiving an anti-fungal medication, assess urinary output for a toddler receiving a chelating agent, provide additional fluids for a toddler receiving sulfa medications)
   h. Provide information and instruction (for example: instruct the parents to keep medications out of the toddler's reach, teach the parents to maintain the toddler with otitis media in an upright position when drinking, instruct the parents to have syrup of ipecac on hand in their household, make referrals to support groups, encourage routine vision and dental checkups)
5. Evaluation: determine the extent to which goals have been achieved
   a. Evaluate, record, and report the patient's response to nursing interventions (for example: barking cough has decreased in frequency, toddler eats and retains iron-rich diet, urine remains cloudy, urine specific gravity is maintained at 1.020, parent gives correct return demonstration of urine test for protein)
   b. Modify the plan of care if necessary (for example: apply additional padding to the siderails for a toddler with hemophilia who has developed ecchymosis, obtain an order for fluid restriction due to increased edema in a toddler with nephrosis, withhold chelating agent for a toddler who has a urinary output of less than 30 ml/hour)

VII. The Preschooler (3–5 years) (10%)

A. Theoretical framework
1. Anatomy and physiology (for example: normal growth patterns, vital signs, developmental milestones, laboratory values, gross and fine motor development, immune system)
2. Common health problems (pathophysiology and clinical manifestations)
   a. Acute health problems
      1) Communicable diseases (including HIV virus)
      2) Tonsillitis
      3) Fractures—casts, traction

          4) Upper respiratory infections
          5) Strabismus
       b. Chronic health problems
          1) Nephrotic syndrome
          2) Juvenile rheumatoid arthritis
          3) Cystic fibrosis
          4) Leukemias
          5) Asthma
          6) Sickle cell anemia
    3. Factors influencing health care
       a. Individual factors (for example: growth and development, nutrition [physiologic anorexia], immunizations, play [cooperative, imaginary playmate], language development, school readiness, presence of birth injuries and congenital anomalies, sexual identity formation, susceptibility to infection)
       b. Safety (for example: motor vehicle accidents, drowning, burns, poisonings, self-induced damage, administration of medications)
       c. Psychosocial factors (for example: initiative vs. guilt [Erikson], fears [real and imagined], concept of death, preparation for hospitalization, fear of mutilation and intrusive procedures, fear of abandonment, loss of control, therapeutic play)

B. Nursing care
    1. Assessment: establish a database
       a. Gather objective and subjective data (for example: vital signs, weight, hydration status, nutritional status, respiratory effort and pattern [expiratory wheezing, nasal flaring], laboratory and diagnostic data [sweat test, urine for protein, sedimentation rate, arterial blood gases, hemoglobin, platelets], elimination patterns, complaints of joint pain and difficulty breathing, verbalization of body image changes)
       b. Assess factors influencing the preschooler's health (for example: cultural differences, siblings, overcrowding, type of shelter, interaction with significant others, effect of hospitalization, susceptibility to infection, exposure to children outside of the home) (see VIIA3)
    2. Diagnosis: identify the patient's actual or potential nursing diagnoses
       a. Analyze and interpret data (see VIIB1)
       b. Identify nursing diagnoses (for example: risk for infection related to immunosuppression, body image disturbance related to the presence of a cast, risk for injury [hemorrhage] related to surgical removal of the tonsils, pain related to tissue ischemia)
    3. Planning: set priorities, identify patient-centered goals (expected outcomes) and select interventions
       a. Set priorities and establish goals (for example: the child will remain free of infection despite leukopenia, the child will verbalize understanding of the need for the cast, the child will not aggravate the operative site, the child will be free of joint pain)
       b. Incorporate individual, safety, and psychosocial factors (for example: select method of medication administration appropriate to patient age, encourage child to role play using hospital equipment, provide choices when appropriate) (see VIIA3)

 c. Select nursing interventions to help the patient meet goals (for example: limit exposure of the child with leukemia to infected children on the unit, demonstrate the use of a cast on a doll, encourage the parents to comfort the child to discourage crying, position the extremities comfortably and in good alignment)
4. Implementation: use nursing interventions to achieve goals
 a. Use nursing measures to promote normal growth and development (for example: encourage role playing; provide a night-light for the child; provide age-appropriate activities, such as puzzles, paints, and crayons; avoid intrusive procedures when possible; encourage parental involvement)
 b. Use nursing measures to promote safety (for example: secure orthopedic apparatus, use correct temperature for thermal devices, use protective isolation to prevent the spread of opportunistic infection)
 c. Use nursing measures to promote oxygenation (for example: organize activities to decrease the child's oxygen needs and promote rest, perform postural drainage on the child with cystic fibrosis, administer nebulizer treatments as ordered)
 d. Use nursing measures to promote nutrition (for example: provide a low-salt diet for the child who is in the acute edema phase of nephrotic syndrome, provide foods high in fiber and fluid for the child who is immobilized)
 e. Use nursing measures to promote healing (for example: decrease activity for a child during the edematous phase of nephrotic syndrome, encourage the intake of fluids for a child during the crisis phase of sickle cell anemia)
 f. Use nursing measures to relieve discomfort (for example: give an oatmeal bath to the child with chickenpox, administer narcotics as ordered to the child in sickle cell crisis, cleanse edematous eyelids with warm saline wipes, establish a plan for pain management)
 g. Use nursing measures specific to prescribed medications (for example: administer pancreatic enzymes with cold food, administer mucolytic agents at least an hour before meals, monitor the platelet count of a child with leukemia who is receiving chemotherapy)
 h. Provide information and instruction (for example: instruct parents to avoid the administration of cough suppressants to a child with cystic fibrosis; instruct the parents of a child with sickle cell anemia to monitor fluid intake during periods of heat, stress, or physical activity; instruct the parents of a child who is receiving chemotherapy about the importance of oral hygiene)
5. Evaluation: determine the extent to which goals have been achieved
 a. Evaluate, record, and report the patient's response to nursing interventions (for example: the WBC of a child who is on chemotherapy remains above 3,000, expiratory wheeze is decreased, pedal pulses are present, extremities are cold to touch, child continues to complain of joint pain)
 b. Modify the plan of care if necessary (for example: request the physician to increase the dose or frequency of analgesics, increase periods of activity for the child as edema subsides, provide longer rest periods for the child whose PO_2 has decreased)

VIII. The School-Age Child (6–12 years) (10%)

A. **Theoretical framework**
  1. Anatomy and physiology (for example: normal growth patterns, growth spurts, vital signs, developmental milestones, gross and fine motor development, prepubescent changes, laboratory values)
  2. Common health problems (pathophysiology and clinical manifestations)
     a. Acute health problems
        1) Skin disorders—insect bites, lice, poison ivy
        2) Acute glomerulonephritis
        3) Rheumatic fever
        4) Appendicitis
        5) Enuresis—primary and secondary
        6) Concussions
        7) Legg-Calvé-Perthes disease
     b. Chronic health problems
        1) Minimal brain dysfunction
        2) Mental retardation
        3) Cerebral palsy
        4) Epilepsy
        5) Diabetes mellitus
        6) Brain tumors
        7) Reye's syndrome
        8) Sensory impairment
  3. Factors influencing health care
     a. Individual factors (for example: growth and development, nutrition [childhood obesity, basic food groups], stress, children who care for themselves after school, organized play, intellectual development, school phobia, sex role identity, play in same-sex groups)
     b. Safety (for example: accidents, bike riding, sports injury, firearms, experimentation with intoxicating substances)
     c. Psychosocial factors (for example: industry vs. inferiority [Erikson]; concept of death; preparation for hospitalization; importance of peers; learning social skills; separation from family, peers, and school during hospitalization; loss of control and enforced dependency during hospitalization; fear of illness; pain and immobility; therapeutic play)

B. **Nursing care**
  1. Assessment: establish a database
     a. Gather objective and subjective data (for example: vital signs, weight, height, hydration status, nutritional status, neurological indicators [headaches, spastic movements, gait, muscle tone, chorea], laboratory and diagnostic data [sedimentation rate, C-reactive protein, ASO titer, creatinine, BUN, albumin, blood glucose], elimination patterns)
     b. Assess factors influencing the school-age child's health (for example: cultural differences, siblings, living conditions, interaction with significant others, stress-related disorders, experimentation with harmful substances, dishonest behavior) (see VIIIA3)

2. Diagnosis: identify the patient's actual or potential nursing diagnoses
    a. Analyze and interpret data (see VIIIB1)
    b. Identify nursing diagnoses (for example: impaired physical immobility related to neuromuscular impairment; risk for injury related to lack of awareness of environmental hazards; risk for altered nutrition: less than body requirements related to decreased insulin level)
3. Planning: set priorities, identify patient-centered goals (expected outcomes) and select interventions
    a. Set priorities and establish goals (for example: child will acquire locomotion within capabilities, child will be free from injury from potentially hazardous factors in the hospital environment, child will demonstrate ability to plan nutrition to achieve normal serum glucose values within one month)
    b. Incorporate individual, safety, and psychosocial factors (for example: encourage the child to tell a story about her illness, provide privacy during treatments, provide a same-sex roommate, explain hospital safety rules) (see VIIIA3)
    c. Select nursing interventions to help the patient meet goals (for example: employ aids that facilitate locomotion such as crutches and braces, reinforce and reiterate to the child what he can do and to what areas of the hospital he may go, have the child list all foods eaten in the last 24 hours, have the child make up a sample lunch menu based on the ADA guidelines)
4. Implementation: use nursing interventions to achieve goals
    a. Use nursing measures to promote normal growth and development (for example: encourage the child to perform small tasks on the unit; provide play to promote a sense of industry such as crafts, board games, and computer games; provide privacy to maintain self-esteem; encourage visits with hospitalized age-mates)
    b. Use nursing measures to promote safety (for example: explain rules of traction safety, demonstrate correct procedure for self-administration of insulin, provide an airway at the bedside of a child with seizures, elevate the head of the bed to reduce intracranial pressure, perform a neurological assessment for a child with a head injury)
    c. Use nursing measures to promote oxygenation (for example: monitor the child's oxygen saturation level; position the child with edema in semi-Fowler's position; remove accumulated secretions for the child with seizure activity; assess the peripheral pulses of a child who is in traction, splints, or a cast; maintain the child on bed rest to reduce oxygen needs)
    d. Use nursing measures to promote nutrition (for example: maintain intake and output, maintain fluid restriction for a child with acute glomerulonephritis, restrict salt in the diet of a child who is edematous, plan a menu using the ADA exchange list, administer feedings through a nasogastric tube if indicated)
    e. Use nursing measures to promote healing (for example: teach skin care to the child with diabetes, maintain splints for a child with Legg-Calvé-Perthes disease, apply lotions to the skin of a child with poison ivy)
    f. Use nursing measures to relieve discomfort (for example: provide a medicated bath for the child with a skin disorder, encourage the child with

polyarthritis to assume a position of comfort, encourage ambulation and splinting for a child following an appendectomy)
- g. Use nursing measures specific to prescribed medications (for example: check for allergies before administering an antibiotic, monitor blood sugar prior to the administration of insulin, use correct technique when administering insulin, monitor vital signs prior to the administration of analgesics, monitor therapeutic levels of anticonvulsant medications)
- h. Provide information and instruction (for example: provide guidance about the use of sports equipment, bicycles, and helmets; teach the child and parent how to perform a finger stick test for glucose, insulin injection, and urine testing; instruct the parents of a child with rheumatic fever that antibiotics must be continued for at least five years; teach children who are allergic to stinging insects to protect uncovered skin and avoid scented products)
5. Evaluation: determine the extent to which goals have been achieved
    - a. Evaluate, record, and report the patient's response to nursing interventions (for example: the child refuses to perform self-injection of insulin, the child is able to use assistive devices correctly, the child reports a decrease in pain, the child has no evidence of head lice, the pedal pulse is present, the child is pale and diaphoretic after insulin administration)
    - b. Modify the plan of care if necessary (for example: teach the parents of a child with diabetes to administer insulin, decrease environmental stimuli, elevate the head of the bed, assess for signs of increased intracranial pressure, monitor vital signs frequently, provide the child with a glass of orange juice and reassess finger stick)

IX. The Adolescent (13+ years) (10%)

A. Theoretical framework
1. Anatomy and physiology (for example: normal growth patterns, height, weight, growth spurts, developmental milestones, secondary sex characteristics, menarche, hormonal changes)
2. Common health problems (pathophysiology and clinical manifestations)
    a. Acute health problems
       1) Acne
       2) Infectious mononucleosis
       3) Sexually transmitted diseases (STDs)
       4) Sexual trauma
       5) Sports injuries
       6) Suicide
       7) Substance abuse
    b. Chronic health problems
       1) Anorexia nervosa and bulimia
       2) Scoliosis
       3) Hypertension
       4) Effects of chronic illness on the adolescent (for example: psychosocial effects on patients who have cystic fibrosis, diabetes, sickle cell anemia, asthma)

3. Factors influencing health care
   a. Individual factors (for example: nutrition [normal requirements, obesity, fad diets], contraception, need for privacy, body image, age-appropriate activities, rate of growth, independence, sexual experimentation, body image, lifestyle changes related to chronic illness, cultural variations)
   b. Safety (for example: accidents, sports injuries, contraception, risk-taking behaviors)
   c. Psychosocial factors (for example: identity vs. role confusion [Erikson], interpersonal relationships [parents, peers], body image, preparation for hospitalization, loss of control in decision making, separation from peers, therapeutic play, peer control)

B. Nursing care
   1. Assessment: establish a database
      a. Gather objective and subjective data (for example: vital signs, intake and output, dietary habits, laboratory and diagnostic data [hemoglobin, hematocrit, Dextrostix, urine pH, VDRL, vaginal cultures, specific gravity], reports of pain [sickle, scoliosis])
      b. Assess factors influencing the adolescent's health (for example: diet fads, hormonal changes, sexual development, body image, sexual awakening, exposure to drugs and alcohol, need for independence) (see IXA3)
   2. Diagnosis: identify the patient's actual or potential nursing diagnoses
      a. Analyze and interpret data (see IXB1)
      b. Identify nursing diagnoses (for example: impaired skin integrity related to corrective devices; pain related to genital lesions secondary to herpes infection; body image disturbance related to fear of obesity; altered nutrition: less than body requirements related to self-starvation, risk for injury related to acute depression)
   3. Planning: set priorities, identify patient-centered goals (expected outcomes) and select interventions
      a. Set priorities and establish goals (for example: the adolescent's skin will remain intact when the corrective device is worn, the adolescent will have reduced pain when voiding, the adolescent will verbalize positive indicators of body image, the adolescent will gain weight at the rate of 0.1 kg per day, the adolescent will verbalize a decrease in suicidal thoughts)
      b. Incorporate individual, safety, and psychosocial factors (for example: prescribed diets, secondary sex characteristics, menarche, growth spurts, effects of hormonal changes, self-image) (see IXA3)
      c. Select nursing interventions to help the patient meet goals (for example: monitor the skin surfaces that are in contact with assistive devices, encourage the adolescent to use a sitz bath with warm water, encourage the adolescent to verbalize feelings about self, weigh the adolescent at regular intervals under standard conditions, remove all potentially dangerous objects from the adolescent's belongings)
   4. Implementation: use nursing interventions to achieve goals
      a. Use nursing measures to promote normal growth and development (for example: provide choices while giving care, provide time with peers, arrange for the adolescent to have use of a telephone, assist the adolescent with scoliosis to select clothing that complements the brace)

    b. Use nursing measures to promote safety (for example: observe the patient's behavior before and after peer visits, use asepsis to prevent transmission of communicable disease, locate the patient's room near the nurse's station, instruct the patient with mononucleosis to avoid contact sports, teach the adolescent who is sexually active about the proper use of condoms)
    c. Use nursing measures to promote oxygenation (for example: provide oxygen to an adolescent with respiratory depression, increase fluid intake to promote the circulation of RBCs for an adolescent with sickle cell anemia, monitor oxygen saturation levels for an adolescent with respiratory depression)
    d. Use nursing measures to promote nutrition (for example: encourage a diet high in protein and iron, use behavior modification techniques for the adolescent with anorexia, maintain a consistent approach in implementing the nutritional regimen for an adolescent with an eating disorder, include calcium-rich foods in the diet of an adolescent who is immobilized following spinal fusion)
    e. Use nursing measures to promote healing (for example: encourage the adolescent to wear the Milwaukee brace for 23 hours a day, teach the adolescent with a skin condition about correct cleansing techniques and medical asepsis, teach the adolescent with diabetes about proper care of minor infections)
    f. Use nursing measures to relieve discomfort (for example: acknowledge the adolescent's expression of feelings of sadness, administer pain medication prior to providing respiratory hygiene to an adolescent with spinal fusion, wash the perineal area with nonperfumed soap and tepid water)
    g. Use nursing measures specific to prescribed medications (for example: teach the adolescent to apply antiviral ointment to genital lesion, ascertain the patient's pregnancy status prior to the administration of metronidazole hydrochloride [Flagyl], stress the need to avoid sun exposure and apply sunscreen for a patient who is taking retinoic acid for acne, instruct the adolescent to apply antifungal vaginal medication at bedtime)
    h. Provide information and instruction (for example: discuss contraceptive options and the need for regular medical follow-up; encourage the family of an adolescent with an eating disorder to attend counseling sessions; discuss safer sex practices with the adolescent who is sexually active; instruct the adolescent about the undesirable effects of fad and crash diet programs; teach the adolescent with diabetes mellitus how to adjust food, activity, and insulin; make referrals to support groups and community services)
5. Evaluation: determine the extent to which goals have been achieved
    a. Evaluate, record, and report the patient's response to nursing interventions (for example: the adolescent shows no evidence of infection in the reproductive tract, the adolescent has gained one pound in the last week, the adolescent will not interact with others on the unit, patient becomes dizzy when sitting upright after surgery, evidence of skin breakdown present)
    b. Modify the plan of care if necessary (for example: encourage one-to-one activities with staff to establish trust, encourage the adolescent who is recovering from surgery to sit up for short periods, apply padding to the brace where it is in contact with reddened areas, refer the patient to the orthotist for adjustment)

Sample Questions: Maternal & Child Nursing (assoc.)

1. The nurse instructs a patient who is in her 36th week of pregnancy about measures to relieve the discomfort caused by varicose veins. Which patient statement indicates that she understands these measures?
   1) "I avoid crossing my legs when sitting."
   2) "I practice pelvic rocking in the evenings."
   3) "I perform Kegel's exercise six times daily."
   4) "I massage my legs before bedtime."

2. The nurse is caring for a patient who is receiving magnesium sulfate intravenously for severe preeclampsia. Which evidence would be most indicative of an overdose of this medication?
   1) respirations of 10/min
   2) generalized tremors
   3) hot, dry skin
   4) excitability

3. Which information should the nurse provide to a patient who is having labor augmented by an oxytocin (Pitocin) infusion?
   Expect the contractions to
   1) increase in frequency and decrease in duration.
   2) increase in frequency with little time for rest.
   3) increase in intensity, but decrease in frequency.
   4) increase in intensity and duration.

4. Which action should the nurse include when planning comfort measures for a patient who recently delivered and is experiencing afterpains?
   1) Maintain the fluid intake and massage the fundus.
   2) Provide a warm blanket and administer an analgesic medication as ordered.
   3) Reposition the patient frequently and take the vital signs q4h.
   4) Provide ice packs to the perineum and encourage early breast-feeding.

5. Approximately 12 hours following vaginal delivery of a 7 lb infant, the nurse notes that a patient's fundus is firm and located slightly above the umbilicus in the midline. How should the nurse interpret these data?
   1) Uterine atony is present.
   2) A boggy uterus is present.
   3) Normal involution is occurring.
   4) Subinvolution is occurring.

6. A patient who is breast-feeding her newborn complains that her breasts are tender and engorged. Which suggestion should the nurse make?
   1) Expose the nipples to the air for 30 minutes after nursing.
   2) Take the prescribed narcotic analgesic every four hours.
   3) Take a warm shower prior to nursing.
   4) Apply cold packs to the breasts after nursing.

Sample Questions: Maternal & Child Nursing (assoc.)

7. A newborn is exhibiting excessive salivation, gastric distention, drooling, and slight cyanosis. Which problem should the nurse suspect?
    1) cleft palate
    2) cystic fibrosis
    3) esophageal atresia
    4) pyloric stenosis

8. Which assessment data indicate that a four-week-old newborn is developing within normal limits?
    1) The birth weight has doubled.
    2) The Moro reflex is no longer present.
    3) The head circumference has increased by 3 cm.
    4) The infant grasps a rattle placed in the hand.

9. The preoperative nursing care plan for a newborn with tracheoesophageal fistula should include which measure?
    1) Suction the infant regularly, to remove excessive mucus.
    2) Provide the infant with a pacifier, to satisfy her sucking needs.
    3) Place the infant's head lower than her feet, to facilitate the drainage.
    4) Hold the infant upright while feeding her, to prevent aspiration.

10. The nurse assesses a newborn at one hour of age and collects the following data: weight 7 lb 4 oz; P 150, R 45, and T of 97° F axillary; and acrocyanosis. Based on these data, the nurse should take which action?
    1) Remove the infant's clothing except the diaper and place him in a warming unit.
    2) Suction the mouth and nares of the infant and swaddle him in a light blanket.
    3) Place the newborn on his abdomen in an open crib.
    4) Bathe the newborn and place him in an open crib.

11. The mother of a six-month-old infant says to the nurse, "We don't have to worry about our baby getting into any poisons. I keep them all out of the baby's reach." Which response by the nurse is most appropriate?
    1) "You are wise to place poisons out of your baby's reach."
    2) "Tell me more about where you store medicines and poisons."
    3) "Other parents should be told about these precautions."
    4) "I will make a note about that in your baby's chart."

12. The nurse instructs the parent of a nine-month-old infant about common childhood illnesses and their management. Which response by the parent indicates that the nurse's instruction has been effective?
    1) "I won't give my baby aspirin if he has signs of flu or chickenpox."
    2) "It's okay to take my baby to the day-care center if he shows signs of chickenpox."
    3) "I still have some questions about the importance of baby immunizations."
    4) "If my baby ever contracts a childhood illness, I'll feel like it is my fault."

Sample Questions: Maternal & Child Nursing (assoc.)

13. A two-year-old child is receiving chelating medication for lead poisoning (plumbism). Which manifestation indicates a possible side effect of the medication?
    1) glycosuria
    2) hyperkalemia
    3) hypocalcemia
    4) polyuria

14. Which menu selection by the parents of a 30-month-old child who has celiac disease indicates the need for further instruction regarding their child's diet?
    1) cornflakes with milk
    2) chicken and rice
    3) oatmeal raisin bran cereal
    4) rice pudding

15. What is the rationale for maintaining a preschooler who is in sickle cell crisis on bed rest?
    1) to minimize oxygen consumption
    2) to prevent bacterial infection
    3) to reduce oxygen tension
    4) to correct respiratory acidosis

16. A seven-year-old child is brought to the emergency department with intractable vomiting and lethargy. Her parents state that she had a cold several days earlier and was given aspirin. The nurse should take which actions?
    1) Start oxygen, insert an IV of hypertonic glucose, and notify the physician.
    2) Place the child in a safe, quiet area, and notify the physician.
    3) Observe the child periodically and report any noticeable changes to the physician.
    4) Place the child on her side, start oxygen, and notify the physician.

17. What is the physiological reason adolescents often feel fatigued during their growth spurt?
    1) The heart and lungs grow more slowly than the rest of the body.
    2) The trunk grows faster than the extremities.
    3) The bones grow more slowly than the muscles.
    4) The small muscles grow faster than the large muscles.

18. Which contraceptive measure also provides some protection against sexually transmitted diseases?
    1) cervical cap
    2) condoms
    3) oral contraceptives
    4) contraceptive foam

19. A patient who is in the first trimester of pregnancy reports that she has experienced intermittent nausea for the past several days. Which suggestion should the nurse make?
    1) Eat no more than three meals a day.
    2) Eat the largest meal of the day in the morning.
    3) Eat small, frequent meals spaced throughout the day.
    4) Take a brief walk immediately after eating.

Sample Questions: Maternal & Child Nursing (assoc.)

Recommended Resources

Bobak, I., Lowdermilk, D., & Jensen, M. (1995). Maternity nursing *(4th ed.). St. Louis: Mosby.*

Carpenito, L. (1997). Nursing diagnosis: Application to clinical practice *(7th ed.). Philadelphia: J.B. Lippincott.*

Ladewig, P., London, M., & Olds, S. (1998). Maternal-newborn nursing care: The nurse, the family, and the community *(4th ed.). Menlo Park, CA: Addison Wesley.*

Pillitteri, A. (1995). Maternal and child health nursing *(2nd ed.). Philadelphia: J.B. Lippincott.*

Wong, D.L. (1997). Whaley & Wong's Essentials of pediatric nursing *(5th ed.). St. Louis: Mosby.*

Study Guide
Maternity Nursing (559)

Credit Hours: 3
Question Type(s): Multiple-choice
Credit Level: Lower

The information in this study guide is valid until Summer 2001.
If you will be taking the examination after that date, be sure to check for a new edition of this guide before you complete your preparation for the exam.

General Description of the Examination

The Maternity Nursing examination measures knowledge and understanding of maternity nursing and care of the newborn. It is based on material usually taught in a course in maternity nursing at the associate degree level.

The examination requires you to possess knowledge and understanding of the theoretical framework related to each content area. The examination further requires you to apply this knowledge by using the nursing process (assessment, diagnosis, planning, implementation, and evaluation) to provide nursing care to the family during the childbearing cycle.

Content Outline

The detailed content outline for Maternity Nursing is identical to the first four content areas of the Maternal & Child Nursing (Associate Level) examination on pages 564–573. The chart below indicates the percent allotted to each content area.

Content Area	Percent of Examination
I. Antepartal Care	30%
II. Intrapartal Care	20%
III. Postpartal Care	30%
IV. The Newborn	20%
Total	**100%**

Sample Questions: Maternity Nursing

1. The nurse instructs a patient who is in her 36th week of pregnancy about measures to relieve the discomfort caused by varicose veins. Which patient statement indicates that she understands these measures?
   1) "I avoid crossing my legs when sitting."
   2) "I practice pelvic rocking in the evenings."
   3) "I perform Kegel's exercise six times daily."
   4) "I massage my legs before bedtime."

2. The nurse is caring for a patient who is receiving magnesium sulfate intravenously for severe preeclampsia. Which evidence would be most indicative of an overdose of this medication?
   1) respirations of 10/min
   2) generalized tremors
   3) hot, dry skin
   4) excitability

3. Which information should the nurse provide to a patient who is having labor augmented by an oxytocin (Pitocin) infusion?
   Expect the contractions to
   1) increase in frequency and decrease in duration.
   2) increase in frequency with little time for rest.
   3) increase in intensity, but decrease in frequency.
   4) increase in intensity and duration.

4. Which action should the nurse include when planning comfort measures for a patient who recently delivered and is experiencing afterpains?
   1) Maintain the fluid intake and massage the fundus.
   2) Provide a warm blanket and administer an analgesic medication as ordered.
   3) Reposition the patient frequently and take the vital signs q4h.
   4) Provide ice packs to the perineum and encourage early breast-feeding.

5. Approximately 12 hours following vaginal delivery of a 7 lb infant, the nurse notes that a patient's fundus is firm and located slightly above the umbilicus in the midline. How should the nurse interpret these data?
   1) Uterine atony is present.
   2) A boggy uterus is present.
   3) Normal involution is occurring.
   4) Subinvolution is occurring.

6. A patient who is breast-feeding her newborn complains that her breasts are tender and engorged. Which suggestion should the nurse make?
   1) Expose the nipples to the air for 30 minutes after nursing.
   2) Take the prescribed narcotic analgesic every four hours.
   3) Take a warm shower prior to nursing.
   4) Apply cold packs to the breasts after nursing.

7. A newborn is exhibiting excessive salivation, gastric distention, drooling, and slight cyanosis. Which problem should the nurse suspect?
    1) cleft palate
    2) cystic fibrosis
    3) esophageal atresia
    4) pyloric stenosis

8. Which assessment data indicate that a four-week-old newborn is developing within normal limits?
    1) The birth weight has doubled.
    2) The Moro reflex is no longer present.
    3) The head circumference has increased by 3 cm.
    4) The infant grasps a rattle placed in the hand.

9. The preoperative nursing care plan for a newborn with tracheoesophageal fistula should include which measure?
    1) Suction the infant regularly, to remove excessive mucus.
    2) Provide the infant with a pacifier, to satisfy her sucking needs.
    3) Place the infant's head lower than her feet, to facilitate the drainage.
    4) Hold the infant upright while feeding her, to prevent aspiration.

10. The nurse assesses a newborn at one hour of age and collects the following data: weight 7 lb 4 oz; P 150, R 45, and T of 97° F axillary; and acrocyanosis. Based on these data, the nurse should take which action?
    1) Remove the infant's clothing except the diaper and place him in a warming unit.
    2) Suction the mouth and nares of the infant and swaddle him in a light blanket.
    3) Place the newborn on his abdomen in an open crib.
    4) Bathe the newborn and place him in an open crib.

Recommended Resources

Bobak, I., Lowdermilk, D., & Jensen, M. (1995). Maternity nursing (4th ed.). St. Louis: Mosby.

Carpenito, L. (1997). Nursing diagnosis: Application to clinical practice (7th ed.). Philadelphia: J.B. Lippincott.

Ladewig, P., London, M., & Olds, S. (1998). Maternal-newborn nursing care: The nurse, the family, and the community (4th ed.). Menlo Park, CA: Addison Wesley.

Pillitteri, A. (1995). Maternal and child health nursing (2nd ed.). Philadelphia: J.B. Lippincott.

Study Guide
Adult Nursing (554)

Credit Hours: 8 **Credit Level: Upper**
Question Type(s): Multiple-choice

The information in this study guide is valid until Summer 2001.
If you will be taking the examination after that date, be sure to check for a new edition of this guide before you complete your preparation for the exam.

General Description of the Examination

The Regents College Examination in Adult Nursing measures knowledge and understanding of the health and nursing care of young, middle-aged, and older adults. It is based on material normally taught in an upper-division sequence of courses in medical-surgical nursing or adult nursing at the baccalaureate level.

The examination tests for a knowledge and understanding of the physiological, developmental, psychological, social, cultural, and spiritual dimensions of health and illness in adults. It tests for the ability to use the nursing process in a variety of settings to deliver health care to adults with actual or potential health problems.

Use of the Nursing Process Dimension in this Content Outline

The nursing process dimension indicates the stage of the nursing process to which the content of the item is predominantly related. Items are classified as relating to Assessment, Analysis, Planning, Implementation, or Evaluation.

For the purposes of this examination, the stages of the nursing process are defined as follows:
  A. *Assessment* is the process of gathering and synthesizing data about the client's health status.
  B. *Analysis* is the identification of the client problem (nursing diagnosis) and the determination of the expected outcomes (goals) of client care.
  C. *Planning* is the formulation of specific strategies to achieve the expected outcomes.
  D. *Implementation* is the carrying out of nursing care designed to move the client toward the expected outcomes.
  E. *Evaluation* is the appraisal of the effectiveness of the nursing interventions relative to the nursing diagnosis and the expected outcomes.

The material included in Area I serves as a foundation for the material covered in Areas II-X.

Content Outline

Content Area	Percent of Examination
I. Core Concepts	10%
II. Nursing Management of Clients with Cardiovascular System and Hematologic System Dysfunction	10%
III. Nursing Management of Clients with Respiratory System Dysfunction	10%
IV. Nursing Management of Clients with Urinary System Dysfunction	10%
V. Nursing Management of Clients with Reproductive System Dysfunction	10%
VI. Nursing Management of Clients with Endocrine System Dysfunction	10%
VII. Nursing Management of Clients with Gastrointestinal System Dysfunction	10%
VIII. Nursing Management of Clients with Sensory System and Neurological System Dysfunction	10%
IX. Nursing Management of Clients with Musculoskeletal System Dysfunction	10%
X. Nursing Management of Clients with Immune System and Integumentary System Dysfunction	10%
Total	**100%**

I. Core Concepts (10%)

A. Theories about adulthood—E. Erikson, R.J. Havighurst, D.J. Levinson

B. Individual differences in health behaviors—physical, developmental, psychological, social, cultural, and spiritual dimensions of health and illness

C. Stress response
   1. Physiological response (for example: fight-or-flight response, neuroendocrine response)
   2. Psychological response (for example: anxiety, fear, panic)
   3. Patterns of coping and adaptation

D. Pain
   1. Theories of pain mechanism (for example: specificity theory, gate control theory)

2. Types of pain (for example: superficial, deep, referred, phantom limb, acute, chronic)
   3. Treatment modalities (for example: medications, imagery, behavior modification, modes of medication administration)

E. **Fluid and electrolyte imbalance**
   1. Disturbances in homeostasis (for example: fluid overload and deficiencies, metabolic and respiratory acidosis and alkalosis, electrolyte disturbances)
   2. Manifestations (for example: hyperpnea, tetany, confusion, EKG changes)
   3. Treatment modalities (for example: fluid and electrolyte replacement therapy, medications, dietary modifications)

F. **Shock**
   1. Types—cardiogenic, hypovolemic, distributive
   2. Pathophysiology—compensatory, progressive, refractory
   3. Manifestations (for example: changes in renal function, acid base balance, perfusion, cardiac output, level of consciousness, fluid dynamics)
   4. Treatment modalities (for example: respiratory support, fluids, medications, hemodynamic monitoring, perfusion assistive devices)
   5. Complications (for example: adult respiratory distress syndrome [ARDS], disseminated intravascular coagulation [DIC], prerenal failure)

G. **Technology management in the hospital and at home**
   1. Respiratory support
   2. Parenteral therapy (for example: central line management, total parenteral nutrition, chemotherapy, vasoactive medication)
   3. Enteral feeding tubes (for example: gastrostomy, nasogastric, jejunostomy)

II. Nursing Management of Clients with Cardiovascular System and Hematologic System Dysfunction (10%)

This area focuses on topics such as hypertension, ischemic heart disease, congestive heart failure, valvular disorders, thrombophlebitis, peripheral vascular disease, aneurysm, inflammatory and infective heart disease, dysrhythmias, anemias, blood dyscrasias.

A. **Assessment** (for example: identifying cardiovascular risk factors, assessing physical and behavioral manifestations and responses, interpreting laboratory and diagnostic test results, monitoring dysrhythmias, assessing response to surgery and diagnostic procedures)

B. **Analysis** (for example: identifying relevant nursing diagnoses/collaborative problems, establishing priorities among client's problems, determining appropriate goals and outcome criteria)

C. **Planning** (for example: formulating specific strategies for decreased cardiac output, activity intolerance, anxiety, fluid volume excess, risk for infection, impaired tissue integrity, self-esteem disturbance, altered comfort, altered tissue perfusion, and prevention of complications)

D. **Implementation** (for example: assisting with activities of daily living; promoting effective coping strategies; teaching about self-care, medication management, self-monitoring techniques, and risk factor modification; supervising the administration of blood products; implementing the medical plan)

E. **Evaluation** (for example: evaluating response to intervention or therapy; appraising level of knowledge; validating the client's perception of the effectiveness of intervention;

evaluating patterns of pain and response to pain therapy; evaluating response to diuretics, cardiotonics, antiarrhythmics, antihypertensives, chemotherapy, thrombolytic therapy, pacemakers, internal defibrillators, cardiac catheterization and related procedures, and surgery)

III. Nursing Management of Clients with Respiratory System Dysfunction (10%)

This area focuses on topics such as asthma; inflammatory and infective respiratory diseases, such as pneumonia and tuberculosis; pneumothorax; chronic obstructive pulmonary disease; cor pulmonale; pulmonary embolism; acute respiratory failure; sleep apnea; cancer of the larynx and lung.

A. **Assessment** (for example: identifying respiratory risk factors; assessing physical and behavioral manifestations; interpreting laboratory and diagnostic test results, such as arterial blood gases and pulmonary function tests)

B. **Analysis** (for example: identifying relevant nursing diagnoses/collaborative problems, establishing priorities among client's problems, determining appropriate goals and outcome criteria)

C. **Planning** (for example: formulating specific strategies for ineffective airway clearance, ineffective breathing pattern, impaired gas exchange, altered lifestyle, anxiety, activity intolerance, and prevention of complications)

D. **Implementation** (for example: assisting with maintenance of adequate airway; assisting with activities of daily living; medication management; promoting effective coping strategies; teaching about self-care, self-monitoring techniques, dietary adjustments, and lifestyle changes; implementing the medical plan)

E. **Evaluation** (for example: evaluating response to intervention or therapy; appraising level of knowledge; validating the client's perception of the effectiveness of intervention; evaluating response to antibiotics, corticosteroids, bronchodilators, chest tubes, oxygen therapy, and surgery)

IV. Nursing Management of Clients with Urinary System Dysfunction (10%)

This area focuses on topics such as cystitis; pyelonephritis; obstructive uropathies, such as benign prostatic hyperplasia; renal calculi; acute and chronic renal failure; renal trauma; urinary incontinence; glomerulonephritis; cancer of the bladder.

A. **Assessment** (for example: identifying risk factors for urinary and renal dysfunction, assessing physical and behavioral manifestations, interpreting laboratory and diagnostic test results, assessing incontinence patterns)

B. **Analysis** (for example: identifying relevant nursing diagnoses/collaborative problems, establishing priorities among client's problems, determining appropriate goals and outcome criteria)

C. **Planning** (for example: formulating specific strategies for fluid and electrolyte imbalance, altered comfort, altered urinary elimination, body image disturbance, and prevention of complications)

D. **Implementation** (for example: assisting with management of urinary catheters and urinary diversion; assisting with activities of daily living; promoting effective coping strategies; teaching about self-care, medication management, self-monitoring techniques, dietary adjustments, and lifestyle changes; implementing the medical plan)

E. Evaluation (for example: evaluating response to intervention or therapy; appraising level of knowledge; validating the client's perception of the effectiveness of intervention; evaluating response to antibiotics, antihypertensives, diuretics, dialysis, and surgery)

V. Nursing Management of Clients with Reproductive System Dysfunction (10%)

This area focuses on topics such as sexually transmitted diseases; pelvic inflammatory disease; endometriosis; premenstrual syndrome; perimenopausal problems; impotence; cancer of the ovaries, cervix, endometrium, and breast; cancer of the testes and prostate.

A. Assessment (for example: identifying risk factors for reproductive system dysfunction, assessing for physical and behavioral manifestations, identifying high-risk behaviors for sexually transmitted diseases, interpreting laboratory and diagnostic test results)

B. Analysis (for example: identifying relevant nursing diagnoses/collaborative problems, establishing priorities among client's problems, determining appropriate outcome criteria)

C. Planning (for example: formulating specific strategies for self-esteem disturbance, body image disturbance, knowledge deficit, altered sexuality patterns, self-protection and protection of partners, altered comfort, and prevention of complications)

D. Implementation (for example: promoting effective coping strategies; teaching about self-care, medication management, self-monitoring techniques, and lifestyle changes; promoting optimal sexual health; implementing the medical plan)

E. Evaluation (for example: evaluating response to intervention or therapy; appraising level of knowledge and adherence to self-monitoring practices; validating the client's perception of the effectiveness of intervention; evaluating response to hormonal agents, antibiotics, chemotherapy, radiation therapy, and surgery)

VI. Nursing Management of Clients with Endocrine System Dysfunction (10%)

This area focuses on topics such as diabetes mellitus, thyroid dysfunction, parathyroid dysfunction, pituitary dysfunction, adrenal dysfunction.

A. Assessment (for example: identifying risk factors for endocrine system dysfunction, assessing for physical and behavioral manifestations, interpreting laboratory and diagnostic test results)

B. Analysis (for example: identifying relevant nursing diagnoses/collaborative problems, establishing priorities among client's problems, determining appropriate goals and outcome criteria)

C. Planning (for example: formulating specific strategies for activity intolerance, sleep pattern disturbance, altered nutrition, knowledge deficit, risk for infection, impaired skin integrity, altered fluid volume, altered role performance, ineffective coping, altered body image, and prevention of complications)

D. Implementation (for example: promoting effective coping strategies; teaching about self-care, medication management, self-monitoring techniques, dietary adjustments, and lifestyle changes; implementing the medical plan)

E. Evaluation (for example: evaluating response to intervention or therapy; appraising level of knowledge; validating the client's perception of the effectiveness of the intervention; evaluating response to hypoglycemic agents, hormonal agents, and surgery)

VII. Nursing Management of Clients with Gastrointestinal System Dysfunction (10%)

This area focuses on topics such as inflammatory and infective disorders of the gastrointestinal tract; constipation; eating and absorption disorders; obesity; bowel obstruction; hiatal hernia; ulcers; cholelithiasis; pancreatitis; cirrhosis; inflammatory bowel disease; hepatitis; abdominal trauma; cancer of the mouth, esophagus, stomach, pancreas, liver, colon, and rectum.

A. Assessment (for example: identifying risk factors for gastrointestinal system dysfunction, assessing for physical and behavioral manifestations, interpreting laboratory and diagnostic test results)

B. Analysis (for example: identifying relevant nursing diagnoses/collaborative problems, establishing priorities among client's problems, determining appropriate goals and outcome criteria)

C. Planning (for example: formulating specific strategies for preparation for diagnostic testing, altered comfort, fluid volume deficit, altered nutrition, altered bowel elimination, impaired skin integrity, knowledge deficit, self-esteem disturbance, and prevention of complications)

D. Implementation (for example: assisting with activities of daily living; helping clients manage ostomy care; promoting effective coping strategies; teaching about self-care, medication management, self-monitoring techniques, dietary adjustments, and lifestyle changes; providing nutritional support; implementing the medical plan)

E. Evaluation (for example: evaluating response to intervention or therapy; appraising level of knowledge; validating the client's perception of the effectiveness of intervention; evaluating response to anticholinergic agents, histamine receptor inhibitors, antacids, antiemetics, antidiarrheals, cathartics, enteral and parenteral nutrition, diagnostic or therapeutic endoscopic procedures, and surgery)

VIII. Nursing Management of Clients with Sensory System and Neurological System Dysfunction (10%)

This area focuses on topics such as glaucoma, cataracts, retinal detachment, corneal disorders, inner ear dysfunction, Meniere's disease, otosclerosis, headaches, cerebrovascular accident, intracranial aneurysms, degenerative neurological diseases, brain and spinal cord trauma, seizure disorders, Guillain-Barré syndrome, inflammatory neurological disease, Lyme disease, Parkinson's disease, multiple sclerosis, Alzheimer's disease, myasthenia gravis, brain tumors.

A. Assessment (for example: identifying risk factors for sensory system and neurological system dysfunction, assessing for physical and behavioral manifestations, interpreting laboratory and diagnostic test results)

B. **Analysis** (for example: identifying relevant nursing diagnoses/collaborative problems, establishing priorities among client's problems, determining appropriate goals and outcome criteria)

C. **Planning** (for example: formulating specific strategies for impaired physical mobility, visual and auditory impairment, self-esteem disturbance, risk for injury, impaired skin integrity, impaired swallowing, altered elimination, sensory/perceptual alteration, impaired verbal communication, altered thought processes, self-care deficit, and prevention of complications)

D. **Implementation** (for example: assisting with activities of daily living and rehabilitation; promoting effective coping strategies for client and family; teaching about self-care, medication management, self-monitoring techniques, and lifestyle changes; helping client achieve optimal level of functioning; providing a safe environment; implementing the medical plan)

E. **Evaluation** (for example: evaluating response to intervention or therapy; appraising level of knowledge; validating the client's perception of the effectiveness of intervention; evaluating response to anti-Parkinsonian agents, antispasmodics, anticholinergics, analgesics, anticholinesterase inhibitors, miotic agents, osmotic diuretics, corticosteroids, anticonvulsants, and surgery)

IX. Nursing Management of Clients with Musculoskeletal System Dysfunction (10%)

This area focuses on topics such as fractures, rheumatoid arthritis, osteoarthritis, osteomyelitis, osteoporosis, cervical and lumbar disc disease, carpal tunnel syndrome, amputations, osteogenic sarcoma, metastatic lesions.

A. **Assessment** (for example: identifying risk factors for musculoskeletal system dysfunction, assessing for physical and behavioral manifestations, interpreting laboratory and diagnostic test results)

B. **Analysis** (for example: identifying relevant nursing diagnoses/collaborative problems, establishing priorities among client problems, determining appropriate goals and outcome criteria)

C. **Planning** (for example: formulating specific strategies for impaired physical mobility, risk for injury, risk for falls, knowledge deficit, altered lifestyle, body image disturbance, altered comfort, self-care deficit, sleep pattern disturbance, and prevention of complications)

D. **Implementation** (for example: assisting with activities of daily living and rehabilitation; teaching about self-care, medication management, self-monitoring techniques, and lifestyle changes; helping with exercises, transfer techniques, cast care, prostheses, traction, supportive devices, and assistive devices for mobilization; implementing the medical plan)

E. **Evaluation** (for example: evaluating response to intervention or therapy; appraising level of knowledge; evaluating adherence to exercise regimen; validating the client's perception of the effectiveness of intervention; evaluating response to nonsteroidal anti-inflammatory agents, corticosteroids, muscle relaxants, analgesics, and surgery, such as total joint replacement, laminectomy, fusion, arthroscopy)

X. Nursing Management of Clients with Immune System and Integumentary System Dysfunction (10%)

This area focuses on topics such as allergies; immunological deficiencies, such as acquired immunodeficiency syndrome (AIDS); systemic lupus erythematosus; tissue transplantation and rejection; inflammatory and infective dermatological disorders; burns; wounds and ulcers; skin cancers.

A. Assessment (for example: identifying risk factors for immune system and integumentary system dysfunction, assessing for physical and behavioral manifestations, assessing wound characteristics, assessing stages of wound healing, interpreting laboratory and diagnostic test results)

B. Analysis (for example: identifying relevant nursing diagnoses/collaborative problems, establishing priorities among client's problems, determining appropriate goals and outcome criteria)

C. Planning (for example: formulating specific strategies for anxiety, ineffective breathing pattern, altered elimination, risk for infection, impaired tissue integrity, fluid volume deficit, knowledge deficit, anticipatory grieving, social isolation, impaired social interactions, body image disturbance, and prevention of complications)

D. Implementation (for example: assisting with activities of daily living; medication management; assisting with environmental control and avoidance of allergens; assisting with prevention of infection; assisting with therapeutic baths, soaks, and topical medications; promoting effective coping strategies; promoting optimal sexual health; teaching about self-care, self-monitoring techniques, and lifestyle changes; implementing the medical plan)

E. Evaluation (for example: evaluating response to intervention or therapy; appraising level of knowledge; validating the client's perception of the effectiveness of intervention; evaluating response to antihistamines, immunotherapy, antibiotics, immunosuppressants, skin care regimens, grafting, and reconstructive surgery)

Sample Questions: Adult Nursing

1. Which finding indicates adequate fluid volume in a client with hypovolemic shock?
   1) urinary output of at least 0.5 ml/kg/hr
   2) urine pH greater than 7.5
   3) urine specific gravity of 1.090
   4) negative urine glucose

2. Which factor is likely to contribute to the development of diarrhea in a client on continuous tube feeding via jejunostomy?
   1) rapid rate of feeding
   2) excess water in feeding
   3) improper tube placement
   4) low-fiber formula

3. The nurse should suspect hypocalcemia when the client exhibits which signs?
   1) tingling of the fingers, muscle spasms, and tetany
   2) night blindness, tachycardia, and weakness
   3) pale mucous membranes, shortness of breath, and lethargy
   4) bleeding tendencies, thirst, and hypotension

4. Which abnormal heart sound in a client recovering from a myocardial infarction should lead the nurse to suspect the onset of heart failure?
   1) split S_1
   2) gallop rhythm
   3) ejection click
   4) pericardial friction rub

5. Which finding in a client's lower extremities should lead the nurse to suspect venous insufficiency?
   1) pallor
   2) tenderness to touch
   3) swollen joints
   4) leathery skin texture

6. The nurse assesses that a client with lung cancer is exhibiting prolonged bleeding at a venipuncture site. The nurse should suspect that the client is developing which complication?
   1) anemia
   2) acute respiratory failure
   3) metastasis to the lymph nodes
   4) disseminated intravascular coagulation

7. The nurse teaches a client with venous insufficiency how to prevent the recurrence of venous stasis ulcers. Which client comment at the next clinic visit indicates an understanding of the nurse's teaching?
   1) "Support hose with the same pressure gradient on the entire leg are the best kind for me."
   2) "When I sit down, I try to alternate pressure by crossing and uncrossing my legs."

Sample Questions: Adult Nursing

       3) "I take walks often and go swimming at least three times a week."
       4) "My support hose keep creeping down, so I hold them up with round garters."

8. Which data indicate a possible pneumothorax in a client who has had a thoracentesis?
   1) diminished breath sounds and dyspnea
   2) blood-tinged sputum and dullness on percussion
   3) flail chest and crackles on auscultation
   4) paradoxical chest movement and inspiratory stridor

9. A client receiving preoperative instructions about a total laryngectomy asks the nurse to explain esophageal speech. Which information should the nurse include?
   1) The client can start to learn esophageal speech immediately after the surgery.
   2) The client starts learning esophageal speech by practicing controlled belching.
   3) Esophageal speech is clearly understandable from the beginning.
   4) Esophageal speech is easy to learn and most clients are proficient by discharge.

10. The nurse teaches a client's family how to administer oxygen to the client prior to nasotracheal suctioning. The nurse can conclude that the teaching was effective if a family member states which reason for giving oxygen first?
    1) It will decrease the discomfort of suctioning.
    2) It will make it easier to cough and get secretions out during the procedure.
    3) It will replace what is suctioned out when the tube is in the lungs.
    4) It will provide an extra supply so there is enough in the bloodstream during suctioning.

11. Which data should the nurse expect when taking a health history from a client diagnosed as having acute pyelonephritis?
    1) recent urethral catheterization
    2) long-standing hypertension
    3) chronic urinary tract infections
    4) recent influenza

12. Which measure should the nurse implement when a client is experiencing respiratory difficulty during peritoneal dialysis?
    1) Slow the flow rate and elevate the head of the client's bed.
    2) Maintain the client in a supine position and encourage coughing and deep breathing.
    3) Drain the fluid immediately and assess the client's vital signs.
    4) Provide oxygen as needed and encourage the client to perform relaxation exercises.

13. The nurse teaches a client with acute renal failure about follow-up care. Which client statement indicates that the nurse's teaching was successful?
    1) "I need to take antibiotics to avoid infections."
    2) "I need to decrease my protein intake to protect my kidneys."
    3) "I will have periodic laboratory tests to monitor my progress."
    4) "I will drink at least one gallon of fluid per day."

Sample Questions: Adult Nursing

14. A female client who has a vaginal yeast infection complains of itching and burning of the vulva and perineum. What should the nurse suggest to the client to promote comfort?
    1) Apply antibiotic cream.
    2) Empty the bladder frequently.
    3) Wear cotton underwear.
    4) Douche every morning.

15. When assessing the nutritional status of a client with premenstrual syndrome, the nurse should ask the client about her intake of which of the following?
    1) supplemental fat-soluble and water-soluble vitamins
    2) natural diuretics, such as grapefruit
    3) foods high in protein and low in fat
    4) coffee, tea, and chocolate

16. The nurse is teaching a client who has had a vaginal hysterectomy. Which is a common complication that the client should know how to manage?
    1) difficulty in voiding
    2) loss of appetite
    3) gastrointestinal upset
    4) excessive fatigue

17. Which instruction should the nurse include in a discharge plan to prevent lymphedema in a client who has had a mastectomy?
    1) Sleep on the affected side or on your back for eight weeks.
    2) Measure arm circumference weekly at four inches above and four inches below the elbow.
    3) Use your hand, arm, and shoulder on the operative side to perform activities of daily living.
    4) Follow a diet low in sodium and take a diuretic every day.

18. Which is an appropriate short-term goal for a client with Cushing's syndrome? The client will
    1) gain weight.
    2) restrict activity.
    3) allow others to assist with hygiene.
    4) avoid people with colds or the flu.

19. The nurse has begun discharge planning with an active adolescent client who has been newly diagnosed with diabetes requiring insulin therapy. Which concept should the nurse include in the teaching plan?
    1) The client should eat more food during periods of increased exercise.
    2) It is not necessary to monitor glucose levels before and after strenuous exercise.
    3) The client should choose the thigh site for insulin injections prior to exercise.
    4) The client should use a higher than usual dose of insulin before aerobic exercise.

Sample Questions: Adult Nursing

20. Which finding indicates the effective maintenance of fluid balance in a client with diabetes insipidus?
    1) urinary output of 3–4 L/day
    2) urine specific gravity of 1.010
    3) pulse rate of 100–110
    4) blood pressure of 90/64

21. Which findings should the nurse expect when assessing a client with hyperthyroidism?
    1) lethargy and constipation
    2) dry scaly skin and cold extremities
    3) weight loss and increased appetite
    4) periorbital pallor and frequent blinking

22. What is the primary purpose of administering histamine antagonists to a client with gastritis?
    1) to neutralize gastric acids
    2) to inhibit acid production by the gastric mucosa
    3) to relieve pain caused by gastric inflammation
    4) to decrease inflammation of the gastric mucosa

23. Which strategy for dietary management should the nurse include in a home care plan for a client who has had a gastric resection?
    1) Maintain a fat-free diet for bowel regularity.
    2) Promote liberal intake of fluids with and between meals.
    3) Increase carbohydrate intake with meals.
    4) Serve six small high-protein meals per day.

24. The nurse has taught the family of a client with pancreatitis about home care related to total parenteral nutrition (TPN). Which activity by a family member indicates an understanding of how to prevent the most common complication of this therapy?
    1) washing the hands carefully
    2) testing for protein in the urine
    3) recording daily weights
    4) troubleshooting mechanical problems in the pump

25. A client is being discharged following a corneal transplant. The nurse should instruct the client and caregivers to report which early manifestation of graft rejection?
    1) blind spot in the visual field
    2) decrease in vision
    3) diplopia
    4) excess tearing in the eye

26. The nurse teaches a client with multiple sclerosis strategies to enhance bladder control. Which statement by the client indicates that the nurse's teaching was effective?
    1) "I'll reduce my fluid intake."
    2) "I'll take my antihistamine medication as scheduled."
    3) "I'll catheterize myself several times a day."
    4) "I'll eat a diet high in protein."

Sample Questions: Adult Nursing

27. Which action should the nurse take to prevent hip dislocation in a client who has had a total hip replacement?
    1) Turn the client to the affected side.
    2) Keep the client's hip in abduction.
    3) Maintain hip flexion of the affected leg to less than 30°.
    4) Use a two-person lift when getting the client out of bed.

28. The assessment of pallor, pulselessness, and paresthesia in the affected extremity of a client in skeletal traction should alert the nurse to which possible complication?
    1) fat embolus
    2) neurovascular damage
    3) osteomyelitis
    4) deep venous thrombosis

29. Which finding should the nurse expect in the health history of a female client diagnosed with osteoporosis?
    1) recent weight gain
    2) prolonged immobility
    3) taking an estrogen replacement
    4) increased calcium in the diet

30. The nurse is reviewing the results of laboratory tests for a client who has AIDS. Which finding should alert the nurse that the client is at risk for a serious opportunistic infection?
    1) negative polymerase chain reaction
    2) decreased amount of human immunodeficiency virus
    3) 2:1 ratio of T-helper cells to T-suppressor cells
    4) $CD4^+$ lymphocyte count of 350–450 cells/µl

31. If a client who has had a renal transplant develops fever, elevated BUN level, hypertension, and graft tenderness, the nurse should suspect which complication?
    1) infection
    2) renal failure
    3) kidney rejection
    4) fluid overload

32. The nurse is teaching a client how to prevent the spread of pediculosis capitis to other family members. Which strategy would be the most effective?
    1) Wash the bedclothes daily.
    2) Use antibacterial soap and shampoo.
    3) Use topical corticosteroids to control pruritus.
    4) Do not share hats and scarves.

33. When providing emergent treatment for an open skin wound, the nurse should use which substance to clean the wound?
    1) warm tap water
    2) sterile isotonic solution
    3) half-strength hydrogen peroxide
    4) alcohol swabs

Sample Questions: Adult Nursing

Recommended Textbooks

Lewis, S. et al. (1996). Medical-surgical nursing: Assessment and management of clinical problems *(4th ed.). St. Louis: Mosby.*

This text covers general nursing concepts related to the adult client and nursing assessment and management of medical surgical problems. The nursing process is a major organizing theme. The text provides a brief review of anatomy and physiology before describing assessment and common diagnostic studies for each body system. The nursing role in management of diseases and disorders of body systems includes information related to health promotion and maintenance, acute intervention, and chronic and home care. Study aids include learning objectives and multiple choice review questions and answers, case studies with critical thinking challenges, and ethical and research content.

OR

Smeltzer, S., & Bare, B. (1996). Brunner & Suddarth's Textbook of medical-surgical nursing *(8th ed.). Philadelphia: J.B. Lippincott.*

This comprehensive text is organized into 17 sections with a total of 66 chapters. Charts and tables are used extensively to highlight key information. Each chapter focuses on the nursing process and concludes with critical thinking exercises and an extended list of references and bibliography. The appendix details diagnostic studies and their meaning. The text includes an IBM-compatible self-study disk.

Additional Textbooks
Beare, P.G., & Myers, J.L. (1998). Adult health nursing. *(3rd ed.). St. Louis: Mosby.*

This well-illustrated text contains 60 chapters covering health deviations common to adult clients. Each chapter includes "clinical alert" sections which highlight major areas of nursing concern or common client complications. Critical thinking questions are included at the end of each chapter to assist the student in learning essential material. The text contains a thorough explanation of the physiologic aspects of each disease. A home care guide is included in the planning aspects of clinical care.

Shannon, M.T. et al. (1995). Govoni & Hayes Drugs and nursing implications. *(8th ed.). Norwalk, CT: Appleton & Lange.*

This 1,200 page text provides a comprehensive, easy-to-follow guide for drug therapies. The index includes both general categories of mechanism of action and specific generic and trade names. The format is simple, yet thorough, and includes appropriate, research-based implications for nursing care.

Study Guide

Maternal & Child Nursing (457) (baccalaureate)

Credit Hours: 8
Credit Level: Upper
Question Type(s): Multiple-choice

The information in this study guide is valid until Summer 2001.
If you will be taking the examination after that date, be sure to check for a new edition of this guide before you complete your preparation for the exam.

General Description of the Examination

The Regents College Examination in Maternal & Child Nursing (baccalaureate) measures knowledge and understanding of health and illness as it pertains to maternal and child nursing and to the psychodynamics of family functioning. It is based on material taught in an upper-level sequence of courses in maternal and child nursing at the baccalaureate level.

The examination tests for a knowledge of the physical, emotional, and psychosocial concepts relevant to the health care of the childbearing and childrearing family. It tests for the ability to utilize the nursing process in the delivery of health care to the individual and family in a variety of settings, and for the ability to apply principles of normal growth and development to nursing management.

Content Outline

Content Area	Percent of Examination
I. Nursing Management of the Childbearing Family and the Childrearing Family	10%
II. Nursing Management of Normal Pregnancy	25%
III. Nursing Management of the Family with a High-Risk Pregnancy and the Family with a High-Risk Neonate	20%
IV. Nursing Management of the Well Child and Family	20%
V. Nursing Management of the Ill Child and Family	25%
Total	**100%**

Content Outline (continued)

Nursing Process: All steps of the nursing process—assessment, analysis, planning, implementation, and evaluation—will be represented in approximately equal proportions in the actual exam questions.

Content Area	Percent of Examination
I. Assessment	20%
II. Analysis	20%
III. Planning	20%
IV. Implementation	20%
V. Evaluation	20%
	Total 100%

NOTE: *In content areas IV and V, a health problem listed as an example for a particular age group may also be applicable in other age groups.*

I. Nursing Management of the Childbearing Family and the Childrearing Family (10%)

A. The family (for example: changing family roles and lifestyles, single-parent families, alternative families)

B. Social and cultural aspects (for example: delayed childbearing, family at the poverty level, sexuality, specific ethnocultural beliefs, adolescent pregnancy)

C. Ethical and legal considerations (for example: artificial insemination, surrogate parent, abortion, in vitro fertilization, sterilization, Pregnant Patient's Bill of Rights, Bill of Rights for Children and Teens, United Nations Declaration)

D. Biological aspects of human reproduction (for example: reproductive anatomy and physiology, conception, contraception, embryology, fetology)

E. Fertility and infertility (for example: crisis intervention for couples who are infertile, diagnostic testing and treatment, effect of pharmacokinetics on fertility)

F. Prepregnancy counseling (for example: chromosomal and multifactorial abnormalities, identification of families at risk)

II. Nursing Management of Normal Pregnancy (25%)

A. Nursing management during the antepartal period
  1. Psychosocial changes of pregnancy (for example: individual and family response to pregnancy, developmental tasks of the expectant family, sexuality during pregnancy, body image and self-concept changes, role changes, fantasies and fears about the unborn child, concerns about labor)

2. Biophysical changes of pregnancy (for example: signs and symptoms of pregnancy, physiologic changes, minor discomforts, warning signs of pregnancy complications, pharmacokinetics)
3. Anticipatory guidance (for example: childbirth education classes; birthing alternatives; parenting classes; changing family structure; use of community resources; education about smoking, alcohol use, medications, substance abuse, teratogens)
4. Nutritional needs of pregnancy (for example: recommended daily nutritional requirements, vitamin and mineral supplements, nutritional risk factors, sociocultural influences on diet)
5. Assessment of maternal and fetal well-being (for example: ultrasonography; alpha-fetoprotein testing; Leopold's maneuvers; laboratory studies such as toxoplasmosis, rubella, cytomegalovirus, herpes virus [TORCH]; enzyme-linked immunosorbent assay [ELISA] testing; alcohol and drug screening; screening for gestational diabetes; Pap smear; blood type, hematocrit, and hemoglobin; urinalysis)

B. **Nursing management during the intrapartal period**
1. First stage (for example: database assessment, factors affecting onset, contractions, vital signs, mechanism of labor, medications, external and internal fetal monitoring, supportive care, IV therapy, fluid intake, induction of labor, epidurals, use of prostaglandins)
2. Second stage (for example: pushing techniques, vaginal or cesarean birth, vaginal birth after cesarean [VBAC], episiotomy, medications, anesthesia, emotional response, supportive care, Apgar scoring, immediate gross assessment and physical care of neonate)
3. Third stage (for example: placental expulsion, parent-infant interaction, medications, initial breast-feeding)
4. Fourth stage (for example: assessment of mother, including fundus, vital signs, lochia, voiding, fluid status, possible lacerations, episiotomy, cesarean site, emotional response; medications)

C. **Nursing management during the postpartal period**
1. Psychosocial changes (for example: attachment process, unmet expectations, parenting, changing family systems and roles, postpartum depression)
2. Biophysical changes (for example: hormonal changes; changes in fundus, lochia, breasts, bladder, bowel, perineum, extremities, nutritional status; need for medications; postoperative care)
3. Anticipatory guidance for self-care at home (for example: body image changes, rest and activity level, fatigue, physical changes, personal hygiene, need for follow-up care, sexual activity, contraception, sterilization, integration of new family member, breast-feeding, nutrition during lactation, formula feeding, comfort measures)

D. **Nursing management of the normal neonate and family**
1. Biophysical changes (for example: body system adaptations; transitional assessment [periods of reactivity]; complete physical assessment, including neurological status and gestational age; Brazelton Neonatal Behavioral Assessment Scale; screening tests)
2. Anticipatory guidance (for example: handling; positioning; bathing: cord care;

circumcision care; education about normal conditions and appearance of the newborn, including skin variations, reflexes, and sleep patterns; breast-feeding; formula feeding; concerns about infant feeding; elimination patterns; parent-infant attachment)

III. Nursing Management of the Family with a High-Risk Pregnancy and the Family with a High-Risk Neonate (20%)

A. The family with a high-risk pregnancy
 1. Antepartal period
    a. Identification of the client at risk (for example: age, parity, multiple gestation, nutritional status, economic status, health status, environmental hazards, family violence)
    b. Assessment of fetal well-being (for example: amniocentesis, alpha-fetoprotein testing, chorionic villi sampling, nonstress testing, oxytocin challenge testing, contraction stress testing, ultrasonography, biophysical profile, maternal assessment of fetal activity)
    c. High-risk conditions (for example: hemorrhagic conditions of early and late pregnancy; incompetent cervix; ABO incompatibility; Rh isoimmunization; pregnancy-induced hypertension [PIH]; cardiac conditions, diabetes mellitus, hyperemesis gravidarum; toxoplasmosis, rubella, cytomegalovirus, herpes virus [TORCH]; chlamydia; HIV; acquired immunodeficiency syndrome [AIDS]; substance abuse; trauma)
 2. Intrapartal period
    a. Assessment of fetal well-being (for example: fetal distress, external monitoring, internal monitoring, fetal pH testing)
    b. High-risk conditions (for example: dystocia, hemorrhage, hypertension, premature rupture of membranes, preterm labor, prolapsed cord, multiple birth, infection, hydramnios, ruptured uterus, fetal malpresentation)
 3. Postpartal period
    a. High-risk conditions (for example: hemorrhage; hypertension; infection; preexisting health problems; emotional problems, including grief and bereavement; uterine atony; uterine inversion; disseminated intravascular coagulation [DIC]; hemolysis, elevated liver enzymes, and low platelet count [HELLP] syndrome)
    b. Anticipatory guidance (for example: breast-feeding of the high-risk neonate, use of community resources, implications of high-risk status for future pregnancies)

B. The family with a high-risk neonate
 1. Biophysical changes (for example: complete physical assessment, including neurological status and gestational age; maladaptive body system responses; screening and diagnostic tests; effect of maternal conditions)
 2. High-risk conditions (for example: very low birth weight [VLBW], intrauterine growth retardation [IUGR], preterm, postterm, HIV, maternal substance abuse, hypoglycemia, thermoregulation, sepsis, respiratory distress syndrome [RDS], apnea, necrotizing enterocolitis [NEC], bronchopulmonary dysplasia, retinopathy of prematurity, hyperbilirubinemia)
 3. Anticipatory guidance (for example: orientation to neonatal intensive care

unit, care and feeding of the high-risk infant, vulnerable child syndrome, passive skin-to-skin contact [kangaroo care], promotion of parent-infant attachment, use of community resources)

IV. Nursing Management of the Well Child and Family (20%)

A. The infant
1. Growth and development (for example: physical, cognitive, psychosocial)
2. Nutritional needs (for example: recommended daily allowances, introduction of solid foods, weaning, sociocultural influences on diet)
3. Health promotion (for example: developmental screening, vision and hearing screening, immunizations, fluoride supplements, iron supplements)
4. Common health problems (for example: colic, fever, diarrhea, food intolerances, eczema, gastroesophageal reflux, apnea)
5. Anticipatory guidance for parents (for example: teething, sleeping patterns, sensory stimulation, speech development, prevention of nursing caries, safety, prevention of shaken baby syndrome, selection of day care)

B. The toddler
1. Growth and development (for example: physical, cognitive, psychosocial, moral, social)
2. Nutritional needs (for example: recommended daily allowances, physiologic anorexia, self-feeding, serving size, finger foods)
3. Health promotion (for example: screening for lead levels and anemias, vision and hearing screening, dental care, developmental screening, immunizations)
4. Common health problems (for example: anemia, upper respiratory infections, ear infections, parasitic infections, poisonings)
5. Anticipatory guidance for parents (for example: play, discipline and limit setting, temper tantrums, toilet training, speech development, safety, prevention of child abuse)

C. The preschooler
1. Growth and development (for example: physical, cognitive, psychosocial, moral, social)
2. Nutritional needs (for example: recommended daily allowances, ritualistic food behaviors)
3. Health promotion (for example: vision and hearing screening, developmental screening, immunizations)
4. Common health problems (for example: communicable diseases, tonsillitis [tonsillectomy, adenoidectomy], speech problems, strabismus)
5. Anticipatory guidance for parents and child (for example: play, sibling rivalry, masturbation, safety, child maltreatment, implication of day care for child)

D. The school-age child
1. Growth and development (for example: physical, cognitive, psychosocial, moral, social, self-esteem)
2. Nutritional needs (for example: recommended daily allowances, nutritional habits)
3. Health promotion (for example: vision and hearing screening, dental care, developmental screening, scoliosis screening, encouraging good health habits)

4. Common health problems (for example: communicable diseases, minor accidents, obesity, enuresis, bites and stings, allergies, school phobia)
5. Anticipatory guidance for parents and child (for example: safety, substance abuse, dishonest behavior, children who care for themselves after school; monitoring activities, including television viewing; injury prevention; early recognition of depression)

E. **The adolescent**
1. Growth and development (for example: physical, cognitive, psychosocial, moral, social, self-esteem)
2. Nutritional needs (for example: recommended daily allowances; eating habits, including snacking and irregular mealtimes; peer influences)
3. Health promotion (for example: vision and hearing screening, dental care, scoliosis screening, breast self-examination [BSE] or testicular self-examination [TSE], immunizations)
4. Common health problems (for example: acne, obesity, male and female reproductive system alterations)
5. Anticipatory guidance for parents and child -for example: peer and family relationships; risk-taking behaviors; substance abuse; sex education, including sexually transmitted diseases [STDs], contraceptive measures, AIDS awareness; motor vehicle safety

V. **Nursing Management of the Ill Child and Family— Nursing responsibilities related to pain management, therapeutic play, medication administration, fluid and electrolyte balance, safety, reaction to hospitalization and illness, legal and ethical issues, preparation for home care, and schooling (25%)**

A. **The infant**
1. Major health problems (for example: cleft lip, cleft palate, pyloric stenosis, esophageal atresia, gastroenteritis, bronchiolitis, developmental dysplasia of hip, clubfoot, Hirschsprung's disease, hydrocephalus, myelodysplasias, genetic disorders, congenital heart disease, nonorganic failure to thrive, HIV, AIDS, sepsis)
2. Family and infant's response to health problems (for example: coping mechanisms, coping with sudden infant death syndrome [SIDS], caring for the technology-dependent infant, attachment disorders)

B. **The toddler**
1. Major health problems (for example: foreign body aspiration; sickle cell disease; nephrotic syndrome; cystic fibrosis; cerebral palsy; meningitis; accidents, such as burns and poisoning; croup; seizures; Kawasaki disease; lead poisoning; celiac disease; autism; abuse)
2. Family and child's response to health problems (for example: chronic illness, fears of bodily injury and harm)

C. **The preschooler**
1. Major health problems (for example: hearing and vision problems, acute

glomerulonephritis, neoplastic disease, pneumonia, Wilms' tumor, developmental delays, child with special needs, epiglottitis, acute appendicitis)
    2. Family and child's response to health problems (for example: reaction to developmental delays or terminal illness, magical thinking)

D. The school-age child
    1. Major health problems (for example: diabetes mellitus, hemophilia, epilepsy, asthma, acute rheumatic fever, multiple trauma, learning disabilities, attention-deficit hyperactivity disorder, Reye's syndrome, Lyme disease, child with special needs, juvenile rheumatoid arthritis)
    2. Family and child's response to health problems (for example: coping mechanisms, self-care)

E. The adolescent
    1. Major health problems (for example: suicide; sexually transmitted diseases; pelvic inflammatory disease [PID]; papilloma; scoliosis; sports injuries; Osgood-Schlatter disease; mononucleosis; hepatitis; substance abuse; eating disorders; pregnancy; immunological disorders, including lupus; osteosarcomas; ulcerative colitis; Guillain-Barré syndrome)
    2. Family and child's response to health problems (for example: coping mechanisms, self-care)

Sample Questions: Maternal & Child Nursing (bacc.)

1. Which client statement is typical of a member in a newly formed blended family?
   1) "My relationships with family members are about the same."
   2) "I've had to develop new ways of functioning in my new family."
   3) "Few additional decisions have been necessary with the new family structure."
   4) "Having more family members has decreased my stress."

2. A client who is expecting her first baby asks the nurse to explain why there is fluid surrounding the baby during pregnancy. Which client statement indicates understanding of the nurse's teaching related to the purposes of amniotic fluid?
   The fluid
   1) ensures a safe delivery.
   2) keeps the baby's lungs open.
   3) provides a cushion to protect the baby.
   4) helps keep the baby's heartbeat regular.

3. Which instruction should be included in a teaching plan regarding preconception health measures?
   1) The couple should maintain their current lifestyle and daily activities.
   2) The woman should use appetite suppressants to achieve an ideal weight for her body build and height.
   3) The couple should plan genetic counseling if they are over the age of 25.
   4) The couple should determine if they are exposed to any environmental hazards in their work or community.

4. A client at 16 weeks gestation has gained 12 pounds during the pregnancy. The client says that she is too fat. Which is the most appropriate nursing intervention?
   1) Explain that the fetus will require most of the client's caloric intake.
   2) Refer the client to a nutritionist for information on low-calorie foods.
   3) Assess the client's knowledge of weight gain and nutrition in pregnancy.
   4) Provide the client with pamphlets on weight control in pregnancy.

5. A pregnant client is making her first antepartum visit. Which assessment approach will provide the nurse with the most useful information about the client's nutrition?
   1) Request the client to bring a one-week dietary account with her to the next visit.
   2) Have the client complete a nutritional questionnaire during the visit.
   3) Discuss the client's diet in the past 24 hours and typical dietary patterns.
   4) Ask the client to describe her family's nutritional patterns.

6. A new mother who is breast-feeding is diagnosed with nonpurulent mastitis. Which instruction should the nurse give to the mother concerning breast-feeding?
   1) Continue to breast-feed if the discomfort is tolerable.
   2) Stop breast-feeding at once because of the risk of cross-infection.
   3) Only give the baby milk that has been mechanically expressed.
   4) Allow the baby to nurse longer because the increased vessel dilatation facilitates healing.

Sample Questions: Maternal & Child Nursing (bacc.)

7. A client in the second stage of labor says that her water has broken. Which action should the nurse implement first?
    1) Perform a Nitrazine paper test.
    2) Assess the fetal heart rate.
    3) Change the wet bed linens.
    4) Chart the assessment data.

8. In assessing a term neonate immediately after birth, the nurse finds that the anterior fontanelle is soft and pulsates with each heartbeat. Which action should the nurse take?
    1) Observe the fontanelle for color changes.
    2) Consult with the physician immediately.
    3) Check for signs of increased intracranial pressure.
    4) Do nothing since this is a normal finding.

9. What should the nurse teach new parents about caring for the umbilical cord?
    1) Call the health care provider when the cord falls off.
    2) Cover the cord area snugly with the diaper.
    3) Wipe the cord area with alcohol two or three times a day.
    4) Give tub baths to ensure adequate cleansing of the cord area.

10. A nonstress test is performed to assess fetal well-being in a pregnant client. Which test result would indicate a healthy fetus?
    1) one or two fetal movements in an hour
    2) acceleration of the fetal heart rate when the fetus moves
    3) deceleration of the fetal heart rate when the uterus contracts
    4) no variability in the fetal heart rate during uterine contractions

11. A gravida 5, para 4 client at 34 weeks of gestation comes to the emergency department with painless vaginal bleeding. Why is a vaginal examination contraindicated for this client? A vaginal examination may
    1) tear a low-lying placenta.
    2) stimulate Braxton Hicks contractions.
    3) introduce an infection into the birth canal.
    4) cause premature rupture of the membranes.

12. A multipara in labor is receiving oxytocin (Pitocin) IV. She is 4 cm dilated and the baby is at station –2. External fetal heart and uterine contraction monitors are being used. The nurse notes several variable decelerations on the strip. What is the appropriate nursing intervention?
    1) Administer IV analgesia.
    2) Ambulate the client.
    3) Change the client's position.
    4) Increase the Pitocin infusion.

Sample Questions: Maternal & Child Nursing (bacc.)

13. Which finding should the nurse expect when assessing a neonate who is large for gestational age?
    1) birth weight at the 90th percentile
    2) Epstein's pearls
    3) head circumference at the 75th percentile
    4) skin desquamation

14. The nurse is providing anticipatory guidance about engorgement to a new mother who is breast-feeding. The nurse should include which instruction?
    1) Restrict maternal fluid intake.
    2) Obtain medical intervention since an infection may have occurred.
    3) Breast-feed less frequently during the time the breasts are engorged.
    4) Express some milk prior to breast-feeding to facilitate the baby's ability to latch on.

15. The nurse is planning to teach new mothers in a well-baby clinic about immunizations for their infants. Which information is most important for the nurse to include?
    1) the reason for spacing the immunizations over time
    2) the controversies concerning risks and benefits of immunizations
    3) the necessity of adhering to a schedule for immunizations during the first five years of life
    4) the legal requirement that all school-age children be immunized

16. Which behavioral manifestation in an eight-month-old infant should lead the nurse to suspect bilateral acute otitis media?
    1) rolling the head from side to side
    2) scratching the cheeks
    3) feeding voraciously
    4) sucking on the fingers

17. Which suggestion by the nurse would be most helpful to parents who complain about their four-year-old child's ritualistic food behavior?
    1) Avoid unfamiliar foods.
    2) Eliminate between-meal snacks.
    3) Involve the child in the preparation of food.
    4) Promote mealtimes as a social activity.

18. The parents of a child who has chickenpox ask when their child can return to school. The nurse's reply should be based on which information?
    Communicability ends when
    1) the first lesion appears.
    2) the fever subsides.
    3) all the lesions have disappeared.
    4) all the lesions have crusted.

Sample Questions: Maternal & Child Nursing (bacc.)

19. The chances that an adolescent with obesity will adhere to a weight reduction diet will most likely be increased if the nurse does which of the following?
    The nurse
    1) models good eating habits for the adolescent.
    2) discusses ways to incorporate favorite foods into the adolescent's meals.
    3) refers the adolescent for nutrition counseling.
    4) reviews the food pyramid and healthy eating habits with the adolescent.

20. The nurse teaches the parents of an infant with congestive heart failure the correct procedure for administering digoxin. Which client statement indicates that the nurse's teaching was effective?
    1) "If we miss a dose, we'll give the next dose as soon as possible."
    2) "If the baby vomits after taking digoxin, we'll give a second dose."
    3) "If the baby doesn't like the digoxin, we'll mix it in his bottle."
    4) "We'll plan to give the digoxin one hour before or two hours after meals."

21. Which diagnostic sign should the nurse expect to find in a toddler at the beginning of the acute phase of Kawasaki disease?
    1) abrupt onset of high fever that responds to antibiotics
    2) oropharyngeal reddening or "strawberry" tongue
    3) a vesicular systemic rash, accentuated in the perineum
    4) increased irritability and inconsolableness

22. A child who has lead poisoning is undergoing chelation therapy. Which nursing intervention is of primary importance?
    1) Record intake and output accurately.
    2) Locally apply warm soaks to the injection sites.
    3) Apply a local anesthetic prior to administering injections.
    4) Monitor vital signs every eight hours.

23. In the initial assessment of a child with glomerulonephritis, the nurse should expect which findings?
    1) hematuria and petechiae
    2) hypertension and proteinuria
    3) flank pain and fever
    4) oliguria and glycosuria

24. The nurse is evaluating the response of a child with asthma to asthma therapy. Which signs will appear first if the child's condition is improving?
    1) increased abdominal skin turgor and shallow respirations
    2) increased blood flow to the nail beds and lips
    3) decreased pulse and blood pressure
    4) decreased rhonchi and wheezes

25. Which behavior places an adolescent at risk for Osgood–Schlatter disease?
    1) repetitive jumping
    2) substance abuse
    3) sexual activity
    4) automobile driving

Sample Questions: Maternal & Child Nursing (bacc.)

Recommended Resources

The examination development committee recommends that you obtain both of the resources listed below:

Olds, S., London, M., & Ladewig, P.W. (1996). Maternal newborn nursing: A family-centered approach *(5th ed.). Menlo Park, CA: Addison-Wesley.*

This text covers theoretical and therapeutic nursing foundations in the care of the childbearing woman and her family. It provides broad coverage of family needs within the context of normal as well as abnormal adaptation. Critical thinking scenarios provide practice with decision-making criteria in commonly occurring practice situations. Key terms and points are highlighted throughout the text. A workbook that provides review exercises is available.

Wong, D. (1999). Whaley and Wong's Nursing care of infants and children *(6th ed.). St. Louis: Mosby.*

This text covers theoretical and therapeutic interventions for the child within the context of normal growth and development and family interaction, as well as deviations from normal system functioning. The text provides broad coverage of individual, family, and community influences on health/illness states. Key terms are highlighted throughout the text. A study guide is also available for this text.

Study Guide
Psychiatric/Mental Health Nursing (503)

Credit Hours: 8 **Credit Level:** Upper
Question Type(s): Multiple-choice

The information in this study guide is valid until Summer 2001.
If you will be taking the examination after that date, be sure to check for a new edition of this guide before you complete your preparation for the exam.

General Description of the Examination

The Psychiatric/Mental Health Nursing examination measures knowledge and understanding of the theoretical/therapeutic foundations for psychiatric mental health nursing practice, and tests the application of this knowledge and understanding to the nursing care of clients, using the nursing process as an organizing framework. Within this framework, the client system is defined as the individual, the family, the small group, or the community, with major emphasis on the individual.

The examination is based on material typically taught in an upper-division sequence of courses in psychiatric/mental health nursing at the baccalaureate level.

Content Outline

Content Area	Percent of Examination
I. Theoretical/Therapeutic Foundations for Psychiatric/Mental Health Nursing Practice	25%
II. Nursing Assessment and Nursing Analysis	25%
III. Nursing Planning and Nursing Implementation	30%
IV. Nursing Evaluation	20%
Total	**100%**

I. Theoretical/Therapeutic Foundations for Psychiatric/Mental Health Nursing Practice (25%)

A. History of psychiatric/mental health nursing
1. Contributions of significant leaders
   a. Linda Richards
   b. Dorothea Dix
   c. Harriet Bailey
   d. Ida Orlando
2. Important historical events
   a. Concept of therapeutic community—as discussed by Maxwell Jones
   b. Introduction of psychotropic drugs
   c. Community mental health movement
   d. Introduction of CAT scan, PET scan, and MRI

B. Psychobiological theories, psychological theories, and nursing theories
1. Psychobiological—genetics, biogenic amines
2. Intrapersonal—as discussed by Sigmund Freud, Erik Erikson, Carl Rogers, and Dorothea Orem
3. Interpersonal—as discussed by Harry Stack Sullivan and Hildegard Peplau
4. Cognitive—as discussed by Aaron Beck and Jean Piaget
5. Systems, family, and communication—as discussed by Virginia Satir, Murray Bowen, Salvador Minuchin, and Jay Haley
6. Behavioral, stress, and crisis—as discussed by B.F. Skinner, Hans Selye, Gerald Caplan, and Donna Aguilera
7. Sociocultural and phenomenological—as discussed by Thomas Szasz, R.D. Laing, and Madeleine Leininger

C. Nurse-client relationship with the individual, the family, the small group, and the community
1. Characteristics of the nurse in the nurse-client relationship (for example: empathy, warmth, genuineness, objectivity, self-awareness, acceptance)
2. Phases in the relationship
   a. Preorientation or pregroup
   b. Orientation or initial
   c. Working
   d. Termination
3. Tools used in the nurse-client relationship
   a. Communication skills
      1) Modes of communication, i.e., verbal, nonverbal, metacommunication
      2) Therapeutic techniques and barriers to therapeutic communication (for example: clarification, validation)
   b. Interviewing techniques
      1) Structure of the interview
      2) Mutual goal setting
      3) Roles of the participants
4. Roles of the nurse in the nurse-client relationship
   a. Caregiver
   b. Health teacher

       c. Change agent
       d. Client advocate
       e. Role model
   D. **Treatment modalities**
       1. Individual psychotherapy
       2. Group therapy (for example: types of groups, group process)
       3. Milieu therapy
       4. Family therapy
       5. Behavior therapy
       6. Somatic therapies (for example: psychotropic drug therapy, electroconvulsive therapy, biofeedback, relaxation techniques)
       7. Crisis intervention
   E. **Professional accountability and liability related to ethical, legal, and research issues**
       1. Confidentiality
       2. Standards of practice
       3. Right to receive and/or refuse treatment
       4. Voluntary/involuntary commitment
       5. Patient's Bill of Rights
       6. Documentation
       7. Right to die

II. Nursing Assessment and Nursing Analysis (25%)

Nursing Assessment—the process of gathering and synthesizing data about the client's health status in relation to the client's functional health patterns

Nursing Analysis—the identification of the nursing diagnosis (client problem) and the determination of the expected outcomes (goals) of client care

   A. **Of the functional client system**
       1. The individual as client system
       For example, assessing: coping strategies, cultural/ethnic/spiritual factors, support systems, defense mechanisms, physiological health, developmental level, normal grieving
       2. The family as client system
       For example, assessing: developmental life cycle, communication patterns, roles, power structure, multigenerational patterns, cultural/ethnic/spiritual patterns, support systems
       3. The small group as client system
       For example, assessing: task and maintenance functions, roles, norms, communication patterns, stages of group development, cohesion, task accomplishment
       4. The community as client system
       For example, assessing: demographics, cultural/ethnic/spiritual patterns, services, environmental factors, political/power structures, economic factors

   B. **Of the dysfunctional client system**
       1. The individual as client system
           a. For example, assessing: impaired coping strategies, impaired support

systems, impaired defense mechanisms, negative impact of cultural/ethnic/spiritual factors, impaired physiological health (acute and chronic illness), impaired developmental level, impaired grieving
- b. For example, assessing: alterations of mood (mood disorders), potential for violence to self and others (suicide, battering, rape), alterations in thought processes (schizophrenic disorders), dysfunctional behavior in response to stress and anxiety (anxiety disorders, somatoform disorders, dissociative disorders, immunological disorders, personality disorders), potential for substance abuse (substance abuse disorders), altered patterns of sexuality (sexual dysfunction and sexual disorders), altered patterns of nutrition (eating disorders), cognitive impairment (organic mental disorders and mental retardation)
2. The family as client system
For example, assessing: alteration in communication (as in double bind), alteration in parenting (as in child abuse or elder abuse), alteration in role function (as in parentified child), inappropriate developmental life cycle stage (as in teenage pregnancy), dysfunctional power structure (as in codependency), inadequate support systems, negative impact of cultural/ethnic/spiritual patterns, dysfunctional multigenerational patterns (as in substance abuse and suicide)
3. The small group as client system
For example, assessing: inability to move beyond the expected conflict stage, developmental arrest at any stage of group process, dysfunctional roles, dysfunctional norms, dysfunctional communication patterns, lack of cohesion, inability to accomplish tasks
4. The community as client system
For example, assessing: underserved populations (as in individuals who are homeless and mentally ill), environmental hazards, overcrowding, underutilization of services, negative impact of cultural/ethnic/spiritual patterns

III. Nursing Planning and Nursing Implementation (30%)

Nursing Planning—the formulation of specific strategies to achieve the expected outcomes

Nursing Implementation—the carrying out of nursing plans designed to move the client toward the expected outcomes

A. For the functional client system
1. The individual as client system
For example, promoting and supporting: coping strategies, cultural/ethnic/spiritual factors, support systems, defense mechanisms, physiological health (including dignified death), developmental level, normal grieving
2. The family as client system
For example, promoting and supporting: appropriate stage of life cycle development, healthy communication patterns, healthy role patterns, appropriate power structures, positive cultural/ethnic/spiritual patterns, appropriate support systems, healthy multigenerational patterns
3. The small group as client system
For example, promoting and supporting: appropriate task and maintenance

functions, functional norms, role appropriate behavior, healthy communication patterns, appropriate stages of group development, cohesion, task accomplishment
    4. The community as client system
    For example, promoting and supporting: positive cultural/ethnic/spiritual patterns, adequate services, healthy environmental factors, responsive political/power structures, adequate economic factors

B. **For the dysfunctional client system (see IIB for specific dysfunctions)**
    1. The individual as client system
        a. For example, planning and treating: impairments related to coping strategies, cultural/ethnic/spiritual factors, support systems, defense mechanisms, physiological health (acute and chronic illness), developmental level
        b. For example, planning and treating: impairments related to alterations in mood, thought processes, sexuality, cognition, nutrition, violent behavior, stress and anxiety, substance abuse, grieving
    2. The family as client system
        a. For example, planning and treating: alterations in communication, parenting, role function
        b. For example, planning and treating: inappropriate developmental life cycle stage, dysfunctional power structure, inadequate support systems, negative impact of cultural/ethnic/spiritual patterns, dysfunctional multigenerational patterns
    3. The small group as client system
        a. For example, planning and treating: small group inability to move beyond the expected conflict stage, developmental arrest at any stage of group process
        b. For example, facilitating: functional roles, functional norms, appropriate communication patterns, appropriate stages of group development, cohesion, task accomplishment
    4. The community as client system
        a. For example, planning and treating: the negative impact of cultural/ethnic/spiritual patterns, underserved populations, environmental hazards, overcrowding
        b. For example, promoting: adequate utilization of services, responsive political/power structures, advocacy and lobbying

IV. Nursing Evaluation (20%)
Nursing Evaluation—the appraisal of the effectiveness of the nursing interventions relative to the nursing diagnosis and the expected outcomes

A. **Of the functional client system**
    1. The individual as client system
    For example, evaluating the maintenance of: coping strategies, positive cultural/ethnic/spiritual factors, support systems, defense mechanisms, physiological health, developmental level, normal grieving behaviors
    2. The family as client system
    For example, evaluating the maintenance of: appropriate stage of life cycle development, healthy communication patterns, healthy role patterns,

appropriate power structures, positive cultural/ethnic/spiritual patterns, appropriate support systems, healthy multigenerational patterns
3. The small group as client system
For example, evaluating the maintenance of: appropriate task and maintenance functions, functional norms, role appropriate behavior, healthy communication patterns, appropriate stages of group development, cohesion, task accomplishment
4. The community as client system
For example, evaluating the maintenance of: positive cultural/ethnic/spiritual patterns, adequate services, positive environmental factors, responsive political/power structures, adequate economic factors

B. Of the dysfunctional client system (see IIB for specific dysfunctions)
1. The individual as client system
   a. For example, evaluating improvement and/or residual dysfunction related to: coping strategies, negative impact of cultural/ethnic/spiritual factors, support systems, defense mechanisms, physiological health (acute and chronic illness), developmental level, bereavement
   b. For example, evaluating improvement and/or residual dysfunction related to: alterations in mood, thought process, sexuality, cognition, nutrition, violent behavior, stress and anxiety, substance abuse, grieving
2. The family as client system
For example, evaluating improvement and/or residual dysfunction related to: alterations in communication, alterations in parenting, alterations in role function; inappropriate developmental life cycle stage, dysfunctional power structure, inadequate support systems, negative impact of cultural/ethnic/spiritual patterns, dysfunctional multigenerational patterns
3. The small group as client system
For example, evaluating improvement and/or residual dysfunction related to: small group inability to move beyond the expected conflict stage, developmental arrest at any stage of group process, roles, norms, communication patterns, stages of group development, cohesion, task accomplishment
4. The community as client system
For example, evaluating improvement and/or residual dysfunction related to: cultural/ethnic/spiritual patterns, underserved populations, environmental hazards, inadequate utilization of services, unresponsive political/power structures, advocacy and lobbying

Sample Questions: Psychiatric/Mental Health Nursing

1. Which statement by a client who is having a crisis should take priority for nursing intervention?
    1) "I finally moved my family into a house of my very own and I am wondering if I can afford the payments."
    2) "I have a best friend who listens to my problems but she is on vacation."
    3) "My fiancé of six years just called off our engagement."
    4) "My 10-year-old daughter is spending her first summer away from me at camp."

2. What is the primary task of the orientation stage of the nurse-client relationship?
    1) to solve problems
    2) to establish therapeutic goals
    3) to explore past difficulties
    4) to evaluate progress

3. A young man calls a crisis center hotline stating that he can no longer cope with his problem and that he is falling apart. Which would be the nurse's most therapeutic initial response?
    1) "What do you think would help you?"
    2) "Everyone has their bad days."
    3) "Tell me about your situation."
    4) "How do you usually handle stress?"

4. What should the nurse do when a client becomes silent during a nurse-client interaction?
    1) Suggest that the client share her thoughts.
    2) Direct the conversation to a less intimidating topic.
    3) Terminate the interaction with the client.
    4) Ask the client a nonthreatening question.

5. Which response by the nurse leader can enhance norm setting for a group and promote a feeling of safety and support?
    1) "We've heard you discuss this before, Mr. Jones."
    2) "Questions should be addressed to me."
    3) "What do you see as your worst problem at home?"
    4) "It is important to give everyone a chance to participate."

6. What is the basic premise of family therapy as a treatment modality?
    1) The family needs help in dealing with the behavior of the member who is the client.
    2) The family needs help in understanding the developmental needs of the member who is the client.
    3) The member with the presenting symptoms needs special support from the therapist.
    4) The member with the presenting symptoms signals the presence of pain in the whole family.

Sample Questions: Psychiatric/Mental Health Nursing

7. In which of the following situations does the nurse have just cause to physically restrain a client?
   1) An older adult client with newly diagnosed Alzheimer's disease is wandering the halls in the early evenings.
   2) A client newly admitted with mania refuses medication and throws a plate and a chair.
   3) An adolescent client who is agitated begins to argue loudly with another client about the use of the television.
   4) A client with depression who was recently removed from suicide precautions says, "I still feel like hurting myself."

8. Which statement is characteristic of a client who is experiencing a resolution of grief?
   1) "His death reminds me of my brother's death last year."
   2) "I won't forget him, but I have the children to think of now."
   3) "He was so wonderful. Everyone loved him."
   4) "I'm going to keep his ashes in an urn so I can't forget him."

9. The use of which assessment technique would be the best way for the community mental health nurse to identify a community's strengths?
   1) spending a day in the community health center observing the clients who come there
   2) talking with long-time residents about what they like about the community and why they stay
   3) collecting demographic data from census tract information
   4) reviewing newspaper editorials to identify concerns and trends

10. The nurse is assessing a client with possible depression. Which finding in the client's history would indicate a predisposition to depressive disorders?
    The client's
    1) adoptive mother had a diagnosis of bipolar disorder.
    2) biological mother had a diagnosis of bipolar disorder.
    3) adoptive father was treated for reactive depression.
    4) biological father was treated for reactive depression.

11. A client with alcoholism states that he drinks only when he is frustrated by the behavior of his three adolescent children. Which defense mechanism is the client using?
    1) denial
    2) projection
    3) rationalization
    4) sublimation

12. During a group meeting, the nurse observes that one of the members tends to view problems in terms of right and wrong. Which dysfunctional group role is being assumed by this client?
    1) complainer
    2) monopolizer
    3) moralist
    4) victim

Sample Questions: Psychiatric/Mental Health Nursing

13. After a destructive tornado occurs in a community, which event should indicate to the nurse that community-wide crisis intervention is needed?
    1) The number of homes put up for sale increases.
    2) Many parents report that their children have nightmares and sleep disturbances.
    3) The local weather bureau receives increased requests for information on tornado precautions.
    4) The school board changes the policy on fire drills to include tornado drills.

14. Which nursing intervention should be given priority to meet the recreational needs of an adolescent client who attends the community mental health center adolescent program?
    1) Schedule frequent one-to-one discussion sessions between the nurse and the client.
    2) Provide the client with equipment for an activity of the client's choice.
    3) Arrange activities that will promote peer group interaction.
    4) Ask the activities therapist to meet daily with the client.

15. Which strategy should have priority in the nursing care plan for a single parent to meet the parent's emotional needs?
    1) Introduce the client to community socialization programs.
    2) Assess the client's support system.
    3) Encourage the client's involvement in recreational activities.
    4) Provide pamphlets about single parenting.

16. Why should the nurse allow a newly admitted client with obsessive-compulsive behavior to complete rituals?
    Because the client
    1) has not yet learned alternative coping mechanisms
    2) will become psychotic if prevented from completing the rituals
    3) will not develop trust in the nurse who prevents rituals from being completed
    4) needs to know that the staff is accepting of this behavior

17. Which strategy should the nurse include in the plan of care for a client with Alzheimer's disease who is experiencing apraxia?
    1) Give simple, sequential directions using both verbal and nonverbal communication.
    2) Use color-coded signs so the client can find the bathroom.
    3) Use clocks and calendars and other orienting devices.
    4) Administer prn antianxiety medication when the client becomes confused.

18. A married woman with three school-age children is caring for her 80-year-old father in her home. She reports feeling overwhelmed with her responsibilities and says, "I feel like everyone wants something from me." The nurse should give priority to which intervention in the plan of care for this family?
    1) Assist family members to clarify their expectations of each other.
    2) Encourage the woman to find a nursing home for her father.
    3) Suggest that the husband and children perform more household chores.
    4) Arrange for a live-in aide to care for the client's father.

Sample Questions: Psychiatric/Mental Health Nursing

19. A client who describes himself as a recreational cocaine user denies the seriousness of his cocaine use when confronted by his family. Which would be the most healthy family response?
    1) Continue the discussion when everyone is calmer.
    2) Give the client one more chance to quit by himself.
    3) Acknowledge their inability to change his behavior.
    4) State that they will contact the authorities if they find any cocaine.

20. During the second meeting of an outpatient group, a client tries to change the rules of the group. Which is the nurse's most therapeutic intervention?
    1) Treat the client's disruptive behavior matter-of-factly.
    2) Ignore the client's manipulative behavior.
    3) Have the client restate personal expectations in relation to group goals.
    4) Arrange an individual session with the client.

21. Which client statement best indicates that nursing interventions directed toward motivating the client to change behavior have been effective?
    1) "I can't stand this pain any longer."
    2) "I wish I felt better."
    3) "I just can't seem to pull it together."
    4) "I want someone to help me."

22. The nurse is evaluating nursing care for a client with depression. Which finding is the most significant indicator of therapeutic progress?
    The client's
    1) speech has slowed and become more logical.
    2) need for sleep has decreased.
    3) self-concept has become more positive.
    4) appetite has increased.

23. A client is admitted to a psychiatric unit after taking an overdose of barbiturates. On the day after admission, which client behavior is most significant in evaluating whether the client's risk for committing suicide has increased?
    The client
    1) no longer talks about suicide.
    2) verbalizes angry feelings.
    3) socializes with a group of other clients.
    4) becomes more cheerful and outgoing.

24. The nurse is evaluating a client who is in the manic phase of bipolar disorder and who is on a regimen of lithium carbonate. Which indicates an adverse reaction to the medication?
    1) orthostatic hypotension
    2) vomiting and diarrhea
    3) involuntary movements of mouth and jaw
    4) rigidity of posture

Sample Questions: Psychiatric/Mental Health Nursing

25. Which comment by a group member should the nurse evaluate as being appropriate behavior during the orientation stage of group development?
    1) "Let me tell you about my problem with my mother-in-law."
    2) "It would be easy to say my problems are due to my ex-husband."
    3) "I thought the group leader was supposed to help us out."
    4) "This group is OK, but I still have a lot of problems."

Recommended Resource

Stuart, G., & Sundeen, S. (1998). Principles and practice of psychiatric nursing *(6th ed.). St. Louis: Mosby.*

This text covers theoretical/therapeutic foundations, the psychiatric client (dysfunctional client), and mental health issues (functional client). It provides good coverage of family, group, and community. DSM-IV is integrated throughout the clinical chapters. Study aids include learning objectives and a topical outline at the beginning of chapters, key terms highlighted, and key points summarized at the end of chapters.

Additional Resources

Haber, J., Krainovich-Miller, B., McMahon, A.L., & Price-Hoskins, P. (1997). Comprehensive psychiatric nursing *(5th ed.). St. Louis: Mosby.*

This text covers theoretical/therapeutic foundations, the psychiatric client, and has a limited mental health focus. It provides adequate coverage of family and group and has a limited community focus. DSM-III is integrated throughout the clinical chapters. Study aids include objectives and key terms at the beginning of chapters, key terms italicized, and key points highlighted at the end of chapters.

Rawlins, R. et al. (1993). Mental health-psychiatric nursing: A holistic life-cycle approach *(3rd ed.). St. Louis: Mosby.*

This text covers theoretical/therapeutic foundations, the psychiatric client, and mental health issues. It provides adequate coverage of family and group and has a limited community focus. DSM-III is integrated throughout the clinical chapters, which are organized in terms of behavioral concepts, rather than diagnostic categories. (This may be confusing to some students.) Study aids include objectives, key words, and concepts at the beginning of chapters.

Stanhope, M., & Lancaster, J. (1996). Community health nursing: Promoting health of aggregates, families, and individuals *(4th ed.). St. Louis: Mosby.*

This text primarily focuses on community and providing care to aggregates, families, and individuals through community nursing practice. Pertinent chapters for this examination include mental health issues, violence, HIV, homeless, developmental stages, group, family, and substance abuse. Study aids include objectives, chapter outline, and key terms at the beginning of chapters, key terms italicized, and key concepts summarized at the end of chapters.

Varcarolis, E. (1998). Foundations of psychiatric-mental health nursing *(3rd ed.). Philadelphia: W.B. Saunders.*

Sample Questions: Psychiatric/Mental Health Nursing

This text covers theoretical/therapeutic foundations, the psychiatric client, and has a limited mental health focus. It provides adequate coverage of group, but has no family and community chapters. DSM-IV is integrated throughout the clinical chapters, which are organized according to the degree of anxiety. Study aids include objectives, key terms, and outline at the beginning of chapters, and self-study exercises at the end of chapters.

Wilson, H., & Kneisl, C. (1996). Psychiatric nursing *(5th ed.). Menlo Park, CA: Addison-Wesley.*

This text covers theoretical/therapeutic foundations and the psychiatric client. It does not cover mental health issues. It provides good coverage of family and group and has a limited community focus. DSM-IV is integrated throughout the clinical chapters. Study aids include competencies at the beginning of chapters, key words italicized, and chapter summaries at the end of chapters.

Answer Rationales

The information in parentheses after the item number shows the location of the material in the content outline. The key (correct answer) is indicated by a ★ and bold text.

Abnormal Psychology

1.(IB) 1) Medical definitions describe psychological disorders as diseases that require treatment.
2) Personal discomfort definitions focus on the client's feelings of distress.
3) Social definitions describe disorders in terms of a failure to conform to cultural norms and expectations.
★4) Statistical definitions consider any rare or infrequently occurring behavior to be abnormal.

2.(IC)**★1) Epidemiological studies are specifically designed to assess the frequency of a disorder within a population. Case studies are often useful for generating hypotheses about cause and effect relationships, but are rarely used for testing these hypotheses systematically.**
2) Correlational studies do not permit definitive cause and effect conclusions to be drawn because the researcher does not systematically manipulate the variables.
3) Experimental studies require a researcher to randomly assign participants to conditions and systematically manipulate independent variables.
4) Observational studies do not permit cause and effect relationships to be determined because the researcher records naturally occurring events in the environment. The researcher does not systematically manipulate variables.

3.(IIIA) 1) Although the concept of anxiety threshold is discussed by many personality theorists, it does not play a key role in the relationship between psychodynamic therapists and patients.
★2) Transference, the tendency of the patient to view the therapist as similar to an important figure in the patient's life (e.g., a parent), is believed by psychoanalysts to be necessary for therapeutic improvement.
3) Empathy is a Rogerian concept that refers to a therapist's ability to relate to a client's feelings.
4) A response hierarchy is a component of the systematic desensitization technique used by behavior therapists.

4.(ID2) 1) Freud considered conscious experience to be very limited, involving only a small part of the personality.
2) The preconscious refers to memories and thoughts that can be brought to consciousness, but are not currently at the conscious level.
3) The superego refers to the moral standards of an individual instilled by one's family and culture in childhood.
★4) Freud argued that the primary motivation for behavior stems from the id urges, which are entirely unconscious.

5.(ID3/4) 1) Cognitive-behavioral therapists tend to focus on current, rather than historical, factors.
★2) Cognitive-behavioral therapists believe that abnormal behaviors result from faulty thoughts and assumptions that a person uses continually.
3) Insight into unconscious motives is emphasized by psychodynamic therapists.
4) Hypnosis is usually used by psychodynamic therapists seeking to understand unconscious motives.

6.(IIM2)**★1) Instability in mood, self-concept, and interpersonal relationships is one of the central features of borderline personality disorder.**
2) Inflexibility and perfectionism are behaviors typically observed in individuals with obsessive-compulsive personality disorder.
3) Although constant attention seeking is sometimes seen in patients with borderline personality disorder, this behavior is more typical of individuals with histrionic personality disorder.
4) Callousness in interpersonal relationships is a primary feature of both narcissistic and antisocial personality disorders.

7.(IE1) 1) Avoidant personality should be diagnosed on Axis II, major depression on Axis I.
2) Hypertension should be noted on Axis III (general medical conditions).
★3) Major clinical disorders are diagnosed on Axis I, personality disorders on Axis II, and general medical conditions on Axis III.
4) Hypertension should be noted on Axis III, major depression on Axis I, and avoidant personality on Axis II.

8.(IF2) 1) Judgments by clinicians are often subjective and frequently there is low agreement among clinicians regarding the diagnosis of symptoms.
★2) The MMPI was designed to be a reflection of empirical research. Only items that were shown to differentiate between psychiatric and control groups were included on the test.
3) The MMPI was intended to be atheoretical regarding the cause and treatment of disorders.
4) The MMPI is not linked to the DSM system.

9.(IIA1)**★1) Agoraphobia, the fear of situations from which escape would be difficult or embarrassing, or in which help would be difficult to obtain in the event of a panic attack, is a common consequence of panic disorder.**
2) Cardiovascular disease is not a common complication of panic disorder.
3) Bipolar disorder is not a complication of panic disorder.
4) Migraine headaches are not a complication of panic disorder.

10.(IIA2)**★1) Classical conditioning occurs when an initially neutral stimulus (for example, a dog) is paired with a powerful stimulus (for example, a bite/pain) so that the neutral stimulus acquires the ability to provoke a response (for example, fear).**
2) Operant conditioning focuses on how consequences (for example, reinforcement) shape behavior.

3) Cognitive dissonance occurs when a person simultaneously holds two contradictory beliefs or ideas.
4) Social learning refers to the acquisition of responses through the observation of others.

11.(IIA3) 1) Compulsions are ritualistic behaviors that an individual repeatedly and uncontrollably presents.
2) Delusions are false beliefs that distort reality and are commonly experienced by people suffering from schizophrenia.
3) Illusions are perceptual tricks or distortions.
*4) Obsessions are defined as persistent, irrational thoughts or impulses.

12.(IIC) 1) Although patients with conversion disorder and somatization are sometimes depressed, depression is not specific to either of these two conditions.
2) Neither somatization disorder nor conversion disorder are classified as dissociative disorders.
3) Although loose associations are commonly observed in schizophrenia and in the manic phase of bipolar disorder, they are not commonly observed among patients with somatoform disorders.
*4) Both conversion disorder and somatization disorder are classified as somatoform disorders. Somatoform disorders are conditions characterized by the presence of physical symptoms that suggest, but that cannot be explained by, a medical condition.

13.(IID) 1) The personalities in multiple personality disorder are not believed to be loosely organized or incomplete.
*2) The personalities in multiple personality disorder are believed to be both distinct and well-developed.
3) The personalities in multiple personality disorder are believed to possess highly organized emotional processes.
4) The personalities in multiple personality disorder are believed to possess highly organized thought processes.

14.(IIC) 1) Individuals with hypochondria are more likely to be vigilant for the onset of new symptoms than are individuals with conversion disorder.
2) Individuals with conversion disorder appear to be almost indifferent to their symptoms.
*3) The key diagnostic feature of conversion disorder is the presence of physical symptoms that have no apparent physical cause.
4) Clients with hypochondria are more concerned with the potential of illness than are those diagnosed as having conversion disorder.

15.(IID) 1) Depersonalization is a condition in which a person feels separated from her/his body or perceives a gross distortion of the body or its parts.
*2) Dissociative fugue is characterized by physical flight and the adoption of a new identity.
3) Somnambulism refers to sleep walking.
4) Dissociative identity disorder is diagnosed when a person appears to display two or more distinct personalities.

16.(IID) *1) Depersonalization refers to the feeling that one is separate from one's body.
2) Hearing voices is an example of a hallucination.
3) This statement signifies that the client is experiencing suicidal thoughts.
4) This statement is likely to be made by a person diagnosed with either transsexualism or gender identity disorder.

17.(IIE)*1) Asthma is the most common childhood stress-related disorder.
2) Hypertension (high blood pressure) is likely to have its onset in adulthood.
3) Migraines are not frequently observed in children.
4) Ulcers are likely to have their onset in adulthood.

18.(IIG2)*1) Research with men who have been diagnosed with either voyeurism or exhibitionism often indicates that they are socially withdrawn.
2) Most men who engage in voyeurism or exhibitionism do not report feelings of anger.
3) Most men who are diagnosed with either voyeurism or exhibitionism are heterosexual.
4) Research evidence suggests that most men who engage rn voyeurism or exhibitionism are socially withdrawn.

19.(IIG2) 1) Transsexualism refers to a disorder in which individuals seek to change their physical sex.
2) Hypoactive sexual desire disorder refers to an abnormal lack of interest in engaging in sexual activity.
3) Frotteurism refers to a disorder in which individuals achieve sexual arousal by rubbing up against unsuspecting others.
*4) Transvestitism refers to a disorder in which a person experiences a recurrent desire to wear clothing of the opposite sex so that the person may become sexually aroused.

20.(IIB) 1) Implosion, a variant of imaginal flooding, is not used in the treatment of bipolar disorder.
*2) Lithium carbonate is one of the standard pharmacological treatments for bipolar disorder.
3) Psychoanalysis has not been found to be effective in the treatment of bipolar disorder.
4) Although electroconvulsive therapy (ECT) is sometimes used with patients who have bipolar disorder and are experiencing depression, it is not a standard or first-choice treatment for bipolar disorder.

21.(II-I1) 1) Overinclusiveness refers to the tendency to erroneously treat different stimuli as though they belong to the same category.
2) Delusions of grandeur refer to irrational and persistent beliefs that one is all-powerful or extremely important to the world. These beliefs are sometimes expressed by some clients who are diagnosed as having schizophrenia or another psychotic disorder.
*3) Neologisms are invented words that some clients with schizophrenic symptoms create and use.
4) Thought broadcasting refers to the delusional belief that others can hear one's private thoughts.

22.(IIK2) 1) Separation anxiety disorder has not been shown to be related to either low birth weight or malnourishment.
2) No relationship has been reported between conduct disorder and low birth weight or malnourishment.
3) Anorexia nervosa is an eating disorder that is most likely to have its onset in adolescent girls who have not

experienced either low birth weight or previous malnourishment.
*4) Low birth weight and malnourishment have been shown to be causes of poor brain development which can result in mental retardation.

23.(IIJ) 1) Delirium is characterized by a disturbance in consciousness and awareness accompanied by changes in cognition that cannot be accounted for by memory loss.
2) Although patients with Alzheimer's disease sometimes develop paranoid delusions, these delusions are not a defining feature of Alzheimer's disease.
*3) Dementia is characterized by the presence of multiple and severe cognitive deficits, especially memory loss. Dementia is the primary feature of Alzheimer's disease.
4) Dysthymia, a chronic form of depression, is not a key feature of Alzheimer's disease.

24.(IIIA) 1) Most therapists do not believe that the client's capacity to feel physically attractive is highly related to the client's level of social skills.
2) Therapists who believe that the client is unable to openly express anger would typically use the technique of assertiveness training.
*3) These techniques are designed to increase the frequency of social behaviors displayed by the client. They would most likely be used by a therapist who believes the depression is caused by a lack of reinforcement from other people.
4) Therapists who believe that the client's depression is due to an inability to focus on the problems of others would use techniques designed to increase the client's empathy.

25.(IIIA)***1) Antipsychotics, which include phenothiazines, are the standard pharmacological treatment for schizophrenia.**
2) Monoamine oxidase inhibitors are sometimes used to treat depression and certain anxiety disorders, but are not used in the treatment of schizophrenia.
3) Stimulants are most commonly used in the treatment of attention-deficit hyperactivity disorder, but are not used in the treatment of schizophrenia.
4) Tricyclics are commonly used in the treatment of depression, but are not typically used in the treatment of schizophrenia.

Anatomy & Physiology

1.(IA2) 1) The coronal plane divides the body into ventral (anterior) and dorsal (posterior) planes.
2) The frontal plane is the same as the coronal plane.
*3) The sagittal plane divides the body in half along the vertical (longitudinal) axis, thus dividing into right and left halves.
4) The transverse plane divides the body into superior and inferior halves.

2.(IIB) 1) Hydrogen becomes weakly positive.
2) Oxygen forms a stable atom in the water molecule.
3) Oxygen's electronegativity remains the same within the water molecule.
*4) Hydrogen and oxygen have different electronegativities, resulting in an unequal sharing of electrons.

3.(IIIC2) 1) An aponeurosis is a broad sheetlike tendon that connects muscle to other muscle or to bone.
2) A fascicle is a bundle of muscle or nerve cells surrounded by a connective tissue membrane.
3) A ligament is composed of dense regular collagen fibers with some elastin. A ligament connects bone to bone.
*4) A tendon is a cordlike structure composed of dense regular collagen fibers. A tendon connects muscle to bone.

4.(IIID1/2) 1) Actin and myosin interact to promote muscle contraction in all muscle tissue.
2) Branching muscle fibers allow for sequential and rhythmic contraction associated with cardiac muscle.
*3) The refractory period is the period during which muscle contraction cannot be initiated.
4) Low extracellular calcium inhibits proper muscle contraction.

5.(IVA1/4) 1) Association neurons connect sensory and motor neurons.
Postganglionic neurons transmit impulses from preganglionic fibers to the target organ.
*3) Motor neurons carry impulses from the central nervous system to a series of effectors, i.e., muscles or glands.
4) Sensory neurons transmit impulses from sense organs to the central nervous system.

6.(IVA6a) 1) Voluntary eye movements are controlled by the oculomotor and trochlear cranial nerves.
*2) The cerebellum coordinates motor function with the cerebrum through three paired bundles of nerve fibers known as the cerebellar peduncle.
3) Regulation of autonomic body functions is done by the autonomic nervous system comprised of the sympathetic and the parasympathetic divisions.
4) Regulation of emotions is largely in the domain of the hypothalamus and limbic system.

7.(IVA6) 1) Brain function depends upon adequate blood supply and not on the corpus callosum.
Abstract thought is controlled by higher centers in the cerebral cortex.
*3) The corpus callosum consists of commissural fibers carrying information between the right and left cerebral hemispheres.
4) Autonomic function is associated with brain stem activity.

8.(IVB2b) 1) Loudness is dependent upon sound intensity. The greater the sound intensity, the greater the vibration of the basilar membrane which leads to increased transmission of nerve impulses to the brain.
2) Each ear receives the vibrating signal from slightly different positions. Discriminating the direction of sound is done by the temporal lobes of the brain.
*3) The basilar membrane is narrower and stiffer at the base of the cochlea where high-frequency (high-pitched) sounds produce maximum vibration and greater transmission of nerve impulses to the brain.

4) Low-frequency sounds cause maximum vibration at the apex of the cochlea where the basilar membrane is wider and more flexible.

9.(IVC) 1) Less calcium will be lost in the feces.
2) Less calcium will be excreted in the urine.
★3) Osteoclasts are bone-dissolving cells that release calcium into the bloodstream.
4) Bone will be broken down in an attempt to raise blood calcium levels.

10.(VA2) **★1) The QRS wave reflects the spread of the impulse throughout the ventricles, forcing blood into the aorta and pulmonary artery.**
2) The P wave represents the spread of an electrical impulse through the atria and their subsequent contraction.
3) The T wave represents repolarization of the electrical tissue and the P wave represents the beginning of the next cardiac cycle.
4) Right after the T wave, the heart is at rest.

11.(VA2a) In early atrial diastole, the atria are filling with blood from the venous system.
Atrial systole involves contraction of the atria, forcing blood into the ventricles.
In early ventricle diastole, the ventricles are receiving blood from the atria.
★4) In ventricular systole, the ventricles are contracting and forcing blood into the aorta and pulmonary artery.

12.(VA2b) 1) An increased stroke volume increases the amount of blood ejected from the ventricle.
2) A more rapid heart rate increases the amount of blood forced out of the heart.
3) As more blood returns to the heart, more blood is subsequently ejected.
★4) The parasympathetic nervous system has an inhibitory effect on cardiac function.

13.(IVC3e) 1) Alpha cells produce glucagon which raises blood sugar.
★2) Beta cells produce insulin which lowers blood sugar.
3) Delta cells secrete somatostatin which inhibits the secretion of insulin and glucagon.
4) F-cells secrete hormones which regulate the release of pancreatic digestive enzymes.

14.(VA4b) 1) See 4).
2) See 4).
3) The sympathetic nervous system stimulation of the adrenal medulla releases epinephrine and norepinephrine which will cause an increase in cardiac output and an increase in stroke volume.
★4) The sympathetic nervous system stimulation of the adrenal medulla releases epinephrine and norepinephrine which will cause an increase in cardiac output and vasoconstriction in visceral blood vessels resulting in an increase in peripheral resistance.

15.(VC2) 1) Acute pancreatitis results from severe insults to the pancreas.
2) Cirrhosis is a hardening of the liver tissue.
★3) Gastric juices are rich in hydrochloric acid, which causes irritation in the gastric mucosa.
4) Peritonitis is an inflammation of the peritoneum and is usually the result of infection.

16.(VB2d) 1) The basic rhythm of respiration is regulated by the medullary rhythmicity center which is located in the medulla oblongata.
2) Constriction of terminal bronchioles is caused by histamine.
3) Inspiration is part of the medullary rhythmicity center in the medulla oblongata and is stimulated by high CO_2 levels, low O_2 levels, and falling pH levels.
★4) Stretch receptors are found within the bronchioles and lung tissue. When the receptors are stretched, nerve signals are sent via the vagus nerve to the apneustic center and medullary rhythmicity center and further inspiration is inhibited. Therefore, the Hering-Breuer reflex protects the lungs from overinflation damage.

17.(VIB/C)**★1) This represents the path by which the blood filtrate passes on the way to the final production of urine.**
2) The loop of Henle transports the filtrate from the proximal convoluted tubule to the distal convoluted tubule.
3) The collecting tubule represents the end of the filtration process.
4) The collecting tubule represents the end point of the pathway.

18.(VD2) 1) Acetic acid is formed when pyruvic acid is decarboxylated and joined with CoA to enter the mitochondria during aerobic oxidation when the oxygen supply is adequate.
2) During aerobic oxidation, citric acid is formed in the mitochondria when the acetyl group of acetic acid is joined with oxaloacetic acid.
★3) When oxygen is inadequate, pyruvic acid is reduced by two hydrogen ions to form lactic acid. Lactic acid can be transported to the liver to be reformed into glucose or pyruvic acid.
4) Pyruvic acid is the end product of anaerobic glycolysis.

19.(VID1)**★1) Aldosterone from the adrenal cortex increases the retention of sodium and triggers the loss of potassium.**
2) ADH from the posterior pituitary triggers the retention of water by the kidneys.
3) Thyroxine from the thyroid gland regulates cell metabolism.
4) Cortisol from the adrenal cortex elevates blood sugar and reduces inflammation.

20.(VID&E)**★1) A decrease in blood volume leads the nephron juxtaglomerular cells to release renin. Renin converts angiotensinogen to angiotension I. Angiotension I is converted to angiotension II in the lung. Angiostatin II stimulates the adrenal cortex to release aldosterone.**
2) Cortisol is stimulated by pituitary ACTH.
3) Glucagon is produced in the alpha cells of the islets of Langerhans and is stimulated by epinephrine.
4) Insulin is produced in the beta cells of the islets of Langerhans and is stimulated by high blood glucose levels.

21.(VIIB) 1) Since bicarbonate absorbs H+, acidity will be reduced. Increased acidity is caused by an increase in H+.
***2) Increased pH is caused by a reduction of available H+. Bicarbonate absorbs H+, reducing the available H+ and causing pH to increase.**
3) Bicarbonate is a component of the carbonic acid-bicarbonate buffer system. The more bicarbonate available, the greater the opportunity to absorb H+ and prevent a fall in pH.
4) Bicarbonate is a plasma solute. Any increase in solutes will increase osmolarity.

22.(VIIIB7) 1) Prolactin has no connection with the posterior pituitary.
2) Prolactin triggers the development of lactiferous ducts.
3) The milk let-down reflex is a product of oxytocin release.
***4) Impulses from a suckling infant induce an increase in prolactin production and more milk production.**

23.(VIIIB5a) 1) A corpus albicans is a degenerated corpus luteum that has lost its capacity to produce progesterone.
2) Follicle cells are involved in producing estrogen and developing the secondary oocyte.
***3) The placenta is able to convert cholesterol to progesterone which is important to maintain the pregnancy after the corpus luteum degenerates.**
4) Thecal cells surround the follicle and are involved in the secretion of steroids.

Ethics: Theory & Practice

1.(IA5) 1) One may obey laws of society without being virtuous. Moreover, not all virtue is regulated by societal laws.
2) Though intelligence and prudence are useful tools in moral decision making, they are not in and of themselves virtuous.
***3) According to Aristotle's "Doctrine of the Golden Mean," moral virtue is a matter of steering a course between excess and deficiency.**
4) Acting nobly and admirably are characteristics of a virtuous person, but are not in and of themselves virtuous.

2.(IA4) 1) The focus of ethical egoism is the individual, not the social unit.
2) Cultural relativism identifies moral worth as conformity to a society's expectation.
3) Kantianism is a deontological theory concerned with the motive for one's actions, not the results.
***4) Utilitarianism describes the moral worth of an action in terms of its consequences for the social unit.**

3.(IA8) 1) This is not a fundamental objection to the theory of intuitionism.
2) In principle, moral behavior is not necessarily pragmatic.
3) In principle, moral behavior does not necessarily maximize pleasure.
***4) A fundamental objection to intuitionism is that intuitions differ from person to person.**

4.(IA4) 1) Ethical egoism permits both broad and narrow views of intrinsic good; utilitarianism is a consequentialist theory that attempts to shape the social unit's future.
***2) Though both are concerned with promoting good, ethical egoism focuses on the individual while utilitarianism broadens the concern to the social unit.**
3) Ethical egoism is concerned with the individual, not with universals; utilitarianism is concerned with consequences, not with duties or inclination.
4) Ethical egoism is concerned with consequences, not feelings; utilitarianism is not based on theology or metaphysical determinism.

5.(IB5) 1) For a Kantian moralist, maximizing social utility is not a moral basis for behavior.
***2) For a Kantian moralist, respect for persons is an inviolable moral principle and to deliberately distort the truth, for any reason, would compromise the dignity of the person.**
3) Kantian ethics is based on duty, not policy.
4) Kantian ethics is based on duty, not inclination.

6.(IB1) 1) Not all forms of distribution are just.
2) Not all rules are just.
***3) The formal principle of justice requires a non-preferential treatment that reflects a sensitivity to both similarities and differences.**
4) Not all forms of society are just.

7.(IB4) 1) This does not define *prima facie* duty because moral considerations are not taken into account.
***2) *Prima facie* means "at first glance." A *prima facie* duty is a duty that a person ought to do, all other things being equal. The distinction between *prima facie* duty and actual duty is designed to reflect the complex moral situations in which people often find themselves. Additional moral considerations may preclude acting according to a prima facie duty.**
3) The concepts of *prima facie* duty and actual duty reflect the process of an initial versus a complete analysis of a situation. They do not dictate the temporal order of prescribed action.
4) *Prima facie* duty is not based on the assistance or interference of others.

8.(IC1) 1) Emotivism is not concerned with whether an action makes anyone feel good.
2) Emotivism denies the possibility that any act is objectively right or wrong.
3) Emotivism does not consider the reasonableness of an act.
***4) Emotivism rejects any rational basis for moral judgment; to say that an act is right is merely expressing one's approval.**

9.(IC1) ***1) Emotivism rejects any rational basis for moral judgment; to say that an act is right or wrong is merely expressing one's approval or disapproval.**
2) Emotivism denies the possibility of moral wisdom.

3) Emotivism does not treat morality as a matter of reason; nor does it allow for a goal of moral perfection.
4) Emotivism is not based on a conflict between the individual's spirit and humanity.

10.(ID1)*1) **In the absence of a normative premise, a normative conclusion requires deriving what ought to be the case from what is the case (i.e., the is/ought problem).**
2) A deductively valid argument with a normative conclusion does not have to contain any non-normative premises.
3) A deductively valid argument with a normative conclusion does not have to contain any factual premises.
4) The context of the argument is irrelevant.

11.(ID3) 1) Maximizing well-being is required only by certain consequentialist theories.
2) Conforming with intuition is required only by intuitionist theories.
3) Expressing one's deepest convictions is irrelevant to the definition of moral judgment.
*4) **Any judgment, to be a moral judgment, must apply equally to all people, circumstances, and occasions.**

12.(ID4)*1) **According to Plato's *Republic*, immorality and injustice reflect an undesirable lack of harmony within the self and society.**
2) Plato does not advocate morality as a mechanism to gain control of others.
3) Plato values being moral over seeming to be moral.
4) If there is no distinction between is and ought, all morality loses its prescriptive edge.

13.(IIB) 1) Because Nurse Beamer emphasizes respect for persons, Nurse Beamer's reasoning is most clearly associated with Kantianism.
2) Because Dr. Carrigan emphasizes an approach which would maximize utility in this particular situation, Dr. Carrigan's reasoning is most clearly associated with act utilitarianism.
*3) **Because Dr. Johnson argues that "the long-term benefits for the human race surely outweigh any disadvantage which may apply to this particular case," Dr. Johnson's reasoning is most clearly associated with rule utilitarianism.**
4) Dr. Osborne supports trying to save the fetus, but does not provide any reason for doing so other than the fact that "we can."

14.(IIB)*1) **Because Nurse Beamer emphasizes respect for persons, Nurse Beamer's reasoning is most clearly associated with Kantianism.**
2) Because Dr. Carrigan emphasizes an approach which would maximize utility in this particular situation, Dr. Carrigan's reasoning is most clearly associated with act utilitarianism.
3) Because Dr. Johnson argues that "the long-term benefits for the human race surely outweigh any disadvantage which may apply to this particular case," Dr. Johnson's reasoning is most clearly associated with rule utilitarianism.
4) Dr. Osborne supports trying to save the fetus, but does not provide any reason for doing so other than the fact that "we can."

15.(IIB) 1) Susan and the fetus are unable to make a decision; therefore, neither is an autonomous individual.
2) This option does not focus on what Marie would want.
*3) **Individual autonomy is the ability to make decisions for oneself. What would Marie want? To ask that is to focus on individual autonomy.**
4) An approach which emphasizes individual autonomy will leave the decision up to Marie, not to the hospital.

16.(IIB) 1) Egoism seeks to maximize benefit for the individual agent. Profession does not matter.
*2) **Based on the assumption that teachers provide significant benefit to society, utilitarianism will assign greater moral weight to saving her life.**
3) Divine Command theory is based on the will of God. Profession does not matter.
4) Kantianism bases moral decisions on universal criteria. Profession does not matter.

17.(IIB)*1) **Dr. Johnson wants to do the experimental transplant. Dr. Osborne wants to maintain somatic function in Susan. The two are not in conflict.**
2) Since Dr. Johnson wants to do the experimental transplant while Dr. Carrigan wants to transplant Susan's heart to Marie, the two are in conflict.
3) Since Dr. Osborne wants to maintain somatic function in Susan while Dr. Carrigan wants to transplant Susan's heart to Marie, the two are in conflict.
4) Since Dr. Johnson treats Marie as an expendable experimental subject while Nurse Beamer objects to treating people as objects, the two are in conflict.

18.(IIB) 1) What happens to Susan after the fetus matures? Taking Susan off life support after her fetus has matured could be construed as a form of euthanasia.
*2) **A strong opponent of all forms of euthanasia (active and passive) would support keeping Susan on life support indefinitely.**
3) Since Susan can be maintained on life support, failure to do so simply to procure her heart for transplantation could be construed as a form of euthanasia.
4) A strong opponent of euthanasia will not allow decisions based on personal belief.

Foundations of Gerontology

1.(IE) 1) In a cross-sectional design, different age groups are compared at the same time on the variable of interest. A cross-sectional analysis does not account for the numerous period and cohort differences that exist when intelligence is measured in persons of different ages.
*2) **A longitudinal design is best for studying the way intelligence varies with age. In a longitudinal design, a single cohort is measured periodically over a number of years. This analysis provides information about changes that occur with age.**
3) In period analysis, there is no way to measure intelligence. Period analysis is used to determine how historical events that took place in a person's life influenced the person.

4) In a time series analysis, two or more cross-sectional comparisons are made at different times of testing. See 1).

2.(IE) 1) A cross-sectional design studies various groups of people and measures specific parameters of all groups at the same time. There is no measurement taken at a later time.
***2) A longitudinal design specifies a group of persons whose parameters are measured repeatedly over a period of time to eliminate the effects caused by such factors as the time when the person grew up or the education they received.**
3) A period analysis looks at the effects of the historical period on a person when that person was a particular age.
4) A time series analysis examines several cross-sectional analyses done at different time periods.

3.(IIB1) 1) Birthrates are not the deciding factor in the sex ratio.
2) See 1.
***3) Males have a higher mortality than females at all ages in part for genetic reasons and in part for environmental and societal reasons.**
4) The mortality rate for females is lower than for males at every age.

4.(IIB3) 1) Although health care is an area facing great pressure, the number of older people in the United States needing special housing is small. Over 20 million older adults live in their own homes.
***2) Health care and income are the public systems facing the greatest pressure from growth in the population of older people. Census data shows that one out of every eight people in the United States is over the age of 65. As people age, their health needs increase at the same time that typical annual income declines by 30 to 50 percent following retirement.**
3) Although transportation may be a problem for some groups of older people, for most older adults transportation is not an area facing great pressure. Housing is not a great problem since most older people live in their own homes.
4) Transportation and education are not areas facing great pressure. Most older adults live in their own homes. Although more older adults are continuing some form of lifelong learning today than ever before, it is still primarily younger groups who are engaged in full-time educational pursuits.

5.(IIA2) 1) See 3).
2) See 3).
***3) The dependency ratio is defined as the number or proportion of retirement-age persons divided by the number or proportion of working-age persons.**
4) See 3).

6.(IIC) 1) The decline in birthrates and death rates will lead to an increase in the number of persons alive.
***2) As jobs require more technical training, more people will complete high school.**
3) Political activity remains high from middle age well into older age.
4) The health status of older persons has improved over time, not worsened.

7.(IIIA)**1) Manifestations of aging are the result of an individual's genetics and the environment in which the individual grows and develops. Since there is essentially an infinite number of combinations resulting from this interaction, the outcome of the aging process is highly variable among different persons.**
2) Older people are living longer and larger numbers are available for studies. As life expectancy continues to increase and greater numbers of people live to older ages, there is likely to be a continued increase in the number of older persons who can be studied.
3) Although funding for research is highly competitive, significant amounts of money have been allocated over the years to areas of research on aging, particularly for biomedical research.
4) Senescence, or normal aging, refers to the time-related biological processes that affect all persons. There is no general disagreement regarding this definition.

8.(IIIA4) 1) The aging process affects all members of a species.
2) Aging has a negative effect on an organism, whereas the positive effects are the result of the growth or developmental phase.
3) Functional changes affect persons of all ages.
***4) Aging is an internally controlled process, not something that is dependent upon some factor in the environment.**

9.(IIIC3/IIIH1) 1) Free radicals are unstable oxygen molecules that are produced more rapidly with exercise and have the potential to damage the body.
***2) Antioxidants will reduce the number and activity of the free radicals and may have an impact on life expectancy.**
3) A low-calorie, high-protein diet will do nothing to alter the production of free radicals or their effects in the body.
4) Life expectancy is determined in part by genetics with a major component that is environmental.

10.(III-I)**1) A person who is involved in the planning is more likely to feel in control and more likely to experience fewer negative effects.**
2) The speed with which the relocation is accomplished is not important.
3) Similarities and differences between the facilities may affect the reaction to the move and can be either positive or negative.
4) Even if the person's needs are anticipated and met, the critical issue is the degree of involvement of the older person.

11.(IVA3) 1) Stimuli are processed more slowly as the nerve conduction velocity decreases, synaptic delay increases, and muscle contraction time lengthens.
2) Complex tasks may be performed differently, but unless there is disease or a disability, the older person can still perform complex tasks.
3) Trial and error is a method used by younger persons and typically takes longer to accomplish the complex task.
***4) Strategies help the person who is older to shortcut the complex task and perform the task more effectively and efficiently.**

12.(IVB3) 1) In early adult transition, Erikson would suggest, the main issue is the development of intimacy versus isolation.
2) During midlife transition, the person is preparing for the generativity versus stagnation issues that Erikson identified.
3) During middle adulthood transition, the issue for Erikson is generativity versus stagnation; generativity is the ability to support others, especially persons who are older as well as making a contribution to the larger world.
*4) **In late adulthood, the issue for Erikson is ego integrity versus despair, that is, when one sees one's life as having meaning or not.**

13.(IVC2) 1) Activity theory suggests that people who maintain high levels of activity have a high degree of satisfaction with their lives.
2) In age stratification theory, the population is divided into age-based categories (for example, youth, adulthood, middle age, and old age). This theory does not offer suggestions on any aspect of life satisfaction in aging.
*3) **Disengagement theory suggests that it is natural for people who are older to gradually withdraw from society and for society to withdraw from people who are older. Since this is an expectation on both sides, the person whose life activities decrease perceives this as a normal and a positive situation and, therefore, experiences a high degree of satisfaction.**
4) Exchange theory suggests that people try to maximize rewards and minimize costs in their interactions with other people.

14.(IVD3)*1) **Medication is often seen as the only means one has of dealing with this issue in an older person.**
2) Psychotherapy may be effective but is not often considered because it is long term.
3) Group therapy is not necessarily going to be effective for a chronic mental disorder.
4) Nutritional modification has very little impact on a chronic mental disorder.

15.(VB3) 1) Age stratification is the division of the population into age-based categories (for example, youth, adulthood, middle age, and old age).
*2) **Double jeopardy refers to the limitations imposed upon individuals by being a member of a historically underrepresented group and by being old. Race and ethnicity are powerful determinants of the quality of life in old age.**
3) Ethnocentrism is an anthropological concept suggesting that one cultural or ethnic group is inherently better than another.
4) New ageism is a term that stereotypes older people as needing assistance.

16.(VC) 1) Disabilities may have an impact on whether a person continues to work, but do not contribute to a move to a retirement community.
2) Retirement communities are not necessarily low-cost housing. If they have services attached, they may be more expensive than stand-alone housing.
3) Public transportation is generally not an issue.
*4) **Retirement communities tend to be homogeneous and for many persons, this is a very attractive feature that few other housing options offer.**

17.(VD4) 1) An extended family does not include friends or neighbors.
*2) **In an extended family, family members over several generations or with several different levels of relationship (aunts, uncles, brothers, sisters, etc.) interact with each other and provide reciprocal services as needed. The interactions are mutually beneficial and take place on a frequent basis because the members of the family live near each other.**
3) Just the opposite is true. Older people enjoy their frequent interactions with adult children and may play a significant role in the lives of their grandchildren. It is also true that older people may provide just as much support to their adult children as they receive.
4) The overwhelming preference of older adults is to live in their own homes. Living independently, even in widowhood, is extremely important.

18.(VD1a) 1) The Age Discrimination in Employment Act was passed in 1967.
2) The Older Americans Act was passed in 1965.
*3) **The Social Security Act was passed in 1935.**
4) The Medicare Health Insurance Program was passed as an amendment to Social Security in 1965.

19.(VID) 1) Community involvement is something that is a part of the person's life history. For some, involvement may rise with retirement when there is more time to be involved.
2) Family relationships may be enhanced with the additional time.
3) Health does not fail in those who retire in good health.
*4) **Income generally drops 40% or more for all but the most wealthy of persons who retire.**

20.(VID2)*1) **Retirement was designed to reduce the number of older workers in the workforce during the Depression. It is still used as a way to reduce workforce participant numbers.**
2) General retirement programs are established to move persons out of the workforce regardless of whether or not they did a good job.
3) Persons who retire are not too old to work. Many persons resume working after retiring.
4) Disability insurance, not retirement programs, covers persons who can no longer work due to physical disorders.

21.(VIIA) 1) Studies suggest that persons who are older are slightly more likely to hold an opinion about a current policy issue than are persons who are younger.
2) There does not appear to be a shift from one party to another as persons age, nor is there necessarily a move toward becoming more conservative.
3) With more time and more experience, persons who are older may be a larger percentage of the persons holding office, not a smaller percentage.
*4) **Persons who are older do vote more regularly than do persons who are younger.**

22.(VIIC1) 1) Red tape, although an issue, is not a major problem for most persons who receive SSI benefits.
2) The income level is set at the federal level, so there is no state-to-state variation.
3) Although there is a reluctance to accept help in any form, this is not the major reason for fewer people applying for SSI than are entitled to receive it.
*4) SSI is not well publicized and many people do not know it exists or that it is something for which they might be eligible.

23.(VIIC2) 1) Medicaid pays for far more nursing home care than does Medicare. Medicare has a severe limit on payments for this form of extended care.
*2) Medicare begins at 65 while Medicaid is available to persons who meet various income guidelines regardless of their age.
3) The Social Security Trust Fund finances the Medicare program; Medicaid is paid for from general tax revenues.
4) Medicaid requires no co-payment; Medicare does require a co-payment.

24.(VIID1c) 1) Medicare is an entitlement program that is based only on the age of the individual.
2) Senior Nutrition Program provides nutritious low-cost meals for senior citizens. The program also provides companionship when done in a congregate setting. No set price is charged; a voluntary donation is requested. The only requirement is to be 60 or over, or have a spouse over 60.
3) Social Security is an entitlement program. People must work and pay taxes into Social Security to get benefits. Most people need 10 years of work to qualify for Social Security benefits.
*4) Supplemental Security Income (SSI) is a federal program of public assistance to older people. All SSI applicants have to demonstrate that their income from other sources falls below the prescribed minimum in order to qualify. This is a means test.

25.(VIIIB) 1) Anger is the second stage in Kübler-Ross's theory in which the dying person recognizes that denial can no longer be maintained. The issue now becomes "Why me?" and anger, resentment, and rage may be expressed directly.
2) Bargaining is the third stage in which the person hopes that death can be postponed or delayed. The person negotiates, often with God, to try to delay death for some period of time.
3) Denial is the first stage in which the person is completely unwilling to accept that he or she is going to die. The person's reaction is, "It simply is not going to happen. Someone has made a mistake."
*4) Depression is part of the fourth stage in which the person mourns her or his death and feels a sense of loss. This period of depression helps the person who is dying to accept the certainty of death.

Life Span Developmental Psychology

To keep you from relying on question position rather than knowledge, the sample questions for this examination were <u>not</u> presented in chronological (content outline) order.

1.(IIC1) 1) The Lamaze method is applicable to both home and hospital births.
2) The Lamaze method was designed to reduce the use of anesthetics, it does not eliminate the use of anesthetics or cesarean sections.
*3) The central aspect of the Lamaze method is to reduce a patient's apprehension and awareness of labor pains by breathing and relaxation training.
4) Underwater births are not part of the Lamaze method.

2.(XB)***1) In the acceptance stage, the person recognizes impending death; preparations for a funeral are often part of this stage.**
2) In the bargaining stage, the person sets distant deadlines, such as an event a year away, to forestall death.
3) In the denial stage, the person disputes the diagnosis or acts as though unaware of impending death.
4) In the depression stage, the person is sad and despondent but has not reached acceptance or planned for the inevitable death.

3.(VB5)***1) ADHD is characterized by short attention span, distractibility, and high levels of physical activity.**
2) Dysgraphia is a learning disability in which a person is unable to write. Although the handwriting is messy, this child can write.
3) Dyslexia is a learning disability in which a person is unable to decode text. This child's reading ability is not indicated.
4) Emotional disturbance is a general category that does not refer to a specific pattern of symptoms.

4.(IB3a) 1) In a cross-sectional design, different groups of participants who are of different ages are studied. This study has one group of participants who are the same age.
2) In an experimental design, some aspect of the participants' experience is changed (the independent variable is manipulated). In this study, the infants are observed; there is no manipulation of an independent variable.
*3) In a longitudinal design, a group of participants is studied over a long period of time. In this study, one group of infants is studied over a five-year period.
4) In a sequential design, different age groups are studied over a long period of time, and new groups are added. In this study, only one group is studied.

5.(IXB1) 1) Lower hormone levels do not cause shortness of breath.
*2) The reduced cardiovascular efficiency characteristic of this age would directly cause shortness of breath during a strenuous activity such as running.
3) A decline in agility may occur with aging and could cause falls, but is not a direct cause of shortness of breath.

4) Slower neural conduction may occur with aging and may affect the speed of fine motor and cognitive tasks, but is not a direct cause of shortness of breath.

6.(IVA5) ***1) Accidents account for approximately half of the deaths of preschool children in the United States.**
2) Diarrhea is not a serious problem in the United States because of the clean water and food supply.
3) Diphtheria is no longer a major cause of death since children in the United States are routinely immunized against diphtheria in infancy.
4) Pneumonia is routinely cured with antibiotics in the United States.

7.(VIC4) 1) The authoritarian parenting style is associated with compliant or rebellious adolescent behavior, but is not usually associated with independent decision making by adolescents.
*2) The authoritative parenting style is associated with adolescents who are self-reliant, responsible, and make decisions independently.
3) The permissive parenting style is associated with adolescents who tend to be less mature and responsible.
4) The restrictive parenting style is associated with adolescents who are compliant or resistive to authority, but do not make decisions independently.

8.(VB1) 1) A child at the concrete operational stage will understand the concept of conservation, but will perform conservation best when he or she actually observes the procedure rather than just hears about it.
2) A child at the preoperational stage cannot mentally reverse a transformation and would say that the taller glass now has more water.
*3) A child at the concrete operational stage can observe a change in a quantity and mentally reverse it, and so will be able to understand that the quantity of water remains the same.
4) A child at the preoperational stage cannot understand that the quantity remains the same even when seeing the procedure demonstrated.

9.(IIA6) 1) There is no evidence that a shared prenatal environment is a critical determinant in the similarity between identical twins.
*2) Identical twins come from the same ovum and sperm, and therefore have identical genetic structure. Genetic code accounts for the IQ and personality trait correlations among twins reared in separate environments.
3) Phenotype refers to outward physical appearance. Phenotypes are usually not identical, even in genetically identical twins.
4) In identical twins, 100% of their genes are identical.

10.(VIB2) 1) Rather than experiencing excessive self-esteem, many adolescents experience a loss of self-esteem at puberty.
2) Adolescence is often marked by increased risk-taking, rather than a fear of taking risks.
3) Concrete operational thinking is associated with middle childhood; in adolescence, there is typically a transition to formal operations, and this transition is related to adolescent egocentrism.
*4) Imaginary audience refers to the adolescent's belief that others are avidly watching and evaluating the adolescent's behavior.

11.(XD) 1) Although the death of a loved one may affect the status and role of the survivor, it is not the same as the survivor's emotional response to the loss.
2) Burial rituals are a part of traditional bereavement but they do not necessarily address the survivor's emotional response to the loss.
3) Grief is a normal, rather than abnormal, reaction to the death of a loved one.
*4) Grief is an individual's emotional response to a loss, such as the death of a loved one.

12.(VIIC1) 1) Levinson's is a stage theory of adulthood, in which periods of change alternate with periods of stability; adulthood is not one long, stable period.
2) Levinson argues that adulthood is marked by periods of stability during which there is little change; adulthood is not a process of continuous change.
3) In Levinson's theory, when changes occur, they are gradual, not rapid.
*4) Levinson's study found that stable periods alternate with transitional periods and that both periods are years in duration.

13.(IVB3) 1) Functional grammar is a working knowledge of appropriate word order and sentence structure.
2) Overextension is the tendency in early childhood to overapply morphological and grammatical rules to exceptional situations (e.g., "foots" instead of "feet").
*3) Telegraphic speech is the stage when a child can combine words into sentences, but leaves out words and parts of words that are not essential to the meaning (for example, "Mommy go store"). The term "telegraphic" refers to telegrams that charged by the word, so only the essential words were included.
4) Underextension is the failure to apply grammatical and morphological rules in appropriate situations.

14.(IA3) 1) Vocal language learning is not possible in infants who are unable to hear language being spoken.
*2) Maturation refers to development that is based on a person's genetic blueprint and is, therefore, basically unaffected by the presence or absence of environmental input. Babbling begins when the infant is physically able to make sounds, and is an example of maturation.
3) Modeling is a form of learning in which the child imitates the behavior of another person. Early babbling by infants is related to maturation; it is not related to infants imitating behavior. A child who cannot hear cannot imitate babbling or any other speech sounds.
4) Reinforcement refers to strengthening a behavior through a pleasurable consequence. When infants who are deaf babble, their babbling is maturational rather than being affected by reinforcement.

15.(VIIIA1) 1) Both females and males experience some hearing loss as they age.
2) Males experience more hearing loss than females as they age.
*3) Males experience more hearing loss than females because of physiological factors.

4) Females do not experience more hearing loss than males as they age.

16.(IC2) **1) Autonomy vs. shame and doubt is Erikson's second stage, ages 1 to 3. During this stage, children assert their own will; a two-year-old wants to "do it myself." When parents continue to do everything for children, the children may doubt their abilities and develop shame and doubt.**
2) Industry vs. inferiority is Erikson's stage corresponding to middle childhood. Children can use their increased cognitive and physical abilities in this stage to develop new skills and complete tasks. Experiences of failure during this stage may lead to a sense of inferiority.
3) Initiative vs. guilt is Erikson's stage of early childhood, ages 3 to 5. During this stage, children may try many new things although they may not successfully complete as many tasks as in the industry stage. Children in very strict environments that do not support curiosity and exploration may develop guilt.
4) Trust vs. mistrust is Erikson's stage of infancy. An infant who is nurtured learns to trust the world through being fed and held with affection. An infant who is neglected experiences the world as an untrustworthy place.

17.(IIIB1d)***1) Plasticity is the ability to change and adapt. Early in life, the brain has some potential to adapt to injuries by having different areas of the brain take over the functions of damaged areas.**
2) The brain's ability to change and adapt decreases with age.
3) Some growth in brain cell projections occurs in middle age; however, the greatest period of brain plasticity occurs in infancy and childhood.
4) Brain plasticity is not constant throughout the life span, it is greater earlier in life.

18.(IIIA1) 1) In the Babinski reflex, the toes fan out when the sole of the foot is stroked.
2) The Moro reflex is a startle response in which the arms fling out and then join together, the skin flushes, and crying may occur.
3) The plantar reflex occurs when the sole of the foot is irritated and the toes contract. It indicates neurologic health.
*4) The stepping reflex occurs when the infant is held upright with the feet touching a surface. Both legs move in a pattern similar to walking although the infant cannot support her weight.

19.(VIIIC1b)***1) Longitudinal studies by Costa and McCrae and others have found five basic personality clusters (extroversion, openness, agreeableness, conscientiousness, and neuroticism) that remain stable throughout adulthood in most individuals.**
2) Adult experiences have not been shown to dramatically change personality traits in adulthood.
3) Personality traits are less stable in childhood as the major characteristics are still developing.
4) Most people's personality traits are resistant to change in late adulthood.

20.(IB2b) 1) Age is not a variable in this study since all the children are preschoolers at the onset of the study.
*2) The researcher is measuring the effects of the program by looking at grades. Grades are used as the test or measure of the outcome. When studying the effects of a variation in experience on a resulting behavior, the resulting or outcome behavior is the dependent variable.
3) The type of preschool program is the independent variable. The researcher is trying to find out how the variation in programs, the independent variable, affects later school grades, the dependent variable.
4) Placement in elementary school is not being systematically examined in this study.

21.(IIIB2a) 1) Conservation is an aspect of concrete operational thinking that develops around the ages five to seven, not in infancy.
2) Double-blind studies are used to assess the effects of interventions such as drug treatments, when neither the participants nor the researchers know who has the real treatment and who has the placebo.
3) Equilibration studies would be designed by a Piagetian researcher to test the stability of a child's cognitive schemas.
*4) Habituation is a decreased response to a repeated stimulus. In studying infant perception with this technique, when a visual or sound stimulus is presented repeatedly, the infant will show decreased interest. When a different stimulus is presented, if the infant shows renewed interest, we know that the infant perceives the stimuli as different.

22.(IXD3) 1) Autonomy versus shame and doubt is Erikson's second stage, age 1 to 3, when children develop increased control of their bodies and behavior and want to do more things for themselves.
*2) Integrity versus despair is Erikson's stage of late adulthood. In successful aging, one can reflect on one's life as having had meaning; conversely, despair involves the feeling that life was meaningless.
3) Intimacy versus isolation is Erikson's stage of early adulthood during which individuals struggle to develop mature relationships.
4) Generativity versus stagnation is Erikson's stage of middle adulthood in which the developmental goal is to provide for the next generation, through parenting, mentoring at work, and other future-oriented activities.

23.(VIIIC2) 1) Identity versus role confusion occurs during adolescence as the individual seeks to develop a work identity. For most people, this is an event that occurs prior to the occurrence of parenthood.
*2) Generativity versus stagnation is Erikson's stage of middle adulthood in which the developmental goal is to provide for the next generation, through parenting, mentoring at work, and other future-oriented activities.
3) Integrity versus despair is Erikson's stage of late adulthood. In successful aging, one can reflect on one's life as having had meaning; conversely, despair involves the feeling that life was meaningless.
4) Intimacy versus isolation is Erikson's stage of early adulthood during which individuals struggle to develop mature relationships.

24.(VIC2) 1) Gilligan notes that many women are less concerned with rules and laws than they are with caring for others and maintaining good relationships.
2) Gilligan's theory explicitly rejects the view that good moral decision making must be solely concerned with the rights of individuals. Instead, Gilligan argues that women tend to focus on what is best for many people.
3) Cognitive development can influence moral decision making, but it is not the central factor discussed by Gilligan.
*4) According to Gilligan, women most value the maintenance of good relationships and open lines of communication when they strive to resolve moral dilemmas.

25.(IC4) 1) This statement describes a later stage, concrete operations, when a child can solve logical problems if the objects represented in the problems are present.
2) This statement describes the beginning of concept formation that occurs in infancy during the sensorimotor stage.
*3) This statement describes the preoperational stage in which children begin to pretend and to relate past experiences to present ones and to think symbolically.
4) This statement describes the formal operational stage when abstract thought develops.

26.(IIA7) 1) The triple X pattern (having three X chromosomes) results in females with normal physical appearance and mental retardation.
2) PKU is a disorder caused by a recessive gene that prevents the infant from metabolizing a protein. Left untreated, PKU results in mental retardation.
3) Klinefelter's syndrome occurs in males who have an extra X chromosome which results in underdeveloped testes and enlarged breasts.
*4) The question describes the physical and cognitive signs of Turner syndrome which occurs in females who are missing an X chromosome, making their chromosomal pattern XO instead of XX.

27.(VIC1) 1) Achievement of identity occurs after a crisis has been resolved and a commitment to an identity has been made.
2) Diffusion is experienced by individuals who have not experienced a crisis nor made a commitment. This stage involves the development of a sense of accomplishment, proficiency, and work ethic.
3) Foreclosure occurs when a person makes a commitment to an identity before going through a crisis or searching process.
*4) Moratorium involves experiencing a crisis that prompts an individual to actively seek a psychological identity. The adolescent would search for the aspects of ethnic identity that mean the most to her or him, and continue to look for definitions of this identity.

28.(IXA) 1) In the cross-linkage theory, aging and death occur because tissues become less elastic as cellular proteins become bound to each other, and, therefore, the efficiency of cell function is reduced.
2) In endocrine theory, hormonal changes lead to aging and death.
*3) In Hayflick theory, there is a genetically set limit to the number of times tissue cells can regenerate. When that limit is reached, organs cease to function and death occurs.
4) In wear-and-tear theory, death occurs because organs wear out and cease to function as a result of age and usage.

29.(IIIA2)*1) Within moments of birth, infants can turn their head in the direction of a sound.
2) See 1).
3) See 1).
4) See 1).

30.(VIIC1)*1) While Erikson focused on psychosocial stages, Vaillant's longitudinal study put more emphasis on career development and choices.
2) Early adult transition is a stage in Levinson's description of adult development.
3) Keeping the meaning is a phrase used in the context of Erikson's stage of generativity versus stagnation.
4) Postformal thought is a stage of development proposed by research in cognitive development in adulthood. Postformal thought is a more contextual form of thinking than formal thought.

31.(IVB2) 1) Chomsky's theory focused on language acquisition and transformational grammar.
2) Piaget's approach to cognitive development emphasized the child as an independent explorer who learns from her or his own experience rather than from adult intervention.
3) Skinner focused on behavioral learning and rejected the constructs of cognitive development.
*4) Vygotsky found that children can solve problems with adult assistance when the problems are just beyond their level of proficiency. He called this the "zone of proximal development." Vygotsky's approach to learning involves more social intervention than the others.

32.(VIIIB2)*1) Fluid intelligence refers to the capacity to learn new material. Cross-sectional research finds that this ability peaks in early adulthood and then gradually declines.
2) Crystallized intelligence refers to factual knowledge, specific skills, and abilities affected by experiences. Research has shown that this remains stable or increases with age.
3) Research has shown that fluid intelligence begins to decline after young adulthood.
4) Crystallized intelligence remains stable or increases with age.

33.(VB3) 1) Intelligence quotient refers to scores obtained on an intelligence test.
*2) Metacognition refers to the knowledge children acquire about their abilities, thought processes, and memories.
3) Operational thought refers to the use of logical thought processing.
4) Self-awareness is a broad term that extends to children's knowledge of their personalities, social skills, and other characteristics.

34.(IIC2) 1) The cervix begins to dilate in the first stage of labor.

2) The placenta is expelled during the third stage of labor, after the baby is delivered.
*3) **The second stage of labor begins when the baby's head emerges and continues until the baby completely emerges.**
4) The amniotic sac breaks during the first stage of labor.

35.(VIIB1) 1) Concrete operational thought, age 7 to 11, is rooted in the present and does not involve abstract, relativistic, or integrative thinking.
*2) **Postformal thought can emerge in adulthood. It is more relativistic and contextual than formal thought. A postformal thinker has the experience to decide what problems are important and to weigh different theories that may account for a set of facts.**
3) Preoperational thought is illogical, intuitive, and tied to the here-and-now. No relativistic thinking is possible during this stage, age 2 to 7.
4) Sensorimotor thought develops in infancy and is rooted in sensation and physical action. It is nonsymbolic and concrete. Abstraction, relativism, and integration are not possible during this first year of life.

Microbiology

1.(IB3) 1) Algae are classified as eukaryotes.
*2) **The archaeobacteria are classified as prokaryotes because they lack a nucleus, nuclear membrane, and organelles. Archaeobacteria also have other properties consistent with the prokaryotes.**
3) Protozoans are classified as eukaryotes.
4) Yeasts are classified as eukaryotes.

2.(IC)*1) **The Gram stain is called a differential stain because it separates (differentiates) one group of bacteria from another group.**
2) The lipid granule stain does not separate bacteria into groups. It allows viewing of the structures within the cells.
3) The negative stain does not separate bacteria into groups. It is used to show clear bacteria on a dark background.
4) The simple stain does not separate bacteria into groups. It is used to stain bacteria.

3.(IIA) *1) **Spore formation in the bacteria is limited almost exclusively to members of the genera *Bacillus* and *Clostridium*.**
2) Bacteria of the *Erwinia* genus do not produce spores.
3) Bacteria of the *Pseudomonas* genus do not produce spores.
4) Bacteria of the *Salmonella* genus do not produce spores.

4.(IIB1)*1) ***Euglena gracilis* is considered autotrophic because it uses its photosynthetic pigments to synthesize its own food materials.**
2) Heterotrophic refers to an organism that uses preformed organic matter for food.
3) Parasitic refers to an organism that uses living preformed organic matter.
4) Saprophytic refers to an organism that uses nonliving preformed organic matter.

5.IIB3 1) The pour plate method would be inappropriate because the organism of interest is too rare.
2) This is an inappropriate method because not all species grow on minimal media.
*3) **The enrichment medium increases the relative percentage of the organism of interest when the population streak plate method is used afterward.**
4) The organism of interest is too rare for the streak plate method to be used directly.

6.IID3*1) **Conjugation requires cell-to-cell contact and would be blocked by the barrier.**
2) Generalized transduction utilizes phage that can fit through the barrier.
3) Specialized transduction utilizes phage that can fit through the barrier.
4) Transformation uses DNA that can fit through the barrier.

7.IID4*1) **The RNA polymerase would always find an open promoter/operon region.**
2) The repressor never binds to DNA.
3) The repressor never binds to DNA under the conditions described.
4) Operons are turned off when the repressor is bound. This cannot happen because the repressor is a mutant.

8.IIE 1) Information about the extent of recombination is not required.
2) The curve gives no indication of the location of virion particles.
*3) **The curve indicates the number of phage particles.**
4) The curve shows the number of viruses released, but provides no information on the phylogeny of viruses.

9.(IIIB) 1) Desiccation is not a reliable form of sterilization because it has low sporicidal activity.
2) Pasteurization is not a reliable form of sterilization because it has virtually no sporicidal activity.
*3) **Pressurized steam is used for sterilization in the autoclave where it penetrates tough bacterial spores and destroys them quickly.**
4) Ultraviolet light is not a reliable form of sterilization because it has low sporicidal activity.

10.IIIB3 1) Bacteria cells are not blood, so hemolysis does not occur.
*2) **Small temperature increases lead to denaturation of some proteins.**
3) Lipids are more resistant to moist heat than are proteins.
4) Water remains with a cell until driven off at increasingly higher temperatures.

11.IIIB4 1) Infrared radiation is not strong enough to induce the production of oxygen radicals.
*2) **Ionizing radiation is powerful enough to ionize water by causing atoms to change to ions.**
3) Ultraviolet light is not strong enough to induce the production of oxygen radicals.
4) Visible radiation is not strong enough to induce the production of oxygen radicals.

12. IIID 1) The practice of adding antibiotics to animal feed may actually reduce the cost of feed as animals gain weight faster.
2) The practice may lead to an oversupply of antibiotics needed for human beings.
3) The practice lowers the antibiotic resistance of the animals to disease.
*4) **The practice preferentially allows the growth of bacteria strains that are resistant to drugs used to treat human infections.**

13. (IVA1b)*1) **The intestine of most human beings contains a population of nonpathogenic *Escherichia coli* as part of its normal flora.**
2) *Pseudomonas aeruginosa* is not commonly located in the intestine. It is a possible pathogen in individuals who are immunocompromised.
3) *Staphylococcus aureus* is not commonly located in the intestine. It is found in the nose and on the skin.
4) *Vibrio cholerae* is not commonly located in the intestine. It is a pathogen and the agent of cholera.

14. (IVB1d) 1) Catalase is not found in tears or saliva and has no effect on the cell walls of bacteria.
2) Coagulase is not found in tears or saliva. It is an enzyme produced by staphylococci that forms blood clots.
*3) **Lysozyme is normally found in tears and saliva and destroys the cell walls of gram-positive bacteria.**
4) Penicillinase is not found in tears or saliva. It is an enzyme produced by some penicillin-resistant bacterial species.

15. IVB1*1) **Lysozyme weakens the cell wall by rupturing peptidoglycan layers.**
2) Their pH is not basic enough to break the cell wall.
3) Oxygen is diffused, not deprived, through tears.
4) The ionic strength is increased due to NaCl in tears.

16. IVC2 *1) **IgM antibodies are the primary response to exposure to an antigen.**
2) IgG antibodies appear 24 to 48 hours after the primary response to exposure to an antigen.
3) Recent exposure to antigens does not induce the production of IgG.
4) There is no known disorder that only produces IgM.

17. (IVC3b)*1) **Vaccination is an artificial means of introducing antigens to the body, and since the body produces its own antibodies, the immunity is active.**
2) Artificially acquired, passive immunity results from an injection of antibodies.
3) Naturally acquired, active immunity results from an episode of disease.
4) Naturally acquired, passive immunity results from antibodies passed from mother to child across the placenta.

18. VA*1) **The pneumococcal strain is not recognized as foreign and therefore is not endocytosed.**
2) Pneumococci have cell walls that are recognized by phagocytes.
3) Exotoxin does not target phagocytes.
4) Endotoxins are only produced by gram-negative bacteria.

19. VA2 1) A beta-hemolytic infection is commonly associated with high-grade fever.
2) These organisms, which can inhabit the mucous membranes of the upper respiratory tract, are not characterized by skin rashes.
3) This organism is the causative agent of "walking pneumonia," and generally does not produce the signs described in the newborn.
*4) **Rubella often goes undetected and can produce the signs described in the newborn if contracted in the first trimester of pregnancy.**

20. VA3 1) Adenoviruses generally cause the common cold, characterized by swelling of the lymph nodes, or meningitis.
*2) **This causative organism is a dimorphic fungus that can appear in yeastlike form in macrophages, where it can multiply.**
3) Both the tuberculin and acid-fast tests are negative, so this organism is not the causative agent.
4) This bacterium is a spirochete, a corkscrew-shaped bacterium.

21. VB1 1) Cardiomyopathy is a disorder of the heart muscle and is often of unknown etiology.
2) Endotoxin is associated with typhoid fever, meningitis, and urinary tract infections, not cholera.
*3) **Because of the loss of fluids in persons with cholera, the blood becomes so viscous that vital organs cannot function properly.**
4) In renal failure, abrupt reduction of renal function is accompanied by progressive retention of waste compounds and is not associated with cholera.

22. VC1 1) The acidity of the reproductive tract inhibits infectivity, it does not enhance it.
*2) **The disease in females is more insidious than in males.**
3) The use of condoms would help prevent disease transmission.
4) Treatment is the same for females and males.

23. VIA 1) Coliforms may be pathogenic and can cause diarrhea and opportunistic urinary tract infections.
2) Bacteriophages do not affect human beings.
*3) **Coliforms are indicator organisms for detecting human waste in water.**
4) Although coliforms cause disease, the disease is not usually fatal.

24. (VD1a) 1) Smallpox vaccination develops after an injection of cowpox viruses.
*2) **Tetanus toxoid is used in the DPT immunization to develop immunity against tetanus.**
3) A toxoid is not used to render immunity to tuberculosis. A preparation of live bacteria called BCG is used.
4) A toxoid is not used to render immunity to typhoid fever. Treated bacteria are used.

25. VIC2 1) A small, slowly growing cell would slow the process and provide more chance for contamination.
2) Low temperatures would cause the microorganism to grow more slowly.
*3) **Antibiotics are secondary metabolites that are easy to retrieve if in an appropriate growth medium.**
4) Polysaccharide makes purification of a compound difficult.

26.(VIC1) 1) Malolactic fermentation is not involved in the conversion of ethanol in wine to acetic acid.
2) This condition does not lead to ethanol production.
3) See 2).
*4) When wine is exposed to the air (under aerobic conditions), acid-forming bacteria use the oxygen to convert the ethanol in wine to acetic acid.

Pathophysiology

1.(IA1) *1) Atrophy refers to the decrease in the size of cells and their differentiated functions. An example is endocrine atrophy which occurs when endocrine signals are interrupted or when hormonal support is withdrawn.
2) Dysplasia refers to the disorganized appearance of cells due to abnormal size, shape, and arrangement.
3) Hyperplasia refers to an increase in the number of cells within a tissue, leading to an increase in the size of the tissue or organ. An example is enlargement of breast tissue during pregnancy or lactation.
4) Hypertrophy refers to an increase in cell mass leading to enlargement of a tissue. It is stimulus-related and an adaptive response. An example is thickening of the myocardium of the ventricular wall.

2.(IA3) 1) Cardiac cells demonstrate an increase in size, not in the number of cells.
*2) Hyperplastic growth is dependent upon mitotic cell division which increases the number of cells. This is most often seen in epithelial tissues.
3) Hyperplastic growth is not seen in nerve cells.
4) Skeletal muscle cells demonstrate an increase in size, not in the number of cells.

3.(IC2) 1) The mating of two carriers (heterozygous) results in a two-in-four chance of producing an offspring who carries the disease. It is possible, therefore, that not all the children will be carriers.
*2) Cystic fibrosis is an autosomal recessive disorder. The mating of two carriers (heterozygous) results in a one-in-four chance of producing an offspring affected with the disorder, and a two-in-four chance of producing an offspring who carries the disease. The chance of having an offspring who is neither a carrier nor is affected with the disorder is one-in-four.
3) It is possible to have an offspring who is neither a carrier nor is affected with the disorder.
4) There is a one-in-four chance of having an offspring who is affected with the disorder.

4.(IIA2) *1) Corticosteroids promote healing in skin disorders by suppressing inflammation and reducing erythema, edema, and pruritus.
2) Corticosteroids reduce the pruritis associated with some skin disorders but have no analgesic effect. Antipyretics, such as acetaminephen, are often used to relieve local discomfort of skin disorders.
3) Corticosteroids inhibit collagen formation.
4) Treatment with corticosteroids impairs the immune response and increases the risk of infection.

5.(IIA2) 1) There is no documented evidence that steroid hormone activity leads to malignant melanoma.
*2) The increased incidence of malignant melanoma is attributed to greater sun exposure. An increased frequency of malignant melanoma in the Sunbelt States of the US supports the role of ultraviolet (UV) light as a cause of this tumor.
3) Long-term antibiotic therapy is not associated with malignant melanoma.
4) There is no correlation between fungal skin infections and the incidence of malignant melanoma.

6.(IID3) 1) Myxedema (advanced hypothyroidism) is characterized by facial puffiness, nonpitting edema, and altered mental state.
2) Myasthenia gravis, an autoimmune neuromuscular disorder, is characterized by diplopia, ptosis, increasing weakness with activity, and possible respiratory failure.
3) Hashimoto's disease (lymphocytic thyroiditis) is characterized by an enlarged thyroid gland.
*4) Graves' disease is characterized by hyperthyroidism thyromegaly (goiter), thyrotoxicosis, and exophthalmos.

7.(IID4) *1) Anaphylactic reactions (type I hypersensitivity) are associated with angioedema, bronchial wheezing, and cutaneous itching.
2) Cytotoxic reactions (type II hypersitivity) occur in transfusion reactions and hemolytic disease of the newborn.
3) Immune complex reactions (type III hypersitivity) are seen in serum sickness, arthritis, and vasculitis.
4) Delayed hypersensitivity (type IV) develops over time and is seen in Guillain-Barré syndrome and contact dermatitis.

8.(IIIA5) 1) This pattern describes third degree or complete heart block.
2) This pattern describes Mobitz type II second degree heart block.
3) This pattern describes first degree heart block.
*4) This pattern describes Mobitz type I (Wenckebach type I) second degree heart block.

9.(IIIC1) 1) The cardiac cycle refers to the repetitive contraction and relaxation of the heart muscle.
2) Myocardial conduction refers to the conduction of the electrical impulse in the myocardium.
*3) Preload, afterload, contractility, and the heart rate are hemodynamic parameters that influence cardiac output.
4) Atrial systole is atrial contraction.

10.(IIIF1) 1) The foramen ovale refers to the opening between the two atria of the heart in the fetus. It normally closes shortly before or after birth. If it remains open or patent, it is referred to as an atrial septal defect.
2) A ventricular septal defect occurs in the septum between the left and right ventricle. It permits blood to flow from the left to the right ventricle and to recirculate through the pulmonary artery and the lungs.
*3) Transposition of the great arteries is a fetal anomaly in which the aorta arises from the right ventricle and the pulmonary artery arises from the left ventricle, and there is no communication between the systemic and pulmonary circulations.

4) In atrial septal defect there is an abnormal opening between the atria that increases the flow of oxygenated blood into the right side of the heart. In ventricular septal defect, there is an opening below the septum that separates the ventricles and permits blood to flow from the left to the right ventricle and to recirculate through the pulmonary artery and the lungs.

11. (IIIG2) 1) Myocardial infarction is characterized by chest pain and serial ECG abnormalities. Friction rub is not present.
2) Angina pectoris is characterized by chest pain associated with intermittent myocardial ischemia. Transient ECG changes occur. Friction rub is not present.
3) Cardiac tamponade caused by an accumulation of pericardial fluid results in external compression of the heart chambers reducing stroke volume. Clinical manifestations include dull chest pain, diminished ECG amplitude, and muffled heart sounds. Pericardial friction rub is not present.
*4) **Acute pericarditis is characterized by chest pain, friction rub, and ECG abnormalities. Systemic effects of inflammation and pericardial damage lead to stretching and rubbing of the viseral and pericardial layers.**

12. (IVA2) *1) **Bronchiectasis is characterized by recurrent infection and inflammation of bronchial walls which leads to persistent dilation of bronchi and bronchioles.**
2) Emphysema is characterized by destructive changes in the alveolar walls with enlargement of the distal air sacs.
3) Chronic bronchitis is defined as hypersecretion of the bronchial mucosa with a production cough for greater than three months.
4) Cystic fibrosis is an autosomal recessive disorder of the exocrine glands that is characterized by the production of an abnormally thick obstructive mucus.

13. (IVF3) *1) **Since the most common site of infection with tuberculosis is the lungs, transmission occurs from the inhalation of contaminated droplets produced when an infected person coughs or sneezes.**
2) Contaminated blood can transmit diseases such as hepatitis and HIV.
3) Fecal-oral contamination can transmit diseases such as salmonella and *E. coli* food poisoning.
4) Sexual contact can transmit diseases such as gonorrhea, herpes simplex, trichomonas, and HIV.

14. (VA2) 1) Addition or retention of sodium leads to the development of fluid volume excess.
*2) **The removal of a sodium-containing fluid from the body leads to extracellular fluid volume deficit.**
3) Excess aldosterone secretion would promote sodium retention leading to the development of fluid volume excess.
4) Inadequate excretion of sodium and water would promote fluid volume excess.

15. (VC1) *1) **A pH below normal (7.35–7.45) and PaCO$_2$ above normal (35–45 mm Hg) indicates primary respiratory acidosis. Anion gap 8 mEq/L is within normal limits (less than 15 mEq/L), thus eliminating metabolic acidosis. PaO$_2$ 65 mm Hg represents hypoxemia.**
2) Although pH 7.2 represents acidosis, the elevation of the anion gap to 25 mEq/L indicates metabolic acidosis. The decrease in PaCO$_2$ indicates partial compensation since the lungs will hyperventilate to eliminate excessive carbonic acid in an attempt to restore the pH to normal.
3) Elevated pH (greater than 7.35–7.45) and decreased PaCO$_2$ indicates respiratory alkalosis. The normal anion gap indicates no metabolic acidosis component.
4) Although the PaCO$_2$ is elevated, the presence of pH 7.5 indicates an alkalotic abnormality.

16. (VE2) 1) As renal disease advances and GFR falls to about 25% of normal, phosphate is retained by the kidneys. Phosphate retention does cause the depression of serum calcium levels, but there will be decreased phosphate excretion by the kidneys.
2) Phosphate retention causes depression of serum calcium levels and interference with vitamin D3 activation by the kidneys. As renal function decreases, low serum calcium and high phosphate levels stimulate parathyroid activity resulting in bone resorption of calcium and phosphate.
*3) **As renal disease advances, there is progressive disruption of calcium phosphate interrelations. Phosphate is retained when the GFR declines to 25%. There are decreased serum calcium levels secondary to phosphate retention and interference with vitamin D$_3$ activation by the kidneys.**
4) With advancing renal disease, phosphate retention causes depression of serum calcium levels or hypocalcemia.

17. (VG2) 1) Chlamydia typically produces discharge.
2) Gonorrhea typically produces purulent discharge and painful urination.
*3) **During the early stages of syphilis, a painless ulcerative lesion, or chancre, develops at the site of entry of the spirochete.**
4) Nonspecific urogenital infections typically produce inflammation and pain.

18. (VIA2) 1) Tachycardia, hyperthermia, urticaria, with pain and spasm below the level of the lesion, are not associated with autonomic dysreflexia.
2) Flaccid paralysis of all skeletal muscles and absence of deep tendon reflexes are associated with spinal shock. Hypoventilation occurs with spinal cord injury above C5.
3) After a complete spinal cord injury, paresthesia occurs below the level of injury. Hypotension is a symptom of spinal shock. In autonomic dysreflexia, pallor and goose bumps occur below the level of the lesion.
*4) **Hypertension, bradycardia, and severe headache, with sweating and flushing of the skin above the level of the lesion are symptoms typical of autonomic dysreflexia. The stimulus that triggers autonomic dysreflexia is often a full bladder.**

19. (VIG4) 1) Endogenous opioids and enkephalins decrease the pain response. Anything that interferes with or inhibits their action would not relieve pain.
2) Morphine antagonists would increase the awareness of painful sensations.
3) Substance P is a neuropeptide that promotes pain transmission.
*4) **The effect of acupuncture and TENS can be explained by the gate control theory which sug-**

gests that large fiber stimulation decreases the pain response.

20.(VIH2) 1) Synovitis or inflammation of the synovial membrane is seen later in the degenerative disease process.
★2) Since articular cartilage has a limited capacity for repair and regeneration, trauma or stress can predispose the development of degenerative joint disease.
3) The epiphyseal plate or growth plate is not affected in degenerative joint disease.
4) Alterations in the joint cavity occur later in the degenerative disease process.

21.(VIIA4) 1) An increase in intrathoracic pressure would prevent the hernia from sliding upward.
★2) An increase in intra-abdominal pressure, such as assuming a supine position, disrupts the competency of the gastroesophageal junction, causing it to slide above the diaphragm into the thoracic cavity.
3) A decrease in intra-abdominal pressure would not be associated with an exacerbation of a hiatal hernia.
4) A decrease in intrathoracic pressure would have no effect on a hiatal hernia.

22.(VIIB2) 1) The mucosa of the small intestine appears flat in celiac disease. Mucous membrane edema is seen in inflammatory processes.
2) Hyperplasia of lymphoid tissue is not associated with celiac disease.
★3) Celiac disease is characterized by defects in metabolism as a result of gluten intolerance. There is damage to the surface epithelium of the small intestine and atrophy of the villi.
4) Increased cellular production of gastric secretions can promote peptic ulcer disease.

23.(VIIG5) 1) Administration of hypotonic saline would exacerbate the hyponatremia and fluid volume overload associated with SIADH.
2) Infusion of 0.9% sodium chloride isotonic solution may be used to raise the serum sodium level, but it may not be sufficient enough to treat the severe hyponatremia associated with SIADH.
3) Antidiuretic hormone is secreted from the posterior pituitary gland. Administration of posterior pituitary extract would exacerbate the clinical situation.
★4) Fluid restriction is the treatment for SIADH. This treatment should result in a loss of body weight and an increase in serum osmolality.

24.(VIIH5) 1) Low levels of ACTH indicate adrenocortical hyperfunction.
2) High levels of T_4 and T_3 indicate hyperthyroidism.
3) Low levels of parathyroid hormone indicate parathyroid hypofunction.
★4) TSH, thyroid-stimulating hormone, is elevated in thyroid hypofunction.

25.(VIIJ) 1) There is no evidence that avoiding caffeine has any effect on individuals with ovarian cysts or endometriosis.
2) Avoiding caffeine is not typically included in the treatment of mastitis or amenorrhea.
★3) The methylxanthines, including the related alkaloid caffeine, increase metabolic activity in the breast. Decreasing caffeine in the diet has been effective in helping to alleviate breast tenderness and pain associated with fibrocystic breast disease and premenstrual syndrome (PMS). In addition, women with PMS are advised to avoid stimulants, such as caffeine, to help alleviate symptoms associated with anxiety.
4) Avoiding caffeine is not included in the treatment of pelvic inflammatory disease and leiomyomas.

26.(VIIIA) 1) Gout is a metabolic disorder that is associated with deposition of uric acid in bony and connective tissues.
2) Rheumatoid arthritis is an inflammatory disorder of the joints and synovial tissues.
★3) Joint pain, fever, morning stiffness, proteinuria, and a red rash across the bridge of the nose and cheeks are symptoms of systemic lupus erythematosus, an autoimmune disorder that affects multiple organ systems.
4) Ankylosing spondylitis involves the entire spine. There is morning stiffness with marked limitation of motion. There is no associated fever or facial rash.

27.(VIIIB) 1) Decreased pH and decreased HCO_3^- indicate an uncompensated metabolic acidosis. $PaCO_2$ 45 is normal and indicates that the patient is not yet hyperventilating as a compensatory mechanism to restore the pH to normal.
★2) Elevated pH 7.48 and decreased $PaCO_2$ 30 indicates respiratory alkalosis. Hyperventilation is a cause of this acid-base imbalance.
3) $PaCO_2$ 60 and pH 7.20 indicate respiratory acidosis. Elevated $PaCO_2$ indicates alveolar hypoventilation leading to retention of CO_2. PaO_2 60 indicates hypoxemia.
4) Elevated pH 7.51 and elevated HCO_3^- 33 indicate metabolic alkalosis. $PaCO_2$ 52 indicates the lungs are compensating by retaining CO_2 through hypoventilation in an attempt to restore the pH to normal.

28.(VIIIC) 1) Urea levels are decreased in liver disease.
2) A high-carbohydrate diet is given to provide the patient with calories. Protein is restricted to inhibit its breakdown into ammonia.
★3) Reduction of serum ammonia levels is essential in the treatment of hepatic encephalopathy to slow its progression. Treatment to eliminate ammonia-producing substances from the GI tract includes administering neomycin and lactulose and reducing dietary protein intake.
4) Prevention of secondary infection is important since it can precipitate hepatic encephalopathy by increasing tissue metabolism which increases ammonia production; however, it is not the ultimate goal of treatment.

Psychology of Adulthood & Aging

1.(IA) 1) Biological age compares a person's physical state to that of persons of different ages. A 40-year-old in an excellent state of health and fitness would have a

young biological age compared to her or his chronological age. This question, however, does not mention the person's health status.
2) Chronological age is a person's age in years. A 40-year-old would be considered middle-aged.
3) Psychological age refers to capacities such as memory, intelligence, feelings, and motivation that a person uses to adapt to changing environmental demands. The question does not give enough information to know whether or not this person is psychologically functioning as a young person.
★4) Social age refers to a person's roles in relation to other members of society. Since most first-year college students are 17 or 18 years old, this 40-year-old individual's social age could be considered as young.

2.(IA) 1) Early retirement is nonnormative; retirement at 65 would be normative.
★2) A normative age-graded event is an event that happens to many individuals during a particular age period. Reaching menopause at 50 is a normative age-graded event because it occurs in most women between 45 and 55 years of age.
3) Winning a lottery is a nonnormative event because it is unusual and it is not related to different age periods.
4) Testing positive for AIDS is a nonnormative event.

3.(IB) 1) Age-segregated congregate housing refers to planned housing with services such as meals and recreation. Relatively few people over age 65 live in this type of housing.
2) Only about 5% of people over age 65 live in institutional settings.
3) Retirement communities are a growing form of age-segregated congregate housing, but only a small percentage of people over age 65 live in these communities.
★4) The vast majority of people over age 65 live in their own homes or apartments.

4.(IIA) 1) Age changes and cohort are not confounded because all the participants are going through the age changes together.
2) Cohort and selective dropout are not confounded. Although there can be a problem with selective dropout over the course of a longitudinal study, cohort is constant.
3) Time of measurement and cohort are not confounded. Time-of-measurement effects can occur in longitudinal research, for example if the age group all experience wartime or economic changes, but time of measurement is not a confound because all the participants experience the same time effects.
★4) Age changes and time of measurement are confounded in longitudinal research because it can be difficult to separate the effects of age (such as being a young adult) from the effects of historical events (such as being young during the Vietnam War).

5.(IIB)**★1) An important component of research ethics is that participants must be informed of risks that might influence their participation in the research study.**
2) If compensation is offered, a subject is usually paid for participating whether or not he or she decides to continue with the study.

3) For informed consent to be meaningful, subjects must understand what they are agreeing to do; therefore, attention to language or cultural barriers is vital.
4) Informed consent must be obtained from subjects prior to their participating in the research.

6.(IIIA) 1) In Costa and McCrae's model, conscientiousness means being organized, deliberate and rule-following. We do not have this information about Mark and Dorothy.
2) In Costa and McCrae's model, extroversion means the tendency to be outgoing, assertive, and active. We do not have this information about Mark and Dorothy.
★3) In Costa and McCrae's model, neuroticism means the tendency to be anxious, moody, and self-punishing. Mark fits this description while Dorothy does not.
4) In Costa and McCrae's model, openness to experience refers to curiosity and imagination. We do not have this information about Mark and Dorothy.

7.(IIIB) 1) According to Erikson, autonomy versus shame and doubt is the struggle of early childhood. The young child is working on gaining control of her or his body, behavior, and surroundings and doing more things for herself or himself.
2) According to Erikson, generativity versus stagnation is the struggle of middle adulthood in which the focus shifts to concern for the next generation (generativity) or feelings of self-absorption (stagnation).
★3) According to Erikson, integrity versus despair is the struggle of older adulthood. An older adult who looks back at her or his life and concludes that it has been worthwhile achieves integrity. One who feels life was a waste of time develops despair.
4) According to Erikson, intimacy versus isolation is the struggle of early adulthood. The young adult, having struggled with identity, is ready to form a close mutual relationship.

8.(IIIC) 1) Disengagement theory suggests that reduced involvement with society in aging is normal and healthy; it does not associate loneliness and depression with social withdrawal.
2) Disengagement theory suggests that one reason withdrawal from society is a natural development is that declines in health (rather than better health) make continued participation difficult.
★3) Disengagement theory suggests that older adults who withdraw from society are satisfied because they have met personal and societal expectations.
4) Disengagement theory suggests that older adults choose to withdraw from society rather than being ignored or forced out of social life.

9.(IVA)**★1) Presbycusis is the condition associated with aging of progressive hearing loss for high-pitched sounds. It results from changes in the inner ear: sensory (atrophy and degeneration of hair cells), neural (loss of neurons in the auditory pathway), metabolic (diminished supply of nutrients to the cochlea), and mechanical (atrophy and stiffening of vibrating structures in the cochlea).**
2) Presbyopia is a reduction in near vision.

3) Presbystatis is a loss of balance and equilibrium.
4) Tinnitus is a constant ringing in the ears.

10.(IVA) 1) Calcium and vitamin D have no effect on night sweats.
*2) **Calcium and vitamin D are needed to prevent osteoporosis.**
3) Calcium and vitamin D have no effect on preventing pregnancy.
4) Calcium and vitamin D are unrelated to the development of Alzheimer's disease.

11.(IVA)*1) **Hayflick found that cells can divide a maximum of approximately 50 times before the genetic material of the resulting cells is too damaged to reproduce. The 110-to-120-year life span is extrapolated from the cell divisions needed to keep the human body functioning.**
2) Wear-and-tear theory suggests that aging is caused by cumulative damage. The theory does not predict a maximum life span.
3) Free radicals are components of cell metabolism that can damage cells through reactions with other substances. The impact of free radicals on the life span has not been predicted.
4) Cross linkage is the formation of bonds between proteins in cells. Harmful levels of cross linkage, including oxidation, occur in cells during aging. This process affects individuals at different rates and does not predict a maximum life span.

12.(IVB)*1) **An individual who is actively involved in the decision to move into a nursing home will adjust better to the move since personal choice increases the sense of control.**
2) When the individual is not the one making the choice, the individual will have more difficulty adjusting to the nursing home.
3) See 2). Also, having time to accept the idea may increase the individual's apprehension about the move.
4) Details and pictures may be helpful, but having an active role in the decision is more likely to help the individual's adjustment.

13.(IVB) 1) Exercise has known health benefits and retards the aging process, but it is not the most significant factor in improving health.
*2) **Smoking cessation would do more to improve health in the United States than any other behavior change.**
3) Better diet has known health benefits, but quitting smoking would have a greater impact on improving health.
4) Stress reduction can benefit health, but quitting smoking would have a greater impact on improving health.

14.(VA) 1) At any age, the sensory store is of very short duration (a fraction of a second). This level of processing is not significantly age related.
2) Iconic memory is another term for sensory store and this level of processing is not significantly age related.
3) Long-term memory shows the least decline in old age.
*4) **Manipulating information in short-term memory shows the most significant decline in old age.**

15.(VB)*1) **Crystallized intelligence refers to knowledge of words, facts, and procedures for completing familiar tasks. As more information is acquired each year a person lives, crystallized intelligence is most likely to increase with age.**
2) Fluid intelligence refers to thinking ability applied to relatively novel problems and timed tasks. It involves fluency and flexibility of thinking and speed of processing. Fluid intelligence shows a greater decline with age than crystallized intelligence.
3) Full-scale intelligence refers to the total IQ score on an individual IQ test. Full-scale IQ does not increase with age.
4) A performance score is the part of an individual IQ test that requires working with puzzles, pictures, and spatial information. Most of these tasks are timed for speed as well as accuracy. This part of an IQ score declines more with age than parts that use verbal information and are untimed.

16.(VB) 1) Logical hypothetical-deductive reasoning is the main feature of formal thought, a stage that occurs in adolescence and precedes postformal thought.
2) Distinguishing mental symbols from real objects is a feature of the early stage of preoperational thought that begins in young children.
3) A person capable of postformal thought may believe some truths are absolute, but the person is not using postformal thought when committing to absolute truths.
*4) **When using postformal thought, a person considers the context and frame of reference of an idea. This kind of postformal thinking recognizes the subjective element in knowledge. For example, in evaluating scientific theories, a postformal thinker realizes that more than one theory may account for a set of facts, and that facts are collected by methods that may affect their interpretation.**

17.(VIA) 1) Older men who are close to retirement age are less affected by job loss because the job loss can be viewed as an early retirement and financial responsibilities are often decreased in late adulthood.
*2) **Middle-aged men are most affected by job loss. They have more financial responsibilities and work is often an important part of their identities. It may also be more difficult for middle-aged men to find new jobs than it is for young men.**
3) Young men are often more flexible in their career plans and tend to have fewer financial responsibilities than middle-aged men, so job loss tends to be less traumatic for them.
4) Job loss affects age groups differently.

18.(VIA) 1) Most people retire before age 65.
2) The percentage of males age 65 or older working full time has decreased.
*3) **The percentage of people choosing early retirement has increased.**
4) The percentage of people choosing early retirement has increased.

19.(VIB) 1) The distant type of grandparenting has little contact with grandchildren. This couple is involved with their grandchildren.
*2) **These grandparents represent the formal type of grandparenting. They provide occasional child**

care and show affection and concern, but do not assume primary parenting roles.
3) The fun seeker type of grandparenting is characterized by informal playfulness with the grandchildren. This couple does not represent the fun seeker type of grandparenting.
4) The surrogate type of grandparenting occurs when grandparents assume some or all parenting activities, become full-time primary caregivers, or provide daily care when parents are at work. This couple does not assume the parenting role.

20.(VIB) 1) Empty nest refers to the situation in which middle-aged parents are alone after the last child has left the home.
2) Kinkeepers of the family, usually women, are the ones who plan social activities, send cards and letters, and generally keep the family in touch with one another.
3) Revolving door refers to the situation in which adult children leave the parental home and later return, often due to circumstances such as job loss or marital breakdown.
*4) **The sandwich generation refers to the situation in which middle-aged persons, especially women, are providing care for their own children as well as for their parents.**

21.(VIIA) 1) The hospice movement is not involved with assisted suicide.
2) Hospice principles discourage extreme interventions to prolong life in a person who is dying.
*3) **The primary principles of hospice care are to preserve the dignity and relieve the pain in the person who is dying.**
4) Hospice care generally begins when attempts to cure a disease are no longer deemed to be effective. Surgical care, chemotherapy, and other interventions used in hospitals are not part of hospice care.

22.(VIIB)*1) **Insisting that a mistake was made is an example of denial, the first stage in Kübler-Ross's stages of dying.**
2) Becoming very depressed is part of the fourth of Kübler-Ross's stages, after bargaining and before acceptance.
3) Accepting the diagnosis and planning for death is an example of acceptance, the last of Kübler-Ross's stages.
4) Becoming angry is the second of Kübler-Ross's stages.

23.(VIIIA)*1) **Age has been found to be unrelated to life satisfaction.**
2) Income is a significant factor in life satisfaction. People with higher incomes report more life satisfaction, when other factors are held constant.
3) Marital status is a significant factor in life satisfaction. Married people as a group report higher life satisfaction, when other factors are controlled.
4) Social support is a significant factor in life satisfaction at all ages.

24.(VIIIB) 1) Alzheimer's disease is characterized by plaques and tangles in neurons and, eventually, by accelerated cell loss.
*2) **Multi-infarct dementia is a loss of cognitive ability due to the cumulative effects of a series of small strokes, or transient ischemic attacks.**
3) Parkinson's disease is caused by the deterioration of the neurons in the midbrain that produce the neurotransmitter dopamine.
4) Pseudodementia is an apparent loss of cognitive ability due to depression.

25.(VIIIB) 1) No treatment presently exists to reverse the symptoms of Alzheimer's disease.
2) Multi-infarct dementia may be halted from progressing by treating the risk factors of stroke such as hypertension and by rapid intervention when a transient ischemic attack occurs. The damage to the brain, however, cannot be reversed.
*3) **Nutritional deficiencies such as a vitamin B_{12} deficiency can lead to dementia symptoms that are reversible when nutritional supplements are taken.**
4) Pick's disease is a form of brain degeneration. It is not reversible.

26.(VIIIC) 1) Cognitive therapy focuses on irrational beliefs that are causing a person's anxiety or depression.
2) Sensory training is used with people who are very regressed to stimulate the senses by exposing the person to various smells, tastes, textures, sounds, and visual stimuli.
*3) **Remotivation therapy draws on past skills and interests to rekindle interest in the world.**
4) Reality orientation is used with individuals who are confused to orient them to place and time with the use of large calendars, verbal reminders, and visual cues.

Research Methods in Psychology

1.(IA2) 1) Correlation refers to the degree of relationship between two variables.
2) Observation refers to the systematic noting and recording of events.
3) Publication refers to the write-up of a research paper.
*4) **Replication refers to the repeating of research procedures to verify that the outcome obtained is the same as in the previous research experiment.**

2.(IC2) 1) "Correlational" is not a model of hypothesis formation. Correlation refers to the degree of relationship between two variables.
2) The "deductive" model of hypothesis formation is the process of reasoning from general principles to make predictions about specific cases.
*3) **The "inductive" model of hypothesis formation is the process of reasoning from specific cases to more general principles.**
4) "Scientific" does not refer to a specific model of hypothesis formation.

3.(IIA2) 1) Although by debriefing individuals the researcher does follow APA scientific guidelines, this is not the primary reason for the debriefing.
2) Debriefing is conducted to protect the participants, not to protect the institution and the department.
3) The researcher is legally responsible for what happens to the participants in a study.
*4) **Debriefing participants by explaining the true nature and purpose of the study will eliminate or**

minimize the harmful effects of any deception used in the study.

4.(IIA3)***1) Obtaining informed consent ensures that participants are fully informed about the possible risks and benefits of participating before they decide whether to be in the study.**
2) The APA publishes guidelines for conducting ethical research, but it does not review and approve individual studies.
3) Payment to participants does not ensure that they will not experience harmful effects from the research.
4) Conducting a less risky pilot study would not make a risky experiment more acceptable.

5.(IIC) 1) Failing to obtain informed consent is unethical, but it does not constitute fraud.
2) Conducting a risk/benefit analysis is an important step in ensuring that the study is ethical, but it is not related to fraud.
***3) Fraud involves deliberately omitting or falsifying data so that the research results come out the way the researcher wants.**
4) Debriefing is an important step in ensuring that the study is ethical, but it is not related to fraud.

6.(IIIA1) 1) A case study is a descriptive record of an individual's experiences/behaviors as noted by an observer. A case study would be an inappropriate method for a study about adolescents' attitudes.
2) An experimental study involves manipulating variables. It is not appropriate to manipulate variables when studying attitudes about smoking.
3) The observation method is inappropriate for this topic because it is difficult to directly observe attitudes.
***4) The survey method is an appropriate way to obtain information about people's attitudes by simply asking them. In addition, surveys allow the researcher to gather data about experiences, feelings, thoughts, and motives that are hard to observe directly.**

7.(IIIA2) 1) Position preference is not just selecting answers at random.
***2) Position preference is a type of response style that involves always choosing the response in a certain position, such as the last option, when in doubt about the right answer.**
3) Responding to the manifest content of the question, the plain meaning of the words that actually appear on the page, is another type of response style.
4) How conservatively a person answers the questions is not related to position preference.

8.(IIIA3a) 1) In convenience sampling, participants are selected based on who is most readily available. The odds of selecting any one individual are not known.
2) In nonprobability sampling, the odds of selecting any one individual are not known.
***3) In probability sampling, subjects are selected in such a way that the odds of their being in the study are known.**
4) In quota sampling, participants are selected using predetermined criteria to reflect the makeup of the population. Quota sampling is a type of nonprobability sampling. The odds of selecting any one individual are not known.

9.(IIIA3b)***1)In quota sampling, researchers select samples based on predetermined quotas that are intended to reflect the makeup of the population. Since quota sampling is not random, the sample may not be truly representative of the population. Quota sampling is low in external validity.**
2) The size of the sample does not affect the validity of the findings based on the use of quota sampling.
3) Quota sampling does not involve selecting alternate participants.
4) The size of the sample does not affect the validity of the procedure when quota sampling is used.

10.(IIIB2c) 1) Bidirectional causation means that the variables may cause each other.
2) Causal modeling is the creation and testing of models that may suggest cause and effect relationships among variables.
3) Multiple correlation is defined as statistical intercorrelations among three or more variables.
***4) The third variable problem is an alternative explanation in correlational research. It is the term used to specify when a correlation between two variables of interest may be the result of an unknown or unmeasured variable that is associated with both measured variables.**

11.(IIIB2a)***1) A correlation between two variables does not imply that one variable causes the other variable.**
2) Even if a positive relationship exists between two variables, correlation does not prove causation.
3) Even if a negative relationship exists between two variables, correlation does not prove causation.
4) Even if a significant relationship exists between two variables, correlation does not imply that they are causally related.

12.(IIIC2b/c)***1) Because cross-sectional studies involve comparing more groups than longitudinal studies, they require more subjects.**
2) Longitudinal designs require more time because participants are followed over a long period of time to see how they change.
3) There is a higher attrition rate in longitudinal designs because participants are followed over a long period of time and some may drop out along the way.
4) Neither cross-sectional nor longitudinal studies permit causal inferences to be drawn.

13.(IIIC2d) 1) A case study is a descriptive record of an individual, not a group. It would not be an appropriate design for this situation.
2) A cross-sectional design compares participants who are at different stages of development. It would not be an appropriate design for this situation.
3) The observational method is one way to collect data, but it does not take advantage of the fact that the researcher is forewarned about the event.
***4) A pretest/posttest design allows the researcher to take measures before and after the program is implemented to see if the program had any effect on racial tension.**

14.(IIID2)*1) **A case study involves an in-depth investigation of an individual's experience and behaviors by a researcher. It does not involve groups of subjects or manipulation of conditions, as do 2), 3), and 4).**
2) A correlational study examines the degree of relationship between two traits, behaviors, or events.
3) A quasi-experimental design is used to assess the effects of different experimental manipulations, but without the use of random assignment of subjects to the conditions.
4) An experimental design is used to assess the effects of different experimental manipulations, with the use of random assignment of subjects to the conditions.

15.(IIID3) 1) This is an example of a participant-observer study in which the researcher actually becomes part of the group being studied.
2) This is an example of naturalistic observation in which behaviors are observed as they occur spontaneously in natural settings.
*3) **This is an example of an archival study in which the researcher examines data that has already been collected for other purposes.**
4) This is an example of a case study in which an individual is described in great detail.

16.(IVA1) 1) The independent variable is manipulated by the experimenter. It is not held constant.
*2) **If manipulating the independent variable brings about a change in the dependent variable, then the experimental hypothesis is supported.**
3) The dependent variable is measured by the experimenter. It is not held constant.
4) The dependent variable is measured and the independent variable is manipulated.

17.(IVA1) 1) The difference in concerns refers to changes in the dependent variable, expressed concerns.
2) Expressed concerns is the dependent variable.
3) The pregnant women are the participants.
*4) **The researcher is examining whether the trimester of pregnancy affects expressed concerns; therefore, trimester of pregnancy is the independent variable.**

18.(IVA3d) 1) Other scales of measurement may also include negative numbers.
*2) **Only a ratio scale has a true zero point.**
3) Both ratio and interval scales have equal intervals between the values.
4) The same statistical tests can be used for both interval and ratio scales of measurement.

19.(IVA4b) 1) The level of agreement between observers is an issue of reliability, not validity.
2) See 1).
*3) **Interrater reliability refers to the degree of agreement between different observers or raters.**
4) Test-retest reliability refers to the consistency between an individual's scores on the same test taken at two or more different times.

20.(IVA5b)*1) **Content validity refers to whether the content of a measure (such as a questionnaire) reflects the content of what is being measured (such as driving safety). This type of validity is** often determined with the help of subject matter experts who judge the measure.
2) External validity refers to how well the findings of an experiment generalize to people and settings that were not tested directly.
3) Face validity refers to the degree to which a manipulation or measurement technique is self-evident.
4) Internal validity refers to the determination that the changes in behavior observed across treatment conditions in the experiment were actually caused by the independent variable.

21.(IVB2) 1) The mechanical malfunction is an extraneous variable, but it has not affected all the groups.
*2) **An extraneous variable is any factor that is not the main focus of the experiment and is not intentionally manipulated. The mechanical malfunction is an extraneous variable, and since it has affected only one of the groups, it is a threat to internal validity.**
3) This question describes the effect of an extraneous variable on one of the groups; it does not discuss the independent variable.
4) The question describes the effect of an extraneous variable on one of the groups; it does not discuss the dependent variable.

22.(IVB2) 1) If the dependent variable varies as a result of changes in the independent variable, this is an indication that the experiment has worked, not that it is confounded.
2) If the dependent variable fails to vary as a result of changes in the independent variable, this is an indication that the experiment has not worked, not that it is confounded.
*3) **If an extraneous variable varies systematically with the independent variable, the study is confounded because it is not clear which variable is responsible for any changes in the dependent variable.**
4) If an extraneous variable fails to vary systematically with the independent variable, this means that the study is not confounded.

23.(IVB2) 1) Confounding occurs when an extraneous variable varies systematically with the independent variable. Kitty litter color is an extraneous variable, but cat's gender does not vary in the study.
*2) **Kitty litter color and kitty litter scent are confounded. Color and scent vary systematically with one another, so it is impossible to tell whether color or scent is responsible for the cat's preference for one kitty litter over the other.**
3) Confounding occurs when an extraneous variable varies systematically with the independent variable. Although scent is an independent variable, frequency of use is a dependent variable.
4) Confounding occurs when an extraneous variable varies systematically with the independent variable. Frequency of use is a dependent variable and cat's gender does not vary in the study.

24.(IVB3c) 1) Ensuring an appropriate number of subjects in the study group has no effect on maturation.
2) Assuring that all subjects are from the same age group has no effect on maturation.

*3) Maturation refers to any internal changes in participants that might affect the dependent variable. Minimizing the duration of the experiment (the time between administering pretest and posttest measures) will minimize the amount of change that could occur.
4) Treatment ordering effects are not relevant to maturation.

25.(IVC3d)***1) External validity refers to the degree to which we can generalize the results of a study to other people and settings. The use of aggregation, multivariate designs, nonreactive measurements, field experiments, and naturalistic observations can enhance a study's external validity.**
2) The measures listed in the question do not affect the operational definitions of the variables.
3) The measures listed in the question do not affect the reliability of the measures.
4) The measures listed in the question do not affect the statistical power.

26.(VA) 1) A between-subjects design can be used regardless of the populations that are included in the study.
2) Participants are placed into experimental conditions by the researcher. Participants normally do not choose which condition they will be in.
3) If participants are each assigned to at least two levels of the independent variable, it is a repeated-measures design.
*4) If each participant is randomly assigned to one level of the independent variable, it is a between-subjects design.

27.(VA1a)***1) Using random assignment eliminates any systematic bias that might cause the groups to differ at the beginning of the study.**
2) Random assignment is not necessary for manipulating independent variables.
3) Random assignment does not protect the privacy of participants.
4) Random assignment involves assigning participants to experimental conditions, not sampling participants from the population.

28.(VA1b) 1) In a mixed design, within-subjects and between-subjects variables are combined in a single experiment. In this question, there is only a between-subjects variable.
2) In a multiple-independent-group design, subjects are randomly assigned to more than two conditions. In this question, only two conditions are present.
*3) In a two-matched-groups design, the groups are matched on a variable (such as age) that is believed to be highly related to the dependent variable.
4) In a factorial design, two or more independent variables are studied simultaneously. In this question, there is only one independent variable, familiarity of music.

29.(VA2a) 1) In a mixed design, within-subjects and between-subjects variables are combined in a single experiment. In this question, there are two between-subject variables.
2) In a two-matched groups design, the groups are matched on a variable that is believed to be highly related

to the dependent variable. In this question, there is no matching variable in the study.
*3) In a between-subjects factorial design, there is more than one independent variable (drug level and time of day) and each participant is assigned to only one condition.
4) In a within-subjects factorial design, each participant is assigned to more than one condition. In this question, each participant is assigned to only one condition.

30.(VB1b) 1) This is not a between-subjects design because each participant experiences more than one experimental condition.
*2) This is a within-subjects one independent variable design because each participant experiences more than one condition, and sleep deprivation is the only independent variable.
3) See 1).
4) This is not a multiple independent variable design because there is only one independent variable, sleep deprivation.

31.(VB2b) 1) History effects occur when events outside the experiment may have caused changes in the dependent variable.
*2) If the conditions are presented in the same order to all participants, participants may have a higher score in the later conditions because they have had a chance to practice, not because of the change in the independent variable.
3) Selection effects occur when there are preexisting differences between the participants in different conditions that may be responsible for their different responses to the independent variable.
4) Mortality effects occur when more participants drop out of one condition than another.

32.(VB3) 1) Block randomization is a technique that involves random assignment of subjects to conditions, but ensures that equal numbers of subjects are in all conditions. It does not control for progressive error.
*2) Counterbalancing is a technique for controlling order effects by distributing progressive error across the different treatment conditions of the experiment.
3) Random assignment is a technique for assigning subjects to treatment conditions so that each subject has an equal chance of being assigned to each treatment condition. It does not control for errors that occur as the experiment progresses.
4) Statistical regression is a naturally occurring phenomenon in which extreme scores tend to regress toward the mean during retesting. It is a source of error, not a technique for controlling error.

33.(VC1)***1) *ABA* is the design being used. *A* represents a phase of the experiment in which measures are taken while no treatment is being administered. (The number of problem behaviors is counted.) *B* represents a phase where measures are taken while treatment is being administered. (The number of problem behaviors is counted while the child undergoes therapy.) Then *A* is repeated.**
2) *BAB* is not correct. See 1).
3) *ABAB* is not correct. See 1).
4) *ABABA* is not correct. See 1).

34.(VIA2) 1) See 2).
*2) **Of the three measures of central tendency (mean, median, mode), the mean is the most sensitive to, and drawn toward, extreme scores such as those occurring in the lower tail of the distribution in the illustration. The median is affected to a lesser degree than the mean. The mode is not affected at all. Therefore, in a negatively skewed distribution such as the one illustrated, the mean would be the lowest value, the median would be the next lowest, and the mode would be the highest.**
3) See 2).
4) See 2).

35.(VIB) 1) Although it is true that the full-time students sampled found the facilities more useful than the part-time students sampled, this statement does not involve any statistical inference.
*2) **Statistical inference refers to making a statement about the population and all its samples based on what we see in the samples we have. Based on the samples of part-time and full-time students in this study, inferences are being made about how all part-time and full-time students at the college feel about the facilities.**
3) It may be true that the full-time students sampled have more opportunity to use the facilities than the part-time students sampled, but the study did not measure this factor.
4) It may be true that the full-time students at the college have more opportunity to use the facilities than the part-time students at the college, but the study did not measure this factor.

36.(VIB4a)*1) **This is a one-way design because only one independent variable (amount of caffeine) is involved. It is a between-subjects design because each participant experiences only one experimental condition.**
2) This is not a repeated-measures design because each participant experiences only one experimental condition.
3) This is not a two-way design because only one independent variable (amount of caffeine) is involved, not two.
4) This is not a two-way design because only one independent variable (amount of caffeine) is involved, not two. It is not a repeated-measures design because each participant experiences only one experimental condition.

37.(VIC2) 1) Replication does not affect how the variables interact with one another in the study.
2) Replication does not affect how the participants will react during the study.
3) Replication does not affect internal validity (the degree to which a researcher is able to state a causal relationship between the independent and dependent variables).
*4) **Replication, or repetition of the experiment with other populations or in other settings, allows the researcher to determine how generalizable (or externally valid) the research findings are.**

38.(VIIA) 1) An article in a popular magazine is not written in a scientific writing style.
2) An editorial in a newspaper is not written in a scientific writing style.
*3) **A research report is written in a scientific style, as is a study published in a medical journal.**
4) An essay in a textbook is not written in a scientific writing style.

39.(VIIB2) 1) Because the abstract is a summary of the report, it would be very difficult to write it before any of the other sections have been written.
2) Because the abstract includes a description and interpretation of the results, it could not be written before the data have been analyzed.
3) Although the abstract appears on the page following the title page, it is usually written after the report is completed.
*4) **The abstract is a summary of the research report and should be written last, after the entire report has been written.**

40.(VIIB4) 1) Characteristics of the sample are described in the participants subsection.
*2) **A description of everything that happened to the participants in the experiment in chronological order is included in the procedure subsection.**
3) Statements of findings are included in the results section.
4) A review of the literature is included in the introduction.

Statistics

1.(IIA1)*1) The mean is the sum of the set of values (1 + 1 + 2 + ... + 11 = 55) divided by the number of values (11): $\frac{55}{11} = 5$
2) 2 is the mode of the data set.
3) 6 is not the mean.
4) 4 is the median of the data set.

2.(IIB1)*1) Since the variance is zero, there is no variation. All the values are the same (all the test scores are 82), so the range is zero.
2) 50 is the midpoint of the test scale.
3) 82 is the mean of the test scores.
4) 100 is the range of the test scale.

3.(IIC3d) 1) 45 is the 12th ranked measure; therefore, it is not the median. 45 is the mode of the set of data.
2) 45.5 is not the 13th ranked observation; therefore, it is not the median.
*3) The rank of the median is $\frac{n+1}{2} = \frac{(25+1)}{2} = 13$.

The median is the 13th ranked observation. The 13th ranked observation is 47.
4) 49 is not the 13th ranked observation; therefore, it is not the median.

4.(IID4) 1) The standardized score of 55 is
$$\frac{(55-70)}{4} = -3.75.$$

*2) The formula for the standardized score is
$z = \frac{(x-\mu)}{\sigma}$. The standard score of 60 is

$\frac{(60-70)}{4} = -2.5$.

3) The standard score of 65 is $\frac{(65-70)}{4} = -1.25$.

4) The standard score of 80 is $\frac{(80-70)}{4} = 2.5$.

5.(IIE4) Assuming that $k \neq 0$,
1) the mean will be increased by $\frac{k}{n}$ if k is positive.
2) the median will change as every number is shifted by k units.
3) the mode will change because every value in the data set is changed.
*4) **the range will remain unchanged. The lowest and highest observations will change by the same amount, so the difference will remain the same.**

6.(IIIA,C) 1) This scatterplot shows a weak positive relationship; therefore, the correlation coefficient is a small positive number, but is not closest to zero.
2) This scatterplot shows a strong positive relationship; therefore, the correlation coefficient is a positive number close to one.
3) This scatterplot shows a strong negative relationship; therefore, the correlation coefficient is a negative number close to -1.
*4) **This scatterplot shows a random pattern relationship; therefore, the correlation coefficient is a number closest to zero.**

7.(IIIB)*1) **Because the slope = 1/2 = 0.5, for each two-unit increase in x there is a one-unit increase in y.**
2) Here, x and y are incorrectly reversed.
3) The value of $\bar{y}$ is actually 3 units less than $0.5\bar{x}$.
4) The correlation between x and y is positive because the slope of the regression line is positive.

8.(IIIC) 1) The slope of the regression line is negative, so the correlation must be negative.
*2) **The slope is negative and all points fit the line perfectly. This is a perfect negative linear relationship; correlation coefficient $r = -1$.**
3) When the points fit the line perfectly, the correlation can only be 1.00 or -1.00.
4) See 3).

9.(IVA1a) 1) $54 = (2)(3)(3)(3)$ which does not represent the number of any three-letter combinations.
2) $676 = (1)(26)(26)$ which represents the number of three-letter combinations where the first letter is W only or R only.
*3) **$1352 = (2)(26)(26)$ which represents the number of three-letter combinations where the first letter must be a W or a K.**
4) $17,576 = (26)(26)(26)$ which represents the number of any three-letter combinations.

10.(IVB2a) 1) $0 = P(A \text{ and } B)$.
2) If A and B are independent, then $P(A \text{ and } B) = P(A)P(B) = (.4)(.5) = .2$.
3) If A and B are independent, then $P(A \text{ or } B) = P(A) + P(B) - P(A \text{ and } B) = .7$.
*4) **Since A and B are mutually exclusive, then $P(A \text{ or } B) = P(A) + P(B) = .4 + .5 = .9$.**

11.(VA1a) 1) This is not a probability distribution because it has a negative entry.
2) This is not a probability distribution because it has two negative entries.
*3) **A probability distribution must satisfy these rules: $P(x)$ can only be between 0 and 1 inclusive, and the sum of the $P(x)$ values must be equal to 1. This distribution satisfies both rules.**
4) This is not a probability distribution because the sum of $P(x)$ values is not 1.

12.(VA2d)*1)
$$m = np = 60\left(\frac{1}{6}\right) = 10; = s = \sqrt{np(1-p)}$$
$$= \sqrt{60\left(\frac{1}{6}\right)\left(\frac{5}{6}\right)} = \sqrt{8.33} = 2.89$$

2) $\mu = np = 60\left(\frac{1}{6}\right) = 10; 8.33 = (2.89)^2 = $ the variance.

3) 30 and 3.87 are the mean and standard deviation of a binomial distribution with $n = 60$ and $p = 60$ and $p = \frac{1}{2}$

4) 30 and 15 are the mean and variance of a binomial distribution with $n = 60$ and $p = \frac{1}{2}$.

13.(VB2f) *1) $P(fail) = P(x < 70) = P\left(z < \frac{70-75}{5}\right)$
$$= P(z < -1) = .1587 \approx .16$$

2) $.34 = P(70 < x < 75)$
3) $.68 = P(70 < x < 80)$
4) $.84 = P(x > 70) = P(pass)$

14.(VIA2) 1) When the population is divided into stratified groups, it is a stratified sample.
2) When the sample consists of every nth subject, it is a systematic sample.
3) When the sample uses only subjects that have been screened for common traits, it is a judgment or nonprobabilistic sample.
*4) **When samples of the same size have the same probability of being selected, it is a simple random sample. Each set of n units has an equal chance of being selected.**

15.(VIB3) 1) 12 is the standard deviation of the population.
*2) **The standard error of the sample means is**
$$\frac{s}{\sqrt{n}} = \frac{12}{\sqrt{36}} = 2.$$
3) 36 is the sample size.
4) 72 is the mean of the population.

16.(VIC) 1) Cluster sampling is based on the random selection of clusters of elements from a population.
2) In simple random sampling, every possible sample of a given size has the same chance of being selected.
3) In stratified random sampling, first the population is divided into strata, then a random sample is selected from each stratum.

*4) This is a classic case of systematic sampling. The first item (#16) is randomly chosen. Then items are chosen at fixed intervals (every 25th).

17.(VIIA) 1) A change of sample size will change the length of the confidence interval for the population mean.
*2) A change of sample mean will change the midpoint of the confidence interval for the population mean.
3) A change of sample standard deviation will change the length of the confidence interval for the population mean.
4) A change of confidence level will change the length of the confidence interval for the population mean.

18.(VIIA1)*1) Increasing the confidence level and decreasing the sample size will increase the length of the confidence interval.
2) Decreasing the confidence level and increasing the sample size will decrease the length of the confidence interval.
3) Increasing both the confidence level and the sample size may increase or decrease the length of the confidence interval.
4) Decreasing both the confidence level and the sample size may increase or decrease the length of the confidence interval.

19.(VIIA2c) Use t because sample size is small.

1) $27.75 \pm 3.51 = \bar{x} \pm z_{.025} \dfrac{s}{\sqrt{n}}$

2) $27.75 \pm 4.60 = \bar{x} \pm z_{5,.025} \dfrac{s}{\sqrt{n}}$

*3) $n=5, \bar{x}=27.75, s^2=16$. The 95% confidence interval for the true mean is

$\bar{x} \pm t_{4,.025} \dfrac{s}{\sqrt{n}} = 27.75 \pm 2.776 \dfrac{4}{\sqrt{5}} = 27.75 \pm 4.97$.

4) $27.75 \pm 14.02 = \bar{x} \pm z_{.025} \dfrac{s^2}{\sqrt{n}}$

20.(VIIB3)*1) $(2430, 2620) = (2525 - 95, 2525 + 95)$. The number of students enrolled is a binomial distribution with $n = 5490$, $p = .46$, which is approximately normally distributed with mean = $np = 2525$ and standard deviation = $\sqrt{np(1-p)} = 37$.

Therefore, a 99% confidence interval for the number of students who will enroll is $2525 \pm (z._{005})(37) = 2525 \pm (2.57)(37) = 2525 \pm 95$.
2) $(2453, 2597) = (2525 - 72, 2525 + 72)$
$= 2525 \pm (z_{.005})(37)$
3) $(2465, 2585) = (2525 - 60, 2525 + 60)$
$= 2525 \pm (z_{.025})(37)$
4) $(0.443, 0.477) = \left(\dfrac{2430}{5490}, \dfrac{2620}{5490}\right)$ is the 99% confidence interval for the proportion of students who enroll.

21.(VIIIA2) 1) $.044 = P(z > 1.71)$. This is the P-value of a one-sided test.
2) $.05 = P(z < -1.645)$ or $P(z > 1645)$. This is the P-value of a one-sided test when $z = 1.645$.
*3) $.087 = 2(1 - .9564) = 2P(z > 1.71)$. This is the P-value of the test.

4) $.10 = 2P(z > 1.645)$. This is the P-value of a two-sided test when $z = 1.645$.

22.(VIIIC2)*1) Since the population variances are unknown but are assumed to be equal, test statistic t and pooled variance calculated from the sample variances should be used.
2) This test procedure is only for normal populations with unknown and unequal variances.
3) This test procedure is only for large sample sizes and populations with unknown and equal variances.
4) This test procedure is only for large sample sizes and populations with unknown and unequal variances.

23.(VIIIB2) 1) This conclusion means accept H_0.
2) This conclusion means do not accept H_a.
*3) This conclusion means accept H_a. The critical value $z_a = z_{0.5} = 1.645$. $z = 2.8 > 1.645$. Therefore, we reject H_0 and accept H_a.
4) This conclusion means do not claim $p > .80$.

24.(VIIID) 1) 0.7 is not closest to 1.15.
*2) $\hat{p}_1 = .47$, $\hat{p}_2 = .38$, $\hat{p} = \dfrac{(.47)(82)+(.38)(78)}{82+78}$

$= \dfrac{39+30}{160} = \dfrac{69}{160} = .43$.

Therefore, the observed value for the z test is

$\dfrac{\hat{p}_1 - \hat{p}_2}{\sqrt{\hat{p}(1-\hat{p})\left(\dfrac{1}{n_1}+\dfrac{1}{n_2}\right)}} = \dfrac{.47 - .38}{\sqrt{.43 \star .57\left(\dfrac{1}{82}+\dfrac{1}{78}\right)}}$

$= \dfrac{.09}{\sqrt{.006131}} = \dfrac{.09}{.0783} = 1.15$

3) 1.6 is not closest to 1.15.
4) 2.53 is not closest to 1.15.

25.(VIIIE2) 1) The chi-square test for goodness of fit is used to determine whether observed data fit a theoretical distribution.
*2) The chi-square test for independence of effects is most appropriate. "Men and women have different preferences" suggests a test of independence.
3) Means are <u>not</u> being compared.
4) See 3).

World Population

1.(IB) 1) Brazil does not have the population base to make it the most populated country by the year 2050.
2) China has the largest population today, but it has a relatively low fertility rate.
*3) India's high fertility rate will cause it to become the world's most populous country by the year 2050.
4) The United States has both a low birth rate and a low death rate that results in a low growth rate.

2.(IB) 1) A low mortality and low fertility pattern is associated with economically developed countries.

*2) A low mortality and high fertility pattern is associated with most economically developing countries.
3) A high mortality and low fertility pattern rarely occurs anywhere.
4) A high mortality and high fertility pattern is uncommon because mortality has declined substantially throughout the world in recent decades.

3.(IIA) ***1) Malthus specifically mentioned delaying marriage as a means of controlling population growth.**
2) Raising wages may lead to an increase in fertility rather than a decline in fertility.
3) Although subsidized education would have an indirect effect on fertility, Malthus believed deferring marriage would directly affect population growth.
4) Taxing wealthy incomes would have little or no impact on overall fertility rates, since people who are wealthy constitute only a small percentage of any country's population.

4.(IIB) 1) Darwin was not concerned with class differences as a factor in economic development.
2) Malthus focused on the relationship between food resources and population growth.
*3) Marx emphasized the importance of class differences in his economic and historical works. He argued that the consequences of capitalism are overpopulation and poverty for the majority with a few elite capitalists reaping the benefits of development. In a socialist (classless) society, population growth would be readily absorbed by economic development with no side effects.
4) Mill is best known for his work on the nature of liberty.

5.(IIE) 1) Boserup's work is associated with the argument that population growth may stimulate economic development.
*2) Easterlin argued in his relative income hypothesis that relative economic well-being and economic upward mobility will lead to greater fertility and larger families.
3) Omran's work is associated with historical demographic patterns.
4) Ravenstein's work is associated with a classic theory on migration.

6.(IIIA1) ***1) CBR is defined as the total number of live births in a given year divided by the total midyear population, multiplied by 1,000.**
2) GFR is defined as the total number of live births in a given year divided by the total number of woman in the childbearing ages, multiplied by 1,000.
3) GRR is defined as the number of daughters that a female just born may expect to have in her lifetime, assuming that birth rates stay the same and ignoring her chances of survival through her reproductive years.
4) TFR is defined as an estimate of the average number of children that would be born alive to each woman if the current age-specific fertility rates remained constant.

7.(IIIA3) 1) This is not a formula for measuring fertility.
*2) The CWR is a census-based measure of fertility, calculated as the ratio of children aged 0–4 to the number of women aged 15–49, multiplied by 1,000.
3) See 1).
4) See 1).

8.(IIIA6) 1) The CWR is concerned with the total number of children aged 0–4, both female and male.
2) The GFR is concerned with the total number of live births, both female and male, in a given year.
*3) The GRR is concerned with female births, only.
4) The TFR is concerned with the average number of children, both female and male, that would be born to each woman if the current age-specific birth rates remained constant.

9.(IVA2) 1) Census data, only does not provide the data on mortality needed to calculate the ASDR.
2) Vital registration data, only does not provide the age-specific data needed to calculate the ASDR.
*3) Both census and vital registration data are required to calculate the ASDR. The number of people of a given age and sex who died in a given year is obtained from the vital registration data, and the total population of people of that age and sex is obtained from the census data.
4) Sample survey data do not include the total population and population pyramids are visual presentations of the age-sex distribution of a society.

10.(IVB2) 1) Accidents are a relatively minor cause of death in the United States.
2) Communicable diseases such as influenza are not a major factor in mortality rates in the United States.
*3) Degenerative illnesses such as heart disease are the major cause of death in the United States.
4) Homicides are a very minor cause of death in the United States.

11.(III,IV) 1) Country A has the highest crude death rate, highest crude birth rate, highest infant mortality rate, and highest total fertility rate. These demographic rates are characteristic of an economically developing country.
*2) Country B has the lowest crude birth rate, a low crude death rate, the lowest infant mortality rate, and the lowest total fertility rate. These demographic rates are characteristic of an economically developed country.
3) Country C has a high crude birth rate, a low crude death rate, a high infant mortality rate, and a high total fertility rate. These demographic rates are characteristic of an economically developing country.
4) Country D has a reasonably low crude birth rate, the lowest crude death rate, a very low infant mortality rate, and a total fertility rate that is almost at replacement level. These demographic rates are characteristic of a newly industrialized country that is at the verge of achieving demographic transition.

12.(III,IV) ***1) The annual growth rate is calculated by subtracting the crude death rate from the crude birth rate, dividing by 1,000, and multiplying the result by 100 to express it as a percent. Country A clearly has the highest annual growth rate of 3% calculated as $((50 - 20)/1,000) \times 100 = 3.0\%$.**
2) The annual growth rate for Country B is $((11 - 10)/1,000) \times 100 = 0.1\%$.

3) The annual growth rate for Country D is ((20 − 5)/1,000) X 100 = 1.5%.
4) The annual growth rate for Country E is ((29 − 6)/1,000) X 100 = 2.3%.

13.(III,IV)*1) Country A has the highest crude death rate, highest crude birth rate, highest infant mortality rate, and highest total fertility rate. These demographic rates are characteristic of a sub-Saharan African nation.
2) Country B has the lowest crude birth rate, a low crude death rate, the lowest infant mortality rate, and the lowest total fertility rate. These demographic rates are characteristic of an economically developed country.
3) Country C has a high crude birth rate, a low crude death rate, a high infant mortality rate, and a high total fertility rate. These demographic rates are characteristic of an economically developing country. Country C's extremely low mortality rate is not associated with a Sub-Saharan African country.
4) Country E has a high crude birth rate, a very low crude death rate, a medium infant mortality rate, and a high total fertility rate. Country E's extremely low mortality rate is not associated with a Sub-Saharan African country.

14.(III,IV)*1) Country A has the highest total fertility rate of all the countries listed. A high total fertility rate is indicative of a society having traditional gender roles where women have substantially less power than men.
2) Country B is likely to have the greatest gender equality given its very low total fertility rate.
3) Country D appears to be moving toward gender equality given its fertility rate of 2.3.
4) Country E's fertility rate indicates a country with traditional gender roles; however, Country E's data is not as conclusive as Country A's.

15.(III,IV) 1) The natural increase is the difference between the crude birth rate and crude death rate, divided by 1,000, and multiplied by 100 to express it as a percent. Country A has the highest natural increase of 3.0%.
*2) Country B has the lowest natural increase of 0.1%.
3) Country D has a natural increase of 1.5%.
4) Country E has a natural increase of 2.3%.

16.(VB3) 1) Migration ratio is calculated as follows:
Net migration   X 1,000
Births−deaths
*2) This formula calculates the crude net migration rate.
3) In-migration rate is calculated as follows:
Total in-migrants   X 1,000
    Total midyear population
4) Out-migration rate is calculated as follows:
Total out-migrants   X 1,000
    Total midyear population

17.(VC1) 1) Climate is an underlying factor in some migration but it is not considered to be the major determinant.
*2) Employment opportunities appear to be the primary motivation for migration today.

3) Family influences migration patterns but it is not the major determinant.
4) Availability and cost of housing are also important influences but they are not the major determinants.

18.(VC2) 1) People who have not completed high school are the least likely to migrate.
2) People who have completed high school, only are more likely to migrate than people who have not completed high school but are less likely to migrate than people who have attended or completed college.
3) Some college education influences migratory patterns but not to the same degree as it does for people who have graduated from college.
*4) People who have completed college are the most likely to migrate due to greater employment opportunities.

19.(VC3) 1) Dual labor market theory attempts to explain why different groups of workers are willing to work for different wage scales within a society.
2) Neoclassical economic theory argues that migration is a process of labor adjustment caused by differences in the supply and demand for labor.
3) Network theory examines how employment patterns are influenced by family and social networks.
*4) World systems theory examines the economic relationships between the developed and developing nations of the world.

20.(VIA)*1) China instituted a one-child policy and was successful in reducing the general fertility rate.
2) India does not have a one-child policy and has not reduced the general fertility rate.
3) Japan has a low fertility rate without a one-child policy.
4) Thailand has reduced the general fertility rate without a one-child policy.

21.(VIB)*1) Due to its higher fertility rate, India will surpass China as the world's most populous country.
2) India's population base and growth rate is much higher than that found in the United States.
3) Given current trends, there is no indication that India's fertility rates will drop sharply.
4) India does not attract large numbers of immigrants.

22.(VIC)*1) Sub-Saharan African nations have the highest fertility rates in the world; therefore, Africa's share of the world's population will substantially increase.
2) Given China's relatively low fertility rate, Asia's share of the world's population will decline.
3) Given the decline in fertility rates that many Latin American societies are experiencing, Latin America's share of the world's population will decline.
4) Given current demographic patterns, Western Europe will experience a net decline in population.

23.(VIC) 1) Higher educational status for men is not consistently associated with lower fertility rates.
2) Lower educational status for men tends to lead to higher fertility rates.
*3) Higher educational status for women is strongly associated with lower fertility rates.

4) Lower educational status for women tends to lead to higher fertility rates.

24.(VIIB1) 1) The CPI measures the cost of basic goods and services. It does not measure a nation's income.
2) Stock market performance does not measure a nation's income.
3) The GRR is the proportion of all births that are female. It does not measure a nation's income.
*4) The GNP measures the total goods and services produced by a society and is the most commonly used measure of a nation's income.

25.(VIIB2) 1) Capitalists generally argue that population growth may stimulate economic development.
2) Nationalists generally argue that population growth stimulates economic development.
*3) Neo-Malthusians view population growth as a barrier to economic development.
4) Neo-Marxists view the unequal distribution of resources, not population growth, as the major detriment to economic development.

26.(VIIB3) 1) Core nations are not self-sufficient in energy sources and have to import large quantities of oil.
2) Core nations have both high incomes and high rates of consumption.
3) By attracting immigrants from economically developing countries, core nations have lower emigration and higher immigration rates.
*4) Core nations dictate economic terms to the rest of the world and peripheral and semi-peripheral nations are dependent upon decisions made by the core nations.

27.(VIIB3) 1) Marxists would argue just the opposite of this statement.
2) Marxists would be highly critical of this elitist approach to population.
3) This statement reflects the Malthusian perspective.
*4) This statement reflects the classic Marxist perspective of examining social structure, both political and economic, to understand development.

28.(VIIC2) 1) This statement describes a political reaction to an economic policy. It does not describe the green revolution.
2) This statement does not describe the green revolution.
*3) The green revolution is the name given to the development of enriched varieties of wheat and rice.
4) This statement describes the conversion of landmass for agricultural purposes. It does not describe the green revolution.

29.(VIID1) 1) Immigration policies were not discussed at the 1994 conference.
2) China's fertility policy was not part of the 1994 Conference.
3) High mortality rates as a means of reducing population is neither reasonable nor an ethical policy to implement for population control. This policy was not discussed at the 1994 conference.
*4) Women's roles were a central theme of this conference. The Program of Action emphasized the empowerment of women, gender equality, and reduction of infant and maternal mortality rates.

30.(VIIE2) 1) Advertising expensive cars in the mass media constitutes a mass marketing campaign not aimed at any one particular group.
*2) Starting a college radio station that plays only Top 40 songs targets college students, a specific market segment.
3) Using population data to determine the number of televisions to stock at an appliance store is an example of market research.
4) Hiring department store salespersons with different ethnic and racial backgrounds establishes a broader-based appeal.

Human Resource Management

1.(IA2) 1) An organization's strengths and weaknesses must be determined in light of the organization's mission and goals; therefore, they are determined in the second phase of the strategy formulation.
2) Part of the second phase of the strategy formulation is the determination of an organization's external opportunities and threats.
*3) The first step in strategy formulation is definition of the organization's mission and goals. The mission and goals will define the boundaries and dimensions of the internal and external analyses.
4) Assessing the knowledge, skills, and abilities of employees is part of the third phase.

2.(IA) 1) A reluctance to take risks is not associated with any business strategy.
2) Companies that follow a cost leadership strategy require employees who focus on short-term results.
3) Companies that follow a cost leadership strategy require employees with high concern for quantity.
*4) Companies that follow a differentiation strategy require employees with high tolerance for ambiguity. A differentiation strategy involves setting a company's products and services apart from its competitors; therefore, the company must be highly creative in its approach to the market. This means frequent changes in products and services and requires an employee tolerance for ambiguity.

3.(IIB3) 1) The ADA does not require employers to identify why a job should be done.
*2) The ADA requires employers to make reasonable accommodations that will allow individuals who are disabled to perform essential functions of the job. Therefore, essential job tasks must be included in job descriptions.
3) Generic job descriptors would not identify the essential job functions and tasks for individual jobs; therefore, compliance with the ADA would be impossible.
4) The ADA addresses the issue of essential job functions and does not make any reference to the reasonability of job descriptors.

4.(IIC1)*1) **The four-fifths rule states that, to avoid disparate impact, applicants in the underrepresented group should have at least an 80% chance of being selected as applicants in the majority group. In this question, the selection ratio for whites is 50% (35 selected out of 70 applicants; 35 divided by 70 = 50). The selection ratio for blacks must be 80% of the selection ratio for whites, or 40% (80% × 50% = 40%). Forty percent of the 30 black applicants equals 12 (30 x 40% = 12). Twelve black applicants should be selected to avoid disparate impact.**
2) See 1).
3) See 1).
4) See 1).

5.(IID2) 1) A BFOQ is used when a job requires that one of the protected categories of sex, race, or national origin must be used in hiring people, such as a locker room attendant in a women's locker room.
2) An EEO-1 report is an annual report required by regulatory agencies. It is designed to show how well organizations are complying with fair employment laws and regulations.
3) A quota system involves hiring a specific number or percentage of individuals based on a protected category, for example, hiring a specific percentage of women from the applicant pool based on their sex, only. This is a potentially illegal practice.
*4) **An affirmative action plan is a document that includes four parts: a utilization analysis, an availability analysis, identification of problem areas, and a listing of corrective actions (including specific goals and timetables) to be undertaken to resolve problem areas.**

6.(IIIB1) 1) A forecast of external supply is determined by labor market surveys on unemployment and employment rates of various job categories.
2) A forecast of business activity is an estimate of the future business activity based on the current business activity of the company, and is used as one factor in estimating demand.
3) A forecast of labor demand is estimated from future business activity and any significant organizational changes in the company's business plan, such as downsizing.
*4) **A forecast of the internal labor supply of the company is based on a workforce analysis of how many people are currently in job categories and recent employee movements through retirements, promotions, transfers, voluntary turnovers, or terminations.**

7.(IIIB1) 1) The Delphi technique is not a statistical technique.
2) The nominal group technique is not a statistical technique.
3) The labor force participation rate is not a statistical technique.
*4) **The transitional matrix is a statistical technique that describes the probability of employees changing jobs during a specific time period.**

8.(IVB1) 1) Since the content of narrative interviews is not controlled and their job relevance is not assured, neither validity nor reliability can be assumed.
2) Nondirective interviews are simply a conversation and their job relevance cannot be guaranteed; therefore, validity is highly questionable.
*3) **Questions in a structured interview are planned and each applicant is asked the questions in the same manner; research has proven these interviews have the highest reliability and validity.**
4) Since questions in an unstructured interview are not planned, there is no consistency between interviews; therefore, there is no reliability.

9.(IVB1)*1) **Negligent hiring occurs when an employer hires a new employee who subsequently causes injury to another person, and the employer should have known about the new employee's propensity to commit injurious acts from the employee's past record. Reference checks can minimize the risk of negligent hiring because they supply objective historical information.**
2) Honesty tests are subjective; they do not provide objective information about the new employee's past record. New employees can lie about their past on these tests.
3) Job experience questionnaires only supply information on previous jobs, dates, and positions held. Job experience questionnaires do not contain information about a person's propensity to injure others.
4) Ability tests measure a person's ability to do the job. Ability tests are not related to a person's propensity to injure others.

10.(IVC1) 1) Job analysis is a technique for determining the tasks and responsibilities for a given job, as well as the knowledge, skills, and abilities required to perform that job.
*2) **Utilization analysis is a report of the percentages of men, women, and members of historically underrepresented groups employed by an organization. It is the first step in determining if the company is in compliance with Title VII of the Civil Rights Act, and is required in the annual EEO-1 report sent to the federal government.**
3) Availability analysis is a report of the numbers of men, women, and members of historically underrepresented groups within the relevant labor market from which an organization draws its employees.
4) Yield ratio analysis reports the numbers of applicants who successfully progress from each phase of the selection process to the next compared to the numbers who originally entered each phase.

11.(IVC2) 1) Title VII of the Civil Rights Act of 1964 prohibits discrimination on race, sex, and national origin. It does not address medical examinations.
2) The ADEA prohibits discrimination on age (over 40). It does not address medical examinations.
3) The Vocational Rehabilitation Act of 1973 requires employers who have federal contracts to take affirmative action toward qualified individuals who have disabilities. It does not address medical examinations.
*4) **The ADA outlaws the use of medical examinations prior to the issuance of a job offer. This is one of the most important provisions of the ADA in protecting people with disabilities from being discriminated against in the hiring process.**

12.(VA2) 1) Customers only see one aspect of employees' job behaviors and some employees are never seen by

customers. Therefore, evaluating the success of a performance appraisal system based on endorsement by customers would be erroneous.
*2) **Acceptance by employees is critical to the success of a performance appraisal system.**
3) Performance appraisal systems are not used in determining pension levels.
4) Performance appraisal systems are not used to assess profitability which is a company-level measure based on revenues and expenses.

13. (VA3) 1) BARS do not involve setting goals. BARS is a method built on identifying critical incidents of job performance to define different levels of performance on the dimensions of the job.
2) The critical incident technique does not involve the joint setting of goals.
*3) **MBO begins with the establishment of mutually acceptable goals by the employee and the employee's supervisor.**
4) Assessment centers focus on multiple methods of evaluating job performance using simulated tasks such as in-basket exercises, role playing, and leaderless group discussions.

14. (VA6) 1) Decision-making training shows supervisors good strategies to use in making decisions and helps them to identify inferential mistakes inference supervisors often make in appraising employee performance.
2) Observation training shows supervisors how to improve the manner in which they observe behavior and to identify important behaviors that affect employee performance.
*3) **Rater error training shows supervisors common errors that are made in evaluating employee performance and discusses techniques for avoiding errors.**
4) Frame-of-reference training attempts to reduce inter-rater error by developing a common frame-of-reference (or perspective) among raters who are evaluating employee performance.

15. (VB3) *1) **Greater work satisfaction is one of the four personal and work outcomes of the job enrichment approach to job redesign. Job enrichment focuses on increasing the meaningfulness and complexity of boring jobs.**
2) Job enrichment will most likely increase training requirements since it increases the complexity of the job tasks.
3) Physical requirements are not addressed by the job enrichment approach.
4) Increased performance feedback is one of the five aspects of the process of job enrichment. Therefore, it is not an advantage or outcome of the process.

16. (VIA2) *1) **An apprenticeship is job training under the direction of an experienced employee.**
2) Action learning involves classroom instruction, an applied learning project, and classroom presentation of project results.
3) Behavior modeling is a technique for teaching interpersonal skills, not job training.
4) Cooperation training focuses on interpersonal skills, not job training.

17. (VIA2) 1) An organizational analysis is used to determine where in the organization individuals need to be trained.
2) Performance evaluations are used to determine how well a specific employee is carrying out the tasks that comprise a job.
*3) **An individual analysis is used to determine the current skills and knowledge of the employees to be trained.**
4) Job analysis is used to establish what the individual knowledge, skills, and abilities are for a particular job.

18. (VIC1) 1) Career planning provides self-assessment and goal setting for any individual's career; it is not limited to employees being considered for higher-level managerial positions.
2) Management forecasting refers to the process of determining what the supply and demand will be for management positions in the future but it does not assess who will fill those positions.
*3) **Succession planning is part of the supply analysis done in human resource planning. It is a systematic and documented plan for replacement of managerial employees by identifying employees at lower levels who are judged to have managerial potential.**
4) Trend analysis reports the patterns of employees movement into, within, and out of an organization.

19. (VIE2) 1) Insisting that management shut down a dangerous work site is not one of the five rights granted to employees under OSHA, and would be in violation of the employment contract for most companies.
*2) **Requesting an OSHA inspection of a potentially unsafe working condition is one of the five rights granted to workers under OSHA.**
3) Having the employer pay damages for exposure to dangerous substances is not one of the five rights granted to employees under OSHA.
4) Having OSHA remove dangerous substances is not one of the five rights granted to employees under OSHA and would be outside the authority of the OSHA inspector.

20. (VIIA1) 1) Since only jobs within the company are evaluated, external equity cannot be determined using job evaluation. External equity involves comparing similar jobs in different companies.
2) Individual equity focuses on whether individuals feel that their compensation is fair relative to their contribution when compared to others performing the same job in the same company.
*3) **Job evaluation is the primary tool for assessing internal equity, the fairness of compensation between jobs within the same company.**
4) Interorganizational equity is another term for external equity. See 1).

21. (VIIA1) *1) **A wage and salary survey provides information on the wage and salary levels by job category of an organization's competitors. The survey is done to determine the external equity of the organization's compensation system.**
2) The employees' level of satisfaction would be determined by an employee opinion poll or attitude survey focused on satisfaction with pay policies.

3) Internal equity of jobs would be determined by a job evaluation study.
4) Internal equity of pay would be determined by a job evaluation study, followed by an examination of each person's salary in relation to the salary range.

22.(VIIB2)★1) **Gainsharing plans are incentive systems in which productivity gains are shared with the employees in terms of financial rewards. The primary focus is on productivity improvement.**
2) Gainsharing plans are often found in unionized companies.
3) Gainsharing plans would be a weak bargaining trade-off since both the company and the employees share jointly in productivity gains.
4) Turnover and absenteeism rates are not related to gainsharing plans.

23.(VIIIB1) 1)The AAA maintains a list of qualified arbitrators for the settlement of grievances, but it has no say in union representation elections.
★2) **The Wagner Act of 1935 established the NLRB. One of the NLRB's major functions is to determine the appropriate bargaining unit for a union representation election.**
3) The DOL is the federal agency that administers labor legislation, but it has no say in union representation elections.
4) The FMCS maintains a list of qualified arbitrators for the settlement of grievances, but it has no say in union representation elections.

24.(VIIIC2)★1) **During a union campaign, management may present its opinion about the ramifications of unionization. This is one of the most important management activities specifically permitted under the NLRA.**
2) Under the NLRA, management is expressly forbidden from interfering with any workers right to unionize.
3) Under the NLRA, the questioning of employees individually about their union preferences is an unfair labor practice.
4) Under the NLRA, management making promises contingent upon the rejection of a union is an unfair labor practice.

25.(VIIID1) 1)Integrative bargaining seeks solutions that benefit both management and the union. It is a win-win negotiation.
★2) **Distributive bargaining focuses on dividing a fixed economic pie between management and labor. The resources are fixed so that if one party gains, then the other must lose. It is a win-lose negotiation.**
3) Multiemployer bargaining involves the union negotiating with more than one employer at the same time, as is done in the auto industry. The negotiation can be win-lose or win-win.
4) Intraorganizational bargaining refers to the fact that there are more than two parties to any labor-management negotiation. Employees with high seniority may have entirely different demands than do newer employees. It can involve both win-lose and win-win negotiation.

Labor Relations

1.(IA3) 1) Industrial unions are organized by industry, not by political jurisdictions. Most laws that cover industrial union activities are federal rather than state or local.
2) Craft unions are organized by trade, not by political jurisdictions. Most laws that cover craft union activities are federal rather than state or local.
★3) **Public-sector unions are organized according to political jurisdictions and most of the laws and policies that cover their union activities are state and local. Public-sector union membership remains stable, maintaining their political influence.**
4) Private-sector unions deal primarily with private companies, not elected public officials. The laws that govern their relations with their employers are generally made at the national, rather than state or local level. Private-sector union membership is declining, reducing their political influence.

2.(IB2) 1) The AFL supported the war effort and the government.
2) The CIO did not exist until after World War I.
3) The KOL had disappeared by World War I.
★4) **The IWW was a revolutionary federation that opposed World War I and called for the overthrow of capitalism in the United States.**

3.(IC2) 1) Autocratic governance is the equivalent of a dictatorship, which is contrary to the laws stipulating how unions must be governed.
2) Bureaucracy is a form of organizational structure, not a governance process.
★3) **In the democratic governance of a union, power, authority, and legitimacy arise from the consent of the governed. The law requires that union officers be elected in free elections.**
4) Theocratic governance is directed by divine guidance. Unions are not religious organizations.

4.(IC2) 1) Union members do not have to attend 50 percent of local meetings to obtain strike benefits.
2) Bargaining unit members do not have to vote for the union to receive strike benefits.
3) Bargaining unit members do not have to show support for union leadership to receive strike benefits.
★4) **Unions can terminate or reduce strike benefits for individual members who work for other employers or do not perform their strike duties.**

5.(IIB1) 1) The Norris-LaGuardia Act prohibited federal courts from issuing injunctions against lawful union activities.
★2) **The Taft-Hartley Act added a list of unfair union practices to the unfair management practices contained in the Wagner Act.**
3) The Wagner Act was a pro-labor act that included only unfair management labor practices.
4) Under the Clayton Act, unions were no longer subject to antitrust restrictions.

6.(IIB2)★1) **Right-to-work laws prohibit union membership as a condition of employment.**

2) Under right-to-work laws, contract clauses requiring union membership as a precondition to employment are prohibited.
3) An agency shop allows an employee to decline union membership but still pay dues and fees. An agency shop would be prohibited under right-to-work laws.
4) This legal principle was not established under right-to-work laws.

7.(IIB2)***1) The employer is forbidden to give financial assistance to a union because this would undermine the union's independence in representing its members.**
2) The employer has the right to make the case against voting for the union but cannot threaten employees for voting for the union or promise a specific benefit for voting against the union.
3) The employer can speak to individuals about the advantages of not joining a union under the same conditions as detailed in 2).
4) The employer is required by law to consider a union demand, but not to accede to it.

8.(IIB2) 1) An arbitrator's issuance of a binding decision on the contract is not an appropriate remedy for a company that refuses to bargain in good faith.
2) The NLRB is limited in its remedial powers and does not have the authority to make a binding decision on the contract.
***3) When a violation of good faith bargaining is found, the NLRB can order the violator to cease and desist bad faith bargaining and to comply with the law or be subject to fines.**
4) NLRB decisions can be appealed to the courts; however, the initial step is for the NLRB to issue a cease-and-desist order.

9.(IIC1) 1) The National Labor Relations Act governs labor relations in the private sector.
***2) The Civil Service Reform Act governs labor relations in the federal government.**
3) The Taft-Hartley Act is an amendment to the National Labor Relations Act and pertains only to the private sector.
4) The Landrum-Griffin Act primarily governs the internal governance practices of private sector unions.

10.(IIIC) 1) Professional employees are protected by the act.
2) Plant guards are nonsupervisory employees who are protected by the act.
3) Major-league baseball players are nonsupervisory employees who are protected by the act.
***4) Supervisory employees are considered management and are not protected by the act.**

11.(IIIC) 1) Market constraints affect the number and types of employees, but not the community of interests among those employed.
2) The jurisdiction of the union will determine which union is interested in organizing a group of workers, not whether all of those workers have a community of interest for purposes of collective bargaining.
3) The number of employees is not a relevant concern in the determination of the appropriate bargaining unit.
***4) Community of interests refers to the mutuality of interest among employees in bargaining for wages, hours, and working conditions and is frequently used by the NLRB to determine the appropriate bargaining unit.**

12.(IIIE)***1) Strikers continue to be members of the bargaining unit even while on strike, therefore, they have a right to vote in the election.**
2) Not allowing strikers to vote would violate their rights as members of the bargaining unit.
3) The right to carry out a legal strike is protected for all workers in all situations by the National Labor Relations Act.
4) The National Labor Relations Act is enforced by the National Labor Relations Board, not by the courts.

13.(IIIE1) 1) Contract settlement is an agreement between management and the union representing the employees on the terms of the contract.
***2) Union organizing is the process by which a union is either granted or not granted the right to represent employees in collective bargaining with management. It begins with an authorization card campaign. The intermediate steps are: the union requests a representation election if more than 30% of employees sign the authorization card; the NLRB determines the bargaining unit; the NLRB holds an election. Union organizing is concluded with the NLRB's certification of the election results.**
3) A corporate campaign is a tactic used by unions to bring pressure on management during an organizing campaign or collective bargaining.
4) Good faith bargaining is the legal requirement that management and the union seriously attempt to arrive at a settlement during collective bargaining.

14.(IVD) 1) If product demand is low, management has less pressure to settle because it is not worried about losing market share during a strike.
2) The same condition would prevail as in 1). In addition, management would have replacement workers available during a strike if it chose to hire them.
***3) Given that product demand is high, competitors exist who can meet the demand, and few replacement workers are available, the company risks losing market share if its employees strike.**
4) The lack of competitors able to supply the high demand during a strike means that the company can take a strike without losing market share.

15.(IVE2) 1) Wage rates are a distributive bargaining issue.
***2) Integrative bargaining occurs when both parties attempt to resolve common concerns such as an employee alcohol treatment program.**
3) Amount of vacation is a distributive bargaining issue.
4) Overtime pay rate is a distributive bargaining issue.

16.(IVE2)***1) Distributive bargaining occurs when the goals of the two parties conflict. It encourages threats, bluffs, and secrecy. It is the most adversarial approach to collective bargaining.**
2) Integrative bargaining occurs when both parties attempt to resolve common concerns. This approach encourages trust, an understanding of the other negotiators' real needs and objectives, and emphasizes commonalities between the parties instead of differences.

3) Intraorganizational bargaining occurs when management and union negotiators try to reach accord within their own organizations. Union and management negotiators often have more difficulty with members of their own negotiating teams than with one another.
4) Mandatory bargaining is not an approach to collective bargaining. It is the requirement of the National Labor Relations Act that the union and management bargain in good faith over wages, hours, and working conditions.

17.(IVF3) 1) An agency shop would not be preferred because it does not require that all employees in the bargaining unit become members of the union, only that they pay the union a fee for services.
*2) **A union shop is preferred because it requires that all employees in the bargaining unit become members of the union.**
3) An open shop would not be preferred because it does not require employees of the bargaining unit to join the union or to pay fees for services.
4) The maintenance of membership clause would not be preferred. It provides a window at the expiration of a collective bargaining agreement in which employees can withdraw from membership in the union.

18.(IVF3) 1) A closed shop requires workers to be members of a union before they can be employed in the bargaining unit. A closed shop is almost always illegal.
2) A maintenance of membership clause requires employees of the bargaining unit to remain members of the union until the contract expires.
3) An open shop requires no payment to the union.
*4) **Under an agency shop, employees of the bargaining unit do not have to join the union but they have to pay for the services the union provides for them, such as grievance administration and collective bargaining.**

19.(IVG1) 1) Striking workers have no rights to their old jobs unless the company agrees to take them back in the contract settlement.
*2) **After the strike is over, the striking employees are effectively on layoff status and have recall rights according to seniority when the company needs them.**
3) The Department of Labor is not involved in strike resolution.
4) The company first decides what categories of worker it wants to recall, but then workers are recalled by seniority.

20.(VB1)*1) **A grievance is an employee's concern over a perceived violation of the labor agreement. The employee's grievance is submitted to the grievance procedure for resolution.**
2) Labor law is law passed by federal and state legislatures and primarily governs the relations between unions and employers.
3) While a complaint at the workplace may be a grievance, not all complaints are grievances. Complaints may not involve a violation of the labor agreement and may not be submitted to the grievance procedure for resolution.
4) Past practice refers to a specific and identical action that has been continually employed over a number of years to the recognition and satisfaction of both parties.

Although a violation of past practice may represent a grievance, it does not define a grievance.

21.(VB3) 1) The union is required to process the grievance. The union must only take it forward as far as the union believes it has merit, but not as far as arbitration which is the final step in the grievance procedure.
2) The union is required to provide an adequate defense for a grievant.
*3) **Fair representation requires that the union represent all of the bargaining-unit employees, members and nonmembers, in both contract negotiation and administration, including the use of the grievance procedure, at the union's expense.**
4) The grievant is not required to pay the expenses.

22.(VC3) 1) The arbitrator is a third-party neutral employed by the union and management to make a binding decision on an employee's grievance.
2) The employee is the party who has grieved the discharge and does not have the burden of proof that the discharge was for cause.
*3) **Since the employer has brought charges against an employee resulting in the discharge, the employer has the burden of proof to show that the discharge was for cause.**
4) In a discharge arbitration hearing, the role of the union is to defend the employee who was discharged.

23.(VIB1) 1) Eighty-five percent of the workers newly hired at NUMMI were former General Motors (GM) employees. In the expansion of the Saturn plant, an agreement was negotiated to hire additional employees from employees laid off at other GM plants. Thus, a large percentage of the workforce had previously worked in a unionized environment.
2) At both NUMMI and Saturn, the original workforce was not employees who had been laid off. A subsequent agreement at the Saturn facility between GM and the UAW allowed for the hiring of additional employees from a group of GM employees who had been initially laid off.
*3) **At NUMMI and Saturn, one of the incentives for the union to allow management more flexibility was a management commitment to spend more money on employee training.**
4) The number of production job classifications was not increased.

24.(VIB3)*1) **Joint labor-management committees attempt to resolve noncontractual problems through cooperative efforts outside of formal contract negotiations.**
2) Processing grievances is guided by the grievance procedure as detailed in the collective bargaining agreement.
3) Setting wages is done through the collective bargaining process and the specific wage rates for given job classifications are typically covered in the collective bargaining agreement.
4) Disciplining employees involves managerial actions that are taken against an employee who has violated organizational rules.

Organizational Behavior

1.(IC) 1) A confounding variable varies systematically with the independent variable. There is no confounding variable in this study.
2) A dependent variable is the response affected by the independent variable. The dependent variable in this study is attendance.
*3) An independent variable affects the dependent variable and causes a change in it. The independent variable in this study is job satisfaction which affected employees' attendance during snowstorms.
4) A moderating variable is considered a contingency factor. There is no contingency variable in this study.

2.(IIB4) 1) When facing opposition, presenting only one side of a policy is less effective than presenting both sides.
2) Management should focus on the policy, not on the topic.
*3) By promoting the positive aspects of the policy while acknowledging that there are negative aspects, management will be more successful in changing employee attitudes.
4) See 2).

3.(IIB5) ***1) When turnover and absenteeism are high, a low average level of satisfaction may indicate an organization-wide problem.**
2) When productivity is high, the average level of employee satisfaction is less likely to be a problem.
3) Level of employee satisfaction is less important in predicting turnover for employees with higher performance levels since the organizations make a great effort to keep them.
4) When the majority of employees display a low level of effort, variables other than the average level of employee satisfaction are probably more important.

4.(IIC3) 1) Consensus compares a person's behavior with the behavior of others faced with the same circumstances. This supervisor did not compare the person with others.
*2) Consistency refers to the particular behavior of one person over time. This supervisor is focusing on the consistency of one employee's performance over time.
3) Distinctiveness refers to determining whether a person behaves in the same way in different situations. This supervisor is focusing on the employee's performance, not on the situation.
4) Stereotyping involves making judgments based on a person's membership in a group. There is no evidence of stereotyping by this supervisor.

5.(IID1) ***1) Classical conditioning is an involuntary passive response (happiness or fond memories) to a conditioned stimulus (picture on a calendar) that is associated with an unconditioned stimulus (fond memories on a farm during one's youth).**
2) Operant conditioning is a voluntary behavior that is followed by an application or removal of a consequence.
3) Social learning is learning through observation of others or through direct experiences.
4) Behavior modification is the application of operant procedures to modify an individual's behavior.

6.(IIE3c) ***1) Employees' ability to perform and their acceptance of the goals are prerequisites to the achievement of high-standard goals. There is no evidence that the goal has been accepted by employees and some evidence that the goal is resented; therefore, the goal acceptance appears to be the problem.**
2) Difficult goals will lead to a higher performance, but only when they are accepted by employees.
3) Goals must be specific. The goal to increase production by 20 percent was specific so it was not a factor in the failure of Willamson's performance goal.
4) The failure of Williamson's performance goal was not related to her employees' belief in their capabilities to perform, since at one point their performance increased by 5 percent.

7.(IIE3b) 1) The performance goal system was not implemented for truck drivers.
2) Increasing their hourly wage by 5 percent does not address the employees' concern for procedural justice, the fairness of the process of distributing rewards.
*3) Developing a piece-rate system for them is relevant to the employees' concern for procedural justice, the fairness of the process of distributing rewards.
4) Assigning additional duties to the machine operators will not change the process that Williamson is using to determine the distribution of rewards among the truck drivers. Adding additional duties will only increase the machine operators' perception that the system is unfair since they believe they are not being paid for all the work they already perform.

8.(IIE3b) 1) Demonstrating that a pay-for-performance system will not guarantee that everyone will make more money does not address the machine operators' complaints about the system.
2) An increase in the piece-rate amount by 5 percent for the small increase in performance does not guarantee that the machine operators will make as much as they did before.
3) Adjusting the performance goal from a 20 percent increase to a 10 percent increase will not guarantee that the machine operators will make as much as they did before.
*4) Ensuring that all operators will make at least as much money as they did before will greatly increase the acceptance of the system. If the machine operators earn at least as much as they did before, they will have far fewer objections to the system.

9.(IIE4e) 1) Pay-for-performance systems do not guarantee a consistent income.
2) Pay-for-performance systems are generally unrelated to the benefits package.
*3) It is a widely held belief that compensation systems which are oriented toward individuals are most effective.
4) The pay-for-performance plan that was implemented was an individual plan, not a group plan.

10.(IIIA2c) 1) A bulletin is an example of an impersonal medium and has the lowest channel richness.

★2) Of the communication mediums listed, electronic mail has the highest channel richness.
3) A letter has lower channel richness than electronic mail.
4) A memorandum has lower channel richness than electronic mail.

11.(IIIA4)**★1) An all-channel network that allows all group members to actively communicate with each other leads to a high level of satisfaction among the members.**
2) A formal chain network in which members must rigidly follow the formal chain of command leads to a moderate level of member satisfaction.
3) A grapevine is not a formal communication network.
4) In a wheel network, the leader acts as the central conduit for all the group's communication and member satisfaction is not as high as in all-channel network.

12.(IIIB5) 1) Taking charge and setting goals is a thruster-organizer role.
2) Communicating information to outsiders is a role of an explorer-promoter.
3) Gathering information for decisions is the role of a reporter-advisor.
★4) Supporting group members is a typical role of an upholder-maintainer.

13.(IIIC3d) 1) Stating a position clearly before the group makes a decision will increase the likelihood of groupthink because group members will be reluctant to disagree with a manager.
2) Encouraging group members to reach consensus as quickly as possible will increase the likelihood of groupthink by not taking the time to fully explore alternatives.
3) Asking group members to avoid reexamining alternatives to decisions will increase the likelihood of groupthink by not allowing for a realistic appraisal of the alternatives.
★4) Encouraging group members to voice objections about the group's course of action will decrease the likelihood of groupthink by allowing the group to fully explore alternatives to a course of action.

14.(IIIC3e)**★1) The voting behavior of the council members is an example of groupshift. Groupshift is a shift from the direction the group originally favored to a more extreme position.**
2) Cohesiveness refers to how attracted members are to each other and how motivated they are to stay in the group.
3) The degree of involvement of the group members is not discussed in this question.
4) Social facilitation refers to the effect that the presence of others has on an individual's performance on a task.

15.(IIID3) 1) Quality circle programs do not involve the entire organization.
2) Although quality circle programs may eventually result in higher customer satisfaction, their primary focus is not customer satisfaction.
3) Upper management is not a direct participant in a typical quality circle program.
★4) Empowering employees to solve problems in their area of responsibility is central to a quality circle. A typical quality circle program provides employees with opportunities to become involved and share the responsibility for identifying, reviewing, and recommending appropriate solutions for quality problems.

16.(IIIE2) 1) Research has not indicated that physical traits can distinguish leaders from nonleaders.
2) Research has not identified a set of traits common to all leaders.
★3) Research indicates that although there are some unique traits that contribute to effective leadership, these traits will not be found in all leaders on a consistent basis.
4) Research has not differentiated effective leaders from ineffective leaders.

17.(IIIE4b)**★1) When followers are able and willing to perform their jobs, delegating is the most effective leadership style.**
2) Participating is most effective when followers are able and unwilling.
3) Selling is most effective when followers are unable and willing.
4) Telling is most effective when followers are unable and unwilling.

18.(IIIE4c) 1) Graen's leader-member exchange theory focuses on the in-groups and out-groups that form between leaders and their subordinates.
2) Hersey and Blanchard's situational theory focuses on the follower's readiness.
3) Fiedler's contingency theory focuses on the match between a leader's style and the degree of situational favorableness.
★4) House's path-goal theory focuses on the extent that a leader's behavior motivates effective performance based on subordinate need satisfaction.

19.(IVA) 1) An adhocracy has little formalization and authority is decentralized.
★2) A bureaucracy is characterized by standardization. It is departmentalized and formalized. Authority and decision making are centralized.
3) A matrix structure combines functional and product departmentalization and has much less standardization than a bureaucracy.
4) A simple structure is a flat organization without the many layers of a bureaucracy.

20.(IVB1)**★1) Ceremonies that are used to recognize employees whose performance and behavior is consistent with corporate mission and values are considered the artifact of the organization's culture. Artifacts are the most tangible form of a work environment's culture.**
2) Basic assumptions are the unspoken underlying tenets of the organization's culture.
3) Socialization is a process in which new employees are transformed from outsiders to accepted members of the organization.
4) Latent refers to factors or items that exist, but are not visible within the organization's culture.

21.(IVC4) 1) The systematic study of employee behavior on a case-by-case basis is not associated with action research.

2) Executive actions that are needed to solve organizational problems are unrelated to action research.
*3) **Collection and analysis of data for the purpose of organizational change are the fundamentals of action research.**
4) The systematic study of opportunities and threats in the organizational environment describes a SWOT analysis, which is typically part of strategic planning.

22.(IVC4) 1) A quality circle group is unlikely to be directly affected by the change, so having a quality circle implement the change will not help to reduce resistance to the change.
*2) **Allowing employees affected by the change to participate in the change process will help to reduce the employees' resistance and increase their commitment to implementation of the change.**
3) There may be resistance or resentment to a change implemented by an outside agent who will not be affected by the change.
4) There is no evidence that having an interdepartmental team implement the change will help reduce resistance to the change.

23.(IVD2) 1) Whether feedback is provided or not is unrelated to technostress.
2) Resentment and jealousy of a coworker is unrelated to technostress.
3) Failure to follow through on a promise due to budget constraints is unrelated to technostress.
*4) **Technostress is stress that is caused by new information technology. The frequent breakdown of the new software application is a potential cause for technostress.**

24.(VB) 1) Individualism refers to the extent to which people concentrate on caring for themselves and their immediate family.
*2) **According to Hofstede, employees with high power distance show a great deal of respect for authority and are less likely to disagree with an authority figure.**
3) Quality orientation emphasizes assertiveness. Assertive people are comfortable expressing their disagreements with others.
4) Uncertainty avoidance deals with the extent to which people feel threatened by uncertain and ambiguous situations.

25.(VC) 1) Identifying the organization's distinctive competencies is one of the important aspects of reengineering.
*2) **Reengineering means completely breaking a process or system down and designing a new and better version. By automating an outdated process, the process will remain the same.**
3) Assessing the organization's core processes is an important aspect of reengineering.
4) Reorganizing horizontally by process is an important aspect of reengineering.

Production/Operations Management

No content area codes for these questions are available at this time.

1. 1) A manufacturer of packaged goods produces goods only and is not a service organization.
2) A bank with 24-hour automatic teller machines provides a service but it does not produce goods.
3) A fire department is a service organization but it does not provide goods.
*4) **A restaurant is a service organization that provides goods (food and beverages) and service (prepares and serves the food and beverages).**

2. 1) Facility location decisions can and often do have a profound effect on competitive advantage (e.g., locating near a major market, thereby reducing lead times and transportation costs).
2) Facility location decisions affect distribution costs and also affect costs of transporting supplies and raw materials, labor costs, and consumer convenience (for retail operations).
3) Facility location decisions do affect operations at lower levels of the organization in many ways, including lead times for customers and lead times from suppliers, availability of labor, ability to expand, and more.
*4) **Good facility location decisions can effectively position each element of the production-distribution system so that the contribution of each element is maximized.**

3. 1) See 2).
*2) **A critical path is defined as the path with the longest duration (the longest path).**
3) See 2).
4) See 2).

4. 1) This statement is false. Exponential smoothing requires very little data storage.
*2) **This statement is true. Simply changing the value of the smoothing constant changes the weighting pattern.**
3) This statement is false. Exponential smoothing cannot compensate for and will lag a trend.
4) This statement is false. Exponential smoothing cannot compensate for and will lag seasonal variations.

5. 1) See 2).
*2) **Compute the average of the last three periods:**
$$F_7 = \frac{140 + 120 + 130}{3} = 130.0$$
3) See 2).
4) See 2).

6. 1) Managers try to design quality into processes so that control charts are not needed.
2) Managers try to design quality into processes so that inspection is not needed.
*3) **A major concept of total quality control is that quality is everyone's responsibility.**
4) Total quality control includes striving for no defectives.

7. 1) See 3).
2) See 3).
★3) Compute the Economic Order Quantity, Q:

$$Q = \sqrt{\frac{2\,(\text{annual demand})\,(\text{order cost})}{\text{Annual holding cost}}}$$

$$= \sqrt{\frac{2\,(10{,}000)\,(20)}{10}} = 200 \text{ units}$$

4) See 3).

Reading Instruction in the Elementary School

1.(IC) 1) Schema is not a teaching strategy.
2) Schema is not a modeling process.
3) Schema is not a method of organizing an assessment program.
★4) Schema is a mental structure within an individual that provides the means for organizing life experiences into acquired knowledge.

2.(IE) **★1) Knowledge of inventive spelling provides teachers with valuable information about children's writing development. This knowledge also helps teachers understand children's awareness of letter-sound associations.**
2) Inventive spelling is a developmental stage in learning to write, it is not related to classroom research.
3) Inventive spelling is a well-documented developmental process in learning to write and is not a trend.
4) Patterned word recognition does not address the importance of understanding students' inventive spelling.

3.(IH) **★1) Learning to read and write are processes facilitated by the integration of all of the language arts. Children learning English as a second language should be immersed in reading and writing activities as soon as they begin school.**
2) Waiting for a survival vocabulary to develop will unnecessarily slow second language learning.
3) Children's listening and speaking ability will grow more rapidly when they are simultaneously exposed to reading and writing.
4) Reading and writing instruction should not be delayed until after students have developed a 200–300 word listening/speaking vocabulary.

4.(IIA) **★1) "Clk" is correct. An emergent writer first focuses on consonant sounds in a word and does not typically represent vowel sounds in a word.**
2) "Cluk" is not correct. See 1).
3) "Coc" is not correct. See 1).
4) "Cok" is not correct. See 1).

5.(IIB) 1) Following instructions or directions has no relationship to the term directionality.
★2) Directionality is the ability to follow the way print is arranged on a page, top to bottom, left to right.
3) Directionality does not refer to the case of letters.
4) Directionality has no connection to the sequencing of sounds, it relates to the sequencing of print.

6.(IIC) 1) Phonic generalizations are not needed when using a dictionary. Dictionaries provide users with definitions and phonetic pronunciation of words.
★2) Phonic generalizations are used in learning to: pronounce words when reading; help students to identify words they cannot read; produce an approximation of a difficult word which students can then self-correct if the word is already in their speaking/listening vocabulary.
3) English has many irregularities in phoneme-grapheme correspondence.
4) Phonic generalizations are not used to develop memory skills.

7.(IIF) 1) Oral reading can be effectively used to learn about decoding, but not retellings.
★2) The goal of reading is to construct meaning from print. Retellings display and provide useful information about the students' understanding of what they have read.
3) Retellings do not relate to assessing phonemic awareness (distinguishing phonemes in a given word).
4) Self-corrections occur while reading a text. Retellings are completed after reading. Miscues give teachers information about children's oral reading processes, but retellings provide information about their comprehension.

8.(IIIA) 1) Since *jumped* does not look like *huddled*, the student is not relying on the graphic cuing system.
2) Orthographic refers to the written spelling system. The miscue, *jumped*, reflects little relationship to the word *huddle*.
3) Since *jumped* has little sound relationship to *huddled*, the student is not relying on the phonic cuing system.
★4) The student uses syntactic knowledge to produce the miscue. The student has substituted a verb for a verb. This miscue, *jumped*, fits grammatically in the sentence and sounds like it could be the correct reading for *huddled*.

9.(IIIA1) **★1) Centimeter is correct because the soft *c* sound is heard in this word, and this is similar to other soft *c* sounds such as *city*, *cell*, *civil*, and *cycle*.**
2) Chair is incorrect because the sound of *c* in chair is part of the digraph *ch*. Digraphs are two letters forming a single sound. Other examples of words with the *ch* digraph are *chin*, *chap*, *catch*, and *chow*.
3) Considerate is incorrect because the *c* in considerate represents the hard sound of *c*, and this is similar to words with other hard sounds of *c* such as *cap*, *cop*, *confer*, and *current*.
4) Match is incorrect because the *c* in match is part of the digraph *ch*. See 2).

10.(IIIC) 1) Semantic mapping is not used for word recognition.
2) Since the purpose of a semantic map is to visually represent concepts, semantic mapping has no direct connection to becoming an independent reader.
★3) Semantic mapping provides a visual display of the relationship among concepts and helps readers understand how words they know can be used in new contexts.

4) A semantic map graphically displays vocabulary and does not usually include or stress a dictionary definition of words.

11.(IVA1) 1) An emphasis on dictionary usage would not improve comprehension because dictionary definitions lack social context and often do not lead to a clear understanding of the way words are used in context.
2) Memorization of new vocabulary items has limited value because only a small number of words would be successfully remembered. Moreover, to know words well, students need to experience them in a variety of written contexts.
3) Writing vocabulary in a notebook is a mechanical task and does not focus on the development of meaning.
*4) Prior knowledge is the foundation for all vocabulary learning and comprehension. Students must relate prior knowledge to the process of reading in order to understand vocabulary and comprehend text.

12.(IVA4) 1) Metacognitive ability means knowing about and regulating thinking processes. Students may be able to identify stated and implied ideas but not be aware of how they do it.
2) Clear thinking is important to reading, but it is not metacognitive.
*3) Metacognitive ability involves self-awareness and regulation of the reading process. Readers and writers are metacognitive when they use their awareness of the reading process to select and employ particular reading and writing strategies.
4) Interpreting an author's message based on background experience is not metacognitive since students may not be aware of how they made the interpretation.

13.(IVA5) 1) Since posting a list of strategies does not show how to use the strategies, modeling has not occurred.
2) Pausing between sentences is not a strategy for developing comprehension.
3) Spelling new words is not a strategy for developing comprehension.
*4) Thinking aloud after sentences are read is an effective strategy for modeling comprehension processes.

14.(IVA5) 1) Although an understanding of narrative structure is important for comprehension of story material, it is not aesthetic reading.
2) Discussing a text in small groups is not a part of the definition of aesthetic reading.
3) Self-monitoring behaviors are critical to metacognitive processes, but they are not aesthetic reading.
*4) Aesthetic reading refers to experiencing, thinking, and feeling while reading.

15.(IVB2) 1) This does not define genre.
2) See 1).
*3) Genre refers to types and categories of literature such as fiction, nonfiction, biography, mystery, and science fiction.
4) See 1).

16.(VA2) 1) Silent reading is effective for developing overall reading ability, but it is not a component of the language experience approach.

2) Retelling is an effective strategy for developing and assessing comprehension, but it is not a component of the language experience approach.
3) Practice reading and sharing are effective learning experiences, but they are not components of the language experience approach.
*4) Recording personal stories and using them for reading material are central components of the language experience approach. An advantage of this approach is that students' language and life experiences are explicitly incorporated into classroom literacy lessons.

17.(VA3) 1) Clymer points out that many phonic generalizations are inconsistent and not useful.
*2) Clymer advocates teaching only the few phonic generalizations that are consistent and useful.
3) Clymer does not advocate teaching phonics at all grade levels.
4) Clymer advocates teaching the few phonic generalizations that are consistent rather than those that have exceptions.

18.(VA4)***1) A literature circle is a group of students discussing a piece of literature. The students sit in a circle and share and discuss their responses to a piece of literature that has been read by all the group members.**
2) Dramatic performance of literature is not a literature circle.
3) Creating a semantic web is not a literature circle.
4) Reading and retelling is not a literature circle.

19.(VB8) 1) The cloze procedure requires students to fill in words that have been systematically deleted from a reading selection.
*2) The K-W-L study method includes three steps that provide the student with the opportunity to complete all the processes mentioned in the question. *K* asks the students to question what they already *know* about a topic; *W* requires that they must generate ideas for what they *want* to learn; and *L* indicates that they review and summarize what they have *learned*.
3) Retelling requires a student to read and then recall what was read.
4) A story grammar is a structure for a story including such elements as plot, character, and setting.

20.(VC3a) 1) Phonetic analysis refers to identifying words by their sounds. Phonetic analysis does not help readers understand word elements.
2) Semantic mapping is a visual display of the relationship among concepts. It is not used to understand elements within words.
*3) Structural analysis helps readers understand word parts that convey meaning, such as the *s* in boys and the *ed* in look*ed*.
4) Syntactic analysis refers to an analysis of how words are ordered in sentences.

21.(VD5) 1) Although it will add to fluency and confidence in writing, diary writing does not require students to read, reflect, or question what they have read.

2) Free writing is a teaching strategy for developing writing fluency, but it does not require students to read, reflect, or question what they have read.
3) A learning log is a summary of what a student has learned. A log does not require students to read. A log can be used, for example, to record a learning activity such as a science experiment.
*4) A response journal requires students to read, write a personal response, reflect, and question what they have read. Response journals help students build fluency and confidence in their writing.

22.(VIA4) 1) Waiting for children to demonstrate independent work skills is not an effective guideline. The most effective way for children to learn independent work skills is through guided practice reading and writing.
2) Proficiency in reading and writing is promoted by engaging in independent reading and writing; postponing these activities may postpone proficiency.
3) While students can profit from sharing their work, it is never desirable for teachers to require sharing. This could defeat the purpose of establishing independent reading and writing.
*4) Designated time periods are essential for establishing and maintaining independent reading and writing.

23.(VIB1) 1) In guided reading, the teacher helps students with the silent reading process. Teacher guidance is missing from this response.
2) This is a description of literature circles and teacher guidance is missing from this response.
*3) Guided reading occurs in the presence of a teacher. Teachers help students before silent reading by questioning and prompting them about anticipated text content.
4) This teaching strategy helps students with prediction and word identification. It is not guided reading.

24.(VIB4) 1) Oral and written language learning is dynamic and interactive, not linear.
2) Curriculum integration allows for both breadth and depth of learning.
*3) Curriculum integration allows key concepts to be studied from the vantage point of different subject areas. Children learn key concepts and how the concepts relate to other concepts through authentic literacy activities.
4) Although scheduling of the elementary subjects changes because of curriculum integration, the overall allocation of time remains the same.

25.(VID1)***1) In the Small, Small Pond is an illustrated story about the environment of a pond over the four seasons of the year.**
2) Owl Moon is a story about a father and son who go owling in the midst of winter. Only winter is mentioned.
3) Smokey Night is a story about the Los Angeles riots and a boy who loses his cat in a building fire. The seasons are not related to this book.
4) Tar Beach is a story about a young girl who dreams of flying over New York City during a summer evening. Only summer is mentioned.

26.(VID1) 1) In Dear Mr. Henshaw, a favorite teacher receives letters from the protagonist about problems in coping with his parents' divorce and adjusting to a new school. It is not about racism and prejudice.
2) In The Girl Who Loved Wild Horses, a Native American girl chooses to live among the wild horses where she is truly happy and free. It is not about racism and prejudice.
3) The Giver takes place in the future and describes a society that lives in a controlled environment and embraces conformity. It is not about racism and prejudice.
*4) Maniac Magee is an excellent book choice for a unit on racism and prejudice. The book is about a boy who is orphaned and white and who faces prejudice while living with a family who are black.

27.(VIIB3) 1) A teacher-student conference is helpful for learning about a student's interests, literacy history, book choices, etc. It is not the best method to gain information about a student's oral reading level.
*2) A running record is an assessment tool for learning about a student's oral reading level. It requires the student to orally read from the classroom reading material as the teacher carefully observes.
3) A literature discussion addresses a student's response to reading. It does not provide information about a student's oral reading level.
4) A standardized test will reveal how a student performs in relation to other students of similar age or grade. A standardized test is not useful for providing information about oral reading level.

28.(VIIB3) 1) Interviews are not part of an IRI.
*2) An IRI consists of a series of graded passages of increasing difficulty that students read orally and silently.
3) A sampling of students' work over time is not part of an IRI.
4) An IRI does not include a series of checklists that assess language qualities and traits. Some IRIs do include checklists to assess oral and silent reading behaviors.

29.(VIIB6) 1) Informal assessment, such as an IRI, does not provide normative data for the purpose of making comparisons.
*2) Norm-referenced assessment compares the abilities (for example, reading) of students with other national samples.
3) Portfolio assessment is an individualized assessment tool and does not provide comparison information to other students.
4) Teacher-made assessment provides useful information about student performance on classroom literacy activities. However, this information cannot be used to make comparisons with students in other classrooms throughout the country.

30.(VIIC) 1) The cloze procedure, replacing words that have been deleted, provides teachers with a quick and limited view of reading abilities. It is not associated with authentic assessment.
2) An IRI, which consists of a series of graded passages of increasing difficulty, is not associated with authentic assessment.
*3) Portfolios are associated with authentic assessment because they contain actual classroom material and tasks completed by students. A literacy portfolio might contain a list of books which have been read,

an audiotape of a retelling, a written response to a book, photographs of books projects, etc.
4) A standardized test is administered to a group for the purposes of measuring achievement and comparing students to national samples. It is not associated with authentic assessment.

Nursing Concepts 1

1.(IA) 1) Demonstration represents an intervention rather than an assessment of the patient's response to nursing care.
2) Explanation represents an intervention rather than an assessment of the patient's response to nursing care.
*3) Evaluation involves an assessment to determine if nursing intervention have been effective in helping clients to achieve the patient outcome/goal.
4) Discussions of expected outcomes would be part of the planning phase, after a diagnosis has been established.

2.(IA1c) 1) see 4)
2) see 4)
3) see 4)
*4) Establishing an expected outcome/goal should be the first step in the planning phase so that nursing actions to achieve the goal can be identified.

3.(IB1b)*1) To be used effectively in the nursing process, data must be validated through a process that includes obtaining additional subjective and objective data.
2) Data collection precedes analysis, planning, and implementation.
3) See 2)
4) See 2)

4.(IB2e)*1) Effective breathing patterns are required to meet the most basic physiological need for air. Any problem that interferes with oxygenation can potentially cause death if not dealt with immediately.
2) Fatigue is associated with the need to rest, a physiological need that can be deferred without the same consequences as 1).
3) Altered nutrition is associated with the need for food, a physiological need that can be deferred without the same consequences as 1).
4) Fluid volume deficit is associated with the need for fluid, a physiological need that can be deferred without the same consequences as 1).

5.(IB3a) 1) See 3)
2) A nursing diagnosis identifies a health problem and is not a goal.
*3) A goal (expected outcome) is a measurable patient behavior as opposed to a nursing action. A goal can be used to evaluate the effectiveness of a plan.
4) See 3)

6.(IIB1) 1) In the right sidelying position, the head and shoulders are not elevated. This position does not allow maximal lung expansion.

2) In the supine position with the head on a pillow, the head and shoulders are not elevated. This position does not allow maximal lung expansion.
*3) Sitting up and leaning forward on the arms allows the patient free movement of the diaphragm and maximal lung expansion to facilitate respiration.
4) The head of the bed should be elevated 45°–90° to allow for maximal lung expansion.

7.(IIB1b) 1) It is unrealistic to try to eliminate all stress. Stress can be positive and can provide a stimulus for change.
*2) Knowing the patient's previous experience with stress can be useful in predicting how the patient will react to stress in the hospital. This information will assist the nurse in implementing a plan of care to help reduce the patient's stress.
3) The patient does not necessarily need to develop new coping mechanisms.
4) A private room may be impractical and is not the most effective method of stress reduction.

8.(IIB5a)*1) This patient response indicates a knowledge deficit and a need for further information and clarification by the nurse.
2) This patient response indicates understanding of the nurse's teaching objectives.
3) See 2).
4) See 2).

9.(IIIA4d)*1) Because of the injurious physical and psychological effects of restraints, they should only be applied as a last resort to maintain physical safety.
2) A patient who is restrained will still require frequent observation. Restraints are associated with injuries.
3) Confusion does not necessarily mean that the patient requires restriction of physical activity to maintain safety. Restraints can also lead to increased confusion.
4) The need for restraints is determined by patient behaviors, not family request.

10.(IIIB3a)*1) Wound healing places additional demands on the body. Patients require a diet rich in protein and vitamin C. Collagen is a protein formed from amino acids. Vitamin C is needed for synthesis of collagen. Collagen adds tensile strength to the wound.
2) Although people who exercise regularly tend to have good circulation and heal quickly, this is not the most effective intervention.
3) Dressing changes require sterile technique to prevent wound infection.
4) Bed rest is not a factor in promoting wound healing. The effects of immobility may adversely affect wound healing.

11.(IIIB1d) 1) Weak rapid pulse occurs as a result of fluid volume deficit.
2) Rapid respiratory rate occurs as a result of fluid volume deficit.
3) Dry mucous membranes and decreased salivation result from fluid volume deficit.

*4) Decreased skin turgor is associated with fluid volume deficit.

12.(IIIB4b) 1) Syrup of ipecac will induce vomiting. Vomiting of certain poisons will cause further tissue destruction.
2) Dilution with milk is only indicated for certain poisons.
3) Vomiting of certain poisons will cause further tissue destruction.
*4) The poison control center will provide accurate information about specific antidotes or other treatments for an identified poison.

13.(IIIB4d)***1) Scatter rugs may easily slip on tile floors, causing falls.**
2) A step stool should be used to safely reach for something on a shelf.
3) Cleaning solutions should be properly labeled and stored away from the reach of young children, not from responsible adults.
4) A gas stove with a properly working pilot light does not pose a danger.

14.(IVA3c) 1) This patient is not the most susceptible to infection because the patient does not have increased risk factors for infection. Risk factors related to infection include inadequate nutritional status, age (neonates and older adults), altered skin integrity, altered immune response, and high stress level.
2) See 1).
3) See 1).
*4) Older adults have an increased risk of developing serious infections. With aging, there is a decrease in the function of the immune system and slowed response to antibiotic therapy. Respiratory problems predispose an older adult to infections such as pneumonia.

15.(IVB1b)***1) A laceration is an open wound in which tissues are torn and wound edges are often jagged. The depth of the wound varies. An inflammatory response is the body's reaction to a wound and the resulting tissue injury. There is vasodilatation of surrounding capillaries, and exudation of serum and white blood cells into damaged tissues. This results in localized warmth and swelling (edema).**
2) Purulent drainage is a sign of wound infection.
3) Severe pain is an indication of underlying problems such as fracture or torn meniscus.
4) Swelling and pain would prevent full movement of the knee joint.

16.(IVB5a) 1) The amount of drainage depends on the location and extent of the wound. During the early stage of wound healing, the inflammatory response results in an exudate that escapes from the wound. This drainage is serous or serosanguineous and will gradually decrease.
2) Within seven to ten days a wound that is healing normally fills with epithelial cells and the edges close.
3) In the inflammatory stage there is an increase in white blood cells. This stage lasts about three days. A continually increased WBC could be a symptom of infection which usually becomes apparent three to seven days after injury or surgery.

*4) Edema occurs during the inflammatory stage of wound healing. The blood supply to the wound increases, bringing with it substances and nutrients needed in the healing process. The area appears inflamed and edematous as a result. This phase lasts three to four days, then the edema subsides and the proliferative stage of wound healing occurs.

17.(VA3b) 1) See 4)
2) See 4)
3) See 4)
*4) Vision is the most important sense for safe administration of medication. Loss of visual acuity may make it difficult for the older adult to read the drug name and instructions on the prescription label so that the risk for errors is increased.

18.(VB4a)***1) The Z-track method of administering intramuscular injections allows subcutaneous tissue to form a seal so that medication remains in the muscle and does not seep back into the subcutaneous tissue where it could cause irritation.**
2) The method keeps the medications in the muscle so it does not reduce pain at the injection site.
3) The action of the drug is not affected by the administration method.
4) The rate of absorption is not affected by the administration method.

19.(VB4e) 1) See 2).
*2) Two tablets will contain the 0.25 mg of medication (0.125 + 0.125 = 0.25) the physician ordered.
3) See 2).
4) See 2).

20.(VIA1f) 1) This response represents false reassurance and does not focus on the patient's concerns.
*2) This response is an open-ended statement and provides an opportunity to further discuss patient concerns.
3) This response does not address the patient's feelings.
4) See 1).

21.(VIB2a) 1) Altered health maintenance is a state in which an individual is at risk of a disruption in health because of an unhealthy lifestyle or lack of information. The patient's symptoms do not support this diagnosis.
2) Altered thought processes is a state in which an individual experiences a disruption in reality orientation, problem solving, judgment, and comprehension. The patient's symptoms do not support this diagnosis.
*3) Impaired verbal communication is a state in which an individual experiences a decreased ability to speak, but can understand others. The patient's behavior and difficulty in verbalizing supports the diagnosis of impaired verbal communication.
4) Ineffective individual coping is a state in which an individual is unable to manage internal or environmental stressors. Although this patient is experiencing frustration, the diagnosis of impaired verbal communication is more appropriate.

22.(VIB4a) 1) This response represents false reassurance and does not focus on the patient's concerns.

2) This response denies the patient's feelings and may cut off further communication.
*3) This response uses reflective technique, validates what was said, and encourages the patient to discuss concerns.
4) See 2).

23.(VIB4a) 1) This response appears to probe for information and may cut off communication.
*2) This response is an open-ended statement that encourages the patient to elaborate, clarify, and describe thoughts and feelings.
3) This response has a negative focus, appears to probe for information, and may cut off communication.
4) This statement invites a yes or no response and does not encourage verbalization of feelings.

Nursing Concepts 2

1.(IA4b) 1) Severe dehydration is associated with an elevated BUN because long-standing significant fluid volume deficit reduces the glomerular filtration rate and interferes with clearance of nitrogenous wastes through the kidney.
2) Urinary obstruction causes an increase in tubular resorption of urea, thus increasing the BUN.
*3) Urea nitrogen is an end product of protein and amino acid catabolism. Insufficient protein intake decreases catabolism and decreases BUN.
4) Prolonged immobility increases the rate of protein breakdown and increases the amount of nitrogenous end product excreted in the urine.

2.(IA2d) 1) Vitamin D plays an integral role in calcium metabolism.
2) The mechanisms responsible for prostaglandin production are not fully understood but vitamin C is not considered a stimulating factor.
*3) Vitamin C acts as a reducing agent, thus promoting the absorption of iron in the small intestine.
4) Vitamin K affects prothrombin formation and blood clotting.

3.(IA5e) 1) Fatigue is a symptom of iron deficiency anemia, not a side effect of iron therapy.
2) Fever is not a side effect of iron therapy.
3) Fat absorption is not related to iron therapy.
*4) Common side effects of iron therapy are nausea, vomiting, and indigestion, because iron aggravates the stomach mucosa.

4.(IB4a) 1) This lunch is not high in iron. Tuna is high in protein, sodium, and potassium. Chocolate pudding is high in sodium and potassium.
2) This lunch is not high in iron. Cheese is high in protein and sodium. Tossed salad and raw apple are high in potassium.
*3) This lunch is high in iron. Eggs, dried apricots, and spinach are high in iron.
4) This lunch is not high in iron. Hamburger is high in protein, carbohydrates, and fat. French fries are high in potassium.

5.(IIA5b)***1) Bulk-forming laxatives promote the normal mechanism of defecation. They act by absorbing water and forming a soft bulky mass which stretches the intestine and stimulates reflex peristaltic waves leading to defecation.**
2) Prolonged use of emollient laxatives will inhibit vitamin C absorption.
3) Saline laxatives are used for complete bowel evacuation.
4) Stimulant laxatives irritate intestinal mucosa and cause cramps.

6.(IIIA5d) 1) The dorsal recumbent (back-lying) position causes difficulty in insertion of the rectal tube and interferes with the flow of solution.
*2) The left lateral (left sidelying) position is most conducive to allowing the solution to flow along the natural curve of the sigmoid. The sigmoid extends in an s-shape from the rectum to the descending colon in the left side of the abdomen.
3) The right sidelying position will decrease the flow of solution by gravity.
4) The prone (lying face downward) position is impractical.

7.(IIIA2) 1) Bradycardia, abnormally slow pulse rate, is not a clinical manifestation of hypoxia. In hypoxia, the heart rate increases in a compensatory effort to deliver more oxygen to the tissues.
2) Cyanosis indicates the presence of 5 grams or more of unoxygenated hemoglobin per 100 ml in the blood and the surface blood capillaries are dilated. Cyanosis is a late sign of hypoxia.
3) Hypertension (rather than hypotension) is a common early indicator of hypoxia.
*4) Tachypnea, an increase in rate and depth of respiration, is an early indicator of hypoxia.

8.(IIIB2b) 1) Use of absorbent pads has no effect on bladder control.
2) Use of absorbent pads has no effect on dysuria (painful or difficult voiding).
*3) Use of absorbent pads decreases skin irritation by absorbing wetness and leaving a dry surface.
4) Use of absorbent pads has no effect on the intervals between voiding. Bladder training programs are used to help patients postpone voiding.

9.(IIIB2a)***1) Dyspnea, reduction in a person's physiological capacity to endure activities to the degree desired or required, is a major defining characteristic of activity intolerance.**
2) Flaccid muscles suggest impaired physical mobility or limited ability for physical movement, not a reduced physiological capacity to tolerate movement.
3) History of a lack of exercise does not constitute an altered physiologic response to activity and does not necessarily indicate a reduced physiological capacity to endure activity.
4) Sleeping for long periods of time does not constitute an altered physiological response to activity and does not necessarily indicate a reduced physiological capacity to endure activity.

10.(IIIB4a) 1) Productive coughing clears sputum from the respiratory tract but does not affect the viscosity of the sputum.

*2) Humidified air keeps the airway moist and decreases the viscosity of sputum.
3) Frequent oral hygiene does not affect the viscosity of sputum.
4) Bed rest will increase the viscosity of sputum.

11.(IIIB4) 1) A nasal cannula delivers a low concentration of oxygen, 24–45%.
2) A non-rebreather mask delivers the highest concentration of oxygen, 95–100%.
3) A simple mask is a low-flow system and delivers an oxygen concentration of 40–60%.
*4) A Venturi mask is a high-flow system that delivers oxygen precisely within 1%, from 24–50%.

12.(IIIB5) 1) There are many noninfectious causes of impaired gas exchange. Freedom from infection is not an indicator of a patient's status relative to gas exchange.
2) Although normal nail bed color indicates absence of cyanosis, arterial blood gas monitoring is the best evidence of improved gas exchange.
3) Clear breath sounds indicate the absence of abnormal or adventitious sounds due to air passing through narrowed or fluid filled airways or to an inflamed pleura. It does not indicate the status of gas exchange.
*4) In arterial blood gas monitoring, levels of oxygen, carbon dioxide, and pH are measured. These are the most complete and accurate indicators of gas exchange.

13.(IVA1)***1) Sodium ions help maintain blood volume and interstitial fluid volume by regulating water balance.**
2) Acid-base balance is controlled by the concentration of hydrogen ions in the body.
3) Carbohydrate metabolism is affected by digestion.
4) Factors in regulating enzyme activity are temperature, pH, and concentration of substrate.

14.(IVA4a) 1) Infants have a greater amount of insensible fluid loss because of their higher metabolic and respiratory rates.
2) Infants have a higher metabolic rate than adults.
3) The normal range of serum potassium is the same in infants as in adults.
*4) Because the infant has a relatively larger body surface area than an adult, a proportionately larger volume of fluid can be lost through the infant's skin and this places the infant at risk for fluid volume deficit.

15.(IVA4a)***1) The decreased percentage of body fluid that occurs with age is due to increased adipose tissue.**
2) Fluid filtration rate is decreased in older adults.
3) Intracellular fluid volume is decreased in older adults.
4) There is no age-related change in the viscosity of body fluid.

16.(IVA5c) 1) Loop diuretics do not cause an increase in appetite.
2) Loop diuretics do not cause blurred vision.
*3) Postural hypotension is a common side effect of loop diuretics.
4) Loop diuretics do not cause edema.

17.(IVB1c) 1) Orthostatic hypotension, not hypertension, occurs with a decrease in intravascular fluid volume.
2) Hypoventilation is breathing that is insufficient to meet the metabolic need for oxygen and the need for carbon dioxide removal from the blood. It is a pathologic rather than an adaptive event.
3) Pyrexia may be a result of dehydration and may increase loss of body fluids.
*4) Tachycardia, an increase in heart rate, is one of the first signs of hypovolemia. Tachycardia is an attempt to increase blood flow to the kidneys and aid in water and electrolyte regulation.

18.(IVB1d) 1) Crackles in lung bases are a sign of fluid volume excess.
*2) The patient's laboratory results indicate fluid volume deficit. A dry, furrowed tongue is a clinical manifestation of fluid volume deficit.
3) High blood pressure is associated with fluid volume excess.
4) Slow, bounding pulse is associated with fluid volume excess.

19.(IVB4b) 1) A rate of 14–15 gtt/min is too slow and would take longer than 12 hours to be absorbed.
*2) A rate of 20–21 gtt/min is correct.

$$\text{Drops/minute} = \frac{\text{Total infusion volume} \times \text{drops/mL}}{\text{Total infusion time in minutes}} = \frac{1{,}000 \times 15}{720} = 20.8$$

3) A rate of 26–27 gtt/min is too fast and would take less than 12 hours to be absorbed.
4) A rate of 30–31 gtt/min is too fast and would take approximately 6–8 hours to be absorbed.

20.(IVB5a) 1) Since bowel sounds with diarrhea are hyperactive, an improvement would be a decrease in bowel sounds.
*2) Since muscle weakness is a complication of persistent diarrhea, an increase in muscle strength would be a positive outcome.
3) Decrease in urinary output is a complication of persistent diarrhea.
4) Decrease in tissue turgor is associated with fluid volume deficit.

21.(VA1) 1) The object should be carried close to the center of gravity.
2) Use of the major muscle groups such as the upper and lower arms prevents muscle strain and injury. The object should not be supported on one shoulder only.
3) The object is too heavy if its weight is 35 percent or more of a person's body weight.
*4) The object should be held close to the body so that the line of gravity falls within the base of support, achieving greater stability.

22.(VA4b) 1) Atelectasis refers to the collapse of an alveolus, a lobule, or larger lung unit. It is unrelated to fluid intake.
2) Orthostatic hypotension is a drop in systolic pressure when the patient moves from a lying to a sitting or standing position. Increased fluid intake will not significantly decrease the risk of orthostatic hypotension.
3) Proteinuria is a sign of kidney damage. Increased fluid intake may enhance kidney damage.
*4) Increased fluid intake will dilute crystal formation and prevent the formation of renal calculi.

23.(VB2b) 1) This is an intervention, not a goal.
2) See 1).
*3) A patient who is unable to move freely is at risk for skin breakdown. The dependent body parts are exposed to pressure, reducing the circulation to affected body parts which can result in the formation of pressure ulcers. An important goal for this patient is that the patient will experience no skin breakdown.
4) See 1).

24.(VB4c)***1) A contracture is a permanent shortening of a muscle. Passive range-of-motion exercises are done to prevent contractures and maintain joint flexibility.**
2) Passive range-of-motion exercises improve joint mobility but do not decrease muscle pain.
3) Passive range-of-motion exercises will maintain joint flexibility but will not restore joint function.
4) Passive range-of-motion exercises will maintain joint flexibility but will not prevent joint weakness from recurring.

25.(VB4c) 1) Orthostatic hypotension is unrelated to the dietary intake of calcium and protein.
2) Performing passive range-of-motion exercises does not prevent orthostatic hypotension.
*3) Orthostatic hypotension is characterized by a decrease in blood pressure when a person assumes a standing position. It is the result of peripheral vasodilatation without a compensatory rise in cardiac output. A gradual change of position stimulates renin (a kidney enzyme) which prevents a dramatic drop in blood pressure.
4) Although elevating the legs will inhibit venous pooling and will enhance circulation, it is not the most effective nursing intervention for preventing orthostatic hypotension.

26.(VIA4c)***1) Milk and cheese are dietary sources of the amino acid L-tryptophan which is thought to help induce sleep.**
2) This is not associated with ingestion of dairy products.
3) See 2)
4) See 2)

27.(VIB3b)***1) A warm shower before bedtime promotes relaxation and fosters sleep.**
2) Tea, as a bedtime snack, should be avoided because tea contains the stimulant caffeine which will interfere with the ability to fall asleep.
3) Physical exercise should be avoided two hours prior to bedtime.
4) Daytime napping should be discouraged since it can disrupt normal sleep patterns.

28.(VIB5b)***1) Patients with sleep pattern disturbances need to develop a regular daily routine to help establish sleeping patterns and avoid disruption of biorhythms.**
2) Falling asleep within thirty minutes is a positive outcome; there is no need to revise the plan of care.
3) Use of relaxation techniques is a positive outcome; there is not need to revise the plan of care.
4) Feeling less irritable is a positive outcome; there is no need to revise the plan of care.

Nursing Concepts 3

1.(IA1) 1) Duration is a characteristic of pain which is noted by use of the word "continuous."
2) Intensity is a characteristic of pain which is noted by use of the phrase "8 on 1 to 10 scale."
3) Location is a characteristic of pain which is noted by use of the words "abdominal" and "incisional area."
*4) Onset, a characteristic of pain describing when it began, is not included in the note.

2.(IA2) 1) NSAIDs inhibit prostaglandin synthesis and interrupt the pain signal at the peripheral level.
2) Opioids bind to receptors in the dorsal horn, inhibit release of neurotransmitters, and interfere with the relay of the pain signal across the synapse.
3) Anesthetics and anticonvulsants block ion channels and prevent generation of the pain signal.
*4) Noradrenergic agonists attach to alpha2 noradrenergic receptors in the dorsal horn, thereby modulating the ascending pain signal.

3.(IB5a) 1) A child may talk with a visitor and smile, despite being in pain. Children frequently deny pain to persons other than parents, perhaps because of fear of what will be done if they admit to pain.
2) Children react to, and cope with, pain in many different ways depending on their temperaments. Using a video game as a distraction from pain may be a learned coping mechanism.
*3) Because children tend to be honest with parents in regard to pain, a statement to a parent regarding the relief of pain is considered to be valid.
4) Children who have a dry mouth or who are thirsty may sip clear fluids or suck on ice pops regardless of presence or absence of pain.

4.(IIA2a) 1) Fatigue is a psychogenic cause of erectile dysfunction but level of exercise itself is neither an organic nor a psychogenic cause.
2) Elevated cholesterol level is a documented risk for coronary artery disease but not for erectile dysfunction.
*3) Endocrine diseases such as diabetes, pituitary tumors, and hypo- and hyperthyroidism are among the organic causes of erectile dysfunction.
4) Erectile dysfunction is unrelated to understanding of the normal sexual response cycle.

5. (IIB1e) 1) Rapid plasma reagin (RPR) is a serological test most often used for premarital and prenatal screening for syphilis.
2) Darkfield examination of serous exudate from a moist lesion is done to check for the presence of T. pallidum, the causative organism of syphilis.
3) The Pap test, as used in gynecology, is primarily a screening test for cancer of the cervix. It can detect infection but is not organism specific.
*4) The preferred method for diagnosing gonorrhea in women is by means of a cervical culture which is 80% to 90% accurate in diagnosing the infection.

6.(IIB2b) 1) Counseling is not a priority of patient management in the acute phase of rape trauma syndrome; it is

in the reorganization phase that the survivor may benefit from counseling.
2) The survivor must feel safe before she can cooperate with the collection-of-evidence procedures, which may in themselves be traumatic to her.
***3) The first priority when admitting and examining a rape survivor is a key nursing action in the reorganizational phase of recovery, not the acute phase.**
4) Establishment of a trusting relationship between the nurse and the rape survivor is a key nursing action in the reorganization phase of recovery, not in the acute phase.

7.(IIIA3c) 1) Not all people of a specific group have the same health care needs, beliefs, or values.
2) Different cultures interpret direct eye contact differently, so it is not always appropriate.
***3) The provision of translator services for non-English speaking patients promotes culturally congruent care.**
4) The nurse accepts and complies with the patient's wishes regardless of the patient's cultural background.

8.(IIIB2a) 1) Rash, cough, and fever are not indicative of alcoholism.
2) Employment status would be unrelated to the described symptoms.
3) Food preferences would not be related to the symptoms described. Food allergies may cause a rash or cough but would not result in a fever.
***4) Rates of immunization and routine screening are low among Native Americans. Therefore, the nurse would be concerned about the risk for tuberculosis and pneumonia.**

9.(IVB1) 1) To be a patient advocate means to speak/act on behalf of the patient. Supporting the family in their decisions is not advocating for the patient.
***2) The patient advocate role requires the nurse to protect the patient's human and legal rights. Basic to this function is ensuring that the patient has access to knowledge for informed decision making and is treated in a respectful manner.**
3) Providing the patient with information about advance directives is a part of the nurse's responsibility as a patient advocate but is only a small part.
4) Educating the patient and the family about care needs is part of the nurse's teaching role.

10.(IVB3b) 1) Not all patients with chronic illness require home health care.
***2) Chronic illness is associated with limitations and the need for adaptation. Prioritizing self-care activities helps ensure that the most critical tasks of daily living can be accomplished within the patient's limitations.**
3) Chronic illness management is a collaborative process among the patient, the family, and the health care providers.
4) Patients with chronic illness may need to recognize that their lifestyle is irrevocably altered by their illness. However, telling the patient about this does not assist the patient in planning daily living.

11.(VA2b) 1) Healthy People 2000 does not include the goal of creating a list of community resources to which patients may be referred.
***2) One of the three major goals for the health of the American public identified in Healthy People 2000 is "to reduce health disparities among populations."**
3) Prevention of unintentional injuries is identified as a priority, but not a goal, in Healthy People 2000.
4) Use of computerized diagnostic tools is not addressed in Healthy People 2000.

12.(VB5c) 1) Halfway houses provide food, shelter, clothing, health care counseling, and job placement services.
***2) Shelters address the battered woman's immediate need for safety.**
3) Missions provide services and programs to the homeless.
4) Respite care provides temporary relief to unpaid caregivers living in a patient's home.

13.(VB3a) 1) Altered bowel elimination may occur in any patient on opioid therapy or prolonged bed rest.
2) Altered nutritional status may occur in a variety of patient situations, such as in a patient with nausea and vomiting, altered level of consciousness, dysphagia, etc.
3) Patients with pain, activity intolerance, or perceptual/cognitive impairment may not be able to dress, feed, or bathe themselves.
***4) Hospice care provides treatment for patients who are terminally ill, with an emphasis on palliative rather than curative care.**

14.(VIA1a1)***1) Auscultation of fetal heart tones is a positive sign of pregnancy.**
2) Factors other than pregnancy, such as stress, infection, and fatigue may also elevate the temperature.
3) Maternal perception of fetal movement, or quickening, is a possible sign of pregnancy, but a woman may interpret sensations such as flatulence as fetal movement.
4) Absence of menses for two consecutive months is a possible sign of pregnancy, but stress, anemia, or illness can also cause amenorrhea.

15.(VIA7c) 1) Smoking irritates the bronchi and may cause hyperplasia, not thinning of the bronchial walls.
***2) Women who smoke have higher rates of perinatal loss. Smoking places stress on the fetus from hypoxia and creates severe changes in the inner walls of the placental capillaries and major arteries. These vascular changes may account for placental insufficiency and reduced exchange of nutrients and oxygen.**
3) Smoking is an irritant which increases, rather than decreases, mucus production.
4) Smoking is not associated with uterine fibroid formation.

16.(VIA1b1c) 1) Pushing with each contraction is not a sign that labor is imminent. The patient may feel pressure and have the urge to push before complete cervical dilatation.
2) The fundus does not rise further above the umbilicus as labor progresses.
***3) Crowning is a sign of imminent delivery. Crowning indicates that the fetal head is maintaining the perineal opening and is no longer forced back upwards by the pelvic floor muscles.**

4) Contractions increase in length, duration, and frequency as labor progresses.

17.(VID5c)***1) Engorgement is a result of insufficient emptying of the alveoli due to poor sucking or infrequent or inadequate nursing. If engorgement causes problems with breast-feeding, the patient should be taught to express a few drops of milk before putting the infant to breast.**
2) Substituting formula is not appropriate because engorgement will become worse with inadequate or infrequent sucking.
3) Use of nipple shields will not help the infant latch onto an engorged breast.
4) Rolling the nipple between two fingers is done to make a flat or inverted nipple more prominent.

18.(VIA1a2) 1) Tidal volume increases during pregnancy.
2) Heart rate increases during pregnancy.
***3) Blood volume increases to transport nutrients to the placenta and to meet maternal needs.**
4) Although urinary frequency may occur, urinary output does not increase.

19.(VIC1h) 1) Hyperbilirubinemia has no direct effect on the cardiovascular system.
2) Hyperbilirubinemia has no direct effect on the gastrointestinal system.
***3) Untreated hyperbilirubinemia is toxic to the brain and will result in permanent neurological sequelae.**
4) Hyperbilirubinemia has no direct effect on the respiratory system.

20.(VIC1h) 1) Genetic predisposition is not a factor in neonatal hemorrhagic disease.
2) Immune system disorder is not a factor in neonatal hemorrhagic disease.
3) Hemolysis of red blood cells causes hyperbilirubinemia, not hemorrhagic disease.
***4) Hemorrhagic disease of the newborn results from a deficiency of vitamin K-dependent clotting factors. Vitamin K is produced in the bowel by means of bacterial flora that are initially low in the newborn. Vitamin K is administered to newborns shortly after delivery to prevent hemorrhagic disease.**

21.(VIIA2)**1) The most common symptom of retinal detachment is a sudden, painless change in vision such as flashes of lights, a shower of spots, or a sensation of a curtain being pulled down over part of the visual field.**
2) Periorbital edema is associated with trauma and with hyperthyroidism.
3) Purulent discharge is associated with infections such as conjunctivitis and keratitis.
4) Excessive tearing is associated with inflammation such as ectropion, entropion, or chalazion.

22.(VIIA2b) 1) Drainage from the ear may be seen following rupture of the tympanic membrane.
***2) Pain is related to the pressure from purulent exudate on the tympanic membrane.**
3) Tinnitus is a manifestation of Meniere's disease or other inner ear disorder.

4) Vertigo is related to a disorder of balance and the vestibular system of the inner ear.

23.(VIIB2a) 1) Adverse effects of niacin include headache, drowsiness, insomnia, and assorted gastrointestinal, genital, urinary, and musculoskeletal symptoms; they do not include tinnitus.
2) Tinnitus is associated with hypertension and other systemic disorders such as arteriosclerosis, anemia, and hypothyroidism.
***3) Tinnitus is a classic symptom of mild salicylate intoxication (salicylism), a condition which usually occurs after repeated administration of large doses of drugs containing aspirin.**
4) Tinnitus may occur with chronic ear infection but does not necessarily accompany any middle ear infection.

24.(VIIIA3) 1) Endometriosis is not an infective condition; endometritis is an infection.
2) Endometriosis is hormone dependent, active as long as the ovaries are active. Atrophy in the reproductive system occurs when hormone production declines.
3) Endometriosis is characterized by multiple cystic nodules lined with endometrial tissue, not by fibrotic tumors.
***4) Endometriosis is a condition in which endometrial tissue, which undergoes proliferative and secretory changes in response to estrogen and progesterone, is found in locations outside the uterus.**

25.(VIIIA6a) 1) BUN is a measure of renal function; abnormal renal function is not a contraindication to estrogen replacement therapy.
2) Elevated cholesterol is associated with an increased risk of coronary artery disease and myocardial infarction; estrogen is believed to protect against coronary artery disease and myocardial infarction. Thus, elevated cholesterol may suggest the use of estrogen replacement therapy, not contraindicate it.
3) Elevated creatinine indicates impaired renal function, which is not a contraindication to estrogen replacement therapy.
***4) Elevated serum bilirubin occurs in liver disease when damaged liver cells are unable to clear normal amounts of bilirubin from the blood. Liver disease contraindicates estrogen replacement therapy.**

26.(VIIIB3b)**1) General postoperative care following abdominal surgery includes the use of elastic pressure stockings, leg exercises, and early ambulation to prevent deep vein thrombosis.**
2) IV fluid replacement is standard for up to 24 hours after surgery or until the patient is stable and tolerating oral fluids. Following general anesthesia, nausea and vomiting is common; therefore, large amounts of oral fluids would be contraindicated.
3) Early ambulation and turning and positioning every two hours should be encouraged to prevent cardiopulmonary complications.
4) The protocol for assessing vital signs is followed unless the patient becomes hemodynamically unstable or complications arise.

Differences in Nursing Care: Area A (modified)

1.(IB1)***1) Increase in the respiratory rate (respiratory rate of 26), tachycardia (pulse of 120), and weakness with exercise are physiological signs of activity intolerance related to insufficient oxygen secondary to chronic obstructive pulmonary disease (COPD).**
2) The patient with COPD would have tachypnea (not bradypnea) and an increased respiratory rate.
3) Pursed-lip breathing is a compensatory mechanism that a patient with COPD uses to help with expiration. Fatigue can result from numerous causes and PCO_2 of 40 is normal.
4) Nasal flaring, ineffective cough, and dyspnea are signs of acute respiratory distress. They are not signs of activity intolerance related to oxygen insufficiency in a patient with COPD.

2.(IB1) 1) It is normal for the heart rate to increase gradually.
2) It is normal for the heart rate to increase with activity.
3) It is normal for the heart rate to slow with rest as long as the pulse does not become bradycardic.
***4) Any sudden slowing of the pulse rate should be reported immediately since it may indicate a pacemaker malfunction.**

3.(IB5) 1) Weight is not critical information to report for this patient.
***2) Since digitalis therapy has a direct influence on the heart rate, heart rate must be reported. The most serious side effect of digitalis therapy is the development of dysrhythmias and the presence or absence of dysrhythmias should be reported.**
3) Blood pressure is not critical information to report for this patient.
4) Urinary output is not critical information to report for this patient.

4.(IB4) 1) This action is not appropriate. Administering the Lasix would deplete the already low potassium and dietary replacement would not adequately compensate. Medical intervention is required.
2) This action is not appropriate. Administering the ordered dose would deplete the already low potassium. The physician should be notified first before giving the medication.
3) This action is not appropriate. Although it is correct to withhold the medication, the nurse would need an order to repeat the laboratory test and repeating the test will not resolve the hypokalemia. The nurse needs to consult with the physician.
***4) This action is appropriate. Withholding the medication prevents further loss of potassium. The physician needs to be consulted before the medication is given.**

5.(IB4) 1) Humidity is used to counteract the dry, irritating effects of oxygen, and does not affect the viscosity of the secretions.
***2) Increasing fluids provides adequate hydration, which thins secretions and makes them easier to expectorate.**
3) Postural drainage uses gravity to help remove secretions from the lungs, but it does not decrease the viscosity of the secretions.
4) IV fluids are only necessary when the patient is unable to take PO fluids.

6.(IA1) 1) Administration of vitamin B_{12} will not directly improve tissue oxygenation. Vitamin B_{12} is administered orally to treat nutritional vitamin B_{12} deficiency and parenterally to treat pernicious anemia.
2) Administration of vitamin C will not directly affect tissue oxygenation. Vitamin C is essential for the formation of collagen. It promotes wound healing, promotes iron absorption, and reduces susceptibility to infection.
***3) The infusion of packed red blood cells will improve tissue oxygenation by providing hemoglobin to transport oxygen to the tissues.**
4) Since plasma does not contain any oxygen-carrying blood components, the infusion of plasma will not improve tissue oxygenation.

7.(IB3) 1) Encouraging fluids will not decrease fatigue, dyspnea, or other symptoms of anemia.
2) The patient with anemia fatigues easily and frequent ambulation should not be included in the care plan.
***3) Providing frequent rest periods must be included in the care plan for a patient with anemia. Measures to conserve energy prevent undue fatigue that results from poor oxygen delivery to the tissues.**
4) Providing a high-protein diet will not restore tissue oxygenation.

8.(IB3)***1) Oxygen consumption should be minimized to prevent sickling of the red blood cells. When blood oxygen levels increase, most sickle cells resume normal shape. Maintaining bed rest decreases oxygen demand.**
2) Bed rest will not prevent bacterial infection.
3) Bed rest will not reduce oxygen tension. Oxygen saturation levels need to be increased in sickle cell anemia.
4) Bed rest will not correct respiratory acidosis. Respiratory acidosis results from hypoventilation; sickle cell anemia does not cause hypoventilation.

9.(IB5) 1) Isometric exercises are contraindicated in patients with angina. These exercises cause an increase in the cardiac workload. Each time an isometric exercise is stopped, a large amount of venous return enters the heart—this can stress a diseased heart.
2) Patients with angina must avoid physical exercise immediately after a meal. A temporary increase in blood flow to the GI tract following meals may cause angina with exercise.
3) Patients with angina can bend and the lifting of light objects is acceptable.
***4) Nitroglycerine reduces myocardial oxygen consumption which will decrease ischemia and relieve anginal pain. Since nitroglycerine will increase the patient's tolerance for activity, it should be taken before such activities as sexual intercourse.**

10.(IA4)***1) Atropine sulfate will be given because it blocks vagal stimulation, causing an increased heart rate.**

2) Lidocaine is not used for ventricular asystole. Lidocaine is used to suppress some ventricular dysrhythmias and will not stimulate the heart to beat.
3) Morphine will not correct ventricular asystole. Morphine is an opioid analgesic used to manage severe pain.
4) Inderal is never used to treat asystole. It is a beta-adrenergic blocking agent used to treat hypertension or angina.

11.(IB1) 1) Spoon-shaped fingernails are seen with iron deficiency anemia.
*2) Smooth, sore, red tongue is a classic sign of pernicious anemia.
3) Inflamed, swollen joints are seen with sickle cell anemia.
4) Petechiae on the face and neck are seen with thrombocytopenia.

12.(IB1) 1) Tension pneumothorax increases intrathoracic pressure and compromises venous return to the heart, which causes a decrease in cardiac output. This decreased cardiac output makes the pulse weak, not bounding.
2) Tension pneumothorax decreases cardiac output and therefore causes hypotension, not hypertension.
3) Edema is not related to pneumothorax. Peripheral edema results from expansion of fluid in the interstitial space and is related to cardiac disease, renal disease, tissue trauma such as burns, and osmotic pressure changes.
*4) Profuse diaphoresis is an indication that a tension pneumothorax is developing. Other characteristics of tension pneumothorax are hypotension, tachycardia, air hunger, and cyanosis.

13.(IIB4) 1) Teaching the patient about esophageal speech preoperatively is not correct. It does not address the patient's immediate postoperative needs because esophageal speech cannot be taught until at least one week following surgery.
*2) Telling the patient that paper and pencil (or a magic slate board) will be given for communication in the immediate postoperative period is correct. It addresses the patient's concern about how needs will be conveyed to others.
3) Tracheoesophageal puncture cannot be created during laryngectomy surgery.
4) Learning sign language is not practical and may cause unnecessary stress for the patient. Other means of communication are more appropriate.

14.(IIA4) 1) Nausea and vomiting may alter the patient's fluid and electrolyte balance, but will not directly increase vulnerability to infection.
2) Pulmonary fibrosis results in formation of scar tissue in the connective tissue of the lung and will not directly increase vulnerability to infection.
*3) With bone marrow suppression, white blood cell production decreases, leaving the patient vulnerable to infection.
4) Cardiotoxicity may result from antineoplastic agents, but it does not increase vulnerability to infection.

15.(IIB3) 1) Patients with stomatitis should be taught to follow a soft, bland diet, not a regular diet. Bland, room temperature foods are less irritating than regular foods. Fastidious oral care is essential.
2) Liquids, hard candy, and ice chips do not provide adequate protein or calories and should not be used as snacks. Appropriate snack foods should be high in nutritional value as well as soothing to the mouth.
3) Patients receiving chemotherapy are only kept NPO if a serious GI disorder is diagnosed. Patients receiving chemotherapy are encouraged to maintain adequate oral nutrition.
*4) Patients should be taught to brush their teeth with soft toothbrushes to minimize trauma and to use soothing mouthwashes with normal saline.

16.(IIA2) 1) Infants with pyloric stenosis appear hungry and willingly feed; their sucking reflex is not poor.
2) Bowel movements are usually normal.
3) The feeding never enters the intestine, so the emesis does not contain bile.
*4) Visible gastric peristaltic waves occur as the gastric musculature forcefully tries to empty through the pyloris.

17.(IIA1)***1) Untreated basal cell carcinoma is characterized by invasion and erosion of the adjoining tissues.**
2) Basal cell carcinoma does not mutate to a malignant melanoma.
3) The lesions of basal cell carcinoma grow slowly and because of this the center becomes indurated and sometimes crusted. There is no inflammation in the underlying tissue.
4) Basal cell carcinoma rarely metastasizes.

18.(IIA3d)***1) Dietary intake of fat is associated with increased colon cancer risk. Dietary fats increase production and bowel concentration of cholesterol and bile acids that are converted to carcinogen-promoting compounds by fecal bacteria. Also, high fat intake slows digestion and allows more time for carcinogens to be absorbed by the intestine.**
2) Diets high in fiber reduce cancer risks by increasing roughage as well as providing anticancer compounds such as those found in cruciferous vegetables.
3) Diets low in protein do not cause an increased risk of colon cancer. Although adequate protein is necessary for normal cellular growth and wound healing, low levels do not cause an increased risk for colon cancer.
4) Diets low in iron do not influence the risk of colon cancer. Low iron levels will result in hypochromic, microcytic anemia, but that is not a risk factor for colon cancer.

19.(IIA2d) 1) Fat intolerance, belching, and flatulence are usually seen in patients with chronic pancreatitis and are not typically seen in patients with pancreatic cancer.
*2) Hyperglycemia is a result of insulin deficiency from impairment of the beta cells on the islets of Langerhans which occurs with pancreatic cancer. Mid-abdominal pain results from pressure by the growth on surrounding tissues and organs. Profound weight loss results from several factors associated with the cancer. Meals often aggravate abdominal pain, causing patients to decrease their food intake. Patients may also suffer from anorexia.

3) Vomiting, burning epigastric pain, and diarrhea are signs of gastrointestinal abnormalities and are not signs of pancreatic cancer.
4) Weight loss, not weight gain, is a sign of pancreatic cancer. Lower abdominal pain and polycythemia are not associated with pancreatic cancer.

20.(IIB3a) 1) Although adequate calcium intake helps to build and maintain bone tissue, normal blood clotting, nerve transmission, and muscle action, excessive calcium intake will not benefit the patient with cancer.
2) Although fiber is important to gastrointestinal motility, increasing fiber will not improve the nutritional status of the patient with cancer.
3) Although iron is required for hemoglobin synthesis and oxygen transport, there is no benefit for the patient with cancer in exceeding the normal recommended dietary amount.
*4) High protein intake is essential to maintain proper nutrients and tissue development for patients with advanced cancer. The tissue protein synthesis that is vital for cellular regeneration and tissue building requires amino acids and nitrogen. Efficient protein use depends on adequate intake of proteins to build tissue and to prevent the tissue wasting common in cancer patients. Cancer patients have an increased need for protein, calories, vitamins, and minerals to meet the demands of the disease.

21.(IIB1a) 1) First pregnancy after the age of 30 is not associated with an increased risk for cervical cancer, although it is a minor risk factor for breast cancer.
2) Late menopause is not associated with an increased risk for cervical cancer, although it is a minor risk factor for breast cancer.
*3) A major risk factor for cervical cancer is multiple sex partners. Multiple partners increase the potential for being exposed to the human papilloma virus that is a major risk factor for cervical cancer.
4) Multiple pregnancies alone do not predispose a woman to cervical cancer. However, multiple sex partners pose a definite risk of cervical cancer.

22.(IIB1a) 1) Alpha-fetoprotein (AFP) is a blood test used to screen for certain birth defects and chromosomal anomalies in pregnant women. Decreased levels of AFP may indicate Down syndrome, but are not associated with prostate cancer.
2) Carcinoembryonic antigen (CEA) serum levels are used to detect and monitor colon cancer, not prostate cancer.
3) Erythrocyte sedimentation rate (ESR) is a blood test that is used to diagnose various inflammatory conditions such as rheumatoid arthritis.
*4) The prostate gland releases a substance called prostate-specific antigen (PSA) which is measured by a blood sample. Levels of PSA increase with prostate cancer and decrease when prostate cancer is in remission.

Differences in Nursing Care: Area B

1.(IA1a[4])***1) Delusional thought patterns may be part of the clinical manifestations of the manic phase.**
2) Psychomotor activity is extensive. The patient constantly goes from one activity to another.
3) There is a decreased need for sleep.
4) The patient is not passive in communication. In the manic phase, the patient becomes more talkative and demanding of peoples' attention.

2.(IA1d) 1) The patient with schizophrenia has minimal affective response or emotional reaction.
*2) The patient with schizophrenia may demonstrate an indifference or a disinterest in the environment, leading to emotional apathy.
3) The patient with schizophrenia experiences an inability to trust, panic anxiety, and withdrawal into self. Euphoria is not a clinical manifestation.
4) The patient with schizophrenia has diminished emotional expression. Sadness is not one of the diagnostic criteria.

3.(IA1e[2]) 1) Suspiciousness is a characteristic of paranoid personality disorder.
2) Patients with personality disorders are unable to identify their own feelings and needs or to understand how to meet those needs.
3) Patients with passive-aggressive personality disorder feel misunderstood, are scornful and argumentative, and use a hostile-submissive pattern of interaction.
*4) Patients with passive-aggressive personality disorder display manipulative or devious behavior when dealing with stress or conflict. The individual's resentment, anger, or hostility is masked by an outward appearance of compliance.

4.(IA4i[1d])***1) Blurred vision is a sign of severe lithium toxicity, fine hand tremors are an expected effect, and diarrhea is an early sign of toxicity.**
2) Neutropenia, palpitations, and drowsiness are side effects of antipsychotic drugs.
3) Psychological dependence, ataxia, and depression are side effects of the benzodiazepine class of antianxiety drugs.
4) Akathisia, tardive dyskinesia, and delusions are side effects of antipsychotic drugs.

5.(IA2c) 1) This behavior represents denial, which the patient uses to escape an unpleasant reality.
*2) This behavior represents dissociation, the separating of a traumatic event from awareness and memory.
3) This behavior represents repression, the process of excluding unacceptable feelings from conscious awareness.
4) This behavior represents suppression, the conscious denial of a disturbing thought.

6.(IB2b)***1) To begin working with a patient who is suspicious, the nurse must first establish trust and reduce the patient's anxiety.**
2) See 1).
3) See 1).

4) See 1).

7.(IB2b) 1) Medication, prescribed to relieve stress and avoid sleep deprivation, does not directly address the issue of high risk for self-directed violence.
2) The best protection against suicide is one which provides for a therapeutic relationship between the client and the nurse.
3) Cognitive improvement is a sign of rational thinking but does not prevent self-directed violence.
*4) **A short-term goal for the patient who is suicidal is to make a no-suicide contract with the nurse covering the next 24 hours.**

8.(IB2c)*1) **Victims of abuse are at high risk for injury. Assurance of safety is the most important goal.**
2) Understanding the psychodynamics will not do anything to stop the cycle of abuse.
3) This implies that the abuse was somehow the fault of the victim and ignores the issue of safety.
4) See 2).

9.(IB4b) 1) Isolation allows the patient's hallucination to continue, while talking with someone can help to minimize the hallucination.
2) Antianxiety medications are not effective for hallucinations.
*3) **Focusing on activities that are presently occurring will keep the patient busy and divert attention away from the hallucination.**
4) The nurse should not argue about or deny the hallucination.

10.(IB4e) 1) Insisting that the patient stop the handwashing ritual will escalate the patient's anxiety.
2) Restricting access to the sink will increase the patient's frustration, anxiety, and panic.
*3) **Providing extra time to accommodate for the handwashing ritual will prevent panic. The patient needs a structured schedule of activities, including time for rituals.**
4) Postponing the handwashing ritual will increase the patient's anxiety level.

11.(IB4g)*1) **An untoward side effect of antipsychotic medication is a blockage in dopamine that can lead to muscular and motor rigidity such as in Parkinson's disease. Administering an antiparkinsonian medication will have an anticholinergic effect and relieve acute dystonic reactions.**
2) Antipsychotic medication should be reduced gradually over a two- or three-week period.
3) These are not expected side effects, but an adverse reaction to medication.
4) Antipsychotic therapy is titrated from a low dosage and then the dosage is increased to produce a therapeutic response.

12.(IIA2i) 1) The patient with diabetes insipidus has skin which tends to be warm and dry.
2) With diabetes insipidus, fluids are excreted rather than retained due to the lack of vasopressin.
*3) **The patient with diabetes insipidus excretes a large volume of urine with low specific gravity and an elevated serum sodium level. Hypernatremia may be a result of dehydration and will lead to poor skin turgor.**
4) Pruritis is not a clinical manifestation of diabetes insipidus.

13.(IIA4a) 1) Corticosteroid therapy may result in muscle wasting, not in tremors.
2) Corticosteriod therapy may result in increased blood sugar levels, not in increased potassium. Hyperkalemia is a sign of Addison's disease, not of treatment effects.
*3) **Corticosteroid therapy suppresses inflammation and autoimmune reactions that curtail the body's immune response and increase the risk of infection.**
4) Corticosteroid therapy results in sodium retention, fluid retention, and weight gain.

14.(IIB1a[3]) 1) Loosening the dressing is indicated when a patient reports fullness or pressure at the incision site.
2) It is impractical to lift the patient off the bed.
*3) **Rolling the patient to the side would allow blood to flow by gravity to the sides and back of the neck.**
4) Bleeding will not be seen in the posterior pharynx.

15.(IIB1a[4])*1) **In chronic renal failure, there is a decreased secretion of erythropoietin. This results in impaired red blood cell formation, causing fatigue and leading to activity intolerance.**
2) Increased serum magnesium is common in chronic renal failure.
3) In chronic renal failure, metabolic acidosis occurs and the kidneys cannot excrete the excessive acid. The treatment is to administer bicarbonates.
4) The increase in serum phosphate that occurs in renal failure does not affect activity level.

16.(IIB4d) 1) Chvostek's sign is a test for hypocalcemia which occurs during the oliguric phase.
2) In the diuretic phase, the blood volume is decreasing and the veins would not be distended.
3) Trousseau's sign is a test for hypocalcemia which occurs during the oliguric phase.
*4) **In the diuretic phase, potassium is excreted producing hypokalemia and dysrhythmias.**

17.(IIB4f) 1) Continued medication is necessary to keep the patient symptom free.
2) Palpitations and diaphoresis should be reported to the health care provider and may indicate that the dosage needs to be reduced.
*3) **A regular schedule for medication administration assures constant blood level of the hormone and prevents symptoms of undermedication.**
4) It is recommended that the medication be taken before breakfast.

18.(IIIA2a) 1) Hyperglycemia is not associated with hepatic encephalopathy.
2) Hyperkalemia is not associated with hepatic encephalopathy.
3) Hypernatremia is not associated with hepatic encephalopathy.
*4) **Elevated ammonia levels cause hepatic encephalopathy. Ammonia is formed in the**

intestines from the breakdown of protein by intestinal bacteria and converted to urea in the liver. Hyperproteinemia will increase ammonia production.

19.(IIIB1a[3]) 1) Bilirubin levels should be monitored but alterations are not life threatening.
2) Skin color should be monitored but alterations are not life threatening.
3) Urinary output should be monitored but alterations are not as life threatening as hemorrhage.
*4) **Assessing vital signs monitors the patient for bleeding and hemorrhagic shock, which is a life-threatening emergency.**

20.(IIIB1b) 1) Anorexia does not cause itching. A patient with hepatocellular jaundice may develop anorexia, but this does not cause itching.
2) Ascites affects skin integrity because of the edematous tissue, but is not a significant cause of itching.
*3) **Jaundice causes severe itching due to the accumulation of bile salts in the skin.**
4) Malnutrition does not cause itching.

21.(IIIB2a) 1) The patient with pancreatitis is most likely to have diarrhea or frequent, frothy, and foul smelling stools rather than constipation.
2) Pancreatitis results from mechanical obstruction, not destruction, of the bile ducts.
*3) **The patient with pancreatitis has frequent bouts of severe abdominal and back pains that cause splinting and an ineffective breathing pattern.**
4) Sensory deficits are not a clinical manifestation of pancreatitis.

22.(IIIB3b)*1) **The patient with liver dysfunction cannot absorb vitamin K, has impaired clotting factors, and has thrombocytopenia, thus increasing the risk of bleeding. Small gauge needles are used to decrease the risk of bleeding.**
2) Bathing with soap should be avoided to prevent removal of natural oils, since dryness and itching are common problems.
3) With liver disease, hypertension, not hypotension, is common due to obstruction to blood flow through the portal venous system.
4) Physical restraints are counterproductive and increase agitation.

23.(IIIB4b) 1) Monitoring intake and output is important, but pain relief has higher priority.
*2) **Irritation and edema of the inflamed pancreas stimulate the nerve endings causing severe abdominal pain. Relieving the patient's pain should receive priority.**
3) The patient's position should be changed frequently, but pain relief should be given priority.
4) Lab values should be monitored, but pain relief takes priority.

24.(IIIB4f) 1) A high-fat diet is not appropriate for the patient with cirrhosis since fat accumulates in the liver tissue and causes cellular destruction.
2) A high-fiber diet would not contribute to the management of ascites.
3) A high-carbohydrate diet should be followed to restore glycogen reserves and to meet the energy needs of the disease process.
*4) **A low-sodium diet reduces fluid retention, edema, and ascites.**

25.(IIIB5a) 1) Increased urination and nausea are symptoms of diabetes mellitus.
*2) **Sweating and shakiness are symptoms of hypoglycemia and should be reported so that insulin dosage, diet, or exercise can be adjusted.**
3) Unusual thirst and rapid breathing are symptoms of hyperglycemia.
4) Dry skin and fruity breath odor are signs of hyperglycemia.

26.(IVA2a) 1) Squatting does not significantly affect blood pressure.
2) Squatting decreases peripheral circulation.
3) Squatting does not affect peripheral resistance.
*4) **Squatting increases the systemic vascular resistance, which will decrease venous return to the heart and will diminish symptoms.**

27.(IVB1a[1]) 1) With Hirschsprung's disease, the stool is not greasy, but ribbonlike or watery. Greasy stools are associated with celiac disease.
*2) **With Hirschsprung's disease, the muscle of the bowel lacks nerve innovation, which leads to absences of peristalsis and results in chronic constipation.**
3) Projectile vomiting is not a clinical manifestation of Hirschsprung's disease.
4) Hirschsprung's disease is a megacolon disorder and does not affect the respiratory system.

28.(IVB1a[3])*1) **Meningomyelocele involves herniation of the spinal cord with sensory and motor dysfunction corresponding to the level of the spinal anomaly.**
2) Respiratory paralysis is not a clinical manifestation as the anomaly involves the lower motor neuron.
3) There is no pain associated with movement because of a loss of motor and sensory function.
4) This is a lower motor neuron anomaly and does not affect the pharyngeal, laryngeal, or oral muscles.

29.(IVB5a) 1) Chicken salad is not low in phenylalanine.
*2) **Fruit salad has no protein; therefore, it has no phenylalanine.**
3) An egg salad sandwich has a high level of phenylalanine.
4) Peanut butter has a high level of phenylalanine.

Differences in Nursing Care: Area C

1.(IA3)*1) **Adolescents frequently deny having an STD due to the perceived stigma and possible threat to emotional relationships.**
2) Adolescents often do not seek medical attention early.
3) Adolescents frequently do not openly discuss symptoms of STDs due to social and peer pressure.

4) Adolescents are often not willing to accept teaching from a health care provider.

2.(IB1) 1) Increased activity will increase peristalsis but will not cause diarrhea; decreased activity will decrease peristalsis and leave the patient prone to constipation.
*2) Diarrhea can be caused by various classifications of drugs. Taking antibiotics can result in a superinfection of the intestinal tract, resulting in diarrhea.
3) The amount of fluid intake over the last 24 hours would not be a cause of diarrhea.
4) An abdominal assessment of the patient should be completed by the nurse, but it will not provide information regarding the cause of the diarrhea.

3.(IB3) 1) The patient with a urinary tract infection (UTI) should take showers rather than tub baths to prevent bacteria from entering the urethra and bladder.
*2) The patient with a UTI should increase fluid intake to dilute urine and lessen the irritation on the bladder mucosa.
3) The patient with a UTI should void after intercourse, but it is not necessary to abstain from intercourse.
4) Vitamin C is not included in the therapeutic management of a UTI.

4.(IA3) 1) There is no defect in the B lymphocyte population.
2) There is a decreased number of T lymphocytes.
*3) An opportunistic infection is the result of a decrease in the T-helper cell population. The virus infects these cells and uses the cells for reproduction.
4) Hyperactivity of the humoral response is not a cause of these infections.

5.(IB5b) 1) The medication should be taken at the same time each day to ensure equal spacing between doses.
2) Prothrombin levels should be monitored.
*3) Nonsteroidal anti-inflammatory agents such as ibuprofen may induce gastric irritation and possible bleeding. Therefore, ibuprofen should not be taken by a patient on warfarin sodium therapy.
4) Swimming three times a week for exercise is an excellent activity that would not place the patient at risk for bleeding.

6.(IA4) 1) Tetanus toxoid provides active immunity.
2) Tetanus toxoid has no antibacterial effect.
*3) Tetanus toxoid stimulates antibody production and provides active immunity.
4) Tetanus toxoid does not neutralize bacterial toxins; it provides active immunity.

7.(IB4) 1) Crusts may be removed, but the itching will not be relieved.
2) A four-year-old may not have the cognitive ability to reason the cause and effect of scratching.
*3) Applying pressure to the pruritic areas will provide relief and will reduce the need for scratching.
4) Applying medicated powders is not recommended.

8.(IA4)***1) The multiple-puncture skin test is used to screen large groups of individuals. This test is not used to establish a definitive diagnosis of tuberculosis.**
2) The Mantoux test and the chest X ray are used to establish a diagnosis of tuberculosis.
3) Drug sensitivity is not determined by the screening and diagnostic tests used to determine tuberculosis exposure.
4) The treatment modality for tuberculosis is a preestablished medication regimen.

9.(IA4) 1) Emotional lability is not a side effect of amphotericin B.
2) Pulmonary edema is not a side effect of amphotericin B.
3) Renal impairment can be a side effect of amphotericin B and cause hypokalemia, not hyperkalemia.
*4) The nurse must monitor the patient taking amphotericin B for evidence of anaphylactic shock, such as shaking and chills.

10.(IIB1) 1) Abdominal assessment is not a priority.
2) Cardiac assessment is not a priority.
*3) Neurovascular assessment is a priority. Trauma from frostbite results in freezing of the tissues causing neurovascular damage. The feet, hands, nose, and ears are most frequently affected.
4) Respiratory assessment is not a priority.

11.(IIB5) 1) Moderate wound drainage is not a desired outcome for a rigid cast dressing.
*2) Uniform compression of the stump is the desired outcome for early fitting for a prosthesis.
3) A rigid cast dressing will not prevent phantom pain.
4) Adequate circulation to the distal part of the leg is necessary. Care is taken so there is no constriction of the circulation.

12.(IIB1) 1) If the sutures are intact in the epithelium, the wound is healing by primary intention.
2) If the wound edges are well approximated, the wound is healing by primary intention.
3) A wound healing by secondary intention does have drainage.
*4) In a wound healing by secondary intention, granulated tissue forms into connective tissue and fills in the affected area.

13.(IIB1) 1) Drooling may be present but it is not specific to the ingestion of a caustic substance.
2) Since there is severe pain in the mouth, swallowing is difficult and painful.
3) Tinnitus is a clinical manifestation of acute aspirin poisoning.
*4) Caustic substances cause chemical burns in the mucosa of the mouth and throat, leaving the mucosa white and swollen.

14.(IIA4)***1) Soaking the burned area briefly in cold water is recommended.**
2) Application of ointments, salves, or oils is contraindicated.
3) If the burned area is left open, there may be bacterial contamination and further pain from the air contact with the burn.
4) Rinsing the burned area may cause further tissue damage.

15.(IIB2) 1) Difficulty swallowing is a concern but it is not the priority.
*2) **Following a tonsillectomy, the patient who is swallowing frequently should be assessed for possible hemorrhaging. This diagnosis should be given priority.**
3) Acute pain related to the tonsillectomy is an appropriate nursing diagnosis but it is not the priority.
4) Anxiety may be a concern but it is not the priority.

16.(IIB4) *1) **Administering a cool sponge bath will reduce the body's temperature and should be done as rapidly as possible.**
2) Assessing for hyperkalemia is not necessary for heatstroke.
3) The temperature is monitored continuously by inserting a probe into the rectum or esophagus.
4) A cool environment is necessary to reduce body temperature.

17.(IIA4) *1) **Amphojel reacts with gastric acid to decrease acidity.**
2) Amphojel has no effect on gastric motility. Central nervous system depressants reduce gastric motility.
3) Amphojel has no effect on inhibiting histamine. H$_2$ receptor antagonists such as cimetidine (Tagamet) block the action of histamine.
4) Amphojel does not inhibit the production of gastric acid. Omeprazole (Prilosec) inhibits the gastric acid pump.

18.(IIIA2) 1) Seizure activity can occur as a result of brain injury, but it is not the first sign of altered neurological status related to brain injury.
2) Poor pupillary response is a later sign of increased intracranial pressure (IIP) related to brain injury.
3) Widening pulse pressure is a serious development related to increased intracranial pressure (IIP) that can result from brain injury, but it is not the first sign.
*4) **A change in the level of consciousness is the first sign of altered neurological status related to brain injury and is indicative of increased intracranial pressure (IIP).**

19.(IIIB1) *1) **Claustrophobia would be a significant finding since the patient undergoing an MRI lies on a platform that is moved through a narrow tube-like machine.**
2) Blood pressure in the patient with hypertension will be monitored, but it is not considered significant when preparing the patient for an MRI.
3) No dye is used for an MRI.
4) Impaired vision would create the need for a more descriptive patient orientation, but it is not a contraindication for an MRI.

20.(IIIB5) 1) Capillary refill time of less than five seconds is a normal finding.
*2) **Complaint of pain on movement of the toes is a sign of neurovascular compromise of the affected extremity and a sign of compartment syndrome.**
3) Palpable dorsalis pedis pulse is a normal finding.
4) Toes that are warm to the touch is a normal finding.

21.(IIIB5) 1) The purpose of intermittent self-catheterization by the patient with a spinal cord injury is not to determine post-voiding residual. If the patient could void, there would be no need for intermittent self-catheterization.
2) The amount of urine obtained after each catheterization is variable and no minimal amount is predetermined as acceptable.
3) The absence of dribbling between catheterizations does not necessarily indicate that the patient is performing the procedure correctly.
*4) **The patient is taught self-catheterization using aseptic technique. Urinary tract infections are a serious complication of poor self-catheterization aseptic technique.**

22.(IIIA4) 1) Antihypertensives reduce blood pressure.
2) Calcium channel blockers increase myocardial oxygen supply.
*3) **Corticosteroids reduce cerebral edema by acting as an anti-inflammatory.**
4) Vasodilators reduce blood pressure.

23.(IIIB4) 1) Limiting the intake of carbonated beverages has no effect on exacerbations of multiple sclerosis.
*2) **Avoiding emotionally stressful situations is very important. Exacerbations are associated with periods of emotional and/or physical stress.**
3) Limiting exposure to persons with viral infections is not necessary.
4) Increasing the number of hours of sleep at night is not necessary.

24.(IIIB1) 1) Urate crystals may be found in the urine with a number of conditions that have an increased cell turnover.
2) Tophi (crystalline deposits in articular tissue) can be aspirated but not palpated.
3) A biopsy of surrounding tissue will not confirm the presence of gout.
*4) **The finding of urate crystals in a symptomatic joint cavity confirms the presence of gout.**

25.(IIIA4) 1) This does not describe decerebrate posture.
2) See 1).
*3) **Decerebrate posture results from damage or trauma at the midbrain. The arms and legs are extended, with pronation of the hands and feet.**
4) See 1).

Occupational Strategies in Nursing

1.(IIIB2) 1) Continuing to only monitor the patient would be a breach of duty; it is the responsibility of the nurse to seek needed medical care.
2) Asking another physician to examine the patient would be inappropriate since this physician would have no right to direct the patient's treatment.
3) Reporting to the medical board is not appropriate since it has not been determined that there was a breach of duty.
*4) **Any deviation from medical care that poses a threat to the well-being of a patient must be**

reported to the nursing administration so that appropriate care can be provided.

2.(IIIC2)★1) **The primary purpose of the Patient Self-Determination Act is to allow patients to be involved in health care decisions including decisions about treatments intended to preserve life.**
2) Although the act includes informing patients about what types of care are available if they become incapacitated, it is not the primary purpose of the act.
3) The act is not limited to older adults.
4) Legislation cannot ensure that family members will agree on treatment for a patient who is terminally ill.

3.(IIIB3) 1) This action is not ethical. A patient has the right to make a decision free from persuasion by the nurse.
★2) **These actions by the nurse are the defined skills used for solving ethical dilemmas.**
3) This action is not ethical. The nurse should respect the physician's right to stand by a decision.
4) This action is not ethical. Dealing with the family circumvents the patient who has the right to determine care and treatment.

4.(IIA4) 1) The ANA-PAC is nonpartisan and does not support any one political party.
★2) **The major purpose of the ANA-PAC is the improvement of the health care delivery system via political action.**
3) The ANA-PAC encourages nurses to be politically active but this is not its primary goal.
4) The ANA-PAC offers financial support to political candidates who demonstrate positive attitudes toward health care reform but this is not its primary goal.

5.(IIA3) 1) Removing furniture from the room will not contain costs.
2) Reusing safety razors would have little effect on cost containment, and since safety razors can become dull, reusing them could cause injury to the patient.
3) Ordering large quantities of a new medication might control costs, but it is not appropriate since medications have an expiration date.
★4) **Disposable equipment is expensive and is meant for single use. Using permanent equipment is a positive cost-containment measure.**

6.(IIIA2) 1) Describing a patient's behavior as cheerful is referred to as subjective data. Subjective data can be described only by the patient and is based on opinion, not fact.
2) This is subjective data. See 1).
3) This is subjective data. See 1).
★4) **If the nurse describes the patient as "tearful," then the nurse can see the tears. This is objective data that can be obtained by physical assessment or observation.**

7.(IVB1) 1) Montag's report did not address the issue of baccalaureate education being the minimum requirement for entry into professional practice.
2) Montag's report did not emphasize the need for nursing research in basic nursing education.
★3) **Montag's report described the nursing curriculum as an integrated program of general education and nursing credits, with the community college as the educational setting.**
4) Montag's report did not propose a selective admission policy for nursing programs.

8.(IIID4)★1) **Continuing education has made nurses more accountable for clinical competence, which is required by the Code for Nurses.**
2) Continuing education has not discouraged nurses from renewing their licenses.
3) Nurses who have been inactive often pursue continuing education prior to seeking employment, but continuing education is not responsible for more inactive nurses returning to the workforce.
4) Burnout in nurses is most effectively reduced by stress-reduction methods, not by continuing education.

9.(IVD2) 1) This is an example of team nursing.
2) This is an example of functional nursing.
★3) **This is an example of primary nursing, in which a registered nurse is responsible for the total care of a number of patients from admission to discharge.**
4) This is an example of team nursing.

10.(IIB2) 1) This patient should be admitted to an acute care hospital.
2) This patient would best be serviced by an ambulatory care center.
3) This patient needs supportive care.
★4) **A day-care center would provide this patient with activities such as social interaction, reorientation programs, and exercise.**

11.(IIIB2) 1) This action is inappropriate because it negates the right of a patient to know their own diagnosis.
2) This action is inappropriate because the nurse avoids the issue of the patient's right to know.
★3) **This action is appropriate. The Patient's Bill of Rights states that a "patient has the right to... relevant, current and understandable information concerning diagnosis, treatment, and prognosis."**
4) This is not the appropriate action.

12.(IVC1) 1) Management and supervision of a nursing unit is an educational outcome of baccalaureate nursing.
2) Leading a team composed of RNs and LPN/LVNs requires extensive management skills beyond the scope of associate degree nursing.
3) Community nursing is an educational outcome of baccalaureate nursing.
★4) **The associate degree nurse is prepared to administer technical bedside care to a group of patients.**

13.(IA2)★1) **Prior to the Civil War, there was no organized structure for administering care to people who were ill or wounded. The Civil War focused attention on the needs of health care delivery and by 1862, hospitals with medical and nursing staff became the providers of care to people who were ill and wounded.**
2) The Depression did little to focus attention on the needs of health care delivery.

3) The Industrial Revolution did little to focus attention on the needs of health care delivery.
4) The Revolutionary War did little to focus attention on the needs of health care delivery.

14.(IIIA1) 1) Providing guidelines for nursing education is not the purpose of the ANA *Standards*.
2) Nursing licensure requirements are enacted by state law.
★3) Improving nursing is the purpose of the ANA *Standards*. The ANA *Standards* provide a means to evaluate the quality of nursing practice and assist in assuring the public that quality nursing care is being delivered.
4) Promoting unity within the profession is not the purpose of the ANA *Standards*.

15.(IIA4) 1) Nurses do not have exclusive knowledge of matters related to health care.
2) Nurses' opinions may be valued by legislators but this is not why writing letters is important.
★3) Nurses can share their experiences in letters to legislators and influence health legislation.
4) Nursing licensure is a state right and is not dependent upon elected political power.

16.(IIID5) 1) The American Hospital Association monitors the quality of hospital care offered to the public.
2) The American Nurses Association is concerned with nursing practice and certification.
★3) The National League for Nursing offers voluntary accreditation to nursing education programs.
4) The National Council of State Boards of Nursing promotes public policy related to the safe and competent practice of nursing.

17.(IIIB1) 1) Appealing to the nurse's conscience will not assist in clarifying the issue.
2) Modeling is a technique used for developing self-esteem.
3) Reflecting is a technique used in therapeutic communication.
★4) Values clarification allows nurses to define their own individual values and choose an action that is congruent with these values.

18.(IIIA1) 1) The nurse is expected to have the knowledge and judgment to recognize if the doctor's order is correct. If the order is incorrect, and the nurse carries it out, the nurse can be held accountable.
★2) Sound institutional standards can be an adequate defense in allegations of professional liability.
3) Acting consistently according to personal values will not necessarily protect the nurse from litigation if the nurse's personal values are in conflict with a standard of practice.
4) Accepting responsibility as a patient advocate is important but it may not provide legal protection from liability.

19.(IB) 1) Montag developed an educational model that created an additional entry level into the practice of professional nursing.
★2) Montag's educational model envisioned the technical nurse being educated at junior and community colleges.
3) Montag's model may have complicated the distinction between the technically and professionally prepared nurse.
4) Montag's project was privately funded by the W.K. Kellogg Foundation.

20.(IVD5) 1) This situation is not an example of managed care. Managed care is a method that is designed to promote and deliver care at the patient's bedside in an acute care setting.
★2) This situation is an example of case management. Case management is a nursing care delivery method that provides care across the health care continuum, progressing from home, to hospital, to clinic, to home.
3) This situation is not an example of primary nursing. Primary nursing is a method in which one nurse is responsible for the complete care of a group of patients 24 hours a day, seven days a week.
4) This situation is not an example of team nursing. Team nursing requires a team approach for delivering nursing care with the team leader being a professional nurse.

21.(IVD6) 1) This is an example of the opposite of differentiated practice.
★2) This is an example of differentiated practice which allows nurses to assume roles and responsibilities commensurate with their level of educational preparation and experience.
3) This is not an example of differentiated practice.
4) This is not an example of differentiated practice.

22.(IVE10)**★1) The nurse is resistant to the change because the nurse was not available to be involved in the change process.**
2) In this situation, resisting change is not related to a lack of research on the need for the change.
3) The question does not indicate that this new charting procedure would increase the amount of paperwork.
4) Lack of familiarity with the new forms might create some resistance, but lack of involvement in the decision-making process is a much stronger factor in creating resistance.

23.(IIIC2) 1) Assault is the attempt or threat to touch another person.
2) Battery is the willful touching of a person that may or may not cause harm.
3) Negligence is the failure to act as a reasonably prudent nurse would act and criminal negligence is negligence that was in violation of criminal law. Even though this nurse has been negligent, the nurse has not committed a crime.
★4) This nurse is guilty of malpractice. Malpractice is negligence by a specially educated professional person in the performance of her or his duties.

24.(IIIC2) 1) A nurse is not qualified or educated to ensure that the person is of sound mind.
2) The nurse is not responsible for recording the names of those individuals who are present when the will is signed.
★3) The nurse is responsible for recording an assessment of the patient's physical and mental status in the patient's record at the time the patient signs the will.
4) The nurse is not responsible for confirming that the will was drawn up by an attorney.

25.(IIID3)**1)** **Nursing certification is the validation that a nurse has met minimum standards of competency in a specialty area.**
2) Mandatory licensure of nurses is an attempt to ensure safe nursing care for the public.
3) Licenses are legal permits that allow individuals to practice a profession.
4) Licensing determines the minimum standards to practice a profession.

Health Restoration: Area I

1.(IF) 1) Although carbonic acid decreases in respiratory alkalosis, it is not a compensatory mechanism.
2) Human oxygen needs do not normally decrease.
3) Metabolic alkalosis is characterized by a high plasma bicarbonate level that leads to respiratory changes. It is not a result of the respiratory changes.
*4) The lungs attempt to compensate for the excess bicarbonate by retaining carbon dioxide and this results in increased partial pressure of carbon dioxide.

2.(IF) 1) Normal urine specific gravity is between 1.010 and 1.025. Urine specific gravity of 1.040 is evidence of concentrated urine, a manifestation of fluid volume deficit, and would not indicate effective therapy.
2) Hemoconcentration could be manifested by a hematocrit greater than normal as the red blood cells become suspended in a decreased plasma volume and, thus, would not indicate effective therapy.
*3) Normal skin turgor reflects adequate hydration and is an indication of effective therapy.
4) Low blood pressure can be a manifestation of fluid volume deficit and is not an indication of effective therapy.

3.(IC) 1) Although constipation may occur because of the use of epidural analgesia, it is not the most important problem to be managed postoperatively.
*2) Clients receiving epidural analgesia postoperatively are at risk for respiratory depression. The most important intervention is to monitor respirations.
3) Epidural analgesia usually decreases blood pressure.
4) Although the heart rate may decrease with the administration of epidural analgesia, the primary intervention is respiratory assessment.

4.(IIA1) 1) In asystole, cardiac standstill, there is an absence of ventricular activity on the electrocardiogram, including no QRS complexes. There are QRS complexes on this strip.
2) In atrial fibrillation, the ventricular rate can vary widely (50–180 bpm) and the ventricular rhythm is usually irregular. An irregular baseline on the electrocardiogram (fibrillatory waves) occurs between usually normal QRS complexes. The irregular baseline does not appear on this strip.
*3) The QRS complex of premature ventricular contractions is usually wide and bizarre on the electrocardiogram (as seen on this strip) and the rhythm is irregular when the premature beat occurs.
4) In sinus tachycardia, the electrocardiogram would show a heart rate of greater than 100 bpm and the rhythm would be normal.

5.(IIA4)***1) With heart failure, cardiac output is diminished, perfusion is not adequate, and congestion of the lungs and periphery may develop. This is the primary problem and the goal is to reduce the workload of the heart.**
2) Breathing patterns may be altered related to fatigue, but the primary concern is to decrease the workload of the heart.
3) The client may be at risk for impaired skin integrity, but the primary diagnosis is decreased cardiac output.
4) Family processes may be altered, but the primary diagnosis is decreased cardiac output.

6.(IIA1) 1) The normal resting heart rate for a six-month-old who is awake is 80–150.
*2) Vomiting is the earliest sign of digoxin toxicity.
3) Tetany is not an indicator of digoxin toxicity.
4) Hypertension is not an indicator of digoxin toxicity.

7.(IIIA1) 1) Bronchial breath sounds heard over the tracheal area are normal.
*2) Bilateral decreased breath sounds in the lung bases may indicate inadequate lung expansion which may lead to atelectasis.
3) The absence of adventitious breath sounds is a normal finding.
4) Vesicular breath sounds are normal findings in the lung bases.

8.(IIIA4)***1) Heparin is the anticoagulant approved for preventing new clot formation.**
2) Anticoagulant therapy will not dissolve an existing embolus.
3) The client is usually positioned with the head of the bed elevated.
4) Blood transfusions are not used in the treatment of pulmonary embolus.

9.(IIIA3)***1) Confusion or altered thought processes occur early in the presence of hypoxia.**
2) Constricted pupils are not a sign of hypoxia.
3) Cyanosis is a late and unreliable sign of hypoxia.
4) Enlarged liver is not a sign of hypoxia.

10.(IIIA) 1) Fever and tachypnea, often seen with pneumonia, cause an increase in insensible water loss and the client may become dehydrated. Fluid restriction would not be a therapeutic dietary intervention.
2) The client with pneumonia may have a poor appetite and there is no need to restrict sodium or fat.
*3) Adequate hydration may help in thinning secretions which can then be more easily removed by coughing.
4) A mechanically soft diet high in vitamin A is not indicated for pneumonia.

11.(IVA3)***1) Allopurinol (Zyloprim) is used to prevent hyperuricemia secondary to chemotherapy in many clients with cancer.**
2) Furosemide (Lasix) is used to promote renal excretion of the drug, not to manage fluid retention.

3) Phenytoin (Dilantin) is not routinely administered to clients with leukemia who are receiving standard chemotherapy.
4) Heparin (Liquaemin Sodium) is contraindicated in the presence of thrombocytopenia.

12.(IVB5) 1) This statement reflects accurate information and does not necessitate additional teaching.
★2) Additional teaching is needed. Radiation therapy and alkylating agents can cause decreased fertility and sterility. Sperm banking prior to initiation of treatment is often an option. Counseling may also include waiting at least one year to assess if the cancer is in remission before starting a family.
3) See 1).
4) See 1).

13.(IVA1) 1) These are not typical symptoms of lymphoma.
★2) Weight loss, fever, and night sweats are classic symptoms of lymphoma.
3) See 1).
4) See 1).

14.(VA5) 1) The normal PaO_2 is 80–100 mm Hg. A PaO_2 of 60 mm Hg indicates low oxygenation.
2) Blood pressure of 80/60 is low; normal blood pressure is 120/80.
★3) Urinary output of 30–50 ml/hr in an adult is considered evidence of adequate replacement.
4) Urine specific gravity of 1.450 is concentrated and indicates hypovolemia.

15.(VA4) 1) The drug container does not need to be protected from light.
★2) Clients receiving dopamine need continuous EKG monitoring to observe for dysrhythmias.
3) The IV will not be discontinued because additional fluid and medications will need to be infused.
4) A large vein is selected to infuse a greater volume of fluid and medication at a faster rate.

16.(VA3) 1) The client is positioned with the head of the bed elevated 30–45° but this is not the primary intervention.
2) Maintenance of effective respiratory function would take precedence over starting an IV. Fluids may be restricted with head trauma.
★3) Maintaining an open airway should receive priority to maintain oxygenation and tissue perfusion.
4) Cerebrospinal fluid loss might occur in some types of head trauma but maintenance of effective respiratory function would be the primary intervention.

17.(VIA5) 1) Alcohol is not recommended for a client with cirrhosis to prevent further complications and promote liver healing.
2) Diuretics should be administered early in the day so that the drug can be dissipated before bedtime to avoid interruption of the client's sleep. Eating bananas might help if a potassium-wasting diuretic is prescribed. Eating meat and eggs would help to improve the client's general nutritional status.
★3) Clients on diuretics should be advised against self-medication with over-the-counter drugs, such as laxatives or cathartics that enhance potassium loss, or antacids that contain sodium. Diuretics should be taken according to prescribed guidelines to avoid further fluid and electrolyte complication.
4) Baked chicken and poached eggs are low-sodium foods.

18.(VIA5) 1) Thyroid hormone replacement is generally a lifelong therapy. In most cases, medication is continued even after symptoms improve.
2) Chest pain is not a normal side effect of Synthroid and the health care provider should be notified immediately to rule out any cardiac problems.
★3) Synthroid should be taken at the same time every day, preferably in the morning to avoid interfering with sleep.
4) Any change in sleeping pattern needs to be reported to the health care provider to evaluate if the medication dosage needs to be adjusted.

19.(VIA1)**★1) Extreme fatigue is related to a decrease in thyroid hormone resulting in a decreased metabolic rate.**
2) Diarrhea is a symptom of hyperthyroidism. The client with hypothyroidism often complains of constipation.
3) Heat intolerance is a symptom of hyperthyroidism. The client with hypothyroidism often complains of being cold, even in a warm environment.
4) Muscle tremors are a symptom of hyperthyroidism.

20.(VIA1) 1) Nausea and vomiting is not a common symptom of hypoglycemia. It is more likely seen with the hyperglycemia of diabetic ketoacidosis.
★2) When the client with diabetes mellitus is treated with insulin, hypoglycemia can occur. In mild hypoglycemia the symptoms are sweating, tremors, tachycardia, palpitation, nervousness, and hunger.
3) Tachypnea and dehydration are symptoms of diabetic ketoacidosis.
4) Ketonuria and malaise are symptoms of diabetic ketoacidosis.

21.(VIIA5)**★1) Dizziness is a side effect of Benadryl. Clients may need to be reminded not to drive or work with machinery.**
2) Dry mouth can be produced by Benadryl, but it is an inconvenience, not a potential problem.
3) Difficulty falling asleep is not usually a side effect of Benadryl; drowsiness is more common.
4) Increased alertness is not a side effect of Benadryl.

22.(VIIA1) 1) Although enhancing self-concept is a viable goal, it is not the priority goal for a child with newly diagnosed juvenile rheumatoid arthritis.
2) Although promoting socialization is a viable goal, it is not the priority goal for a child with newly diagnosed juvenile rheumatoid arthritis.
★3) Reducing discomfort should be given priority in the management of juvenile rheumatoid arthritis. The goal is to provide as much relief as possible with medication and therapy to help the client cope.
4) Although encouraging self-care is a viable goal, it is not the priority goal for a child with newly diagnosed juvenile rheumatoid arthritis.

23.(VIIA2) 1) Diarrhea is not a common finding in a client with systemic sclerosis.
*2) Dysphagia may indicate disease progression involving the esophagus and may indicate complications related to drinking, eating, and swallowing.
3) Although malaise can be a common finding in systemic sclerosis, it is not as potentially serious as dysphagia.
4) Although pain is a common symptom related to inflammation, fibrosis, and sclerosis of connective tissue, dysphagia is of greatest concern because it can result in choking or aspiration.

Health Restoration: Area II

1.(IA5)***1) Since the client is noncompliant with the daily medication regimen, a long-acting medication is indicated as an alternative. Prolixin in an injectable form can be given every seven to twenty-eight days.**
2) Inconsistent administration of this antipsychotic medication will result in less than prescribed blood levels and probable symptom recurrence.
3) See 2).
4) See 2).

2.(IA) 1) Taking a walk with the nurse indicates beginning acceptance of interaction, but since there is no verbal interaction, it is not the best indicator of trust.
2) Attending unit activities with the nurse indicates a higher involvement in interaction than walking since the client is participating in a group activity, but since self-disclosure is not required, it is not the best indicator of trust.
3) Sitting with the nurse in the day area indicates the lowest level of interaction and trust since the client does not have to be verbally or actively involved; therefore, this behavior is not a good indicator of trust.
*4) Discussing past life experiences with the nurse indicates the highest level of personal interaction, self-disclosure, and personal involvement with the nurse; therefore, this behavior is the best indicator of trust.

3.(IA4) 1) This intervention focuses on the physical complaint and fails to demonstrate an understanding of the psychodynamics of a client with a panic disorder.
2) This intervention is not appropriate since the physical and psychological symptomatology indicate that the client is unable to focus on detailed instructions or tasks.
3) See 2).
*4) The primary goal is to decrease the client's anxiety. This intervention meets the goal by altering the client's interaction with the environment in a timely and therapeutic manner.

4.(IA3) 1) Encouraging small frequent feedings is unrealistic. With the increase in psychomotor activity in a client with mania, the client may be too busy to eat even small regular meals.
2) Providing three meals daily is unrealistic. With the increase in psychomotor activity in a client with mania, the client may be too busy to eat regular meals.
*3) Allowing frequent nutritious finger foods which the client can eat while standing or moving best decreases the risk of malnutrition. This intervention takes into consideration the increase in psychomotor activity in clients with mania.
4) Administering nutritional supplements can augment a diet, but supplements alone will not provide a well-balanced diet.

5.(IIA1) 1) Withholding medication is unsafe. Anticonvulsant medication is the primary component of seizure control and must be administered consistently to maintain therapeutic blood levels.
*2) The client should be instructed to reduce stress, maintain adequate rest, and avoid alcohol use to avoid precipitating factors for seizure activity.
3) Following a seizure, the level of consciousness and degree of orientation will improve within several hours to 24 hours.
4) Assuming the supine position will not prevent occlusion of the airway.

6.(IIB2) 1) This action is unsafe. Washing down solid foods with liquids should be avoided as it may cause choking and aspiration in a client with amyotrophic lateral sclerosis (ALS).
2) This action is unsafe. Dry foods are hard to chew and swallow. The client with ALS has a loss of tongue coordination, making it difficult to move solids back toward the pharynx. Due to impaired pharyngeal motility, inadequately chewed food may become lodged in the esophagus and cause choking.
3) This action is unsafe; to facilitate swallowing, the client with ALS needs to be in an upright position with the neck slightly flexed.
*4) This is the best action. A client with ALS experiences a progressive weakening in muscles used to swallow food, thus a longer time span in an upright position after eating is needed to facilitate swallowing and prevent aspiration.

7.(IIA4) 1) This action is inappropriate as the client with expressive aphasia usually understands what is said but is unable to respond verbally.
*2) Since the client with expressive aphasia understands what is said but is unable to verbally communicate, a picture board enables the client to point to the activity or object desired.
3) Correcting errors may be potentially detrimental as the client is aware of the deficit and may become frustrated and angry.
4) Teaching facial muscle exercises is inappropriate for a client with expressive aphasia.

8.(IIA2)***1) The goal in caring for a client with early Parkinson's disease is to maintain the client's usual activities for as long as possible.**
2) Diarrhea is not a common problem with Parkinson's disease. Medication and reduced activity usually lead to constipation.
3) Looking at alternative living arrangements is not appropriate for a client with early Parkinson's disease. Most clients with Parkinson's disease who adhere to the prescribed regimen can maintain their independence.
4) The client with Parkinson's disease has difficulty swallowing and usually requires a soft diet with think liquids. Supplemental high-calorie, high-protein feedings may be needed.

9.(IIIA2) 1) Pyloric stenosis usually develops in the first few weeks of life; it is not a congenital anomaly.
2) This diagnosis does not pertain to pyloric stenosis.
*3) Restoring hydration and electrolyte balance is the primary emphasis of preoperative care for an infant who is vomiting due to pyloric stenosis.
4) This diagnosis does not pertain to pyloric stenosis.

10.(IIIA4)*1) Use of strict aseptic technique decreases the chance of developing peritonitis in a client who is receiving intermittent peritoneal dialysis.
2) Monitoring the client's lungs and pulse after receiving dialysis will not prevent peritonitis.
3) Moving the client from side to side during drainage will facilitate outflow of the solution but it will not prevent peritonitis.
4) Calculating fluid balance is not related to preventing peritonitis.

11.(IIIB3) 1) Limiting fluids will dehydrate the client; fluids should be given at regular intervals throughout the day.
*2) Reminding the client to go to the bathroom will assist in reducing functional incontinence.
3) Keeping a commode or bedpan near the client's bed is not necessary since the client is ambulatory.
4) Using adult undergarments only addresses the symptom of the functional incontinence, wetness. It does not address the cause of the incontinence.

12.(IVB) 1) This intervention is not a strategy for preventing the transmission of pinworms.
2) See 1).
*3) Since the bed linen is frequently contaminated with pinworms, frequent and careful washing of bed linen helps to minimize transmission to other family members.
4) See 1).

13.(IVC4) 1) See 4).
2) See 4).
3) See 4).
*4) The parent needs to be informed that the child is in the communicable stage and should be taken home. The period of communicability for varicella is approximately one day before the rash appears to six days after the rash appears, when all the vesicles have crusted.

14.(IVA5) 1) In the acute phase, the child with osteomyelitis would be on complete bed rest with immobilization of the affected extremity. A leg splint would be part of the immobilization.
2) In the acute phase, the child with osteomyelitis would not be allowed to use a wheelchair since the child is on complete bed rest.
*3) Pain in the limb is a classic sign of osteomyelitis. The occurrence of pain when moving the affected limb indicates that the child is still in the acute phase.
4) Performing range-of-motion exercises is not indicated. During the acute phase, movement of the affected leg will cause the child discomfort.

15.(VA4) 1) This is an unsafe intervention. Bearing down and performing the Valsalva maneuver are contraindicated. The client would be taught open glottal breathing techniques.
*2) Penicillin prophylaxis is indicated for this client to prevent heart damage.
3) It is not necessary to place the client on bed rest following delivery.
4) Breast-feeding is not a contraindication for this client.

16.(VA2) 1) This urinary output is too low and indicates that the mother is dehydrated or in shock.
2) Since the degree of placenta previa may change rapidly, the absence of vaginal bleeding is not an indication of effective intervention.
*3) The FHR and maternal vital signs are within normal limits and indicate effective care. Since placental tissue is exposed in placenta previa, increasing the risk of infection, vital signs need to be monitored frequently. Also, the fetus is at risk for intrauterine compromise and needs to be monitored frequently.
4) The maternal vital signs indicate impending shock; the FHR, when maternal vitals are taken into consideration, indicates fetal distress.

17.(VB5) 1) There is insufficient data to determine if nursing interventions have been inadequate.
*2) Shock and disbelief are characteristic grief responses to the diagnosis of trisomy 21.
3) The mother's verbalizations about her feelings are not unusual and do not indicate that further referrals are needed at this time.
4) There is insufficient data to determine if there is a lack of bonding with the neonate.

18.(VIA2) 1) Itching is not related to neurological complications.
*2) Numbness and tingling of the toes are common signs of nerve damage.
3) Weak femoral pulse may indicate circulatory impairment, not neurological complications.
4) Warm, puffy toes are common findings following a fracture; they are not related to neurological complications.

19.(VIA4) 1) Adduction of the affected leg beyond the body's midline can cause dislocation of the hip.
2) See 1).
*3) Slight abduction with hip flexion less than 90° prevents possible dislocation.
4) Hip flexion beyond 90° can cause dislocation.

20.(VIA5) 1) Heat therapy is not indicated.
2) Splints rather than an elastic bandage are used after sutures are removed.
3) Active extension and flexion of the fingers is encouraged to promote circulation.
*4) Application of cold reduces swelling.

Health Support A: Health Promotion & Health Protection

1.(IC) 1) A client who is truly concerned about confidentiality is not more likely to divulge binge drinking to the nurse than to the doctor.
2) Active euthanasia involves intervention that hastens death. This is not a plausible explanation for the client's reluctance.
3) Binge drinking may be a reaction to poor quality of life, but it is inconsistent with seeking a better quality of life.
*4) The client is seeking to maintain his individual lifestyle without advice or interference from the physician.

2.(IIE) 1) Loyalty in meeting one's obligations to the family occurs in Kohlberg's conventional stage.
*2) Avoiding punishment is the principal reason for obedience in Kohlberg's preconventional stage.
3) The need to be good in one's own eyes and in the eyes of others occurs in Kohlberg's conventional stage.
4) The desire to treat others as one wishes to be treated occurs in Kohlberg's conventional stage.

3.(IIB) 1) Practice sessions should be limited to five or 10 minutes; 15 minutes is too long a period.
2) Telling the toddler his behavior is unacceptable will only make matters worse and achieve nothing.
3) This toddler is within normal parameters and his behavior is not unusual.
*4) It is most important that the parent be reassured that the child falls within normal parameters.

4.(IVA) 1) Encouraging the avoidance of conflict minimizes the client's feelings.
2) A nurse should not agree just to be compliant; it is important to explore the client's feelings.
3) The nurse is interested in this client and, while the family is important, the client's feelings must be considered first.
*4) Allowing the client to express her feelings will give her a sense of self-worth and help her to realize that her perceptions may be valid.

5.(IVA) 1) The physician or nurse practitioner may reduce milk intake to a pint (16 ounces) a day with calcium lactate or a quart with aluminum hydroxide gel, but eight ounces is not an adequate daily intake of milk for the pregnant client.
*2) Practicing dorsiflexion of the feet will stretch affected muscles.
3) Toe pointing or extension of the foot may actually cause leg cramps.
4) Aluminum hydroxide gel may actually be prescribed to absorb phosphorus and eliminate it through the gastrointestinal tract to correct a potential imbalance in the calcium/phosphorus ratio.

6.(VB) ***1) DTP is a killed vaccine that is not shed and therefore is safe for the sibling of an immunocompromised child to receive.**
2) An HBV immunization is inappropriate at this time.
3) An MMR immunization is inappropriate at this time.
4) TOPV is a live vaccine and is inappropriate to give to a sibling of an immunocompromised child living in the same household.

7.(VA)***1) Crying is the primary way an infant communicates.**
2) Crying at this time has a reflexive quality that is usually related to physiological needs.
3) Infants cry up to 1-1/2 hr per day and most infants have an unexplained period of fussiness daily.
4) Crying periods are actually on the increase at one month of age. The peak tends to occur around three months.

8.(VIA) 1) Prevention of dental caries involves the elimination of the bedtime bottle, but a bottle of water may be substituted for sweet liquids.
2) If water is fluoridated above 0.7ppm, oral supplements are not recommended.
*3) Young children can participate in toothbrushing, but parents need to thoroughly brush all teeth. Young children are usually only able to brush the mandibular occlusive surface (lower arch, top surface) and the front labial surface (outer or lip side). The most effective cleaning is done by parents.
4) Sweets are less damaging if consumed immediately after a meal rather than as a snack between meals.

9.(VIIA)***1) This is the age where rules are very important and games allow the school-age child to have more control.**
2) Team play does involve competition.
3) School-age children are quite involved in hobbies and other complex activities.
4) School-age children are becoming more interested in creative activities and the organizing of collections, not less interested.

10.(VIIB)***1) Red ring-shaped lesions are early symptoms of Lyme disease.**
2) Skin-colored vesicles are not symptoms of Lyme disease.
3) Raised track-like burrowing lesions are symptoms of mites.
4) Pink papules on the palms and soles are not symptoms of Lyme disease.

11.(VIIA) 1) The adolescent already knows the rules and the need for strict observance; it is the source of the stress.
2) Exercise will provide temporary stress reduction, but the stress will return in the strict family environment.
3) Outside employment may provide some relief for the adolescent, but it doesn't deal with the basic problem.
*4) Power struggles in the family will continue to produce stress until a compromise is negotiated.

12.(IXB)***1) Perception of the barriers and benefits of a health behavior is one of several factors used to predict the likelihood that a client will engage in the behavior.**
2) Pender's model is not based on fear as a motivator for health behavior.
3) Using avoidance to increase motivation for health behavior is not consistent with Pender's model.

4) Collecting data about individual perceptions and modifying factors precedes health education in Pender's model.

13.(IXB) 1) To achieve daily consumption of 1200 mg of calcium, most women need to include food groups other than dairy products and use calcium supplements.
2) Obtaining a baseline bone density test will not prevent the development of osteoporosis.
*3) **For the premenopausal woman, 1200 mg of calcium daily is recommended.**
4) While calcium is present in green leafy vegetables it is bound with oxalic acid, which makes the calcium unavailable to the body.

14.(XB)*1) **The prostate specific antigen (PSA) blood test and digital rectal exam (DRE) should begin at age 40 annually for all males.**
2) The recommended age for beginning digital rectal exams (DREs) is 40, according to the American Cancer Society Cancer Screening Guidelines.
3) A negative transrectal ultrasound (TRUS) does not prevent cancer.
4) Seeing a doctor after the symptoms occur will not prevent prostate cancer or detect cancer earlier.

15.(XA) 1) Ego integrity vs. despair is the stage of old age where one assesses life to have been either rewarding (maintaining ego integrity) or hopelessly unfulfilling (leading to despair).
*2) **Generativity vs. stagnation is the Eriksonian stage when middle-aged families must cope with their concern for children, parents, and the environment. Failure to address these concerns leads to stagnation.**
3) Identity vs. role confusion is the period when adolescents begin to discover who they are and what they will do with their lives; the risk is not finding a place in this life.
4) Intimacy vs. isolation is the stage of the young adult who is seeking to establish an intimate relationship or risk isolation.

16.(XIA) 1) Frequency of sexual contact by itself is not a risk factor for disease.
*2) **Use of proper precautions against STDs is an important primary prevention strategy to avoid disease, regardless of age.**
3) Physiological changes may warrant counseling by the nurse, but are not as important as disease prevention counseling.
4) The number of sexual partners is a risk factor, but secondary to using disease precautions.

17.(XIB) 1) The presence of others is not sufficient protection for a client with decreased sensation to temperature.
*2) **Use of a thicker barrier against heat will protect against accidents from diminished sensation.**
3) Skin lotion does not affect the skin's ability to feel heat.
4) A water heater set at 130° F would be considered too hot.

18.(XIB) 1) Calling the client's family will not necessarily result in the client receiving the needed care.
2) Keeping the client busy does not address the depression and suicide risk indicated by the client's statement.

*3) **This statement is indicative of high risk for suicide and requires intervention by a mental health professional.**
4) Reminiscing is not a treatment for possible suicide.

Health Support B: Community Health Nursing

1.(IA) 1) The ANA *Standards* are general principles that are not just for physical care.
*2) **The ANA *Standards* do provide criteria for evaluating the quality of care delivered.**
3) The ANA *Standards* do incorporate general principles of nursing.
4) The state, rather than the professional organization, has the legal authority to regulate nursing practice.

2.(ID) 1) Organizing care by other providers is a coordinator role.
*2) **Assessing and identifying client health needs and planning to meet them is a case-management role.**
3) Scheduling a case conference is a coordinator role.
4) Transmitting client information to other providers is a coordinator role.

3.(ID)*1) **Informed lobbying through professional organizations is most likely to have impact on the larger community (that is, the nation).**
2) This is an example of a local action.
3) This is an example of the nurse acting as a change agent.
4) This is the referral resource role of the nurse.

4.(IIE) 1) Effect is an aspect of outcome evaluation.
*2) **Efficiency is the aspect of process evaluation that measures the use of resources.**
3) Effort is the aspect of process evaluation that measures the amount of effort expended in the program.
4) Impact is an aspect of outcome evaluation.

5.(IIB) 1) There is no data in the situation regarding fraud or the number of Medicaid clients involved.
2) There is no data in the situation regarding an increase in health problems.
3) There may be a need-service match for non-Medicaid clients, but the diagnosis of concern relates to the needs of Medicaid clients.
*4) **The situation portrays inadequate resources (need-service mismatch) to meet Medicaid clients needs.**

6.(IIB/C) 1) This could be an example of primary or tertiary prevention, but it is not secondary.
2) This could be an example of primary or tertiary prevention, but it is not secondary.
*3) **Bone density is a type of screening which is an example of secondary prevention.**
4) This could be an example of primary or tertiary prevention, but it is not secondary.

7.(IIB) 1) Crime potential is a component of community assessment, not diagnosis, and is not amenable to nursing action.
2) Street maintenance is not a nursing priority.
*3) **The nurse's primary responsibility in community health is to intervene in health problems.**
4) The inference is not logical, nor is the problem solvable by the nurse.

8.(IIB)*1) **An aging population has an increased need for health services related to the presence of chronic illness.**
2) Need for leisure-time programs is not especially related to age.
3) Need for educational opportunities does not increase with aging.
4) Although there may be a need for retirement planning services, this is not an area of nursing responsibility.

9.(IIIB) 1) This is an example of compliance with beliefs of the dominant culture, not of cultural accommodation.
*2) **Cultural accommodation is the modification of health care services in keeping with the client's cultural background.**
3) This is a referral that may or may not be culturally appropriate.
4) This relates to accommodating needs of individuals and is not culturally driven.

10.(IIIB) 1) Smaller doses of psychotropic medications are generally required by persons of Asian background.
2) Asian religious groups are not expecially likely to prohibit taking specific medications.
3) This statement is too global for the situation.
*4) **Clinical experience has documented the observation that Asian clients may experience extrapyramidal effects.**

11.(IVB) 1) Biological factors are an element of Dever's model that corresponds to host-related factors in the epidemiologic triad model.
2) Lifestyle factors are an element of Dever's model that corresponds to the social environment in the epidemiologic triad model.
*3) **Identification of health care system as a separate concern is unique to Dever's model.**
4) This is incorrect because only agent, host, and environment are mentioned.

12.(IVD)*1) **Lyme disease, which is tickborne, occurs more frequently in the summer, because it is related to the life cycle of the tick and to human exposure.**
2) Immunization is being developed but is not in widespread use.
3) Lyme disease is not transmitted person to person.
4) All ages are at risk for contracting Lyme disease.

13.(VA) 1) Diabetes is not primarily an environmental health concern.
2) Collecting soil samples is not a realistic nursing action.
*3) **Year 2000 Health Objective 11.13 states "increase to at least 30 the number of states requiring informing prospective buyers of the presence of lead-based paint . . . in all buildings offered for sale."**
4) Scheduling health fair activities related to hypertension does not meet an environmental health objective.

14.(VB)*1) **Boiling water has been shown to be effective in eliminating bacterial contamination.**
2) Eliminating groundwater contamination is a long-term solution that is the primary responsibility of the town engineer.
3) Lobbying legislators requires a long period of time and others in the community will become ill unless immediate action is taken.
4) Providing medication is not legally within the nurse's role and will only treat the symptoms; the problem will not be resolved.

15.(VA) 1) Ionizing radiation occurs naturally in soil and rock.
2) Natural radiation may be harmful to human beings.
*3) **Radon accounts for 55% of human exposure to ionizing radiation.**
4) Natural radiation may contribute to illness but is not clearly established as a direct cause.

16.(VIB) 1) Screening should have been part of determining the problem. It is not an initial response to the findings.
*2) **Once a problem has been identified, the next appropriate step would be to identify any contributing factors.**
3) This action is an appropriate one; however, it occurs after an initial response to determine the factors.
4) This is not an initial step for the nurse to take.

17.(VIC) 1) Simply informing the community will not resolve the problem of inadequate emergency care.
2) Careful planning and coordination are essential to providing successful emergency services; planning should not be delayed.
3) Lobbying for a new hospital is a long-term solution, but does not address the immediate problem.
*4) **Research has shown that early hours of care are critical to successful outcomes, and protocols assist the nurse to take effective actions.**

18.(VIA) 1) A problem has already occurred; hence making referrals is secondary prevention.
*2) **Immunization is an example of primary prevention.**
3) Screening is an example of secondary prevention
4) Preventing recurrence is an example of tertiary prevention.

19.(VIIA)*1) **Cocaine use may cause weight loss, disrupted sleep and eating patterns, irritability, and hallucinations.**
2) Vision and hearing are not affected by long-term cocaine use.
3) Memory is not affected by long-term cocaine use.
4) The oral cavity is not affected by cocaine use, although the nasal passages are.

20.(VIIF)*1) **Families of terminally ill children need additional support in coming to terms with the eventuality of death.**
2) The family is ultimately responsible for this decision about whether to resuscitate; nurses should not impose their own view.

3) Becoming involved in a cancer support group is appropriate earlier in the child's illness.
4) Teaching options for pain control should have been a priority throughout the child's illness, not just at the terminal phase.

21.(VIIB) 1) Improving local health department services is not a *Healthy People 2000* objective.
2) The nutrition objective relates to all school-age children, not specifically to those in poverty.
3) There is no national health goal related to guaranteed annual income.
★4) National health goal 8.3 emphasizes access to preschool programs for all disadvantaged children.

22.(VIIC)**★1) Exposure to hazardous environmental conditions is neglect.**
2) Physical abuse occurs when a child is intentionally subjected to force.
3) Child maltreatment is a broader category that includes intentional neglect or abuse.
4) Medical neglect occurs when interventions necessary to the child's health are withheld.

Professional Strategies in Nursing

1.(IA2) 1) The US army did not create a nursing corps until 1901.
2) Although women from religious orders did work as nurses during the Civil War, most of the nurses who volunteered were lay women.
★3) As a result of the care nurses gave to wounded soldiers during the Civil War, the public recognized the need for nurses.
4) The American Red Cross was not created until 1882.

2.(IA2) 1) Awareness of the need to incorporate cultural diversity concepts into nursing curricula did not emerge until many years later.
2) Nursing theory development did not emerge until the 1960s.
3) Nursing research by nurses did not emerge until the 1960s.
★4) The use of trained nurses in military hospitals during the Spanish-American War led to the creation of the Army Nurse Corps in 1901.

3.(IB5) 1) This was not the purpose of the 1970 study *An Abstract for Action*.
★2) The purpose of the 1970 study *An Abstract for Action* was to improve health care delivery by analyzing and improving nursing and nursing education.
3) See 1).
4) See 1).

4.(IIA2) 1) A retrospective chart audit is conducted after care has been given; therefore, it is not the best option for monitoring the process of providing care.
2) The purpose of data collected via audits is to obtain aggregate data and to analyze trends, not to evaluate performance by individuals, teams, or nursing units.

3) Identifying documentation deficiencies is not the primary purpose of a retrospective chart audit.
★4) Retrospective chart audits are conducted after nursing care has been delivered and are used to obtain aggregate data about client outcomes.

5.(IIB2) 1) Physicians do not determine the legal scope of nursing practice.
★2) State practice acts authorize state boards of nursing to issue rules and regulations governing the practice of nursing, which includes determining the legal scope of nursing practice.
3) Journal articles would be a secondary less reliable source and would not be legally binding.
4) The nurse administrator has no legal authority to make such a determination.

6.(IIB3) 1) Assault is the sense of threat of harm. This situation does not involve assault.
2) Battery is bodily harm. This situation does not involve battery.
3) Fraud is an intentional deception or attempt to cheat the client. This situation does not involve fraud.
★4) This situation does involve negligence. Negligence is the omission of an act (for example, not fully explaining a procedure to the client) that any reasonable person in the same position would perform.

7.(IIB3) 1) As a witness to a will, the nurse should not read its contents.
★2) It is a personal decision by the nurse to agree to witness the signing of the will. If the nurse does witness a will, it is critical to document the client's apparent mental condition at the time.
3) There is no professional standard concerning witnessing a will. It is a personal choice by the nurse.
4) Hospital policies vary from institution to institution. The nurse would need to check on a hospital's policy before automatically assuming it is against hospital standards.

8. 1) The *Patient's Bill of Rights* does not address incompetent practice.
(IIC2) 2) The *Patient's Bill of Rights* focuses on clients while the *Code for Nurses* focuses on nurses.
★3) Both the *Patient's Bill of Rights* and the *Code for Nurses* begin with statements emphasizing the respectful treatment of clients and this theme continues throughout both documents.
4) The *Code for Nurses* does not address the client's right to information.

9.(IIC6)**★1) The principle of distributive justice involves treating people with the same needs equally and people with different needs differently. The nurse applies distributive justice by including the emergency case in today's schedule since the emergency case has an urgent need, and by postponing the case with the least need to another day.**
2) Not adding the emergency case denies the high priority the case deserves and is not an application of distributive justice.
3) Randomly eliminating a client without considering the client's need is not an application of distributive justice.

4) Reducing visiting time with each client to make time for a new client is not an application of distributive justice since the clients have different needs requiring different amounts of time.

10.(IIC7)*1) Evaluating merits of research protocols is not an ethical function of an IRB.
***2) An institutional review board (IRB) reviews research projects and functions as an advocate for potential subjects (clients) to protect them from being deprived of personal rights and dignity.**
3) An IRB is more concerned with the potential benefits to subjects than to the institution.
4) A separate ethics committee would deal with ethical concerns related to clients.

11.(IIIA1)**1) As nurses become more accountable for the outcomes of nursing practice through such mechanisms as shared governance, they demonstrate more autonomy over their practice.**
2) A person can have a professional attitude without autonomy.
3) A person can be a change agent without being autonomous.
4) Fee-for-service provider reimbursement is unrelated to autonomy in nursing practice.

12.(IIIA2) 1) In Benner's model, the entry-level nurse (or advanced beginner) has not developed the ability to prioritize that is necessary to thoroughly understand the nursing process.
2) In Benner's model, the entry-level nurse (or advanced beginner) is capable of applying theory to practice.
3) Benner's model focuses on how the nurse carries out critical thinking, not on technical skills.
*4) Benner's model emphasizes that progression to the level of expert can be accomplished only through extensive experience.

13. (IIIA2)1) This task is typical of Kramer's stage 1, gaining proficiency in skills and routines.
2) This task is typical of Kramer's stage 4, conflict resolution.
*3) This task is typical of Kramer's stage 2, social integration. The new graduate tries to fit in with the new work group while also trying to maintain the high standards and values learned in school.
4) This task is typical of Kramer's stage 3, moral outrage.

14.(IIIB3)**1) According to Neuman's model, this nursing action is an example of tertiary prevention which focuses on restabilization and prevention of recurrence after treatment.**
2) According to Neuman's model, this nursing action is an example of secondary prevention.
3) See 2).
4) According to Neuman's model, this nursing action is an example of primary prevention.

15.(IIIB3)**1) Martha Rogers' model emphasizes that there is a science unique to nursing that serves as the basis of nursing practice.**
2) This statement describes Orem's model.
3) This statement describes Roy's model.
4) This statement describes Henderson's model.

16.(IIIC1) 1) This is not the purpose of case management.
2) This describes the purpose of differentiated practice.
*3) The purpose of case management is to ensure that clients' health care needs are met in an efficient, cost-effective manner.
4) This describes the purpose of primary nursing.

17.(IIIC2) 1) This situation is not an example of the nurse acting as a client advocate.
*2) The nurse is acting as a collaborator by including the client and family members in the development of a care plan for the client. By working with the client and family, the nurse gains their help and cooperation to achieve client outcomes.
3) This situation is not an example of the nurse as an educator.
4) This situation is not an example of the nurse as an independent practitioner.

18.(IIIC2) 1) Developing unit policies and procedures is the nurse manager's responsibility.
*2) The clinical nurse specialist (CNS) is a clinical expert with CNS certification in a particular specialty and is best used as a resource for client care situations beyond the usual scope of nursing staff, such as with the most difficult client.
3) Evaluating nursing staff is the nurse manager's responsibility.
4) Updating the care plans is the nursing staff's responsibility.

19.(IIID2) 1) The nurse earns the respect of physicians through job performance, not by obtaining a degree.
2) Being a role model by pursuing further education does not guarantee that the staff nurses will attribute any expertise to the nurse who is pursuing the advanced degree.
*3) By acquiring advanced knowledge of administrative theory and strategies, the nurse increases her or his chances of being hired in an administrative (line) position with associated position power.
4) A master's degree in nursing administration would focus on management content, not on clinical skills.

20.(IVA2) 1) Awareness of need is only the first step in affecting change in the health care delivery system.
*2) Health care delivery is influenced by public policy. To influence public policy nurses must become active in its development.
3) Delivery of health care involves more than just nursing.
4) Involvement at the policy level will have a greater impact than participation in individual projects.

21.(IVB1) 1) HMOs were created in response to escalating hospital costs and profits, not losses.
2) Facilitating reimbursement for physician claims was not a factor related to the development of HMOs.
*3) HMOs promote health by emphasizing preventive treatment, thus decreasing the need for more expensive health care services, thus lowering costs.
4) HMOs do not necessarily increase access to health care since not all people are employed where HMOs are options or can afford HMO fees as private individuals.

22.(IVB1)*1) Nurse practitioners function as primary providers focusing on health promotion. This function fits well with the goal of HMOs—to keep people healthy and health care costs down.
2) Nurse practitioners would be responsible for both individual and group client education in an HMO.
3) Screening telephone calls would be underutilization of a nurse practitioner.
4) Routine client workups would be done in the clinic setting of an HMO, not in a hospital.

23.(IVB1) 1) HMOs do focus on health promotion and maintenance, but it is done primarily to keep costs down and is not the primary reason for their existence.
2) One of the major criticisms of HMOs is that they do not provide comprehensive health care.
*3) The Health Maintenance Organization Act of 1973 funded the development of HMOs as one strategy to control spiraling costs of health care.
4) The focus on using nonphysician health care providers developed as a result of HMOs and other cost-containment strategies; it was not the impetus.

Research in Nursing

1.(IA)*1) As noted in the *Code of Federal Regulations*, an element of informed consent is "a description of any reasonably foreseeable risks or discomforts to the subject."
2) Consent may be obtained by research assistants and may be written, verbal, or in the case of questionnaires implied when the subject returns the completed instrument.
3) Most research subjects do not receive financial compensation.
4) The researcher should answer all subjects' questions about a study and the consent form should tell the subject who to contact for answers to questions.

2.(IB) 1) Deductive reasoning moves from the general to the particular.
*2) Inductive reasoning moves from the particular (observations of infants crying at change of shift) to the general (the formulation of a theory).
3) With intuition, a researcher follows and acts upon a "hunch."
4) With trial-and-error, one solution is tried and then another until an effective solution is found.

3.(IC) 1) Nursing is still not recognized as a profession equal to medicine.
*2) Conversion of the NCNR to the NINR gave nursing research recognition equal to that of the other national health institutes.
3) Funding is based on priorities set by the Institute not on the size of the study.
4) Funding is based on national priorities rather than on local health problems.

4.(ID) 1) A well-written literature review is a summary and a critique; it is not a series of quotations.
2) A well-written literature review contains mostly primary sources.
3) A well-written literature review is based on critical analysis and synthesis, not on opinion.
*4) A well-written literature review notes gaps and inconsistencies in an existing knowledge base to establish the need for the present study.

5.(ID) 1) A critical evaluation of a theory is written by a person other than the individual who developed the theory; therefore, it is a secondary source.
2) A monograph on educational perspectives is an individual's opinions about the topic; therefore, it is a secondary source.
*3) A doctoral dissertation is written by the person who conducted the research; therefore, it is a primary source.
4) A textbook on clinical skills is written by a person to summarize the current knowledge base; therefore, it is a secondary source.

6.(IE) 1) Data are collected after the research problem has been developed and refined.
2) Instruments cannot be selected until the problem has been developed and refined.
*3) A review of the literature is a critical element in developing and refining a research problem.
4) Data analysis is conducted after the research problem has been developed and refined.

7.(IIA) 1) The hypothesis has one independent variable (preoperative instruction) and one dependent variable (perception of hospitalization); therefore, it is simple rather than complex.
*2) The hypothesis predicts that hospitalization will be perceived more positively by clients who receive preoperative instruction; therefore, it is directional.
3) The hypothesis predicts that clients who receive preoperative instruction will perceive hospitalization more positively; therefore, it is directional rather than nondirectional.
4) The hypothesis predicts a relationship between the independent and dependent variables; therefore, it is a research, rather than a statistical or null, hypothesis.

8.(IIB)*1) History is a threat to internal validity when an event (such as introduction of a new nurse manager) that is not the independent variable may affect the dependent variable.
2) Mortality is a threat to internal validity when subjects are lost from a study.
3) Selection bias is a threat to internal validity when steps are not taken to ensure that a sample is representative of the population.
4) Testing is a threat to internal validity when the same test is used as a pretest and a posttest.

9.(IIC) 1) Cluster sampling involves successive random sampling that progresses from large units to small units.
2) Quota sampling involves identifying the strata of the population and the nonrandom selection of subjects to proportionally represent the strata in the sample.
3) Simple random sampling involves listing all elements of the population and using a table of random numbers to select the sample.

*4) Systematic sampling involves listing all elements of the population and selecting every "kth" unit (in this case every third subject).

10.(IIC) 1) The nature of the sites may put a practical limitation on how large a sample could be, but not on how large the sample should be.
2) The number of data collectors has no influence on the size of the sample required for a study.
3) The convenience of the sampling does not affect the sample size needed.
*4) **The study design and associated power analysis provide the sample size needed.**

11.(IID) 1) Interviews allow for greater depth and more complex data to be collected than questionnaires.
2) Interviews allow researchers to clarify respondents' answers.
*3) **Questionnaires are less costly than interviews, allowing for a larger, more diverse sample.**
4) Verbally asking questions in interviews can control the sequence in which subjects respond.

12.(IIE)*1) **The Celsius scale ranks temperature with equal intervals between the numbers. Since the zero point is arbitrary, the Celsius scale is an interval level of measurement.**
2) The nominal level of measurement simply classifies objects or events into categories.
3) The ordinal level of measurement shows relative ranking of objects or events, but the intervals between assigned numbers are not equal.
4) The ratio level of measurement shows rankings of events or objects on a scale with equal intervals between numbers and an absolute zero point.

13.(IIIA) 1) A study to determine if a relationship exists between two variables (prenatal care and Apgar scores of newborns) requires a quantitative design.
*2) **A study being conducted to describe or explore a lived experience (the experience of delivering a stillborn infant at term) requires a qualitative design.**
3) A study being conducted to survey a population for information (number of clients with contraceptive failure who attend a prenatal clinic in one year) requires a quantitative design.
4) A study being conducted to determine if a relationship exists between two variables (self-esteem and maternal attachment in adolescents) requires a quantitative design.

14.(IIIB)*1) **Ethnography focuses on scientific descriptions of cultural groups, such as older African American adults living in rural areas.**
2) Phenomenology focuses on learning about the meaning of a human experience as it is being lived.
3) Grounded theory focuses on developing a theory about basic social processes.
4) The historical method focuses on understanding the past so that it can guide the present and future.

15.(IIID) 1) External validity deals with generalizing study findings to additional populations and is an issue in quantitative research.
2) Instrument reliability requires that the data be in a quantitative form.
3) Creativity of design is not a consideration in determining scientific rigor.
*4) **Credibility, auditability, fittingness, and confirmability are used to determine the truth, accountability, faithfulness, and accuracy of the findings in qualitative research.**

Fundamentals of Nursing

1.(IA3b) 1) Assault is a threat or an attempt to make bodily contact with another person without that person's consent. This nurse actually touched the patient.
*2) **Battery is assault carried out and includes the willful, angry, and violent touching of another person's body or clothes. Administering an injection after a patient has refused it is a classic example of battery.**
3) The nurse's action is not an invasion of privacy. An example of invasion of privacy is breach of confidentiality.
4) A misdemeanor is a classification of a crime; it is not in itself a type of offense.

2.(IC) 1) Beliefs are individually held attitudes and are not the rules of a profession.
*2) **Ethics are the rules or principles that govern professional conduct; ethics are the expected, publicly stated standards of a particular group.**
3) Morals are personal standards of right and wrong, not the standards of a group.
4) Values are the beliefs of an individual, not the rules of a profession.

3.(IIB) 1) The stage of resistance occurs later in an illness, as the body adapts.
*2) **Stress activates the sympathetic nervous system, causing the findings.**
3) The inflammatory response is a localized response to tissue injury or infection.
4) The local adaptation syndrome occurs when one part of the body responds to an injury.

4.(IIIB2a)1) Diaphoresis is a systemic response to fever and infection.
2) Fatigue is a systemic response to infection.
3) Fever is a systemic response to infection.
*4) **Swelling occurs when blood vessels dilate to increase blood flow to localized infectious agents.**

5.(IIIB1b)1) This would have no effect on a patient's risk for infection.
2) See 1).
*3) **A tetanus booster should be repeated every ten years in adults, so this patient is susceptible to tetanus, that is, at risk for infection.**
4) The patient did receive the polio vaccine, even though it was late, so the patient is immune to polio and not at risk for infection.

6.(IIIB2c)1) A full bag of standing urine is a medium for bacterial growth.
2) The drainage system should remain intact. Breaking the connection allows a portal for bacteria to enter the system.

3) Clamping the tubing promotes stasis of urine in the bladder.
*4) Positioning the tubing correctly promotes drainage and limits urinary stasis, thereby limiting bacterial growth.

7.(IIIB2a)1) Diminished breath sounds place a patient at risk for impaired gas exchange, not physical injury.
2) Hyperactive bowel sounds do not place a patient at risk for physical injury.
*3) A weak right hand grasp indicates the patient has altered mobility, placing the patient at risk for physical injury.
4) Bilateral ankle edema is an indicator of fluid volume excess which does not place a patient at risk for physical injury.

8.(IIIC1b)1) Massaging the site following the injection is not recommended because it may force the medication back into the needle track and cause irritation.
2) The Z-track method is used for intramuscular injections, not subcutaneous injections.
*3) Changing the needle prior to the injection ensures that no medication clings to the needle as it is inserted through the subcutaneous tissue into the muscle where it is injected.
4) The medication should not be administered rapidly. It is injected slowly and the needle is allowed to remain in place for 10 seconds after injecting the medication.

9.(IIIC2a)1) Absorption is the process by which a drug is transferred from its site of entry to the bloodstream.
2) Distribution is the movement of a drug throughout the body. The rate of distribution depends on perfusion and capillary permeability of the drug. Distribution usually does not involve the liver.
3) Excretion is the removal of a drug from the body. The kidneys excrete most drugs.
*4) Metabolism is the breakdown of a drug into inactive form. Liver disease may interfere with this process.

10.(IIID2d)1) A small amount of oil on the skin will help to moisturize.
*2) Oil is a slippery substance and can cause falls in the bathtub.
3) Alternating the use of bath oil with a skin lotion is personal preference and not a priority instruction for the patient.
4) The oil can be applied any way the patient likes. This is not a priority instruction.

11.(IVB1a)1) The patient will not return to the stage from which she was awakened.
*2) After being awakened, a patient begins the sleep cycle at stage one and progresses through all of the stages.
3) See 2).
4) See 2).

12.(IVC1c)1) The inability to endure or complete daily activities is not life threatening.
2) Poor gastrointestinal elimination is not life threatening.
*3) Loss of respiratory functioning may become a serious threat to health.
4) Urinary problems have a lower priority than do pulmonary problems.

13.(IVD1c)1) Tylenol is not associated with gastric bleeding.
2) Codeine is a narcotic analgesic and is not associated with gastric bleeding.
*3) Indocin is a nonsteroidal anti-inflammatory agent (NSAID). NSAIDs have been associated with gastric irritation and bleeding. Indocin is especially difficult to tolerate and should be used cautiously, if at all, in older adults.
4) Demerol is a narcotic analgesic and is not associated with gastric bleeding.

14.(IVD2c)***1) Providing an analgesic before the onset of pain is preferable. If the nurse waits for the patient to report pain, a larger dose may be required.**
2) Pain may vary in intensity from moment to moment and different pain relief measures may be required to control pain.
3) The choice of pain relievers is based on the patient's report of pain. Report of mild pain may require a different analgesic than more severe pain.
4) Pain therapy should not increase discomfort or harm the patient. In a trusting relationship, the nurse should manage the patient's pain regardless of the time intervals.

15.(VA2b)***1) Butter, being of animal origin, contains saturated fat.**
2) Margarine contains monounsaturated fat.
3) Olive oil contains monounsaturated fat.
4) Peanut oil contains monounsaturated fat.

16.(VIIB1b)1) Dyspnea, feeling short of breath, is not a positive response to oxygen therapy.
*2) Eupnea, normal, effortless breathing, is a positive response to oxygen therapy.
3) Hyperpnea, an increased depth of respiration, is not a positive response to oxygen therapy.
4) Orthopnea, the inability to breathe except in an upright position, is not a positive response to oxygen therapy.

17.(VIIIA1)***1) Loss of fluid makes the blood more concentrated and results in an increased hematocrit.**
2) Leukocytosis is an elevated WBC and is evidence of infection, not fluid volume deficit.
3) Distended neck veins are an indicator of fluid volume excess.
4) Peripheral edema is an indicator of fluid volume excess.

18.(VIIIB1b)1) A 5% dextrose in water is a sodium-free solution and would not be used for a patient with hyponatremia.
2) A 5% dextrose in 0.45% NaCl solution only contains half as much sodium as does normal blood and would not be used for a patient with hyponatremia.
*3) A 5% dextrose in 0.9% NaCl is normal saline and would provide additional intake of sodium for a patient with hyponatremia.
4) Lactated Ringer's solution is an isotonic solution used primarily for maintaining or replacing volume.

19.(VIIIB3b) 1) See 2).
*2) The standard formula for calculating IV flow rate is:

$$\frac{volume\ (mL) \times drop\ factor(gtt/mL)}{time\ in\ minutes}$$
$$\frac{1,000 \times 10}{600} = 16.66\ .$$

3) See 2).
4) See 2).

20.(VIIIB3c) 1) Calculating the volume of salt in the patient's diet does not teach the patient how to limit sodium in the diet.
2) Giving the patient a list of foods to avoid may provide information regarding foods high in sodium, but it does not teach the patient how to read and interpret food labels.
3) Giving the patient a set of preplanned menus does not allow for flexibility in the diet and patients often have difficulty complying with strict plans.
*4) Sodium is found in many foods and the patient must know how to read and interpret food labels in order to calculate a daily intake. The patient can then include personal preferences in the dietary plan, which should improve compliance with limiting sodium.

Maternal & Child Nursing (associate) and Maternity Nursing

1.(IB5a)***1) Crossing the legs at the knees compresses blood vessels and impedes venous return which contributes to varicosities.**
2) Pelvic rocking is used to improve abdominal muscle tone.
3) Kegel's exercises are used to strengthen the perineum.
4) Massage is contraindicated; it could cause an embolus.

2.(IB5a)***1) Toxic doses of magnesium sulfate result in hypotonia and respiratory failure. The respiratory rate must remain above 12/min.**
2) Muscle tone is reduced when central nervous system (CNS) depressants such as magnesium sulfate are used. Tremors would not be observed.
3) Hot, dry skin is not a sign of toxicity for magnesium sulfate.
4) The patient becomes sedated when a CNS depressant is used. Excitability would not be observed.

3.(IIB4g)1) Pitocin increases both the frequency and the duration of uterine contractions.
2) Short rest periods between contractions compromise the fetus. Short rest periods are not an acceptable outcome of using Pitocin to augment labor.
3) A decrease in the frequency of contractions is counterproductive in augmenting labor.
*4) Pitocin acts on oxytocin receptor sites in uterine myofibrils. Pitocin causes the contractions to become intense and longer in duration, thus facilitating labor progress.

4.(IIB3c)1) Massaging the fundus will cause increased discomfort since uterine muscles are tender after delivery.
*2) Providing warmth causes vasodilation and provides immediate comfort to the patient who may shiver from the exertion of labor. Administering an analgesic will relieve pain from the uterine afterpains and perineal edema.
3) Repositioning the patient and assessing vital signs will not relieve afterpains.
4) Providing ice packs will not relieve afterpains. Early breast-feeding causes a release of oxytocin and will increase afterpains.

5.(IIIB2a)1) Atony is failure of the uterus to remain firmly contracted. This patient's fundus is firm.
2) A boggy uterus is a soft uterus. This patient's fundus is firm.
*3) These data indicate normal involution. Twelve hours postpartum the nurse would expect the uterus to be firm and located slightly above the umbilicus in the midline.
4) Subinvolution is failure of the uterus to return to a nonpregnant state. Twelve hours postpartum is too soon to make this assessment.

6.(IIIB4f)1) Exposing the nipples to air promotes healing, but has no effect on breast engorgement.
2) A narcotic analgesic would be passed to the infant in the breast milk and is contraindicated.
*3) The application of heat by taking a warm shower stimulates the letdown of milk and relieves engorgement.
4) The application of cold reduces the metabolism of tissues and would inhibit the production of milk.

7.(IVA2a)1) Cleft palate does not cause excessive salivation or gastric distention.
2) Cystic fibrosis affects the exocrine glands; drooling is not exhibited.
*3) A newborn with esophageal atresia exhibits excessive salivation, gastric distention, drooling, and cyanosis.
4) Pyloric stenosis, caused by hypertrophy of the sphincter, is exhibited by projectile vomiting.

8.(IVB1a)1) The birth weight doubles at five months of age.
2) The Moro reflex is present until approximately six months of age.
3) The head circumference increases about 1.5 cm per month during the first six months of life.
*4) The infant's hand clenches on contact with a rattle at one month of age.

9.(IVB3c)***1) Suctioning accumulated secretions must be done frequently to prevent aspiration pneumonia.**
2) Providing a pacifier will encourage the infant to swallow saliva and choke.
3) The infant's head must be kept upright so that fluid in the esophageal pouch can be suctioned and to prevent aspiration of gastric secretions.
4) The infant cannot be fed orally until the fistula has been repaired.

10.(IVB4e)*1) **The newborn's temperature is subnormal. The newborn needs to be warmed to minimize oxygen consumption and hypoglycemia. All other data are within normal limits.**
2) Acrocyanosis is normal in the newborn and suctioning is not required. Swaddling the newborn in a light blanket will not warm him sufficiently.
3) The newborn should be placed on the back or side.
4) The newborn should not be bathed until the temperature is stable and within normal limits.

11.(VB1b)1) This response by the nurse does not elicit further information from the mother.
*2) **This response by the nurse elicits more information about the placement of poisons in anticipation of the infant's beginning to creep, stand, and walk.**
3) See 1).
4) See 1).

12.(VB5a)*1) **The parent understands that aspirin should not be given to a child with flu or chickenpox due to the link between Reye's syndrome and the administration of medications containing salicylates.**
2) The parent does not understand that a child with signs of a communicable disease should not be placed in contact with children who are healthy.
3) The parent would not need to ask further questions if the nurse's teaching was effective.
4) The parent does not understand that many childhood illnesses are unavoidable and their occurrence is not related to parental negligence.

13.(VIB4g)1) Glycosuria is not a side effect.
2) Hyperkalemia is not a side effect.
*3) **Hypocalcemia is a possible side effect. Serum calcium must be monitored.**
4) Polyuria is not a side effect.

14.(VIB5b)1) Corn is an acceptable substitute grain food.
2) Rice is an acceptable substitute grain food.
*3) **Gluten, which is found in oatmeal and wheat bran, is contraindicated.**
4) Rice is an acceptable substitute grain food.

15.(VIIB3b)*1) **Bed rest for a child in sickle cell crisis reduces the child's activity, which maximizes tissue oxygenation and minimizes oxygen consumption.**
2) Bed rest will not prevent infection in a child in sickle cell crisis.
3) The symptoms of sickle cell crisis are unrelated to oxygen tension.
4) The hypoxia of sickle cell anemia results in metabolic acidosis, not respiratory acidosis.

16.(VIIIB4b) 1) The child is not in respiratory distress and a hypertonic glucose IV solution could cause dehydration and hyperglycemia.
*2) **The nurse should suspect that the child has Reye's syndrome. Reye's syndrome can cause cerebral edema, combativeness, and disorientation; therefore, a safe quiet area is needed, as well as immediate medical intervention.**
3) The child needs intensive, immediate care.

4) Vomiting and lethargy are not indicators of oxygen need.

17.(IXA1)*1) **The slower growth of the heart and lungs in adolescents reduces blood flow and oxygen supply which leads to fatigue.**
2) The extremities elongate first, followed by trunk growth.
3) The bones grow faster than muscles.
4) All muscles grow at approximately the same rate.

18.(IXA3a)1) The cervical cap does not protect against organisms entering the body through lesions in the vagina or around the vaginal orifice or perineum.
*2) **Condoms collect the ejaculate so that it does not come into contact with perineal, vaginal, or cervical tissue.**
3) Oral contraceptives prevent ovulation; they do not protect against bacterial and viral infections.
4) Contraceptive foam is a spermicidal agent; it does not protect against bacterial or viral infections.

19.(IB4d)1) Eating only three meals a day allows the stomach to empty and may promote nausea and gastric distention.
2) The patient should avoid large meals which can cause stomach distention.
*3) **Spacing food intake throughout the day in small frequent meals avoids complete emptying of the stomach and maintains blood glucose levels, thus alleviating nausea.**
4) Exercise will not alleviate nausea and it can decrease blood glucose levels.

Adult Nursing

1.(IF4)*1) **Urinary output of at least .05 ml/kg/hr indicates adequate fluid volume.**
2) Urine pH is not related to fluid volume.
3) Elevated urine specific gravity indicates fluid volume depletion.
4) Normal negative urine glucose is not related to fluid volume.

2.(IG3)*1) **Rapid rate of feeding can cause diarrhea due to distention and increased osmolarity.**
2) Excess water in feeding will decrease osmolarity, decrease diarrhea, and increase urine output.
3) Improper tube placement could lead to respiratory complications or vomiting.
4) Low-fiber formula is more likely to lead to constipation.

3.(IE2)*1) **Tingling of the fingers, muscle spasms, and tetany are indicative of decreased calcium. Calcium is needed for nerve transmission and muscle contraction.**
2) Night blindness, tachycardia, and weakness are not related to calcium deficit.
3) Pale mucous membranes, shortness of breath, and lethargy are not related to calcium deficit.
4) Bleeding tendencies, thirst, and hypotension are not related to calcium deficit.

4.(IIA) 1) A split S₁ is a rare finding and does not indicate congestive heart failure (CHF).
★2) Gallop rhythm (presence of an S₃) is indicative of fluid volume overload and CHF.
3) An ejection click is indicative of valvular disease.
4) A pericardial friction rub is indicative of pericarditis.

5.(IIA) 1) Pallor is a symptom of an arterial obstruction, not of venous insufficiency.
2) Tenderness to touch is not a symptom of venous insufficiency.
3) Swollen joints are a symptom of inflammatory joint problems, not of venous insufficiency.
★4) Leathery skin texture is typical of the chronic skin changes in venous insufficiency.

6.(IIB) 1) Although prolonged bleeding may result in anemia, it is not a sign of anemia.
2) Bleeding is not a sign of acute respiratory failure.
3) Although lung cancer may metastasize to the lymph nodes, prolonged bleeding is not a sign of metastasis.
★4) Disseminated intravascular coagulation with resultant clotting abnormalities is frequently secondary to malignancy.

7.(IIE) 1) Support hose with the same pressure gradient will not promote venous return.
2) Crossing the legs even for short periods of time decreases venous return and should be avoided.
★3) Exercise such as walking and swimming improves the effect of the skeletal muscle pump on venous return.
4) Round garters may seriously decrease venous return and should not be used.

8.(IIIA)**★1) Diminished breath sounds and dyspnea result from air in the pleural cavity and indicate a possible pneumothorax.**
2) Air in the pleural cavity does not cause blood-tinged sputum; dullness on percussion is due to fluid in the chest cavity.
3) Flail chest occurs in an open chest; crackles result from delayed reopening of the small airways.
4) Paradoxical chest movement occurs with an open chest and inspiratory stridor is caused by airway obstruction.

9.(IIID) 1) The surgical site must be significantly healed before the speech therapist can help the client learn esophageal speech.
★2) Practicing controlled belching is the first step toward learning esophageal speech. Air is swallowed and trapped in the esophagus. When the trapped air is released in a controlled belch, the pharyngoesophageal segment vibrates and produces sound.
3) Due to the difficulty of controlling the sound produced, esophageal speech is usually difficult to understand.
4) Only about 10% of clients will develop fluent esophageal speech.

10.(IIIE) 1) Administering oxygen is not related to the comfort of suctioning.
2) Administering oxygen has no effect on the effort required to cough.
3) Administering oxygen before suctioning will not replace oxygen that is in the lungs.
★4) Administering oxygen before suctioning increases the amount of oxygen in the bloodstream. The client will be better able to tolerate the decrease in oxygen flow that occurs during suctioning.

11.(IVA) 1) Pyelonephritis is not related to bladder catheterization.
2) Pyelonephritis is not related to hypertension.
★3) Pyelonephritis is an infection of the kidney that most commonly is secondary to repeated bladder infections.
4) Pyelonephritis is most commonly bacterial, not viral.

12.(IVD)**★1) Slowing the infusion rate of the dialysate and raising the head of the bed allow the fluid to distend the lower abdomen. Taking pressure off the diaphragm provides more time for the client to become accustomed to the increased abdominal pressure.**
2) Placing the client in a supine position would increase upward pressure and increase the respiratory difficulty.
3) Draining the fluid is an emergency measure taken only if the client was experiencing severe respiratory difficulty.
4) Providing oxygen and encouraging relaxation will not decrease pressure on the diaphragm, which is causing the respiratory difficulty.

13.(IVE) 1) Prophylactic antibiotic therapy is not appropriate.
2) Severe reduction in protein intake is not necessary and may cause catabolism of body proteins, especially if enough calories are provided.
★3) Periodic laboratory tests are done to monitor recovery of renal function and to ensure appropriate further treatment.
4) Drinking one gallon of water daily would severely tax the impaired kidneys' ability to maintain water balance and would place the client at high risk for hypervolemia.

14.(VD) 1) Antibiotic therapy is a risk factor for the development of yeast infections.
2) Emptying the bladder will not affect a vaginal yeast infection.
★3) Cotton underwear decreases the risk of developing specific vaginal infections by keeping the perineum cool and dry.
4) Frequent douching is a risk factor for the development of vaginal infections.

15.(VA) 1) Intake of supplemental vitamins may actually decrease premenstrual syndrome.
2) Intake of natural diuretics may alleviate the premenstrual symptom of water retention.
3) High-protein, low-fat diets have not been linked to symptoms of premenstrual syndrome.
★4) Coffee, tea, and chocolate contain caffeine which has been implicated in premenstrual syndrome.

16.(VD)**★1) Difficulty in voiding is a common complication of a vaginal hysterectomy.**
2) Loss of appetite is not a common or expected complication.
3) GI upset is not a common or expected complication.

Answer Rationales: Adult Nursing   701

4) Excessive fatigue is not a common or expected complication.

17.(VC) 1) Sleeping on the affected side promotes pooling of lymphatic fluid and should be avoided.
2) Measuring arm circumference will monitor the development or progression of lymphedema but will not prevent its development.
***3) Passive and active range of motion promotes lymphatic drainage and will help to prevent the development of lymphedema.**
4) Use of diuretics will not alter lymphatic drainage.

18.(VIB) 1) The client is likely to have gained weight due to water retention and fat deposition. Weight loss or stabilization is a more appropriate goal.
2) Activity restriction is not recommended as it can lead to further muscle wasting.
3) The client should be encouraged to provide her or his own self-care needs. Moderate activity decreases the complications of immobility and helps improve self-esteem.
***4) The client should avoid people with colds or the flu. High levels of circulating corticosteroids cause an immunosuppressive effect, placing the client at high risk for infection.**

19.(VIC) ***1) Exercise improves insulin utilization and glucose uptake by muscles; therefore, without additional glucose sources, the client may develop hypoglycemia. Eating extra food during periods of increased activity will provide the required glucose.**
2) It is very important for the client to monitor glucose levels before and after strenuous exercise to maintain glucose levels in the optimal range.
3) The client should avoid using the thigh for insulin injections prior to exercise because the increased muscle activity will increase the absorption rate of insulin.
4) Increasing the insulin dose before exercise will cause more rapid depletion of the body's glucose levels and may lead to hypoglycemia.

20.(VIE) 1) Urinary output of 3–4 L/day is excessive and may be indicative of fluid volume deficit.
***2) Urine specific gravity of 1.010 is normal and provides evidence that the kidneys are concentrating urine appropriately.**
3) A pulse rate of 100–110 is a compensatory mechanism and may be the result of hypokalemia related to diabetes insipidus.
4) A blood pressure of 90/64 is low and may be the result of hypokalemia related to diabetes insipidus.

21.(VIA) 1) Lethargy and constipation are signs of hypothyroidism.
2) Dry, scaly skin and cold extremities are signs of hypothyroidism.
***3) Weight loss and increased appetite are signs of hyperthyroidism.**
4) Periorbital pallor and frequent blinking are not associated with hyperthyroidism.

22.(VIIB) 1) Histamine antagonists do not neutralize gastric acid; they inhibit the secretion of gastric acid.
***2) The major action of histamine antagonists is inhibiting acid production by the gastric mucosa.**
3) Histamine antagonists do not treat gastric inflammation.

4) See 3).

23.(VIID) 1) A fat-free diet will further limit absorption of fat-soluble vitamins and is not advised.
2) Fluids taken with meals can increase gastric distension and the ìdumpingî of hypertonic fluid into the intestine, initiating the symptoms of dumping syndrome.
3) Increased carbohydrate intake with meals can lead to postprandial hypoglycemia and is contraindicated.
***4) Serving six small high-protein meals daily decreases the volume of food which enters the intestine and decreases the risk of dumping syndrome, especially if meals are eaten without drinking fluids.**

24.(VIIE) ***1) Handwashing is the single most effective means of preventing infection which is the most common complication of central lines and total parenteral nutrition (TPN).**
2) Testing the urine for protein evaluates kidney function but does not prevent complications of TPN.
3) Recording daily weights helps to evaluate the effectiveness of TPN but does not prevent complications.
4) Troubleshooting mechanical problems in the pump does not prevent infection.

25.(VIIID) 1) A blind spot is not related to graft rejection.
***2) Decrease in vision is often the first sign of graft rejection.**
3) Diplopia is not related to graft rejection.
4) Excessive tearing is not related to graft rejection.

26.(VIIIE) 1) Reducing fluid intake will not alter bladder control, but may increase constipation and risk of urinary tract infections due to stagnant urine in the bladder.
2) Antihistamines will not alter bladder control.
***3) Self-catheterization several times daily will ensure complete emptying of the bladder to prevent urinary retention and bladder atony in multiple sclerosis.**
4) A high-protein diet will have no effect on bladder control.

27.(IXD) 1) The client should not lie on the affected side without by the surgeon's approval, generally several weeks after surgery.
***2) The affected hip must remain in an abducted position to prevent prosthesis dislocation.**
3) Hip flexion should not be less than 45–60 degrees.
4) One person is needed to help the client protect the affected side when getting out of bed.

28.(IXA) 1) Fat emboli result in damage and symptoms to other organs, not to the affected extremity.
***2) Pallor, pulselessness, and paresthesia are signs of neurovascular damage.**
3) Fever and increased white blood cells are signs of osteomyelitis.
4) Pain, swelling, and localized warmth are signs of deep vein thrombosis.

29.(IXA) 1) Recent weight gain is not associated with osteoporosis.
***2) Prolonged immobility is a risk factor for osteoporosis.**
3) Estrogen replacement decreases the risk of osteoporosis.

4) High calcium intake decreases the risk of osteoporosis.

30.(XB) 1) A positive polymerase chain reaction indicates HIV activity.
2) Decreased amount of HIV indicates a decreased risk of opportunistic infection.
3) A 2:1 ratio of T-helper to T-suppressor cells is the normal healthy ratio and does not indicate risk for opportunistic infection.
★4) A CD4+ count below 500 places the body at risk for opportunistic infection.

31.(XB) 1) Hypertension and graft tenderness are not signs of infection.
2) Fever and graft tenderness are not signs of renal failure.
★3) Fever, elevated BUN, hypertension, and graft tenderness are indicators of renal graft rejection.
4) Fever and graft tenderness are not signs of fluid overload.

32.(XB) 1) Washing bedclothes daily will not affect the spread of pediculosis capitis to other family members.
2) Using antibiotic soap and shampoo will not affect pediculosis; a special shampoo containing pyrethrin or benzene hexachloride is needed.
3) Topical steroids may help the pruritus briefly but will not kill the pediculi nor prevent their spread.
★4) The sharing of headgear (hats and scarves) is the prime means of spreading pediculosis. Headwear should never be shared with others.

33.(XD) 1) Warm tap water is not sterile and may introduce chemicals such as chlorine or bacteria. It is also hypotonic and may cause further damage to the wound.
★2) A sterile isotonic solution will promote washing away of debris or bacteria and will not further damage the tissue.
3) Half-strength hydrogen peroxide is too strong an oxidizing agent to use on an open wound.
4) Alcohol swabs are drying and may also further damage the tissue.

Maternal & Child Nursing (baccalaureate)

1.(IA) 1) Relationships change in a blended family. They do not stay the same.
★2) Forming a blended family challenges members to develop new ways of functioning.
3) Members of a blended family have many additional decisions to make to meet the needs of all members.
4) Stress in members of a blended family increases with the intermingling of their values and goals.

2.(ID) 1) Although amniotic fluid provides protective qualities, it does not ensure a safe delivery.
2) Although amniotic fluid aids in lung development, it does not keep the lungs open.
★3) Amniotic fluid provides a protective cushion for the fetus.
4) Amniotic fluid does not regulate fetal heart rate.

3.(IF) 1) This is not correct because it assumes that the couple's current lifestyle is a healthy one.
2) The woman's ideal weight should be maintained by a combination of a balanced diet and exercise and not by the use of appetite suppressants.
3) Genetic planning is not recommended for the couple until age 35.
★4) Identification of environmental hazards is an important consideration for the couple in the preconceptual period.

4.(IIA) 1) Additional calories are required for both the mother and the fetus.
2) Dieting is not recommended during pregnancy.
★3) Assessment of the client's knowledge is always a priority before teaching can be implemented.
4) Weight control is not recommended during pregnancy.

5.(IIA) 1) Although a one-week dietary account offers a great deal of information, it does not reveal dietary patterns.
2) A questionnaire does not reveal dietary patterns.
★3) Discussing a 24-hour recall and typical dietary patterns will yield a general dietary history that the nurse can use to make recommendations.
4) A family's nutritional patterns do not necessarily reflect the individual member's dietary patterns.

6.(IIB) **★1) Breast-feeding can be continued; it is not contraindicated in the case of non-purulent mastitis if the discomfort is tolerable.**
2) It is not necessary to stop breast-feeding.
3) See 2).
4) Recommending that the mother allow the baby to nurse longer is not necessary.

7.(IIB) 1) Confirmation of amniotic fluid by a Nitrazine test is not a priority.
★2) Assessment of fetal heart rate is the priority after rupture of the membranes due to the possibility of prolapse of the umbilical cord.
3) Changing the bed linen is a comfort measure and is not a priority.
4) Although charting the event is important, it does not take priority over assessment of the fetal heart rate.

8.(IID) 1) See 4).
2) See 4).
3) See 4).
★4) No action is needed since a soft pulsating fontanelle is a normal finding.

9.(IID) 1) It is not necessary to notify the health care provider when the umbilical cord falls off.
2) It is not necessary to cover the cord as leaving the umbilical area open to the air aids in drying.
★3) Cleansing the cord with alcohol aids in drying has an antiseptic effect.
4) Tub baths are contraindicated until the umbilical cord has fallen off.

10.(IIIA) 1) Fetal movements, alone, are not indicative of a healthy fetus.
★2) Acceleration of the fetal heart rate associated with fetal movement is a sign of fetal well-being.

3) Deceleration of the fetal heart rate during uterine contractions is not a reassuring sign.
4) No variability of the fetal heart rate is not a reassuring sign.

11.(IIIA)*1) **A vaginal exam could tear the placenta and cause further bleeding and fetal distress.**
2) Stimulation may cause additional bleeding; however, this is not the primary reason.
3) Since the question does not indicate that the membranes have ruptured, the client is not at risk for infection.
4) Although premature rupture of the membranes is a risk, tearing of the placenta poses the greatest risk.

12.(IIIA)1) IV analgesia will not alleviate variable decelerations.
2) Ambulation has not been shown to alleviate variable decelerations.
*3) **Changing the client's position is the appropriate intervention to relieve variable decelerations.**
4) Increasing the Pitocin infusion will stimulate the contraction pattern, but will not alleviate the variable decelerations.

13.(IIIB)*1) **Large-for-gestational-age neonates have birth weights at or above the 90th percentile.**
2) Epstein's pearls are a common variation found in neonates of varied gestational age and weight.
3) Head circumference is not associated with large-for-gestational-age neonates.
4) Skin desquamation is not a finding associated with large-for-gestational-age neonates.

14.(IIIC)1) Restricting fluids does not prevent engorgement.
2) Medical intervention is not necessary since engorgement is a normal phenomena.
3) Breast-feeding should be done more frequently when the breasts are engorged.
*4) **With engorgement, manual expression of a small amount of milk will facilitate the baby's ability to latch on.**

15.(IVA) 1) Explaining why immunizations are spaced over time is not the most important information for the nurse to provide.
2) Explaining the controversies concerning risks and benefits is not the most important information for the nurse to provide.
*3) **Explaining that it is critical to obtain immunizations on a regularly scheduled basis is the most important information for the nurse to provide.**
4) Explaining that legal requirements for immunizing children must be met is not the most important information for the nurse to provide.

16.(IVB)*1) **Rolling the head from side to side is a clinical manifestation of otitis media.**
2) Scratching the cheeks is not a clinical manifestation of otitis media.
3) Infants with otitis media generally have a loss of appetite and feed poorly.
4) Sucking the fingers is not a clinical manifestation of otitis media.

17.(IVC) 1) Avoiding unfamiliar foods does not address the ritualistic food behavior.
2) Nutritionally balanced snacks should be part of the diet for a four-year-old.
*3) **Involving the child in food preparation will meet the child's need for control and will promote the child's interest in trying new foods.**
4) Children are not ready to view mealtime as a social activity until they are five years old.

18.(IVD) 1) Communicability is greatest when the first lesions appear.
2) The amount of time that a fever is present varies and does not affect communicability.
3) Communicability ends long before all the lesions have disappeared.
*4) **Communicability ends when all the lesions have crusted.**

19.(IVE) 1) Role modeling by the nurse is not the most effective method since adolescents tend to eat with their peers.
*2) **Incorporating healthy dietary habits into the adolescent's current eating habits is the most effective long-term intervention.**
3) Nutritional counseling is not meaningful to many adolescents.
4) The food pyramid is not meaningful to many adolescents.

20.(VA) 1) Whether or not to give the missed dose of digoxin depends on how much time has elapsed. The next dose should be given at the regular time.
2) If the baby vomits after taking the drug, it is difficult to determine the amount of drug that was absorbed. It is not correct to give another dose.
3) Mixing digoxin with food is not recommended since the amount of the drug taken may vary with the formula intake.
*4) **Administering digoxin before or after meals assures accurate assessment of drug intake.**

21.(VB) 1) The clinical symptoms of Kawasaki disease do not respond to antibiotics.
*2) **Oropharyngeal redness or ìstrawberryî tongue is a classic sign of Kawasaki disease.**
3) A perineal rash is not associated with Kawasaki disease.
4) Irritability is not associated with Kawasaki disease.

22.(VB)*1) **Chelation therapy is potentially nephrotoxic; adequate intake and output are necessary for lead excretion.**
2) Warm soaks are of little comfort for the painful injection.
3) A local anesthetic should be mixed with the chelation therapy.
4) Vital signs should be monitored more frequently than every eight hours to assess for dehydration.

23.(VC) 1) Petechiae are not common in glomerulonephritis.
*2) **Hypertension and proteinuria are classic signs of glomerulonephritis.**
3) Flank pain and fever are not found in the initial assessment of a child with glomerulonephritis.
4) Glycosuria is not associated with glomerulonephritis.

24.(VD) 1) Skin turgor is unrelated to an improving condition in a child with asthma. Shallow respirations would indicate impaired respiration.
2) Increased blood flow to the nail beds and lips is not an initial sign of improvement in a child with asthma.
3) Pulse and blood pressure are not indicators of an improving condition in a child with asthma.
*4) Decreased rhonchi and wheezes indicate relaxation of the bronchioles and improved aeration and, therefore, indicate that the child's condition is improving.

25.(VE)***1) Repetitive jumping causes pressure and inflammation on the ligaments and joints in the legs, placing the client at risk for Osgood-Schlatter disease.**
2) Substance abuse is not associated with the onset of Osgood-Schlatter disease.
3) Sexual activity is not associated with the onset of Osgood-Schlatter disease.
4) Automobile driving does not place undue stress on the ligaments and joints of the lower extremities.

Psychiatric/Mental Health Nursing

1.(IB6) 1) Moving to a house may cause stress, but the family finances can be managed.
2) The best friend's absence is temporary, she will return from vacation.
*3) Ending an engagement is a primary nonanticipated event and represents a permanent loss.
4) Sending a child to camp is an anticipated event and is a part of a normal developmental phase.

2.(IC2) 1) Solving problems is a task of the working stage.
*2) Mutual identification of therapeutic goals is the primary task of the orientation stage.
3) Exploring past difficulties is a task of the working stage.
4) Evaluating progress is an ongoing task throughout the entire nurse-client relationship, but it primarily occurs in the termination stage.

3.(IC3) 1) This response will not identify the precipitating event/current stressor that led the client to believe he is unable to cope.
2) This response is nontherapeutic. It conveys little understanding of, or respect for, the client's feelings and, therefore, hinders communication.
*3) The first step of crisis intervention is assessment, with an initial focus on identifying the precipitating event. This response uses a broad, open-ended question to elicit a detailed client response.
4) This response will not provide data into what happened that has led the client to believe he is unable to cope.

4.(IC3)***1) Suggesting that the client share her thoughts gives the client a chance to think and talk about what is on her mind at that time.**
2) Redirecting the conversation is nontherapeutic. It allows the client to avoid conflict.
3) Terminating the interaction is nontherapeutic and punitive.
4) See 2).

5.(ID2) 1) This response is challenging and neither addresses norms nor promotes a feeling of safety and support.
2) This authoritarian response would not promote a feeling of safety and support.
3) This personal question addressed to one member would not promote a feeling of safety and support.
*4) This response helps bring the group together, gives each member a feeling of equal importance, and promotes a feeling of safety and support.

6.(ID4) 1) The member with the presenting problem is not the source of all family problems.
2) The developmental needs of the member who is the client can be addressed without the need of family therapy.
3) The therapist needs to be equally supportive of all family members.
*4) The entire family is feeling stressed, and the member who is the client is merely the one who has developed overt symptoms.

7.(IE2) 1) This client is not exhibiting violent behavior; therefore, alternative strategies such as medication or psychosocial intervention may be effective.
*2) This client is exhibiting violent behavior. The primary indication for using restraints is the control of violent behavior that is either self-directed or directed toward others and that cannot be controlled by medication or psychosocial strategies.
3) See 1).
4) See 1).

8.(IIA1) 1) This response does not necessarily indicate grief resolution and may indicate unresolved issues that can complicate the current loss.
*2) The ultimate outcome of uncomplicated grief reaction is realization that the object of one's love no longer exists and emotional investment is withdrawn. The client is focusing on loved ones who are still part of the client's life, without negating the loss.
3) This response indicates idealization, in which only perceived or actual positive attributes of the person are seen. Since this response is not realistic, it does not indicate grief resolution.
4) This response indicates a delayed grief reaction in which living memories are projected onto an object.

9.(IIA4) 1) By observing clients in a community health center, the nurse is not having direct contact with the clients. Also, this is a limited population since only clients seeking health care services would be seen.
*2) Longtime residents are most familiar with the positive as well as the negative aspects of living in a community.

3) Collecting demographic data lacks the personal and interpersonal feelings the nurse can assess by talking to residents.
4) Concerns and trends described in newspaper articles do not provide a comprehensive picture of a community.

10.(IIB1) 1) Genes are not inherited from adoptive parents.
★2) There is a genetic predisposition to depressive disorders.
3) See 1).
4) Reactive depression is due to a life event and is not inherited.

11.(IIB1) 1) The client acknowledges his drinking; therefore, he is not using denial.
2) The client is not saying someone else has a drinking problem; therefore, he is not using projection.
★3) The client is offering a superficially logical explanation for his unacceptable behavior; the client is using rationalization.
4) Alcohol abuse is not a socially approved behavior; therefore, this is not sublimation.

12.(IIB3) 1) A member in the role of complainer focuses on the negative and discourages problem resolution.
2) A member in the role of monopolizer attempts to control the group by constantly talking.
★3) A member in the role of moralist tends to view everything as right or wrong, without looking at all the factors that affect an issue.
4) A member in the role of victim tends to attribute problems as being the fault of others, without looking at their own role in the problem.

13.(IIB4) 1) The number of homes up for sale is not necessarily an indication of a crisis.
★2) Nightmares and sleep disturbances in children indicate that something very frightening has occurred and crisis intervention is needed.
3) Requesting information on tornado precautions is a safety measure in a tornado-prone area.
4) Including tornado drills in schools is an additional safety measure in a tornado-prone area.

14.(IIIA1) 1) Focusing on the individual nurse-client relationship does not meet the client's recreational needs nor does it meet the adolescent developmental task of forming appropriate peer group support.
2) The client's choice of activities may not meet the adolescent developmental task of forming appropriate peer group support.
★3) Arranging activities with the client's peers meets the primary adolescent developmental task of appropriate peer group support.
4) Meeting with the activities therapist does not meet the adolescent developmental task of developing appropriate peer group support.

15.(IIIA2) 1) Social programs may not meet the emotional needs of the client. This type of intervention may be indicated after a client's support system is determined to be inadequate.
★2) Single parents are at high risk for the development of emotional difficulties and assessment of the parent's support systems is the nurse's priority.

3) Recreational activities will not necessarily meet the emotional needs of the client.
4) Providing literature will not necessarily meet the emotional needs of the client.

16.(IIIB1)**★1) The nurse should not force a client who is severely anxious into a situation that the client is unable to handle, nor should the nurse remove the client's defense mechanisms before the client learns alternative coping mechanisms.**
2) Interference with a ritual leads to increased anxiety, not to a loss of reality testing.
3) The most characteristic client response to preventing a client from completing rituals would be anger.
4) The client needs to know that the staff accepts the client, but not the dysfunctional behavior.

17.(IIIB1)**★1) The client who has Alzheimer's disease with apraxia is unable to perform purposive movement and use objects properly; therefore, giving the client simple, sequential directions would be helpful.**
2) Color-coded signs will not help the client find the bathroom.
3) Orienting devices will not help the client perform purposive movements.
4) Administering an antianxiety medication when the client is confused does not treat apraxia.

18.(IIIB2)**★1) Assisting family members to clarify their expectations of each other will help the family make a plan for shared responsibilities so that the woman will not feel overburdened.**
2) Finding a nursing home might be a last resort, but alternatives need to be tried first.
3) The arrangement for sharing work needs to be made by the family, rather than the nurse telling the family what to do.
4) Having a live-in aide might not be financially possible nor be an acceptable option for the family.

19.(IIIB2) 1) Discussion by the family cannot change the client's behavior.
2) Since the client perceives himself as not having a problem, he is unlikely to quit even if given one more chance.
★3) Most family theories are based on the belief that family members can only change their own behavior, not the client's behavior. This is a basic principle of most self-help groups that deal with addictive behaviors.
4) Though contacting authorities is a positive action that fosters accountability, it would probably lead the client to become angry and more secretive.

20.(IIIB3) 1) Treating the client matter-of-factly will not change the behavior.
2) Ignoring the manipulative behavior will not change the behavior.
★3) Restating personal expectations will help the client realize how the client's needs fit in with those of the other group members.
4) The client's problem behavior needs to be addressed in the presence of the group.

21.(IVA1) 1) An expression of pain does not indicate that the client is motivated to change behavior.
2) The wish to feel better does not indicate that the client is motivated to change behavior.
3) This statement does not indicate that the client is motivated to change behavior.
*4) Asking for help indicates that the client is motivated to accept and use help to get better.

22.(IVB1) 1) Slow speech may indicate continued depression. Although logical speech may indicate improvement, many clients with depression manifest logical speech patterns. This finding does not indicate progress.
2) A decreased need for sleep does not indicate therapeutic progress.
*3) Self-concept in clients with depression is almost always negative. A more positive self-concept definitely indicates improvement.
4) Some clients with depression eat excessively; therefore, increased appetite alone cannot be used as a definite indication of improvement.

23.(IVB1) 1) No longer talking about suicide may show that the client's suicidal ideation has decreased.
2) Verbalizing angry feelings probably indicates a decreased suicide risk since the client is expressing anger.
3) Socialization is helpful for clients with depression and may be a sign that the client is feeling better.
*4) It is unusual for a client with depression to show marked improvement so soon. This behavior often means that the client has made a new plan for another suicide attempt.

24.(IVB1) 1) Orthostatic hypotension is not a side effect of lithium.
*2) Vomiting and diarrhea are common adverse reactions to lithium.
3) Tardive dyskinesia is not a side effect of lithium.
4) The Parkinsonian syndrome, which includes rigidity of posture, is not a side effect of lithium.

25.(IVB3) 1) This remark is too personal for the orientation stage when group members hardly know one another.
2) See 1).
*3) In the orientation stage, group members often expect the leader to solve everyone's problems.
4) The orientation stage is too early for a group member to expect the group to be solving the member's problems.

Committee List

Abnormal Psychology

Kathleen Crowley-Long, PhD (State University of New York at Albany, Educational Psychology, 1987), Chair, Department of Psychology and Associate Professor, The College of Saint Rose

Mary Ann Flynn-Bush, PhD (University of Illinois, Counseling Psychology, 1988) Professor of Psychology, Nazareth College

Timothy M. Osberg, PhD (State University of New York at Buffalo, Clinical Psychology, 1982) Professor of Psychology, Niagara University

Anatomy & Physiology

Harvey Cramer, MS (Syracuse University, Biology, 1975) Adjunct Professor of Biology, Utica College of Syracuse University

Michael J. Raley, PhD (Albany Medical College, Physiology and Cell Biology, 1998) Assistant Professor, Albany College of Pharmacy

Joel Reicherter, MS (Long Island University, 1968) Associate Professor of Biology, State University of New York College of Technology at Farmingdale

Ethics: Theory & Practice

Frederick Kaufman, PhD (University of Virginia, Philosophy, 1984) Associate Professor and Chair of the Philosophy Department, Ithaca College

Wade Robison, PhD (University of Wisconsin, Philosophy/Law, 1968) Ezra A. Hale Chair in Applied Ethics, Rochester Institute of Technology

Paul Santilli, PhD (Boston College, Philosophy, 1976) Professor of Philosophy, Siena College

Douglas Shrader, Jr., PhD (University of Illinois at Chicago, Philosophy, 1979) Professor and Chair of the Philosophy Department, State University of New York at Oneonta

James H. Young, EdD (State University of New York at Buffalo, Educational Foundations, 1969) Educational Consultant

Foundations of Gerontology

K. Della Ferguson, PhD (Kansas State University, Psychology, 1979) Associate Dean, Utica College of Syracuse University

Richard H. Machemer, Jr., PhD (University of Vermont, Animal Science—Physiology, 1976)
Professor of Biology and Gerontology, St. John Fisher College

William F. Price, PhD (Oregon State University, Adult Education—Gerontology, 1978)
Chair, Department of Social Science and Professor of Gerontology, North Country Community College

Life Span Developmental Psychology

Ellen C. Banks, EdD (Harvard University, Human Development, 1974)
Professor and Chair, Daemen College

Kathleen Crowley-Long, PhD (State University of New York at Albany, Educational Psychology and Statistics, 1987)
Associate Professor, The College of Saint Rose

Jack Demick, PhD (Clark University, Psychology, 1981)
Professor and Chair, Suffolk University

John S. Klein, PhD (Columbia University, Human Learning & Cognition, 1982)
Associate Professor, Castleton State College

Beverly A. Slichta, MS (Oklahoma State University, Psychology, 1974)
Academic Dean, Erie Community College

Jonathan Stone, PhD (New York University, Psychology, 1975)
Professor, Dutchess Community College

Microbiology

I. Edward Alcamo, PhD (St. John's University, Microbiology, 1971)
Professor of Microbiology, State University of New York College of Technology at Farmingdale

Mark Gallo, PhD (Cornell University, Microbiology, 1991)
Assistant Professor, Niagara University

Jean A. Douthwright, PhD (University of Rochester, Biophysics, 1980)
Professor of Biology, Rochester Institute of Technology

Pathophysiology

Linda A. Adamchak, DC (Western States Chiropractic College, Chiropractic/Clinical Studies, 1988)
Assistant Professor, Hudson Valley Community College

Marilyn Belli, MS, RN (University of Rochester, Medical-Surgical/Cardiopulmonary Nursing, 1983)
Assistant Professor, Utica College of Syracuse University

Wilfrid DuBois, PhD (Boston University, Endocrinology, 1982)
Associate Professor, D'Youville College

Joan P. Frizzell, PhD (University of Pennsylvania, Nursing, 1997)
Assistant Professor, LaSalle University

Karim Mehrazar, PhD, MT (ASCP) (UHS/Chicago Medical School, Immunology, 1990)
Assistant Professor, Morgan State University

Dudley G. Moon, PhD (Albany Medical College of Union University, Physiology & Cell Biology, 1983)
Professor, Albany College of Pharmacy

Psychology of Adulthood & Aging

Ellen C. Banks, EdD (Harvard University, Human Development, 1974)
Professor of Psychology, Daemen College

K. Della Ferguson, PhD (Kansas State University, Psychology, 1979)
Professor of Psychology, Utica College of Syracuse University

Karl Kosloski, PhD (University of Nevada-Reno, Social Psychology, 1984)
Associate Professor of Gerontology, University of Nebraska at Omaha

Hedva J. Lewittes, PhD (Stanford University, Psychological Studies, 1976)
Associate Professor of Psychology, State University of New York College at Old Westbury

Robin K. Montvilo, PhD (Fordham University, Psychology, 1972)
Associate Professor of Psychology, Rhode Island College

Christina S. Sinisi, PhD (Kansas State University, Psychology, 1993)
Assistant Professor of Psychology, Charleston Southern University

Research Methods in Psychology

Lori-Ann Bonvino Forzano, PhD (State University of New York at Stony Brook, Experimental Psychology, 1992)
Assistant Professor, SUNY at Brockport

Paula Goolkasian, PhD (Iowa State University, Experimental Psychology, 1974)
Professor, University of North Carolina–Charlotte

Rondall Boo-Hock Khoo, PhD (Pennsylvania State University, Experimental Psychology, 1990)
Assistant Professor, Western Connecticut State University

Kathryn LaFontana, PhD (University of Connecticut, Social Psychology, 1995)
Assistant Professor, Sacred Heart University

Jennifer Myers, PhD (University of Michigan, Developmental Psychology, 1992)
Visiting Assistant Professor, University of Michigan at Ann Arbor

James H. Reynolds, PhD (Syracuse University, Psychology, 1961)
Professor Emeritus, Colgate University

Statistics

Gary Egan, MA (State University of New York at Binghamton, Mathematics, 1984)
Assistant Professor, Monroe Community College

Lifang Hsu, PhD (University of California at Santa Barbara, Mathematical Statistics, 1983)
Associate Professor, Le Moyne College

Wesley Jordan, EdD (Columbia University, Mathematics Education, 1976)
Professor, Pace University

Gary Kulis, MA (State University of New York at Binghamton, Mathematics, 1988)
  Instructor, Mohawk Valley Community College

Malcolm Sherman, PhD (University of California, Berkeley, Mathematics, 1964)
  Associate Professor, The University at Albany

World Population

Sanjoy Chakravorty, PhD (University of Southern California, Urban and Regional Planning, 1992)
  Assistant Professor, Temple University

William Egelman, PhD (Fordham University, Sociology, 1979)
  Professor, Iona College

David Elliott, PhD (University of Oregon, Sociology, 1984)
  Area Coordinator for Cultural and Historical Studies and Mentor, Center for Distance Learning, Empire State College (SUNY)

Ezekiel Kalipeni, PhD (University of North Carolina at Chapel Hill, Geography/Demography, 1986)
  Assistant Professor, University of Illinois at Urbana–Champaign

Yuhui Li, PhD (The Ohio State University, Sociology, 1990)
  Assistant Professor, Rowan University

John Macisco, PhD (Brown University, Sociology, Population, 1966)
  Professor of Sociology, Fordham University

English Composition

Sandra Jamieson, PhD (State University of New York at Binghamton, English, 1991)
  Director of Composition, Drew University

Roxanne Mountford, PhD (Ohio State University, Rhetoric and Composition, 1991)
  Assistant Professor, University of Arizona at Tucson

Mary O'Reilly, PhD (Princeton University, English, 1972)
  Professor, Rider University

Beulah Spangler, PhD (University of North Carolina at Chapel Hill, English & American Literature, 1982)
  Professor, Peace College

Rosemary Winslow, PhD (The Catholic University of America, English Language and Literature, 1984)
  Associate Professor, The Catholic University of America

Robert Yagelski, PhD (Ohio State University, Rhetoric and Composition, 1991)
  Assistant Professor, The University at Albany

American Dream

Michael Kiskis, DA (State University of New York at Albany, American Literature, 1986)
  Associate Professor of American Literature, Elmira College

Richard Leveroni, PhD (State University of New York at Albany, Sociology/Education, 1984)
   Professor, Department of Humanities & Social Sciences, Schenectady County Community College

Gary McLouth, DA (State University of New York at Albany, American Literature, 1985)
   Associate Professor, American Literature & Journalism, The College of Saint Rose

Joanna Zangrando, PhD (George Washington University, American Studies, 1974)
   Professor and Chair, American Studies, Skidmore College

History of Nazi Germany

Kenneth J. Blume, PhD (State University of New York at Binghamton, History, 1984)
   Associate Professor of Humanities and Head of Division of Humanities and Social Sciences, Albany College of Pharmacy

Mark Walker, PhD (Princeton University, History, 1987)
   Professor of History, Union College

Religions of the World

William Grimes, PhD (University of North Carolina at Chapel Hill, Philosophy, 1969)
   Associate Professor of Philosophy, The University at Albany (Retired)

W. Bruce Johnston, PhD (State University of New York at Albany, Philosophy, 1980)
   Chair, Philosophy and Religious Studies, The College of St. Rose

Richard Leveroni, PhD (State University of New York at Albany, Sociology and Education, 1984)
   Professor, Department of Humanities and Social Sciences, Schenectady County Community College

Human Resource Management

Bonni Perroh Baker, MA (The Ohio State University, Health in the Workplace & Health Counseling, 1986)
   Associate Professor, Siena College

Daphne H. Bruce, MBA (Rochester Institute of Technology, General Management, 1977)
   Major Professor, Roberts Wesleyan College

Michael J. Gent, PhD (Texas Christian University, Organizational/Social Psychology, 1978)
   Associate Professor, Canisius College

LaVerne H. Higgins, PhD (University of Oregon, Human Resource Management/Organizational Behavior, 1994)
   Assistant Professor, Le Moyne College

Michael Kavanagh, PhD (Iowa State University, Industrial-Organizational Psychology, 1969)
   Professor, The University at Albany

Barbara-Jayne Lewthwaite, MBA (St. John's University, Executive Management, 1979)
   Associate Professor, Centenary College

Labor Relations

Gregory G. Dell'Omo, PhD (University of Wisconsin-Madison, Industrial Relations, 1987)
   Associate Professor, Saint Joseph's University

Ronald L. Filippelli, PhD (The Pennsylvania State University, History, 1969)
Professor of Labor and Industrial Relations, The Pennsylvania State University

Ira B. Lobel, JD (Catholic University, Law, 1974)
Commissioner, Federal Mediation and Conciliation Services

Scott R. Lyman, PhD (Virginia Polytechnic Institute and State University, Labor Relations/Human Resource Management, 1992)
Assistant Professor, Marist College

Nancy G. Lynch, MBA (State University of New York at Buffalo, Human Resources, 1995)
Adjunct Faculty, Labor Relations and Human Resource Management, State University of New York at Buffalo

John Watson, PhD (St. Louis University, Management, 1972)
Professor, St. Bonaventure University

Organizational Behavior

Marjorie Adams, DBA (George Washington University, Organizational Behavior and Development, 1987)
Associate Professor, Morgan State University

Rowland Baughman, DBA (George Washington University, Organizational Behavior, 1975)
Professor of Management, Central Connecticut State University

Cherlyn Granrose, PhD (Rutgers, Psychology, 1981)
Professor, The Claremont Graduate School

Michael Scozzaro, PhD (University of Akron, Industrial/Organizational Psychology, 1992)
Assistant Professor of Psychology, Buffalo State College

Ahmad Tootoonchi, PhD (U.S. International University, Leadership and Human Behavior, 1986)
Associate Professor, Frostburg State University

Monica Zeigler, MS (Pace University, Education/Administration, 1993)
Associate Director of Freshman Studies, Pace University

Production/Operations Management

Michael Bommer, PhD (The Wharton School of Commerce & Finance, Statistics & Operations Research, 1971)
Professor of Management, Clarkson University

Peter Duchessi, PhD (Union College, Administration & Engineering Systems, 1981)
Associate Professor of Management Science, The University at Albany

Leo Dworsky, MBA (Boston University, Industrial Management, 1962)
Associate Professor of Business Administration, The College of Saint Rose

Douglas Lonnstrom, PhD (Rensselaer Polytechnic Institute, Urban Environmental Studies, 1984)
Associate Professor of Mathematics for Business/Statistics, Siena College

William J. Stevenson, PhD (Syracuse University, Business, 1971)
Associate Professor of Business, Rochester Institute of Technology

Business Policy & Strategy

William K. Holstein, PhD (Purdue University, Economics, 1964)
   Professor, Distinguished Service, The University at Albany

L.L. Jayaraman, PhD (University of Pennsylvania, Operations Research, 1978)
   Associate Professor, Montclair State College

Herbert Sherman, PhD (The Union Institute, Management, 1988)
   Management Consultant

John Watson, PhD (St. Louis University, Management and Organizational Behavior, 1974)
   Professor, St. Bonaventure University

Reading Instruction in the Elementary School

Maria Ceprano, PhD (State University of New York at Buffalo, Reading/Research and Evaluation, 1980)
   Chair, Department of Reading, State University of New York College at Buffalo

Virginia Goatley, PhD (Michigan State University, Educational Psychology/Literacy, 1995)
   Assistant Professor, The University at Albany

Peter McDermott, PhD (State University of New York at Albany, Reading, 1981)
   Associate Professor, The Sage Colleges

Carole S. Rhodes, PhD (New York University, Teaching and Learning, 1990)
   Associate Professor, Pace University

Dorothy Troike, PhD (Syracuse University, Reading Education, 1977)
   Professor, State University of New York College at Cortland

Nursing Concepts 1 and 2

Leona Bishop, MS, RN (Russell Sage College, Nursing Education, 1971)
   Professor, Hudson Valley Community College

Joanne Bonesteel, MS, RN (Boston College, Medical-Surgical Nursing, 1984)
   Nurse Educator, Regents College

Patricia Irons, MA, RN (Columbia University, Nursing Education, 1961)
   Professor and Chairperson in Nursing, Queensborough Community College

Marianne Lettus, EdD, RN (State University of New York at Albany, Program Development and Evaluation, 1990)
   Associate Dean of Nursing, Regents College

Mary Ann Hellmer Saul, PhD, RN (Adelphi University, Nursing, 1986)
   Professor, Nassau Community College

Margaret Warshaw, MA (New York University, Nursing, 1970)
   Director of Nursing, County College of Morris

Nursing Concepts 3

Nancy Donahue, MS, RN (State University of New York at Albany, Education Administration, 1983)
   Associate Professor of Nursing, Columbia-Greene Community College

Tana Durnbaugh, EdD, RN,CS (Illinois University, Nursing Education, 1985)
   Professor, Nursing Department, College of Lake County

Judy Kaplan, PhD, RN (New York University, Nursing Research, 1993)
   Assistant Professor of Nursing, Nassau Community College

Marianne Lettus, EdD, RN (State University of New York at Albany, Program Development and Evaluation, 1990)
   Associate Dean of Nursing, Regents College

Frances Monahan, PhD, RN (New York University, Nursing, 1980)
   Professor and Chairperson of Nursing, Rockland Community College

Differences in Nursing Care: Area A (modified)

Nancy Fairbanks Bond, MS, RN (Russell Sage College, Medical-Surgical Nursing, 1971)
   Professor Emeritus, State University of New York Agricultural & Technical College at Morrisville

Elaine Davi, MS, RN (Catholic University of America, 1981)
   Assistant Professor of Nursing, Hudson Valley Community College

Edna Gardenier, EdD, RN (State University of New York at Albany, Educational Administration, 1990)
   Professor and Coordinator of Nursing Department, Dutchess Community College

Frances Monahan, PhD, RN (New York University, Nursing, 1980)
   Professor and Chairperson of Nursing Department, Rockland Community College

Elaine Muller, EdD, RN (Columbia University, Higher Education, 1989)
   Professor of Nursing, Queensborough Community College

Kristine Ring-Wilson, MS, RN (Russell Sage College, Parent-Child/Teaching, 1974)
   Nurse Educator, Regents College

Michele Morgan Woodbeck, MS, RN (Russell Sage College, Medical-Surgical Nursing, 1979)
   Assistant Professor of Nursing, Hudson Valley Community College

Differences in Nursing Care: Area B

Civita Allard, MS, RN (Russell Sage College, Nursing Education, 1985)
   Associate Professor, Mohawk Valley Community College

Leona Bishop, MS, RN (Russell Sage College, Nursing Education, 1964)
   Professor, Hudson Valley Community College

Patricia R. Cook, PhD, RN (University of South Carolina-Aiken, 1995)
   ADN Program Director, University of South Carolina-Aiken

Nancy Donahue, MS, RN (Russell Sage College, Nursing Education, 1969; State University of New York at Albany, Educational Administration, 1983)
   Associate Professor, Columbia-Greene Community College

Barbara Marckx, MS, RN (University of Colorado, Medical-Surgical Nursing, 1964; Syracuse University, Psychiatric-Mental Health Nursing, 1993)
   Professor, Broome Community College

Marilyn Stapleton, MS, RN, C (Russell Sage College, Nursing Education, 1982)
   Nurse Educator, Regents College

Dolores Vaz, MEd, MSN, RN (Nursing Education, University of Rhode Island, 1983)
   Professor of Nursing, Bristol Community College

Differences in Nursing Care: Area C

Marlene Benson, MS, RN (State University of New York Binghamton, Family Nursing, Gerontology, 1987)
   Associate Professor, Broome Community College

Toni Doherty, MS, RN (Western Connecticut State University, Adult Health, 1991)
   Assistant Professor, Dutchess Community College

Patricia Jablonski, MS, RN (Russell Sage College, Medical-Surgical Nursing, 1980)
   Instructor in Nursing, Hudson Valley Community College

Debra Jeffs, MS, RN, C (Russell Sage College, Parent-Child Nursing, 1992)
   Nurse Educator, Regents College

Dicey O'Malley, EdD, RN (State University of New York at Albany, Program Development and Evaluation, 1984)
   Associate Professor and Chairperson, Hudson Valley Community College

Mary Schinner, MS, RN (State University of New York at Buffalo, Adult Health, 1972)
   Dean of Health Sciences, Trocaire College

Occupational Strategies in Nursing

Joea Bierchen, EdD, RN (University of Florida, Curriculum and Instruction/Educational Leadership, 1981)
   Professor Emeritus, St. Petersburg Junior College

Patricia Irons, MA, RN (Columbia University, Nursing Administration, 1961)
   Professor and Chairperson in Nursing, Queensborough Community College

Suzanne Kreuzer, MS, RN (State University of New York at Buffalo, Adult Health Nursing, 1981)
   Associate Professor, Trocaire College

Marianne Lettus, EdD, RN (State University of New York at Albany, Program Development and Evaluation, 1990)
   Associate Dean of Nursing, Regents College

Esther McEvoy, MS, RN (Russell Sage College, Medical-Surgical Nursing, 1969)
   Professor and Chairperson, Maria College

Dicey O'Malley, EdD, RN (State University of New York at Albany, Program Development and Evaluation, 1984)
   Associate Professor and Chairperson, Hudson Valley Community College

Health Restoration: Area I

Glenda Kelman, MS, RN (Russell Sage College, Medical-Surgical Nursing, 1974)
   Associate Professor of Nursing, The Sage Colleges

Deborah L'Herault, MS, RN (Russell Sage College, Cardiology Nursing & Nursing Education, 1991)
Assistant Professor of Nursing, University of Vermont

Bridget Nettleton, EdD, RN (State University of New York at Albany, Educational Administration and Policy Studies, 1996)
Nurse Educator, Regents College

Lynn Nichols, MS, RN (University of Pennsylvania, Medical-Surgical Nursing, 1968)
Associate Professor of Nursing, State University of New York College at Plattsburgh (Retired)

Teresa Pistolessi, PhD, RN (The University at Albany, Education, 1996; Russell Sage College, Parent-Child Nursing, 1972)
Assistant Professor of Nursing, The Sage Colleges

Dennis Ross, PhD, RN (Case Western Reserve University, Nursing, 1992)
Professor of Nursing, Castleton State College (deceased)

Health Restoration: Area II

Elizabeth Ayello, PhD, RN (Adelphi University, Medical Surgical Nursing, 1994)
Clinical Assistant Professor of Nursing, New York University

Bridget Nettleton, EdD, RN (State University of New York at Albany, Educational Administration and Policy Studies, 1996)
Nurse Educator, Regents College

Gail Sanzone, MS, RN (University of Maryland, Adult Psychiatric/Mental Health Nursing, 1976)
Adjunct, The Sage Colleges

Gladys Scipien, MS, RN (Boston University, Maternal-Child Health Nursing, 1969)
Associate Professor of Nursing, University of Massachusetts

Ann Sedore, PhD, RN (Syracuse University, Adult Education, 1988)
Chief Nursing Officer/Senior Hospital Administrator, University Hospital, Syracuse

Marie Winterkorn, MS, RN (Russell Sage College, Parent/Child Nursing, 1987)
Assistant Professor of Nursing, State University of New York College at Plattsburgh

Health Support A: Health Promotion & Health Protection

Anne Doyle, MSN, RN (Hunter College, Psychiatric/Mental Health Nursing, 1969)
Retired from City College, City University of New York

Gloria Gelmann, EdD, RN (Columbia University, Family and Community Education, 1982)
Associate Professor of Nursing, Seton Hall University

Glenda Kelman, PhD, RN (New York University, Nursing Theory and Research, 1997)
Associate Professor of Nursing, The Sage Colleges

Barbara Pieper, PhD, RN (Adelphi University, Community Health Teaching, 1992)
Associate Professor of Nursing, The Sage Colleges

Health Support B: Community Health Nursing

Linnea Jatulis, PhD, RN (State University of New York at Albany, Program Development and Evaluation, 1989)
Retired from The Sage Colleges

Ramona Mae Leslie, MS, RN (Russell Sage College, Medical–Surgical Nursing, 1975) Nurse Educator, Regents College (retired)

Cecilia Mulvey, PhD, RN (Syracuse University, Community Health, 1986)
Associate Professor of Nursing, Syracuse University, Maxwell School of Nursing

Paula Scharf, PhD, RN (New York University, Nursing Research and Theory Development, 1986)
Associate Professor of Nursing, Pace University

Ann Weitzel, MS, RN (University of Rochester, Community Health Nursing, 1980)
Assistant Professor of Nursing, State University of New York College at Brockport

Professional Strategies in Nursing

Gail Hagenah, MS, RN (State University of New York at Buffalo, Child Health, 1976)
Assistant Professor of Nursing, State University of New York College at Brockport

Linnea Jatulis, EdD, RN (State University of New York at Albany, Program Development and Evaluation, 1989)
Retired from The Sage Colleges

Rachel Pollow, PhD, RN (University of Texas at Austin, Educational Administration, 1984)
Associate Professor of Nursing, State University of New York College at Plattsburgh

Deborah Sopczyk, MSN, RN (State University of New York at Buffalo, Child Health, 1979)
Nurse Educator, Regents College

Kay Viggiani, MS, RN (Syracuse University, Medical–Surgical Nursing and Gerontology, 1987)
Associate Professor of Nursing, Keuka College

Lee Xippolitos, PhD, RN (State University of New York at Stony Brook, Psychiatric–Mental Health Nursing, 1985)
Clinical Associate Professor of Nursing, State University of New York at Stony Brook

Research in Nursing

Susan Bastable, EdD, RN (Columbia University, Curriculum and Instruction in Nursing, 1979)
Associate Professor, State University of New York Health Science Center College of Nursing, Syracuse

Dorothy Gilbert, PhD, RN (Columbia University, Anthropology, 1977)
Associate Professor, School of Nursing, University of Massachusetts at Amherst

Rona Levin, PhD, RN (New York University, Nursing, 1981)
Professor and Director, Division of Health Sciences, Felician College

Veta Massey, PhD, RN (University of Texas at Austin, Nursing, 1989)
Dean, Division of Nursing, Baptist College of Health Sciences

Susan Schmidt, PhD, RN (University of Cincinnati, Epidemiology, 1994)
Associate Professor and Epidemiologist, Xavier University

Deborah Sopczyk, MSN, RN (State University of New York at Buffalo, Child Health, 1979)
Nurse Educator, Regents College

Fundamentals of Nursing

Toni Doherty, MS, RN (Western Connecticut State University, Adult Health, 1990)
Assistant Professor, Dutchess Community College

Loretta Kloda, MS, RN (University of Rochester, Nursing, 1964)
Professor, Monroe Community College

Mary Schinner, MS, RN (State University of New York at Buffalo, Adult Health, 1972)
Dean of Health Sciences, Trocaire College

Michele Morgan Woodbeck, MS, RN (Russell Sage College, Medical-Surgical Nursing, 1979)
Assistant Professor, Hudson Valley Community College

Maternal & Child Nursing (associate) and Maternity Nursing

Civita Allard, MS, RN (Russell Sage College, Nursing, 1985)
Associate Professor, Mohawk Valley Community College

Patricia Jablonski, MS, RN (Russell Sage College, Medical-Surgical Nursing, 1980)
Assistant Professor, Hudson Valley Community College

Ann Dylis Knauf, MS, RN (Russell Sage College, Parent-Child Nursing, 1986)
Assistant Professor, Maria College

Nancy Latterner, MA, RN (New York University, Parent-Child Nursing, 1971)
Professor, Nassau Community College

Anne Tucker Rose, MS, RN (Russell Sage College, Maternal-Child Health, 1971)
Associate Professor, Hudson Valley Community College

Adult Nursing

Zara Brenner, MSN, RN, CS (University of Rochester, Medical/Surgical Nursing, 1977)
Assistant Professor of Nursing, State University of New York College of Brockport; Clinical Nurse Specialist, The Genesee Hospital

Sandy Burgener, PhD (Wayne State University, Nursing Research: Gerontology, 1989)
Associate Professor of Nursing, Indiana University

Linda Copel, PhD (Texas Woman's University, Nursing: Research & Theory Development, 1984)
Associate Professor of Nursing, Villanova University

Wendy Nelson, MSN (University of Cincinnati; Burn, Trauma, and Emergency Nursing, 1982)
Assistant Professor, The Sage Colleges

Ann Sedore, PhD, RN (Syracuse University, Adult Education, 1988)
    Chief Nursing Officer/Senior Hospital Administrator, University Hospital, State University of New York at Syracuse

Maternal & Child Nursing (baccalaureate)

Gloria Gelmann, EdD, RN (Columbia University, Family and Community Education, 1982)
    Associate Professor of Nursing, Seton Hall University

Kathleen Haubrich, PhD, RNC (University of Cincinnati, Nursing and Health, 1995)
    Associate Professor, Miami University of Ohio

Teresa Pistolessi, PhD, RN (State University of New York at Albany, Education 1996)
    Assistant Professor, The Sage Colleges

Nancy Troy, PhD (New York University, Theory Development and Research in Nursing, 1986)
    Assistant Professor, Wayne State University

Marie Winterkorn, MS, RNC (Russell Sage College, Parent/Child Nursing, 1987)
    Assistant Professor of Nursing, State University of New York College at Plattsburgh

Psychiatric/Mental Health Nursing

Anne W. Doyle, MSN, RN, C (Hunter College, Psychiatric/Mental Health Nursing, 1969)
    Associate Professor of Nursing, City College, City University of New York (Retired)

Mary C. McLaughlin, EdD, RN (Teachers College, Columbia University, Curriculum and Teaching, 1985)
    Assistant Professor of Nursing, Adelphi University

Tanya E. Ratney, EdD, RN (Boston University, Educational Leadership, 1985)
    Associate Professor of Nursing, Fitchburg State College

Gail Sanzone, MS, RN, CS (University of Maryland, Adult Psychiatric/Mental Health Nursing 1976)
    Adjunct, The Sage Colleges